CRIMINOLOGY

Explaining Crime and Its Context

seventh edition

Stephen E. **BROWN**
Western Carolina University

Finn-Aage **ESBENSEN**
University of Missouri, St. Louis

Gilbert **GEIS**
University of California, Irvine

Criminology: Explaining Crime and Its Context, Seventh Edition

Brown, Stephen E.
    Criminology: explaining crime and its context -- 7th Ed. / Stephen E. Brown, Finn-Aage Esbensen, Gilbert Geis
        Includes bibliographical references and index.
        ISBN 978-1-4224-6332-1 (softbound)

Library of Congress Control Number: 2010923132

Cover design by Tin Box Studio, Inc./Cincinnati, Ohio

EDITOR Janice Eccleston
ACQUISITIONS EDITOR Michael C. Braswell

To MiSuk, Stephanie, and Cory.

—SEB

To Dana, Thor, Heidi, and Eva-Rosa.

—FE

In memory of Dolores Tuttle Geis and Robley Elizabeth Geis.

—GG

Preface

Our challenge in preparing the seventh edition of *Criminology: Explaining Crime and Its Context* centered on paring back what, by the sixth edition, had grown into a 600+ page book. It seemed a daunting task to the three of us, as authors, because explaining crime is an expansive charge. There is such an array of information that we feel can strengthen the criminological foundation of our students, yet it needs to be manageable within the structural confines of an academic term. Much to our delight, the theoretical boundaries of criminology have blossomed over the span of this text's evolution. Ergo, it was time to trim back and prioritize our burgeoning content.

We had the good fortune of guidance in this attenuating process from several colleagues who have used this text in their own classrooms. While we bear responsibility for final decisions in the process, we rest assured that the final product is much sounder than it would have been without their guidance. Hearty thanks are extended to the following criminologists:

Karen Booyens	University of Pretoria
Kimberly Detardo-Bora	Marshall University
Paul Klenowski	Clarion University of Pennsylvania
William Lugo	Eastern Connecticut University
Stephen Tibbetts	California State University - San Bernardino
Charles Tittle	North Carolina State University

Throughout the years, our efforts to present the evidence and stimulate critical thought regarding a range of criminological perspectives, both seasoned and emerging, have benefited from the comments of far too many students and colleagues to list. For those who have contributed, we extend hearty thanks. Specifically for their help on this edition, we would like to acknowledge Terrance (T.J.) Taylor at the University of Missouri - St. Louis for his thoughtful comments and camaraderie, as well as Dena Carson and J. Michael Vecchio for their assistance. Thanks also to Diane Christenson, Marilyn Washler, and Patricia Edwards, all at the University of California - Irvine for all of their help.

Table of Contents in Brief

Table of Contents

PART I

Foundations for Criminology

The opening unit of this text provides a foundation for the study of criminology as conceptualized by the authors. The goal is to explore the crime problem, its context, and, especially, the causes of crime. Unfortunately media presentations of crime and efforts to control it present a distorted reality of crime as a simple phenomenon (Anderson et al., 2009).* Nothing could be further from the truth; understanding crime is far from a simple task. To the contrary, it is extremely complex and challenging. The subtitle of this text, "explaining crime and its context," summarizes that premise. It is the goal of this book to delineate the complex context in which crime emerges. Crime can only be understood by considering the broad social context from which it emanates.

Theories or more simply, explanations of crime, serve as the central thesis. While many criminologists do more than develop theories of crime, it is those explanations that provide the foundation for all other criminological endeavors. Predicting criminality and policy development should logically be rooted in some explanatory framework. This text examines a number of frameworks for explaining crime and, therefore, is suggestive of many strategies for addressing it.

In defining crime and criminology, these initial chapters draw attention to three important issues that should be kept in mind throughout the remainder of the book. First is the *relativity of crime*. What is considered a crime varies by time, place, and who is doing the defining. Examination of crime in the context of diverse cultures from around the world illustrates, perhaps most vividly, the importance of the concept of relativity in understanding crime and deviance. In that sense criminology is inherently cross-cultural. While the focus within the book is more on U.S. criminological thought, material from a range of cultures is included to bolster a broader understanding of crime, deviance and social control. It turns out that the relativity of crime is a fruitful concept for understanding the continual redefinition of crime within our own cultures.

---

*Anderson, J.F., N.J. Mangels & A.H. Langsam (2009). "The Challenges of Teaching Criminological Theory: Can Academia Deliver What the Media Promises?" *Criminal Justice Studies*, 22:223-236.

1

The prevalence of the *scientific method* in the field of criminology serves as a second thesis. At the heart of criminology to most, but not all criminologists, is the idea that it is a science. Indeed, Chapter 1 discusses criminology as the scientific study of the causes of crime. Most of the explanations for crime examined within this text, as well as tests of their validity, are based on scientific research. While some coverage is extended to alternative approaches to knowledge about crime, the emphasis on scientific study reflects the scholarly emphasis of the field.

Finally, the impact of *ideology* on explanations of crime and on crime policy is a cornerstone of this book. A conscious effort has been made to highlight the role of ideology by presenting a wide range of explanations of crime rooted in five dominant paradigms, as well as emerging perspectives on crime. The intent is to offer a balanced perspective on the field of criminology, while obviating neglect of gender subordination, violent white-collar crime, family violence, and other socially harmful behaviors that are often excluded from examination.

1
Crime and Criminology

Crime and criminals capture the attention of nearly everyone. The public fascination with these matters has not escaped the news and entertainment media. The large following of "On the Record with Greta Van Susteren," aired on Fox News Network, and the "Nancy Grace" show, carried by Cable News Network, reflect the widespread fascination with these topics. Sometimes people romanticize criminals so that outlaws like Robin Hood and Jesse James become folk heroes. Other criminals, or alleged offenders, are demonized and become outlets for anger, fear and other emotions. In yet other scenarios, those claiming to be victims are vilified.

At the heart of this fascination with crime-related issues lay some intriguing questions: Why do people commit these crimes? How should we respond? Why is one behavior a crime and not some other behavior? We might exclaim about some outrageous but legally permissible behavior: "There oughtta be a law!" While the public is intrigued, criminologists address these issues in a more systematic manner. A *criminologist* is "one who studies crime, criminals, and criminal behavior. One who attempts to determine the causes of crime" (Rush & Torres, 1998:52). But what is *crime* and how serious are different forms of it? Consider each of these brief scenarios, and rank-order them from most to least serious. After doing so, consider your rationale for the rank you gave each, and then compare your rankings to those of several classmates. Are they different? If so, how and why?

- George points a .38 caliber revolver at the cashier in a liquor store, and yells, "Put all the money in the bag!"

- Karen and Mary smoke marijuana a couple of evenings a week in their college dormitory room while listening to CDs. They laugh a lot.

- Executives hide the fact that their corporation is losing large sums of money. They pay themselves huge bonuses, while encouraging employees to invest more. Ultimately, the corporation declares bankruptcy, resulting in thousands of employees losing their jobs and retirement benefits.

3

- Stuart is a middle manager in a large corporation and is involved with planning a merger with a smaller company. Knowing that the stock value of the other business will be dramatically increased by the merger, he gives his fiancée, Anna, $40,000 to invest for him in its stock.

- A group of automobile executives discusses a faulty brake system in a car model that was marketed last year. They knew that the brake system could contribute to a number of accidents that can result in serious disabilities and loss of lives. They conclude that they will not recall the vehicles because it is more profitable not to do so, based on the number of lawsuits that their company can expect to lose versus the cost of the recall. As a result, 14 people die in crashes the following year that are attributed to faulty brakes.

- "Snake" and "Slim" take great pride in their tough persona. They like to fight and feel this earns them respect or neighborhood "rep." They equally value degrading people whom they regard as different from themselves. In living out these psychological needs they frequently consume large volumes of alcohol and seek out young men whom they believe to be gay as targets for physical assaults. One Saturday night their savage beating of a college student, while screaming sexual orientation epithet's results in hospitalization of a young man with three with three cracked ribs, a broken nose and multiple abrasions.

- Abby is a teenager with a two-year-old son. She lives with Manley, her 22-year-old boyfriend, who burns her son with cigarettes and urinates on the burnt flesh. She has seen him do this several times, but has never reported it to the authorities because, she says, she loves Manley. After the injuries were reported by a teacher, authorities had the boy examined by a physician who reported that several of the scars on his arms and legs were permanent, but that he was otherwise in good health.

- Jake is a third-year police officer. He has heard that a local gang member, Frederic "Big" Johnston, has raped several young girls in his neighborhood. There has never been physical evidence to support these rumors and no one living in the neighborhood has ever complained to police. Jake, however, feels that after three years of police work he has a good read of street toughs. He finds "Big" alone in an alley one night, gives him a severe beating with his nightstick, and expresses to him in extremely vulgar language what he plans to subject Big to if he hears more rumors of his sexual victimization of young girls.

- Dustin works as a mechanic in a car dealership. The owner tells his mechanics that to earn their full salary they must replace at least five sets of shock absorbers each week. He routinely (and falsely) tells female customers (who he assumes know little about cars) that their cars need new shocks. Consequently, Dustin always meets his quota and gets full pay. In fact, his boss approaches him after he has worked there several months and tells him: "You're the kind of man we want on our team. Starting with the next paycheck you've got a twenty percent pay raise. You have a good future with us."

- Dr. Hippocrates likes to buy a new Mercedes each year, and prefers to pay cash. When the new model appears on the market he finds that he is short of cash. He tells the parents of each child brought to him that month with a sore throat that a tonsillectomy is necessary. He performs seven such operations at a charge of $1,650 each.

- Sharon is a 23-year-old in her second year as a high school science teacher. She begins meeting Jim, a 14-year-old freshman after school to have sex in her apartment.

- Buford has been dating Carol for the past two semesters. They regularly go out two or three times a week, and often engage in heavy petting. One Friday night, in severe weather conditions, Buford drives Carol several miles out into the country and says, "It's been long enough. Now you put out or get out."

- Alvin is a small farmer in a financially distressed region. He knows that he will go bankrupt if the tomatoes, his only cash crop, are unsuccessful again this year. They become infested with beetles and he is afraid that legal treatments will not help. He dusts his crop with DDT, knowing that it is a dangerous and illegal pesticide.

- Jennifer lies about her income on an application for food stamps so that she will be eligible. Her income is barely over the minimum because she took a second job so she could afford dance lessons for her daughter.

Let's consider your ranking of the "seriousness" of the above scenarios. Which did you find most and least serious? How did your seriousness rankings compare to those of other students? This exercise should raise a number of questions. First, in order to rank the seriousness of the behaviors, this term must be operationally defined. Most typically, crime or wrongdoing will be defined in terms of harm rendered. How do we determine what behaviors are most harmful? Comparing your views with those of others, you may find a lot of disagreement. Harm is a construct that often is in the eyes of the beholder. Rarely, however, is harmfulness the exclusive criterion for assessing misconduct. Other values are usually injected. For example, there are classes of people such as children, the elderly and disabled, to whom extra protection is extended under the law. What groups from these scenarios arguably merit special or extended protection? Why?

Second, note that there is wide variation in how the criminal justice system would respond to the scenarios. Not all are crimes in all jurisdictions, nor will there be criminal justice intervention in all of the portrayed acts even where the behaviors are criminalized. Others on the list are likely to be aggressively pursued by the criminal justice system, but still may not be thought of by you as matters that should be the business of criminal law. In other words, you will likely conclude that these scenarios include examples of both excluded harms and overcriminalized behaviors. What arguable examples of each do you see? These scenarios represent both sides of the *relativity of crime* (or law), a major thesis in this book. Stated succinctly, all of us do not agree on what ought to be treated as crime and what should not. Our perceptions of wrongdoing will vary along lines of gender, religion, race, social class and many other circumstances (Mitchell, 1998). Ultimately, however, moral assessments of behavior will shape our response, resulting in some being treated as crimes while other behaviors are not. The general public, special interest groups and criminal justice personnel will have varying degrees of influence in this process of designating certain behaviors as criminal.

Third, offenses in the scenarios may reflect characteristics with which you or other students empathize. Conversely, others may seem to you obnoxious or revolting behaviors. Should all who bring harm to others be held equally accountable or should the offender's circumstances and characteristics be taken into account? Does it matter if the offender is rich or poor, healthy or unhealthy, or has led an easy or deprived life? That is, should we only consider the act (crime) or should we also consider characteristics of the offender in ranking seriousness? Figure 1.1 summarizes some of the questions raised in assessing crime seriousness.

FIGURE 1.1
Common Criteria for Assessing Crime Seriousness

Harm Inflicted:	What is the objective level of harm caused by the behavior?
Status of Victim:	Does the victim merit special protection by the law?
Moral Judgments:	What and whose moral judgments will influence the criminalization of behaviors and activation of the criminal justice process?
Offender Characteristics:	What is the role of the background and circumstances of offenders?

Dealing with the "crime" of a society is a trying task. On the one hand, an important philosophical question is whether the criminal law reflects the interest of members of the society at large or what criminologists call a *consensus* model. That is, does a consensus underlie our law's definition of what behaviors are criminal or is our law a reflection of *conflict* whereby the state serves the interest of some at the expense of others? Public opinion, therefore, is relevant in the sense that American ideology endorses a consensus model of government. We expect the law to reflect the views of our citizenry. On the other hand, criminologists oftentimes become frustrated with a public policy path in the crime arena that is largely uninformed and subject to manipulation by politicians and the media. Most criminologists appreciate the complexity of the crime problem. Certainly most would agree that crime is at least as difficult to address as are health care, the economy and foreign policy. As law professor Samuel H. Pillsbury (1995:313) states:

> Can we imagine major legislative decisions on health policy without careful consultation of doctors, insurance executives, and health care administrators? How about resolving monetary policy without extended commentary from financial experts and economists? What about foreign policy without diplomats and intelligence or military experts?

Yet, crime initiatives are debated and adopted with minimal criminological consultation. The criminal justice expert seems to occupy a special—and especially lowly—place in policy debates. Elliott Currie (1999:15) aired concern with the gap between what criminologists have learned and the direction of crime policy in America. This concern was echoed in two presidential addresses to meetings of the American Society of Criminology. In lamenting a counterproductive "theory and policy divide" at the 2003 meeting, John Laub (2004) illustrated the disdain that many politicians have displayed toward academe in general, and criminology in particular. He quoted former Georgia Governor Zell Miller, for example, dramatically separating criminal justice policy from criminological knowledge:

> Nobody can tell me from some ivory tower that you take a kid, you kick him in the rear end, and it doesn't do any good. I do not give a damn what they [academic researchers) say (cited in Laub, 2004:16).

Former Arizona Governor Fife Symington (prior to his 1997 bank fraud conviction) similarly expressed his anti-criminological sentiments, proclaiming:

> I was not hired to be Arizona's chief social theorist. I was not sent here to sit meditating on Freud or on the latest 'root causes' of criminal behavior. The criminal law deals not with theories but with thugs (cited in Welch et al., 1998:234).

Addressing the 2004 meeting of the American Society of Criminology, Frank Cullen (2005) also fretted that many feel "that criminology is largely irrelevant" and therefore urged intensified effort to disseminate criminological knowledge. He went on to say that "as scientists, we have a form of knowledge—scientific knowledge—that has a special legitimacy" and that "engaging in rigorous science increases the chances that criminology will make a difference" (2005:27).

The problem is that a large chasm separates the scientific findings of criminologists and the stances taken by political leaders. As Travis Pratt (2008:44) has observed, "the most methodologically rigorous available research demonstrates that policies such as 'three strikes' laws... have little to no appreciable impact on crime rates." One critic (Austin, 2003) asserted that this is due to the inferior quality of criminological research but most see other causes. To reduce the gap between criminological knowledge and criminal justice policy Pratt (2008) argues that criminologists must strive to communicate a complex body of scientific knowledge in straight forward language that is understandable to policy makers and their constituents. Similarly, Marvell and Moody (2008) recommend that the complex research designs used by criminologists be standardized by a credible board of experts. Clearly, however, both gaining credibility and translating complex scientific findings to politically palatable policy statements remain quite a challenge for criminology.

Criminology as Science

As illustrated in the preceding section, "crime" is a relative phenomenon, conveying different thoughts and meanings to different people. Thus criminology is not a field readily reducible to a concise definition. A starting point, however, is Edwin Sutherland's classic delineation of the tripartite boundaries of *criminology* as "the study of the processes of making laws, breaking laws, and reacting towards the breaking of laws" (Sutherland & Cressey, 1974:3). Such a broad definition however, has the disadvantage of being unmanageable in a single text. This book, therefore, is more generally oriented toward criminology as a scientific endeavor to explain crime (the breaking of laws), while acknowledging the importance of making law and reacting to law violation.

Two essential components of a science are its theoretical and its methodological branches. *Theory* represents an effort to explain or make sense of the world, thus revolving around the "why" of crime, criminalization, and similar concerns. *Methodology* refers to the techniques or methods that criminologists use as they attempt to determine the "whys" of crime (see Chapter 3). Theory and methods are integrally related in the *scientific method* of studying crime. Theories are developed to explain observed facts, while observations are undertaken to test theories. But some of those committed to a scientific criminology object to an "empirical scientism" that they believe has elevated methodology above theory, contributing to what they see as the demise of the criminological imagination (Williams, 1984). The coverage within this book of an array of recent efforts to explain crime suggests much vitality in terms of criminological theorizing. Despite dominance of the scientific view, some criminologists advocate a broader base including, for example, a humanistic approach to understanding crime. This more expansive conception of how to seek knowledge is championed within a critical criminology that focuses on how the power elite define crime to suit themselves. Jack Gibbs reflected the deep chasm between some consensus and conflict theorists when he retorted that the principal contribution of these critical criminologists has been "hot air":

> Entirely apart from invidious comparisons, how can social and behavioral scientists differ from social critics, philosophers, revolutionaries, theologians, journalists, social workers, and historians? If sociologists and criminologists cannot answer that question

satisfactorily, the two fields do not deserve survival. I have no difficulty in answering: social and behavioral scientists can strive for empirical theories and assess those theories largely in terms of predictive power (1987:3-4).

In a rejoinder, Ray Michalowski countered:

> There are many criminologies and many criminologists. . . . If we are to create a viable and vibrant criminology the time has come for us to accept the diversity of our subject and for criminologists of different epistemological and theoretical persuasions to talk seriously with one another, not at or past one another (1987:18).

While there is a consensus among criminologists that the scientific method is at the heart of understanding crime and criminal behavior, the exchange above exemplifies the diversity of views that exist within the field. The debate over the appropriate role of the scientific method in criminology is rooted in ideological differences. This is another issue central to understanding the field.

Ideology within Criminology

Ideology refers to a set of beliefs or values that all of us develop, usually unconsciously, about the way that the world is or ought to be. Ideologies underlie religious, political, social and moral positions. The resulting views serve as guiding biases in all manner of social relations. "An ideology. . . . serves the interests of one segment of a society more than all other segments . . ." (Curra, 2000:6). The benefits may accrue to one gender, a particular ethnic group, a certain religion, a political group and so forth. It is within this larger framework shaping political and religious ideology that a bias regarding our view of crime and criminals emerges. It is not that ideology *per se* is a bad thing. To the contrary, it is vital, and inevitable, that we be bound by a set of beliefs. We should, however, strive to recognize what those values are. Moreover, we should be willing to carefully assess them.

Political ideology may be conceptualized as falling on a continuum, ranging from left wing (politically liberal) to right wing (politically conservative). Each position on the continuum is associated with values that have dramatic implications for defining and responding to the crime problem. Current debate reflects relatively clear ideological lines regarding crime issues. Figure 1.2 contrasts a sampling of conservative and liberal views. For criminologists, the division is largely between various "control" (see Chapter 8) and deterrence (see Chapter 5) theorists on the one hand and social structure/support theorists (see Chapter 7) on the other. The broad strategy of the former is to seek ways to exert control over offenders, while the structuralists/support theorists identify ways to provide more adequate opportunities for those whose environments press them toward crime. As Frank Cullen and his colleagues (1999:189) explain it, the popularized control perspective "requires doing something to a person rather than for a person. Control theories thus can easily be tilted in a repressive direction."

The conservatives, however, begin with the assumption that the offender is flawed or morally defective. The conservatives call for placing more people in prison for longer periods of time, while more liberal leaning criminologists advocate enhancing social supports for those most at risk for delinquent or criminal behavior.

FIGURE 1.2
Conservative Versus Progressive/Liberal Crime Ideology

Conservative	Progressive
• Advocate broad use of death penalty	• Oppose use of death penalty
• Favor low age of criminal responsibility for juveniles	• Favor higher age of criminal responsibility for juveniles
• Favor high levels of incarceration for drug users	• Favor minimal levels of incarceration for drug users
• Favor mandatory and minimum prison sentences for many crimes	• Generally opposed to mandatory and minimum prison sentences
• Favor long prison sentences for many types of crime and criminals	• Favor reserving long prison sentences for selected crimes and criminals
• Favor use of criminal laws to control vices	• Generally oppose the use of criminal laws to control vices
• Favor harsh prison conditions	• Favor humane and comfortable prison conditions

---

Religious orientations fall on a similar continuum that also bears a strong relation to views of crime and punishment. Christian fundamentalism, at one end of the continuum, has often been found to be associated with more punitive attitudes toward offenders (e.g., Grasmick et al., 1993; Stack, 2003; Vogel & Vogel, 2003). Examining subjects at this end of the religious continuum, James Unnever and his colleagues (2005) found that those who reported more time spent in religious activities and more rigid religious views were more likely to support the death penalty. Similarly, their respondents who interpreted the Bible more literally tended to support harsher courts. Conversely, they observed that those who scored higher on measures of compassion and whose image of God as more gracious, as opposed to harsh and judgmental, were less supportive of both capital punishment and harsher courts. While these relations are complex, for example varying across regions and ethnicity, there is clearly a strong linkage between religious ideology and understanding of crime and criminals.

Because bias, or close-mindedness, often permeates ideology, advocates of both conservative and liberal-based crime policies typically cling to a singular view. Ling Ren, Jihong Zhao & Nicholas Lovrich (2006) contrasted the two ends of the ideological spectrum and went on to empirically assess the success of crime reduction programs rooted in both. To the chagrin of ideologues, they found that increased expenditure on police activity (consistent with conservative ideology) and on community development (congruent with liberal premises) both were associated with lower rates of violent crime. They recommended "that an effective public policy on crime control should combine the merits of both the conservative and the liberal perspectives on crime" (2006:28). Unfortunately, however, few are likely to heed their advice.

There are many obstacles to reducing the impact of ideological bias. Many practitioners, legislators and academicians are unaware of or underestimate their own biases. One of the text authors, for example, recently encountered a categorical denial of the existence of ideological differences in debating academic issues with a colleague. Thinking that open acknowledgment of their different ideological premises might help clarify the impasse, the author was bemused when confronted with an angry denial. The pair was wed to competing perspectives, but one was unwilling or unable to recognize this. While such denials are sometimes malicious attempts to hide self-interest, they are perhaps more often evidence of a failure to comprehend the power of our own socialization experiences. That process itself might be understood through principles of learning theory that are delineated in Chapter 8. As a science, criminology often is assumed to be value-free, but separating values from intellectual inquiry is not an easy task.

The biases emanating from ideology have boundless consequences. Policy is typically advocated to pursue ideological ends rather than to effectively deal with crime. Perusing the listing in Figure 1.2, for example, identifies the moral/political views that all too often determine the policy positions to which individuals subscribe. Particularly revealing of the dominance of ideology over sound policy deliberation are the reversals of positions that emerge under politically volatile circumstances. To illustrate, a litmus test for conservatives is often a pro-prosecution and victim advocacy role, while for liberals it is more typically one of protecting constitutional rights of the accused and emphasis on the doctrine of "presumption of innocence." In the unique and highly publicized case of rape allegations directed toward members of the Duke University lacrosse team in the spring of 2006, however, dramatic position reversals of scores of "experts" were clearly the result of shifting stereotypical images of victims and offenders. Given an alleged lower-class minority victim, with a stigmatized "stripper" identity and accused perpetrators from privileged white segments of society, many conservatives shifted to a staunch defense of the presumption of innocence. Liberals, on the other hand, altered course to embrace aggressive prosecution. The change of heart among both conservatives and liberals illustrated, in Curra's (2000:6) words, that "ideology . . . serves the interest of one segment of society over all other segments." It seems that this case, like many other matters in the criminal justice process, revolved around ideology. Unfortunately, Walter Miller's (1973:142) assertion decades ago that "[I]deology is the permanent hidden agenda of criminal justice" continues to ring true. E.J. Williams and Matthew Robinson (2004) recognize that ideological bias is at the foundation of competing criminological paradigms. They conclude, however, that a widespread failure to acknowledge the influence of ideology has undermined the legitimacy of academic programs in criminal justice. They urge that ideology be brought to the forefront of criminal justice academe and, like Ling Ren and colleagues (2006), call for more balance in assessing of ideological premises. Analyses of such scholars suggest that ideologically based name-calling is not only unbecoming, but impedes our progress in understanding the crime problem and determining what actions may be most helpful in addressing it.

Yet another consequence of ideology within criminology is that gender historically has been ignored, part of a general problem of gender subordination, under which issues pertinent to females have been neglected and misrepresented. Some criminologists attribute that neglect to a paucity of female offenders and conclude that it was understandable given that crime is primarily a male problem. Others, however, attribute it to male domination of criminological theory and the criminal justice apparatus. Yet ideological bias is readily apparent in both the manner in which females have been treated in our justice system and in how theoreticians have addressed gender. Historically, women have been subordinated under criminal law and subjected to discrimination within the criminal justice system. Explanations of female offenses by criminologists and other social scientists have been sexualized, reflecting the stereotypical views of women in a patriarchal society.

The changing definition of crime, or relativity of law, is largely driven by ideology. Relativity and ideology are deeply intertwined. Ideological leanings impact not only our understanding of the causes of crime and response to it, but even the operational definition of crime. Crime cannot be defined independent of an ideological framework, and consequently, any definition of crime will favor some groups over others. Clearly then, how crime is defined is of paramount importance.

The "Crime" in Criminology

Defining criminology only as "the scientific study of crime" leaves unanswered a pivotal question, "What is crime?" Definitions of crime offered by criminologists vary widely along a continuum. Representative of the narrower end of this definitional continuum is Paul Tappan's highly *legalistic definition*:

> Crime is an intentional act in violation of the criminal law (statutory and case law), committed without defense or excuse, and penalized by the state as a felony or misdemeanor. In studying the offender there can be no presumption that . . . persons are criminals unless they also are held guilty beyond a reasonable doubt of a particular offense (1947:100).

This perspective reduces the subject matter of criminology to a subset of those actions or inactions proscribed by criminal law, consisting of only those behaviors successfully processed by the criminal justice system. It excludes behavior that is not criminalized, detected, or reported to law enforcement authorities and successfully prosecuted. All contemporary criminologists view this as an exceedingly restrictive definition. Criminology has rejected such a rigid legalistic definition of its province of study. Edwin H. Sutherland, widely regarded as the dean of American criminology during its formative years, introduced the concept of white-collar crime, which substantially broadened the boundaries of the field. Articulating a modified legalistic definition, Sutherland maintained:

> The essential characteristic of crime is that it is behavior which is prohibited by the State as an injury to the State and against which the State may react, at least as a last resort, by punishment. The two abstract criteria generally regarded by legal scholars as necessary elements in a definition of crime are legal description of an act as socially harmful and legal provision of a penalty for the act (1949:31).

Sutherland noted, however, that "[a]n unlawful act is not defined as criminal by the fact that it is punished, but by the fact that it is punishable" (1949:35), and thereby challenged Tappan's notion that study must be restricted to convicted offenders. He argued that white-collar crime meets such a legalistic definition because it is punishable (by fines, injunctions, etc.); even though less punitive and stigmatizing processes have been developed to soften the consequences of illegal behaviors by powerful persons. Sutherland maintained that white-collar crimes were real crimes, both in the behavioral and the legalistic sense, but that they were being diverted into a distinct category of behavior by legislative fiat that provided for "differential implementation of the law" (1949:42). Sutherland thereby expanded the realm of criminology to focus on the law in action.

Representative of the next position on the continuum, and pushing toward a broader definition of criminology, are the works of Hermann Mannheim and those of Thorsten Sellin. Mannheim (1965) firmly rejected the value of law in delineating criminological boundaries, identifying all antisocial behavior as the subject matter. Similarly, defining criminology as the study of violations of conduct norms, only a subset of which are embodied in the criminal law at any given place and time, Sellin concluded:

> The unqualified acceptance of the legal definitions of the basic units or elements of criminological inquiry violates a fundamental criterion of science. The scientist must have freedom to define his own terms, based on the intrinsic character of his material and designating properties in those materials which are assumed to be universal (1938:21).

Such definitions are defended, in part, because they are not biased in favor of the legal status quo. More legalistic criminologists maintain, however, that state definitions of the crime problem may be objectively studied, while broader definitions tend to reduce criminology to the study of deviant behavior, with each criminologist individually judging which acts merit attention.

The broadest criminological conceptualization of crime emanates from the critical camp of criminologists. Similar labels applied to this perspective are *new* and *radical criminology*. From this perspective, crime and deviance are also considered synonymous. This approach broadens criminological theory, however, by contending that political and economic forces play the key role in generating crime and deviance. These factors, termed the "political economy of crime," are said to form the backdrop for both the crime problem and the structure of reactions to it. What behaviors are subject to criminalization and decriminalization are believed to be contingent on the power structure of society.

"New" criminologists find the more restrictive definitions of the criminological domain shortsighted because they depoliticize criminology. Materialism, forced production, division of labor, and other features of capitalism are said to create a political and economic environment that necessitates criminalization of deviance. This, it is argued, should be the focus of criminological study. Sutherland's examination of white-collar crime, for example, "was informed hardly at all by an examination of the ways in which white-collar infractions were (and are) functional to industrial-capitalist societies. . . ." (Taylor et al., 1973:273-274). Rather, Sutherland focused on the disparities of law in action, contending that white-collar crime was "real crime," that is, a violation of the legal code. In contrast, new criminologists have asserted:

> A criminology which is not normatively committed to the abolition of inequalities of wealth and power, and in particular of inequalities in property and life-chances, is inevitably bound to fall into correctionalism [reforms failing to address underlying problems]. And all correctionalism is irreducibly bound up with the identification of deviance with pathology. A fully social theory of deviance must, by its nature, break entirely with correctionalism . . . because . . . the causes of crime must be intimately bound up with the form assumed by the social arrangements of the time. Crime is ever and always that behavior seen to be problematic within the framework of those social arrangements: for crime to be abolished, then, those social arrangements themselves must also be subject to fundamental social change (Taylor et al., 1973:281-282).

Herman and Julia Schwendinger (1975) are representative of this view of the boundaries of the crime problem. They maintain that the definitional premises of criminologists such as Sutherland, and even Sellin, overlooked social injuries induced by the elite who control the state. Though Sellin broadened criminological parameters to envelop violation of legal and extralegal conduct norms, his assumption that "no conduct norm without a sanction can be imagined" (1938:34) left unquestioned the social injuries perpetrated by political and economic elites who are able to dictate the structure of established institutions. Thus the usual definition of the terms of criminological inquiry may leave many issues of harmful social conduct unexamined. Economic "violence" denying work, living quarters, decent wages, child care, and health care are rarely included in the realm of criminological inquiry except under this radical perspective. The Schwendingers offered an alternative humanistic definition of crime founded upon the notion of human rights.

Redefinition of crime on the basis of human rights requires explication of the content of such rights, who violates them, how, and why. Human rights, the Schwendingers declared, are "the fundamental prerequisites for well-being, including food, shelter, clothing, medical services, challenging work and recreational experiences, as well as security from predatory individuals or repressive and imperialistic social elites" (Schwendinger & Schwendinger, 1975:133-134). Both individuals and institutions may infringe upon these rights. Many behaviors widely prohibited by criminal law are subsumed under this definition, while many human rights violations typically excluded from the criminal law also are embraced. Primary among the latter in the Schwendingers' view, and for them of far greater magnitude than most social harms addressed by criminal codes, are racism, sexism, imperialism, and poverty. By analogy, they asked:

> Isn't it time to raise serious questions about the assumptions under-lying the definition of the field of criminology, when a man who steals a paltry sum can be called a criminal while agents of the State can, with impunity, legally reward men who destroy food so that price levels can be maintained whilst a sizable portion of the population suffers from malnutrition? (1975:137)

Commenting on U.S. military conflicts, William Chambliss (2004:242-243) contended:

> In all my work with counterintelligence in Korea I learned how U.S. soldiers murdered and raped Korean civilians during the war . . . today in Iraq we see the same or worse crimes being committed against Iraqi prisoners, citizens and suspected terrorists . . . the fact is that these are crimes of the state and should be high on the list of crimes to be researched and explained by criminologists.

Criminologists such as the Schwendingers and Chambliss argue that the discipline should cease serving as defenders of state institutions that are often criminal (by the human rights definition) and instead ought to become guardians of human rights.

Definitional parameters of criminology, it can be seen, reveal sharp contrasts that have dramatic implications for what criminologists do and do not study. Figure 1.3 reviews the continuum of definitions that have been discussed. This text examines a diversity of issues, consistent with the entire range of definitional approaches and reflects the variety of endeavors constituting contemporary criminology.

FIGURE 1.3
Continuum of Crime Definitions

		Definitional Approach				
	Legalistic	Modified Legalistic	Normative		New	
Representative(s) of the Approach	Tappan	Sutherland	Sellin	Mannheim	Taylor, Walton & Young	Schwendingers
Definition of Crime	Judicially determined violation of criminal law	Socially harmful act with provision for penalty by the state	Violations of conduct norms	Antisocial behavior	Deviance subjected to	Violations of human rights criminalization
Preferred Focus of Criminology	Adjudicated criminals	White-collar offenders and reactions to them	Variety of of norm violations and reactions to them	Variety of behaviors judged anti-social and reactions to them	Political and economic fac-tors that shape state responses to deviance	Imperialism, racism, sexism, and poverty

One telling criticism of a strict legalistic definition of criminological parameters is that the law in action departs substantially from law in books. The legalistic definition avoids the issue of reactions and nonreactions of the justice system to criminal conduct. Most criminologists, however, view reactions to law violations as critically germane to criminological inquiry, contending that discretionary actions and inactions of justice system personnel shape both the crime problem and the criminal population.

An even more poignant criticism of the legalistic perspective is that the restricting of attention to criminalized behaviors generates an artificial categorization of behavior. That is, the law is relative; some harmful behaviors are legal, while some innocuous actions are illegal. For example, the U.S. Surgeon General concluded that the addictive nature of tobacco rivals that of heroin. Tobacco use leads to the loss of more than 400,000 lives annually in the United States, compared to some 566 deaths attributed to heroin in a single year (Trebach, 1982). Yet production, sales, and possession of heroin are criminalized, while tobacco growth is supported by government subsidies. In an analogous example reviewed by Michael Lynch and Paul Stretesky (2001), Congress reacted to 250 assault rifle homicides with quick legislation, while failing to address more than 10,000 deaths attributed to pesticide exposure. The law, then, is a phenomenon that shrinks and expands through the political process.

Largely because it is a relative phenomenon, conceptualizing crime is a complex task (Henry & Lanier, 2001). As Robert Bohm (1986:195) has explained, "All definitions of crime, legal or otherwise, include actions or inactions that arguably should be excluded and exclude actions or inactions that arguably should be included." This idea raises many questions: Why is it legal to smoke tobacco, but not marijuana? Why is abortion legal, but not euthanasia (mercy killing)? Why is property inheritance protected by law, but not expropriation of property to facilitate equitable distribution of wealth? What other behaviors might one contend should be criminalized or decriminalized? Many criminologists, for example, believe that avoidable, but legal, killings and injuries exceed manyfold those prohibited by criminal law (Box, 1983; Brown, 1986; Reiman, 1990; Robinson, 2004). Such forms of violence include behavior as diverse as corporate production of avoidable environmental toxins, fostering unsafe working conditions, marketing unsafe products, and performing unnecessary surgery. Increased criminalization and prosecution in these areas is called for by some criminologists. An examination of 15 cases of physicians prosecuted for violent crimes in the course of their work serves as evidence that some progress toward this goal is being realized (Liederbach et al., 2001). They found no cases of this sort prior to 1986, and the majority of cases that were prosecuted occurred in 1995 or later.

The "overreach of the criminal law," a phrase coined by Norval Morris and Gordon Hawkins (1970), is an opposing concern. The concept is derived from the premise that the law "is an inefficient instrument for imposing the good life on others" (1970:2), and when it addresses what are termed "victimless crimes," these crimes without victims represent occurrences for which no complainant is forthcoming (see chapter 9). The crime usually consists of a voluntary exchange of services or substances such as prostitution and drugs. Also subsumed under the victimless rubric are behaviors offensive to some "moral entrepreneurs" (Becker, 1963), but that do not involve exchange of legally proscribed services or contraband such as public drunkenness. Owing to the absence of a complainant, victimless crime legislation is largely unenforceable and such laws often set into motion a self-fulfilling prophecy of criminal behavior. A high school student may be labeled "delinquent" for committing a victimless offense, be cut off from the "good" kids, forced to find friends among outsiders, and with them may get into trouble that otherwise would have been avoided. On this basis, many criminologists campaign for decriminalization of a number of "victimless" behaviors.

Crime, however defined, is a relative phenomenon. Behaviors criminalized, as well as those regarded as deviating from nonlegal norms, vary widely across time and locales. Abortion, an act which at one time was prohibited in American legal codes, now is legal (decriminalized) under many circumstances, but under the Robert's court could possibly be once again criminalized. In a comparable time frame, marital rape has been criminalized in most states. While the content of criminal law has shifted, so have public perceptions of the crime problem. Increasingly spurned have been violent white-collar offenses (Cullen et al., 1982), drunk driving (Gusfield, 1981; Kingsnorth et al., 1993), and family violence (Gelles, 1972; Pfohl, 1977; Tierney, 1982), while tolerance of many heterosexual practices (once illegal) has grown in recent years so that such practices are now the norm (Goode, 1984) and campaigns of gay and lesbian groups are expanding the legal rights of homosexuals. Legal and extralegal norms vary even more widely across cultures, meaning that we should be "asking always whether this or that theoretical statement or generalization in criminology is culture-bound or whether in fact it has universal applicability" (Geis, 1987:7-8).

Paradigms in Criminology

What is done in criminology is determined not only by the definition of crime, but by the theoretical orientation or "school of thought" that is followed. There are a number of competing theoretical perspectives, sometimes termed *paradigms*, within criminology. As Robert Chaires and B. Grant Stitt (1994), note, the paradigm selected by criminologists tends to reflect particular ideological biases, because underlying each paradigm are sets of untestable assumptions. All theories are then constructed on this unverifiable foundation. The concept of paradigm is often used very loosely and defined differently. Thus there is considerable variation in results when criminologists attempt to classify theories by paradigmatic categories. Some identify more, but five major paradigms have dominated thinking about crime: rational choice, positivism, interactionism, critical criminology, and theoretical integration. Chapters in Part II are devoted to theories affiliated with each of these paradigms. Just keep in mind that this is only intended as a very general conceptual scheme for identifying differences between theoretical perspectives.

Though largely neglected in American criminology until relatively recently, the *rational choice* paradigm has provided the basis for much criminological inquiry. The deterrence doctrine (examined in detail in Chapter 5) has served as its focal point. The legitimacy of criminal law, from this perspective, is a given, with the issue only being how to dissuade people from violating it. That goal is achievable because, it is assumed, people are rational and able to make decisions regarding their own behavior. The question is how to structure and administer sanctions for outlawed behavior.

The *positivistic* paradigm dominated American criminology for most of the twentieth century. It assumes that forces beyond the control of individuals, rather than rational decisions, determine criminal behavior. Suppose you attend a party at which someone covertly drops acid (LSD) in the punch and you do something really bizarre after consuming it. The force that determined your deviant behavior (i.e., ingestion of the laced punch) was beyond your control. Although legal responsibility for conduct is a separate matter, the positive criminologist is seeking causal explanations. Causal forces, for positivists, may originate with biogenic sources (see Chapter 6), criminogenic social structures (see Chapter 7), or deficient social processes, such as poor family interaction (see Chapter 8). All positivistic theories are founded on the assumption that crime is generated by forces that are largely beyond the realm of individual choice. They also accept the criminal label as nonproblematic, asking only what caused the behavior and not why the behavior is criminalized. Many theories rooted in the positivistic paradigm empathize with offenders, maintaining that social, biological, or other pathologies are responsible for their conduct. The premise that the conduct itself is criminal, however, is uncritically accepted.

The *interactionist* paradigm (explained in Chapter 9), revolving around the actions and reactions of persons and groups, may focus on any deviant or criminal behavior, but has particularly provided the theoretical framework for study of victimless crimes (see Chapter 13). Criminologists subscribing to this paradigm tend to analyze state definitions of crime and the operation of social control agencies such as the police. State definitions of crime are received with skepticism because at the heart of the perspective is the belief that no acts are inherently deviant. Instead, it is thought that acts become deviant only because the reactions of others so label them. Social control agencies are particularly likely to enhance negative labeling of behaviors that otherwise might be dismissed as only mildly deviant, rather than as criminal. These labels may then be incorporated as part of the self-concept of the labeled person, leading to additional (secondary) deviance. Labeling thus generates a self-fulfilling prophecy that propels its subject into a spiral of deviance.

Critical criminology, including new, radical, and Marxist perspectives, is a paradigm that provides a broad definition of the crime problem. It goes further than the interactionist paradigm by rejecting state definitions of crime, asking why relatively powerless wrongdoers are so much more subject to criminalization than the powerful ones. Its focus includes the full range of deviance, with particular attention accorded crimes of the powerful. This paradigm is examined in Chapter 9.

Integration of various approaches rests on the belief that optimal explanations of crime can be derived from combinations of two or more theoretical perspectives rather than by exclusive use of a single one. Integration does not imply any particular definitional orientation to crime. Integrationists argue that singular theoretical models have stagnated, but that integration holds potential for a paradigmatic revolution

(Swigert, 1989). Advocacy for combining theories rests on an assumption that the many competing theories "merely reflect differences in focus or emphasis rather than fundamentally opposed views of the world" (Hirschi, 1989:39). Critics maintain that integration will yield "theoretical mush" by so diluting the characteristics and assumptions of independent theories that their individual explanatory powers will be reduced (Akers, 1989). Some criminologists also object that integration of distinct theories fails to generate new theoretical insight, much less a new paradigm. Specific integrated theories of crime are discussed in Chapter 10, but the approach has become so widespread that it is characteristic of many theoretical perspectives that have earned their own place in theoretical nomenclature. Life-course criminology (reviewed at the end of Chapter 10), for example, has become so popular and is such a broad perspective that some criminologists refer to it as a paradigm.

Figure 1.4 summarizes the five primary paradigms that provide the perspectives from which explanations of crime are sought. Each is explored in some detail in the chapters specified in the right-hand column. As with definitional diversity, each paradigm or perspective contributes to our understanding of crime, and each serves as a point of departure for many significant contributions to contemporary ideas about criminal behavior.

FIGURE 1.4
Paradigmatic Framework for Examining Crime

Paradigm	Explanation For Crime	Crime Focus	View Of Criminalization	Reference Chapters
Rational Choice	Individuals are able to make rational, calculating choices regarding behavior. Criminal choices are made when advantageous.	Any criminalized behavior.	State definitions of crime are unchallenged.	5
Positivism	Many distinct pathological conditions may be the genesis of criminal behavior	Any deviant or criminal behavior, but most often those traditionally perceived as relatively serious.	State definitions of crime tend to be uncritically accepted.	6, 7, 8
Interactionism	Reactions of persons and groups to particular behaviors result in some being labeled criminal.	Victimless crimes.	State definitions of and reactions to crime are critically analyzed.	9, 13
Critical	Power elite define crimes and operate agencies of social control in their own interest, preserving their position in society.	Crimes of the state and powerful individuals.	State definitions of crime are rejected.	9
Integration	Crime can best be explained by combining two or more theoretical perspectives.	Varies with theories incorporated.	Varies with theories incorporated.	10

Policy and Criminology

Criminologists for many decades were inclined to view the field as a rather pure social science pursuit of truth. There has long been a healthy criminological skepticism that seeking to answer policy questions threatened to compromise and corrupt the field. The fear was that efforts to inform policy would invite ideological bias. Herbert A. Bloch and Gilbert Geis, for example, described criminology "as a field oriented to the understanding of criminal behavior . . . and not necessarily as a pursuit dedicated to the reduction of crime" (1962:12). The renowned Edwin Sutherland (Sutherland & Cressey, 1974) clearly viewed policy matters as secondary to theoretical explanations for criminal behavior. In recent years, however, the tides have shifted in a direction of closer linkage between the work of criminologists and policy development.

The first four issues of the 2009 volume of *The Criminologist*, the official newsletter of The American Society of Criminology (ASC), published lead articles discussing that organizations growing role in advocacy of criminal justice policy (Blumstein, 2009; Clear, 2009; LaFree & Huffman, 2009; Liberman, 2009). The ASC has experienced its' own controversy on this point. To date the organization has endorsed only two specific policy positions. The first, pronounced in 1989, was to oppose capital punishment. One of the authors of this text (Brown) was editing the *The Criminologist* at the time and received a strident letter from Ernest van den Haag, a staunch proponent of capital punishment, resigning his membership in protest. Indeed, it is difficult for an organization comprised of thousands of criminologists to take specific policy stances because "the fundamental knowledge base in our field is much thinner than we would like" (Blumstein, 2009:3). In 2007 ASC adopted its second specific policy position, the view that UCR data should not be employed in ranking the safety of American cities. Although this position is less controversial, several ASC leaders have argued that the organization should avoid specific policy positions. Akiva Liberman (2009) contends that the organization should limit its advocacy to the process of testing policies through application of scientific experiments or what he calls "evidence-generating policies." Carter Hay (2009) similarly suggests that crime control policy should be routinely informed by theoretically driven program evaluations and longitudinal (across time) data. Alfred Blumstein (2009:4) suggests that the organization should limit "its advocacy role to those policies that accrue to the benefit of the field rather than to endorse public policies" and both Todd Clear (2009) and Gary Lafree & Katharine Huffman (2009) maintain that theory and research should be driving ongoing inquiry. Clear adds (2009:5) that these efforts should be "free from expectation that it necessarily bases its agenda on whatever program priorities exist in the justice's [Department of Justice] current program initiatives, or whatever program interest excites the field at the moment."

Virtually all criminologists agree that our knowledge and expertise have not contributed to policy as they should. By demanding theoretical consistency and strict scientific evaluation it is agreed that we can improve societal success in contending with the crime problem. As with any other field reliant upon scientific advances, this will require greater investments. Sadly, however, dental research is funded at a level eight times higher than all research on crime and justice matters combined

(Blumstein, 2009). We will have to do much better than that if we are to understand and ultimately reduce the crime problem in the United States. Undoubtedly, similar neglect plagues crime control research in other parts of the world. It will be necessary to shed the ideological blinders that frequently drive crime and justice policies and draw upon the scientific knowledge base of criminology if we are to more effectively contend with matters of crime and social control.

Summary

Crime is a subject of great interest to people. Many firmly believe that they understand the causes of crime and what ought to be done about it. Yet despite some surface agreement (consensus) about the ranking of crimes by "seriousness," more careful research reveals many differences (conflict) in public views on crime issues. Perhaps neither of the polar arguments about what underlies criminal law, conflict or consensus, is entirely accurate. Moreover, views of crime shift dramatically across time and space. Crime, in other words, is a relative phenomenon. The shifts them-selves are largely driven by ideology, often injecting biases that lead to emotional exploitation of the public by politicians and the media.

Depending upon their ideological leanings, criminologists vary considerably in the methods they employ, what they see as the goal(s) of criminology, what constitutes "crime," and the paradigm or theoretical perspective that guides their work.

While most criminologists view the field through a social science lens, calling for empirical testing of theories, some advocate qualitative approaches, arguing that observing statistical patterns may miss the human, or even spiritual, element of crime. More mainstream criminologists counter that the discipline must be able to predict conditions that will lead to crime and that denial of the importance of that predictive

FIGURE 1.5
Fundamental Issues in Criminology

Issue	Description
Ideology	Basic beliefs or values, usually formed early in life, and through which people filter information
Relativity of Crime	The variation in conception of what behavior is criminal from one time, place or context to another
Paradigm	A general framework or orientation, including some basic assumptions, on which theories are based
Scientific Method	An approach to the study of phenomenon that incorporates both theory and observation
Consensus	A belief that the law reflects the interest of most people in society more or less evenly
Conflict	A belief that the law disproportionately reflects the interest of a powerful minority within society

power is a reflection of ideological bias. They ask, what is criminology to do if not explain what conditions will lead to crime? While this text includes discussions of works from a variety of methodological perspectives, it reflects the dominance of the scientific approach.

Most criminologists think that their work should lead to insight regarding the causes of crime and hopefully have implications for crime prevention. Some heavily emphasize the importance of crime etiology, while others place more concern on practical implications for crime prevention. The trend in recent years, however, has been to seek a stronger tie between the scientific studies of criminologists and public policy.

Four conceptual definitions of crime for setting the parameters of criminology were reviewed in this chapter. Conceptions of crime fall along a continuum from relatively narrow to quite broad. One of the major themes of *Criminology: Explaining Crime and Its Context* is the relativity of crime, as is emphasized in the "normative" definition.

This book is organized around five paradigms for explaining crime: free will or rational choice, positivism, interactionism, the critical perspective, and integration. It is very important that you develop an ability to contrast these theoretical orientations in terms of how they tend to define crime, how they explain it, and their policy implications.

You should also consider what type of crime might best be explained by each theoretical approach. An effort has been made to present the various paradigms in a way that will broaden your thinking about the causes of crime and, most importantly, will impress upon you the complexity of criminological matters. As one of the authors routinely notes in his course syllabus, "the only erroneous understanding of crime is that it is a simple issue. Our hope is to sensitize you to the complexities of the problem so that as professionals in the field, and/or informed citizens, you will never fall prey to the 'dumb and dumber' approach of contemporary politicians in your understanding of criminal behavior."

Some other themes of this book should be clear from reading the introductory chapter. First, there is a conscious intent to take full account of gender issues in crime. Criminological works are always colored by the ideological biases of the times, as will be seen in many of the theories discussed in chapters ahead. Thus sexism has crept, or oftentimes jumped, into the accounts offered for crime. In hopes of contributing to the movement to engender criminology, the gender implications of various theories are frequently examined. Emphasis is also placed on the assumptions underlying theories and their policy implications. Finally, consistent with emphasis on the relativity of crime, examples are drawn from cultures around the world. Crime can be better understood by considering diverse social contexts. Technological changes are rapidly shrinking the globe and these changes must be incorporated in the criminological enterprise.

Key Terms and Concepts

Conflict
Consensus
Crime
Criminologist
Criminology
Critical Criminology
Ideology
 Integration
Interactionism
Legalistic Definition (of Crime)

Methodology
New Criminology
Paradigm
Positivism
Radical Criminology
Rational Choice
Relativity of Crime
Scientific Method
Theory

Key Criminologists

Hermann Mannheim
Herman Schwendinger
Julia Schwendinger

Thorsten Sellin
Edwin Sutherland
Paul Tappan

References

Akers, R.L. (1989). "A Social Behaviorist's Perspective on Integration of Theories of Crime and Deviance." In S.E. Messner, M.D. Krohn & A.E. Liska (eds.) *Theoretical Integration in the Study of Deviance and Crime*. Albany, NY: State University of New York Press.

Austin, J. (2003). "Why Criminology Is Irrelevant." *Criminology & Public Policy*, 2:557-564.

Becker, H.S. (1963). *Outsiders: Studies in the Sociology of Deviance*. New York, NY: The Free Press.

Bloch, H.A. & G. Geis (1962). *Man, Crime, and Society*. New York, NY: Random House.

Blumstein, A. (2009) "What Role Should ASC Take in Policy Advocacy?" *The Criminologist*, 34,3:1-4.

Bohm, R.M. (1986). "Crime, Criminal and Crime Control Policy Myths." *Justice Quarterly*, 3:193-214.

Box, S. (1983). *Power, Crime, and Mystification*. New York, NY: Tavistock.

Brown, S.E. (1986). "The Reconceptualization of Violence in Criminal Justice Education Programs." *Criminal Justice Review*, 11:34-42.

Chaires, R.H. & B.G. Stitt (1994). "Paradigmatic Concerns in Criminal Justice." *Journal of Crime and Justice*, 17(2):1-23.

Chambliss, W. (2004). "On the Symbiosis between Criminal Law and Criminal Behavior." *Criminology*, 42:241-251.

Clear, T. (2009). "ASC's Policy Efforts." *The Criminologist*, 34,4:1-5.

Cullen, F.T. (2005). "The Twelve People Who Saved Rehabilitation: How the Science of Criminology Made a Difference." The American Society of Criminology 2004 Presidential Address. *Criminology*, 43:1-42.

Curra, J. (2000). *The Relativity of Crime*. Thousand Oaks, CA: Sage.

Currie, E. (1999). "Reflections on Crime and Criminology at the Millennium." *Western Criminology Review*, 2:1-15. (Online)

Dunaway, G.R. & F.T. Cullen (1991). "Explaining Crime Ideology: An Explanation of the Parental Socialization Perspective." *Crime & Delinquency*, 37:536-554.

Geis, G. (1987). "Musings on Cross-Cultural Criminology." *The Criminologist*, 12:1, 4, 7 & 8.

Geis, G. & R.F. Meier (1978). "Looking Backward and Forward: Criminologists on Criminology as a Career." *Criminology*, 16:273-288.

Gelles, R.J. (1972). *The Violent Home*. Beverly Hills, CA: Sage Publications.

Gibbs, J.P. (1987). "An Incorrigible Positivist." *The Criminologist*, 4(4):1, 3 & 4.

Grasmick, H.G., R.J. Bursik & B.S. Blackwell (1993). " Religious Beliefs and Public Support for the Death Penalty for Juveniles and Adults." *Journal of Crime and Justice*, 16:59-86.

Hay, C. (2009). "Examining the Key Causes of crime in Terms of Their Potential Responsiveness to Policy Manipulation." *The Criminologist*, 34,1:5-8.

Gusfield, J.R. (1981). *The Culture of Public Problems: Drinking, Driving and the Symbolic Order*. Chicago, IL: University of Chicago Press.

Henry, S. & M. Lanier (2001). *What Is Crime? Controversies over the Nature of Crime and What to Do About It*. Lanham, MD: Rowan & Littlefield.

Hirschi, T. (1989). "Exploring Alternatives to Integrated Theory." In S.E. Messner, M.D. Krohn & A.E. Liska (eds.) *Theoretical Integration in the Study of Deviance and Crime*. Albany, NY: State University of New York Press.

Kingsnorth, R.F., L. Alvis & G. Gavia (1993). "Specific Deterrence and the DUI Offender: The Impact of a Decade of Reform." *Justice Quarterly*, 10:265-288.

LaFree, G & K. Huffman (2009). "The ASC Goes to Washington: How and Why Now?" *The Criminologist*, 34,2:1-4.

Laub, J.H. (2004). "The Life Course of Criminology in the United States: The American Society of Criminology 2003 Presidential Address." *Criminology*, 42:1-26.

Liberman, A.M. (2009). "Advocating Evidence-Generating Policies: A Role for The ASC." *The Criminologist*, 34,1:1-5.

Liederbach, J., F.T. Cullen, J.L. Sundt & G. Geis (2001). "The Criminalization of Physician Violence: Social Control in Transformation?" *Justice Quarterly*, 18:301-321.

Lynch, M.J. & P. Stretesky (2001). "Toxic Crimes: Examining Corporate Victimization of the General Public Employing Medical and Epidemiological Evidence." *Critical Criminology*, 10:153-172.

Mannheim, H. (1965). *Comparative Criminology*. Boston, MA: Houghton Mifflin.

Marvell, T.B. & C.E. Moody (2008). *"Can and Should Criminology Research Influence Policy? Suggestions for Time-Series Cross-Section Studies,"* 7:359-365.

Michalowski, R.J. (1987). "Reply to Gibbs." *The Criminologist*, 12(6):12, 18.

Miller, W.B. (1973). "Ideology and Criminal Justice Policy: Some Current Issues." *Journal of Criminal Law and Criminology*, 64:141-162.

Morris, N. & G. Hawkins (1970). *The Honest Politician's Guide to Crime Control*. Chicago, IL: University of Chicago Press.

Pfohl, S. (1977). "The Discovery of Child Abuse." *Social Problems*, 24:310-324.

Pillsbury, S.H. (1995). "Why Are We Ignored? The Peculiar Place of Experts in the Current Debate About Crime and Justice." *Criminal Law Bulletin*, 31:3-28.

Pratt, T. (2008). "Rational Choice Theory, Crime Control Policy, and Criminological Relevance." *Criminology & Public Policy*, 7:43-52.

Reiman, J.H. (1990). *The Rich Get Richer and the Poor Get Prison*, Third Edition. New York, NY: Macmillan Publishing Company.

Ren, L., J. Zhao & N.P. Lovrich (2006). "Liberal vs. Conservative Public Policies on Crime: What Was the Comparative Track Record in the 1990s?" Paper presented at the Annual Meeting of the Academy of Criminal Justice Sciences, Baltimore, MD.

Robinson, M.B. (2002). "An Analysis of 2002 ACJS Papers: What Members Presented and What They Ignored." *ACJS Today*, 22,4:1-6.

Robinson, M.B. (2004). *Why Crime? An Integrated Systems Theory of Antisocial Behavior*. Upper Saddle River, NJ: Prentice Hall.

Rush, G.E. & S. Torres (1998). *The Encyclopedic Dictionary of Criminology*. Incline Village, NV: Copperhouse Publishing.

Schwendinger, H. & J. Schwendinger (1975). "Defenders of Order or Guardians of Human Rights?" In I. Taylor, P. Walton & J. Young (eds.) *Critical Criminology*. Boston, MA: Routledge and Kegan Paul.

Sellin, T. (1938). *Culture Conflict and Crime*. New York, NY: Social Science Research Council.

Stack, S. (2003). "Authoritarianism and Support for the Death Penalty: a Multivariate Analysis." *Sociological Focus*, 36:333-352.

Sutherland, E.H. (1949). White Collar Crime. New York, NY: Dryden.

Sutherland, E.H. & D.R. Cressey (1974). *Criminology*, Ninth Edition. Philadelphia, PA: J.B. Lippincott.

Swigert, V.L. (1989). "The Discipline as Data: Resolving the Theoretical Crisis in Criminology." In S.E. Messner, M.D. Krohn & A.E. Liska (eds.) *Theoretical Integration in the Study of Deviance and Crime*. Albany, NY: State University of New York Press.

Tappan, P.W. (1947). "Who Is the Criminal?" *American Sociological Review*, 12:96-102.

Taylor, I., P. Walton & J. Young (1973). *The New Criminology: For a Social Theory of Deviance*. New York, NY: Harper Colophon Books.

Tierney, K.J. (1982). "The Battered Women Movement and the Creation of the Wife Beating Problem." *Social Problems*, 29:207-220.

Trebach, A.S. (1982). *The Heroin Solution*. New Haven, CT: Yale University Press.

Unnever, J.D., F.T. Cullen & B.K. Applegate (2005). "Turning the Other Cheek: Reassessing the Impact of Religion on Punitive Ideology." *Justice Quarterly*, 22:304-339.

Vogel, B.L. & R.E. Vogel (2003) "The Age of Death: Appraising Public Opinion of Juvenile Capital Punishment." *Journal of Criminal Justice*, 31:169-183.

Welch, M., M. Fenwick & M. Roberts (1998). "State Managers, Intellectuals, and the Media: A Content Analysis of Ideology in Experts' Quotes in Feature Newspaper Articles on Crime." *Justice Quarterly*, 15:219-241.

Williams, E.J. & M. Robinson (2004). "Ideology and Criminal Justice: Suggestions for a Pedagogical Model." *Journal of Criminal Justice Education*, 373-392.

Young, J. (1986). "The Failure of Criminology: The Need for a Radical Realism." In R. Mathews & J. Young (eds.) *Confronting Crime*. London, UK: Sage Publications.

2
The Relativity of Law and Crime

Just as our understanding of crime and deviance are relative, changing across time and space, so is the content of criminal law. Criminalization of behaviors is a political process and, therefore, the content of criminal codes varies. This chapter establishes a criminological framework by examining the concept of criminal law and its creation. It will become clear that criminal law, and thus official recognition of "crime" and "criminals," is entirely relative to time and space.

The Concept of Law

Law provides the baseline for formal social control. From a *consensus* perspective, law is thought to contribute to fair and orderly functioning within complex societies. From a *conflict* vantage point, law serves to preserve existing power relationships. Whichever perspective one subscribes to, law is a large, substantive mass that can be subdivided into criminal, civil, and administrative components. Each is designed to control behavior, but there are important differences among them.

Crimes may be acts of commission (i.e., a prohibited act such as rape or intentional marketing of unsafe products) or acts of omission (i.e., failure to perform a required act such as filing an income tax return or providing proper care to a child in one's custody). Under *criminal law* there is no crime unless the conduct prohibited or required is enunciated in the federal or state criminal code in clear and precise language. The code must also specify sanctions that may be applied as a consequence of violations. *Felonies* are the most serious offenses, punishable by execution or by imprisonment for one year or more. *Misdemeanors* may be subject to incarceration in jail for a period up to 11 months and 29 days. The least serious category of crimes are violations (sometimes called infractions or offenses), punishable by relatively small fines.

Every crime consists of specific elements that must be proved beyond a reasonable doubt to support a conviction. The *actus reus*, or "guilty act," is the physical element in a crime. It is comprised of conduct that is prohibited or of failure to act in a manner required by the criminal law. The *mens rea*, or "guilty mind," is the mental element of crime, generally termed intent. Intent ordinarily is an essential element of crime, although in some cases it may be inferred or there may be strict liability. A common example of the latter is statutory rape. The law forbids sexual intercourse with a person under a specified age, typically 18, whether or not the relationship is consensual. Figure 2.1 presents common law definitions of several major felonies.

These descriptors of criminal law do not apply to *civil law* violations (torts). The heart of the distinction between criminal and civil law involves a difference of purpose. Civil law makes no provision for penal sanctions, though it can mandate compensation. Likewise, civil law does not require the same degree of specificity as criminal law. Civil law may even be retroactive, a situation constitutionally forbidden in criminal law. Most distinctively, criminal law in theory addresses wrongs that injure society at large, while civil law violations are legal wrongs against individuals. The following two scenarios are illustrative:

- An acquaintance asks to borrow your car. You agree to loan it after she assures you that it will be properly maintained. She then drives it a long distance, severely damaging the engine as a consequence of failure to add oil. The repairs cost you $500.

- An acquaintance asks to borrow your car, but you decline to loan it. She takes the car without your permission, driving it a long distance and severely damaging the engine as a consequence of failure to add oil. The repairs cost you $500.

In both cases you have suffered and you could likely recover your $500 expense through a civil suit for damages, at least if the offender is solvent. Such a civil proceeding would place you (Smith), the injured party or plaintiff, against the offending party or defendant (Jones). The case would be designated Smith versus Jones, or in the usual form of *Smith v. Jones*. In the second scenario, the state could also prosecute Jones for violating a criminal statute prohibiting auto theft. This criminal court proceeding would be titled The State versus Jones (*State v. Jones* or *People v. Jones*) and would be distinct from your civil action.

Although a single act may involve both criminal and civil liability, the legal actions emanate from different kinds of harm. A wronged individual may sue for damages based on the notion that the state, through civil law, will serve as the arbiter of personal disputes in order to see that they are resolved in a fair manner. Criminal proceedings, however, rest on the premise that the accused has violated the rights of the community at large and has failed to meet a social obligation of all residents. In this sense, a criminal wrong is an injury to society.

The highly publicized O.J. Simpson case illustrates the dual liability, criminal and civil, that a person may face. In 1995, Simpson was acquitted of criminal homicide charges resulting from the stabbing deaths of his ex-wife Nicole Brown Simpson and her friend Ronald Goldman. In a subsequent civil case, however, Simpson was ordered to pay $25 million for the wrongful deaths. Similarly, Robert Blake, the star of the 1970s "Baretta" television show, was acquitted of murdering his wife, Bonnie

FIGURE 2.1
Common Law Definition and Elements of Major Crimes

Crime	Definition	Elements
Murder	unlawful killing of a human being by another human being with malice aforethought	1. unlawful killing 2. a human being 3. by another human being 4. with malice aforethought
Rape	the act of having unlawful carnal knowledge by a man of a woman, forcibly and against her will	1. unlawful 2. carnal knowledge (or sexual intercourse) 3. by force or fear, and 4. without the consent or against the will of the female
Robbery	felonious taking of money or goods of value with intent to steal from the person of another, or in his presence, against his will, by violence or putting him in fear	1. trespass 2. taking 3. carrying away 4. personal property 5. property of another 6. with intent to steal 7. from the person or presence of another 8. by violence or intimidation
Assault	unlawful offer or attempt to injure another, with apparent present ability to effectuate the attempt under circumstances creating a fear of imminent peril	1. an attempt or offer 2. with force and violence 3. to cause immediate physical injury to another 4. with apparent present or immediate ability
Battery	unlawful touching of the person of another by the aggressor or by some substance put in motion by him	1. unlawful 2. application of force 3. to the person of another
Kidnapping	forcibly detaining another against his or her will to unlawfully obtain ransom, or lawfully restraining another and forcibly moving the person imprisoned to another place	1. detaining another 2. by force 3. without his or her consent 4. without legal cause, and 5. moving him or her to another place or to unlawfully obtain ransom
Arson	willful and malicious burning of the dwelling house or outbuilding within its curtilage	1. burning 2. a dwelling house (or outbuilding within its curtilage) 3. house must belong to or be occupied by another person, and 4. burning must be done or caused maliciously
Burglary	breaking and entering the dwelling house of another in the nighttime with the intent to commit a felony therein	1. a breaking 2. an entry 3. a dwelling house 4. of another 5. in the nighttime 6. with intent to commit a felony therein

Source: Adapted from J.C. Klotter & J.M. Pollock (2006). *Criminal Law,* Eighth Edition. Newark, NJ: Lexis-Nexis Matthew Bender.

Bakley, but ordered to pay $30 million in a wrongful death suit. Such an outcome is confusing to many who want to conclude that the "facts" are known; the person is guilty or innocent. What cases like those of Simpson and Blake turn on, at least in part, is the standard of evidence required. A criminal conviction requires "proof beyond a reasonable doubt," while a civil judgment requires a "preponderance of evidence." The difference is substantial. To think of it in numerical terms, the weight of evidence that needs to be established for civil versus criminal liability is on the order of 50.1 as compared to 99+ percent. Other evidentiary standards vary as well. Intent is generally required in criminal, but not in civil, proceedings. Protection against self-incrimination operates in criminal proceedings, but a person may be compelled to testify in civil cases. And, as the Simpson case highlighted, the potential sanctions differ considerably. Criminal law sanctions include fines, probation, incarceration, and (in 38 states, the Federal system, and the military) capital punishment. Civil remedies, however, are limited to financially compensating or otherwise providing relief for the plaintiff. Such distinctions between types of law are summarized in Figure 2.2.

FIGURE 2.2
Summary Dimensions of the Branches of Law

	Criminal	Civil	Administrative
Victim/Complainant	State (society at large)	Individual	State (society at large)
Legality	No crime without specific law	May be broad or retroactive	May be broad or retroactive
Sanction	Fine, incarceration, probation, execution	Payment to the wronged individual	Civil fines, injunctions, closure, seizure, license revocation, criminal action
Conviction/ Judgment Standard	Proof beyond a reasonable doubt	Preponderance of evidence	Administrative determination (or proof beyond a reasonable doubt in criminal actions)
Intent	Required	Not required	Not required

Moreover, a person who is a victim of crime is, at least in principle, obligated to cooperate with the state's prosecution of the offender. Reference to victims "not prosecuting" a crime reflects a common misconception of criminal law. Actually, if a victim is unwilling to provide evidence, the state will likely drop the case. This was not done in the 1993 Detroit case of Darlene Kincer, who pleaded with the judge to drop a charge of assault with intent to murder filed against her boyfriend who, according to witnesses, dragged her with his van, resulting in the loss of an arm, a leg, and her unborn baby. The victim protested that the charges were keeping her and the assailant from patching up their relationship and that her 16-year-old daughter testified against the man only because she did not want a man in her mother's life (*Johnson City Press*, 1993). In this extreme case the judge acted consistent with the theory of criminal law that the assaultive behavior was a wrong against society.

Suppose that your campus is plagued by a serial rapist whose modus operandi (crime method) invariably entails taking women on two dates, both involving no more than tasteful entertainment and pleasant conversation. On the third date, there is forced sex in the offender's apartment. Each victim may have grounds for civil action to seek compensation for emotional trauma and physical harm. The state has an interest in prosecuting the offender to punish him for his action and to avert harm to additional persons. The rapist, like a drunk driver or a thief, is seen as posing a threat to social order. The police officers' and prosecutors' complaint that many rape victims "won't prosecute" illustrates the discrepancy between the law in books and the law in action.

Administrative law combines elements of criminal and civil law. It is based on the delegation of rule-making authority from a legislative body to a regulatory agency. Regulatory agencies have legislative (rule-making), executive (enforcement), and judicial (sanctioning) authority within the boundaries of the powers delegated to them. Civil fines, injunctions, and license suspensions may be administratively imposed or criminal proceedings initiated for violating rules of regulatory agencies. Administrative law emerged only about a century ago, but has grown enormously owing to the perceived need to control business, professional, and corporate activities. There are hundreds of regulatory agencies in the United States, including the Federal Trade Commission, the Securities and Exchange Commission, the Food and Drug Administration, the Internal Revenue Service, and the Environmental Protection Agency.

Conflict or Consensus?

Criminologists seeking to comprehend the forces underlying creation of criminal law largely subscribe to one of two general orientations, though many also favor a blend of the two. The consensus perspective portrays criminal law as a product of social needs and values, while from the conflict tradition, law is seen as the embodiment of the interests of powerful groups. Each tradition includes variations, but the two major themes may be contrasted in terms of their underlying assumptions.

The consensus perspective maintains that criminal law develops and operates in the interest of society at large. Rules and laws are viewed as serving the needs of a majority of the society. The law is deemed to formalize the norms and mores of the community. Emile Durkheim (1893/1933; 1895/1958), an early proponent of this view, conceived of crime as functional to society. Crime, he argued, delineates the boundaries of acceptable behavior and solidifies society in support of those boundaries. Consider, for example, the widespread social condemnation of use of illicit drugs. From the uncompromising messages of school programs such as DARE to the imprisonment of thousands of persons in U.S. prisons and jails, a strong statement is registered that the use of certain types of drugs crosses the boundaries of acceptable behavior. The consensus paradigm focuses on explaining behavior violating normative boundaries and, Durkheim argued, concludes that if no violations occur, society will find it necessary to create new rules so that the boundaries of behavior will be clear.

From the conflict orientation, criminal law is seen as operating in the interest of a wealthy and powerful elite whose desires often conflict with those of members of less privileged groups. Only behaviors contrary to the interests of those elite are criminalized or, at least, are enforced by the law in action. The poor and powerless bear the brunt of legal sanctions, while the elite remain untouched, despite their perpetration of acts harmful to others. Criminologists adopting a conflict perspective focus on explanations of the content of legal codes, that is, on why certain behaviors are made illegal, while others that are equally or more harmful go unattended. Thus the conflict theorist would contend that the heavy criminalization of drugs in the U.S. does not so much set broad social boundaries as it limits availability of mind altering substances to certain classes of people. Those with sufficient resources may avoid law violation by turning to legalized drugs administered through the medical establishment. Moreover, even when violations occur in the upper classes, they are less likely to be processed within the criminal justice system.

Evidence may be marshaled in support of both consensus and conflict perspectives. There is a very strong agreement among virtually all people that acts such as murder and rape (or at least some forms of taking human lives and sexual exploitation) are abhorrent and ought to be severely sanctioned by criminal codes. On the other hand, most people also believe that crimes committed by the elite are treated differently by both the legal codes and in the manner by which they are enforced. This is reflected by the person on the street who reacts to outrageous elite conduct by exclaiming that "rich people can get away with anything!"

Chapters 7 and 8 examine social structure and social process theories of crime that are rooted in a consensual view of society. Consensual theories undergird efforts at social control and provide the basis for tactics to try to keep people within the bounds of "acceptable" behavior. Chapter 9 considers social reaction theories derived from the conflict orientation and explicates the content and the administration of the criminal law in terms of these ideas.

The Relativity of Crime

It should be clear from the introductory chapter that the placement of behaviors along a continuum of social desirability is a vague, perhaps even arbitrary, process. Assessments of any given behavior may vary dramatically across time and space. As John Curra (2000:2) explains it, no human behavior "will be universally judged as improper by all people in all societies . . . at all times." What is defined as laudable behavior at one time may be labeled criminal at another. Behaviors deemed bold or courageous in one place may be regarded as criminal at another. Reactions to behavior often shift more subtly. For example, an act seen as laudable at one time or place may come to be seen as conforming, but not especially admirable, at another. Figure 2.3 illustrates a continuum of the social desirability of behavior, highlighting the most extreme shifts. Movement in and out of the "criminal" end of the continuum is what criminologists refer to as the *relativity of crime*. In an emotional debate over initiating a state lottery to fund education, a Tennessee state Senator unwittingly recognized this principle of law when he quipped, "A few years ago we put people in prison for doing what the state's about to do" (*Johnson City Press*, 2003).

Consider some examples that can be applied to Figure 2.3. In Iraq, prior to the 2003 American invasion and the fall of the Saddam Hussein regime, it was a serious crime to disfigure statues or paintings honoring the Iraqi leader. On the day Baghdad fell, however, such behavior was fostered by the authority of the new occupying American forces and widely perpetrated by crowds of citizens. Similarly, the "Boston Tea Party" was a serious criminal transgression, but soon became a nationally revered act of defiance of "unfair" law. As a general rule, revolutionaries are criminals unless or until their cause wins. George Washington, Fidel Castro, Mao Tse Tung, and Vladimir Lenin—all were largely viewed in their respective countries as heroes but, had their revolutionary efforts failed, they likely would have been executed as criminals.

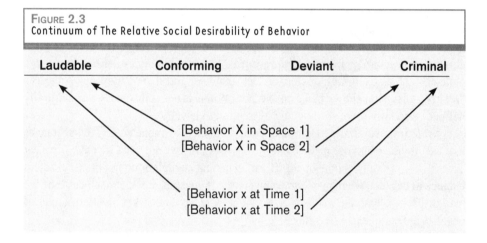

FIGURE 2.3
Continuum of The Relative Social Desirability of Behavior

Relativity across Time

Legal codes vary across time, perhaps because the interests of the elite or powerful change or perhaps because societal consensus alters. Conduct at one time in violation of legal codes may later be decriminalized and, conversely, behavior deemed acceptable later may be criminalized. Until the U.S. Supreme Court's decision in *Roe v. Wade* (1973), abortion was illegal except in a few American jurisdictions where it was permitted if the life of the pregnant woman was in jeopardy. Since 2000, however, The Center for Disease Control (CDC) in Atlanta has reported a little over 800,000 legal abortions annually (CDC, 2008). Tobacco products were freely smoked in virtually all public settings until recent years, but all states now restrict public smoking by statute. Even tobacco producing states like Tennessee and North Carolina have passed legislation broadly prohibiting smoking in restaurants and other public places.

Suicide was once against the law; now the debate centers upon physician-assisted suicide, which is legal in Oregon, but a felony in Michigan. Racial segregation used to carry the force of law in the southern United States, but now discriminatory actions constitute crimes. What used to be considered only "jokes" may now be construed legally as sexual harassment or creating a hostile environment. Even the beating of women by their spouses used to be "acceptable" behaviors within some U.S. state legal codes, providing that the man did not use a stick larger than the diameter of his thumb for the task. Things change so much, as John Curra (2000:14) notes in his excellent work, *The Relativity of Deviance*, that "change is the only real constant." The relativity of crime is the ongoing story of criminal law. The American experience with substance abuse (drugs, alcohol, and tobacco), sodomy, and rape are reviewed below as examples of changes in the law across time.

Substance Abuse

Cultures generally have rules and customs regarding the ingestion of substances into the human body. Consensus across cultures regarding what is acceptable "food" is far from complete. Mere mention of epicurean delicacies from other cultures often elicits groans and perhaps pale countenances. Does the thought of sitting down to a plate of snail, dog, termites, or chicken feet sound delightful, or disgusting? American "reality" television shows bank on the notion that eating substances not culturally defined as foods will be so shocking as to attract viewers.

Aside from cultural perceptions, we are objectively impacted by the substances that we introduce into our bodies. Nutritionists assert, "we are what we eat." If we eat excessively, we can become obese. If we do not eat enough or do not have sufficient balance in our diet, we may become emaciated. If we consume too much caffeine we may display excessive nervousness. Garlic may leave unpleasant breath or a diet of beans may lead to excessive gas.

Persons who flagrantly violate eating norms come to be defined as deviants. Ingesting the wrong substances can dramatically impact how we are seen. Imagine the public reaction in his or her homeland to the Hindu sitting down to a beef steak dinner; the Jewish person devouring a pork sandwich; the vegetarian reaction to their potatoes being fried in animal fat; or the college students discovered by campus police sharing marijuana-sprinkled brownies in their dorm. What we put in our body may be considered deviant by others, and even prohibited by criminal law. Here, we consider drugs, alcohol, and tobacco.

Drugs

Students of criminology, as well as the average citizen, are often unaware that criminalization of drugs is a twentieth-century American creation. Earlier, what we now construe as "drugs" were not dealt with differently than the vast array of other substances that arguably hold some potential for damaging health. What we now think of as "hard drugs" were readily available as medicines and even food additives. Coca-Cola once lived up to the advertisement jingle dubbing it the "real thing" by including cocaine as a stimulating ingredient, later replaced by caffeine (Drug Policy Alliance, 2002a). Our contemporary view of drugs was launched when Congress passed the *Harrison Act* in 1914, effectively criminalizing the sale and possession of opiates. Legislation criminalizing marijuana was in place in 16 states by 1930, and in all states by 1937, when the Federal government passed the *Marijuana Tax Act* (Galliher & Walker, 1977), which, oddly, did not make it illegal to possess marijuana, but did make it an offense not to have paid the exorbitant tax placed on the drug.

The past quarter century has seen a "drug war" based on the idea that law enforcement should aggressively seek to eliminate specified drugs. Consequently, the number of arrests for drug offenses has tripled since 1980, going well beyond 1.5 million annually, while the number of persons incarcerated for drug convictions has increased more than tenfold (King & Mauer, 2002), now exceeding one-half million. Seventy percent of the federal and 20 percent of the state prison population is incarcerated for drug offenses. In 2001, American police arrested 723,627 persons on marijuana charges alone, nearly half of the total arrests for drug crimes (Drug Policy Alliance, 2002c). A Federal Bureau of Prisons survey of state and federal prison inmates incarcerated for drug violations revealed that 58 percent had "no history of violence or high level drug activity" (King & Mauer, 2002:2). The costs of this war in 2003 were estimated at close to $50 billion, averaging $380 per taxpayer (Drug Policy Alliance, 2002b). The illicit drug trade reaps some $400 billion per year in untaxed sales.

According to Erich Goode (2002), the "war on drugs" represents an immense gap between an objective body of knowledge about drugs and a socially constructed image of the problem. As Craig Reinarman (2000:148) expresses it, drug scares "are a form of moral panic ideologically constructed" to assign blame for other social problems. Not unique to drugs, moral panics having been identified as responses to concerns as diverse as witchcraft, communism, child abuse, and alcohol. One of the primary tactics to create a moral panic is a campaign of misinformation. The infamous 1930s film, *Reefer Madness*, exemplifies this in the anti-marijuana campaign, depicting the drug as causing violent behavior. Politicians of that era openly attacked marijuana as a highly addictive drug. The ideologically driven campaign of information distortion continues today. In a 1997 summary of the scientific evidence regarding effects of the substance, Lynn Zimmer and John Morgan (see Chapter 13) identify some 20 common marijuana myths, summarized in Highlight 2.1.

One of the most common marijuana myths is the claim that marijuana is a *gateway drug* or "stepping stone" that leads to later use of hard drugs. The Zimmer and Morgan (1997) review concluded, however, that there is no direct causal link. Many people who use marijuana never go on to use other illegal drugs and there are no physiological factors that would lead them to do so. The observation that most hard drug users tried marijuana first is largely an artifact of the widespread popularity of marijuana and relative rarity of other drugs. Most people consume applesauce before trying caviar, but apples are not said to create a "gateway to caviar." And most sex offenders probably engage in some non-offensive touching of others prior to their assaultive behavior. All are examples of correlation, but not necessarily causality.

HIGHLIGHT 2.1
Myths, Moral Panic, and Marijuana

MYTH	FACT
Science has proven that marijuana is harmful to health.	Evidence leads to a conclusion that, while marijuana use may pose some risk, it does not appear to be great.
Marijuana has no medical benefit.	It has been found effective for treatments associated with glaucoma, cancer, and AIDS.
Marijuana is addictive.	No physical dependence is associated with it.
Marijuana causes people to go on to harder drugs.	There is no causal link between use of marijuana and other drugs.
Marijuana use is extensive because the laws do not sufficiently punish.	Sanctions have dramatically increased in recent years with widespread punishments, including arrests, prison, fines, and probation.
Marijuana causes brain damage.	No human studies have ever supported this claim.
Marijuana drains users of motivation.	While very heavy use of any substance is associated with low achievement, no greater impact has been found with marijuana than with other substances.
Marijuana use impairs memory.	Use of marijuana leads to short-term memory loss as part of the "high." There is, however, no evidence of long-term memory loss.
Marijuana use can lead to mental illness.	Marijuana use does not cause permanent or long-term psychological effects, but can produce psychological effects under its influence.
Marijuana causes aggression and crime.	Marijuana decreases aggression and is not statistically associated with crime, other than the crime of using it.
Marijuana has a widespread effect on sex hormones.	Marijuana may have some impact on fertility.
Marijuana causes birth defects.	There is no consistent evidence of differences between children with and without prenatal marijuana exposure.

HIGHLIGHT **2.1** Continued

MYTH	FACT
Marijuana impairs the immune system.	While there is no evidence of general immune system impairment, findings with tobacco warrant examination of the effects upon persons with compromised immune systems.
Marijuana is more harmful to the lungs than tobacco.	Marijuana smoke does contain carcinogens, but users, on average, consume much smaller quantities.
THC remains in the body and can alter behavior.	THC does remain in fat cells for several weeks, making it easy to detect in urine samples. However, it disappears from brain cells within hours of use.
Marijuana causes automobile accidents.	While some doses of marijuana reduce motor skills, the effect is far less than alcohol. Moreover, marijuana tends to result in more cautious behavior, while alcohol is more like to generate aggressive behavior.
Marijuana is stronger now than it used to be.	Potency appears not to have significantly changed over time.
Marijuana use can be prevented.	The success of American drug prevention programs is very limited.

Adapted from: Lynn Zimmer and John Morgan (1997). "Marijuana Myths, Marijuana Facts: A Review of the Scientific Evidence" New York, NY: The Lindesmith Center.

A welcomed kiss need not be a "gateway to rape" and going on to be a consumer of either caviar or cocaine likely says something about an individual's social background, personality traits, and the like, but nothing directly about apples or marijuana as gateway substances. There is some agreement that illegally using marijuana could provide a social gate to further drug involvement by integrating the user into a criminal subculture. The implication is that marijuana needs to be separated from the market of the harder drugs, something that could most readily be accomplished by decriminalizing it.

The history of marijuana and how it is perceived in the United States provides a remarkable example of relativity of law. Its use has moved from acceptable, or at least tolerated, behavior in the early 1900s to a serious crime by mid-century, only to become less stigmatized in the 1960s and 1970s as middle-class college students took up the habit, followed by still another harsh reversal of the pendulum in the 1980s and early 1990s, and finally greater tolerance and renewed debate for legalization at the close of the twentieth and the early years of the twenty-first century. Since 1996, for example, eight states have passed laws supportive of the medical use of marijuana (Drug Policy Alliance, 2002e).

Use of marijuana has moved about on the deviant/criminal end of the continuum of social desirability for the past three-quarters of a century. The substance continues to reflect conflict among different interest groups. It is difficult to address the topic free of ideological influence.

Alcohol

Increasingly viewed as a "drug" in recent years, "alcohol poisoning kills more people every year than all illegal drugs combined"(Drug Policy Alliance, 2002d). More people are also killed in alcohol-related automobile "accidents" each year than the total recorded in the Uniform Crime Reports as "murders." Alcohol is heavily implicated in a large portion of officially recognized murders. Marvin Wolfgang's (1958) groundbreaking homicide study found that alcohol was present in the offender and/or victim in nearly two-thirds of Philadelphia homicide cases, a finding which has largely held true at different times and places. Alcohol also takes a huge toll in non-vehicular accidents and illnesses. It can be a physically addictive substance and has afflicted millions.

Alcohol has produced death, injury and illness on such a massive scale that it dwarfs the illegal drug problem. Yet the issue is far too complex to simply support the conclusion that "there oughtta be a law" prohibiting alcohol. We had such a law in the form of prohibition mandated by the *Eighteenth Amendment* to the U.S. Constitution (1920 until 1933) and it was a dramatic failure by most measures. Just because something is objectively harmful does not mean that it will be criminalized, nor because something causes little or no harm can it be assumed that it will be legal (Goode, 2001). The relativity of crime/law is, to some degree, a function of other social forces that shape the law. Alcohol is a legal, albeit regulated, substance, and *prohibition* ended because its use was considered acceptable to a large, and powerful, segment of the population. The experiment in prohibition, in fact, is most often explained in conflict terms. It was largely supported by a politically dominant rural, Protestant, native-born constituency and opposed by a growing urban, Catholic, foreign-born population. Legal prohibition is far more effective in homogenous societies. Nonetheless, the U.S. prohibition effort did hold some marginal deterrent effect (see Chapter 5). It succeeded in reducing the overall consumption of alcohol. Its failure lay more in *unintended consequences*, such as increasing consumption of distilled spirits relative to less potent beer and providing organized crime with the classic marketing situation of a commodity in high demand, but legally prohibited.

Despite the scope of problems associated with abuse and the dramatic failure of prohibition, the topic should not be left without pointing to related contemporary trends and misinformation. Alcohol consumption has been increasingly condemned in recent years within certain contexts. There has been a substantial crack down on drunk driving (see Chapter 5) with harsher punishments and lowered blood alcohol content (BAC) levels, the raising of the legal drinking age, and greater restrictions placed on where alcohol can be consumed. These legal changes appear to have influenced social norms as well. The designated driver, for example, is a far more common role now than in years past. Likewise, the college-sanctioned "beer bust" has become a rarity and the faculty member who meets with graduate seminars at off-campus pubs is much more likely to be seen as deviant and to accrue legal liability. In short, a moral panic, albeit on a lesser scale than witnessed by marijuana use, has proliferated. One symptom of this has been an over explanation of crime by attributing unequivocal causal power to alcohol. Many commentators allude to the extraordinarily high rates of alcohol problems in the history of convicted felons and conclude that alcohol causes crime. Causality, however, as reviewed in Chapter 3, is complex. While correlation is a necessary component of causation, it is not sufficient to demonstrate causality. While the correlation is so strong that there is no question that alcohol plays an important role in crime causation, one cannot ignore the widespread use of alcohol entirely independent of crime or the fact that alcohol is merely one of a series of problems that plague most convicted felons.

Tobacco

Within the United States there has been a shift from nearly entirely unregulated public consumption of tobacco, widespread advertising, general availability to youth, and media depictions as glamorous, to the opposite; substantial regulation of public smoking, limits placed upon advertisement, prohibition of tobacco sales to minors, and frequent unfavorable depictions of smoking. Gone are the days when the tobacco industry could openly depict smoking as a healthy habit. Advertising phrases such as "to keep a slender figure," for "healthy nerves," "a flow of energy," "relief from fatigue," and "better digestion" were deployed by the tobacco industry (Blum, 1980) prior to widespread dissemination of knowledge of the harms to smokers and involuntary smokers subjected to second-hand smoke. Nor are tobacco companies of the twenty-first century likely to repeat statements from the pre-1980 era, exposing their intent to "hook" young generations on nicotine, as Highlight 2.2 illustrates.

Tobacco companies finally had to acknowledge publicly that tobacco is a harmful drug, dramatically reshape their rhetoric, and agree to pay a $246 billion settlement to help compensate the states for the health damages caused by the commodity they market. Philip Morris Company, the largest tobacco marketer, conceded in 1999 that its product both causes cancer and is addictive. In 2000, however, the Clinton administration encountered a major setback to regulation of tobacco with a 5 to 4 Supreme Court ruling that the Federal Drug Administration (FDA) lacked authority to do so. Ironically, the FDA has been granted authority to regulate only "safe" drugs, but has concluded that tobacco is an unsafe drug. Thus, the Supreme Court reasoned, in *FDA v. Brown & Williamson Tobacco Corp.* (2000) that the FDA would have no choice but to declare tobacco illegal. As that raises the tumultuous political question of criminalization, the Court concluded, "If they cannot be used safely for any

HIGHLIGHT 2.2
Tobacco Company Strategies for Hooking Kids

> One of the most obvious ways to deliver additional nicotine in a low tar cigarette is to add nicotine from an outside source . . . The problem is one of finding a source of the additional nicotine, and determining how to apply it.
>
> To ensure increased and longer-term growth for CAMEL FILTER, the brand must increase its share penetration among the 14-24 age group . . . Maintenance of the smoking habit demands that smokers receive an 'adequate' dose of nicotine (Blum, 1980).
>
> Some children are so active (hyperkinetic) that they are unable to sit quietly in school and concentrate on what is being taught. We have already collaborated with a local school system in identifying some such children presently in the third grade . . . It would be good to show that smoking is an advantage to at least one subgroup of the population. http://www.health.state.ok.us/program/tobac/doclinks.html

therapeutic purpose, and yet they cannot be banned, they simply do not fit" within FDA parameters. The industry has experienced a precipitous decline in smoking prevalence, from 42.4 percent of the American population in 1965 to 24.7 percent in 1995 (Dreyfuss, 1999). However, what used to be acceptable within the United States remains so in many less developed parts of the world. The American tobacco industry continues many of its old marketing practices outside of the U.S. where such acts remain legal. Vietnam's Ministry of Health reported that at the 1998 Hanoi Tet festival, Philip Morris Tobacco Company provided "a large tent with Marlboro horses to ride on for children, and young, nicely dressed cowboy girls offered single cigarettes free of charge to young boys" (Dreyfuss, 1999). A statement by Essential Action, an anti-tobacco organization, and some 30 women's, girl's, and public health organizations noted, "The tobacco industry is aggressively targeting women and girls in developing countries with seductive advertising that blatantly exploits ideas of independence, power, emancipation, and slimness . . . The launching of Virginia Slims in Hong Kong at a time when less than 2% of Hong Kong women under the age of 40 smoke exemplifies industry attempts to create a market"(Intl-tobacco, 2000). The report noted the bestowing of gift packs for Taiwanese women containing Virginia Slim Light cigarettes and lighters, the use of female pop stars to advertise the products, the low awareness of the hazards of smoking in these international "growth markets," and the wide array of cigarette advertising in these countries. Consequently, rates of female smoking, especially in developing countries, are increasing dramatically, as are the projections of premature smoking-related deaths. The tobacco industry's history of targeting youth, women and the Third World as "growth markets" can be traced back more nearly 30 years (Brown, 1982), but has increased as domestic sales have declined. It is the relativity of law that both causes and allows this. As tobacco has been increasingly defined as a harmful and addictive drug, shifting legal and extralegal responses have reduced conventional domestic markets, resulting in increased industry efforts to pursue nonconventional and less-regulated nondomestic markets. While the health impacts of smoking remain the same, social and legal responses have changed significantly.

Sodomy

Much of the debate regarding criminalization and decriminalization involves activities that, when criminalized, are frequently called *victimless crimes*, owing to the absence of a complaining victim (see Chapter 13). *Sodomy* is a salient example of this variety of crime, and it has been especially conspicuous with the focus on homosexuality. A U.S. Supreme Court decision, *Bowers v. Hardwick* (1986), upheld a Georgia sodomy statute as it applied to homosexuals. That statute declared, "A person commits the offense of sodomy when he performs or submits to any sexual act involving the sex organs of one person and the mouth or anus of another. . . ." (Georgia Code Annotated, 1984). The law provided for one to 20 years of imprisonment.

A Tennessee case was prosecuted shortly after the *Bowers* decision, but based on sodomy interpretations under common law, and thus applying to all persons. Clearly, however, it was being rarely enforced and then only against homosexuals. The incident, occurring on a college campus, involved police investigation of a parked car during late hours, revealing that it was occupied by two men, one of whom was not wearing pants. Both men were arrested and charged with "crimes against nature," interpreted at the time as any form of oral or anal sex. The prosecuting District Attorney General noted in regard to the gay community, "It's high time the gay community realizes it [homosexuality] is not simply an alternate lifestyle—it is a crime." He said he was "concerned about it [homosexuality] in this community. In light of the apparent ease of which I have observed many of these people to engage in homosexual encounters . . . they are endangering everyone by spreading AIDS" (*Johnson City Press*, 1987:3). The two men received five-year sentences, the legal minimum for sodomy or "crimes against nature." The *Bowers* case was overturned in Georgia in 1998, while Tennessee replaced its common law approach with a "Homosexual Acts" provision in the state criminal code in 1989. That legislation was overturned in *Campbell v. Sundquist* (1996).

While in 1960 sodomy was criminalized in all 50 states, the United States Supreme Court took note in *Lawrence v. Texas* (2003) that the number had dwindled to 13 (four, including Texas, were for homosexual sodomy only) and used this as part of their rationale in stating that the *Bowers* decision was wrong. *Lawrence* renounced a law prohibiting sodomy only for homosexuals. Nine states retain anti-sodomy laws, with Virginia having refused to repeal their law in 2004. Yet it is highly doubtful that any prohibition of sodomy among consenting adults in noncommercial relationships can meet the privacy standard set by the court in *Lawrence*. *Highlight 2.3 depicts how* relativity (across time) has shifted sodomy from a criminal act in all 50 states to a constitutionally protected privacy right in a little over 40 years.

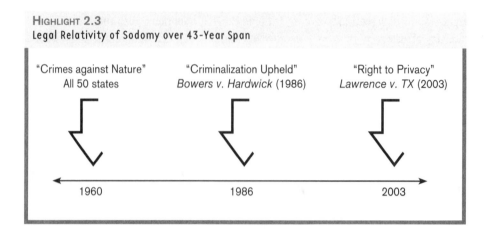

HIGHLIGHT 2.3
Legal Relativity of Sodomy over 43-Year Span

"Crimes against Nature"   "Criminalization Upheld"   "Right to Privacy"
All 50 states   *Bowers v. Hardwick* (1986)   *Lawrence v. TX* (2003)

1960   1986   2003

Rape

Many consider rape as a clear example of consensus—a crime so objectionable that it was a capital (death penalty) crime in America until 1977 when that penalty for rape was invalidated by *Coker v. Georgia* (1977). Yet what constitutes a rape varies widely across time and space. Under common law rape required forcible and non-consensual penetration of a woman's vagina by the penis of a man not her husband. It was legally impossible both for a man to rape his wife and for a man to be a victim of rape. Clearly, however, there have always been both husbands who brutally forced their wives to engage in sexual acts against their will and men who were sexually violated against their will. Such seemingly common sense observations (by today's vantage) played a role in the wholesale reconstruction of American rape laws over the past quarter century. The changes, illustrating the relativity of rape, fell into three broad categories: marital rape, reconceptualization as gender neutral and altering definitions of force and consent.

Under common law women were viewed as property and marriage as a contract that entitled the husband to sexual services of the wife. This influence on the definition of rape persisted until the 1970s. Not until 1976 did the first state redefine forced sexual intercourse with a woman by her husband as rape and the definition of spousal rape remains quite diverse (Hasday, 2000). The case of *State v. Dominy* (1997) in Highlight 2.4 illustrates how bizarrely the legal rationale seems to have evolved in some states, although the spousal exclusion in Tennessee has since been eliminated.

By substituting the penetration of any sexual orifice by any object for the common law penile-vaginal penetration, rape in recent years has been more broadly defined in two senses. First, it now encompasses a wider range of sexual violations. Secondly, it facilitated transition to a gender neutral crime. Rape now recognizes victimized male and female offenders, crimes that previously were legal impossibilities. Consequently, one form of "new" rape, examined below, that has emerged in the public eye involves young male victims and adult female rapists. Such behavior is not new, but was accorded little attention and largely viewed quite differently a couple of decades ago.

State v. Dominy: Spousal Rape Contingent on Dog

The Tennessee State Supreme Court has offered some interpretation of that state's "Limited spousal exclusion" for the crime of rape. Section 39-13-507 of the Tennessee Code Annotated reads:

(a)   A person does not commit an offense under this part if the victim is the legal spouse of the perpetrator except as provided in subsections

(b)(1)   "Spousal Rape" means the unlawful sexual penetration of one spouse by the other where:
    (A)   The defendant is armed with a weapon or any article used or fashioned in such a manner to lead the victim to reasonably believe it to be a weapon;
    (B)   The defendant causes serious bodily injury to the victim; or
    (C)   The spouses are living apart and one (1) of them has filed for separate maintenance or divorce

The facts of the case, originally presented in *State v. Dominy*, 1997 were as follows:

Terry Allen Dominy of Hamilton County, Tennessee, asked his wife to have sexual intercourse with their dog. She refused his demand and he bound her hands and feet with duct tape. He then prompted the dog to have sex with his wife by manipulating it's penis to arousal and placing it in his wife's vagina. The wife said that Dominy had been drinking and smoking dope. She testified that the assault lasted some 10 to 15 minutes with the defendant watching and laughing. He then had intercourse with her himself. He was convicted of aggravated rape and sentenced to three 25-year prison terms.

On appeal Dominy claimed a marital exemption for rape and the Tennessee Court of Criminal Appeals agreed, overturning his conviction. The Tennessee State Supreme Court reversed once again, however, concluding that because the 68-pound German Shepard had snapped at the woman, this constituted the "weapon" necessary under subsection (b)(1)(A) under the Limited Spousal Exclusion. In still another appeal to the state Supreme Court in 2001, the court declared that since Dominy had not originally been charged with spousal rape, even though the prosecutor was well aware that he was married to the victim, the state had forfeited its right to prosecute for that offense. Dominy was set free (*State v. Dominy*, 2001).

The force/consent element of rape also has changed in a number of ways in recent years. One of them is the evolution of statutory rape laws. This offense holds the perpetrator criminally liable even if the sexual activity is purely consensual, indeed, even if the two parties assert deep and abiding love for one another. The legal concept is to protect the victim based upon the logic that they are incapable of formulating reasoned consent due to their young age. Until the 1970s statutory rape could only be committed by a male upon a female and the male offender could be the same age, or younger, than the female victim. Beginning in 1971, however, statutory rape laws began incorporating 2 to 6 year age spans between a younger victim and an older offender, as well as redefining the offense as gender neutral (Cocca, 2002a). Tracing the political process that produced age spanned statutory rape legislation, Carolyn Cocca (2002a) found that conservatives, church groups and anti-abortion activists campaigned against them out of fear that the exemption of similar aged persons from rape liability would license teens for sexual activity. As a result of these political debates different definitions of statutory rape prevailed from state to state, with the age of consent varying from 14 to 18, although most have redefined the crime as gender neutral and incorporated some age span.

Another study undertaken by Cocca (2002b) suggests that the concept of a moral panic can be applied to a recent trend for state's to toughen statutory rape laws to combat teen pregnancies. She contended that while the purported rationale is to protect young girls from older predatory men and to reduce public assistance to unwed mothers, the data belie these goals, revealing that only 8 percent of the fathers of pregnant teens could potentially be subject to prosecution for statutory rape. This is because nearly two-thirds of the child bearing teens are old enough for consensual sex (18 or 19), many of the 15 to 17 year-olds were impregnated by boys of the same age and some are legally married. Thus the real goal arguably is to redefine teen sex in terms that facilitate control of a morally objectionable behavior. Consequently the recent legislative trend has been cast in a light of predatory men victimizing teenage females. The result is statutory rape laws congruent with a conservative agenda of:

> . . . targeting of the poor, pregnant teen and her equally poor and immoral impregnator: few would stand up to defend non-marital adolescent sexuality and pregnancy; the target populations are disempowered by their gender, age, class, race and/or ethnicity . . . (Cocca, 2002b:8-9).

Moral outrage regarding sexual liaison between adolescent males and adult women also fueled the revisions of statutory rape laws. Reviewing the history of California's 1993 legislation, Cocca (2002a) recounted a 1992 case of a 40-year-old woman having sex with eight 14- to 16-year-old boys, generating outrage that she was not eligible for a statutory rape charge. This was followed the next year with publicity surrounding a high school football coach who pressed one of his players into sexual activity with his wife an estimated 1,000 times, conduct again not falling within the bounds of statutory rape as then defined. Later in 1993 California passed legislation that provided both broadened and toughened statutory rape parameters, including jail time even for sexual partners within the three-year span of a person under 16 years of age and a gender neutral provision. Similar legal changes in the state of Washington set the stage for the internationally known case of Mary Kay Letourneau that illustrates a number of issues bound up in the relativity of law.

At the time of her statutory rape case in 1997, Mary Kay Letourneau was 34 years old, and her victim, Vili Fualaau, was 12. At the time Letourneau was a sixth-grade teacher and Fualaau her student. Letourneau had known him since she was his second-grade teacher. She was widely regarded as a model teacher and he as an artistically talented student whom she continued to tutor over the next four years. Letourneau was married and the mother of four children, aged 3 to 12, when Fualaau was assigned to her sixth-grade class. As in her work role, she had an excellent reputation as a mother as well. But important in the eyes of many commentators, Letourneau was struggling with several problems at that time. She and her husband had filed for bankruptcy, openly acknowledged marital strife, and she had suffered a miscarriage. Most significantly, her father, to whom she was very close, succumbed to cancer. Such stresses are sometimes considered sufficient to account for deviant behaviors through "strain" explanations (see Chapter 7). Letourneau was also, however, diagnosed with bipolar disorder (see Chapter 6), a mental illness based upon a chemical imbalance in the brain that is strongly associated with bizarre and irrational behaviors. The diagnosing physician identified classic signs of this mental disorder that she displayed as mania, hypersexuality, and high risk-taking behavior. Letourneau was prescribed Depakote (divalpruex sodium), a milder drug than the lithium that was, at that time, more traditionally used to treat bipolar disorder. And again, she displayed a classic sign of the disease in her later refusal to take the medication and her denial of the disorder. But is it more in order to seek an explanation of her deviance or to consider why the state of Washington chose to brand Letourneau a child rapist? Analysis of this event pits positivism (e.g., strain and mental illness) against interactionism (e.g., labeling).

The concept of relativity is particularly appreciated from the interactionist paradigm. Consider how events unfolded and decide which you find to be the most important question. The young Fualaau was large and exceptionally mature for his age, described by his mother as "an old soul trapped in a young body" (Cloud, 1998:3). He pursued Letourneau sexually, bragged to friends that he would have sex with her and even placed a $20 bet that he would. That bet was won shortly after the school year ended, and just before Fualaau's thirteenth birthday. The sexual relationship continued until February, 1997, when Letourneau was arrested in the principal's office of her school as a consequence of anonymous charges leveled by one of her husband's relatives. To add to the shock of the case, Letourneau was pregnant with the boy's child, who was born in May, 1997. Letourneau was convicted of second-degree child rape and sentenced to seven and one-half years in prison, with all but two-and-a-half months suspended in lieu of her agreement to continue medication for her bipolar disorder and to have no unsupervised contact with minors. Shortly after her release, however, she violated both agreements, again becoming pregnant by Fualaau. She was returned to prison in February, 1998, and completed her original 7 1/2-year sentence in 2005. The two were married later that year in a lavish wedding.

Letourneau saw herself as a victim of the relativity of law. In her earlier words, "When the relationship started, it seemed natural. What didn't seem natural was that there was a law forbidding such a natural thing" (Alexander, 1997:1). As Fualaau then looked at it, "It's unfair. I want Mary to be with me and the kids" (*People Weekly*, 1998:1). While on tour to publicize a book (titled, *One Crime, Love*) released by the couple, Fualaau said that Letourneau was "a victim at the same time they say she's a criminal" (Associated Press, 1998). With her prison time behind her, Letourneau and her husband, Fualaau, are now raising their two daughters. As Greg Olson, author of one of the books about her commented, she has always had a personal need to "prove to the world that this is a love story and not a crime story." Relativity of crime is indeed poignant.

In a 2004 case of striking similarity, 27-year-old Tennessee teacher Pamela Rogers Turner was charged with 13 counts of statutory rape of a 13-year-old male student. As in the Letourneau case, the relationship was revealed by an anonymous tip. Turner also was able to initially avoid prison time through a plea bargain that sent her to jail for 6 months and agreeing to have no further contact with her victim. Within two months of her release, however, she was twice arrested and charged with violating her probation by contacting the boy, placing her at risk, like Letourneau, of having to serve a 7-year prison sentence.

In 2005 another statutory rape case involving a strikingly attractive 23-year-old Florida female teacher and a 13-year-old male student caught national attention. Debra Lafave pled guilty in one county to lesser charges and agreed to three years of house arrest. Charges were dropped in another county because the parents of the boy did not want him to have to testify. Lafave, like Letourneau, was diagnosed with bipolar disorder (see Chapter 6) and stated that she felt the mental disorder "had a lot to do with" her behavior (Fox News, March 22, 2006).

Major procedural changes in prosecuting rape have been incorporated in what are called *rape shield laws*. Historically criminal procedure for the crime of rape was heavily biased against female victims in order to minimize the likelihood of false rape accusations against men. Under common law women were required to physically resist, quickly report the crime and to face hostile questioning in court. These views were evident in the legal and procedural requirements of rape cases until addressed in the rape reform era that began in the 1970s. Rape reform was encouraged, in part, by the widespread view that victims of rape were twice victimized, once by the rapist, and again in court proceedings. The rape victim could expect to be accused of consenting to sex with the rapist, disparaged by defense claims of a pattern of immoral behavior and to be embarrassed by revelation of irrelevant sexual history. Rape shield laws imposed substantial limits on the ability of the defense to introduce information or pursue a line of questioning about the history and character of the alleged victim, swinging the procedural balance in the direction of the victim's interests. The 2003-2004 Kobe Bryant case, however, was viewed by many as a major erosion of rape shield laws. The victim eventually decided that she would not testify and charges were dropped, but not before a lot of derogatory information about her was made public by the defense team and allowed by the judge.

The term *post-penetration rape* was introduced in 1991 (McLellan, 1991) and gained appreciable legal precedent in the recent California *In re John Z* (2003) case. Post-penetration rape occurs when a woman has given her consent to engage in sexual intercourse, but then withdraws the consent during the sex act, and the male partner refuses to immediately withdraw from the activity. While *In re John Z* concluded that a rape has taken place whenever consent is withdrawn during sexual intercourse, but the male participant continues, it has been objected that this redefinition is counterproductive. Some legal theorists have argued that rather than a "rape," this should be designated some other form of sexual assault, as "calling the two scenarios 'rape' confounds the definition of the crime. Moreover, doing so demeans the victims of traditional rape" (Fradella & Brown, 2003:13). Others argue that a rape is a rape is a rape. From the vantage of relativity of crime neither is correct. A rape, or any other crime, is whatever those with the political influence to define it declare at any given time and place.

Relativity across Space

Just as the law is not fixed across time, it varies from one location to another. What is defined as crime may differ dramatically from one country to another or between locations within a specific country. Differences in norms and laws often lead to cross-cultural conflicts. The "ugly American" image may be largely a consequence of an affluent population traveling widely within other cultures, while remaining ignorant of their norms. In some instances, the conflict may be rooted less in ignorance than in *ethnocentrism* (believing that the customs and values of one's own culture are superior to those of others). In some instances, the norm violations will be regarded not only as insulting, but as criminal behavior.

Since the terrorist hijacking and subsequent suicide airline crashes into the World Trade Center on September 11, 2001, attention has focused on the conflict between Islamic extremists and Western culture. This is the highest-profile, contemporary example of the relativity of law across cultures. Those who perpetrate such attacks are labeled "terrorists" in the West, are loathed, and more vigorously pursued than any other type of "criminals." It was labeling them as outlaw terrorist-sponsoring regimes that provided American justification for the invasions of Afghanistan and Iraq. Yet, those same "criminals" are widely regarded as martyrs within Islamic cultures.

The clash between Islamic and Western conceptions of law extends far beyond terrorism and military issues. What is regarded as criminal under fundamentalist Islamic law is often shocking from a Western perspective. The plight of two American aid workers, dimly disguised missionaries, serving in Afghanistan at the time of the September 11 attacks, is illustrative. Dayna Curry and Heather Mercer were arrested by Taliban authorities for being in a private home and preaching Christianity, charges punishable by death under Afghani law at that time. Missionaries were not allowed in the country, so the two women had entered under the auspices of an "aid" organization. However, they had in their possession Bibles, a film about Jesus, a book titled *Sharing Your Faith with a Muslim*, and a paper that documented the frequency of a Christian broadcasting station (Hoover, 2002). The Prime Minister of Australia (two Australian natives were also arrested) bluntly expressed Western reaction, proclaiming "We can't have a situation where the safety and treatment of people who are doing nothing but preaching Christianity are put under threat" (cited in Hoover, 2002). Preaching Christianity, however, is a serious crime in most Islamic countries, although often overlooked by the law in action. In the aftermath of the 2010 Haiti earthquake, 10 American missionaries from an Idaho church found themselves facing kidnapping charges for attempting to move 33 children across the border, to the Dominican Republic. Child trafficking is a pervasive problem in Haiti; a single count of kidnapping carries a possible prison sentence of five to 15 years.

FIGURE 2.4
Relativity of Law across Space: Islamic versus Western Conceptions of Law

- A 1999 report of the execution of an Afghan woman for killing her husband in a domestic dispute detailed the public stoning before thousands of citizens in a stadium. The crowd included many women with their children. Following the execution there were widespread shouts of "God is great!"

- A Nigerian couple was sentenced to death by stoning for "having sex outside of marriage" (*Johnson City Press*, 2002b).

- Reporting another Nigerian stoning sentence for adultery, a 2002 AP report (*Johnson City Press*, 2002c) noted that the rash of such sentences by the Islamic courts represented a struggle between northern, predominantly Muslim states and the predominantly Christian southern states. In this case, the female offender gave birth more than nine months after a divorce. The court delayed her execution until 2004 to allow time for her to nurse her baby.

- In an article titled "Driving While Female," the New York Times (Dowd, 2002) reported on 47 Saudi women who defied the law by driving cars in Riyadh, the capital of Saudi Arabia. Islamic clerics responded to the violation by labeling the women "whores" and "harlots." They lost their jobs and passports, experienced death threats, and had to agree to never speak of their short-lived act of protest. When a Saudi man serving on the King's Consultive Council again raised the issue in 2005, he was soundly repudiated.

- Iran tortured and hung two 16-year-olds and an 18-year-old boy for having gay sex on July 19, 2005. It is estimated that more than 4,000 Iranians have been executed for homosexual behavior since clerical rule was established in 1979.

Figure 2.4 summarizes news reports of other "criminal" behavior that has been harshly dealt with in Islamic countries. These offenses, and Islamic justice responses to them, highlight the crime definition gap between cultures.

Even matters seemingly as innocuous as humor fall within the confines of relativity of crime. What is laughed about in one culture may constitute deviant or criminal words in another. Political figures, for example, traditionally provide fodder for American humor. Whether crude sexual innuendos about former President Bill Clinton or derogatory "Bushisms" belittling President George W. Bush, such caustic commentary is characteristic of American culture. Other cultures, however, view such words as deviant or criminal. Thai culture, for example, regards derogatory humor directed at King Bhumibol Adulyadej as not just disrespectful but criminal. The owner of a Thai-themed Philadelphia lounge was dismayed that her advertisement, incorporating a photo touched up to present the elderly Adulyadej as a hip and funky figure, led to numerous diplomatic protests by the Thai government (*Johnson City Press*, 2002a).

The world witnessed even more serious cultural clashes of humor in 2006. The publication of a series of cartoons in a Danish newspaper sparked diplomatic retaliation, huge demonstrations throughout the Muslim world, boycotts of Danish products, burning of Danish embassies, and loss of lives as demonstrations turned violent. Under Islam any representations of Muhammad are prohibited. The Danish caricatures depicted the Prophet in such unflattering poses as wearing a bomb on his turban and admonishing suicide bombers to stop because the supply of virgins was exhausted. Humor of this sort is viewed as blasphemous by Muslims and is therefore prohibited under Islamic law. One Pakistani cleric announced a bounty in excess of a million dollars for killing the cartoonists who have since been extended security protection by their government.

For their part, most Danes were caught in an unusual quandary. Denmark has long had a reputation as a tolerant country, but also one that places a premium on freedom of expression. They were unaccustomed to seeing their flag burned, being targeted by boycotts and held in disdain by other cultures. Yet the conflict pitted religious tolerance against freedom of expression. The Danish editor, Flemming Rose, who released the cartoons made the case for the latter in this way:

> I think it's problematic when a religion tries to impose its taboos and values on the larger society. When they ask me not to run those cartoons, they are not asking for my respect. They're asking for my submission . . . To me, those cartoons are saying that some individuals have hijacked, kidnapped and taken hostage the religion of Islam to commit terrorism" (Fleishman, 2006:2).

Humor, like all other matters, is relative. What is a laughing matter in one culture may be criminal in another. In short, as we study crime, we must avoid the simplistic thinking that a crime is a crime is a crime. What is a crime depends on where one is, when one is there and what interest groups have sufficient power incorporate their ideologies into the law.

The Criminal Justice System

To understand crime and criminals, it is essential to know something of the process whereby the law is used to officially label people as criminals. We have already seen that not all conduct harmful to society is designated criminal, nor can everything prohibited or required by law be justified under the notions of safety and harm to society. There is no law in most states against failing to help a drowning person, for instance, though this might be easily done. However, it is illegal to gamble at work on a football game—though not in Las Vegas. It is generally legal for a 19-year-old to have a string of sultry love affairs, but not to drink a beer. Crime is relative in the eyes of the beholder and to who has the power to define particular behaviors as crimes. Moreover, the criminal law is applied differentially. Only a very small portion of crimes lead to official action. Typically, a 19-year-old may drink alcoholic beverages with older friends without drawing the ire of the juvenile/criminal justice systems, but on occasion such behavior may be dealt with very severely due to campaigns by moral entrepreneurs or the lodging of a complaint by someone holding a grudge against one of the persons in the drinking group. Understanding discrepancies between the law in books and the law in action helps explain the criminal justice process.

There are important interdependencies between criminal justice and criminology. The focus of criminology is on explaining crime, while criminal justice is more concerned with societal, and particularly official, reactions to crime and criminals. Criminology, consequently, tends to be more theoretical and to include explanations that do not have immediate, or at least not readily adoptable, policy implications. Criminal justice is often more descriptive and is more likely to suggest courses of action for criminal justice practitioners. But the distinction is a matter of emphases, not mutual exclusivity, and many students of crime use these disciplinary labels interchangeably. Academic labels aside, a thorough familiarity with criminal justice is essential to understanding and explaining crime. Conversely, official reactions to crime and offenders cannot be improved without sound theoretical premises.

The most common way to organize knowledge of criminal justice is to do so in reference to its three broad components: police, courts, and corrections (Bernard & Engel, 2001). That approach is taken here, with each component being viewed in terms of four specific goals of criminal justice: (1) deterrence, (2) incapacitation, (3) rehabilitation, and (4) retribution.

Goals of Criminal Justice

Criminal justice is intended to link practice with broader social goals that, in turn, are associated with certain values and assumptions. Some goals are more sensitive to the interests of society; others are more attuned to individual needs. The popularity of each goal varies with the social priorities and elite interests of the time. Generally, as noted above, criminal justice theory explicitly recognizes four formal goals: deterrence, incapacitation, rehabilitation, and retribution. Each involves specific policies, though a particular practice in criminal justice may accommodate two or more distinct goals.

Deterrence (examined at length in Chapter 5) uses punitive sanctions to dissuade persons from committing criminal offenses in the future. The sanctions can be administered either to "teach a lesson" to the convicted offender (*special deterrence*) or to serve as an example to others of the perils of criminality (*general deterrence*). Deterrence theory and policy revolve around modes of punishment delivery, and focus particular attention on police, prosecutorial, and judicial operations. Deterrence, then, has the pragmatic goal of preventing crime by scaring offenders or potential offenders with the threat or the application of punitive sanctions. This goal has been increasingly emphasized since the 1970s.

Incapacitation seeks to reduce or to eliminate the capacity of offenders to commit additional crimes. Capital punishment is the only conclusive means of incapacitating offenders. In the past, criminal transgressors were exiled, in part for incapacitative purposes. The English transported offenders first to America and later to Australia. This measure obviously affected only the capacity to commit offenses in England, not in the locales to which the offenders were sent. Futurists speak of kindred incapacitative schemes that rely on fantastic technology, such as the crystal prisms utilized to exile condemned villains in the motion picture "Superman" saga or the penal space colonies depicted in the motion picture "Star Trek" adventures. Other advocates of incapacitation promote surgical stratagems such as lobotomies and castration, but evidence suggests that such awful incapacitative schemes are not foolproof. Reviewing studies of castrated Danish sex offenders, for instance, Robert Martinson observed of their recidivism that it was "not, interestingly enough, a rate of zero; where there's a will, apparently there's a way" (1974:36).

Imprisonment is the primary criminal justice practice designed to achieve incapacitative goals. There is common sense in the notion that persons imprisoned will be kept from criminal activity. Clearly, however, incarceration is not a completely incapacitative measure because imprisoned offenders may victimize institutional staff and other inmates and, on occasion, escape. A larger concern is whether imprisoned offenders "make up for lost time" by committing crime at a higher rate or of a more serious nature following release than would have been the case had they not been institutionalized. If so, the net incapacitative effect could diminish to zero or even to a negative value. The goal of incapacitation has contributed to increased recourse to prisons in recent years, particularly for offenders labeled "career criminals."

Rehabilitation is designed to change offenders by removing the motivation to engage in criminal behavior. The assumption behind rehabilitation is that behavior can be modified by altering attitudes, values, skills, or constitutional features that cause criminal behavior. Based on a medical model, rehabilitation assumes that appropriate treatments may be prescribed according to the nature of the offender's defect. Rehabilitation may mandate treatment modes as diverse as job training, psychotherapy, and methadone maintenance for heroin addicts.

The goal of rehabilitation dominated the administration of justice from the beginning of the twentieth century until the emergence of an anti-rehabilitation movement in the early 1970s. Rehabilitation was based on optimism that it could lower recidivism rates. At the same time, rehabilitation was considered a compassionate and benevolent response to offenders. In the early 1970s, however, skepticism began to fester, based on disbelief that rehabilitation works, discomfort with the inequities that accompany individualized decisionmaking necessitated by the medical model, and doubt about the accuracy of predictive restraint (e.g., parole) decisions. Rehabilitation and associated policies and procedures (such as probation and parole) in the administration of justice have been de-emphasized in recent years. The issue of the earlier promise of rehabilitation, however, is far from resolved (e.g., Andrews et al., 1990a; 1990b; Cullen, 2005; Logan & Gaes, 1993).

Deterrence, incapacitation, and rehabilitation are all utilitarian goals of criminal justice; the assumption is that they can prevent crime. *Retribution* is based solely on moral reprobation or outrage at criminal misconduct. It involves the punishment of past wrongdoing in order to achieve a moral balance. Retributivists contend that crime, a violation of the rights of others, requires imposition of a penalty that will remove the advantage gained by the offender and restore social equilibrium. Punishment, then, is morally required.

The punishment must also be proportionate to the harm caused or risked, although mercy can be extended once it is acknowledged that the punishment is deserved. Retributivists argue that their position leaves the human dignity of the offender intact.

We punish animals to train them, but humans are punished because they deserve it. As with deterrence, human rationality is presumed. In contrast, rehabilitation assumes that the individual is defective. Most importantly, retributivists assert that their position provides the only justification for punishment. In recent years retribution, sometimes called *just deserts*, has become widely supported as the major goal of criminal justice. Research by Harold Grasmick and his colleagues has identified support of retributive rationale for punishment partially as a function of fundamentalist religious beliefs (Grasmick et al., 1992). The Old Testament reference to "eye for eye, tooth for tooth" (Leviticus, 25:17-22) underlies this belief.

In reinstating capital punishment in *Gregg v. Georgia* (1976) after a four-year court-decreed moratorium, the U.S. Supreme Court explicitly acknowledged retribution as a valid punishment goal. This, however, is a moral question and "no empirical research can tell us if the argument is 'correct' or 'incorrect.' Empirical studies can neither answer the question of what specific criminals (or noncriminals) 'deserve,' nor settle debates over other moral issues surrounding capital punishment" (Radelet & Akers, 1996:1). Deterrence and incapacitation, on the other hand, are goals that can be empirically assessed in relation to capital punishment.

FIGURE 2.5
The Goals of Criminal Justice

Goal	Definition
Deterrence	Prevention of crime by instilling a fear of punishment in potential offenders.
Incapacitation	Prevention of crime by physically eliminating capacity for crime, usually through imprisonment.
Rehabilitation	Preventing additional criminal acts by offenders through elimination of their motives to offend.
Retribution	Punishment of offenders because they deserve it as a consequence of their law violations.

These aims of criminal justice can be complementary. Andrew von Hirsch (1976) argued that just deserts alone might justify a system of punishment, but that the other aims, especially deterrence, are useful supplementary crime control strategies. Similarly, David Fogel (1975), in advocating a retribution-based "justice model" for corrections, acknowledged a role for rehabilitative services, so long as the offenders are volunteers. James Q. Wilson and Richard Herrnstein (1985) saw some virtue in diversity of criminal justice goals and approvingly discussed the merits of retribution along with the usefulness of incapacitation and deterrence.

Incongruities often arise among these goals, however. When should societal interest in deterrence or incapacitation take priority over just deserts? When should the rehabilitative needs of offenders take precedence over protection of society through deterrent or incapacitative measures? Jack Henry Abbott had been in prison some 20 years when he so impressed Norman Mailer with his literary talent that Mailer befriended him and advocated his parole, based largely on a rehabilitative rationale. Before Abbott's release, Mailer wrote these words in his preface to Abbott's book depicting his prison experience:

> It is certainly time for him to get out. There is a point past which any prisoner can get nothing more from prison, not even the pres-ervation of his will, and Abbott, I think, has reached these years. Whereas, if he gets out, we may have a new writer of the largest stature among us . . . (Abbott, 1981:xviii).

Abbott was paroled, and days later murdered a young man working in a restaurant with whom Abbott had a trivial disagreement. Before his release, Abbott had said of freedom:

> I have the right, at least, to walk free at some time in my life even if the odds are by now overwhelming that I may not be as other men (Abbott, 1981:198).

Did Abbott have that right? Or did society and his murder victim have the right to be protected from him? And what of those who are suffering in prison, but would use freedom in a socially acceptable and productive manner? This is the crux of the dilemma in selecting goals for criminal justice. It is not an easy task, and clarity of goals must precede sound policy.

By examining the provisions of legal codes for every state correctional depart-ment, Velmer Burton, Gregory Dunaway, and Renee Kopache (1993) depict the status of formal criminal justice goals. They found that the majority of states have legislatively endorsed more than one goal. Rehabilitation remained the most common goal despite a conservative "get-tough" attitude toward crime that was taking hold at that time. The most recent legislative pronouncements, however, were nonrehabilita-tive. Incapacitation (custody/control) was the second most frequently legislated goal, followed by retribution (punishment/discipline), and deterrence.

Which of these goals is just? According to those who fully appreciate the relativity of crime, a measure of injustice is inevitable. Take the Letourneau/Fualaau affair, for example. If one accepts the premise that Letourneau's actions victimized Fualaau and that she poses a threat to other children, then her seven and one-half years in prison might be justified on grounds of any of these goals. One could argue that she is getting "what she deserves" (retribution), that other children are being protected (deterrence and/or incapacitation), or that she is very sick and needs help (rehabilitation) and should be in a facility equipped to counsel and medicate her. If we do not accept the premise that Fualaau was her victim, even if we find her actions offensive, then the logic of intervening disintegrates. She may be the victim, and the state, the real criminal entity. Philosophical questions aside, what the criminal justice system is supposed to pursue ideally is not necessarily what it pursues in practice, a matter the next section explores.

The Administration of Justice

Justice is administered in America by a "system" comprised of police, courts and corrections, generally referred to as the criminal justice system. Study of criminal justice as a system or process has increased dramatically in recent decades and this system (or process) is intricately linked to criminology. For social reaction theories drawn from the interactionist paradigm these processes are critical. Such understandings of criminal behavior deeply incorporate the actions of criminal justice officials, along with other societal components, in explaining how criminal careers unfold. Likewise, the actions of criminal justice officials are an intricate part of rational choice explanations of criminal behavior. If the formal justice system fails to deliver the necessary criterion for deterrence, for example, the theoretical premise collapses due to an operational failure. The theory could be correct but the mode of delivery is faulty. In short, the connection between criminological explanations of criminal behavior and the operations of the criminal justice system is critical. Echoing Edwin Sutherland's tripartite definition of criminology, some would contend that operation of the criminal justice system is merely subsumed within the criminological domain. While this text is focused on the body of theory or explanations for criminal behavior, further study of criminal justice as a system or process will provide a deeper understanding of the causes of crime.

Summary

Both the content and origins of criminal law are important to the criminologist. Whether it is a product of consensus, meeting the needs of larger society, or whether it serves the interests of the elite in conflict with others is a widely debated issue. It is clear, however, that crime is relative. The content of legal codes varies dramatically across time, as does the law in action. The conceptualization of behaviors as diverse as substance abuse, sodomy, and rape illustrate the problem.

Private wrongs are addressed by civil law, while public wrongs are the subject of criminal law. Criminal procedure is substantially more restrictive because so much is usually at stake. A criminal statute may prohibit the commission of acts (e.g., robbery, rape, and murder) or may require acts and penalize their omission (e.g., filing income tax returns). Such offenses are classified as felonies, misdemeanors, or violations in terms of their perceived seriousness and the range of potential punishments.

Justice is administered by a criminal justice system that is charged with pursuing some combination of deterrence, incapacitation, rehabilitation and retribution. The system is comprised of police, courts and corrections agencies. In practice each exercises a great deal of discretion that introduces additional complexities in efforts to understand crime and criminals. Many criminological perspectives require careful scrutiny of activities within the criminal justice system. To many, studying systems of justice is part of the larger criminological enterprise.

Key Terms and Concepts

Actus Reus
Administrative Law
Civil Law
Conflict
Consensus
Criminal Law
Deterrence
  General
  Special
Due Process of Law
Eighteenth Amendment
Ethnocentrism
Felony
Gateway Drug
Harrison Act (1914)

Incapacitation
Just Deserts
Marijuana Tax Act 1937
Mens Rea
Misdemeanor
Moral Panics
Criminal Justice System
Prohibition
Rape Shield Laws
Rehabilitation
Relativity of Crime (Law)
Retribution
Sodomy
Unintended Consequences (of Prohibition)
Victimless Crimes

Key Criminologists

John Curra

Emile Durkheim

Cases

Bowers v. Hardwick, 478 U.S. 186 (1986)

Campbell v. Sundquist, 926 S.W. 2d 250 (1996)

Coker v. Georgia, 433 U.S. 485 (1977)

FDA v. Brown & Williamson Tobacco Corp., 98-1152 (2000)

Gregg v. Georgia, 428 U.S. 153 (1976)

In re John Z., 29 Cal. 4th 756, 128 Cal. Rptr. 2d 783, 60 P.3d 183 (2003)

Lawrence v. Texas, 539 U.S. 558 (2003)

Roe v. Wade, 410 U.S. 113 (1973)

State v. Dominy, No. 01C01-9512-CC-00404 (Tenn. 1997)

State v. Dominy, 67 S.W.3d 822 (Tenn. 2001)

References

Abbott, J.H. (1981). *In the Belly of the Beast: Letters from Prison.* New York, NY: Random House.

Alexander, K. (1997). "Zero for Conduct: After Bearing the Child of a 13-year-old Student, a Sixth-Grade Teacher May Be Heading for Prison." *People Weekly*, v48 n15. EC: A19823594.

Andrews, D.A., I. Zinger, R.D. Hoge, J. Bonta, P. Gendreau & F.T. Cullen (1990a). "Does Correctional Treatment Work? A Clinically Relevant and Psychologically Informed Meta-Analysis." *Criminology*, 28:369-404.

Andrews, D.A., I. Zinger, R.D. Hoge, J. Bonta, P. Gendreau & F.T. Cullen (1990b). "A Human Science Approach or More Punishment and Pessimism: A Rejoinder to Lab and Whitehead." *Criminology*, 28:419-429.

Associated Press (1998). "Teenage Dad Overjoyed About New Daughter With Ex-Teacher." *Johnson City Press,* October 19.

Becker, H.S. (1963). *Outsiders: Studies in the Sociology of Deviance.* New York, NY: The Free Press.

Bernard, T.J. & R.S. Engel (2001). "Conceptualizing Criminal Justice Theory." *Justice Quarterly*, 18:1-30.

Blum, A. (1980). "Medicine vs. Madison Avenue: Fighting Smoke With Smoke." *Journal of the American Medical Association*, 243:739-40.

Brown, S.E. (1982) "Hidden Assaults and the Tobacco Industry." Paper presented at the annual meeting of The American Society of Criminology, Toronto, Canada.

Burton, V.S., Jr., R.G. Dunaway & R. Kopache (1993). "To Punish or Rehabilitate? A Research Note Assessing the Purposes of State Correctional Departments as Defined by State Legal Codes." *Journal of Crime and Justice*, XVI:177-188.

Caplan, G.S. (1986). "Fourteenth Amendment—The Supreme Court Limits the Right to Privacy." *Journal of Criminal Law and Criminology*, 77:894-930.

CDC (2008). "Abortion Surveillance – United States, 2005" *Surveillance Summaries*, 57 (SS13): 1-32.

Cloud, J. (1998). "A Matter of Hearts." *Time*, v151 n17 EC:A20534677.

Cocca, C.E. (2002a). "The Politics of Statutory Rape Laws: Adoption and Reinvention of Morality Policy in the States, 1971-1999." *Polity*, 35:51-73.

Cocca, C.E. (2002b). ""From 'Welfare Queen' to "Exploited Teen": Welfare Dependency, Statutory Rape, and Moral Panic." *NWSA Journal*, 14:56-80.

Cullen, F. T. (2005). "The Twelve People Who Saved Rehabilitation: How the Science of Criminology Made a Difference." The American Society of Criminology 2004 Presidential Address. *Criminology*, 43:1-42.

Curra, J. (2000). *The Relativity of Deviance*. Thousand Oaks, CA: Sage.

Dowd, M. (2002). "Driving While Female." *New York Times*, Nov. 17.

Dreyfuss, R. (1999). "Big Tobacco Rides East." *Mother Jones Magazine*, Jan./Feb.

Durkheim, E. (1893/1933). *The Division of Labor in Society*, trans. G. Simpson. New York, NY: The Free Press.

Durkheim E. (1895/1958). *The Rules of Sociological Method*, trans. S.A. Soloway & J.H. Mueller. Glencoe, IL: The Free Press.

Drug Policy Alliance (2002a). "Drug By Drug." http://www.lindesmith.org/drugbydrug/cocainecrack

Drug Policy Alliance (2002b). "The Drug War Costs You $380 a Year." alerts@actioncenter.drugpolicy.org

Drug Policy Alliance (2002c). eNewsletter: Oct. 31. alerts@actioncenter.drugpolicy.org

Drug Policy Alliance (2002d). "Drug By Drug: Overview." http://www.lindesmith.org/drugbydrug

Drug Policy Alliance (2002d). "Marijuana: The Facts." http://www.lindesmith.org/marijuana/medical

Erickson, P.G. (1999). "A Persistent Paradox: Drug Law and Policy in Canada." *Canadian Journal of Criminology*, 41:275-284.

Ferrell, W. (2000). http://snltranscripts.jt.org/00/00nbush.phtml

Ferrell, W. (2001). http://snltranscripts.jt.org/01/01mbush.phtml

Fleishman, J. (2006). latimes.com/news, Feb. 9.

Fogel, D. (1975). "We Are the Living Proof..." *The Justice Model for Corrections*. Cincinnati, OH: Anderson Publishing Co.

Fradella, H.F. & K. Brown (2005). "Withdrawal of Consent Post-Penetration: Redefining the Law of Rape." *Criminal Law Bulletin*, 41:3-23.

Galliher, J.F. & A. Walker (1977). "The Puzzle of the Social Origins of the Marihuana Tax Act of 1937." *Social Problems*, 24:367-376.

Georgia Code Annotated A416-6-2 (1984).

Goode, E. (2001). *Deviant Behavior*, Sixth Edition. Upper Saddle River, NJ: Prentice-Hall.

Grasmick, H.G., E. Davenport, M.B. Chamelin & R.J. Bursik, Jr. (1992). "Protestant Fundamentalism and the Retributive Doctrine of Punishment." *Criminology*, 30:21-45.

Gusfield, J.R. (1981). *The Culture of Public Problems*. Chicago, IL: University of Chicago Press.

Hagan, J. (1980). "The Legislation of Crime and Delinquency: A Review of Theory, Method and Research." *Law and Society Review*, 14:603-628.

Hall, J. (1935). *Theft, Law and Society*, Second Edition. Indianapolis, IN: Bobbs-Merrill.

Hasday, J.E. (2000). "Contest and Consent: A Legal History of Marital Rape." *California Law Review*, 88:1373-1325.

Intl-tobacco@essential.org (2000). "Women, Girls and Tobacco: An Appeal for Global Action."

Johnson City Press (2002a). "Lounges Ad Featuring King Draws Thai Diplomat's Ire." Associated Press, June 30, p. 10.

Johnson City Press (2002a). "Reformist Scholar to Be Put to Death for Comments." Nov. 8.

Johnson City Press (2002b). "Couple to Be Stoned to Death for Affair." Aug. 30.

Johnson City Press (2002c). "Stoning Sentences Surge in Nigeria." Sept. 15

Johnson City Press (2003). "Senate OKs Bill Setting up State Lottery." April 24., p. 7.

Johnson City Press (1993). "Judge Rejects Woman's Pleas to Free Attacker." Associated Press November 13, p.12.

Johnson City Press (1987). "Sodomy: Crimes Against Nature Law Pressed." March 29, p. 3.

King, R.S. & M. Mauer (2002). "Distorted Priorities: Drug Offenders in State Prisons." Report of the Sentencing Project, www.sentencingproject.org

Logan, C.H. & G.G. Gaes (1993). "Meta-Analysis and the Rehabilitation of Punishment." *Justice Quarterly*, 10:245-263.

Martinson, R. (1974). "What Works?—Questions and Answers About Prison Reform." *The Public Interest*, (Spring):22-54.

McGarrell, E.F. & T.C. Castellano (1991). "An Integrative Conflict Mode of the Criminal Law Formation Process." *Journal of Research in Crime and Delinquency*, 28:174-196.

McLellan, A. (1991). "Post-Penetration Rape—Increasing the Penalty." *Santa Clara Law Review*, 31:779.

Musto, D.F. (1973). *The American Disease: Origins of Narcotic Control*. New Haven, CT: Yale University Press.

National Center for Health Statistics (2000). http://cdc.gov/nchs/releases/00facts/trends.htm

People Weekly (1998). "Family Man: Teenage Lover of Mary Kay Letourneau Writes Book About Their Romance." EC: 53150648.

Radelet, M.L. & R.L. Akers (1996). "Deterrence and the Death Penalty: The Views of the Experts." *The Journal of Criminal Law and Criminology*, 87:1-16.

Reinarman, C. (2000). "The Social Construction of Drug Scares." In P.A. Adler & P. Adler (eds.) *Constructions of Deviance: Social Power, Context and Interaction*, Third Edition. Belmont, CA: Wadsworth.

von Hirsch, A. (1976). *Doing Justice*. New York, NY: Hill and Wang.

Zimmer, L. & J. Morgan (1997). "Marijuana Myths, Marijuana Facts: A Review of the Scientific Evidence." New York, NY: Lindesmith Center.

3
Production of Crime Statistics

Crime statistics are a vital part of the study of crime. Theories of crime causation often are grounded in crime statistics, and popular and professional perceptions of the extent and distribution of crime are shaped by this information. Public response to crime and criminals is largely based upon views regarding the seriousness and magnitude of the "crime problem." During the 1970s and again in the late 1980s, the United States experienced an increase in both violent and property crime. According to media reports, based on statistics released by the Federal Bureau of Investigation (FBI), crime was growing at alarming rates. Since 1991, however, the crime rate has declined steadily and by 2007, crime was at historically low levels. Contrary to this fluctuation in recorded crime, some criminologists maintain that crime rates have been stable during this historical period. Which of these positions is correct?

This chapter examines the three major sources of crime statistics:

- Uniform Crime Reports (UCR);
- National Crime Victimization Surveys (NCVS);
- Self-Report Data (SRD)

The UCR consist of information collected by local police departments and forwarded to the FBI. The NCVS is conducted jointly by the U.S. Census Bureau and the U.S. Department of Justice. Independent researchers carry out self-report surveys. Other data are obtained from qualitative strategies that include in-depth interviews, observational studies, life histories, and case studies. These latter sources have provided criminology with classic studies of criminal lifestyles. Focusing on an individual or a small group, these qualitative case studies have been largely descriptive; providing detailed information about a wide range of criminal activities: a professional thief (Sutherland, 1937), a professional fence (Klockars, 1974; Steffensmeier, 1986), a drug-dealing community (Adler, 1992), gang members (Campbell, 1991; Decker & Van Winkle, 1996; Miller, 2001), burglars (Wright & Decker, 1994), robbers (Wright

& Decker, 1997), and drug dealers (Jacobs, 1999) among others. Though these works are rich and colorful in their descriptions of individuals, groups, or subcultures, problems of validity and reliability affect the generalizability of descriptive data. Emphasis in this chapter will be upon quantitative sources of crime statistics.

Review of Elementary Research Methodology

A review of elementary research methodology might prove beneficial prior to discussing crime data sources. To facilitate the reading of this and later chapters that review empirical tests of major theoretical propositions in criminology, the following methodological concepts will be considered:

- Independent and dependent variables;
- Correlation and causality;
- Cross-sectional and longitudinal research designs;
- Micro-level and macro-level analyses;
- Sampling;
- Research designs; and
- Validity and reliability.

Generalizability, validity, and reliability are key issues involved in all the social sciences. Research designs attempt to ensure that the work is sound enough so that its findings are not limited to the specific case or cases examined. For example, if we seek to know what causes crime, we could ask people we know why they broke the law. Such an approach will provide some information about why people violate the law, but will it allow us to make generalizations? That is, will it truly explain all criminal acts? In all probability, it will not. Will asking five friends why they drink alcohol even though they are under age provide an explanation of the causes of crime? Such simplistic approaches might strike you as humorous, but many persons base their understandings of crime on such unscientific "research." No wonder so much confusion exists with regard to what to do about crime in society.

How then can the issue of crime causation be studied? First, there are different levels of explanation. The *macro level* attempts to explain crime rates while the *micro level* seeks to understand why individuals commit crime. Macro-level researchers, for instance, might attempt to interpret variations in homicide rates across time or societies, or differences between cities. In such work, the *dependent variable*, the thing to be explained, is homicide rates. The *independent variable*, the thing you believe explains the dependent variable, might be ethnic diversity or the percent of the population living in poverty. Both the independent and dependent variables are measured in terms of a large social unit. The homicide rate usually refers to the number of murders per 100,000 people. Ethnic diversity would be measured in terms of the relative distribution of people identified as white, African-American, Hispanic, Asian, and other, while percent living in poverty would be the percent of the population living below the poverty line ($22,050 for a family of four in 2009). Notice, these three measures do not focus on any one person. Rather, they represent group-level information that can be obtained from the U.S. Census Bureau and from law enforcement records. The macro-level approach assumes that societal factors help to explain individual behavior. This approach will be discussed in greater detail in Chapter 7.

At the micro level, the purpose of research is to explain individual behavior and often involves a social-psychological approach. Instead of trying to explain variations in the homicide rate, a micro-level design would seek to interpret variations in individual behavior. Now the dependent variable would be murder, whether or not an individual committed this act. Independent variables would be individual income (thus allowing classification of an individual as being poor or not poor) and the individual's race. Micro-level measures of this type are usually obtained from individuals through interviews or questionnaires.

An important issue is the extent to which the research can be generalized: that is, can inferences be made beyond the immediate individual or place studied? Generalizability is achieved through sound research design and sampling procedures. Research designs can be considered blueprints that tell the researcher how to proceed, beginning with how units of analysis are to be selected for study.

Much of the early work in criminology and criminal justice relied upon *cross-sectional research designs* in which data are collected at one time point. Public opinion polls or voter preference polls are examples of surveys that interview a cross-section of people about their opinions on a specific topic.

Longitudinal research designs collect information across time. This allows for examination of historical changes. It also allows for establishing correct temporal ordering of variables, an important concern in testing criminological theory. Early self-report studies interviewed youths at one point in time and obtained information about their families, school performance, and their attitudes about a number of things. Simultaneously, the

---

HIGHLIGHT 3.1
Temporal Ordering

Let us assume that we are interested in exploring the relationship between poverty and crime. A survey has been conducted in which respondents have answered the following two questions: "Are you currently employed?" and "During the past year did you break into a building to steal something?" Based on our analysis, we find that people who are unemployed are more likely to report committing a burglary. Now that we have found a correlation between these two variables, does this mean that unemployment causes property crime? No, if anything, these data would be more supportive of the conclusion that breaking into a building to steal something causes a person to lose their job; crime causes unemployment! This cross-sectional example shows the fallacy of asking questions about current statuses and inferring a causal connection to past behavior. To remedy the situation, the question could have been, "Were you employed last year?"

researchers collected information about the youngsters' involvement in criminal activity during an earlier period. The researchers then used current attitudes (independent variables) to explain past criminal activity (dependent variable). This is temporally incorrect. The independent variable needs to occur prior to the dependent variable. Longitudinal research collects information at a minimum of two time periods. Independent variables are obtained in the first measurement and the dependent variable in the second.

To make inferences beyond the specific subjects, some form of *probability* sampling should be used (e.g., simple random, stratified, cluster). This means that every subject or case to which one hopes to be able to generalize has an equal probability of being selected for inclusion in the study. To be able to generalize about the difference in homicide rates between large and small cities, in the example above, the researcher would have to include small and large cities in the sample, and those cities should be drawn from a comprehensive list of all cities. This could be achieved by putting the names of all small cities (i.e., less than 250,000 population) into a hat and selecting five of them for study. Five large cities (i.e., more than 500,000 population) could be similarly selected. This represents a stratified probability sampling procedure in which the population is divided into appropriate categories and then sampled within these strata. In this manner, the study results can be said to be representative of all cities included in the two strata. Simply selecting two cities out of convenience would not produce generalizable data that could necessarily be considered as representative of all small cities.

If, in our macro-level study, we find that cities with wide ethnic diversity and high rates of poverty have higher crime rates, can we conclude that these two variables cause crime? We cannot. Our finding would show that these independent variables are related to, or correlated with, homicide rates. Before we can conclude that they are a cause of the differences in rates, we would have to meet two additional criteria. First, the independent variables must have been measured at a time preceding the measurement of homicide rates. For something to be a cause of something else, it has to occur prior to the thing you are trying to explain. Second, other potential causal factors need to be controlled. Instead of ethnic diversity and poverty causing homicide, geographic location, unemployment, and availability of handguns might be the real explanation of different homicide rates. Without controlling for such potential variables, it is not possible to make causal inferences.

Thus, while there may be a correlation between two things (i.e., the more of one is associated with more of the other), causality entails more than just establishing a relationship. Before it can be said that poverty causes crime, for example, three criteria need to be met: (1) it must be shown that the variables are correlated; (2) temporal ordering must be established (the independent variable must precede the dependent variable); and (3) rival or other potential explanatory factors need to be controlled. Having reviewed these essential elements of research methodology, we turn our attention to crime statistics.

History of Official Crime Statistics

Knowledge about the extent and distribution of crime in the United States prior to the twentieth century was based primarily upon local arrest statistics, court records, and jail and prison data. There had been no systematic attempt to estimate the extent of crime in society at large. Thorsten Sellin, an early commentator on crime figures, cautioned against the use of court and prison records. He wrote that "the value of a crime for index purposes decreases as the distance from the crime itself in terms of procedure increases" (1931:346). Given the reliance upon arrest and trial statistics, no clear picture of the amount of crime in pre-twentieth century America can be formulated.

In 1870, when Congress created the U.S. Department of Justice, it mandated that the Attorney General report crime statistics annually. This reporting, however, did not materialize. Nor did a resolution to the same effect, passed at the 1871 convention of the National Police Association (the forerunner of the International Association of Chiefs of Police, the IACP) have any effect. By the 1920s, police professionals had become concerned about media portrayals of crime waves. This led the IACP to establish a Committee for Uniform Crime Records to develop a procedure for collecting information about the amount of crime across the nation. The task proved particularly complicated because no two states defined all crimes in the same manner. In 1929, a final version of the data collection instrument was distributed to police departments, and a total of 400 agencies submitted their crime reports to the FBI the following January. Comparative criminologists, researchers interested in the study of crime in different countries, currently are confronted with problems similar to those encountered earlier in the twentieth century by American criminologists. Not only do crime definitions differ substantially from one nation to the next, but recording of crime data varies to an even greater degree. In spite of these problems, the field of comparative criminology is expanding as the globalization of the world continues (see, for example, the article by van Dijk & Kangaspunta, 2000).

HIGHLIGHT 3.2
International Crime Data

Since 1970, the United Nations has collected data on crime and the operation of the criminal justice systems of member nations. The first survey results published in 1977 covered the period 1970-1975 and represented data from 64 nations. The United Nations Surveys of Crime and Trends and Operations of the Criminal Justice System (UNCJS) is conducted every five years and the Fifth U.N. survey included reports from 103 nations. Similar to the American UCR, the UNCJS collects information on murder, rape, robbery, assault, and theft. Information on other crimes is also collected but cultural and societal variations in definitions and standards makes analysis of crimes such as bribery, fraud, and drug offenses more difficult. While some claim that there are too many inconsistencies in reporting to make this a useful source of information (Aebi, 2002), others note the value of these data. In support of this latter position, the following standards of the UNCJS are cited: it represents official data from each country; it provides standard definitions and classifications of crimes; it provides regular and ongoing reporting of UN member nations; and it contributes to development of a universal methodology for collecting international crime (Fairchild & Dammer, 2001).

With respect to the Uniform Crime Reports, police departments initially submitted crime data voluntarily; the FBI had no statutory authority to demand compliance. Currently, more than 18,000 law enforcement agencies representing about 95 percent of the nation's population, report to the FBI. Urban residents are somewhat more likely to be included in the UCR data, with 95 percent of the inhabitants of Metropolitan Statistical Areas counted compared to 89 percent of the rural population (U.S. Department of Justice, 2004). This high rate of reporting stems in part from the fact that many states now have the power to demand, with the force of state law, crime statistics from local jurisdictions (Maltz, 1977, 1999). Reporting statistics to the FBI, however, remains a voluntary practice that often has more to do with departmental prestige than it does with coercion. Within the law enforcement subculture, failure to participate in the FBI's Uniform Crime Reports (UCR) system implies that a law enforcement agency is not "professional."

Description of the Uniform Crime Reports

The Uniform Crime Reports consist of two components, Part I (Index) and Part II (non-Index) offenses. Part I offenses include those illegal acts considered to be particularly serious that "occur with sufficient frequency to provide an adequate basis for comparison" (U.S. Department of Justice, 1980:3). Eight crimes comprise the Part I Index crimes. From most to least serious, they are:

1. criminal homicide;

2. forcible rape;

3. robbery;

4. aggravated assault;

5. burglary;

6. larceny-theft;

7. motor vehicle theft; and

8. arson (added in 1979).

Absent from this list are serious crimes such as kidnapping, embezzlement, corporate fraud, and other white-collar offenses. These latter crimes, the FBI argues, occur too infrequently or do not readily come to the attention of the police, and therefore, would not provide a consistent or comparable measure across time or across jurisdictions. As a result of the selection of acts included in the Crime Index, public perception about the nature, extent, and seriousness of illegal behavior becomes biased toward "street" crime.

Crime rates are calculated by dividing the number of crimes committed by the population in a given jurisdiction. This resultant number is then multiplied by 100,000. In this manner, the figure is standardized, enabling comparison of the crime rate per 100,000 population for different localities. A city of 20,000 people with 200 crimes reported to

UCR Guidelines for the Recording of Robbery

3. Robbery
    (Crime against property, score one offense per distinct operation.)
    Definition: The taking or attempting to take anything of value from the care, custody, or control of a person or persons by force or threat of force or violence and/or by putting the victim in fear.
    Robbery is a vicious type of theft in that it is committed in the presence of the victim. The victim, who usually is the owner or person having custody of the property, is directly confronted by the perpetrator and is threatened with force or is put in fear that force will be used. Robbery involves a theft or larceny but is aggravated by the element of force or threat of force.
    In the absence of force or threat of force, as in pocket-picking or purse-snatching, the offense must be classified as larceny rather than robbery.
    However, if in a purse-snatching or other such crime, force or threat of force is used to overcome the active resistance of the victim, the offense is to be classified as strong-arm robbery.
    In analyzing robbery, the following subheadings are used:
    3.a.   Firearm
    3.b.   Knife or cutting instrument
    3.c.   Other dangerous weapon
    3.d.   Strong-arm—hands, fists, feet, etc.
Armed robbery, categories 3.a. – 3.c., are incidents commonly referred to as "stickups," "hijackings," "holdups," and "heists." Robberies wherein no weapons are used may be referred to as "strong-arms" or "muggings."
    In any instance of robbery, score one offense for each distinct operation including attempts. Do not count the number of victims robbed, those present at the robbery, or the number of offenders when scoring this crime.
    In cases involving pretended weapons or those in which the weapon is not seen by the victim but the robber claims to have one in his possession, classify the incident as armed robbery and score it in the appropriate category. If an immediate "on view" arrest proves that there is no weapon, the offense may be classified as strong-arm robbery.

Score One Offense for Each Distinct Operation
3.a. Robbery—Firearm
    Count one offense for each distinct operation in which any firearm is used as a weapon or employed as a means of force to threaten the victim or put him in fear.
3.b. Robbery—Knife or Cutting Instrument
    Score one offense for each distinct operation in which a knife, broken bottle, razor, or other cutting instrument is employed as a weapon or as a means of force to threaten the victim or put him in fear.
3.c. Robbery—Other Dangerous Weapon
    In this category of robbery, enter one offense for each distinct operation in which a club, acid, explosive, brass knuckles, or other dangerous weapon is used.
3.d. Robbery—Strong-Arm—Hands, Fists, Feet, etc.
    This category includes muggings and similar offenses where no weapon is used, but strong-arm tactics (limited to the use of personal weapons such as hands, arms, feet, fists, teeth, etc.) are employed to deprive the victim of his property.

Source: U.S. Department of Justice (1996). *Uniform Crime Reporting Handbook*. Washington, DC: U.S. Department of Justice.

the police, for example, has a crime rate of 1,000 (200/20,000 x 100,000). This crime rate would compare unfavorably to that of a city with 2,000,000 inhabitants and 5,000 crimes reported to the police (a crime rate of 5,000/2,000,000 x 100,000 = 250).

Each year, the FBI attempts to guarantee consistent practices across jurisdictions by distributing to each law enforcement agency a *Uniform Crime Reporting Handbook*, containing guidelines to be followed in recording crimes. Highlight 3.3 provides an example of instructions for recording robbery.

Part II offenses include most other crimes not itemized in Part I. Twenty specific crimes and a catchall "other" category are in this section, including other assaults, embezzlement, vandalism, sex offenses, drunkenness, and status offenses (i.e., juvenile acts, such as truancy, which are defined as criminal only because of the person's age). Information regarding the frequency and distribution of these crimes is rarely reported to the media by the FBI. Therefore, the public rarely learns about the extent of "nonserious" crimes such as hazing and statutory rape (sexual intercourse with a minor).

In addition to information about the number and types of crimes committed and where they occur, the FBI also provides data about characteristics and consequences of crimes, (e.g., degree of injury, monetary loss, and personal characteristics of the victim and offender). This information permits criminologists to examine relationships between variables that could help to explain the causes of crime. As might be expected, crime is not equally distributed in the population; some groups tend to commit (or, at least, get caught engaging in) more illegal acts than others. Explanations for these differentials challenge both theory builders and those seeking to control crime.

The UCR also collects data about law enforcement agencies. This allows planners to evaluate issues such as the effect of police department size on the number of arrests and convictions, the desirability of various types of shift assignments, and hiring trends in law enforcement with regard to sex, race, and educational level. The UCR thus provides a wealth of information not just about crime, but also about aspects of the criminal justice system. The data published in the quarterly and annual reports, however, represent but a fraction of what is gathered. For those interested, UCR data are available online (http://www.fbi.gov/ucr/ucr.htm).

The police, as noted earlier, record crimes differently for Part I and Part II offenses. Part I or Index Offenses consist of crimes known to the police, including both crimes the police themselves discover and crimes reported by citizens. For most offenses, especially property crimes, citizen reports are the major source of information about crime. One study found that only 1.6 percent of the robberies and 0.4 percent of household burglaries were discovered at the scene by the police (Gove et al., 1985). Thus, while UCR data are referred to as "official statistics," the data are primarily a product of police response (reactive behavior) and not of police patrol (proactive behavior).

Given their reliance upon citizen reports, the Part I statistics are the result of a three-stage process:

1.   Citizens must decide whether a crime has been committed;

2.   If citizens determine that a crime has been committed, they must decide whether to report the act to the police; and

3. Once the act has been reported, an officer must decide:

    (a) Whether a crime has occurred;

    (b) How to classify it; and

    (c) Whether to record it.

UCR data, therefore, are several stages removed from the actual crime. Recall Sellin's warning about the value of crime statistics decreasing as one becomes further removed from the crime itself. But remember that reported crime is more proximate to the actual offense than is arrest or conviction.

Part II UCR statistics represent only crimes that result in an arrest. This makes it difficult to compare Part II crimes with Part I offenses. Arrest statistics provide a distorted picture of "nonserious" crimes because only a fraction of crimes known to the police are cleared by an arrest. This again illustrates the importance of trying to obtain data about crime as close to the criminal act as possible.

Strengths of the UCR

Despite various shortcomings, to be discussed in the following section, the UCR are an important source of information about crime in American society. The collaborative effort between the FBI and local, county, and state law enforcement agencies minimizes redundancy. Also, the data offer nationwide crime statistics, which allow for city and regional comparisons. The comparisons are facilitated by the uniform guidelines and definitions provided by the FBI's *Uniform Crime Reporting Handbook*. Presumably, the same criminal act committed in Cullowhee, North Carolina would be recorded in the same manner if committed in Irvine, California. It then becomes possible to compare the relative safety of these two communities as well as to evaluate the performance of the police agencies in solving and preventing crime. The FBI, however, routinely warns against making such comparisons because, despite Handbook advice, law enforcement agencies sometimes employ idiosyncratic methods to record crimes for FBI purposes. In one Ohio city, "stolen" cars were not entered into official records until 24 hours after the initial report. In another Ohio city, about the same size as the first, "stolen" cars were recorded at the time they were reported missing. Not surprisingly, the second city showed a much greater rate of auto theft than the first, though the true rates actually might have been quite similar. Along these same lines, this chapter's Gang Feature highlights the importance of developing consistent criteria for identifying gang members and measuring gang-related crime.

Another advantage of the UCR is that the statistics have been collected and stored since 1930 and are updated monthly. Policy analysts and the public can therefore make annual crime rate comparisons. It also is possible to examine crime trends, be they overall crime rates or rates for specific crimes. For instance, researchers can analyze the crime of rape and compare it to the crime trend in general. In 1960, however, significant changes in recording practices were made that no longer allow direct comparisons with earlier years.

GANG FEATURE

Definitional Issues: Twice as Great, or Half as Great?

What is a gang and what determines whether a crime is gang-related? These are two important question that should be addressed prior to any discussion about gangs. Yet, it is surprising the extent to which these questions are either ignored or readily dismissed. Articles, whether academic or media generated, in which gangs and gang activity are described include a diverse population, often failing to qualify the scope of the topic. Thus, depending upon an author's interest or focus, a gang may be comprised of any, or all of the following: youthful offenders; drug dealing posses; bikers; neighborhood cliques; prisoners; or any other specifically defined group of three (and in some jurisdictions only two) or more individuals whose members engage in criminal activity. These are quite distinct groups and descriptions of one cannot be generalized to the other. In spite of the absence of a common definition of gangs, it is not uncommon to hear or read about gangs, gang members, and gang activity as if these were synonymous terms. While failure to define the groups and activities included in such discussions may result in general confusion about the nature of the problems, there are more serious ramifications from a policy perspective. With respect to gangs and the attention they have drawn in the past 20 years, it is important to be able to identify the magnitude of the problem, both in terms of gang membership and level of gang-related crime. Given the diverse definitions, such simple objectives are difficult to attain. Here we provide an example of definitional differences from law enforcement.

Los Angeles and Chicago are often identified as the two cities with the most pronounced gang presence in the United States. In an interesting project, Cheryl Maxson and Malcolm Klein (1990; 2002) compared "gang-related" homicides in these two cities. This research highlights the difficulty of comparing crime rates among different jurisdictions.

In Los Angeles, both the L.A. Police Department and Sheriff's Department rely upon a "gang member" definition to classify crimes as gang-related. That is, any crime committed by a gang member is considered to be gang-related, i.e., any crime in which either the suspect or victim is on file as an active gang or associate gang member is so classified. The driving force behind this policy, then is the identification of gang members. Both L.A. law enforcement agencies use the following criteria to identify gang members:

- An individual admits to membership in a gang;

- A reliable informant identifies an individual as a gang member;

- An informant of untested reliability identifies an individual as a gang member and it is corroborated by independent information;

- An individual resides in or frequents a particular gang's area and affects its style of dress, use of hand signs, symbols, or tattoos, and associates with known gang members;

- An individual has been arrested several times in the company of identified gang members for offenses which are consistent with usual gang activity;

Additionally, when there are strong indications that an individual has a close relationship with a gang but does not fit the above criteria, that person is then identified as a "gang associate."

In contrast to Los Angeles, the Chicago Police Department utilizes a "gang motive" definition to classify a crime as gang-related. Under this definition, a crime "is considered gang-related only if it occurs in the course of an explicitly defined collective encounter between two or more gangs." Importantly, under this definition, criminal and violent activity engaged in by gang members outside of the gang context is NOT considered gang-related. Clearly, such disparate standards will have substantial effects on the volume of gang-related offenses.

Maxson and Klein (1990, 2002) examined gang homicides in Chicago and Los Angeles.

Gang Feature, *continued*

They found that the Los Angeles homicide rate was reduced approximately 50 percent when the more restrictive gang motive standard was used to classify homicides in that city. In an examination of the relative prevalence of these two definitional approaches, Maxson and Klein (2002) found about an equal number of jurisdictions use each standard. In spite of these different standards, they concluded: "An examination of factors associated with gang member and gang motivated homicides suggest that the qualities of these homicides do not differ dramatically and it is 'appropriate' to make cross-city comparisons about gang and non-gang homicides regardless of definition used" (Maxson & Klein, 2002:182). However, with respect to the prevalence of gang homicides, Maxson and Klein urge caution when comparing homicide rates across different jurisdictions.

Weaknesses of the UCR

An obvious shortcoming of the UCR Crime Index is its emphasis upon conventional street crimes and its exclusion of other serious crime. The UCR definition of serious crime deflects attention from such illegal acts as corporate violence, political crime, and computer fraud. People may be misled into believing that they are most endangered by murderers or robbers, when in fact the personal and financial costs of corporate and political crime far exceed those of conventional street crimes (Simon & Eitzen, 1990; and Kappeler et al., 1993). In their award-winning book *Myths that Cause Crime*, Harold Pepinsky and Paul Jesilow (1984) devoted a chapter to the misconception that white-collar crime is nonviolent. Among the figures they cite are: each year 10,000 lives are lost due to unnecessary surgery and 20,000 persons are killed because of errors in prescribing drugs. The authors point out that numerous birth defects were caused by the premature marketing of Thalidomide by the Richardson-Merrell Company in the 1960s. Chapters 11 and 12 examine more closely the issues of such forms of white-collar crime. The health care debate in 2009 brought attention to the fact that thousands of Americans die each year due to "errors" made by medical professionals.

The UCR also can be a tool for political manipulation. Police administrators sometimes rely upon these data to justify requests for additional money for personnel, equipment, and training. At other times, the Crime Index can be manipulated by a department to indicate exemplary performance (i.e., reducing crime rates or increasing clearance rates). This can be achieved by failing to record some crime reports or by negotiating with offenders to plead guilty to a number of offenses, some of which they may not have committed, in return for a reduced sentence. This most frequently occurs with property offenses, which traditionally have low clearance rates. The police can sometimes solve or "clear" as many as 200 burglaries by bargaining with one suspect. These data become an in-house self-evaluation of police performance.

Several problems also arise from recording practices. While the *Uniform Crime Reporting Handbook* specifies definitions and procedures to be followed, different departments and regions of the country may still adhere to idiosyncratic standards. While it may be accurate to state that "a rose is a rose is a rose," it is not necessarily the case that a rape is a rape is a rape. See, for example, the analysis by Duncan Chappell and his colleagues (1971) of how Boston police reports of rape differ in both vocabulary and style (and particularly in terms of the kinds of acts that are defined as rape) from the reports of Los Angeles police. Cultural standards, level of police professionalism, and staffing patterns can lead to the same behavior being recorded differently in different jurisdictions. Take the case of a 19-year-old female college student who claims that she was raped, beaten, and robbed while hitchhiking home from a fraternity party. Does the officer record this as a rape, a robbery, or an assault? The answer is, it all depends. A chauvinist officer might believe that a woman hitchhiking alone at night is "asking for it," and therefore, the officer might ignore the rape allegation. A different officer may record the event as a rape. (See Chapter 11 for more discussion of rape.) UCR instructions mandate that the crime be tabulated in the most serious category, known as the *Hierarchical Rule*. If the student was robbed and raped, the crimes would appear only as a rape (and not as a robbery), but if she were killed, the crimes would be classified as a homicide (and not as a rape).

Another problem concerns the manner in which crimes are counted. Instructions direct law enforcement agencies to tally each distinct property crime as one offense. If, for example, 10 rooms in a hotel were burglarized, these offenses should be recorded as one burglary, but if 10 apartments in an apartment complex were burglarized, the crimes should be recorded as 10 burglaries. For personal offenses, such as robberies, the number of victims is immaterial for tabulating purposes, as is the number of offenders. If two robbers confront five patrons in a bank, only one robbery is said to have occurred. These definitional rules tend to underestimate the extent of certain offense types and clearly make direct comparison with victimization and self-report surveys inappropriate. For instance, while the UCR procedures would classify the above bank robbery as *one offense*, victimization surveys would identify *five victims* while a self report survey would produce *two offenders*.

Crime rates also can be misleading. Take, for instance, the city of Las Vegas, or any other resort community. These places are inundated by visitors, some of whom inevitably commit crimes. Yet, the crime rate is calculated in terms only of the number of people in the resident population, not in terms of the true total of people that might become either offenders or victims. And because rates are calculated in terms of a jurisdiction's population, serious errors in determining the number of people living in an area—not an uncommon problem—can affect the accuracy of crime rates.

A further criticism of the Crime Index is its reactive nature. Law enforcement agencies rely primarily upon the willingness of private citizens to report crime. Yet, there are numerous reasons why individuals might choose not to report known crimes to the police. One estimate is that only 35 percent of the crimes that take place annually are reported to the police (Harlow, 1986). Reasons most frequently mentioned for not reporting crime are:

- A belief that the event is not important enough to report; and

- A feeling, particularly for violent crimes, that the act is a private or personal matter.

Other reasons include:

- A belief that the police cannot or will not do anything about a report;

- A fear that an individual's own criminal behavior (as in prostitution or drug dealing) may be exposed;

- A fear that a person's or a business's reputation may be damaged by publicity resulting from reporting;

- A fear of reprisal, as in some cases of domestic violence; and

- A disagreement with the legal definition; or

- A belief that the behavior is not wrong or that the criminal act was justified.

A New Look to the UCR: NIBRS—National Incident-Based Reporting System

Given the number of criticisms of the Uniform Crime Reports and the growing complexity and diversity of crime, the National Incident-Based Reporting System (NIBRS) was introduced in 1984 to meet the needs of law enforcement agencies, and incident-level data were being collected by the end of the 1980s (U.S. Department of Justice, Federal Bureau of Investigation [FBI], 2004). NIBRS was developed to address two primary goals:

- to enhance the quantity, quality, and timeliness of crime statistical data collected by the law enforcement community; and,

- to improve the methodology used for compiling, analyzing, auditing, and publishing the collected crime data.

Whereas the traditional UCR system required tallying the number of occurrences of Part I offenses as well as arrest data for Part I and Part II offenses, NIBRS requires more detailed reports and allows for recording of multiple offenses, thus eliminating the Hierarchical Rule which led to recording of only the most serious offense. Agencies using NIBRS collect data regarding individual crime incidents and arrests and submit them in "reports" detailing each incident. This procedure provides much more thorough information about crimes than did the summary statistics of the traditional UCR system.

NIBRS has abandoned the use of Part I and Part II offenses in favor of Group A and Group B classifications. Part I offenses focused on "street offenses" and ignored "suite offenses." Group A is considerably more inclusive of a wide array of criminal activity. Detailed information recorded for each of the 22 Group A offenses include crime circumstances, victim and offender information, arrestee data, and information about the extent of damage to both person and property.

The following offenses are included in Group A:

1. Arson
2. Assault
3. Bribery
4. Burglary
5. Counterfeiting
6. Vandalism
7. Drug Offenses
8. Embezzlement
9. Extortion
10. Fraud
11. Gambling Offenses
12. Homicide
13. Kidnapping
14. Larceny/Theft
15. Auto Theft
16. Pornography
17. Prostitution
18. Robbery
19. Sex Crimes, Force
20. Sex Offenses
21. Stolen Property
22. Weapon Violation

Offenses included in Group B consist of the following:

1. Bad Checks
2. Curfew/Vagrancy
3. Disorderly Conduct
4. DUI
5. Drunkenness
6. Family Offense
7. Liquor Violations
8. Peeping Tom
9. Runaway
10. Trespass
11. All Other

South Carolina was the first state to "pilot" this new program and by 1988, NIBRS was approved for general use (U.S. Department of Justice, FBI, 2006). In 2004, 5,741 agencies (representing 20 percent of the U.S. population and 16 percent of crime statistics collected by the UCR) were represented, and as of 2006, 26 states were NIBRS "certified," 12 were in various stages of testing, and an additional 8 were in various stages of planning and development (FBI, 2006). While the NIBRS data are not a nationally-representative sample of law enforcement agencies or criminal incidents, they are one of the few multi-jurisdictional data sources available for examining offenders, victims, situational characteristics, and police arrest/clearance status in crime incidents.

Strengths of NIBRS

NIBRS provides a number of improvements over existing measures such as the UCR, NCVS, and self-reports. A thorough critique by Maxfield (1999:145) suggests the following benefits of NIBRS over existing alternatives: (1) incident- and victim-level analysis can be disaggregated to local jurisdictions and aggregated to intermediate levels of analysis; (2) incident details supporting analysis of ancillary offenses (drugs, weapons) and crime situations are available;(3) separable individual, household, commercial, and business victimizations are included; (4) data on incidents targeting victims under age 12 are available; (5) a broader range of offense categories, including those affecting abstract victims, are available; (6) allowance for examination of non-household-based individual victims and other incidents that are difficult to measure with household-based surveys; (7) individual-level information about offenders from arrest records and victim reports are available; and, (8) information about the residual status of victims and offenders is included. These advances have a number of practical implications for communities and law enforcement agencies. Faggiani and McLaughlin (1999), for example, demonstrate how local law enforcement agencies can engage in "tactical crime analysis" using NIBRS data by examining local crime patterns and then using this information to strategically target crimes and areas. They also have important implications for researchers who seek to better understand the nature and scope of criminal incidents.

Weaknesses of NIBRS

Maxfield (1999:145-146) also summarizes a number of limitations of NIBRS relative to existing sources of crime data. First, like the UCR, NIBRS data include only crimes reported to police and retained by police recordkeeping systems, thus excluding unreported and unrecorded crimes. Secondly, the inflexibility of the NIBRS specifications creates a considerable reporting burden on participating local agencies. This may explain why NIBRS has been adopted primarily by smaller agencies in smaller states, with the nation's largest cities and agencies lagging behind. Third, different types of agencies have different organizational incentives. The FBI and other national agencies are most interested in a national monitoring system and national-level research application, while local and state submitting agencies are more concerned with local recordkeeping requirements, analysis to support local operations, and conservation of resources for data systems that have local applications. Fourth, the age and complexity of the NIBRS record structure and concomitant size of data files present unfamiliar challenges to researchers, analysts, and computer hardware and software. For example, Dunn & Zelenock's (1999) analyses of 1996 NIBRS data illustrate difficulties associated with analyzing millions of records and the need for powerful computer hardware and software to process the information. Fifth, a number of uncertainties exist concerning the error structure of incident-based measures generally and NIBRS data specifically. Recent examinations have identified some of these limitations and offered methods of correction. For example, Snyder (1999) found that juveniles account for a disproportionate amount of robbery clearances in NIBRS relative to other data sources. Addington's recent work has identified limitations in the NIBRS data concerning murder incidents (Addington, 2004) particularly as they pertain to police clearance rates (Addington, 2006).

Recent Studies Using NIBRS

Despite these limitations, NIBRS provides a promising approach to the study of crime for both researchers and practitioners. Recent examinations by Chilton and Jarvis (1999b) and Rantalla and Edwards (2000) of NIBRS data relative to other sources of crime data have generally found that NIBRS present a suitable complement to more commonly utilized sources such as the NCVS and UCR. Additionally, Akiyama and Nolan (1999) and Dunn and Zelenock (1999) present clear descriptions for users of the data and highlight the remarkable versatility of incident-based measures. This versatility is illustrated as NIBRS data have been used to examine a variety of topics ranging from descriptions of criminal incidents to characteristics of offenders as they pertain to official agency processing (e.g., Addington, 2006; Taylor, Holleran, & Topalli, 2009) to tests of criminological theories. Recent studies have used NIBRS to examine a wide range of crimes, ranging from child abuse (Finkelhor & Ormrod, 2001) and hate crimes (Messner, McHugh & Felson, 2004; Strom, 2001) to intimate partner violence (Thompson, Saltzman & Bibel, 1999; Vasquez, Stohr & Purkiss, 2005) and differences between lethal and nonlethal assaults (Chilton, 2004).

Some concern has been expressed regarding the possible effect on crime rates of this new recording system. Ramona Rantala and Thomas Edwards (2000) conducted an examination of this very issue. They compared crime rates in more than 1,000 agencies that have adopted the NIBRS system and found that while the crime rates under NIBRS were greater, the difference was relatively small. They found that on average the violent crime rate was less than one percent higher and the property crime rate slightly more than two percent higher under NIBRS guidelines compared to the traditional UCR system.

Alternative Measures of Crime

The UCR have been the primary source of crime statistics in the United States for more than 70 years, but there has been a continuous search for alternative and better measures. Two other data sources that rely upon surveys to obtain data on criminal behavior have been developed. Self-report studies request individuals to indicate the type and amount of criminal behavior in which they have engaged. Victimization surveys ask respondents to indicate the types of crimes of which they have been victims. Advocates of these approaches claim that they provide a clearer picture of criminal activity than does the UCR. Others argue that they provide an alternative enumeration.

Self-Report Studies

The history of Self-Report Data (SRD) has been one of methodological improvements. Self-report studies generally have relied upon responses from juveniles and have been influential in the development of theories explaining the etiology (causes) of delinquency. The labeling perspective, for instance (see Chapter 9), was largely influenced by early self-report studies. Likewise, integrated theoretical models and developmental criminology (discussed in Chapter 10) are also tied closely to SRD.

Early self-report studies were conducted by Austin Porterfield (1946) and by James Wallerstein and Clement Wyle (1947). It was not until the work of Short and Nye (1957), however, that self-report measures received serious attention. A description of five major self-report studies highlights not only the methodological improvements made in this data collection technique, but the extent to which this technique has been adopted by criminological researchers, especially during the past 25 years.

Short and Nye (1957)

James F. Short, Jr. and F. Ivan Nye's pioneering work revealed a totally different image of the juvenile delinquent and the extent of delinquency than official records had portrayed. Two different samples of adolescents completed questionnaires: one consisted of youth enrolled in the ninth through twelfth grades in three schools in the state of Washington, while the other was comprised of institutionalized delinquents. Responses to 23 questions inquiring about rule and law violations showed little difference between the two groups. The finding that parents' socioeconomic background and the quality of family life were not related to delinquency was of special significance. This finding contradicted a "truism" about the causes of delinquency: that it is caused by poverty and/or by broken homes.

There were several methodological problems with the Short-Nye scale. The respondents had been requested to identify all those rules and regulations that they had broken since beginning grade school. Response categories were:

1. very often

2. several times

3. once or twice

4. no

Of the 23 rule violations included in the inventory, seven were selected to comprise a delinquency scale. But, the high-school-aged respondents were being asked to recall events that had occurred as long as 10 years earlier, and to indicate approximately how often they had engaged in such behavior. Furthermore, the response categories did not allow the researchers to differentiate adequately between habitual and infrequent "delinquents."

Take, for example, the item "skipped school without a legitimate excuse." In the course of 10 years, an individual may have "skipped" once a year. This is certainly more than once or twice and more than several times. Is it "very often"? It is not possible to differentiate between this respondent and the person that also has skipped school 10 times, but all in the past year.

Another methodological problem raised with the Short-Nye scale is its emphasis upon what can be considered "trivial" offenses. Behaviors such as defying parental authority and skipping school can hardly be equated in terms of seriousness with Part I crimes such as robbery and assault. By including trivial behaviors in their delinquency scales, researchers tend to overestimate the amount of delinquency. This inclusion of what some scholars have referred to as typical adolescent behavior may have contributed to findings such as the absence of a relationship between social class and delinquency (Tittle et al., 1978).

The National Youth Survey (NYS)

A major study utilizing self-report research methods was conducted by Delbert Elliott and his colleagues at the University of Colorado. The National Youth Survey (NYS), begun in 1977, is based on a probability sample of youth in the continental United States (Elliott et al., 1985). The initial sample consisted of 1,726 male and female adolescents. The cohort (the same youths), which was originally between the ages of 11 and 17, was interviewed ten times, annually until 1981 and then again in 1984, 1987, 1990, 1993, and 2002. This last wave provides data about a national sample of young adults from 36 to 42 years of age. Then in 2003, the original respondents, their spouses or partners, their parents, and their children aged 11 and older, were all interviewed.

Unlike prior self-report studies, the NYS measurement of delinquency was geared to approximate the UCR crime categories. Consequently, 40 items were developed that measured all but one of the UCR Part I offenses (homicide) and 60 percent of Part II offenses (see Highlight 3.4).

HIGHLIGHT 3.4

Self-Reported Delinquency and Drug-Use Items as Employed in the National Youth Survey

How many times in the past year have you:

1. purposely damaged or destroyed property belonging to your parents or other family members?
2. purposely damaged or destroyed property belonging to a school?
3. purposely damaged or destroyed other property that did not belong to you (not counting family or school property)?
4. stolen (or tried to steal) a motor vehicle such as a car or motorcycle?
5. stolen (or tried to steal) something worth more than $50?
6. knowingly bought, sold, or held stolen goods (or tried to do any of these things)?
7. thrown objects (such as rocks, snowballs, or bottles) at cars or people?
8. run away from home?
9. lied about your age to gain entrance or to purchase something; for example, lying about your age to buy liquor or to get into a movie?
10. carried a hidden weapon other than a plain pocketknife?
11. stolen (or tried to steal) things worth $5 or less?
12. attacked someone with the idea of seriously hurting or killing him/her?
13. been paid for having sexual relations with someone?
14. had sexual intercourse with a person of the opposite sex other than your wife/husband?
15. been involved in gang fights?
16. sold marijuana or hashish ("pot," "grass," "hash")?
17. cheated on school tests?
18. hitchhiked where it was illegal to do so?
19. stolen money or other things from your parents or other members of your family?
20. hit (or threatened to hit) a teacher or other adult at school?
21. hit (or threatened to hit) one of your parents?
22. hit (or threatened to hit) other students?
23. been loud, rowdy, or unruly in a public place (disorderly conduct)?
24. sold hard drugs, such as heroin, cocaine, and LSD?
25. taken a vehicle for a ride (drive) without the owner's permission?
26. bought or provided liquor for a minor?
27. had (or tried to have) sexual relations with someone against their will?
28. used force (strong-arm methods) to get money or things from other students?
29. used force (strong-arm methods) to get money or things from a teacher or other adult at school?
30. used force (strong-arm methods) to get money or things from other people (not students or teachers)?
31. avoided paying for such things as movies, bus or subway rides, and food?

HIGHLIGHT **3.4** Continued

32. been drunk in a public place?
33. stolen (or tried to steal) things worth between $5 and $50?
34. stolen (or tried to steal) something at school, such as someone's coat from a classroom, locker, or cafeteria, or a book from the library?
35. broken into a building or vehicle (or tried to break in) to steal something or just to look around?
36. begged for money or things from strangers?
37. skipped classes without an excuse?
38. failed to return extra change that a cashier gave you by mistake?
39. been suspended from school?
40. made obscene telephone calls, such as calling someone and saying dirty things?

Source: *Sourcebook of Criminal Justice Statistics* (1989). Table 3.109, pp. 330-331.

The self-report instrument included two separate response sets. Respondents interviewed during January and February were instructed to indicate how many times in the past year ("from Christmas a year ago to the Christmas just past") they had committed each specified offense. If the individual indicated 10 or more times, this was followed with a validity check; respondents were asked whether the behavior was done:

1. once a month
2. once every 2-3 weeks
3. once a week
4. 2-3 times a week
5. once a day
6. 2-3 times a day

Agreement between the two responses could then be checked, and when this was done, a high level of accord was found. The advantage of instructing the youths to answer for the interval between Christmases is that Christmas usually is a salient event that permits the time period to be more clearly identified than would be true if asked about the past year. Furthermore, this time frame enables comparisons to be made between the UCR annual data and self-report results.

Frequency counts allow researchers to examine repeat violators. At the low end of the frequency scale, no differences were found between subgroups (e.g., social class, age, and race). Among high-frequency offenders (those identified as engaging in patterned delinquent behavior); however, differences by race and social class were discovered: lower-class youths and African-Americans appeared more frequently in the high-frequency offender group than whites and middle-class youths (Elliott & Ageton, 1980). Highlighting the importance of replication (i.e., repetition of a previous study to test the reliability of the initial findings), a subsequent analysis utilizing data from the first five years of the NYS (1977-1981) found that once social class was controlled, differences by race disappeared (Huizinga & Elliott, 1987).

Program of Research on the Causes and Correlates of Delinquency

In 1986, the Office of Juvenile Justice and Delinquency Prevention (OJJDP) in the U.S. Department of Justice awarded funds to three research projects to utilize self-report data to examine the causes and correlates of delinquency in high-risk neighborhoods. All three used a core of SRD items that represent a refinement of the NYS items. Two of the projects (Huizinga et al., 1991; Loeber et al., 1991) included children as young as seven in the samples. Prior self-report studies, as noted above, had focused almost exclusively on junior and senior high school youth. Inclusion of the younger cohorts allows for a better determination of early life experiences associated with delinquent or problem behavior. Another methodological issue was the time interval between data collection points. Two of the studies (Loeber et al., 1991; Thornberry et al., 1991) conducted interviews every six months, while the Huizinga et al. research adhered to an annual schedule. The three projects submitted a three-volume report to OJJDP in 1994 (Huizinga et al., 1994b). The project staffs have provided contributions to the understanding of a number of topics including gang behavior (Bjerregard & Smith, 1993; Esbensen & Huizinga, 1993; Thornberry et al., 1993, 2003), gun ownership (Lizotte et al., 1994, 2000; Bjerregard & Lizotte, 1995), victimization (Esbensen & Huizinga, 1991; Esbensen et al., 1999), consequences of arrest (Huizinga and Henry, 2007), and risk factors and resiliency (Huizinga et al., 1994a; Loeber et al., 1995; Thornberry et al., 1995; Kelley et al., 1997; Thornberry et al., 2000).

The Project on Human Development in Chicago Neighborhoods (PHDCN)

The National Institute of Justice and the John D. and Catherine T. MacArthur Foundation have collaborated on an ambitious research endeavor (Farrington et al., 1986; Tonry et al., 1991; Earls & Reiss, 1993). Beginning in 1988, teams of researchers worked on development of a research design and data collection instruments. After six years of planning, the project implemented the research design in 1994 and began collecting data in 1995. A probability sample of 80 Chicago neighborhoods was selected for the longitudinal study. During the first wave of interviews, 6,234 children from seven cohorts (ages 0, 3, 6, 9, 12, 15, and 18 years) were surveyed. Eighty-four percent were successfully re-interviewed during the second wave of data collection in 1997-1998. In addition to the longitudinal study, the PHDCN includes a community survey in which community residents in each of Chicago's 343 neighborhoods are interviewed. Observational studies were also conducted from 1996 through 2000. This project included many of the characteristics, research design and measurement, of the OJJDP projects. One notable addition was the inclusion of the birth cohort; pregnant women whose unborn children were monitored throughout pregnancy and after birth. Another feature of this study was the planned collection of medical data that allowed for testing the role of some physiological factors on crime causation. A number of publications have already been produced by members of the research team conducting this extensive study (e.g., Duncan & Raudenbush, 1998; Sampson & Bartusch, 1998; Raudenbush & Sampson, 1999; Sampson et al., 1999; Morenoff et al., 2001; Sampson, 2002).

The International Self-Report Study

While much of the self-report research has been conducted in the United States, one international effort offers a more global approach to the study of crime. The product of a NATO-sponsored workshop convened in the Netherlands in 1988 (Klein, 1989), this international project led to data collection efforts in 13 countries (Belgium, Canada, France, Germany, Greece, Italy, the Netherlands, Northern Ireland, Spain, Sweden, Switzerland, the United Kingdom, and the United States of America). Every effort was made to use comparable sampling techniques and to employ similar methods of questionnaire administration. As with all comparative research, problems such as language, legal statutes, and cultural variations greatly complicated the undertaking. Preliminary comparisons between the countries have shown a considerable degree of consistency with regard to the correlates of self-reported delinquency (Junger-Tas & Klein, 1994).

Strengths of Self-Report Data

Self-report studies were introduced during the 1940s and 1950s to provide an alternative measure to the UCR. It was argued that a substantial "dark figure" of crime existed, that is, that the police were being informed about or discovering only a relatively small fraction of the crime that was occurring.

UCR data are at least one step removed from the actual crime, and therefore, are subject to bias, distortion, and reporting errors. Self-report studies go straight to the point of investigation, to the perpetrator; they do not rely upon second- or third-hand accounts. It is, therefore, possible to ascertain the amount of "secret deviance" (Becker, 1963) or the "dark figure" of crime (Biderman et al., 1967; Reiss, 1967).

The self-report technique, in addition, is not subject to manipulation or politicization, as are UCR data. The police cannot alter self-report data to suit economic or political needs. In this regard, the self-report data can become a measure of police performance and effectiveness.

Weaknesses of Self-Report Data

Since the first use of self-report data, numerous methodological improvements have been made. While self-report studies have been conducted primarily with adolescent populations, this sample bias has been addressed in recent years. The self-report technique has been used in the study of adult prisoners (e.g., Petersilia et al., 1977; Greenwood & Abrahamse, 1982; Horney & Marshall, 1992; Horney et al., 1995) and this survey method has gained increasing usage with other adult samples, especially as longitudinal samples of youth have been followed into adulthood. Representative of this trend are the NYS, the OJJDP funded Causes and Correlates Program, the Dunedin (New Zealand) Study (Moffitt et al., 2001 and Silva & Stanton, 1996), and the Chicago Neighborhoods study.

Other problems, however, persist. The emphasis upon trivial and status offenses constitutes another major problem. Emphasis upon trivial offenses before the NYS research made it difficult, if not impossible, to draw any meaningful comparisons between official crime rates and self-reported crime rates.

Other criticisms of self-report measures include the time frame under consideration and the response categories provided. The time frame used in the reporting period may affect the validity of the data. It is difficult for respondents to recall accurately events that occurred three, five, or 10 years ago. They may forget or, if the time periods are not clearly identified, respondents may include events that occurred outside of the relevant interval. Telescoping refers to projecting an event outside the time period being studied. A calendar year period, as used in the NYS, better permits comparison with the annual UCR figures. The truncated responses of most self-report surveys do not allow for examination of high frequency offenders and tend to group occasional and frequent offenders. This provided a distorted view of the offending behavior.

Methodological concerns have also been raised. These include:

- Sampling;
- Selective loss;
- Falsification, validity, and reliability;
- Memory decay; and
- Interviewer measurement error.

The majority of self-report studies have utilized limited samples of city, county, or state populations. Such samples may well provide unrepresentative information about the true nature and extent of crime.

The problem of selective loss or sample mortality is closely associated with the sampling issue. Whenever researchers study less than the entire population about which they desire to make inferences, the possibility of sampling error arises. Once a sampling technique and a sample have been selected, researchers must deal with the fact that some people will refuse to participate, while others will be unreachable. To what extent do these non-responses bias the results? Initial loss rates of approximately 25 percent are common. While comparisons can be made based on certain demographic information that may be known about the non-respondents, it is impossible to determine the full extent to which the non-respondents may be similar to or different from survey participants.

Falsification is obviously another important matter. Is it not naive to believe that an individual will admit to a perfect stranger in an interview or on a questionnaire that the individual has engaged in criminal acts? Numerous studies have been conducted to assess the extent of falsification. John Clark and Larry Tifft (1966), using polygraphs in order to try to determine the amount of lying, found very little. Martin Gold (1966) utilized community informants to investigate over-reporting and under-reporting of illegal activity; he concluded that self-reports were valid measures. Others have studied individuals already known to have committed certain offenses or have scrutinized police records in order to verify self-report information (Hirschi, 1969; Elliott & Ageton, 1980; Hindelang et al., 1981). In their review of the literature, Robert Hardt and Sandra Peterson-Hardt (1977) concluded that the self-report method appears to provide valid and reliable measures of criminal activity.

Related to falsification is the role of the interviewer in the data collection process. An interviewer's characteristics and attitudes may affect the reporting of behaviors by respondents. Race, sex, social class, and attitudes all have been examined. This research (Schuman & Converse, 1971; Bradburn & Sudman, 1979) suggests that attempts to match respondents with interviewers who have similar demographic characteristics can reduce response error. In a study of interviewer effect upon self-reported delinquency, however, Esbensen (1983:66) concluded that "the effect of any single variable is likely to be minimal."

Victimization Studies

The development of victimization surveys was sponsored by the President's Commission on Law Enforcement and Administration of Justice in the 1960s (Biderman et al., 1967; Ennis, 1967; Reiss, 1967). The best known of the three major early studies is that by the National Opinion Research Center (Ennis, 1967). This work used a sample of 10,000 households (33,000 individuals) in the continental United States. A household representative answered questions for all of its members, unless there had been a criminal victimization. In that case, the interviewer would question the victim about the incident. These early surveys found that victimization for Index crimes was substantially greater than the crime rate reported by the UCR. The victimization rate for rape, for example, was eight times greater than the UCR figure, while the surveys indicated about five times as many assaults.

Numerous methodological concerns were raised after the initial surveys were completed. They included:

- The time period to be used;

- The likelihood that one member of the household would know of or remember criminal victimizations of others;

- The sample size required to measure crime victimization accurately; and

- The frequency with which such a survey should be conducted.

Pre-tests conducted in 1970 and 1971 answered many of the concerns, such as whether a victim would report a victimization to an unknown interviewer. James Garofalo and Michael Hindelang (1977) conducted a reverse-records check in which a total of 982 victims identified from police records in three cities (Washington, Baltimore, and San Jose) were interviewed by U.S. Census Bureau workers. More than 70 percent reported their known victimization to the interviewers. The rate of reporting specific types of crime varied considerably; 88 percent of the sample reported burglaries, but only 47 percent mentioned assaults. Person-to-person crimes, such as assault and rape, especially those committed by acquaintances, seemed less likely to be reported than were victimizations by strangers. This may be attributable to forgetfulness or repression, but Arnold Binder and Gilbert Geis (1983) suggest that in the case of wife-beating and rape, for instance, a woman may not want to jeopardize her relationship with a husband or boyfriend attacker and, therefore, will not report the crime to interviewers. Only 54 percent of victims raped by a person known to them reported the victimization, for example, while 84 percent of those raped by a stranger mentioned the crime to survey interviewers. A second factor found to affect responses was the time frame. In the San Jose study, 81 percent of the victimizations known to have occurred one to three months prior to the interview were reported, while only 67 percent of those that took place 10 to 12 months earlier were reported to the interviewers.

San Jose and Dayton were used to examine the possible effect of having one household member screen questions (household-respondent method), as opposed to having each household member screen questions about his or her own victimization (self-respondent method). The self-respondent method resulted in twice as many reports of robberies, 50 percent more reports of aggravated assaults, and 20 percent more reports of rape. Thus, the household-respondent method provides a substantial underestimate of criminal victimization.

The National Crime Victimization Survey (NCVS)

The National Crime Victimization Survey (NCVS) (originally known as the National Crime Survey or the NCS) was begun in 1972 under the auspices of the Law Enforcement Assistance Administration (LEAA). It consisted of two separate components, one a sample of American cities and the other a national sample. Other countries have also initiated victimization surveys and in 1988 an ambitious multi-national crime victimization survey was launched. See Highlight 3.5 for an overview of the International Crime Victimization Survey (ICVS) that has now been conducted four times in more than 70 countries.

Between July 1972 and May 1975, studies were carried out in 26 different cities, 13 of which were surveyed twice. Based on a representative probability sample of housing units, approximately 10,000 households with about 22,000 eligible respondents (persons above the age of 12) were surveyed in each city. A separate sample of businesses was also contacted in each city. Anywhere from 1,000 to 5,000 businesses were included, based upon the city size. This study of businesses, however, was later discontinued.

HIGHLIGHT 3.5

The International Crime Victimization Survey

In 1988, three European criminologists, Jan van Dijk, Pat Mahew, and Martin Killias, developed the first large-scale international victimization survey. This initial effort provided the stimulus for the International Crime Victimization Survey (ICVS) which now has successfully collected data four times (1989, 1992-94, 1996-97, 2000, and 2004). To date, this household survey has been conducted one or more times in 72 different countries around the world. The ICVS is similar to the NCVS in that detailed information is collected from individuals concerning their experiences as victims of both property and violent crimes. Telephone surveys are conducted in most nations, but in some countries without widespread use of telephones, household visits are necessary. Data from the first four sweeps of the ICVS have provided some interesting insights to the amount of crime cross-nationally. Long considered an extremely crime-ridden society, the United States of America may not be that different from other nations. Victimization rates for selected crimes and countries are reported for the 1997 ICVS data.

Country	Any Crime	Burglary	Contact Crimes
Argentina	87	28	37
Brazil	68	14	45
Canada	64	19	18
Egypt	69	22	32
England & Wales	63	23	17
China	52	9	13
Germany	62	12	18
Philippines	40	10	11
Poland	61	13	16
Russia	63	17	22
South Africa	64	23	29
Sweden	67	15	19
USA	64	23	20

For the national survey, households and businesses were chosen on the basis of a stratified multi-stage cluster sample, which yielded a sample of 60,000 households containing approximately 136,000 individuals and about 15,000 businesses. Six separate sample units were then selected; members of each subsample were interviewed during successive months. In this manner, the entire sample was interviewed in six months, at which point the cycle was repeated. Each household address was visited a maximum of seven times during three years before it was rotated out of the sample and replaced by a new household address. This procedure produces a panel design that allows the same group of people to be queried over a period of time. It also provides the opportunity to control for the problem of telescoping by comparing the most recently reported victimizations with responses from the previous interview. Budget cuts during the past several years, however, have reduced the sample size of households to slightly more than 40,000 and have increased reliance on telephone surveys to collect the data.

The NCVS, initially supervised by LEAA, is now conducted by the U.S. Bureau of the Census. Victimization statistics are the primary data objective of these surveys, but other information related to crime is also collected. Questions are asked about fear of crime, the perceived decline or improvement of the neighborhood in regard to crime, and about steps that have been taken to protect the household against victimization.

In 1992, the U.S. Department of Justice introduced a redesigned National Crime Victimization Survey (U.S. Department of Justice, 1997c). New screening procedures using detailed cues to help respondents recall crime incidents resulted in considerably higher reported levels of victimization, especially for simple assaults. Of notable interest is the change in the measurement of domestic violence and rape (Bachman & Taylor, 1994). While these types of victimizations were previously obtained through indirect questioning, the redesigned NCVS includes specific questions about these victimizations. To measure domestic violence, respondents are queried about thefts and attacks by someone they know. To measure rape, the respondents are asked: "have you been forced or coerced to engage in unwanted sexual activity by (a) Someone you didn't know, (b) a casual acquaintance, or (c) Someone you know well?" As a result of these types of changes, data collected since 1992 are no longer comparable with data collected in previous years. Highlight 3.6 provides an example of the types of questions asked of respondents in the NCVS.

Strengths of Victimization Surveys

The NCVS had been heralded as the solution to the crime measurement issue, but it also proved far from a perfect enumeration of crime. Nevertheless, the national probability sample of residences allows for comparisons with the UCR data collected by the FBI, and this comparability has been one of the primary uses of the NCVS, a sort of validity check on the UCR. The NCVS, like the UCR, also can be used to study geographical and temporal variations in the crime rate and can provide a basis for evaluating local and national law enforcement practices.

Another major NCVS advantage is that a lot of information is collected about relatively few crimes. The UCR, on the other hand, collects a little bit of information about a lot of crimes. The NCVS approach allows appraisal of financial, psychological, and sociological effects of victimization; for each specific criminal victimization, respondents are requested to supply estimates regarding the cost of materials stolen or destroyed. Due to the NCVS panel design (interviewing the same household over a period of three years), it is also possible to examine the psychosocial effects of victimization upon crime victims over time. How are people's attitudes and behaviors affected by victimization? Is there such a thing as "victim-proneness"? These are questions that can be answered by in-depth interviews.

HIGHLIGHT 3.6

Sample Questions from the National Crime Victimization Survey

INDIVIDUAL'S PERSONAL CHARACTERISTICS		
17. NAME	**18.** Type of interview PGM 4	**19.** Line No.
Last First	401 1 ☐ Per. – Self-respondent 2 ☐ Tel. – Self-respondent 3 ☐ Per. – Proxy 4 ☐ Tel. – Proxy } *Fill 13 on cover page* 5 ☐ Noninterview — *Fill 19-28 and 14 on cover page*	402 _____ Line No.

20. Relationship to reference person	**21.** Age last birthday	**22a.** Marital status THIS survey period	**22b.** Marital status LAST survey period	**23.** Sex	**24.** Armed Forces member	**25a.** Education -highest grade	**25b.** Education -complete that year?	**26.** Attending college	**27.** Race	**28.** Hispanic origin
403	404	405	406	407	408	409	410	411	412	413
01 ☐ Husband 02 ☐ Wife 03 ☐ Son 04 ☐ Daughter 05 ☐ Father 06 ☐ Mother 07 ☐ Brother 08 ☐ Sister 09 ☐ Other relative 10 ☐ Nonrelative 11 ☐ Ref. person	Age	1 ☐ Married 2 ☐ Widowed 3 ☐ Divorced 4 ☐ Separated 5 ☐ Never married	1 ☐ Married 2 ☐ Widowed 3 ☐ Divorced 4 ☐ Separated 5 ☐ Never married 6 ☐ Not inter-viewed last survey period	1 ☐ M 2 ☐ F	1 ☐ Yes 2 ☐ No	Grade	1 ☐ Yes 2 ☐ No	1 ☐ College/ University 2 ☐ Trade/ school 3 ☐ Voca-tional school 2 ☐ Not at all	1 ☐ White 2 ☐ Black 3 ☐ Amer. Indian, Aleut, Eskimo 4 ☐ Asian, Pacific Islander 5 ☐ Other	1 ☐ Yes 2 ☐ No

29. Date of interview ⟶   PGM 5 501 ☐☐ ☐☐ ☐☐ Month   Day   Year

30. Before we get to the crime questions, I'd like to ask you about some of YOUR usual activities. We have found that people with different lifestyles may be more or less likely to become victims of crime.

On average, during the last 6 months, that is, since _____, 19___, how often have YOU gone shopping? For example at drug, clothing, grocery, hardware and convenience stores. *(Read answer categories until respondent answers yes.)*

Mark (X) the first category that applies.

502   1 ☐ Almost every day (or more frequently) 2 ☐ At least once a week 3 ☐ At least once a month 4 ☐ Less often 5 ☐ Never 6 ☐ Don't know

31. On average, during the last 6 months, how often have you spent the evening out away from home for work, school or entertainment? *(Read answer categories until respondent answers yes.)*

Mark (X) the first category that applies.

503   1 ☐ Almost every evening (or more frequently) 2 ☐ At least once a week 3 ☐ At least once a month 4 ☐ Less often 5 ☐ Never 6 ☐ Don't know

32. On average, during the last 6 months, how often have you ridden public transportation? *(Read answer categories until respondent answers yes.)*

Do not include school buses.

Mark (X) the first category that applies.

504   1 ☐ Almost every day (or more frequently) 2 ☐ At least once a week 3 ☐ At least once a month 4 ☐ Less often 5 ☐ Never 6 ☐ Don't know

If unsure, ASK OR VERIFY –

33a. How long have you lived at this address? *(Enter number of months OR years.)*

505 _____ Months (1-11) – *SKIP to 33b* OR 506 _____ Years (Round to nearest *whole year)* – Fill Check Item A

CHECK ITEM A How many years are entered in 33a?

☐ 5 years or more – *SKIP to 36a* ☐ Less than 5 years – *Ask 33b*

33b. Altogether, how many times have you moved in the last 5 years, that is, since _____, 19___?

508 _____ Number of times

FORM NCVS-1 (10-25-95)   Page 9

HIGHLIGHT **3.6** Continued

INDIVIDUAL'S SCREEN QUESTIONS	

36a. I'm going to read some examples that will give you an idea of the kinds of crimes this study covers.

Briefly describe incident(s)

As I go through them, tell me if any of these happened to you in the last 6 months, that is since _____ ____, 19___.

Was something belonging to YOU stolen, such as –

(a) Things that you carry, like luggage, a wallet, purse, briefcase, book –

(b) Clothing, jewelry, or calculator –

(c) Bicycle or sports equipment –

(d) Things in your home – like a TV, stereo, or tools –

(e) Things from a vehicle, such as a package, groceries, camera, or cassette tapes –

OR

(f) Did anyone ATTEMPT to steal anything belonging to you?

MARK OR ASK –

36b. Did any incidents of this type happen to you?

532   1 ☐ Yes – **What happened?**
Describe above
2 ☐ No – **SKIP** to 40a

36c. How many times?

533   _____
Number of times (36c)

40a. (Other than any incidents already mentioned,) since _____ ____, 19___, were you attacked or threatened OR did you have something stolen from you –

Briefly describe incident(s)

(a) At home including the porch or yard –

(b) At or near a friend's, relative's, or neighbor's home –

(c) At work or school –

(d) In places such as a storage shed or laundry room, a shopping mall, restaurant, bank, or airport –

(e) While riding in any vehicle –

(f) On the street or in a parking lot –

(g) At such places as a party, theater, gym, picnic area, bowling lanes, or while fishing or hunting –

OR

(h) Did anyone ATTEMPT to attack or ATTEMPT to steal anything belonging to you from any of these places?

MARK OR ASK –

40b. Did any incidents of this type happen to you?

532   1 ☐ Yes – **What happened?**
Describe above
2 ☐ No – **SKIP** to 41a

40c. How many times?

533   _____
Number of times (40c)

Weaknesses of Victimization Surveys

Caution must be exercised when interpreting NCVS data. Problems include those common to self-report studies (e.g., falsification, telescoping, validity, interviewer effect, and sampling). In addition, idiosyncrasies of the victimization data collection process draw criticism. The household-respondent method, for instance, results in underreporting. This also occurs for rapes and assaults committed by acquaintances. Other procedures result in overreporting; several of these are discussed below.

Cost is also a major problem associated with victimization research. The current NCVS studies of 40,000 households represent a major financial outlay and are to some extent cost-prohibitive.

Several unique methodological issues have been raised concerning NCVS recording practices. Many of the victimizations reported, for example, represent trivial offenses, such as minor assaults that normally would not be considered crimes. Prior to the redesign of the NCVS in 1992, rape was measured indirectly. In the earlier surveys, the woman was not asked if she had been raped. Instead, if she answered "yes" to one of the following questions, "Did anyone threaten to beat you up or threaten you in some way?" or "Did anyone try to attack you in some other way?," then her answer was tabulated as a rape. Such methodological problems may go a long way toward explaining some of the differences in NCVS and UCR findings that are discussed in Chapter 4.

A second recording difficulty is that victimization surveys record crimes perpetrated against individuals and households, employing place of residence as an independent variable. That is, the studies include victimizations that occurred outside of the geographical area of residence. Conversely, they do not measure the victimization of non-residents. This means that persons such as commuters, transients, and tourists, who are included in the UCR data, are not counted in the NCVS figures. This practice distorts the portrayal of the geographical distribution of crime (Skogan, 1976).

Another peculiarity of victimization recording that leads to under-reporting is the use of what are referred to as "series incidents." This offense category includes incidents such as child abuse and spouse abuse, which have no clear-cut beginning or end. In the NCVS, discrete events typically are counted. Therefore, when spouse abuse is reported, it becomes difficult to separate one incident from another. When a father or husband regularly mistreats his children or spouse, for example, is this a single incident or two or three or many more? In such cases, the NCVS uses the series incidence measure. These series incidents are not recorded in the victimization rates. Consequently, the NCVS underestimates the incidence of domestic violence and other crimes that involve a continuing relationship between offender and victim.

Problems shared by the NCVS with the self-report technique revolve around the data collection method. Reliability studies have found that individuals vary in their reporting of victimization, depending upon their educational level and the type of crime committed. "In 1976, for example, persons with college degrees recalled three times as many assaults as those with only an elementary education" (Gove et al., 1985:460). It seems unlikely that the college-educated respondents were assaulted more often; it is more reasonable that they attended to slights and other incidents that those with less education ignored. The majority of assaults reported in victimization surveys are relatively trivial, with many involving no injury. This raises the question of whether an assault or an intended assault, as defined by law, actually occurred (Gove et al., 1985).

Examinations of interviewer impact in self-report studies have indicated little or no significant effect. However, Summer Clarren and Alfred Schwartz (1976:129) concluded: "the upper bound for the number of 'crimes' that could be elicited is limited only by the persistence of the interviewer and the patience of the respondent." Interestingly, the very crimes that tend to be both overreported and underreported (rape, assault, petty theft, and series incidents) are those most affected by the ability and the patience of the interviewers.

Comparison of UCR, SRD, and NCVS Data Sources

The three measures of crime just reviewed paint different pictures of the extent and distribution of crime in the United States. This highlights the importance of understanding the merits of the particular source. According to the UCR, for example, crime increased from 1960 through 1990 and has been declining since 1991, but both the NCVS and SRD suggest relative stability and even a decline since 1973 (Menard, 1987; U.S. Department of Justice, 1997b). Certainly, these contradictory conclusions about crime trends cannot both be valid! But, alas, given the different measurement (e.g., crimes included, populations covered, and recording policies), it is possible that each source is correct in its own particular way. Biderman and Lynch (1991) have provided an excellent critique of the UCR and the NCVS, concluding that once their different methodologies are considered, the findings are not as disparate as it appears.

Robert O'Brien (1985), in providing what is considered by many to be the best review of the three data sources, points out that there are definitional differences between the three. For example, neither the victimization nor the self-report studies include homicide, while the NCVS excludes commercial larceny. With respect to populations covered, the UCR is said to represent 95 percent of the U.S. population, the NCVS is a national probability sample of persons over the age of 12. To date, there is no comparable self-report study of a national probability sample of adults that is conducted on an annual basis.

While the UCR and NCVS allow city comparisons, caution is urged. The UCR records crimes that occur in the city whereas the NCVS measures crimes that happened to city residents. City comparisons using these two data sources, then, are based on different populations and may produce different estimates of crime as well as different descriptions of offenders and victims. Differences also exist with regard to how the data get recorded. Both the NCVS and SRD yield information about actual behavior (i.e., victimization and offending respectively), while the UCR is largely a reactive measure of police response to citizen complaints. Given these differences, one has to ask, "Do these sources actually measure the same phenomenon?" While no clear consensus exists in the field (e.g., O'Brien, 1985; Biderman & Lynch, 1991; Blumstein, Cohen & Rosenfeld, 1991; Menard, 1992), let us consider the example of a convenience store robbery in which five customers are present. The UCR guidelines instruct the police to record this as one criminal event, thus reporting it as one robbery. The NCVS, however, treats the individual as the reporting unit so, if all five victims were participants in the NCVS, then five robbery victims would be tallied. This example illustrates that these two data sources may well measure different aspects of the same phenomenon. To better understand the crime problem and criminal justice response to crime, it is of utmost importance to realize the extent to which the data source shapes the picture of crime. These differences will be discussed more fully in Chapter 4.

Summary

Crime statistics are essential to criminology. Knowledge of the extent and distribution of crime in society shapes both criminological theories and criminal justice policy. This chapter reviewed three major sources of crime data, as well as several other approaches. Crime statistics are inherently quantitative, allowing for computation of crime rates (UCR) or prevalence rates (SRD and NCVS). The data permit researchers and policymakers to examine crime trends and to evaluate the impact of various criminal justice programs.

The Uniform Crime Reports are the result of information supplied by local law enforcement agencies to the FBI. This measure of crime was first collected in 1930 and today represents approximately 95 percent of the nation's population. Most attention is paid to the Part I Index crimes, which include particularly serious and relatively frequently occurring crimes (homicide, rape, robbery, aggravated assault, burglary, larceny-theft, motor vehicle theft, and arson). The FBI tabulates the information sent to it and issues quarterly and annual reports that typically are summarized by the media. These data are largely responsible for the public's perception of the extent of crime in the United States. As with any data, the UCR have both positive and negative aspects associated with their use and interpretation.

Self-report studies, an alternative measure of crime, were introduced during the 1940s. They ask survey respondents to identify illegal or deviant acts they have committed during some specified period. Researchers have continued to improve upon the SRD method and this data source is widely used to test and develop theories of crime.

Victimization studies were introduced in the mid-1960s and provide a third source of information on crime. Similar to the SRD, victimization studies use surveys and ask people directly about crimes that have been committed against them or their households. The National Crime Survey, conducted by the U.S. Census Bureau, provides annual data on the victimization rate for the population at large, as well as for subgroups and for specific areas of the country. As with the self-report method, victimization studies have a number of methodological problems, but they provide a valuable alternative source of information that has improved our understanding of the extent and distribution of crime.

Key Terms and Concepts

Biographies
Causality
Cohort Studies
Comparison Group
Control Group
Correlation
Crime Frequency
Crime Prevalence
Crime Rate
Crime Seriousness Scale
Cross-Sectional Design
Dark Figure of Crime
Dependent Variable
Experimental Group
Hierarchical Rule
Independent Variable
Index Crimes

Levels of Explanation
Longitudinal Designs
Macro Level
Micro Level
National Crime Victimization Survey
Observational Studies
Part I Crimes
Part II Crimes
Probability Sample
Reliability
Self-Report Studies
Stratified Probability Sample
Telescoping
Uniform Crime Reports
Validity
Victimization Surveys

Key Criminologists

Albert D. Biderman
Delbert Elliott
James Garofalo
Michael Hindelang
David Huizinga

Rolf Loeber
F. Ivan Nye
Thorsten Sellin
James F. Short, Jr.
Terence P. Thornberry

References

Addington, L.A. (2004). "The Effect of NIBRS Reporting on Item Missing Data in Murder Cases." *Homicide Studies*, 8:193-213.

Addington, L.A. (2006). "Using NIBRS Murder Data to Evaluate Clearance Predictors: A Research Note." *Homicide Studies*.

Adler, P.A. (1992). *Wheeling and Dealing: An Ethnography of Upper-Level Drug Dealing and Smuggling Community*, Second Edition. New York, NY: Columbia University Press.

Aebi, M. (2002). "Counting Rules as the Main Explanation of Cross-National Differences in Recorded Crime." Paper presented at the Annual Meeting of the European Society of Criminology, Toledo, Spain, September.

Akiyama, Y. & J. Nolan (1999). "Methods for Understanding and Analyzing NIBRS Data." *Journal of Quantitative Criminology*, 15:225-238.

Bachman, R. & B.M. Taylor (1994). "The Measurement of Family Violence and Rape by the Redesigned National Crime Victimization Survey." *Justice Quarterly*, 11:499-512.

Becker, H.S. (1963). *Outsiders: Studies in the Sociology of Deviance*. New York, NY: The Free Press.

Biderman, A.D., L.A. Johnson, J. McIntyre & A. Weir (1967). *Report on a Pilot Study in the District of Columbia on Victimization and Attitudes Toward Law Enforcement*. Washington, DC: President's Commission on Law Enforcement and Administration of Justice.

Biderman, A.D. & J.P. Lynch (1991). *Understanding Crime Incidence Statistics: Why the UCR Diverges from the NCVS*. New York, NY: Springer-Verlag.

Binder, A. & G. Geis (1983). *Methods of Research in Criminology and Criminal Justice*. New York, NY: McGraw-Hill.

Bjerregard, B. & A.J. Lizotte (1995). "Gun Ownership and Gang Membership." *The Journal of Criminal Law and Criminology*, 86:37-58.

Bjerregard, B. & C. Smith (1993). "Gender Differences in Gang Participation, Delinquency, and Substance Use." *Journal of Quantitative Criminology*, 9:329-355.

Blumstein, A., J. Cohen & R. Rosenfeld (1991). "Trend and Deviation in Crime Rates: A Comparison of UCR and NCVS Data for Burglary and Robbery." *Criminology*, 29:237-263.

Bradburn, N.M. & S. Sudman (1979). *Improving Interview Method and Questionnaire Design*. San Francisco, CA: Jossey-Bass.

Campbell, A. (1991). *The Girls in the Gang*, Second Edition. New York, NY: Basil Blackwell.

Chappell, D., G. Geis, S. Schafer & L. Siegel (1971). "Forcible Rape: A Comparative Study of Offenses Known to the Police in Boston and Los Angeles." In J.M. Henslin (ed.) *Studies in the Sociology of Sex*. New York, NY: Appleton-Century-Crofts.

Chilton, R. (2004). "Regional Variations in Lethal and Non-lethal Assaults." *Homicide Studies*, 8:40-56.

Chilton, R. & J. Jarvis (1999). "Using the National Incident-Based Reporting System (NIBRS) to Test Effects of Arrestee and Offender Characteristics." *Journal of Quantitative Criminology*, 15:207-224.

Clark, J.P. & L.L. Tifft (1966). "Polygraph and Interview Validation of Self-Reported Deviant Behavior." *American Sociological Review*, 31:516-523.

Clarren, S.N. & A.I. Schwartz (1976). "Measuring a Program's Impact: A Cautionary Note." In W. Skogan (ed.) *Sample Surveys of the Victims of Crime*. Cambridge, MA: Ballinger.

Decker, S.H. & B. Van Winkle (1996). *Life in the Gang: Family Friend, and Violence*. New York, NY: Cambridge University Press.

Duncan, G.J. & S.W. Raudenbush (1998). "Assessing the Effects of Context in Studies of Child and Youth Development." *Educational Psychologist*, 34:29-41.

Dunn, C.S. & T.J. Zelenock (1999). "NIBRS Data Available for Secondary Data Analysis." *Journal of Quantitative Criminology*, 15:239-248.

Earls, F.J. & A.J. Reiss, Jr. (1993). "Annual Report of the Program on Human Development and Criminal Behavior for the John D. & Catherine T. MacArthur Foundation." Cambridge, MA: Harvard School of Public Health.

Elliott, D.S. & S.S. Ageton (1980). "Reconciling Race and Class Differences in Self-Reported and Official Estimates of Delinquency." *American Sociological Review*, 45:95-110.

Elliott, D.S., S.S. Ageton, D. Huizinga, B.A. Knowles & R.J. Canter (1983). *The Prevalence and Incidence of Delinquent Behavior: 1976-1980*. Boulder, CO: Behavioral Research Institute.

Elliott, D.S., D. Huizinga & S.S. Ageton (1985). *Explaining Delinquency and Drug Use.* Beverly Hills, CA: Sage Publications.

Ennis, P. (1967). *Criminal Victimization in the United States: A Report of a National Survey.* Washington, DC: President's Commission on Law Enforcement and Administration of Justice.

Esbensen, F.-A. (1983). "Measurement Error and Self-Reported Delinquency: An Examination of Interviewer Bias." In G.P. Waldo (ed.) *Measurement Issues in Criminal Justice.* Beverly Hills, CA: Sage Publications.

Esbensen, F.-A., D. Huizinga & S. Menard (1999). "Family Context and Victimization." *Youth and Society*, 31:168-198.

Esbensen, F.-A. & D. Huizinga (1993). "Gangs, Drugs, and Delinquency in a Survey of Urban Youth." *Criminology*, 31:565-589.

Esbensen, F.-A. & D. Huizinga (1991). "Juvenile Victimization and Delinquency." *Youth and Society*, 23:202-228.

Faggiani, D. & C. McLaughlin (1999). 'Using National Incident-Based Reporting System Data for Strategic Crime Analysis." *Journal of Quantitative Criminology*, 15:181-191.

Fairchild, E. & H.R. Dammer (2001). *Comparative Criminal Justice Systems*, Second Edition. New York, NY: Wadsworth.

Farrington, D.P., L.E. Ohlin & J.Q. Wilson (1986). *Understanding and Controlling Crime: Toward a New Research Strategy.* New York, NY: Springer-Verlag.

Finkelhor, D. & R. Ormrod (2001). "Child Abuse Reported to Police." *Juvenile Justice Bulletin* (May). Washington, DC: U.S. Department of Justice, Office of Justice Programs, Office of Juvenile Justice & Delinquency Prevention.

del Frate, A.A. (2002). "Introduction and Overview of the ICVS." Paper presented at the 2nd Annual Meeting of the European Society of Criminology, Toledo, Spain, September 5, 2002.

Garofalo, J. & M.J. Hindelang (1977). *An Introduction to the National Crime Survey.* Washington, DC: National Criminal Justice Information and Statistics Service, Law Enforcement Assistance Administration, U.S. Department of Justice.

Gold, M. (1966). "Undetected Delinquent Behavior." *Journal of Research in Crime and Delinquency*, 3:27-46.

Gove, W.R., M. Hughes & M. Geerken (1985). "Are Uniform Crime Reports a Valid Indicator of the Index Crimes? An Affirmative Answer with Minor Qualifications." *Criminology*, 23:451-502.

Greenwood, P.W. & A. Abrahamse (1982). *Selective Incapacitation.* Santa Monica, CA: RAND Corporation.

Hardt, R.H. & S. Peterson-Hardt (1977). "On Determining the Quality of the Delinquency Self-Report Method." *Journal of Research in Crime and Delinquency*, 14:247-261.

Harlow, C.W. (1986). *Reporting Crimes to the Police.* Washington, DC: The Criminal Justice Archive and Information Network.

Hindelang, M.J., T. Hirschi & J.G. Weis (1981). *Measuring Delinquency.* Beverly Hills, CA: Sage Publications.

Hirschi, T. (1969). *Causes of Delinquency*. Berkeley, CA: University of California Press.

Horney, J. & I.H. Marshall (1992). "Risk Perceptions Among Serious Offenders: The Role of Crime and Punishment." *Criminology*, 30:575-594.

Horney, J., D.W. Osgood & I.H. Marshall (1995). "Criminal Careers in the Short-Term: Intra-Individual Variability in Crime and Its Relation to Local Life Circumstances." *American Sociological Review*, 60:655-673.

Huizinga, D. (1997). "Gangs and the Volume of Crime." Paper presented at the annual meeting of the Western Society of Criminology.

Huizinga, D. & D.S. Elliott (1987). "Juvenile Offenders: Prevalence, Offenders, and Arrest Rates by Race." *Crime & Delinquency*, 33:206-223.

Huizinga, D., F. Esbensen & A.W. Weiher (1994a). "Examining Developmental Trajectories in Delinquency Using Accelerated Longitudinal Designs." In E.G.M. Weitekamp & H.J. Kerner (eds.) *Cross-National Longitudinal Research on Human Development and Criminal Behavior*. Dordrecht, The Netherlands: Kluwer.

Huizinga, D., F. Esbensen & A.W. Weiher (1991). "Are There Multiple Paths to Delinquency?" *Journal of Criminal Law and Criminology*, 82:83-118.

Huizinga, D. & K. L. Henry (2007). "The Effect of Arrest and Justice System Sanctions on Subsequent Behavior: Findings from Longitudinal and Other Studies". In Liberman (Ed.) *The Long View of Crime: A Synthesis of Longitudinal Research*. Springer New York.

Huizinga, D., R. Loeber & T.P. Thornberry (1994b). *Urban Delinquency and Substance Abuse*. Washington, DC: U.S. Department of Justice.

Jacobs, B.A. (1999). *Dealing Crack: The Social World of Streetcorner Selling*. Boston, MA: Northeastern University Press.

Junger-Tas, J. & M. Klein (1994). *International Self-Report Delinquency Survey*. Amsterdam, The Netherlands: Kugler Publishers.

Kappeler, V.E., M. Blumberg & G.W. Potter (1993). *The Mythology of Crime and Criminal Justice*. Prospect Heights, IL: Waveland Press.

Kelley, B.T., D. Huizinga, T.P. Thornberry & R. Loeber (1997). *Epidemiology of Serious Violence*. Washington, DC: U.S. Department of Justice.

Klein, M. (1989). *Cross-National Research in Self-Reported Crime and Delinquency*. Dordrecht: Kluwer.

Klockars, C.B. (1974). *The Professional Fence*. New York, NY: The Free Press.

Lizotte, A.J. M.D. Krohn, J.C. Howell, K. Tobin & G.J. Howard (2000). "Factors Influencing Gun Carrying among Young Urban Males over the Adolescent-Young Adult Life Course." *Criminology*, 38:811-834.

Lizotte, A.J., J.M. Tesoriero, T.P. Thornberry & M.D. Krohn (1994). "Patterns of Adolescent Firearms Ownership and Use." *Justice Quarterly*, 11:51-73.

Loeber, R., S.M. Green, K. Keenan & B.B. Lahey (1995). "Which Boys Will Fare Worse? Early Predictors of the Onset of Conduct Disorder in a Six Year Longitudinal Study." *Journal of the American Academy of Child and Adolescent Psychiatry*, 34:499-509.

Loeber, R., M. Stouthamer-Loeber, W. Van Kammen & D. Farrington (1991). "Initiation, Escalation and Desistance in Juvenile Offending and their Correlates." *Journal of Criminal Law and Criminology*, 82:36-82.

Maxfield, M.G. (1999). "The National Incident-Based Reporting System: Research and policy implications." *Journal of Quantitative Criminology*, 15:119-149.

Maltz, M.D. (1999). *Bridging Gaps in Police Crime Data*. Washington, DC: U.S. Department of Justice.

Maltz, M.D. (1977). "Crime Statistics: A Historical Perspective." *Crime & Delinquency*, 23:32-40.

Maxson, C. & M.W. Klein (1990). "Street Gang Violence: Twice as Great or Half as Great?" In C.R. Huff (ed.) *Gangs in America*. Newbury Park, CA: Sage Publications.

Maxson, C.L. & M.W. Klein (2002). "Defining Gang Homicide: An Updated Look at the Member and Motive Approaches." In J. Miller, C.L. Maxson & M.W. Klein (eds.) *The Modern Gang Reader*, Third Edition. Los Angeles, CA: Roxbury Press.

Menard, S. (1992). "Residual Gains, Reliability, and the UCR-NCS Relationship: A Comment on Blumstein, Cohen, and Rosenfeld." *Criminology*, 30:105-113.

Menard, S. (1987). "Short-Term Trends in Crime and Delinquency: A Comparison of UCR, NCS and Self-Report Data." *Justice Quarterly*, 4:455-474.

Messner, S.F., S. McHugh & R.B. Felson (2004). "Distinctive Characteristics of Assaults Motivated by Bias." *Criminology*, 42:585-618.

Miller, J. (2001). *One of the Guys: Girls, Gangs, and Gender*. New York, NY: Oxford University Press.

Moffitt, T.E., A. Caspi, N. Dickson, P. Silva & W. Stanton (2001). "Males on the Life–Course Persistence and Adolescence–Limited Antisocial Pathways: Follow-Up at Age 26." *Development and Psychopathology*.

Morenoff, J.D., R.J. Sampson & S.W. Raudenbush (2001). "Neighborhood Inequality, Collective Efficacy, and the Spatial Dynamics of Urban Violence." *Criminology*, 39:517-559.

Nye, F.I. (1958). *Family Relationships and Delinquent Behavior*. New York, NY: John Wiley and Sons.

O'Brien, R.M. (1985). *Crime and Victimization Data*. Beverly Hills, CA: Sage Publications.

Pepinsky, H.E. & P. Jesilow (1984). *Myths that Cause Crime*. Cabin John, MD: Seven Locks Press.

Petersilia, J., P.W. Greenwood & M. Lavin (1977). *Criminal Careers of Habitual Felons*. Santa Monica, CA: RAND Corporation.

Porterfield, A.L. (1946). *Youth in Trouble*. Fort Worth, TX: Leo Potisham Foundation.

Rantala, R.R. & T.J. Edwards (2000). *Effects of NIBRS on Crime Statistics*. Washington, DC: U.S. Department of Justice, Office of Justice Programs.

Raudenbush, S.W. & R.J. Sampson (1999). "Econometrics: Toward a Science of Assessing Ecological Settings, with Application to Systematic Social Observation of Neighborhoods." *Sociological Methodology*, 29:1-41.

Reiss, A.J., Jr. (1967). *Studies in Crime and Law Enforcement in Major Metropolitan Areas*. Washington, DC: President's Commission on Law Enforcement and Administration of Justice.

Sampson, R.J. (2002) "Transcending Tradition: New Directions in Community Research, Chicago Style—The American Society of Criminology 2001 Sutherland Address." *Criminology*, 40:213-230.

Sampson, R.J. & D. Bartusch (1998). "Legal Cynicism and (Subcultural?) Tolerance of Deviance: The Neighborhood Context of Racial Differences." *Law and Society Review*, 32:777-804.

Sampson, R.J., J.D. Morenoff & F.J. Earls (1999). "Beyond Social Capital: Spatial Dynamics of Collective Efficacy for Children." *American Sociological Review*, 64:633-660.

Schuman, H. & J.M. Converse (1971). "The Effects of Black and White Interviewers on Black Responses in 1968." *Public Opinion Quarterly*, 35:49-68.

Sellin, T. (1931). "The Basis of a Crime Index." *Journal of Criminal Law and Criminology*, 22:335-356.

Short, J.F., Jr. & F.I. Nye (1957). "Reported Behavior as a Criterion of Deviant Behavior." *Social Problems*, 5:207-213.

Silva, P. & W. Stanton (1996). *From Child to Adult: The Dunedin Multidisciplinary Health and Development Study*. Auckland: Oxford University Press.

Simon, D.R. & D.S. Eitzen (1990). *Elite Deviance*, Third Edition. Newton, MA: Allyn and Bacon.

Skogan, W. (1976). "Crime and Crime Rates." In Wesley Skogan (ed.) *Sample Surveys of Victims of Crime*. Cambridge, MA: Ballinger.

Snyder, H.N. (1999). "The Overrepresentation of Juvenile Crime Proportions in Robbery Clearance Statistics." *Journal of Quantitative Criminology*, 15:151-161.

Steffensmeir, D. (1986). *The Fence: In the Shadow of Two Worlds*. Totowa, NJ: Rowman and Littlefield.

Strom, K.J. (2001). Hate Crimes Reported in NIBRS, 1997-99. *Bureau of Justice Statistics Special Report* (September). U.S. Department of Justice, Office of Justice Programs, Bureau of Justice Statistics.

Sutherland, E.H. (1937). *The Professional Thief*. Chicago, IL: University of Chicago Press.

Taylor, T.J., D. Holleran & V. Topalli (2009). "Racial Bias in Case Processing: Does Victim Race Affect Police Clearance of Violent Crime Incidents?" *Justice Quarterly* 26: 562-591.

Thompson, M.P., L.E. Saltzman & D. Bibel (1999). "Applying NIBRS Data to the Study of Intimate Partner Violence." *Journal of Quantitative Criminology*, 15:163-180.

Thornberry, T.P., M.D. Krohn, A.J. Lizotte, C.A. Smith & K. Tobin (2003). *Gangs and Delinquency in Developmental Perspective*. New York, NY: Cambridge University Press.

Thornberry, T.P., E.H. Wei, M. Stouthamer-Loeber & J. Van Dyke (2000). *Teenage Fatherhood and Delinquent Behavior*. Washington, DC: U.S. Department of Justice.

Thornberry, T.P., D. Huizinga & R. Loeber (1995). "The Prevention of Serious Delinquency and Violence: Implications from the Program of Research on the Causes and Correlates of Delinquency." In J.C. Howell, B. Krisberg, J.D. Hawkins & J.J. Wilson (eds.) *A Sourcebook: Serious, Violent, & Chronic Juvenile Offenders*. Thousand Oaks, CA: Sage Publications.

Thornberry, T.P., M.D. Krohn, A.J. Lizotte & D. Chard-Wierschem (1993). "The Role of Juvenile Gangs in Facilitating Delinquent Behavior." *Journal of Research in Crime and Delinquency*, 30:55-87.

Thornberry, T.P., A.J. Lizotte, M.D. Krohn, M. Farnworth & S.J. Jang (1991). "Testing Interactional Theory: An Examination of Reciprocal Causal Relationships Among, Family, School, and Delinquency." *Journal of Criminal Law and Criminology*, 82:3-35.

Tittle, C., W. Villemez & D. Smith (1978). "The Myth of Social Class and Criminality: An Empirical Assessment of the Empirical Evidence." *American Sociological Review*, 43:643-656.

Tonry, M., L.E. Ohlin & D.P. Farrington (1991). *Human Development and Criminal Behavior: New Ways of Advancing Knowledge*. New York, NY: Springer-Verlag.

U.S. Department of Justice, Federal Bureau of Investigation. (2006). National Incident-Based Reporting System (NIBRS) frequently asked questions [online]. Available at http://www.fbi.gov/ucr/faqs.htm. Retrieved May 30, 2006.

U.S. Department of Justice, Federal Bureau of Investigation. (2004). *Uniform Crime Reporting Handbook*. Washington, DC: US Department of Justice, Federal Bureau of Investigation.

U.S. Department of Justice (1997a). *Criminal Victimization in the U.S.: 1994*. Washington, DC: U.S. Department of Justice.

U.S. Department of Justice (1997b). *Criminal Victimization, 1973-1995*. Washington, DC: U.S. Department of Justice.

U.S. Department of Justice (1997c). *Effects of the Redesign on Victimization Estimates*. Washington, DC: U.S. Department of Justice.

U.S. Department of Justice (1994). *Criminal Victimization in the U.S.: 1993*. Washington, DC: U.S. Department of Justice.

U.S. Department of Justice (1988). *Uniform Crime Reporting: National Incident-Based Reporting System, Volume 1; Data Collection Guidelines*. Washington, DC: U.S. Department of Justice.

U.S. Department of Justice (1996). *Uniform Crime Reporting Handbook*. Washington, DC: U.S. Department of Justice.

van Dijk, J. & K. Kangaspunta (2000). "Piecing Together the Cross-National Crime Puzzle." *National Institute of Justice Journal*, January:34-41.

Vasquez, S.P., M.K. Stohr & M. Purkiss (2005). "Intimate Partner Violence Incidence and Characteristics: Idaho NIBRS 1995 to 2001 Data." *Criminal Justice Policy Review*, 16:99-114.

Wallerstein, J.S. & C.J. Wyle (1947). "Our Law-Abiding Lawbreakers." *Probation*, 25:107-112.

Wright, R.T. & S.H. Decker (1997). *Armed Robbers in Action: Stickups and Street Culture*. Boston, MA: Northeastern University Press.

Wright, R.T. & S.H. Decker (1994). *Burglars on the Job: Streetlife and Residential Break-Ins*. Boston, MA: Northeastern University Press.

4
Distribution of Crime

To try to explain the causes of crime, it is important to know who is committing crime, who is being victimized, and when and where crimes are being committed. This information can also be utilized by criminal justice practitioners to evaluate the effectiveness of crime-fighting techniques and to discover matters requiring greater attention. Similarly, a portrait of criminal activity conveys information about sore points in the social system, and how the system is failing to persuade persons to act in legal ways. Unless you are persuaded that genes are destiny, that is, that criminal activity is predestined for some people, a logical deduction is that each society creates its own criminals.

A number of factors must be considered when discussing the distribution of crime. First, it is essential to determine how many crimes and what types of crimes are being committed; in other words, what is the volume of crime? A second issue is, who is committing the offenses? What are the offenders' social characteristics, i.e., gender, age, race, ethnicity, and social class? The characteristics of victimized individuals and their relationships to offenders are also important. Are they strangers, friends, or relatives? Are they youthful or aged? Other matters of importance in the study of crime are the geographical and temporal distributions. Do crime rates, for example, vary by region of the country and by community size? And what about crime trends over time? And during what times of the year, week, and day do particular crimes most occur? These and other aspects of the distribution of crime are examined in the present chapter.

Volume of Crime: Uniform Crime Reports

The Uniform Crime Reports (UCR) is a major source of information detailing the extent of crime in the United States (see Chapter 3). Published annually by the Federal Bureau of Investigation in the U.S. Department of Justice, these data become available in October for the prior year. Table 4.1 depicts, for 2007, the number of Index crimes reported to and recorded by the police, as well as a breakdown by crime type.

TABLE 4.1
Total Number of Major Crimes Reported to and Recorded by the Police, 2007

United States Population: 293,655,404

	Number	Rate/100,000
Crime Index Total	11,251,818	3,370.5
Violent Crime	1,408,337	466.9
Murder	16,929	5.6
Forcible Rape	90,427	30.0
Robbery	445,125	147.6
Aggravated Assault	855,856	283.8
Property Crime	9,843,481	3,263.5
Burglary	2,179,140	722.5
Larceny Theft	6,568,572	2,177.8
Motor Vehicle Theft	1,096,769	363.3

Source: U.S. Department of Justice (2007). *Crime in the United States, 2007*. Washington, DC: U.S. Government Printing Office.

A total of 11,251,818 Index crimes were recorded in 2007 by reporting law enforcement agencies. Of these, just over 87 percent were property offenses (burglary, larceny-theft, and motor vehicle theft), while less than 13 percent were violent offenses (murder, forcible rape, robbery, and aggravated assault). The distribution in the United States of violent and property offenses is reasonably similar to that found in other industrialized nations.

Historically, the United States has experienced violent crime rates significantly higher than other industrialized nations. The decline in violent crime during the past decade has reduced the disparity between the United States and other industrialized nations. In a cross-national comparison of violent crime rates, for example, Steven Messner and Richard Rosenfeld (2007) report that the rate of robbery is greater in France and England-Wales than it is in the United States. While the disparity in rates has declined, the U.S. violent crime remains well above the average. The U.S. robbery rate for the years 2000 to 2002 of 145.9 robberies per 100,000 residents, while no longer the highest, is more than 60 percent higher than the average rate (89.8) for 15 other industrialized countries. Messner and Rosenfeld maintain that the difference in violence between the U.S. and other countries is further witnessed in the greater likelihood of the use of firearms in robberies (more than 10 more likely in the U.S. than in England and Wales) and homicides. The American homicide rate of 5.9 homicides per 100,000 is five times the average rate of 15 other industrialized nations.

Freda Adler (1983) insists that we should study nations not obsessed with crime in order to determine what socio-cultural factors tend to inhibit criminal activity. She suggested that nations with low crime rates exhibit a greater sense of community and greater congruence in norms than societies showing high crime rates. The lesson from these diverse inquiries is that, though the distribution of violent and property crimes may be similar for industrialized nations, crime rates can vary dramatically from country to country.

The crime rate in the United States of 3,730 means that in 2007, approximately 37 Index offenses were reported for every 1,000 people living in the United States; this figure, however, may be a conservative estimate because offenses sometimes have multiple victims. The FBI "Crime Clock" provides an alternative method of presentation of these crime data. In 2007, a violent crime was committed every 22.4 seconds somewhere in the United States. Someone was murdered every 31.0 minutes, raped every 5.8 minutes, robbed every 1.2 minutes, and assaulted every 36.8 seconds. For property crimes, a burglary was committed every 14.5 seconds, a larceny every 4.8 seconds, and a motor vehicle theft every 28.8 seconds. Put this way, the crime rates seem staggering, especially when we remember that UCR data underestimate the actual volume of crime.

To obtain a more comprehensive picture of the volume of crime, we should also look at UCR Part II offenses. Approximately 12 million arrests were made in 2007 for these crimes, which include drug violations, embezzlement, vagrancy, sexual assaults, and driving under the influence of alcohol or other drugs. Only those crimes resolved by an arrest are tabulated in this category. Underestimation is especially characteristic for offenses that are private in nature and exceptionally difficult to detect, such as gambling, fraud, drug use, and sex crimes. If we assume an arrest rate of 50 percent (which is probably high given the 21 percent clearance rate for Index crimes), this would indicate that there were more than 24 million Part II crimes committed in the United States in 2007. In addition to these Part II offenses, there were almost 12 million Index Offenses reported during the 2007 calendar year; thus, there were in excess of 36 million crimes committed in the United States in 2007. And remember this figure includes only those crimes that come to the attention of the police; additional millions of crimes remain undetected.

Geographical Distribution

Where do these crimes occur? If you are planning to move, what is the safest place in the nation? Table 4.2 provides answers to these two questions by geographical region. In terms of violent crime, avoid the southern states if you want to minimize your odds of being murdered, raped, or assaulted. While these states have 36.6 percent of the population, they account for 41 percent of murders and 44.9 percent of assaults. On the other hand, if you want to reduce the probability that your car will be stolen, stay out of the western states. While these states account for 23 percent of the population, 35.7 percent of all car thefts are recorded in the west. In general, the southern and western states should be avoided if you fear crime. The percent of crimes committed in these states notably exceeds their population percentage. Conversely, the states comprising the northeastern area of the United States are your best bet for reducing the likelihood of becoming a crime victim. While comprising 18.1 percent of the U.S. population, these states account for only 14.5 and 12.2 percent of violent and property crimes respectively.

With respect to community size, metropolitan areas are definitely to be avoided. The crime rate for Metropolitan Statistical Areas (MSAs) is 3,920. For cities and

TABLE 4.2
Geographic Distribution of Crime in the United States, 2007 UCR Data

Region	Percent of the Population	Percent of Violent Crimes	Percent of Property Crimes	Percent of Murders	Percent of Rapes	Percent of Robberies	Percent of Aggravated Assaults	Percent of Burglaries	Percent of Larceny- Thefts	Percent of Auto Thefts
Northeast	18.1	14.5	12.2	13.4	12.0	16.9	13.5	10.5	13.2	9.6
Midwest	22.0	19.4	21.3	19.1	25.3	19.0	19.0	20.6	22.1	18.2
South	36.6	41.1	42.7	45.8	38.8	40.4	44.9	46.7	42.4	36.4
West	23.2	23.1	23.8	21.8	24.0	23.7	22.7	22.2	22.4	35.7

[1] Because of rounding, the percentages may not add to 100.0.

NOTE: Although arson data are included in the trend and clearance tables, sufficient data are not available to estimate totals for this offense. Therefore, no arson data are published in this table.

Source: U.S. Department of Justice (2007). *Crime in the United States, 2007*. Washington, DC: U.S. Government Printing Office.

towns outside MSAs, the rate is even higher, 4,168. Rural areas are by far the safest, with a crime rate of only 1,877. Some people suggest that this difference is attributable to levels of police professionalism that subsequently affect recording practices. The magnitude of the difference in these rates suggests, however, that it is not only, if at all, a matter of idiosyncratic enforcement and recording or under-reporting in rural areas that might explain reported differences in crime rates.

Temporal Distribution

When do crimes occur? When are we most apt to be victimized? Is crime increasing? These are practical questions that are of concern not only to researchers and practitioners, but to all of us. UCR data suggest that while crimes are distributed fairly evenly throughout the year, fewer crimes tend to be committed during the months of January and February. Conversely, slightly more crimes are committed during the warmest summer months (July and August) and during December.

These seasonal fluctuations may be attributable to climatic conditions. People are less mobile and more apt to stay at home during cold, snowy seasons. Thus, fewer opportunities exist to commit crimes. With people remaining at home, for instance, burglars are less likely to find suitable targets. In the hot summer months, people are outdoors more and away on vacations. These factors improve the chances of interpersonal violence among strangers and increase the number of potential unoccupied "hits" for burglars.

During December, more murders, robberies, and burglaries are committed than in any other month. This phenomenon may be closely associated with the pressures and expectations surrounding the holiday season. With the emphasis upon buying gifts, the need for money is heightened. Researchers have also indicated that family holidays such as Christmas lead to increased tension and interpersonal hostility, which are likely to trigger assaults and homicides. Familial and acquaintance interpersonal violence (including homicide, rape, and assault) accounts for more than 50 percent of all such offenses.

Most crimes are likely to be committed during the evening and nighttime hours and over the weekend, especially from Friday evening through Saturday night. For some crimes, such as burglaries, motor vehicle thefts, and larceny-thefts, it is difficult to determine when the crime actually occurred. If someone has been out of town for two weeks and upon returning discovers his or her house burglarized and car stolen, it usually is impossible to determine when during the two-week period the crime occurred. Generally, the crime is considered to have taken place immediately prior to being reported. Consequently, the tabulated figures may not be accurate indicators of the actual time of the offenses.

Fluctuations in crime rates over time have been closely studied. Generally, the discussion focuses on the immediate past and on the American crime scene. Messner and Rosenfeld (1994), for instance, found American homicide rates in excess of eight per 100,000 during the 1920s and 1930s. They then fell below five per 100,000 during the 1950s, only to increase to more than eight homicides per 100,000 during the 1970s and 1980s. During the past few years of the twentieth century, the American murder rate fell, once again, below eight per 100,000 inhabitants. To better understand the current situation, it is beneficial to examine historical and international crime trends. In their historical analysis, Ted Robert Gurr and associates (1977) report finding a U-shaped curve in the rates of criminal violence, with high rates in the early 1800s that declined until the Great Depression and then rose rapidly throughout the twentieth century. More long-term analyses, however, suggest that homicides and assaults are substantially lower now than they were in thirteenth-century England when homicide rates were 10 to 20 times greater than the current rate (Hagan, 1994). Thus, while crime and violence are widely regarded as the number one social problem and one that keeps getting worse, historical data suggest that things have been bad for a long time, and may actually be getting better.

With respect to recent trends, UCR crime totals skyrocketed during the 1960s and 1970s, suggesting a serious crime wave. Figure 4.1 presents a 32-year summary of the number of crimes recorded by the police from 1973 through 2007. Crime rates peaked in 1980, declined steadily until 1984, and then increased each year through 1991. Then, in spite of dire predictions of continuing increases in crime, especially violent youth crime, the crime rate began to decline, falling by 2007 to a lower rate of serious offending than that recorded in 1973. Does this mean that the police did a better job of deterring crime in the early 1980s and the mid to late 1990s? Does it mean that the "get-tough" policies of the past several presidential administrations have been successful? Are such policies as determinant sentencing, "three-strikes" legislation, and mandatory arrest polices responsible for the declining crime rate? Some persons have made such claims, although no evidence has been presented to support them. Or is the trend toward community-oriented policing having its desired effect? What about the role of noncriminal justice factors such as the "booming" economy of the 1990s, the low unemployment rate, or the aging of the American population? Al Blumstein and a number of other colleagues have addressed the declining crime rate in several publications (Blumstein & Wallman, 2000; Blumstein, 2001).

Criminologists had forecast the observed decrease in the crime rate during the early 1980s because they knew that demographic changes associated with the baby boom would lead to a decline in the percentage of individuals in the high-crime committing ages (18-23). It would be only reasonable to assume that this population change would result in lower crime rates. Darrell Steffensmeier and Miles Harer (1987) found that this demographic change accounted for 40 percent of the decrease between 1980 and 1984. Another factor that might explain the decline was the improving national economy and the falling unemployment rate during the 1980s and 1990s.

In March 1985, the California Attorney General convened a conference to discuss why the crime rate was falling. A number of noted scholars gave presentations, with each providing a favorite explanation, ranging from demographic changes to prison policies to early prevention programs. There was little consensus regarding the reasons for the four-year decline in crime rates from 1981 to 1984. One speaker (Geis, 1986:31) noted, however, that the conference should have addressed a different issue: "Why, despite its downward movement, does the crime rate in the United States remain so stunningly high in comparison to that of other advanced nations?" Given the renewed increase in crime rates since 1984, perhaps this was a correct perspective. At the beginning of the new millennium, this question is perhaps even more relevant than it was in 1985, for despite a nine-year decline, the American violent crime rate and the incarceration rate remain higher than those of any other industrialized nation.

Volume of Crime: National Crime Victimization Survey

Victimization rates reported by the National Crime Victimization Survey (described in Chapter 3) suggest that the crime rate is considerably higher than that reported by the UCR. The NCVS estimated that 22.9 million criminal victimizations occurred in 2007, excluding murder, kidnapping, commercial burglary and robbery, as well as victimless crimes such as drug abuse, prostitution, and drunkenness. These last crimes are excluded largely due to the cost of data collection and to the difficulty in securing satisfactory information.

Violent crimes (rape, personal robbery, and assault) accounted for 22.8 percent of the NCVS victimizations (compared to 13 percent in the UCR). The remaining 77.2 percent of reported victimizations involved property crimes, with thefts from households accounting for 58.7 percent of all reported victimizations, burglaries represented another 14.2 percent, and motor vehicle thefts accounted for slightly more than four percent. Table 4.3 provides a summary of the number and percent distribution of victimizations found by the NCVS.

Victimization rates are generally reported per 1,000 persons or 1,000 households. To facilitate comparisons with the UCR, we have converted National Crime Victimization Survey (NCVS) figures to rates per 100,000. The overall victimization rate for violent crimes for people over the age of 12 in 2007 was 2,280; this figure is almost five times the rate reported by the UCR. The NCVS reports property crimes primarily as household victimizations, making comparisons between UCR and NCVS data difficult. The NCVS household crime rate of 14,650, however, was more than four times the UCR crime rate for property victimization. Overall, the NCVS victimization rates are from just under two to more than five times greater than those reported by the UCR.

TABLE 4.3
Personal and Household Crimes, 2007 NCVS Data

Crime Type	Number	Percent of All Crimes	Rate[1]
All Crimes	22,879,700		
Personal Crimes	5,371,200	22.7%	2,150
Violent Crimes	5,177,100	22.8%	2,070
Rape/Sexual Assault	248,300	1.1%	100
Robbery	597,300	2.6%	240
Assault	4,331,500	19.1%	1,730
Personal Theft	194,100	0.9%	80
Household Crimes	17,508,500	77.2%	14,650
Burglary	3,215,100	14.1%	2,690
Theft	13,313,800	58.2%	11,140
Auto Theft	979,600	4.2%	820

[1] Rate per 100,000 persons age 12 and over or per 100,000 households.

Source: Rand, Michael R. (2008). *Criminal Victimization, 2007*. Washington, DC: U.S. Department of Justice.

Geographical Distribution

NCVS data paint a different picture about the geographic distribution of crime than that provided by the UCR. Table 4.4 presents information about the distribution of crime by region and community size. Rural areas, while safer than urban areas, report higher levels of violent crime than do suburban areas although the difference is not as great as noted in the UCR. Part of this discrepancy may be attributed to the recording differences noted in Chapter 3. While crimes occurring in an urban area are reported to the city police department, the victim may well reside in a suburban area. The crime will appear in the UCR data as an urban crime while the NCVS will record this as victimization experienced by a suburbanite. Such recording practices, however, do not explain the discrepancy between UCR and NCVS data with regard to crime rates in different geographical areas. Consistent with the UCR data, the NCVS data indicate that the Northeast has the lowest crime rate. In marked contrast to the UCR, however, the South does not have the highest rate of violent crime; in fact it is only three-fourths the rate of violence reported in the West. What accounts for such disparate findings? Is it a product of the level of police professionalism in these different areas? Is it an artifact of differential reporting of crime by residents of the western states relative to those in the southern states? Which measure (the UCR or NCVS) provides the most accurate picture?

The NCVS also reports that most crimes of violence (robberies and assaults), occur in a public place such as on the street, in a parking garage, or in a commercial building. Rape, on the other hand, is most likely to take place in the victim's home or some other place known to the victim. Furthermore, almost 63 percent of rape victims know their assailants and are victimized in their own homes or at the home of an acquaintance. Victims raped by strangers account for one-third of victims and,

TABLE 4.4
Location and Type of Victimization, NCVS 2005 Data

Location	Crimes of Violence[1]	Household Property Crime[2]
All	2,210	15,400
Northeast	2,020	10,390
Midwest	2,370	15,580
South	1,970	14,680
West	2,590	20,650
Urban	3,140	20,000
Suburban	1,910	14,140
Rural	1,730	12,510

[1] Rate per 100,000 population age 12 and over.
[2] Rate per 100,000 households

Source: U.S Department of Justice (2006) *Criminal Victimization in the United States, 2005*. Washington, DC: U.S. Department of Justice.

unlike the acquaintance rape victims, are more likely to be victimized in a public place such as on a street, in a park or playground, or in a commercial establishment.

Temporal Distribution

Crimes of personal violence, according to NCVS figures, are slightly more likely to be committed during the daytime (53%), although 31 percent occur between 6 p.m. and midnight. Slightly more than one-half (50.5%) of all robberies involving injuries take place during this six-hour period. Household crimes are less likely to be committed at night (33%) than during the daytime (40%), but given the nature of property crime, the time of many crimes cannot be accurately determined (27%).

A different picture from the UCR data is found with respect to victimization trends during the 1970s and 1980s. While some annual fluctuations can be observed between 1973 and 1992, the overall pattern has been quite stable (See Figure 4.2). In fact, the 1992 violent crime victimization rate of 3,210 is virtually the same as the rate of 3,260 recorded in 1973. With the redesign of the NCVS in 1992, historical comparisons became problematic. However, since 1993, when the NCVS violent victimization rate peaked, there has been a steady decline in reported victimizations. This decline in the number and rate of victimizations mirrors the decline reported in the UCR. A similar pattern is evident for property crime rates. Since 1994, household property crime rates have declined more than 50 percent, dropping from 319 per 1,000 households to 146 in 2007.

Volume of Crime: Self-Report Studies

Self-report data (SRD) are not directly comparable to the UCR or NCVS for one important reason: the only national studies conducted to date have been limited to the self-reported behavior of youths and young adults. Self-report studies also employ a different procedure for reporting crime rates than UCR or NCVS. Two measures are currently in use: prevalence rates and frequency rates. Prevalence refers to the number of persons in a population that report one or more offenses of a given type within a specified period. The prevalence rate is typically expressed as a proportion of persons in the population who have reported some involvement in a particular offense or set of offenses. Frequency or individual offending rates (also called lambda) refer to the number of offenses that occur in a given population during a specified time interval. Individual offending rates may be expressed as an average number of offenses per person or as the number of offenses per some population base. While prevalence rates are informative, indicating the number of different persons involved in criminal acts, individual offending rates are more comparable to the UCR and NCVS data.

The best countrywide self-report data are from the National Youth Survey (see Chapter 3). Prevalence rates for youths aged 15 to 21 in 1980 indicate that 65 percent reported committing at least one of the 24 offenses included in a delinquency scale. The prevalence rate for Index offenses was, however, only 12 percent. Individual offend-ing rates for 1980 indicate that an average of 32 offenses were committed per person. The majority of the offenses, however, were status offenses or public disorder crimes. Serious offenses accounted for only one percent of all reported offenses in 1980. Fur-thermore, the individual offending rate for Index offenses was only 0.6 per person. With an adolescent population of approximately 29 million, a prevalence rate of 12 percent suggests that 3.5 million youths commit at least one Index offense per year.

Geographical Distribution

In terms of where crimes are committed, the situation reported in UCR and NCVS data is not found for the NYS data. Both prevalence and frequency rates reveal lower rates of delinquency for rural youth as compared to urban youth, but these differences are not statistically significant. Suburban rates tend to be more similar to the urban than the rural figures. Elliott et al. (1983:90-91) commented that:

> the difference in prevalence rates on the global delinquency scales appeared to reflect higher prevalence rates for urban and suburban youth in relatively nonserious forms of delinquency. The only sys-tematic differences on incidence scales also involved a relatively nonserious offense scale—minor theft. There was little evidence that urban, suburban and rural youth differ with regard to reported incidence or prevalence rates on the serious nonviolent or serious violent offense scales.

Temporal Distribution

The NYS is a longitudinal study in which the same individuals were interviewed from 1977 through 1993. While comparisons can be made over time, a major problem is that changes in the rates may reflect changes in the cohort. As they age, persons begin to engage in different types of behavior. That is, to what extent do temporal changes reflect "maturation effects"? For example, the delinquent behaviors of youths aged 11 to 17, as the cohort was in 1976, may be both qualitatively and quantitatively different from the behaviors of 15- to 21-year-olds in 1980. Given this limitation of the data it is preferable not to make assumptions about temporal patterns.

Distribution of Crime by Gender

A major shortcoming of criminology has been the tendency to exclude females from the field of study. Traditionally, theories of crime have been concerned primarily with the behaviors of males and research has been largely limited to male samples. The exclusion of women has been due in part to the notably low rates of female involvement in crime as indicated by official arrest records (see Table 4.5). Additionally, it was long assumed that females primarily engage in sexual offenses, making their behavior tangential to any serious study of criminality. As a result, the major criminological theories may suffer from a lack of generalizability to females and our understanding of the distribution of crime by gender may be biased. Throughout this text, we will attempt to address this deficiency by calling attention to research and theoretical formulations that include females or focus on females.

Perspectives on Female Crime

Examples of early justifications for excluding females are provided prior to a summary of the gender-crime issue. William Kvaraceus commented that "[t]he majority of delinquent girls, regardless of their reason for referral [to the juvenile court] are in some degree sexually delinquent" (1945:116). Albert Cohen declared that girls were beyond the scope of his theory. He stated:

> The most conspicuous difference between male and female delinquency is that male delinquency . . . is versatile and female delinquency is relatively specialized. It consists overwhelmingly of sexual delinquency (1955:45).

Richard Cloward and Lloyd Ohlin (1960) acknowledged that female gang members existed, but they concluded that they were affiliated with and subordinate to groups of male delinquents. Because the female members were not a real threat on their own, Cloward and Ohlin eliminated women from further consideration in their theoretical work. Females were also readily dismissed in *Causes of Delinquency*, in which Travis Hirschi (1969:35) spelled out his version of social control theory and specifically stated, "In the [data] analysis that follows . . . the females disappear." These theorists, though less concerned with the "immorality" of female offenders, excluded them from serious study. The Gang Feature presented in this chapter refutes this belief among previous criminologists that gang membership is primarily a male phenomenon.

TABLE 4.4
Sex of Offenders by Offense Type, UCR, 2007

UCR Index Offense	Males	Females
Total Arrests	6,150,145	1,968,052
	75.8%	24.2%
Murder and nonnegligent manslaughter	6,519	782
	89.3%	10.7%
Forcible Rape	13,079	133
	99.0%	1.0%
Robbery	64,004	8,351
	88.5%	11.5%
Aggravated Assault	202,588	54,876
	78.7%	21.3%
Burglary	154,607	26,778
	85.2%	14.8%
Larceny-Theft	413,125	275,912
	60.0%	40.0%
Auto Theft	51,382	11,384
	81.9%	18.1%
Arson	7,685	1,409
	84.5%	15.6%

Source: U.S. Department of Justice (2007). *Crime in the United States, 2007*. Washington, DC: U.S. Government Printing Office.

Not all criminologists, however, ignored the criminal activity of women. In *The Criminality of Women* (1961), Otto Pollak argued that crime data underreport female crime. He cited a number of factors for this, including the petty nature of the majority of women's offenses and the likelihood that men who are victims of crimes committed by women do not report them. He also believed that male police officers often face a conflict when dealing with female offenders because of a sense of "chivalry" and preconceived notions about women. As a result, the officers are less likely to suspect and arrest female offenders. Furthermore, the data indicated that women are more likely to be acquitted than men. All told, then, the crimes of women are underreported, less likely to be detected, and even when detected, treated more leniently.

Discussing the masked criminality of the female, Pollak argued that to a large extent this has to do not only with the types of crimes committed by women (illegal abortions, thefts by prostitutes of their customers' possessions, domestic thefts), but also with the innate secrecy of women. He argued that the deceitfulness of women is not only socially induced, but also related to the female physiology. Pollak believed that women acquire the confidence to deceive men through their sexual play-acting, faked sexual response, and menstruation. With the assurance gained in their power to deceive men, women are able to commit crimes that go undetected.

Although there is no apparent support for the work of Pollak, some criminologists accepted his premises. The notion that women are able to conceal their deviance through their legitimate and traditional roles has found its way into a number of studies of female crime. At the same time, Pollak's work has been bitingly criticized by feminist criminologists who find it superficial, misogynistic, and highly overstated. In one of the more subtle critiques, Meda Chesney-Lind and Randall Sheldon (1998) label as "fascinating and contorted" his attempts to explain why "precocious biological maturity" accounts for female but not male sexual delinquency.

Explanations of Female Crime

Studies of women in general increased in the 1970s; this was true in criminology as well. For the first time, substantial numbers of female criminologists entered the field, and many of them focused on the female offender. No longer was the study of the female offender restricted to physical and psychological factors; cultural and social structural variables began to be scrutinized. Criminologists argued that when women break the law, they often do so in their role as women, that is, they go from shoppers to shoplifters and check writers to check forgers.

Dale Hoffman-Bustamonte (1973) emphasized the idea that women are socialized very differently than men. Boys, besides being allowed much greater freedom than girls while growing up, are encouraged to be more aggressive, ambitious, and outgoing. Girls are expected to be nonviolent, hence they do not possess the technical skills to commit violent acts. (Consult also the works of Boocock, 1972 and Schur, 1984.) An example is the reaction parents typically have to their children's participation in fights. For a son involved in a fight, the response may be, "I hope he looks worse than you." Such comments are rarely directed to daughters. Young boys may be discouraged from starting fights, but they are taught not to back down if hit by another boy.

Moreover, in our culture, boys are taught how to fight and that it is appropriate to stop when the opponent is down; this training is not given to young girls. When girls fight, they frequently bite, scratch, and pull hair. This behavior is socially defined as unseemly. Although typically they are not as strong as boys, girls can be much more vicious in fights than boys.

Available data show that when women commit violent crimes, their victims are often relatives or lovers. For homicide, the weapon most often used is a kitchen implement, usually a knife. Even when women commit violent crimes, they utilize gender-specific weapons. In her study of female robbers, Jody Miller (1998) reported that women generally targeted female victims and, when weapons were used, they were more likely to use knives. This choice of weapon is in sharp contrast to male robbers' reliance on guns to intimidate their victims.

As a result of their socialization, girls have less access to illegitimate opportunities than boys. Thus, it is not surprising that girls' criminal behavior occurs at a lower rate than their male counterparts. Given the lack of freedom, opportunity, and training, fewer women become serious offenders.

Role theory, as it presently stands, is a starting point in the development of a feminist criminology. However, as Carol Smart (1976:69) has suggested, "The study of gender roles cannot be, and to be fair, is probably not intended to provide a complete analysis of the [crime] phenomenon." She asserted that role theory must be situated within "a theory which can account for the specifically differentiated roles as well as other features of human activity" (1976:70).

Liberation and Crime

At the same time the women's movement gathered momentum, the crime rate of women appeared to be increasing. As a result, criminologists began examining the link between liberation and crime. In *Sisters in Crime*, Freda Adler (1975:12-13) stated:

> Women are no longer indentured to the kitchens, baby carriages or bedrooms of America. . . . Allowed their freedom for the first time, women . . . by the tens of thousands—have chosen to desert those kitchens and plunge exuberantly into the formerly all male quarters of the working world. . . . In the same way that women are demanding equal opportunity in the fields of legitimate endeavor, a similar number of determined women are forcing their way into the world of major crimes.

Adler connected the rise in female crime with the rise in women's assertiveness brought about by the women's movement. She contended that there were now fewer restraints on women and greater pressure on them from their enhanced positions. Because of this, women were becoming susceptible to the same criminogenic forces that men faced. Therefore, it was likely that with the convergence of role expectations, female crime would begin to resemble male crime. Adler's prediction of an increase in the rate of female involvement in conventional "street crimes" has been realized in official data. Between 1973 and 2007, female arrests for Index offenses increased 48 percent while the male rate declined by 17 percent (see Table 4.6).

While Adler utilized data from case studies to support her position, Rita James Simon (1975) in *The Contemporary Woman and Crime* examined the statistical picture of female crime over a number of decades. To examine the possible effect of the women's movement on the criminality of women, Simon utilized data on the status of women in the labor force, marriage and fertility rates, income, and education, as well as crime statistics. She concluded that some types of crimes (predominantly white-collar offenses) will increase, while other types (violent crimes, in particular) will decrease. These changes, she believed, will occur because of the change in the position of women in society. Furthermore, Simon concluded that as women are accepted into various legitimate fields that have been dominated by men, the criminal justice system will come to deal with women more like men. As a result, women will no longer benefit from "chivalrous" treatment by the police and the courts.

Although the works of Adler and Simon broke new ground, their data and methods of analysis have received considerable criticism. Adler also has been taken to task for assuming that becoming criminal results from being liberated, as the majority of women involved in crime seem to have been influenced very little by the women's movement. Those most touched by the movement tend to be educated and from middle- or upper-class families, while women found in crime statistics tend to be less educated and from the lower class.

Research reported by Helen Boritch (1992) also suggests that Simon and others may have been mistaken in their assumptions that historically, women have been treated more leniently than men by the criminal justice system. Her analysis of court processing from 1871 to 1920 in Middlesex County, Ontario, revealed that women were more likely to receive prison sentences and to incur longer sentences than men.

There continues to be a lack of agreement regarding the rate of female offending and reasons associated with differences in rates of male and female offending. Recent research by Janet Lauritsen, Karen Heimer, and James Lynch (2009), however, reveals that the gender gap in offending is narrowing. Utilizing both UCR and NCVS data, they examined trends in violent offending and victimization from 1973 to 2005. In a response to a critique by Schwartz et al. (2009), Heimer and her colleagues (2009:436) conclude that:

> Males remain more violent than females. Non-lethal violent offend-
> ing has been decreasing for both genders over time. However, the
> decreases have not been of the same magnitude across gender, and
> we observed that the gender gap has narrowed over time. We do not
> find this surprising, given the social and economic changes that have
> occurred in terms of gender (in)equality since the early 1970s.

They suggest that the time has come to "move beyond the debate over whether these changes in offending have occurred and focus research efforts on explaining the reasons for differential changes in female and male rates of violent offending" (Lauritsen et al. 2009:392).

Post-Liberation Explanations

During the past 30 years, a number of researchers and theorists have in fact examined post-liberation explanations of female offending. John Hagan, John H. Simpson, and A. Ronald Gillis (1979, 1985, and 1987) proposed a power-control model of delinquency to explain why girls commit fewer delinquencies. They suggest that daughters are more closely controlled by the patriarchal family than are sons. This control is perpetuated in female peer groups where dependence, passivity, and compliance are reinforced. Furthermore, because women's access to the reward structure of the social system is markedly more restricted than males, Hagan and his associates also link the sexual stratification of crime to the sexual stratification of work.

These ideas have been refined and expanded in a series of articles in which authority in the family and youth power are examined in conjunction with the

GANG FEATURE

Demographic Characteristics of Gang Members

While the gang literature is voluminous, little consensus exists with regard to the nature of gangs, especially with regard to gender and racial composition. The common stereotype is that gangs are primarily a male phenomenon and that females serve largely in an auxiliary capacity. Likewise, media presentations portray gang membership as a minority phenomenon, with non-minority youth virtually absent. Results from recent research suggest that these common assumptions may be erroneous. As discussed in the Gang Feature in Chapter 3, the extent of the gang problem is largely determined by the definition employed. The same applies to the nature and composition of gangs. Different definitions and different methodologies result in different pictures. Much of the gang research has relied on case studies in which researchers observed specific individuals and/or specific gangs identified by knowledgeable informants. These descriptive accounts provide very rich descriptions of these gangs. However, they provide only part of the overall picture. Recent surveys of larger, more general samples of adolescents have included questions about gang involvement and gang activity. These surveys have produced a different picture than the one provided by the case studies. But, again, they provide only part of the picture. Law enforcement data are similar in nature to the information gleaned from case studies. One of the issues is the nature of the sample. In general surveys, both gang and nongang individuals are surveyed. These surveys generally are restricted to younger samples, including respondents as young as 10 years of age. Case studies are usually restricted to gangs and active members, which by default results in older samples, generally 16 and older. It should not be surprising that these different methodologies produce different estimates about the gender and racial composition of gang members.

The police data and case studies reinforce the notion that most gang members are male and from racial minorities. These estimates indicate that more than 90 percent of gang members are male and that 90 to 95 percent of the gang members are minority. Thus, the picture emerges that the gang problem is indeed one that should focus on minority males. A different picture emerges from the general surveys; one that indicates that such attention on minority males is misplaced. These general surveys have found females to account for 30 to 40 percent of active gang youth, more than twice the highest estimates given by case studies and law enforcement data. With respect to race and ethnicity, most of the surveys have been limited to "high-risk" areas and therefore largely comprised of racial and ethnic minorities. One recent survey of 5,935 eighth-grade students conducted in 11 American cities examined the racial and gender composition of delinquent youth gangs (Esbensen & Winfree, 1998). The authors found that 25 percent of the gang members were white and that 38 percent of the gang members were females. As with other general surveys, these estimates differ substantially from the "official" figures. The authors caution that different methodologies (e.g., general surveys compared with case studies), sampling frames (e.g., survey of 13- to 15-year-olds versus observation of 18- to 25-year-old biker gangs), and definitional issues (e.g., restricting gang membership to criminally involved gangs instead of all youth groups), are likely to be the source of these different pictures of gangs. At the same time, they also maintain that it is important to consider all of these sources when assessing the nature and extent of the gang problem and when considering community response to gangs and gang activity.

family's position in the social order. In the estimation of Hagan, Simpson, and Gillis (1985, 1987), it is the presence of power and the absence of control that creates conditions in which delinquency can occur (see also Blackwell, 2000). Given the greater control of women and their lack of power, their lower rate of offending should not come as a surprise.

Research exploring factors associated with adolescent crime, however, have failed to identify different causal or explanatory models for female and male delinquency. Maude Dornfeld and Candace Kruttschnitt studied the effects of family risk factors, such as parental divorce, maternal alcohol abuse, and harsh discipline, and concluded that "while we would not deny that there are gender-specific risk factors . . . we would deny that responses to those risk factors can be predicted solely on the basis of sex" (1992:414). Similarly, results of a multinational longitudinal analysis reported by Avshalom Caspi and his colleagues (1994) indicate that the same three personality scales were correlated with both male and female delinquency.

A growing body of research continues to identify more similarities in the causal explanations of female and male offending than differences. Giordano and Rockwell (2000), for instance, tested the efficacy of differential association theory in explaining serious offending. They found that the social learning concepts of differential association theory were equally applicable to female offenders in their study as they were to male offenders. In a similar vein, Miller (1998) found that, while the actual methods of committing robberies differed between males and females, the motivations underlying the robberies were similar. In their examination of delinquents, Liu and Kaplan (1999) not only found similar patterns of involvement in delinquency, but also identified similar mediating variables exerting the same effect on female and male offending. Esbensen and Deschenes (1998) examined the role of gender in explaining gang membership. They found some modest differences in explanatory models for males and females; the social learning models were quite similar for the boys and girls, but the social control models indicated different explanatory factors explained male and female gang affiliation. In yet another investigation into gender differences, Heimer and DeCoster (1999) explored the effects of familial controls on male and female offending. They found that "girls are less violent than boys mainly because they are influenced more strongly by bonds to family, learn fewer violent definitions, and are taught that violence is inconsistent with the meaning of being female" (1999:303).

UCR Data on Gender and Crime

Many of the reported UCR crimes are never solved, and no information about the offender becomes known. It therefore is necessary to rely upon arrest data for demographic information. This may result in a biased sample in that older, smarter, and occasional offenders probably are less likely to be arrested. Other factors such as sex, race, and social class also may affect police officers' decisions to arrest or not to arrest an individual. Caution must be used, therefore, when employing arrest data to determine the pattern of crime.

Table 4.6 shows that, of the 1,112,485 arrests for Index crimes in 2007, 29 percent were of females. This figure is slightly more than the percentage of females accounting for all arrests (24.2%), suggesting that females, when they commit crimes, are more likely to be arrested for serious crimes than are their male counterparts. In contrast to data from 1973, there appears to have been a major change in the offending levels of women. In 1973, women accounted for only 15 percent of all arrests. Does this change in the percent of arrests accounted for by women reflect a change in female offending? While some may conclude that to be the case, another possibility is that there has been a change in police response to female offenders, with officers increasingly arresting females for offenses that previously would not have resulted in arrest.

TABLE 4.6
Gender of Persons Arrested for Index Offenses in 1973 and 2007 and Percent Change

	1973		2007		% Change 1973-2007	
	Males	Females	Males	Females	Males	Females
All Arrests	5,502,284	997,580	6,498,035	2,028,653		
Percent	84.7%	15.3%	75.8%	24.2%	11.1%	97.3%
Index Crime Total	1,112,485	256,739	997,942	391,791		
Percent	81.3%	18.7%	70.6%	29.4%	-17.9%	48.3%
Violent Crime	260,800	29,582	303,977	66,028		
Percent	89.8%	10.2%	81.7%	18.3%	9.7%	116.8%
Property Crime	851,685	227,157	693,965	325,763		
Percent	78.9%	21.1%	66.4%	33.6%	-26.4%	39.4%

Source: U.S. Department of Justice (2007). *Crime in the United States, 2007*. Washington, DC: U.S. Government Printing Office.

Analysis of crime trends from 1973 to 2007 by gender shows that female rates increased significantly more than did arrest rates for males. Arrests of males for Index offenses are 17.9 percent lower in 2007 than they were in 1973, while female arrests are up 48.3 percent. The increase in violent offending is the most pronounced with arrests of females increasing by 116.8 percent compared to a 9.7 percent increase for males. As discussed above, the base rate for females is significantly lower than the male rate. The absolute increase in male arrests for violent crimes from 1973 to 2007 (43,177) represents two-thirds of the 2007 female violent crime arrest rate (66,028). The question remains, however, does this increase in female arrests reflect an actual increase in female activity or a change in criminal justice processing? In an attempt to examine this issue, David Huizinga and Finn Esbensen (1991) compared data from the 1978 NYS with data from the 1989 Denver Youth Survey. Limiting the NYS sample to urban youth, they examined male and female delinquency rates. Contrary to UCR arrest data, they found the 1989 respondents reported slightly lower rates of offending, although the differences were not statistically significant.

NCVS Data on Gender and Crime

Information regarding the sex of property offenders is unavailable in the NCVS because these offenders are not usually seen by their victims. It is therefore only possible to compare victimization data for crimes of violence in which there is personal contact. The NCVS data reveal a greater level of female participation in violent crimes than does the UCR. The NCVS data indicate that the perceived sex of offenders in single-offender victimizations (that is, the gender of the offender as reported by the victim) is 90 percent male and 10 percent female. This distribution is fairly consistent across offense types; the only exceptions are that rapists tend to be predominately male (99%).

Self-Report Data on Gender and Crime

Although official records indicate that variations in the rates of offending for males and females are significant, self-report data provide a very different picture. In a study of 820 males and females in Oakland, California, Michael J. Hindelang (1971) found that female delinquency was not as specialized as others had claimed. He concluded (1971:533):

> The patterns of female delinquent involvement, although at a reduced frequency, parallel quite closely the pattern of male delinquency. . . . Most and least frequent activities among the males and females are nearly identical. The finding is at odds with the conception of female delinquents as engaging primarily in "sex" delinquencies.

Furthermore, from his re-analysis of 10 self-report data sets, Joseph Weis (1980) concluded that "sex differences are small and the percentages of both sexes involved in a wide variety of offenses are large." Other self-report data indicate the same patterns. Steven Cernkovich and Peggy Giordano's (1979) analysis of a sample from a midwestern community showed similar patterns of delinquent behavior among the sexes, as did Rachelle Canter's (1982) analysis of five panels of the National Youth Survey data. Gender differences are most pronounced for the serious and violent offense categories. For prevalence rates, the male-to-female sex ratios are approximately 3:1 for Index offenses. The ratio for frequency rates is closer to 5:1. Translated into percentages, this suggests that females commit approximately 20 percent of the serious crimes reported by persons aged 15 to 21 years. This figure is quite consistent with NCVS data but twice the rate reported by UCR arrest data. According to SRD data, female offending appears to be very similar to male criminality, except that the former occurs at a less frequent rate.

Distribution of Crime by Age

Next to gender, age is the personal characteristic that appears to be the best predictor of involvement in criminal activity. This is so prevalent that street crime is perceived as being synonymous with youth. Some social scientists have argued that

TABLE 4.7
Age of Persons Arrested, UCR, 2007

	All Ages	Under 16	16-18	19-21	22-24	25-29	30-34	Over 34
All Arrests	10,698,310	788,248	1,371,246	1,442,966	1,150,885	1,505,619	1,047,448	3,391,898
Percent	7.4%	12.9%	13.4%	10.7%	14.1%	9.8%	31.8%	
Index Offenses	1,678,016	196,876	299,095	222,391	156,107	203,219	143,569	456,759
Percent	11.7%	17.8%	13.3%	9.3%	12.1%	8.6%	27.2%	
Violent Crimes	451,071	34,357	61,673	59,356	48,937	66,003	45,976	134,769
Percent	7.6%	13.7%	13.2%	10.9%	14.6%	10.2%	29.9%	
Property Crimes	1,226,945	162,519	237,422	163,035	107,170	137,216	97,593	321,990
Percent	13.2%	19.4%	13.3%	8.8%	11.2%	8.0%	26.4%	
Murder	10,082	234	1,513	1,863	1,474	1,758	940	2,300
Percent	2.3%	15.0%	18.5%	14.6%	17.4%	9.3%	22.8%	

Source: U.S. Department of Justice (2007). *Crime in the United States, 2007*. Washington, DC: U.S. Government Printing Office.

much of what is called criminal or delinquent activity is no more than behavior that is a "normal" part of growing up (e.g., Jolin & Gibbons, 1987). Consistent findings across cultures confirm the age-crime curve. Crime initiation begins in late childhood or early adolescence, increases through the adolescent years, gradually plateaus before declining steadily throughout adulthood. The shape of this curve is remarkably similar across societies, but the age of initiation and the peak years of criminal activity vary to some degree.

In the United States, two different trends are identified in Table 4.7. First, youth under the age of 22 account for a disproportionate number of arrests for Index offenses. According to UCR data, approximately 40 percent of all Index crimes, 41 percent of property crimes, 38 percent of violent crimes, and 48 percent of homicides are committed by persons under the age of 22. Second, with increasing age, the volume of crime decreases, but the decline is greater for property offenses. For instance, property offenses (primarily larceny-theft) account for 83 percent of all Index crime arrests for those under the age of 16 compared to 70 percent of arrests for adults over the age of 34. Thus, relatively speaking, arrests for violent crimes are more common among older groups than they are among the young. These arrest data may partially reflect differential enforcement practices or inexperience on the part of youthful offenders.

Victimization data on the perceived age of offenders in single-offender violent victimizations are consistent with the UCR data: 31 percent of such offenders were under 21 years of age, compared to 30 percent in the UCR data. The NYS data also support the general finding that delinquent behavior increases through early adolescence, reaches a plateau through the late teen years, and then gradually declines through the twenties.

Criminal Careers Debate

During the past 20 years, criminological attention has been paid to the concepts of "criminal careers" and "career criminals." The former assumes that criminal activity is similar to other occupations, with a beginning, a period of activity, and an ending or termination of the career. Career criminal is a term synonymous with the more familiar concept of "habitual offender." The criminal career literature is largely an outgrowth of prediction models and the attempt to identify the costs of crime relative to the costs of incarceration.

The notion of selective incapacitation as a crime-fighting tool gained popularity during the Reagan administration (1984-1992). This policy advocates incarcerating career criminals and other high-rate offenders in order to reduce societal costs (e.g., economic and personal injury costs). For each high-rate offender incarcerated, the number of crimes that would have been committed if that individual were not confined can be estimated. Associated with the policy of locking people up in order to prevent future crimes is the need to be able to predict high-rate offenders and to determine the length of their careers (e.g., will it be necessary to confine these people for life or will they terminate their criminal activity at some earlier point?). One consequence of criminal careers research has been an interest in the relationship between age and level of criminal involvement.

Michael Gottfredson and Travis Hirschi (1986, 1988, and 1990) have been outspoken opponents of the value of the criminal career paradigm, as well as of longitudinal research to conduct evaluative studies of criminal careers. They maintain that the effect of age on crime is invariant. Historical and cross-cultural research, they maintain, shows that the age-crime curve has remained relatively unchanged for 150 years. If, in fact, crime peaks at age 16 or 17 and declines steadily throughout the remainder of the life-cycle, then Gottfredson and Hirschi suggest "maturational reform" best accounts for the decline. Desistance in criminal activity is "change in behavior that cannot be explained and change that occurs regardless of what else happens" (Gottfredson & Hirschi, 1990:136). This is consistent with their belief that criminal behavior is a result of low self-control, which is a relatively stable propensity that varies across individuals and explains differences in rates of criminal activity. Self-control is (or is not) inculcated early in the socialization process and is largely a result of child-rearing practices. To understand the causes of criminal activity, it is necessary to examine early childhood experiences and measure individual self-control. Other factors are of secondary importance.

In contrast to Gottfredson and Hirschi, Alfred Blumstein, Jacqueline Cohen, and David Farrington (1988a, 1988b) are vocal proponents of the criminal career paradigm. They state that criminal careers can be measured in terms of the "longitudinal sequence of offenses committed by an offender who has a detectable rate of offending during some period" (Blumstein et al., 1988a:2). They invoke such terms as initiation or onset, continuity, duration, individual offending rates (or lambda), escalation, desistance, and termination. Longitudinal research is clearly a necessity to study criminal careers. Questions arise concerning the causes of crime, but also of interest are factors associated with increased frequency of crime commission, escalation of the seriousness of offending, and, importantly, desistance of law-violating behavior. Can escalation and termination be explained simply as results of low self-control in the case of the former and maturation in the case of termination? This surely oversimplifies. Blumstein and colleagues cite prior research to support their position that different factors explain the onset and termination of criminal activity and that age is part of this overall criminal career perspective. In Chapter 10 we examine this debate in greater detail.

Distribution of Crime by Race

Race is a third personal characteristic considered to be highly correlated with crime rates. The common notion is that African-Americans and some other minorities are overrepresented in crime statistics, and this indeed does appear to be the case when we examine UCR data. The NCVS data also show a disproportionate number of perceived offenders to be African-American. Most of the self-report studies, however, (including the NYS) do not find the same magnitude of differences in crime rate by race.

Table 4.8 shows that African-Americans, based on arrest statistics, commit violent crimes at a rate considerably disproportionate to the size of their population. While African-Americans comprise less than 15 percent of the American population, they account for 39 percent of arrests for violent crimes, compared to 22.4 percent of offenders in single-offender victimizations in the NCVS. Does this discrepancy between the two data sources represent discrimination within the criminal justice system? A study by Robert Sigler and Melody Horn (1986) found that when the researchers controlled for economic status, race did not appear to have an effect on the likelihood of arrest, although once arrested, African-Americans were more likely to be incarcerated. A number of studies examining sentencing decisions have confirmed the finding that African-Americans are more likely to receive prison sentences, and often harsher ones, than are whites (Chiricos & Crawford, 1995; Everett & Nienstadt,

TABLE 4.8
Distribution of Crime by Race, UCR, 2007

	Total	White	American	Other
Total Arrests	10,656,710	7,426,278	3,003,060	227,372
Percent		69.7%	28.2%	2.1%
Index Crimes	1,672,790	1,095,896	538,758	37,136
Percent		65.5%	33.3%	2.2%
Violent Crimes	449,986	265,108	175,545	9,334
Percent		58.9%	39.0%	2.1%
Property Crimes	1,222,804	830,788	364,213	27,703
Percent		67.9%	29.8%	2.2%

Source: U.S. Department of Justice (2007). *Crime in the United States, 2007*. Washington, DC: U.S. Government Printing Office.

1999; Spohn & Holleran, 2000; Steffensmeier, Ulmer & Kramer, 1998). However, in a recent publication examining sentencing decisions in Pennsylvania, Darrell Steffensmeier and Stephen Demuth (2001) found that Hispanic defendants received the harshest sentences for both drug and nondrug offenses: whites received the least severe treatment with African-American defendants in the middle.

In a comprehensive review of the literature, William Wilbanks (1987) concluded that it is a myth that the criminal justice system is racist. Wilbanks acknowledged that individual cases of prejudice and discrimination occur, but he argued that there is sparse, inconsistent, and contradictory evidence to support a finding of systematic racism against African-Americans in the American criminal justice system. This argument, however, is in direct contrast to the opinions of R. McNeeley and Carl Pope (1981) and the sentencing research that consistently reports that young minority males are at greater risk of being incarcerated than are others, even when offense and prior history are controlled. These authors maintain that the system is racist and discriminates against African-Americans. A theoretical analysis by Ross Matsueda and Karen Heimer (1987) suggested why African-Americans may be represented disproportionately in both the UCR and NCVS statistics. They report that broken homes have a larger impact on delinquency among African-Americans than among other groups. Consequently, African-Americans may be more involved in criminal activities and more likely to be apprehended, as they more often grow up in broken homes.

The NYS data tend to refute the UCR data. With regard to serious and violent offenses, there did not appear to be any racial difference in the rates of crime commission by the fifth year of the study and when social class was controlled, the race relationship disappeared (Huizinga & Elliott, 1987). These findings suggest that some degree of disproportionate minority contact with and processing by the criminal justice system is in effect.

Distribution of Crime by Social Class

An enduring debate in criminology centers on the relationship between social class and crime. This apparently simple issue remains unresolved despite numerous attempts at resolution. Support can be found for both positive and negative relationships between social class and crime. Charles Tittle, Wayne Villemez, and Douglas Smith (1978), based on their meta-analysis of 35 studies, concluded that the link between social class and criminality was a myth. Their article stimulated a proliferation of new research and critical reactions. John Braithwaite (1981), for example, in an ambitious secondary analysis, found that 81 percent of 224 studies reported an inverse relationship between social class and crime (i.e., the lower the social class, the more criminal activity). Introduction of the underclass concept by William Julius Wilson (1987) has spawned further research into this area and the re-emergence of gangs has been linked to the development of an urban underclass—a portion of the population outside the mainstream of the American occupational system (e.g., Hagedorn, 1988; and Vigil, 1988). Charles Tittle and Robert Meier (1990) conducted a critical review of research published during the 1980s and concluded that support of the SES—delinquency relationship was generally weak and inconsistent.

Much of this debate has been spurred by self-report data. Empirical evidence and theoretical works prior to 1960 accepted the relationship between lower class and criminality as an a priori assumption; researchers sought to account for the higher rates of criminal conduct among the lower class. Walter Miller (1958), for example, suggested that the lower class had unique "focal concerns" that placed a cultural value on behaviors resulting in conflict with middle-class beliefs (see Chapter 8). Richard Cloward and Lloyd Ohlin (1960) proposed a set of postulates referred to as "differential opportunity theory" (see Chapter 7). Others suggested that persons in the lower class commit more criminal acts due to their "blocked" opportunities to legitimate means for achieving success. Little empirical evidence existed to dispute the researchers' assumption that the lower class was more criminal.

With the introduction of self-report techniques in the late 1950s and 1960s, new evidence was presented that coincided with the emergence of a new theoretical perspective: labeling theory (see Chapter 9). A number of these studies found no relationship between social class and self-reported juvenile crime. This conclusion supported the argument that it was not that the lower class committed more crime, but rather that this social class-criminality relationship was an artifact of discretionary practices within the criminal justice system. The police, for instance, were more likely to stop and arrest members of the lower class. Similarly, once arrested, lower-class individuals faced a greater likelihood of being convicted and sentenced to prison than did their middle-class counterparts (Evans, 1978; Aaronson et al., 1984).

Not only did these self-report findings fuel a major theoretical debate, but they also raised methodological concerns regarding the measurement of both social class and of criminal activity. Was criminal activity to be defined as the commission of illegal acts or as the official detection and labeling of such acts? Furthermore, should the scope of criminality be confined to the "street crimes" identified in the UCR Index offenses or should there be a broader conception of crime? Answers to these questions will shape, to a large extent, the results of the social class-criminality debate.

There is also the issue of discretionary (or discriminatory) practices within the criminal justice system. To what extent, the labeling theorists would ask, is it possible to discern the difference between behavior and differential response to behavior? Darrell Steffensmeier and Robert Terry (1973) conducted a study of shoplifters and found that the same behavior resulted in different outcomes depending upon the sex and apparent social class of the "criminal." Other studies have reported similar findings, leading to the view that a "Pygmalion effect" or self-fulfilling prophecy may explain the seeming relationship between social class and crime.

The latter question reflects the political nature of crime. When a criminologist or a politician defines crime, that person makes an ideological statement with a number of important implications. If, for example, we define embezzlement, tax evasion, insider trading, and Ponzi schemes as Index offenses, who will the criminals be? Obviously, these are crimes more likely to be committed by members of the middle and upper classes (e.g., Bernie Maddoff) and not by the lower class (see, for example, the recent research reported by Willott et al., 2001). Conversely, if we define serious crime as burglary, robbery, and larceny-theft, then who will the criminals be? The definition of crime has major repercussions for our view of who the criminals are and for how we, as a society, proceed to "fight" crime.

It is no easy task to define social class. If we agree that social class is a composite measure of education, income, and occupation, how do we measure these variables? How do we measure educational attainment: number of years in school, highest grade completed, informal training, or some combination of the preceding? Depending upon the decision, the results may be quite different.

What about income? Does this refer to individual, family, or household income? The researcher also must decide whether to measure gross or net income on a monthly, annual, or possibly even on an average annual basis. A further problem is how to ask questions regarding income. Americans typically find inquiries regarding their income more personal and sensitive than those dealing with either illegal or sexual activity.

On the face of it, it seems obvious that a college dean has higher occupational prestige than a data processor at the computer center. But if you were a researcher interested in determining family social class, how would you decide the social class of a college dean whose husband was a data processor? This is but one issue involved in "operationalizing" concepts such as social class. Another concern is whether to use an individual-, family-, or neighborhood-level measurement of social status.

Given this definitional uncertainty, it is not surprising that neither the UCR nor the NCVS record data regarding the offender's social class. From where, then, does the bulk of this information come? Much of it derives from qualitative and impressionistic opinions formulated into theoretical statements that posit an inverse relationship between social class and criminal behavior. Robert Merton's (1938) pioneering publication is a classic example. Based in part upon empirical observation of who was being arrested and incarcerated, Merton argued that a disjunction between socially accepted means and culturally specified goals was the cause of criminal behavior. He stated that this goals-and-means disjunction was most pronounced among the lower classes. This statement, as will be considered further in Chapter 7, was based upon the belief that all Americans aspire to the same things, but that access to successful achievement of these goals is contingent upon location in the class structure. With everyone seeking wealth, power, and prestige, the members of the lower classes experience the greatest frustration in realizing their dreams. Frustrated lower-class individuals use illegitimate avenues through which to achieve material success.

This theoretical orientation was perpetuated by Miller (1958), Cohen (1955), and Cloward and Ohlin (1960). Empirical studies were relegated the task of post hoc confirmation of these theorists' assumptions. Utilizing samples of prisoners, the studies generally confirmed the theoretical statements. Regardless of how the researchers operationalized social class, the findings were remarkably consistent: the lower classes were disproportionately represented among the inmate population. But, as suggested above, to what extent do these official statistics reflect differential rates of offending or discretionary practices within the criminal justice system? Self-report studies have failed to resolve this argument. While a number of researchers have suggested that the social class-crime relationship is a myth (Tittle et al., 1978; Krohn et al., 1980), others have argued that methodological weaknesses are the source of the confusion (Clelland & Carter, 1980; Elliott & Ageton, 1980; Braithwaite, 1981; Brown, 1985; Tittle & Meier, 1990). Obviously the relationship between social class and crime requires better, more extensive research. In one such recent study, Wright and his colleagues (1999:176) found that socio-economic status has both a positive and a negative effect on delinquency: "low SES promoted delinquency by increasing individuals' alienation, financial strain, and aggression and by decreasing educational and occupational aspirations, whereas high SES promoted individuals' delinquency by increasing risk taking and social power and by decreasing conventional values." This research suggests the importance of examining the mediating variables between social class and behavior.

Victims of Crime

Criminal victimization in the United States, as measured through the earlier version of the NCVS, declined from 1981 through 1992. With the redesign of the NCVS, it is no longer possible to make historical comparisons. Under the revised format of the NCVS, victimizations peaked in 1993 at 43,547,000 and have been falling since; with 22,879,700 victimizations reported in 2007. The UCR, SRD, and limitedly the NCVS provide information about offenders. This information serves as the basis for not only theory development, but also criminal justice policy formation. Knowledge about crime victims is also important for understanding crime and developing measures to effectively deal with crime. Who are these victims? Who is most likely to be victimized? These are questions the NCVS is ideally suited to answer.

Much of the information collected for the NCVS is tabulated by household characteristics. The term household refers to a dwelling unit and its occupants. Household victimization is determined by the occurrence of a burglary, auto theft, or household theft, or is counted if a household member was a crime victim, no matter where the crime occurred. According to the NCVS household survey data, slightly more than one out of every six (15%) American households experienced some form of property crime victimization in 2006. Table 4.9 summarizes the characteristics of victimized households. In general, households with the highest victimization rates were found in the western states, had annual household incomes of less than $7,500, were White and located in urban areas, and were rental units (Catalano, 2005). These victimization rates, however, varied slightly by crime type. Burglary rates, for example, were higher in the lower-income brackets, whereas auto theft was more common among the upper income households.

Household Income

The overall likelihood of property victimization is greatest for households with annual family incomes of less than $7,500. Burglary rates for households with incomes of less than $7,500 (55.7 per 1,000 households) were more than twice the rate for households reporting more than $75,000 annual income (22.4). There was less discrepancy in rates of household theft: 133.2 for households with more than $75,000 annual income compared to 150.3 for those reporting incomes of less than $7,500.

TABLE 4.9
Number of Property Crimes per 1,000 Households, by Race, Hispanic Origin, Income, and other Household Characteristics, 1995 and 2006

Characteristics of household or head of household	Rates of property crime per 1,000 households	
	1995	2006
Race		
White	272.9	156.7
Black	322.3	185.6
Other	292.6	137.7
Hispanic Origin		
Hispanic	364.1	211.7
Non-Hispanic	272.7	154.7
Household Income		
Less than $7,500	290.7	217.3
$7,500 - 14,999	256.1	195.7
$15,000 - 24,999	286.9	183.1
$25,000 - 34,999	283	179.4
$35,000 - 49,999	293.6	166.2
$50,000 - 74,999	317.1	166.8
$75,000 or more	336.1	172.0
Region		
Northeast	223.7	103.9
Midwest	256.3	155.8
South	264.1	136.8
West	387.8	206.5
Residence		
Urban	347.9	194.6
Suburban	267.0	133.0
Rural	218.4	125.1
Home Ownership		
Owned	244.2	136.5
Rented	344.4	192.3

Source: U.S. Department of Justice (1997). *Changes in Criminal Victimization, 1994-1995*. Washington, DC: U.S. Department of Justice, and Rand, Michael R. (2007). *Criminal Victimization, 2006*. Washington, DC: U.S. Department of Justice.

Personal victimizations provide a more consistent picture of crime victims. Those most likely to be victims of violent crimes are the poor; the rate of reported violent crime victimization for all types of personal victimizations decreased with income. As reported in Table 4.10, the rate of personal victimizations for persons in households with incomes of less than $7,500 (64.6 per 1,000 persons age 12 and over) is almost

TABLE 4.10
Number of Personal Crimes per 1,000 Persons, by Victims' Characteristics, 1995, 2006

Victim Characteristic	Personal Crime Rates (per 1,000 persons)	
	1995	2006
Sex		
Male	54.4	27.4
Female	38.5	23.4
Age		
12-15	110.9	47.8
16-19	110.3	52.8
20-24	79.8	45.1
25-34	55.9	36.6
35-49	35.6	20.6
50-64	15.6	13.6
65 or older	6.9	3.9
Race		
White	44.6	23.9
Black	58.4	32.9
Other	43.8	20.4
Two or more	na	69.0
Hispanic Origin		
Hispanic	56.1	28.4
Non-Hispanic	45.0	24.9
Household Income		
Less than $7,500	74.6	64.6
$7,500 - 14,999	49.7	45.9
$15,000 - 24,999	49.2	31.4
$25,000 - 34,999	48.1	34.5
$35,000 - 49,999	45.8	22.5
$50,000 - 74,999	44.1	24.5
$75,000 or more	37.9	14.6
Region		
Northeast	41.1	20.2
Midwest	46.7	23.7
South	39.6	19.6
West	61.5	25.9
Residence		
Urban	59.9	29.7
Suburban	43.5	18.9
Rural	35.5	17.3

Source: U.S Department of Justice (1997). *Changes in Criminal Victimization, 1994-1995*. Washington, DC: U.S. Department of Justice; Rand, Michael R. (2007). *Criminal Victimization, 2006*. Washington, DC: U.S. Department of Justice.

four times the rate of those people living in households with $75,000 or more (14.6). This pattern is consistent for each specific type of crime but is most pronounced for rape/sexual assault (six times greater), aggravated assault (five times greater), and robbery (three times greater).

Geographical Location

Urban households had higher victimization rates per 1,000 households (29.7) than both suburban (18.9) and rural (17.3) households. This pattern was the same for all three types of property crime reported, burglary, motor vehicle theft, and thefts. With regard to personal victimizations, urban areas again had the highest rates for all crime types. With respect to region of the country, the western states are definitely the ones to be avoided from a crime victimization perspective. For both household crimes and personal crimes, the West has rates significantly higher than any other region. The Northeast appears to be the safest region, consistently reporting the lowest rates of victimization.

Race and Ethnicity

Hispanic households (211.7 per 1,000 households) had substantially higher victimization rates than did African-American (185.6) and white (156.7) households. Hispanic households had higher rates of both theft and auto theft but African-American households reported the highest rates of burglary. Personal victimizations displayed a slightly different pattern, with Hispanics reporting a lower rate (28.4 per 1,000 persons aged 12 and older) than African-Americans (32.9) but higher than whites (23.9).

Gender

Males are significantly more likely to commit crime than are females. Likewise, males tend to be victimized more often than females. The difference between male and female victimization rates, however, has decreased steadily. In 1995, males (54.4 per 1,000 persons) reported almost 50 percent more personal victimizations than did females (38.5 per 1,000 persons). By 2006, the male rate was only slightly greater than the female rate of victimization (27.4 versus 23.4). Most of this difference between males and females is attributed to the higher rates of victimization for robbery and aggravated assault among males.

Age

Contrary to popular opinion the elderly are the least likely to be victims of crime. Teenagers are the most likely to experience a personal crime. In fact the victimization rate of 52.8 per 1,000 persons aged 16-19 is 13 times the victimization rate (3.9) for those age 65 and older. For each specific offense type teenagers have the highest risk of victimization. With respect to simple assaults, for example, teenagers are more than twice as likely as 35- to 49-year-olds to be victims, yet 25 times more likely to be victimized than are those persons 65 and older.

Summary

We have described in this chapter the volume and distribution of crime in the United States. Not only is it of interest to criminologists to be aware of geographical, temporal, and social characteristics of crime, it is also vital for criminal justice policymakers to be cognizant of this information. The three dominant sources of crime data, the UCR, the NCVS, and SRD, provide somewhat different pictures about the nature of crime.

The Uniform Crime Reports portray the United States as experiencing a skyrocketing increase in crime throughout the 1960s and 1970s, peaking in 1980, and declining through 1984, before rising again from 1985 through 1991 and declining again since 1992. In contrast, the NCVS data show a relatively stable crime rate through the 1970s and 1980s. Because these two sources may well measure different aspects of crime, it is not surprising that they present different estimates of the volume of crime.

The UCR are limited to crimes recorded by the police, while the NCVS reflect crimes reported to interviewers. These different methodologies may account in part for the discrepancy in numbers. In general, the NCVS and self-report studies list a crime rate from two to 10 times that reported by the UCR. Gove et al. (1985) and others have suggested that these sources are measuring different domains of behavior and, therefore, the sources reach different results.

There is greater agreement with respect to specific characteristics of the distribution of crime and of offenders. The general picture is that crime is concentrated in urban areas, overall crime rates are highest in the West, and most crimes are committed between 6 p.m. and 6 a.m. Criminals are likely to be males under the age of 25. Additionally, African-Americans, according to UCR and NCVS data, are overrepresented in the population of offenders. Self-report data, however, do not support this conception. The same is true for the offender's social class. While neither UCR nor NCVS provide information about the perpetrator's social class, the common assumption has been that members of the lower class commit a disproportionate share of all crimes. Self-report data provide contradictory evidence on this matter. Social class of offenders, thus, remains a hotly debated topic in criminology.

Data from the National Crime Victimization Survey provide a picture of crime victims. Contrary to common stereotypes, the individuals most likely to be victimized are young, African-American and Hispanic males residing in urban areas. Households with the highest probability of victimization are those with six or more occupants, with a Hispanic or African-American head of the household, in urban areas, and with low incomes (this is especially the case for victimization of a violent crime).

Key Terms and Concepts

Age and Crime
Career Criminal
Criminal Career
Escalation
Frequency Rates
Gender and Crime
Geographical Crime Distribution
Individual Offending Rates
Initiation
Lambda

Maturation Effects
Power-Control Theory
Prevalence Rates
Race and Crime
Selective Incapacitation
Social Class and Crime
Temporal Crime Distribution
Termination
Underclass
Victimization

Key Criminologists

Freda Adler
Alfred Blumstein
John Braithwaite
Michael Gottfredson
John Hagan
Travis Hirschi

Steven Messner
Richard Rosenfeld
Rita Simon
Darrell Steffensmeier
Charles Tittle

References

Aaronson, D.E., C.T. Dienes & M.C. Musheno (1984). *Public Policy and Police Discretion: Processes of Decriminalization*. New York, NY: Clark Boardman.

Adler, F. (1983). *Nations Not Obsessed with Crime*. Littleton, CO: Fred B. Rothman.

Adler, F. (1975). *Sisters in Crime*. New York, NY: McGraw-Hill.

Biderman, A.D. & J.P. Lynch (1991). *Understanding Crime Incidence Statistics: Why the UCR Diverges from the NCS*. New York, NY: Springer-Verlag.

Blackwell, B.S. (2000). "Perceived Sanction Threats, Gender, and Crime: A Test and Elaboration of Power-Control Theory." *Criminology*, 38:439-488.

Blumstein, A. (2001). "Why Is Crime Falling—Or Is It?" In Perspectives on Crime and Justice: 2000-2001 Lecture Series. Washington, DC: U.S. Department of Justice, Office of Justice Programs, National Institute of Justice.

Blumstein, A. & J. Wallman (2000). *The Crime Drop in America*. New York, NY: Cambridge University Press.

Blumstein, A., J. Cohen & D. Farrington (1988a). "Criminal Career Research: Its Value for Criminology." *Criminology*, 26:1-36.

Blumstein, A., J. Cohen & D. Farrington (1988b). "Longitudinal and Criminal Career Research: Further Clarifications." *Criminology*, 26:57-76.

Boocock, S.S. (1972). *An Introduction to the Sociology of Learning*. Boston, MA: Houghton-Mifflin.

Boritch, H. (1992). "Gender and Criminal Court Outcomes: An Historical Analysis." *Criminology*, 30:293-325.

Braithwaite, J. (1981). "The Myth of Social Class and Criminality Reconsidered." *American Sociological Review*, 46:36-57.

Brown, S.E. (1985). "The Class-Delinquency Hypothesis and Juvenile Justice System Bias." *Sociological Inquiry*, 55:212-223.

Canter, R.J. (1982). "Sex Differences in Self-Report Delinquency." *Criminology*, 20:373-393.

Caspi, A., T.E. Moffitt, P.A. Silva, M. Stouthamer-Loeber, R.F. Krueger & P. Schmutte (1994). "Are Some People Crime-Prone? Replications of the Personality-Crime Relationship Across Countries, Genders, Races, and Methods." *Criminology*, 32:163-195.

Cernkovich, S.A. & P.C. Giordano (1979). "On Complicating the Relationship between Liberation and Delinquency." *Social Problems*, 26:467-481.

Chesney-Lind, M. & R.G. Sheldon (1998). *Girls: Delinquency and Juvenile Justice*, Second Edition. Belmont, CA: West/Wadsworth.

Chiricos, T.G. & C. Crawford (1995). "Race and Imprisonment: A Contextual Assessment of the Evidence." In D. Hawkins (ed.) *Ethnicity, Race and Crime*. Albany, NY: State University of New York Press.

Clelland, D. & T.J. Carter (1980). "The New Myth of Class and Crime." *Criminology*, 18:319-336.

Cloward, R. & L. Ohlin (1960). *Delinquency and Opportunity*. New York, NY: The Free Press.

Cohen, A.K. (1955). *Delinquent Boys*. New York, NY: The Free Press.

Dornfeld, M. & C. Kruttschnitt (1992). "Do the Stereotypes Fit? Mapping Gender-Specific Outcomes and Risk Factors." *Criminology*, 30:397-419.

Elliott, D.S. & S.S. Ageton (1980). "Reconciling Race and Class Differences in Estimates of Delinquency." *American Sociological Review*, 45:95-110.

Elliott, D.S., D.H. Huizinga, B.A. Knowles & R.J. Canter (1983). *The Prevalence and Incidence of Delinquent Behavior: 1976-1980, National Youth Survey Report Number 26*. Boulder, CO: Behavioral Research Institute.

Esbensen, F. & L.T. Winfree (1998). "Race and Gender Differences Between Gang and Non-Gang Youth: Results from A Multi-Site Survey." *Justice Quarterly*, 15;505-526.

Esbensen, F-A & E.P. Deschenes (1998). "A Multisite Examination of Youth Gang Membership: Does Gender Matter?" *Criminology*, 36:799-827.

Evans, M. (1978). *Discretion and Control*. Beverly Hills, CA: Sage Publications.

Everett, R.S. & B.C. Nienstadt (1999). "Race, Remorse and Sentencing Reduction: Is Saying You're Sorry Enough?" *Justice Quarterly*, 16:99-122.

Geis, G. (1986). "On the Declining Crime Rate: An Exegetic Conference Report." *Criminal Justice Policy Review*, 1:16-36.

Gioradano, P.C. & S.M. Rockwell (2000). "Differential Association Theory and Female Crime." In S.S. Simpson (ed.) *Of Crime & Criminality*. Thousand Oaks, CA: Pine Forge Press.

Gottfredson, M.R. & T. Hirschi (1990). *A General Theory of Crime*. Stanford, CA: Stanford University Press.

Gottfredson, M.R. & T. Hirschi (1988). "Science, Public Policy, and the Career Paradigm." *Criminology*, 26:37-56.

Gottfredson, M.R. & T. Hirschi (1986). "The True Value of Lambda Would Appear to be Zero: An Essay on Career Criminals, Criminal Careers, Selective Incapacitation, Cohort Studies, and Related Topics." *Criminology*, 24:213-233.

Gove, W.R., M. Hughes & M. Geerken (1985). "Are Uniform Crime Reports a Valid Indicator of the Index Crimes? An Affirmative Answer with Minor Qualifications." *Criminology*, 23:451-502.

Gurr, T.R., P.N. Grabosky & R.C. Hula (1977). *The Politics of Crime and Conflict: A Comparative Study of Four Cities*. Beverly Hills, CA: Sage Publications.

Hagan, J. (1994). *Crime and Disrepute*. Thousand Oaks, CA: Pine Forge Press.

Hagan, J., A.R. Gillis & J. Simpson (1985). "The Class Structure of Gender and Delinquency: Toward a Power-Control Theory of Common Delinquent Behavior." *American Journal of Sociology*, 90:1151-1178.

Hagan, J., J. Simpson & A.R. Gillis (1987). "Class in the Household: A Power-Control Theory of Gender and Delinquency." *American Journal of Sociology*, 92:788-816.

Hagan, J., J.H. Simpson & A.R. Gillis (1979). "The Sexual Stratification of Social Control: A Gender-Based Perspective on Crime and Delinquency." *British Journal of Sociology*, 30:25-38.

Hagedorn, J.M. (1988). *People and Folks: Gangs, Crime and the Underclass in a Rustbelt City*. Chicago, IL: Lakeview Press.

Heimer, K. & S. DeCoster (1999). "The Gendering of Violent Delinquency." *Criminology*, 37:277-317.

Heimer, K., J.L. Lauritsen & J.P. Lynch (2009). "The National Crime Victimization Survey and the Gender Gap in Offending: Redux." *Criminology* 47:427-438.

Hindelang, M.J. (1971). "Age, Sex, and the Versatility of Delinquent Involvements." *Social Problems*, 18:522-535.

Hirschi, T. (1969). *Causes of Delinquency*. Berkeley, CA: University of California Press.

Hoffman-Bustamonte, D. (1973). "The Nature of Female Criminality." *Issues in Criminology*, 8:117-136.

Huizinga, D. & D.S. Elliott (1987). "Juvenile Offenders: Offender Incidence and Arrest Rates by Race." *Crime & Delinquency*, 33:206-223.

Huizinga, D. & F. Esbensen (1991). "Are There Changes in Female Delinquency and Are There Changes in Underlying Explanatory Factors?" Paper presented at the annual meeting of the American Society of Criminology.

Jolin, A. & D.C. Gibbons (1987). "Age Patterns in Criminal Involvement." *International Journal of Offender Therapy and Comparative Criminology*, 31:237-260.

Krohn, M.D., R.L. Akers, M.J. Radosevich & L. Lanza-Kaduce (1980). "Social Status and Deviance: Class Context of School, Social Status, and Delinquent Behavior." *Criminology*, 18:303-318.

Kvaraceus, W. (1945). *Juvenile Delinquency and the School*. Yonkers, NY: World Book Company.

Laub, J.H. (1990). "Patterns of Criminal Victimization in the United States." In A.J. Lurigio, W.G. Skogan & R.C. Davis (eds.) *Victims of Crime: Problems, Policies, and Programs*. Newbury Park, CA: Sage Publications.

Lauritsen, J.L., K. Heimer & J.P. Lynch (2009). "Trends in the Gender Gap in Violent Offending: New Evidence from the National Crime Victimization Survey." *Criminology* 47:361-400.

Liu, X. & H.B. Kaplan (1999). "Explaining the Gender Difference in Adolescent Delinquent Behavior: A Longitudinal Test of Mediating Mechanisms." *Criminology*, 37:195-215.

Matsueda, R.L. & K. Heimer (1987). "Race, Family Structure, and Delinquency: A Test of Differential Association and Social Control Theories." *American Sociological Review*, 52:826-840.

McNeeley, R.L. & C.E. Pope (1981). *Race, Crime, and Criminal Justice*. Beverly Hills, CA: Sage Publications.

Menard, S. (1987). "Short-Term Trends in Crime and Delinquency: A Comparison of UCR, NCS, and Self-Report Data." *Justice Quarterly*, 4:455-474.

Merton, R.K. (1938). "Social Structure and Anomie." *American Sociological Review*, 3:672-682.

Messner, S. & R. Rosenfeld (2007). *Crime and the American Dream*, Fourth Edition. Belmont, CA: Wadsworth.

Messner, S. & R. Rosenfeld (1994). *Crime and the American Dream*. Belmont, CA: Wadsworth.

Miller, J. (1998). "Up It Up: Gender and the Accomplishment of Street Robbery." *Criminology*, 36:37-66.

Miller, W.B. (1958). "Lower Class Culture as a Generating Milieu for Gang Delinquency." *Journal of Social Issues*, 14:5-19.

Peterson, D., J. Miller & F.-A. Esbensen (2001). "The Impact of Sex Composition on Gangs and Gang Member Delinquency." *Criminology*, 39:411-440.

Pollak, O. (1961). *The Criminality of Women*. New York, NY: Barnes.

Rand, M.R. (2008). *Criminal Victimization, 2007*. Washington, DC: U.S. Department of Justice, Office of Justice Programs.

Schur, E.M. (1984). *Labeling Women Deviant: Gender, Stigma, and Social Control*. New York, NY: Random House.

Schwartz, J., D. Steffensmeier, H. Zhong & J. Ackerman (2009). "Trends in the Gender Gap in Violence: Reevaluating NCVS and Other Evidence." *Criminology* 47:401-426.

Sigler, R.T. & M. Horn (1986). "Race, Income, and Penetration of the Justice System." *Criminal Justice Review*, 11:1-7.

Simon, R. (1975). *The Contemporary Woman and Crime*. Rockville, MD: National Institute of Mental Health.

Smart, C. (1976). *Women, Crime and Criminology: A Feminist Perspective*. London, UK: Routledge.

Spohn, C. & D. Holleran (2000). "The Imprisonment Penalty Paid by Young, Unemployed, Black and Hispanic Male Offenders." *Criminology*, 38:281-306.

Steffensmeier, D.J. & S. Demuth (2001). "Ethnicity and Judges' Sentencing Decisions: Hispanic-Black-White Comparisons." *Criminology*, 39:145-178.

Steffensmeier, D.J., J. Ulmer & J. Kramer (1998). "The Interaction of Race, Gender, and Age in Criminal Sentencing: The Punishment Cost of Being Young, Black, and Male." *Criminology*, 36:763-797.

Steffensmeier, D.J. & M.D. Harer (1987). "Is the Crime Rate Really Falling? An Aging U.S. Population and Its Impact on the Nation's Crime Rate, 1980-1984." *Journal of Research in Crime and Delinquency*, 24:23-48.

Steffensmeier, D.J. & R.M. Terry (1973). "Deviance and Respectability: An Observational Study of Reactions to Shoplifting." *Social Forces*, 51:417-426.

Tittle, C. & R.F. Meier (1990). "Specifying the SES/Delinquency Relationship." *Criminology*, 28:271-299.

Tittle, C., W. Villemez & D. Smith (1978). "The Myth of Social Class and Criminality: An Empirical Assessment of the Empirical Evidence." *American Sociological Review*, 43:643-656.

van Dijk, J. & K. Kangaspunta (2000). "Piecing Together the Cross-National Crime Puzzle." *National Institute of Justice Journal*. Washington, DC: U.S. Department of Justice.

U.S. Department of Justice (2007). *Crime in the United States, 2007*. Washington, DC: U.S. Department of Justice.

U. S. Department of Justice (1997). *Changes in Criminal Victimization, 1994-95*. Washington, DC: U.S. Department of Justice.

U.S. Department of Justice (1994). *Criminal Victimization in the United States, 1992*. Washington, DC: U.S. Department of Justice

Vigil, J.D. (1988). *Barrio Gangs: Street Life and Identity in Southern California*. Austin, TX: University of Texas Press.

Weis, J.G (1980). *Sex Differences: Study Data Publications*. Seattle, WA: Center for Law and Justice.

Wilbanks, W. (1987). *The Myth of a Racist Criminal Justice System*. Monterey, CA: Brooks/ Cole Publishing.

Willott, S., C. Griffin & M. Torrance (2001). "Snakes and Ladders: Upper Middle-Class Male Offenders Talk about Economic Crime." *Criminology*, 39:441-466.

Wilson, W.J. (1987). *The Truly Disadvantaged: The Inner City, the Underclass, and Public Policy*. Chicago, IL: University of Chicago Press.

Wright, B.R.E., A. Caspi, T.E. Moffitt, R.A. Miech & P.A. Silva (1999). "Reconsidering the Relationship Between SES and Delinquency: A Causation but not Correlation." *Criminology*, 37:175-194.

PART II

Theories of Crime

The first four chapters have provided a foundation for the study of criminology. There is little professional consensus regarding the definition of criminology or the bounds of criminological inquiry, but there are certain elements that most criminologists regard as basic. Crime as it is defined in criminal codes is something with which the criminologist must be conversant. For many criminologists, explaining violations of legal codes is the raison d'être of criminology. Other criminologists view reactions to antisocial or deviant behaviors, whether the behaviors are officially proscribed or not, as central to the field of criminology. It should be stressed that criminology is a science, and as such it is comprised of an empirical and a theoretical component. Measuring crime and related variables, discussed in the preceding two chapters, are major concerns within the empirical domain. The following six chapters turn to the theoretical dimension.

There are basic questions that deserve attention before a review of major theories of crime. These include: "What is theory?" "Why is theory so important to the criminological enterprise?" Students and even criminal justice practitioners often lament that theory is boring and not pertinent to the "real world," that is, to practical concerns. But theory that is alien to the real world is, very simply, poor theory.

The fundamental purpose of theory is to explain things that can be observed. The scientific approach requires that theory be subjected to the test of observation. Propositions that facilitate prediction of the phenomena of interest should be derivable from theories. If a proposed explanation or theory fails the tests of observation and prediction, then it should be rejected. Criminological theories seek to arrive at explanations that account for behavior defined as criminal. If, for example, a theory (assuredly a far-out theory) implicates blue eyes as a causal factor in embezzlement, but blue-eyed persons do not appear disproportionately in representative samples of embezzlers, the theory is discarded. New ideas for the explanation of embezzlement can then be advanced as the scientific interplay of theory and research continue.

Criminologists study crime, criminals, and societal reactions to crime and criminals, accumulating an abundance of facts in the process. These facts should be used as building blocks for theory construction because it is theory that provides meaning to what often seem to be unrelated facts. Theory incorporates propositions that relate two or more concepts in such a fashion that they then can be subjected to the tests of observation and prediction. Thus, the scientific approach is self-correcting in the sense that theories failing to explain and predict should be discarded or revised. Without formal theory development and testing, myths regarding the causes of crime are apt to flourish. This brings us to the pragmatic justification for the study of theories of crime: its implications for crime-related public policy.

First, it is important to recognize that virtually everyone holds some view about the causes of crime and, by implication, about how to prevent, control, and respond to it. College and university students, brick masons, physicians, ministers, nuns, bank presidents, and persons from every walk of life are likely to believe that they know the causes of, and consequently the cures for, criminality. Think of the occasions on which you have heard persons react to discussions of crime or delinquency by exclaiming: "It's in the genes," "They're from the wrong side of town," "They got in with the wrong crowd," or "Those kids need to have their butts kicked." Each of these reactions reflects one or more formal theories. Unfortunately, nonspecialists often adopt simplified explanations and solutions for complex problems such as crime. Such public opinion, whether informed or uninformed, can affect crime control policy, sometimes making things worse rather than improving them.

All criminal justice practitioners embrace some theoretical perspective regarding the causes of crime. These practitioners may not be fully aware that they do this, and their thinking may be ill-formed, but at least in part, their ideas likely guide their behavior. A probation officer, for instance, will be "tough" or "sympathetic" with delinquents depending on his or her beliefs regarding the roots of the misbehavior. The question is not whether criminal justice practice is in need of theory, but rather whether criminal justice policy and practice will be guided by the best possible theory or by theory that is randomly formed, nonsystematic, and unable to pass scientifically rigorous tests. The "real world" of criminal justice turns on theory, but unfortunately, it is often a very poor understanding rather than the best that criminology has to offer. Theory inevitably influences criminal justice policy. A particularly important reason for studying formal criminological theories is to enhance the prospects that sound theory will dominate criminological programs.

Criminology poses many intriguing questions. One of the most absorbing is the age-old question of "Why?" "Why do people commit crime?" "Why do others conform?" "How can we explain or understand crime and criminality?" This section of the text explores a variety of theoretical perspectives on such matters. The theoretical viewpoints are presented in a historical framework. The historical format has merit beyond its organizational value because theoretical notions spawned in a given era often reflect the social, political, and economic character and circumstances of the time. While studying society can tell us much about crime, the reverse is also true.

5

Deterrence and Rational Choice Theories of Crime

One of the most widely debated premises underlying attempts to explain crime, among both criminologists and lay persons, is the role of choice. At issue is the degree to which offenders are or are not driven by rational decisionmaking. Both *deterrence theory* and other explanations falling within the larger *rational choice* paradigm assign a greater role to rational decision making on the part of the criminal offender than do other approaches. Both are rooted in *utilitarianism*, the notion that public policy decisions should maximize pleasure, while minimizing pain among the general citizenry. The assumption of rational calculation among criminals is oftentimes viewed as being directly at odds with other theories of crime, though many criminologists envision rationality as falling more on a continuum than in a dichotomy. Moreover, the value of merging different perspectives (theoretical integration) has increased substantially in recent years.

Classical criminology provides the origin of the concept of deterrence. It represents the first effort to explain crime as a product of natural rather than supernatural forces. At its core is the belief that persons consider the prospects of punitive sanctions before making a decision to commit a crime. This line of thinking provided the rationale for development of contemporary Western criminal justice systems and served as the dominant explanation of crime from the late eighteenth to the late nineteenth century. The last one-third of the twentieth century witnessed a resurgence of the deterrence concept and it continues as a popular theory of crime today.

This chapter begins with an examination of the social context within which classical criminology emerged, a time referred to as the *preclassical* era. The unfolding of classical criminology and its impact is then detailed. The chapter then turns to an examination of the development of contemporary deterrence concepts and the move toward a broader rational choice perspective. The evolution of *routine activities theory* over the past quarter century is reviewed as a leading rational choice perspective that is distinct from deterrence.

Preclassical Views of Crime

Criminology, historically speaking, is a very young field of study. Although norms and regulations of human behavior have always been critical matters in all societies, little intellectual energy was focused on these issues for thousands of years. It was not until the latter part of the eighteenth century that crime was explained as a natural rather than a supernatural phenomenon. Prior to that, crime was attributed to the devil, demons, witches, and various other evil spirits, which were thought to be acting through the offending party.

A major rationale for the application of punishment has been retribution or revenge. In early times, revenge often served as the sole motive for dealing with crime (Schafer, 1976). During periods in which systems of private, kinship, religious, and state-controlled revenge prevailed, little attention was focused on the causes of crime or on how responses to crime might be useful for crime control or prevention. There was nothing in early days that approached formal systems of criminal justice. Revenge served to placate and sometimes to compensate victims of crime.

During the earliest period of private revenge, life was, as Thomas Hobbes (1651/1962:100) described it, ". . . a war, as is of every man, against every man . . . and the life of man, solitary, poor, nasty, brutish, and short." Each individual had to provide for his or her own security and, when that security was violated, the individual had to exact whatever revenge was deemed appropriate and feasible. This state of affairs proved socially dysfunctional, in part because the distinction between victim and offender became blurred. The strength of the party desiring revenge was the only control over the severity of punishment, and the offender was likely to retaliate, thereby setting in motion a spiral of violence.

The problem was intensified when the parties in the revenge cycle were kinship groups rather than individuals. Attacks came to be interpreted as affronts to an entire family, tribe, or clan. Retaliation, in turn, was directed toward any or all members of the offender's kinship group. This widening of the revenge cycle is known as *blood feuding*. What had been a feud between two individuals in an earlier era now became a conflict between kinship groups.

Blood feuds became so disruptive that they posed a threat to the stability of the social order in the Middle Ages. Feudal lords began to capitalize on superstitions regarding the causes of crime and to support a religiously oriented approach to punishing offenders, whom the lords often declared to be possessed. This eliminated the need for private and kinship revenge. These types of revenge were supplanted by punishment in God's name, which was controlled by representatives of the church and state. Punishments were defined as appeasement, not just of the victims, but of God. Those committing crimes were regarded as evil and sinful persons.

Persecution justified by law has been traced as far back as the fourth century A.D. (Newman, 1978), but it reached a pinnacle during the period of the *Holy Inquisition*, which extended from the twelfth century through the eighteenth century. Henry Lea's (1887/1955) massive three-volume work, *A History of the Inquisition of the Middle Ages*, opens with a discussion of the crisis of authority faced by the Roman Catholic Church at the close of the twelfth century. This unsettled condition led to an alliance between church and state that provided the framework for the Inquisition. The historical significance of this age for criminological thought cannot be overstated, as "the inquisitorial process, based upon torture, had become the groundwork of all criminal procedure" (Lea, 1866/1973:86).

The Inquisition took place in most European countries throughout the Middle Ages and led to widespread imprisonment, torture, and execution, which were measures designed to extract confessions and to punish the heretical (Newman, 1978). Actually, the inquisitors and other secular authorities administered the punishments because the Church was prohibited from shedding blood. The words of a thirteenth-century inquisitor, however, reflect the movement's attachment to the Church:

> The object of the Inquisition is the destruction of heresy. Heresy cannot be destroyed unless their defenders and fautors [practitioners] are destroyed, and this is effected in two ways, viz., when they are converted to the true Catholic faith, or when, on being abandoned to the secular arm, they are corporally burned (Lea, 1887/1955, Vol. 1:535).

Secular authorities had no real choice in the matter. If they refused to carry out the inquisitorial sentence and burn the heretics, they themselves were threatened with excommunication and risked being labeled heretical. The title page of *Malleus Maleficarum*, a fifteenth-century witch hunters' manual, notes: "Not to believe in witchcraft is the greatest of heresies" (Kramer & Sprenger, 1486/1928). Most secular authorities, however, were enthusiastic about carrying out their duties "to do with them what was customary to be done with heretics"—that is, to burn them alive (Lea, 1887/1955:537-538).

The cruelty and injustice of the Inquisition represent a horrible chapter in the history of crime and punishment. The witch hunters brought the full machinery of the State to bear on their unfortunate victims. These terrible deeds offer lessons of contemporary significance (Geis & Bunn, 1981). As did witch hunters in the past, do we still have "criminal" scapegoats? Are we still sometimes misled by authorities who define crime in their own interest or out of ignorance, as authorities did in dealing with witchcraft? It was not social deviants or misfits that participated in the torture and killing of thousands of innocent persons labeled "witches." It was respectable members of society, such as the clergy, lawyers, and eminent figures, including the English physician and philosopher, Sir Thomas Browne (Geis & Bunn, 1981). This awful historical episode bears remembering when analyzing contemporary crime and punishment.

As the State assumed full responsibility for crime, brutal punishment became more common, reaching its height in the seventeenth and eighteenth centuries. Death had always been the major method of punishment in the Western world, but it was extended to all felonies in seventeenth-century England (Newman, 1978). Moreover, the death penalty was not administered quickly or humanely. Hanging could produce slow death, with the executioner tugging at the legs of the condemned to finish the job. Gruesome practices were often a part of the criminal process. Although English common law prohibited torture (Langbein, 1977; Heath, 1982), it was sometimes used in Star Chamber proceedings and in the process of *peine forte et dure*, which consisted of stretching the accused on his back and stacking iron weights on him until he died or agreed to plead to the charge. It was important to both the accused and his family that he not plead guilty, for so long as the individual died without pleading, thus remaining unconvicted, his property was passed on to his family. If he were convicted, his property could be confiscated (Maestro, 1973).

Torture in England was never as severe as that employed throughout continental Europe (Newman, 1978). In France, before the Revolution, the accused could be taken from his or her home by the *gendarmerie* (the secret police), tried without any defense, and condemned to death. Paul Lacroix (1963:416) describes the barbaric means of execution by fire used at one time in France:

> [A] stake was erected on the spot specially designed for the execu-
> tion, and round it a pile was prepared, composed of alternate layers
> of straw and wood, and rising to about the height of a man. Care
> was taken to leave a free space round the stake for the victim, and
> also a passage by which to lead him to it. Having been stripped of
> his clothes, and dressed in a shirt smeared with sulphur, he had to
> walk to the center of the pile through a narrow opening, and was
> then tightly bound to the stake with ropes and chains. After this,
> faggots and straw were thrown into the empty space through which
> he had passed to the stake, until he was entirely covered by them;
> the pile was then fired on all sides at once.

Burning alive was the usual punishment for heresy, but even more extraordinary tortures were reserved for perpetrators of what were considered the worst crimes, such as regicide (the killing of a king). The execution of Damiens, the mentally disturbed assassin of King Louis XIV, who was subjected to a variety of preliminary tortures before his *quartering* (described in the second paragraph), vividly illustrates the cruelty of those times:

> In the torture chamber Damiens' legs were placed in devices called
> "boots," which could be squeezed gradually by means of wedges.
> After the insertion of eight wedges at intervals of fifteen minutes,
> every insertion being accompanied by horrible screams, the doctors
> who had been called to be present at the operation decided that it
> was not possible to continue "without the danger of an accident."
> The victim was then taken to the place of execution, in front of
> the Paris City Hall. The site was filled with all the Parisian rabble,
> wishing to enjoy the spectacle. French and Swiss guards kept order
> on all the surrounding avenues. The prisoner was placed on the
> scaffold and tied with ropes applied to his arms and legs. First, his
> hand was burned in a brazier filled with flaming sulphur. He was
> then pinched with red-hot tongs on his arms, his thighs and his
> chest. On his open wounds molten lead and boiling oil were poured.
> This operation was repeated several times and every time the most
> horrible screams came from the wretched creature.

After that, four big horses, whipped by four attendants, pulled the ropes rubbing against the inflamed and bleeding wounds of the patient. The pulling and shaking lasted a full hour. The arms and legs became more and more distended but remained attached to the body. The executioners then cut some of the tendons, and with some more pulling the limbs finally separated. Damiens, despite having lost two legs and one arm, was still breathing and died only when the second arm was detached from his bloody torso. Arms, legs, and body were all thrown into a fire that had been prepared near the scaffold (Maestro, 1973:14-15).

Other means of execution employed well into the eighteenth century included drowning, burying alive, beheading, stoning, and breaking on the wheel. Forms of nonlethal corporal punishment in Europe and the American colonies included the stocks, pillories, whipping, mutilation, and branding. These gruesome preclassical practices served as the catalyst for a powerful reform movement in the understanding of crime and the administration of justice (Scott, 1938/1959).

The Classical School of Criminology

The arbitrary administration of justice and the cruel punishments in medieval Europe, which continued into the eighteenth century, provided fertile ground for the emergence of the classical school of criminology. This school offered the first naturalistic explanation for crime and superseded centuries of interpreting crime as a supernatural phenomenon. The classical school was the dominant perspective for approximately one century, but then fell into disrepute, particularly among American criminologists, with the surge of positivism (described in the following chapter). Many criminologists, however, still highly regard classical thought because it represented a tremendous humanitarian reform. It also provided the fundamental rationale for most criminal codes of the Western world, and in recent years classical thought has reemerged by forming the basis of contemporary rational choice theories of crime.

The classical school of criminology must be interpreted in the context of the Enlightenment, for this school was a product of that larger reform movement. Rationalism, intellectualism, and humanitarianism were pitted against ideas stressing the divine rights of royalty and the clergy (Johnson, 1988). The founding classicists extended the views of the progressive thinkers of that era to the arena of criminal law and its administration. Charles Montesquieu's 1748 publication of *Espirit des lois (The Spirit of the Laws)* was an important prelude to the classical school. This work examined the administration of criminal law and repudiated torture and other abuses. Voltaire's campaign against these widespread injustices also predated the classical school. In 1762, Voltaire successfully lobbied for the rehabilitation (postmortem declaration of innocence) of Jean Calas, a Protestant merchant in Toulouse who had been falsely convicted of murdering his son for planning to convert to the Catholic faith. Calas' son in fact was mentally ill and had committed suicide, but Calas was painfully executed by means of the infamous wheel (Bien, 1960). In that same year, Jean-Jacques Rousseau (1762) published *The Social Contract*, which, along with similar works, formed the basis of the classical school of criminology. The two foremost representatives of classical criminology are Cesare Beccaria and Jeremy Bentham.

Cesare Beccaria— Father of Classical Criminology

Cesare Beccaria (1738-1794) was born in Milan, Italy. He was the oldest of four children in a modestly wealthy aristocratic family. His early education, which he found to be a stifling experience, was at a Jesuit school; his teachers viewed him as moody and disinterested. Mathematics was Beccaria's forte, earning him the nickname "Little Newton" among his peers. At the age of 20, he completed the Doctor of Law degree at the University of Pavia.

Beccaria experienced more than his share of hardships, beginning with his father's refusal to approve his marriage to the woman of his choice. His father placed him under house arrest for three months to dissuade him from marrying Teresa Blasco (Phillipson, 1923/1970). A father at that time had the power to enforce his will under the doctrine of *patria potestas*, a Roman rule that gave fathers virtually unchecked power over the lives of their children. The couple finally wed despite this opposition, but they were forced to live in poverty. Subsequently, however, Beccaria's relations with his family were restored, and he moved back home, where he spent the remainder of his life. Other difficult times in Beccaria's life included the death of Teresa when he was 35, the death of his younger daughter when he was 50, and a succession of suits filed against him by his relatives. Beccaria was shy and modest, so he preferred to avoid the public eye. He was also obese, as he was inordinately fond of fine food and wine.

An important formative point in Beccaria's career came when he joined with two friends, Pietro and Alessandro Verri, to form a literary club, the Academy of Fisticuffs, which met in the Verri home to discuss topics of literary and social interest. Pietro Verri suggested that Beccaria undertake a critical essay on the administration of criminal law. In nine months, Beccaria completed *Dei deliti e delle pene (On Crimes and Punishments)*, which was published in 1764. Slightly more than 100 pages long, the book was written in a straightforward, readable style. Both the author and publisher initially remained anonymous because Beccaria said that he had no desire to become a martyr. These were not times conducive to marching to the beat of a different drummer; the cost of criticizing church and state could be severe.

Cesare Beccaria

On Crimes and Punishments sets forth the central tenets of the classical school of criminology. As the embodiment of an overdue reform movement, it proposed "practically all of the important reforms in the administration of criminal justice and in penology which have been achieved in the civilized world since 1764" (Monachesi, 1972:49). It was an immediate success, and in a short time was translated into French, English, German, Spanish, Dutch, Polish, and a few years later, into Russian, Greek, and other languages. The work was praised by the intellectuals of Beccaria's time, including Voltaire, Diderot, Rousseau, and Hume, though many chose to emphasize Beccaria's utilitarian positions to the neglect of his powerful advocacy of human rights. Traditional jurists and religious zealots defended the system of criminal law that Beccaria attacked; Beccaria became fearful when the inquisitors commissioned a critique of his book. The inquisitors proclaimed that "all sensible people have found that the author of the book *On Crimes and Punishments* is an enemy of Christianity, a wicked man and a poor philosopher" and charged Beccaria with sedition and impiety (Maestro, 1973:64). *On Crimes and Punishments* was placed on the Index of books condemned by the Catholic Church and remained on the list until the abolition of the Index in 1962. Fortunately, the provincial governor interceded on Beccaria's behalf, and the attacks on his work, as so often happens, thrust it further into the public limelight.

In his introduction to Marcello Maestro's biography of Beccaria, Norval Morris observed that the views expressed in *On Crimes and Punishments* "were set deep in established writings" (1973:ix). In particular, social contract theorists such as Hobbes, Locke, Hume, and Rousseau provided a point of departure for Beccaria, who saw punishment as an unfortunate necessity in the prevention and control of crime:

> Laws are the conditions under which independent and isolated men united to form a society. Weary of living in a continual state of war, and enjoying a liberty rendered useless by the uncertainty of preserving it, they sacrificed a part so that they might enjoy the rest of it in peace and safety. . . . Some tangible motives had to be introduced, therefore, to prevent the despotic spirit, which is in every man, from plunging the laws of society into its original chaos. These tangible motives are the punishments established against infractors of the laws (Beccaria, 1764/1963:11-12).

Despite this advocacy of punishment, however, Beccaria first and foremost was a humanitarian legal reformer. He vehemently advocated the principle *nullum crimen sine lege* ("no crime without law") and specified criteria for the enactment and administration of criminal codes. Beccaria staunchly supported the separation of powers between legislative and judicial functions in criminal law. Beccaria (1764/1963:13-14) phrased it in this manner:

> Only the laws can decree punishments for crimes; authority for this can reside only with the legislator who represents the entire society united by a social contract. . . . The sovereign, who represents the society itself, can frame only general laws binding all members, but he cannot judge whether someone has violated the social contract. . . . There must, therefore, be a third party to judge the truth of the fact. Hence the need for a magistrate whose decisions, from which there can be no appeal, should consist of mere affirmations or denials of particular facts.

Moreover, Beccaria argued that, in criminal cases, judges "cannot have the authority to interpret laws, and the reason, again, is that they are not legislators. . . . Nothing can be more dangerous than the popular axiom that it is necessary to consult the spirit of the laws" (1764/1963:14-15). Beccaria was clearly reacting against the abuses of his time, as judicial proceedings were notoriously arbitrary and inconsistent.

Another important vein of classical thought involved the nature of criminal harm. Beccaria asserted that the essence of crime was harm to society. He did not see the law as an instrument for preventing all misdeeds of humankind; he believed that this purpose would be impossible and undesirable. Instead, Beccaria stated that criminal law should be employed only to control behavior that is harmful to society and that punishment can be justified only insofar as it is proportionate to the harm done.

At the heart of classical thought is the notion that "[i]t is better to prevent crimes than to punish them" (Beccaria, 1764/1963:93). Prevention, Beccaria and other classicists argued, was to be accomplished through the mechanism of deterrence, which was founded upon certain assumptions regarding human nature. Deterrence employs threats of punishment to influence behavior. It assumes that people are *rational*, that their behavior is a product of *free will*, and that they are *hedonistic*, that is, that their goal is to increase pleasure and/or to reduce pain. Rational beings are capable of making decisions in a logical, calculating fashion by taking cognizance of the costs and benefits of alternative courses of action. Having free will, they can act as they choose.

If specific assumptions underlying a theory of crime are faulty, the theory itself will lack validity. Are the assumptions undergirding classical deterrence theory tenable? Beccaria and his contemporaries had no doubt that they were, although they never tested their ideas empirically. There is a good deal of "common sense" evidence supporting their assumptions and the concept of deterrence. Much of our day-to-day behavior seems to parallel the model of rational, freely willed, hedonistic behavior. Take a student who arises from bed late one morning (having made an earlier decision to sleep just a bit longer), looks at her watch and, being rational, concludes that she has a choice to make. She can take time for breakfast or she can go to her criminology class. Though she might later attempt to convince her criminology instructor otherwise, after considering the consequences of alternative decisions (e.g., the pleasure of a tasty breakfast versus the pain of hunger), she is free to go to class or to breakfast. The decision seems to involve the rational exercise of free will. The process is hedonistic because it is couched in terms of seeking pleasure (good breakfast and grades) versus avoidance of pain (missing breakfast and attending a supposedly boring criminology lecture).

The deterrence doctrine and its assumptions regarding human nature permeate social relations and institutions. Parents and teachers incorporate the "carrot and the stick" principle to influence the behavior of children. Both the threat of punishment to deter undesirable behavior and the offer of rewards to elicit desired behavior assume that human beings are hedonistic actors. Adults experience the same manipulation from employers who pose threats of disciplinary action and offer promises of pay raises. These tactics can be used to support the assertion that threats of sanctions deter crime. Notice how drivers reduce their speed or come to a complete stop at a stop sign if they see a patrol car there, or consider how teenagers drinking in a park attempt to camouflage their beer cans or wine bottles when they see the police approaching. Despite such validation of deterrence propositions, some criminologists, as scientists, remain skeptical of such evidence. The scientific approach requires that observations be recorded in a systematic manner to avoid the error of "selective observation" (seeing that which supports but overlooking that which contradicts a particular theoretical premise). Common-sense postulates supported by anecdotes often prove to be incorrect (Hagan, 1982). Only in recent years have criminologists begun to assess scientifically the merits of deterrence theory.

Beccaria enumerated three principles of punishment that became the hallmark of classical deterrence doctrine. Assuming that people are rational, hedonistic, and that they exercise free will, it followed for him that crime control is a function of the *certainty, severity* and *celerity* (speed) of punishment. He believed that through proper manipulation of these factors, crime can be prevented. To neglect these principles, or as Beccaria and his contemporaries witnessed in eighteenth-century Europe, to apply them in an arbitrary and inconsistent fashion, is to encourage crime. As people fail to believe in the irrevocable negative consequences of law-violating behavior, they become less likely to conform to legal mandates. Persons that covet the property of another are more apt to steal that property if the prospects of punishment seem relatively low, temporally distant, or not severe.

The first principle of deterrence maintains that, as the perceived certainty of punishment increases, the probability of norm violations declines. Conversely, as Beccaria expressed it, "undoubtedly ignorance and uncertainty of punishments add much to the eloquence of the passions" (1764/1963:17). Laws, he argued, must be very clear and must be consistently enforced.

The second principle of deterrence states that, as the punishment response becomes swifter, the probability of norm violation declines. Conversely, procrastination in regard to punishment increases the probability of norm violations. Beccaria (1764/1963:56) explained the principle in this manner:

> I have said that the promptness of punishments is more useful because when the length of time that passes between the punishment and the misdeed is less, so much the stronger and more lasting in the human mind is the association of these two ideas, crime and punishment; they then come insensibly to be considered, one as the cause, the other as the necessary inevitable effect.

The message is that both prosecution of suspects and punishment of convicted offenders should be conducted expeditiously.

The third principle of punishment in classical deterrence dogma addresses severity. The severity of punishment was accorded less importance than certainty and celerity; Beccaria felt that "the certainty of punishment, even if it be moderate, will always make a stronger impression than the fear of another which is more terrible but combined with the hope of impunity" (1764/1963:58). He maintained that the severity of punishment was justifiable and that it accomplished a desired deterrent effect, but only up to a certain point:

> For a punishment to attain its end, the evil which it inflicts has only to exceed the advantage derivable from the crime. . . . All beyond this is superfluous and for that reason tyrannical (1764/1963:43).

Jeremy Bentham—
Utilitarianism and Classical Thought

Jeremy Bentham (1748-1832) expressed admiration for Beccaria's work and shared many of Beccaria's views, while contributing his own ideas to the classical school. Like Beccaria, Bentham is recognized more for his contributions as a criminal law reformer than as a theoretician. As Gilbert Geis has observed, "the practical results, rather than the theoretical heritage he left behind, stand as major monuments to Bentham. He was not a great philosopher, but he was a great reformer" (1972:66).

Bentham was born in London. He was extraordinarily precocious, reading Latin at four years of age and French soon after. He began the study of law at Oxford at the age of 12, but he was never pleased with his schooling. After a brief encounter with the practice of law, Bentham retreated from the profession of which he was so critical, choosing to devote his life to scholarship. He was a prolific writer, addressing a wide array of subjects.

Bentham displayed a number of eccentricities. He was withdrawn, having few close personal relationships, and he never married, though at the age of 57 he proposed to a woman of many years' acquaintance. He led a regimented life of study and writing, accented by devotion to music, gardening, and animals. His dietary habits were simple, consisting predominately of fruit, bread, tea, and home-brewed ale. His personality, according to Coleman Phillipson (1923/1970), was complex and comprised of "an extraordinary mixture of antithetical characteristics" (1923/1970:150) but also was child-like in many respects. One of Bentham's more remarkable actions was the incorporation of instructions in his will that his body be dissected and the skeleton displayed in a London university, where it sits today, clad as in life and crowned with a wax image of his head.

Odd personal traits aside, Bentham, like Beccaria, responded to the arbitrariness, inconsistency, and cruelty in the administration of justice in his time. He advocated that punishment should not be guided by retribution, but rather by the aim of preventing crime. In agreement with Beccaria, he defined crime as an offense detrimental to the community. At the heart of Bentham's punishment philosophy was utilitarianism, which he referred to as the "greatest happiness principle." According to this principle, actions should be judged according to whether, on balance, they contribute to the happiness and benefit of humankind. Criminal acts detract from the collective happiness and therefore should be prevented. This, Bentham reasoned, can be accomplished because people carefully weigh the costs and benefits of their actions:

> Nature has placed mankind under the governance of two sovereign masters, pain and pleasure. It is for them alone to point out what we ought to do, as well as to determine what we shall do. . . . They govern us in all we do, in all we say, in all we think (1789/1973:66).

This weighing of pleasure versus pain, which Bentham called felicity or hedonistic calculus, can allow the legal system to function as a deterrent of criminal behavior.

By manipulating the pain of punishment, the pleasure stemming from criminal behavior may be outweighed.

A common feature of the classical theorists was their focus on criminal law and their neglect of criminals. This can be understood in the context of the times, as the law was administered in an arbitrary and capricious manner. With this emphasis on statutes and the administration of justice, however, the neglect of the offender detracted from criminological theorizing. The major weakness of Bentham's work was "its total failure to consider criminals as human beings, as live, complicated, variegated personalities" (Geis, 1972:53). Bentham's felicity calculus rested on a series of overly simplistic assumptions regarding human nature. Consequently, while his ideas contributed immensely to the reform of the criminal law and its administration, they fell short as an attempt to explain why criminals violate the law.

Jeremy Bentham

Culver Pictures, Inc.

Impact of Classicism

The classical school represents the emergence of modern criminological thinking, usurping the earlier view that crime is a supernatural phenomenon. Yet in the years following its enunciation, significant deficiencies in this perspective became evident. The simplistic assumptions regarding the motivations of offenders, failure to scrutinize criminals as persons, and neglect of scientific evaluation of classical propositions eventually contributed to bypassing this school of thought in favor of the positivistic explanations of crime to be discussed in the following chapter. The impact of classicism on the practice of criminal justice, however, has never faltered. Many of the operational premises of Western criminal justice systems, and especially the rights accorded the accused, can be traced to the works of Beccaria, Bentham, and other classicists. Criminal law and procedure, as well as penology and policing, were profoundly affected by this reform movement.

Criminal Law and Procedure

Because the classicists focused on the failure of the law to provide a rational framework for the control of criminal behavior, many of their most noteworthy contributions were in the reform of criminal codes and procedures. Legislators such as Sir Samuel Romilly became staunch advocates of legal reform derived from classical principles. Romilly served in the English Parliament from 1806 to 1818, introducing a large number of bills to eliminate barbaric punishments and to facilitate consistency and certainty of punishment. These reforms, however, were not easily accomplished, as witnessed by a portion of an 1813 parliamentary address by Romilly, following defeat of a bill that he had introduced in order to abolish disemboweling and quartering:

> I cannot but confess that I feel some disappointment and much mortification at the resistance to the bill now before us. I had flattered myself that at least in this one instance I should have secured your unanimous concurrence. I certainly did not foresee that in an English House of Commons in the nineteenth century, one voice would have been heard in defense of a law which requires the tearing out of the heart and bowels from the body of a human being, while he is yet alive, and burning them in his sight (Phillipson, 1923/1970:274).

Legal reforms and protections of the accused advocated by the classicists ultimately spread throughout the Western world. In America, such luminaries as John Adams, Benjamin Franklin, and Thomas Jefferson acknowledged a debt to Beccaria. Classical influence is obvious in the French Declaration of the Rights of Man, the English Reform Act of 1832, and the Constitution of the United States. Classical principles include the right of the accused to have a public trial by a jury of peers, the assistance of legal counsel, an opportunity to present evidence on his or her own behalf, and protections derived from the notion that a person is legally innocent of a crime until proven guilty beyond a reasonable doubt. Equally significant are the reductions in the repertoire of corporal punishments, abolition of torture, which became defined as cruel and unusual punishment, and diminution of capital punishment. All of these reforms were stimulated by classical thought. In short, the totality of Western criminal law, including the behaviors proscribed, procedures for prosecution, and the array of punishments for offenders, was revolutionized.

Penology

The classical epoch also infused a wide range of changes in the practice of penology. Until then, incarceration was predominately in two settings. One was the gaols (the British spelling of jail), which were used for relatively short-term detention of persons accused of crimes and awaiting trial, for the condemned awaiting execution or corporal punishment, and for debtors. Conditions in these facilities were awful; those confined were not segregated by age, sex, or reason for incarceration. The other leading mode of confinement was within convict galleys, called hulks. These were dilapidated ships plagued by unsanitary conditions and inadequate food and supplies, resulting in shocking mortality rates. Otherwise, punishment of criminals was corporal or by transportation to such sites as the American colonies and, later, Australia.

Imprisonment under relatively humane conditions, in lieu of these more brutal punishments, was one of the innovations fostered by the classical school. The penitentiary arose, and although conditions were extremely harsh by today's standards (e.g., use of solitary confinement in the Pennsylvania system and enforced silence in the congregate system in New York), they represented a vast improvement over the gaols and hulks. The latter were abolished, as was the practice of transportation, and prisoners generally came to be segregated by age and sex. Even some measure of rehabilitative effort was introduced to facilitate Bentham's "subserviency to reformation," the view that a penalty that reduces offenders' motivation to crime is superior to one that does not.

It was in the context of the move to substitute prisons for existing modes of punishment that Bentham advocated the *Panopticon*, an elaborate prison design. He spent several years and most of his assets seeking to promote this project. In the end, however, the English Parliament rejected it, though some of his ideas filtered to other countries, where they had a limited impact. The Panopticon plan consisted of a circular guard house with wings of cells protruding from it so that guards could maintain observation from that central location along all corridors. This architectural concept is evident in the short-lived Pennsylvania system of prisons. Another major feature, anticipating today's trend toward private management of correctional institutions, was the idea of contract management.

Policing

Reform principles of the classical school of criminology extended into the realm of policing. These reforms took longer, though, because of intense political controversy. In the decade following the death by suicide of Romilly, Sir Robert Peel, serving as Home Secretary, pursued the challenging task of police reform. Modern law enforcement in England and America began with Peel's introduction of the *London Metropolitan Police Act* of 1829. The measure passed both houses of Parliament after several years of adroit political maneuvering by Peel. Widespread resistance had to be overcome because English citizens had a marked distrust of centralized government (Lyman, 1964; Critchley, 1972). Police reforms implemented in France and other continental European countries had increased the power of central government, and the fear was that police power would be similarly used in England. This profuse mistrust of police authority continued after Peel's new police, dubbed "Bobbies" and "Peelers" for their initiator, took to the streets. The public was so antagonistic that "policemen attempting to control traffic were ridden down and lashed with whips" (Critchley, 1972:54). In some instances, Bobbies were killed with impunity. After a few years, however, the new approach to policing, rooted in classical criminology, achieved popularity in London and became the model for police reform throughout England. The same model found its way to America and provided the founding philosophy for municipal policing, which began with the formation of the Boston Police Department in 1838.

At the core of Peel's reform legislation was the goal of deterring crime. In instructions to the first two commissioners of the London Metropolitan Police, Peel stated, "It should be understood, at the outset, that the principal object to be attained is the prevention of crime. . . . The absence of crime will be considered the best proof of the complete efficiency of the police" (Lyman, 1964:133). Following classical propositions, it was believed that crime could be deterred by police patrol. If the police were randomly moving about, dressed in recognizable uniforms, the potential offender would conclude that it was unwise to commit an offense because of the increased risk of apprehension. The higher certainty of punishment would, it was believed, outweigh the benefit to be derived from the offense.

The perception of the police as a deterrent force persisted for nearly 150 years after the Peelian Reform without being seriously questioned. In America, August Vollmer's classic police administration text maintained that patrol "is society's best defense against the criminal. The mere sight of uniformed officials diligently patrolling beats is often sufficient to deter the community's weaker members from committing legal infractions" (1936:217). O.W. Wilson and R.C. McLaren, two more leading authorities on police administration, similarly advocated the deterrent effect of a police presence. They saw patrol as the "backbone" of policing and concluded that "an impression of omnipresence is created by frequent and conspicuous patrol" (1972:320). Over the past three decades, however, police authorities began to consider the deterrent effect of police patrol an open empirical question rather than the essence of crime prevention.

Contemporary Deterrence Theory

Though criminologists largely dismissed the ideas of the classical school early in the twentieth century, neither legislators nor police administrators did. This schism of theory and practice retarded the growth of criminological wisdom. Little effort was made to blend the classical notions of deterrence with dominant sociological perspectives to see if they could explain more crime together than separately. Contributing further to the theoretical schism, deterrence models are the obverse of social reaction (particularly labeling) perspectives (to be examined in Chapter 9). The central thesis of deterrence maintains that punishment diminishes crime, while labeling theory asserts that punishment increases crime. According to deterrence theory, a person's criminal activity will decline as a result of being caught and punished. Labeling theory suggests that the person will be driven by punishment into further crime.

As deterrence theory has matured, becoming more sophisticated and complex, these notions that it is incompatible with other social dynamics has been undermined. Contemporary deterrence theorists have proposed that punishment may deter some, while creating a *backlash effect* for others. Backlash effects are analogous to what labeling theorists postulate; that stiffer penalties will generate more rather than less deviance among some segments of the targeted population. To illustrate, a recent study undertaken by Gary LaFree and his colleagues (2009) found that while both deterrent and backlash effects occurred in response to crackdowns on IRA terrorists in Northern Ireland, the backlash effect was the larger. This is now a broad concern within the counterterrorism community, but there is reason to believe the concept may be applicable across a broad range of offenders. In short, deterrence theory no longer presumes that punishment always yields only positive results, but that it sometimes makes matters worse. What is important is the net effect of enhancing sanctions. So long as punishment responses inhibit more crime than they cause, they may represent a valuable addition to our crime prevention arsenal.

Until recent years, however, such sophisticated and objective analyses of sanctions were not offered by criminologists and other social policy analysts. To the contrary, ideological bias left issues of deterrence ignored for decades. As Jack Gibbs has noted, "With humanitarians supplying moral ammunition, scientists performing as merchants of facts (virtually all pertaining to the death penalty), and social engineers (e.g., psychiatrists, social workers) offering alternatives to traditional punishments, the deterrence doctrine fell into disrepute . . ." (1975:9-10). Ideological predispositions led to empirically unfounded conclusions, some suggesting that deterrence works and some that it does not. At the turn of the twentieth century, Enrico Ferri asserted that "we have but to look about us . . . to see that the criminal code is far from being a remedy against crime, that it remedies nothing" (1901/1968:231). At mid-century, Harry Barnes and Negley Teeters, in their influential criminology text, drew the same untested conclusion, asserting that "the claim for deterrence is belied by both history and logic" (1951:338). In the late 1960s, a leading criminology text continued to offer a similar unsubstantiated assertion to the effect that deterrence "does not prevent crime in others or prevent relapse into crime" (Reckless, 1967:508).

Both exponents and opponents of deterrence theory maintain that their viewpoints are congruent with common sense. Deterrence advocates cite as proof of deterrence the marked reduction in the speed of traffic when vehicles approach a visible patrol car. Deterrence opponents, on the other hand, point to the large number of persons in prison for the second or third time as proof that deterrence does not work. The problem, however, is that "Sometimes common sense is often nonsense" (Hagan, 1982:2). It is not sound to infer from the decelerating vehicles that, in general, "deterrence works," and certainly, the fact that some persons repeatedly violate the law does not repudiate deterrence doctrine. Discussions of deterrence commonly rely on these unwarranted inferences, a fact well illustrated by the wry analysis of Frank Zimring and Gordon Hawkins. They refer to one of their analogies as the *tiger prevention fallacy* (Zimring & Hawkins, 1973:28):

> A man is running about the streets of mid-Manhattan, snapping his fingers and moaning loudly, when he is intercepted by a police officer. This conversation follows:
>
> P.O.:   What are you doing?
> Gtlm: Keeping tigers away.
> P.O.:   Why, that's crazy. There isn't a wild tiger within five thousand miles of New York City!
> Gtlm: Well then, I must have a pretty effective technique!

The issue highlighted by the tiger prevention tale, as Gibbs (1975) stressed, is that deterrence is an inherently unobservable phenomenon. We cannot see that which is prevented, yet absence of the prevented occurrence does not establish a deterrent effect. Contrary assertions, however, are common amo[...]ponents. Conclusions that low levels of deviance can be credited to[...]n reflect the tiger prevention fallacy. While the tiger tale is a fac[...], serious assertions regarding criminal justice successes are somet[...]. One of the text authors often provides an illustrative example wh[...]ice made a pronouncement to the news media in the early days of[...]a popular drug. They assured the media that the locality was unfaz[...]ug. When asked why, the police spokesperson said something to the[...]drug dealers know that we won't put up with it!" The media naiv[...]ridiculous claim, but of course crack later arrived in the small tow[...]n the drug culture for years. The problem finally declined, not bec[...]tivity, but as a consequence of other illegal drugs displacing the crack market. So much for the "crack prevention fallacy!"

Opponents of deterrence often arrive at a similarly flawed, but reversed inferential conclusion. Zimring and Hawkins (1973) have summarized this fallacy as the *warden's survey*. In this analogy, they refer to numerous prison wardens (and others) who have concluded that deterrence does not work based upon their observations of convicted offenders. Their fallacious conclusion is derived from "experience with groups of men who have evidently not been deterred or they would not be in prison" (Zimring & Hawkins, 1973:31). Logically, if deterrence could be observed, it would be located among populations of non-offenders. By this criterion, sanctions could only be judged to be effective deterrents if there were a complete absence of crime.

Criminologists for most of the twentieth century tried to refute the deterrence doctrine with materials that were variations of the warden's survey and with data indicating that murder rates are higher in jurisdictions using capital punishment. Criminal justice practitioners, on the other hand, typically have erred in the direction of the tiger prevention fallacy, exhibiting an unfaltering faith in deterrence theory. Charles Tittle (1980:1) summarized the situation succinctly by noting that "on one hand there was a strong but uncritical belief among the general population and criminal justice practitioners that sanctions do curtail deviance, and on the other hand there was a strong but uncritical belief among academics that they do not."

Criminologists virtually rediscovered the deterrence question about 40 years ago. Johannes Andenaes's (1952; 1966) conceptual analyses served as the harbinger of this re-examination, while the empirical endeavors of Gibbs (1968) and Tittle (1969) fueled an explosion of research activity in the 1970s. It was a unique combination of trends and circumstances that set the stage for this reconsideration of deterrence theory. First, much attention focused on empirical evidence suggesting that rehabilitation, the logical policy derivative of *positive criminology* (see chapter 6), had not succeeded in substantially reducing recidivism. Reviews of rehabilitative programs had concluded as much in the late 1960s and early 1970s (e.g., Bailey, 1966; Wilkins, 1969; Hood, 1971; Kassebaum et al., 1971). Robert Martinson's (1974) generalization that "nothing works" in efforts to rehabilitate offenders helped open the door to deterrence research even wider. In the ensuing decades conceptualization of the concept has made enormous strides.

Conceptualizing Deterrence

The conceptual roots of deterrence lay in the work of Cesare Beccaria and Jeremy Bentham. The theoretical propositions of the utilitarian thinkers see crime as a negative function of the certainty, severity, and speed of punishment. In other words, as punitive responses to crime increase in these three contexts, it is expected that the frequency of crime will decline. Moreover, the concept was proposed as a general theory of crime; that is, an explanation that applies to all people and all types of crime (Exum, 2002). As far as it goes, this assertion seems plausible. The deterrence propositions of rational choice theory, however, have "come a long way" since Beccaria brought them to the forefront (Pratt, 2008: 43).

Certainty. Modern research has focused mostly on the certainty of punishment, the dimension also most emphasized by the early classicists. Quite a substantial body of evidence has emerged that higher certainties of punishment are associated with lower levels of crime. In short, there is a strong consensus that certainty of punishment is the most important of the three elements of punishment. Given that the certainty of punishment deters, however, how much certainty is required? How sure must the potential offender be that punishment will follow to be dissuaded from the prohibited behavior? Some studies of the relationship between crime clearance (arrest) and crime rates show that no deterrent effect exists until arrest probability attains some minimal level (Tittle & Rowe, 1974; Brown, 1978; Brown, 1981). This threshold for the operation of deterrence is called a *tipping level* and adds another layer of complexity to the original deterrence proposition.

Severity. Deterrence theory also suggests that, all else being equal, crime should decrease as punishment severity increases (Andenaes, 1966; Zimring & Hawkins, 1973). Rarely, however, is all else equal. Beccaria and Bentham were cautious about declaring that deterrent effects are contingent upon the severity of punishment. Less is known about the effects of punishment severity, but among the studies completed, most have not supported the deterrence proposition and the consensus has been that the severity of punishment does not matter. A recent study comparing the effects of prison to probation, conducted by Cassia Spohn and David Holleran (2002), is representative. Comparing three groups of felons (drug, drug-involved, and nondrug), they found recidivism was both more frequent and occurred more quickly for all three types of offenders if they were sentenced to prison rather than probation. In other words, rather than a deterrent effect, the more severe punishment (imprisonment) had the opposite impact: a criminogenic or crime-enhancing result. The *criminogenic* effect was even more pronounced among the drug offenders. Spohn and Holleran (2002) concluded that the contemporary punitive emphasis on crime, especially drug crimes, is misguided and counterproductive, given what we are learning about the severity of punishment. Another recent study, however, reached contrary conclusions although it looked at only one type of crime. Greg Pogarsky (2002), in studying the drinking and driving habits of college students, found that the severity of punishment held even more deterrent effect than did the certainty, so long as only "deterrable" subjects were considered. Similarly, Silvia Mendes (2004) has argued that certainty and severity are of equal importance. The Gang Feature of this chapter serves as an

GANG FEATURE

Enhanced Sentencing of Gang Members

In response to gang activity, communities can adopt a number of approaches, commonly categorized as prevention, intervention, and suppression. While some communities incorporate all three strategies into a cohesive response to gangs, most communities have focused their attention on traditional deterrence theory and adopted a suppression approach. From saturation patrols to enhanced sentencing and implementation of vertical prosecution to increased conviction rates, these suppression tactics are based on the assumption that both general and specific deterrence can be achieved by increasing the cost component of the "hedonistic calculus" equation. In this section, we describe one city's suppression efforts.

In 1992, the city of Westminster, California, implemented what has become known as the Tri-Agency Response Gang Enforcement Team (TARGET). Douglas R. Kent and Peggy Smith (1995) detail this approach. It combines the resources of police, probation, and prosecutors in an effort to crack down on "gang leaders and recidivist criminals." Similar to many suppression efforts, the program's primary objectives are:

1. to remove selected hardcore gang members from the community;

2. to gather gang intelligence;

3. to develop innovative techniques for combating gangs; and

4. to develop personnel expertise in gangs and gang crime.

To achieve these objectives, the program consists of a team comprised of personnel from each agency (three police officers, one full-time and one part-time deputy probation officer, one senior district attorney and a D.A. investigator,

and support staff) working under the supervision of a police detective. This team combines each of the justice system's components into one unified team so that "when a crime is committed, however small, the defendant and the case undergo intensive investigation and prosecution for the most serious charges possible" (Kent & Smith, 1995:293).

Attainment of the objectives of the TARGET program is facilitated through two separate strategies: enhanced sentencing procedures and the use of civil abatement laws. The California State Legislature created the Street Terrorism Enforcement Prevention (STEP) Act in the early 1990s. This Act calls for the treatment of gang affiliation as an aggravating circumstance in the sentencing of defendants, active participation in a street gang is considered to be a crime and prosecutors can request enhanced sentences for certain gang-related felonies. Civil abatement laws target the entire membership of a gang. Under such laws, all gang members can be sued in civil court "to abate an area of the city in which they engage in criminal activity." Individual gang members may be served with a court order or general notices may be posted in the area informing gang members that they are prohibited from associating with other gang members in a specified area. Subsequent violation of such court abatement orders constitutes contempt of court and the offending individuals can then be prosecuted in criminal court. Members of the TARGET team work in conjunction to enforce these laws and to reduce gang activity in the city of Westminster.

Given the assumptions of deterrence theory and the interrelationship of certainty, severity, and celerity of punishment, how successful might such suppression programs be? To date, there have not been any published evaluations assessing their impact on gang membership or gang-related activity.

example of public policy focusing on punishment severity in an attempt to deter gang influenced crime and delinquency. This issue of who and what type of crimes might be more deterrable is an interesting topic that we will examine in much more detail later in this chapter.

Speed. If detection and punishment do follow criminal behavior, how quick must the punitive response be to have an effect? The American machinery of justice typically moves very slowly. Might this delay or cancel the effects of a punishment response that is, or is presumed to be, sufficiently certain? Some would suggest that it does, while others have contended that delays in punishment cause further suffering and trepidation, thus actually enhancing deterrent effects. To date, however, few empirical efforts have been undertaken to examine the importance of swift punishment in creating deterrence.

Contemporary Concepts. Another basic conceptual issue concerns the punishment itself. What, in fact, is punishment? Legal sanctions currently in use include fines, denial of privileges such as holding a driver's license, community supervision such as probation, confinement in jails and prisons, and capital punishment. Graeme Newman (1983) maintained that a return to corporal punishment would be a valuable addition to our repertoire of punishments. Others argue for elimination of some current punishments, most notably capital punishment. There are political and cultural limits on the use of sanctions. Although the execution of speeders and subsequent display of their heads beside the posted speed limits in early twentieth-century Peking may have had a significant deterrent impact, most of us probably would not want to resort to such extreme measures to deter speeders (Griffiths, 1970).

If punishment does deter crime, what should we see? There are distinctly different possibilities. It is theoretically possible to completely deter any given individual from any specific form of criminal conduct. If an individual entirely refrains from commission of a criminal act out of fear of legal sanctions, we have *absolute deterrence* (Gibbs, 1975; Tittle, 1980). Remember however, the tiger prevention fallacy, reminding us that the absence of offending behavior by a particular person does not demonstrate absolute deterrence because abstention may be for a variety of reasons other than threat of sanctions. An alternative possibility is for the threat of sanctions to result in less law violation, but not complete conformity to the law. Such a reduction is referred to as *marginal* or *restrictive deterrence*. Reductions may be in the form of less frequent, less conspicuous, or less flagrant violations. A student (or professor), for example, may not park in a prohibited zone every day on the assumption that such frequent and repetitive violation would probably result in a citation. Yet the individual would not be absolutely deterred unless he or she never parked illegally. Similarly, the same student (or professor) may, on the way to campus, drive 50 miles per hour (mph) in a 40 mph zone, but avoid driving 70 mph out of fear that such a flagrant violation would likely result in a speeding citation.

Crime Displacement is another conceptual possibility in the assessment of deterrent effects. This refers to changing the manner of lawbreaking in the face of threats that enhance the perceived certainty or severity of punishment. Displacement represents shifts in times, places and forms of crime (Reppetto, 1976). Increased

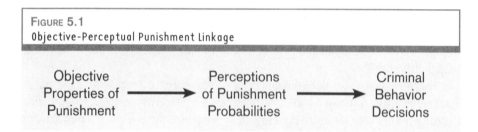

FIGURE 5.1
Objective-Perceptual Punishment Linkage

Objective Properties of Punishment ⟶ Perceptions of Punishment Probabilities ⟶ Criminal Behavior Decisions

deterrent effects for robbery, for example, could lead to increases in other offenses. Rather than ceasing their criminal activity, robbers who conclude that risks of sanctions for robbery have become excessive may become burglars. Robbers who decide that the risks of robbery have become too great at particular hours or in particular neighborhoods may commit robberies at other times or in other places. Consequently, it is important to think in terms of net changes in crime rates that might result from modifications in sanctioning perceptions. If 20 nighttime robberies in a downtown precinct are deterred by focusing efforts on that problem, but 10 more burglaries, five more daytime robberies, and five more suburban robberies occur, crime may have been displaced, but not deterred.

Finally, it is important to emphasize that deterrence consists of a two-part process: first, that individual *perceptions of punishment* certainty and severity are influenced by *objective punishment* properties and, secondly, that increases in the perception of punishment probability and severity decrease the chance of deviant behavior (Scheider, 2001). If, however, individual perceptions of punishment properties are unrelated to objective properties, deterrence efforts are doomed to failure. Thus if potential offenders are less rational than the deterrence framework assumes, or if their assessments of objective punishment prospects are diminished by individual characteristics, deterrent effects will be proportionately diminished. Such underestimating of the objective properties of punishment has been dubbed the *base rate fallacy*. The "base rate" is the expected rate of punishment certainty or severity and the fallacy is ignoring or underestimating that objective level of certainty or severity of punishment. To illustrate, one of the authors often provides the example of convicted offenders using phrases such as, "I thought I was too smart to get caught," or the offender reincarcerated for new offenses declaring "I thought I'd learned where I messed up and wouldn't get caught again." Whether a reflection of an overly optimistic personality or poor judgment skills, such offenders exemplify the base rate fallacy. They conclude that they are exempt from the base odds of getting caught.

Figure 5.1 displays the causal deterrence linkage between objective prospects of punishment (arrests, convictions etc.), perceptions of punishment prospects, and offending behaviors. Unfortunately, recent research has not been kind to this model. Greg Pogarsky and his colleagues (2005), for example, found the process of forming perceptions of punishment risks to be quite complex, noting in particular that it appears to vary across types of offending. Similarly, Kleck et al. (2005) failed to find support for any linkage between macro-level punishments delivered by the criminal justice system and micro-level perceptions of punishment. Without this linkage the logic of general deterrence is undermined.

Matthew Scheider's (2001) experimental work with a sample of college students to assess the base rate fallacy found moderate support in favor of the deterrence hypothesis (that perceptions will be influenced by objective punishment properties) and disfavoring the fallacy. However, it was offense specific. The base rate fallacy was supported for drunk driving and cocaine use. This makes intuitive sense, as college students are likely to have personal knowledge to rely upon for such misconduct (e.g., knowing numerous people who engage in the behaviors without getting caught or facing severe punishment) and thus rely less upon objective information. The support for the first phase of the deterrence (objective punishment prospects driving the perceptual) process, however, supports both the enhancement of punishment and publicizing the message that punishment probabilities and severity are high.

General and Specific Deterrence

Punishment has the potential to deter prohibited behaviors through two distinct processes. Most frequently, when criminologists or criminal justice practitioners speak of deterrence, they refer to general deterrent practices. *General deterrence* involves punitive sanctions (real or perceived) designed to influence the behavior of individuals other than those punished. The sanctioned offender serves as an example to *others* that might contemplate illegal behavior so that, through the rational-calculative process assumed by deterrence theory, additional law breaking is prevented.

Publicity is an essential component of the general deterrence process, for the wider the dissemination of sanctioning information, the greater is the potential impact of that information. Publicity designed to deter unlawful behavior usually takes the shape of media campaigns or informal word-of-mouth. It may communicate accurate information regarding the sanctioning process or utilize distorted messages designed to serve as scare tactics. Further, it may focus on specific offenses (e.g., a message that drug dealers are severely penalized) or general compliance with the law (e.g., a communication that "crime does not pay").

General deterrence theory is a utilitarian scheme with crime-reducing benefits predicated on increasing public perceptions of the certainty, celerity, and/or severity of punishment. One concern is the ethical aspects of punishment. General deterrent effects, many criminologists fear, can be just as readily achieved by punishment of an innocent party that is widely believed to be guilty as by punishment of the factually guilty party. An even more likely scenario is the application of exceptionally severe punishments to offenders that, for reasons unrelated to the gravity of their crimes, have captured the public eye. In both cases, general deterrent effects might be realized, but they would be rooted in actions that are considered unjust from other than a utilitarian vantage point.

Specific deterrence (also called special, individual, and particular deterrence) seeks to discourage the *sanctioned individual* from engaging in future misconduct. Rather than being designed to affect others, it is intended to "teach a lesson" to the criminal. Like general deterrence, specific deterrence is founded on principles of hedonistic calculus (an assumption that human nature leads people to pursue pleasure and avoid pain). The focus, however, is on how punishment actually is experienced rather than publicity about the punishment of others. Apprehension and punishment may lead an offender to an upward reassessment of punishment probabilities, thereby changing his or her cost-benefit calculus and reducing the likelihood of additional crime. Surprisingly, however, a number of researchers (e.g., Pogarsky & Piquero, 2003) have found just the opposite. They suggest that this might be due to (1) a "selection" process, whereby the most committed offenders tend to be caught and (2) a "resetting" phenomenon analogous to that of the gambler believing that their bad luck will not continue. Likewise, the apprehended offender erroneously concludes that they are unlikely to again face arrest and sanction. There are several ways, drawing from other theoretical perspectives, in which efforts to achieve specific deterrence might produce results opposite of those desired. Labeling theory, for example, as previously mentioned, predicts increases in deviant behavior as a consequence of punishment. This is based on the notion that punishment stigmatizes persons, restricting their legitimate opportunities for such things as jobs, associates, and recreation (see Chapter 9). Note, however, that while labeling is essentially the opposite of specific deterrence, it is not necessarily inconsistent with general deterrence. Punishment may increase criminal behavior among those punished, while reducing offenses among the general population that learns about the punishment.

Conceptualizing Deterrence Efficacy: Individuals

The bold assumption of the classical theorists was that *all* persons follow the same calculus in making choices to commit or not commit crimes. While it did not take long to recognize that children and the insane did not fit this thinking, it was not until the new era of deterrence was opened in the closing decades of the twentieth century that criminologists began to recognize that there were many more exceptions. Criminologists now have far more complex conceptual schemes for estimating the effectiveness of sanctions in deterring people from engaging in criminal and delinquent behavior.

Perhaps the greatest shortcoming of classical criminology was a naive and overly simplistic view of human beings. This raises the important question of whether some persons are more deterrable than are others. In recent years, criminologists have identified a host of individual characteristics that might be differentially related to deterrability. For example, persons who place a premium on delayed gratification (i.e., future-oriented) are believed to be more subject to control by sanctioning than present-oriented or impulsive individuals. The impulsive person may reflect less on the consequences of acts and therefore be less affected by them. This bears some resemblance to the concept of low self-control discussed in Chapter 8. Recent research incorporating that concept has indicated that low self-control may be characteristic of persons that are unreceptive candidates for deterrent effects (Piquero & Tibbetts, 1996; Tibbetts & Myers, 1999). These studies have suggested that those with high self-control may be deterrable, at least through informal or shaming mechanisms, while those with low self-control may not be deterrable at all.

Individuals also differ in their penchant for taking risks. Those stimulated by the thrill of risk-taking should be less deterrable than those daunted by risk. Even attitudes toward authority may differentially impact reactions to legal threats. The authoritarian may have more need to comply with rules, thereby being more amenable to control, while the anti-authoritarian "would be likely to view each new threat as an invitation to defiance. . . . Indeed, the attractiveness of a forbidden behavior to an anti-authoritarian may increase as the consequences of apprehension are escalated, because the greater penalty is evidence of a greater challenge attached to the legal threat" (Zimring & Hawkins, 1973:124). Finally, the outlook of the personality may be associated with deterrability. Optimists may underestimate the prospects of apprehension and punishment, and consequently, may be less responsive to deterrent efforts. Pessimists, to the contrary, may overestimate the likelihood of punishment, enhancing their deterrability.

A number of individual factors outside of personality attributes *per se* also appear to be associated with differences in sanction effectiveness, although personality characteristics are closely related to some of these factors. Older persons, for example, owing to their greater stake in the established social order, and perhaps greater experience, tend to be more responsive to sanction threats than younger persons. Second, although relatively little attention has been focused upon deterrability by race, considering the weight assigned to race in other criminological contexts, it is reasonable to suspect possible differences. Both Bishop (1984) and Tittle (1980), for example, found strong empirical support for the notion that African-Americans are more responsive to formal sanction threats than are whites, although it is not clear why this might be the case. One possibility is that African-Americans believe that they will be dealt with more harshly if apprehended and convicted. Brenda Blackwell and her colleagues (1994) also found African-Americans to hold higher perceptions of risks of legal sanctions, but lower perceptions of threats of informal sanctions. Similarly, in their examination of deterrent effects on DUI, Rodney Kingsnorth and his colleagues (1993) did find that punishments were perceived quite differently, depending upon one's location in the social stratification system. Higher-class people were particularly averse to the prospects of spending time in jail. It is, of course, likely that social standing alters ones perceived utility of some types of crime.

We know that gender is the best single predictor of criminality (see Chapter 4), suggesting, to the extent that deterrence factors explain criminal involvement, that females are more responsive to threats of punishment than are males. Evidence regarding the role of gender and formal sanctioning systems, however, has been mixed. In a study of student cheating (Tittle & Rowe, 1973), females were found to be more responsive to sanction threats, and greater special deterrent effects following DUI convictions have been found for females (Kingsnorth et al., 1993). Other studies have found no difference by sex (e.g., Anderson et al., 1977; Finken et al., 1998;) or greater deterrent effects for males (e.g., Silberman, 1976; Bishop, 1984; Miller & Anderson, 1986). This confusion, however, may be resolved by considering the role of informal sanctions in controlling deviance. It has been forcefully argued that women are typically controlled by informal mechanisms, while, for males, it is more often necessary to resort to formal social control (Hagan et al., 1979). Females are more responsive to shaming in patriarchal cultures because they are socialized to be more dependent on the family. "The female is thus always more socially integrated, always more susceptible to shaming by those on whom she is dependent, and never quite as free to make deviant choices as the male" (Braithwaite, 1989:92). It may be that females are far more receptive to deterrent threats than males, but that they occur within the family, prior to any need for intervention on the part of formal agents of social control. Recent studies of gender and sanctions have supported the position that females are more responsive to informal sanction threats (Grasmick et al., 1993; Tibbetts & Herz, 1996), while tests of formal deterrent effects have still failed to show significant and consistent gender differences (Carmichael et al., 2005).

What is at stake for the individual may also be a determining factor in shaping his or her deterrability. What one has the potential to lose through the sanctioning process and what one stands to gain through rule violation may inform their decision-making process. The more one has to lose through sanctioning the more deterrable they should be, and conversely, the more one believes they could gain through deviant means the more difficult to deter they should be. An informative study of cheating among college students reviewed in the next section, for example, found that those with higher grades (more to lose) were more easily deterred, while those with low grades (less to lose) were less deterrable.

Table 5.1 summarizes differential deterrent effects by individual characteristics that have been postulated. A lot of research is needed to arrive at a fuller understanding of these individual differences. What should be clear, however, is that it is far more complex than just assuming all actions taken by all persons are equivalent "choices." Most contemporary deterrence theorists do not accept the classical premise that all persons are alike, but rather recognize a myriad of differences that impact individual deterrability. *Bounded rationality* is a more limited understanding of "the social, physical, and situational context in which criminal decisions are made as well as the offenders' perceptions of the world around them" (Copes and Vieraitis, 2009:242). In short, the contemporary view of rational decision making as bounded incorporates diverse individual differences.

Following the logic that individuals may be more or less deterrable, Greg Pogarsky (2002) has developed a tripartite conceptual schema of deterrability. At one end of the continuum are the *incorrigible*, those who are not significantly affected by threats of punishment. Sex offenders, for example, have notoriously high recidivism rates. They are widely viewed as offenders with psychological or biological disorders that undermine their ability for the rational calculus on which the deterrence doctrine is based. At the opposite polar extreme lie *acute conformists*, individuals who require no threat of punishment to compel conformity because other forces prevent them from violating the rules. Many persons, for example, are deterred by extralegal sources so that threats of legal sanctions are not needed to insure conformity. It is the middle category that Pogarsky identifies as the *deterrable* that are relevant to formal sanction threats. Consequently, he argues that studies of formal sanction threats should limit the search for deterrent effects to this group. Findings may be skewed in research that mixes deterrable subjects with the incorrigible and acute conformists. Another group of criminologists (Wright et al., 2004) came to different conclusions

TABLE 5.1
Deterrent Effects by Individual Characteristics

Individual Characteristics	Deterrability
Future-Oriented/Delays Gratification	High
Present-Oriented/Impulsive	Low
High Self-Control	High
Low Self-Control	Low
Low Risk-Taker	High
High Risk-Taker	Low
Authoritarian	High
Non-Authoritarian	Low
Pessimist	High
Optimist	Low
Older	High
Younger	Low
Black	High
White	Low
(Sparse research)	
Higher Classes	High
Lower Classes	Low
Female	High
Male	Low
Much to Lose & Little to Gain	High
Little to Lose & Much to Gain	Low

in analyzing New Zealanders. They found maximum deterrability among the most crime prone members of their sample, defined primarily by low self-control. Both studies agree that deterrence is irrelevant to conformists, but matters a good deal to some portion of deviants.

Conceptualizing Deterrence Efficacy: Crimes

The classical theorists did not foresee variations in deterrability across types of crime either. The same logic that applies to individuals, however, can be used to analyze varying types of crime. This is helpful because different forms of crime attract different sorts of persons who will vary in terms of the individual characteristics discussed in the previous section. It is likely, for example, that the sex offender will possess more of the traits that render him or her less deterrable than will typically be the case for property offenders.

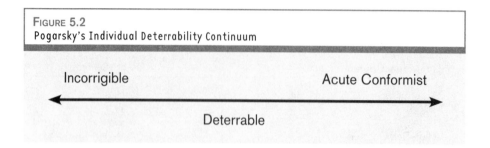

FIGURE 5.2
Pogarsky's Individual Deterrability Continuum

In short, crimes may be conceptually ranked along a continuum from most to least deterrable through an exercise similar to the above examination of individual deterrability. It has been frequently postulated that those crimes that are more rational or "normal" will be more deterrable than those that are less so. The origins of this idea can be traced to classical deterrence theory's assumption that potential offenders are rational and hedonistic. The deterrability of behaviors becomes doubtful to the same degree that the rationality of the behaviors themselves is doubtful. Researchers have found considerable empirical support for this proposition (e.g., Geerken & Gove, 1977). Insider stock trading and child molesting are divergent examples on the rationality continuum. It would be presumed that the potential inside stock trader would give careful consideration to punishment prospects and, if those prospects were perceived as relatively certain and severe, the individual would opt not to commit the crime or to do so less often or less flagrantly. Conversely, potential child molesters would seem to be less capable of conforming to norms governing sexual activity with children even if they perceive the risk of punishment as very likely and severe.

William Chambliss proposed similar deterrability concepts. He defined *instrumental crime* as "instrumental to the attainment of some other goal" and *expressive crime* as one "committed because it is pleasurable in and of itself" (1967:708). The distinction is between gain and passion, with the latter being more difficult to control. The role of emotion in decision-making has continued to occupy a central role among deterrence theorists. Sex crimes, for example, are usually seen as falling far on the emotional or expressive end of the instrumental-expressive continuum. Thus contemporary deterrence/rational choice models suggest that sex crimes should be especially difficult to deter because the emotions that drive the offender are not rational. To the extent that an offense is less rational, it is more difficult to deter. Researchers have, in fact, found some empirical support for the notion that emotion undermines rational decision making among sexual offenders (e.g., Bouffard, 2002; Loewenstein et al., 1997). Various *visceral states* propel people to behave in particular ways, as opposed to their choosing among alternative paths. Obviously, for example, the pedophile does not so much choose to seek out children for sexual activity as they feel driven or compelled to pedophilic sexual outlets. For many pedophiles to "choose" appropriate (legal) adult sexual partners is likely as difficult as it might be for a non-pedophile to choose children as sexual partners or for heterosexuals to elect same sex partners. The emotional constitution for these particular "choices" would be lacking. Consequently, to deter an individual from seeking sexual activity, or any other outlet that is emotionally compelling, is a challenging task to say the least.

Differential deterrent effects have often been noted by theorists regarding crimes against property as compared to those against persons. Property crimes have generally been regarded as most amenable to deterrence, largely because they seem to be more rational and instrumental.

The age-old distinction between crimes, *mala prohibita* and *mala in se* also has been postulated as a differentiating factor in deterrability. The rationale in suggesting that *mala prohibita* offenses are more responsive to threats of legal sanction is that conformity is fully reliant on those formal sanctions, as there are no informal sanctions (Andenaes, 1966). Parking regulations, for example, would not be observed if there were no legal sanctions, according to this argument. No other social control mechanisms would substitute. Offenses *mala in se*, to the contrary, hardly need legal sanctions to forestall widespread violations. "If the threats of legal punishment were removed, moral feelings and the fear of public judgement [sic] would remain as powerful crime prevention forces, at least for a limited period" (Andenaes, 1966:957). Incest, Andenaes notes, is probably not very responsive to legal control, but even in the absence of legal prohibition, few would violate this norm. Many, however, undoubtedly would park where they pleased in the absence of legal regulation.

The locale of the offense may also figure into deterrence. A crime that must be committed in a public setting is likely to be more responsive to legal threats than one that can be perpetrated in private. For example, picking flowers in a public park is probably more readily deterred than assault inside a house. Prostitution by a streetwalker is likewise probably more deterrable than prostitution by a call girl.

The range and force of motivations vary immensely from one type of crime to another. Any of these differences may be related to the prospects for effective deterrence. Table 5.2 summarizes the differentiating factors that have been discussed. In the following pages, we will consider several specific offenses to illustrate the operating principles of deterrence.

TABLE 5.2
Differential Deterrent Effects by Crime

Characteristic of Crime	Deterrability
Rational	High
Irrational	Low
Instrumental	High
Expressive	Low
Property (nonviolent)	High
Persons (violent)	Low
Mala Prohibita	High
Mala in Se	Low
Public	High
Private	Low

Parking Professors. Very early in the onset of renewed criminological interest in the concept of deterrence, William Chambliss (1966) undertook a modest, but interesting, study of a rule-breaking behavior well-known by many professors: faculty violation of campus parking rules. The context of this research was a pattern of flagrant violation of parking regulations by the faculty of a Midwestern university. The rules called for the errant professors to pay one dollar (severity of punishment) for each violation. Additionally, there was no means of regular enforcement (certainty of punishment). A new set of sanctions and enforcement mechanisms were introduced, providing for increases in fines, forfeiture of the right to drive on campus as sanctions for nonpayment, and the towing of unauthorized vehicles. Chambliss studied the response to this "dramatic increase in the certainty and severity of punishment for the violation of parking regulations" (1966:71). Interviewing 43 faculty members, he found that for a 2.5-year period before and after the new policy, 35 percent reported that they had not parked illegally. As nonviolators, they were not candidates for deterrence. Thirteen of the professors, however, reported that they were frequent violators (five or more times) during the period preceding the increased sanctions. Of these, six altered their violation levels to zero, four to one or two, and one to three or four times. Chambliss concluded that "these data indicate clearly that the change in regulations (and the corresponding increase in the certainty and severity of punishment) greatly reduced the number of transgressions and the number of transgressors and served as an effective deterrent" (1966:73). Even the two professors who continued to be frequent violators modified their violations so as to be less flagrant and often (restrictive deterrence). One indicated that his illegal parking now was limited to violations of only a few minutes, while the other reported restricting transgressions to an alley beside his office where he had never received a citation. Although criminologists had discounted deterrence for many decades, it seemed to play a role in deviance and conformity among them (assuming that some of the faculty violators were criminologists!) and their colleagues.

Cheating Students. Charles Tittle and Allan Rowe (1973) conducted another study, also very early in the rediscovery of deterrence. Their investigation sought to determine if moral appeal and/or threat of sanction would reduce classroom cheating among college students. A control group of students and two experimental sociology classes were given a series of weekly quizzes. Unknown to the students, the professors graded the quizzes each time, returning them unmarked at the next class meeting, and then "allowed" the students to grade their own papers. The difference between the professor's and the student's grade was taken as an index of cheating. For each student, the number of questions actually missed (professor's grade) was divided by the number on which cheating was discovered, yielding the percentage of cheating opportunities utilized. For example, if nine questions were actually missed, but the student cheated on three, 33 percent of the cheating opportunities were utilized. These percentages were compared under four classroom circumstances: (1) no professorial pronouncements regarding cheating; (2) a moral appeal to the students that emphasized trust and honesty; (3) a warning that spot checking of quizzes would be initiated in response to complaints of cheating; and (4) an announcement that a cheater had been caught and punished. The experimenters found that cheating increased during the moral appeal phase (though offset by similar and unexplained increases in the control group), but declined significantly in the two threat phases of the course. Cheating college students, like their illegally parking professors, it appears on the basis of this study, can be deterred by credible threats of punishment.

Thirty years later, a similar study (Nagin & Pogarsky, 2003) yielded consistent results and served to reinforce much of what deterrence theorists had learned over three decades. In their experimental design, the researchers recruited students to spend an hour completing a questionnaire for $10. When the students reached the last page, they were instructed that they could double their payment to $20 if they correctly answered at least six of eight trivia questions. Unfortunately, however, they were so difficult that the chances of getting at least six correct were essentially zero! For example, one question required them to identify which of five countries borders Tanzania (it was Zambia). They were then told that the correct answers were on the back of the last page and that they could look to satisfy any curiosity only after they had completed the test. Given that the actual chance of anyone correctly answering at least six questions was near zero, "successfully" doing so was taken as the indicator of cheating. What the researchers wanted to know, of course, was what kind of people cheated and under what circumstances.

The tests were administered to four groups under different circumstances that constituted high and low levels of certainty and severity of punishment. Subjects were also asked to provide certain demographic information and completed various scales assessing past behaviors and personality attributes. Of 256 students, 72 (29%) cheated to acquire the extra $10. The data were then analyzed to determine if experimental conditions (certainty and severity of punishment), demographic differences, past behaviors, and personality traits were associated with the choice to cheat on the trivia questions.

Consistent with dozens of other studies examining a wide range of crime and deviance among many different groups and in many locations, Nagin and Pogarsky found a clear deterrent effect for certainty, but not for severity of punishment. They also found that those who cheated on the quiz reported more past illegal and deviant behaviors (particularly drinking and fighting) than did noncheating respondents. This is important because it suggests that inclinations to cheat on such a minor matter can be generalized to more serious deviance. Consistent with many other studies, they also found that males and those with lower incomes (thus more in need of the extra $10) cheated more and were less deterrable than females or those with higher incomes.

One of the characteristics most associated with cheating is gender. Most studies of academic dishonesty have found more males than females to be cheaters (Gibson et al., 2008). This greater involvement of males is consistent with the distribution of crime by gender, leaving us with the same quandary. Why is male misconduct so prevalent across a wide range of behavioral domains? Focusing on self-reported cheating on college exams, Chris Gibson and his colleagues (2008) found males had lower self-control, while females scored higher on reports of shame and embarrassment. These patterns of internal controls may provide considerable insight regarding gender differentials and the success or failure of deterrent efforts. In sum, however, the deterrability of academic cheating appears to vary widely across student characteristics.

Intimate Partner Violence. Characteristics of the far more serious crime of assaulting a spouse or partner, in contrast to the errant students and professors, suggest low deterrability. The behavior appears to be irrational, expressive, quite violent, and likely to take place in private. Moreover, it is often pointed out that the act historically has been culturally condoned (e.g., Walker, 1979; Brown, 1984) and arguably continues so to some degree. Given a theoretical framework generally suggesting low deterrability, the outcome of the watershed *Minneapolis Domestic Violence Experiment* (Sherman & Berk, 1984) was quite surprising.

The design of this important study provided for random assignment of three police responses to cases of misdemeanor domestic assault: (1) arrest of the offender; (2) separation of the parties; or (3) some sort of advice, including mediation. Police officers responding to domestic violence calls were instructed to intervene as dictated by the color of the form appearing on top of their report pad. Cases were then followed for six months to determine if the assaulters recidivated, as measured by additional reports to the police and periodic interviews with the victims. The lowest rate of repeat assaults (13%) was obtained when the offenders had been arrested, a middle level (18.2%) followed advice or mediation, while the highest incidence of new assaults came after separation. The researchers concluded that "swift imposition of a sanction of temporary incarceration may deter male offenders in domestic assault cases. . . . In short, criminal justice sanctions seem to matter for this offense in this setting with this group of experienced offenders" (Sherman & Berk, 1984:270). Thus, special deterrence was thought to be operating even for this theoretically unpromising type of crime.

The Minneapolis study, in combination with feminist activism and civil suits seeking equal protection of the laws for battered women, had an unprecedented impact on police policy. Arrest became the preferred policy for misdemeanor domestic assault cases in most large U.S. police departments and remains the norm. Arrests of men who had committed misdemeanor assaults against their partners moved from a rarity in 1984 when the study was reported to the typical response well before the close of the decade. Ironically, however, the changes in law have also led to dramatic increases in arrests of women, and have created a sense of ambivalence among some feminist criminologists (Chesney-Lind, 2002).

While the impact of the Minneapolis experiment, combined with other social forces, was rapid and substantial, a series of six replication studies (Omaha, Milwaukee, Charlotte, Colorado Springs, Dade County, and Atlanta) reflected the complexity of the concept of deterrence. Lively debate was stimulated because the conclusions of the evaluators of these six studies were quite divergent. While some found special deterrent effects of arrest, albeit weaker, others did not. Still others found that arrest *increased* recidivism among marginal offenders, those who may have felt they had nothing to lose. In Milwaukee, for example, unemployed suspects were more likely to assault their partners again if arrested (Sherman et al., 1992). Similar results emerged in Omaha (Dunford, 1992) and Colorado Springs (Berk et al., 1992). A recent study analyzing National Crime Victimization Survey (NCVS) data, however, found no evidence that offenders with less to lose would be more likely to repeat the assaults if arrested (Felson et al., 2005).

A number of criminologists have attempted to reanalyze data from this collective set of studies to determine what overall conclusions can be supported. David Sugarman and Sue Boney-McCoy (2000) undertook a meta-analysis, a complex statistical technique for assessing a group of studies, and concluded that there was a deterrent effect overall. Most recently, Christopher Maxwell and colleagues (2002) combined all individual cases (4,032) of males assaulting their partners from five of the six replicating studies. They then analyzed that larger data set, concluding that "there were consistently smaller rates of subsequent victimization and recidivism among the suspects assigned to the arrest treatment versus the nonarrest interventions" (2002:66). Regarding policy direction, they went on to state that their findings "support the continued use of arrests as a preferred law enforcement response for reducing subsequent victimization of women by their intimate partners" (2002:69). Again, however, the recent analysis of the NCVS data (Felson et al., 2005) contradicted the finding that arrest deters. They failed to find significant reductions in recidivism for perpetrators of domestic violence who were arrested.

The evidence for deterring the crime of misdemeanor assaults of women in domestic settings is mixed and complex. The consensus seems to be that there is some special deterrent effect, varying by characteristics of the offender. Unfortunately, differences in deterrability by persons, even when clearly understood, complicate the task of policy development. If arrest deters some assaulters, but escalates the violence of others, police policy for responding to these crimes becomes far more difficult to formulate. Joanne Belknap and K. Douglas McCall (1994) expressed the related concern that focus on the arrest issue has detracted attention from the role of police in referring battered women to shelters and other important resources. Given the current body of evidence, what policies should guide the response of police to misdemeanor assaults of women by their partners?

Policy changes in the arena of police responses to partner battering have been one of the most dramatic within criminal justice in recent decades. The policy directive of most U.S. police departments has shifted from one of arrest avoidance for misdemeanor assault of intimate partners, to a presumptive arrest standard (Brown, 1990). In other words, rather than having to justify an arrest as exceptional, an officer must defend a non-arrest decision when a woman is the victim of a minor assault. The evidence of public support for these changes is mixed. Loretta Stalans (1996) found that 26 percent of Georgia residents favored arrest when the woman suffered "moderate" injuries, but only 1.3 percent when she was not physically injured. She also found that educational levels were positively associated with preference for arrest. A Canadian citizen sample, by contrast (Hilton, 1993), strongly favored arrest. Similar levels of support for arrest were found in a survey of Singapore citizens (Choi & Edelson, 1995). The Singaporean Penal Code, however, does not allow arrest for spousal assaults resulting in only minor injuries.

The Singaporean case serves as an interesting example of the relativity of crime, with current law regarding spousal assaults that produce only "hurt," but not "grievous hurt," being quite similar to the state of American misdemeanor assaults about two decades ago. In contemporary Singapore, and formerly in the United States, a police officer cannot make an arrest for a simple (nongrievous hurt) assault in a domestic

HIGHLIGHT 5.1
Wife-Beating in Kenya: Can It Be Deterred?

Spousal assaults have been the focus of much attention in the U.S. and many other Western countries over the past quarter century. As this chapter discusses, one approach that has been taken in responding to the problem has been to use the punitive sanctions of the criminal justice system in an attempt to deter this type of violent behavior. To be successful, the sanctions of the system must outweigh the informal forces that support the practice, and ultimately, must lead to the evolution of new norms.

Little has been done yet to begin changing a pervasive practice of wife-beating in Kenya. Consequently, it made international news when Agnes Siyiankoi, a member of the southern Kenya Maasai tribe, took her husband to court for beating her. Although illegal, the practice is widespread and culturally condoned. This is rooted in a strong patriarchal culture that views women as the property, first of their fathers, then of their husbands. The authority of males is supported by force, and men who do not beat their wives are viewed as weak. A survey undertaken by the Women's Rights Awareness Program found that nearly 60 percent of their sample of both men and women felt that the women were to blame for the beatings and only 51 percent said that men who beat their wives should be punished.

Ms. Siyiankoi was given in marriage to an older man while still in primary school and suffered 13 years of beatings before pressing the issue in court. Even her mother always urged her to return to her husband, showing the scars resulting from beatings at the hands of her husband and Siyiankoi's father. The beating that led her to file charges was administered with a wooden club and required hospitalization.

Can the practice of wife-beating in Kenya be deterred by criminal sanctioning? In what ways is the Kenyan experience similar to that of the U.S. and other Western countries?

Adapted from G. Mwangi, Associated Press writer, *Johnson City Press*, October 31, 1997:11.

violence case. This lack of authority seems to correlate with negative police attitudes toward victims of domestic assault. Thus in the pre-Reform era, an American police officer reportedly commented to a man who had assaulted his wife: "Well, maybe if I slap my wife around a couple of times, she might behave too." (Paterson, 1979:87). Similarly, though less blatantly hostile toward victims, Singaporean officers recently interviewed by Ganopathy Narayanan (2005:436) suggested that officers should "go for peaceful solution, talk to the man and the woman and try to cool things down for them," while another officer asserted, "You see in a domestic situation, let me tell you, there is no wrong or right, guilty or innocent. Wife pressing charges against husband? That cannot happen!" Highlight 5.1 takes another cross-cultural look at wife battering.

The issue of whether this type of offender can be deterred by threat of legal sanctions has turned out to be far more complex than appeared to be the case as rapid change evolved in the mid and late 1980s. Something, however, seems to have worked, though what it is not clear. Rates of domestic assaults of women declined by 21 percent in the mid 1990s (Holland, 2000). These reductions could reflect deterrent effects resulting from policy changes, normative validation, the greater availability of options to women (e.g., spouse abuse shelters and divorce) or the same factors that have caused other crimes to decline in recent years (e.g., demographic shifts, economic factors or changes in patterns of substance abuse). The recent examination of the NCVS data (Felson et al., 2005) concluded that just reporting the offense to the police, whether by a victim or a third party, had a deterrent effect. As this study did not find a deterrent effect for arrest, this suggests that deterrence is accomplished fairly readily for some. They found deterrent effects more difficult to attain among offenders with prior assault records or alcohol/substance abuse histories. Most likely, it is a combination of these things that have led to progress in combating intimate violence.

Further reflecting the complexity of efforts to deter intimate partner violence, questions have resurfaced in recent years regarding appropriate levels of prosecutorial discretion. At issue is whether prosecutors should pursue all cases of misdemeanor intimate partner violence, generally dubbed "non-drop" policies, or should follow the wishes of the victim. The debate over appropriate sanctions has become so strident that Candace Kruttschnitt concluded that it "has come full circle" (2008:629). On the one hand, it is argued that prosecution deters repeat offenses (special deterrence). On the other hand, however, it is countered that aggressive prosecution can have the unintended consequences of injecting additional strain into the lives of victims (e.g., multiple court appearances), disempowering them (undermining future cooperation with the criminal justice system) and even increase the risk of future assaults for some (Buzawa & Buzawa, 2008). A recent comparison revealed no difference in recidivism rates for domestic assaults in Brooklyn, which has a no-drop policy, and the Bronx, New York, where a there is a victim driven decision regarding the prosecutorial decision (Davis et al., 2008). Mixed evidence regarding deterrent effects, combined with concern about unintended consequences, has led some to conclude that the victim's wishes should be followed. Jo Dixon (2008), for example, suggested that the problem of domestic violence would be better served if the courts made an effort to go beyond mere deterrent effects to address the social roots of the problem. In particular, sanctions "must be coupled with social welfare policies that provide socially marginal populations with employment, housing and child care" (Dixon, 2008: 668).

Another recent direction taken in responding to domestic violence has been the sentencing of offenders to rehabilitative oriented batterer programs. While these programs do monitor the offenders and extend accountability, the rehabilitative goal is at their core and runs counter to the notion of deterrence. However, evaluations have largely been unsupportive of their success in reducing recidivism. A recent assessment of batterer programs in the Bronx, New York, found that offenders who were required to complete the programs displayed the same rates of recidivism as those who were not assigned to them (Labriola et al., 2008). Clearly, however, the popularity of batterer rehabilitative programs in recent years reflects the shifting sands of domestic violence policy.

Homicide. Research regarding the deterrability of murder has been almost entirely limited to the capital punishment debate. As homicide is usually a "crime of passion," it does not seem to be a good candidate for deterrent effects, thus it is surprising that the capital punishment debate has revolved so heavily around deterrence instead of retribution or incapacitation. Moreover, since the U.S. Supreme Court ruling in *Furman v. Georgia* (1972), reinstating capital punishment after a moratorium, its use has steadily grown. A majority of nations no longer include the death penalty in their legal codes, and the United States is the only democratic, industrialized nation that does still allow capital punishment. China, Iran, and Saudi Arabia are the only countries that utilize the death penalty more than the United States (Amnesty International).

Empirical evidence regarding the capital punishment deterrence hypothesis has been accumulating for many decades, beginning with studies by Sutherland (1925) and Sellin (1952). Most of this research has failed to find deterrent effects, with the most notable exception of the findings of economist Isaac Ehrlich (1975). (For a review of this body of research, see Bedau, 1997 and Bailey & Peterson, 1999.) Some research (e.g., see Bowers, 1988; Cochran et al., 1994; Bailey, 1998; Stack, 1998) has even unveiled evidence that executions serve to desensitize some people to the value of human life, actually leading to increases rather than declines in homicide. This finding, antithetical to a deterrent effect of capital punishment, is called the *brutalization effect*.

Once again, however, the most recent research has revealed that the issue of deterrent (and brutalization) effects is quite complicated. Taking advantage of the "natural experiment" opportunity posed by the return of California to the death penalty, John Cochran and Mitch Chamlin (2000), examined weekly homicide rates across seven different categories before and after the state's first post-Furman execution (Alton Harris, in 1992). They found both a deterrent and a brutalization effect, each in only one category of homicide. No relationship was found between execution and any of the other categories. Moreover, the deterrent effect for felony murders was canceled out by the brutalization effect for murders of strangers in argument situations. Thus, capital punishment was found to both decrease and increase later murders at the same time, but most other studies have not found support for either deterrence or brutalization because when all types of homicide are looked at simultaneously, the subcategories with opposite effects tend to cancel one another out. In terms of policy, this finding leaves us rather in the same quandary as do the opposing findings in the domestic violence arena. While punitive sanctions may deter some, they may increase the likelihood of offending for others. The domestic violence focus was on special deterrence, while capital punishment can, by definition (because the offender is dead), only address general deterrence.

Ironically, use of the death penalty has been increasing while evidence of its ineffectiveness has been accumulating. There is a very large chasm between both public opinion and policy versus expert opinion and findings in regard to capital punishment. Public opinion polls in the late 1990s consistently showed that about three-quarters of the population favored capital punishment, but Michael Radelet and Ronald Akers' (1996) survey found that more than two-thirds of police chiefs and three-quarters of criminologists do not see any deterrent effect in the death penalty. It appears, however, that the United States is experiencing a decline in support of the death penalty, not because it does not deter crime, but because new DNA tests have established that innocent people have been executed far more often than was thought. Thus in early

2000, Governor George Ryan suspended capital punishment pending a review of the process and in May, 2000 the New Hampshire state legislature passed a bill abolishing it, though it was repealed by Governor Jeanne Shaheen (Johnson, 2000).

Extralegal Sanctions: Shame and Embarrassment

A basis for conceptualizing extralegal or informal sanctions as a mechanism for deterring aberrant behavior has been in place for some time. Johannes Andenaes (1968) spoke of legal prohibitions functioning as a "moral jolt" awakening offenders or potential offenders to the realization of the extent to which society condemns a particular act. This engenders shame, guilt, or other informal socially induced controls that bring the offender back into conformity or holds the conformist in line. In this manner, criminal sanctions may serve to validate or strengthen norms. Emile Durkheim saw *normative validation* as the principal impact of punishment on crime, arguing that witnessing the official sanctioning of a norm violation reinforces a person's view of that behavior as deviant.

Several relationships between these legal and extralegal forms of sanctions are possible if, in fact, deviant behavior can be deterred. They can have deterrent effects that are independent, contingent on each other, or that interact. Consider, as an example, that Joe or Josephine College was tempted to smoke marijuana for the first time, but after thinking about it, decided that it was not worth the risk. The issue is the nature of the threat that was perceived as making the behavior too hazardous. If the student was deterred by fear of arrest, fines, or a criminal record, formal sanction mechanisms were operative. If, on the other hand, the student opted not to smoke a joint out of concern that his or her parents, coach, criminology professor, or other persons perceived as disapproving would come to know about it, informal sanction threats were the deterring element. If it was reasoned that the police might detect the violation, leading to exposure of the misconduct to those significant others, this suggests that the deterrent effects of informal sanctions are contingent upon formal sanctions. Donna Bishop has summarized this view, suggesting "that the threat of informal sanctioning is the real deterrent and that formal punishment is important only insofar as it triggers informal sanctions" (1984:405). Finally, the would-be deviant might have concluded that legal problems (e.g., court appearance, fines), combined with social disapproval, outweighed the satisfaction that might be derived from getting high. Thus, formal and informal mechanisms would have interacted to achieve deterrent effects.

There is considerable agreement that informal sanction threats accomplish greater deterrent effects than do formal threats. Charles Tittle concluded "that social control as a general process seems to be rooted almost completely in informal sanctioning" (1980:241) and, similarly, Raymond Paternoster and Leeann Iovanni asserted that "formal sanction threats are not important in any immediate or direct sense. It may now be incumbent on deterrence theorists and researchers to consider the development and testing of models of informal social control" (1986:769). The role of informal sanctions in deterrence theory is now being rethought by both theorists and researchers. As Frank Williams has noted, "legal deterrence should be seen as part of a larger framework . . . [I]t is only one form of controlling influence and is inextricably intertwined with other forms of social control" (1985:148).

These early findings of the potency of extralegal sanctions in deterring deviance have led sociologists in particular to develop broader models of control that incorporate extralegal and particularly moral factors. Jack Gibbs (1989) has gone so far as to argue that control should serve as the central notion of sociology, so one might deduce that a sociological approach to explaining crime should be expanded to include extralegal normative violations and controls. The thin, and perhaps arbitrary, line between violation of extralegal and legal norms is quite evident in considering the full gamut of social control attributable to the informal dimension of deterrence. Only a quite small portion of norms are ever assimilated into criminal codes and subjected to legal control. Yet extralegal deterrence may play similar roles in the control of rude and obnoxious, but legal, behavior and in controlling violations of criminal codes. Thomas Scheff (1988) has noted that we rarely have to rely on formal sanctions to accomplish social control. Control is instead maintained by a subtle reward of deference extended by others, instilling the emotion of inner pride, and by the withholding of deference (punishment) that generates the emotion of shame.

Shaming has emerged as perhaps the leading concept in criminological thinking for the informal control of crime and deviance. John Braithwaite (1989), one of the leading theorists to focus on the role of shaming in deterring crime, notes that it may consist of a wide range of social reactions to undesired behavior ranging from "a frown . . . a turning of the back, a slight shaking of the head . . . direct verbal confrontation . . . indirect confrontation by gossip . . . [or] . . . officially pronounced by a judge from the bench" (1989:57-58). Braithwaite, like many other criminologists, has concluded that the prospects of sanctions or shaming being imposed by significant others (e.g., relatives or friends) are much more effective in preventing crime than are the formal threats of the criminal justice system. Moreover, he argues, successful socialization within the family through the vehicle of shaming implants a conscience that will be on duty all of the time, in effect delivering an immediate punishment for every transgression, as opposed to the relatively remote prospects of being caught and shamed for any given violation. Shaming, in other words, builds a conscience or moral awareness which then becomes a more controlling factor than the threat of shaming per se. Braithewaite's theory, however, goes far beyond the bounds of deterrence or even broader rational choice theories of crime. It is a general theory of crime that incorporates elements of opportunity (Chapter 7), control and learning (Chapter 8), and labeling (Chapter 9) theories. While this has become a very popular theory on the conceptual level, to date it has been subjected to very little empirical testing (Hay, 1998). The key concept for crime prevention is to provide a means of reintegration of the offender into the law-abiding community. Its antithesis is stigmatization, or labeling, which is exactly what Terrence Miethe and his colleagues (2000) found in their evaluation of a drug court intended to deter recidivism through shaming.

Harold Grasmick and his colleagues (Grasmick & Bursik, 1990; Grasmick et al., 1993b; Grasmick & Kobayashi, 2002) have extended contemporary informal deterrence theory to draw a distinction between shame, conceptualized as internalized guilt feelings and *embarrassment*, the loss of respect in the eyes of significant others. Their conceptual scheme suggests that these informal sanctions may operate in a manner similar to what classical theorists predicted for formal sanctions. In other words, their deterrence model depicts the potential offender as one who calculates the costs of crime and deviance in terms of the pain of shame and embarrassment, then balances those unpleasant experiences against the perceived gain from the offense.

Research has been revealing with relative consistency that informal sanction threats deter more than the formal. In testing broader rational choice models as an explanation of gender differences in shoplifting and drunk driving, Stephen Tibbetts and Denise Herz (1996) found that perceived threats of shame were the most important factor. Similarly, both Tibbetts and Myers (1999) and the Cochran et al. (1999) studies of academic cheating among college students found shame to be the explanation most supported. Focusing on a more contextually confined form of deviance, lewd behavior at Mardi Gras, David Redmon (2002) failed to find support for deterrent effects of external sources of control in the domains of family, work, and general community. Harold Grasmick and Emiko Kobayashi (2002) hypothesized that informal sanctions in the form of externally based embarrassment would hold greater deterrent effect than internally based feelings of shame in Japanese society due to the Japanese cultural emphasis on collective relations. Examining workplace rule violations within a Japanese hospital, however, shame, not embarrassment, again was the strongest predictor of conformity. If these findings continue to hold up in various cultures and across different types of deviance, criminologists will be more confident about how informal deterrence works. For now, more confidence is placed in internal (shame) sources of control than in external (embarrassment) mechanisms.

A Rational Choice Perspective

The concept of crime deterrence emerged as the centerpiece of the classical school of criminology. Its fundamental propositions remain at the heart of the broader rational choice framework, but as the past several pages illustrate, have experienced a conceptual explosion. While anchored in the original classical deterrence concepts, the contemporary rational choice perspective is far more complex. A recent test of deterrence theory cast in a broader rational choice model, for example, used Bayesian probability theory to assess how individuals calculate their risk of arrests (Matsueda et al., 2006). This model estimates perceptions of punishment probability as a function of baseline risk perceptions that are reformulated in response to numerous sources of new information as well as individual and neighborhood characteristics. Such a detailed model and the statistical techniques used to estimate it are remarkably sophisticated relative to deterrence research just a few years ago and beyond the imagination of the classical founders.

Rational choice expands conventional deterrence research by incorporating many more variables in the reasoning process and by considering choices, not only of potential offenders, but of victims as well. Research regarding the process of choosing crime has revealed it to be a far more complex process than was envisioned by the earlier classical deterrence theorists. Nor do the choices end with choosing or not choosing crime. The offender must decide on the type of crime (Guerette et al., 2004), where and when to commit it, elect a *modus operandi*, determine what to do afterwards and so forth. Conceptualizing robbers as "purposeful foragers," Bernasco & Block (2009), for example, found that the presence of drug and prostitution markets attracted robbers while other community characteristics served to discourage them. Whatever the degree of rationality, choices are an ongoing process among both victims and offenders from the rational choice perspective and these choices are impacted by many different factors. The rational choice perspective has also paved the way for a number of additional practical crime prevention foci. Studies of victimization, defensible space designs, crime displacement, hot spots and routine activities are all highly visible examples within the criminological literature that arguably fall within the rational choice framework. As with more conventional deterrence research, these topics assume that rationality underlies decisions to violate the law, but go on to include other variables. Environmental cues, for example, become important input in the offenders' larger reasoning process. The victim as well serves as a variable within the crime equation and even becomes the primary focus in many theoretical frameworks within the rational choice model. Neither rational choice, however, nor any of its' specific derivatives should be considered a theory of crime in the strictest sense. Rather, they are perspectives that incorporate a choice variable within complicated crime equations.

Routine Activities: Victims and Offenders

Routine Activities Theory, sometimes referred to as a lifestyle approach, was first introduced by Lawrence Cohen and Marcus Felson (1979) to explain escalating official crime rates during the 1970s, but has evolved over the past one-quarter century (see Felson 1994; 1998; 2002). As a rational choice theory, it argues that available opportunities are an important component in crime calculus. Choices in lifestyle on the part of potential victims may create or curtail crime opportunities for the motivated offender. Due to this focus on the lifestyle or routines of victims, many criminologists argue that routine activities is really not a theory of crime at all, but a theory of victimization. In recent years, however, criminologists have increasingly applied the concept to offenders as well. A person's lifestyle may expose them to opportunities or experiences that increase their odds either of engaging in criminal behaviors or of being victimized.

At the heart of routine activities are three premises, often referred to as the *crime triangle*. It is when these three elements are present at any point in space and time that a crime occurs. Thus the crime is seen as an "event" that requires both victim and offender roles. The lifestyle of either, or both, can help explain the occurrence or nonoccurrence of criminal events. The first component necessary for a crime is the presence of *motivated offenders*. The early de-emphasis on motivation explains why routine activities was construed as a theory of victimization rather than of offending. No attention was extended to what motivated offenders. It was assumed that there is an ample supply and that these motivated offenders would commit crime whenever viable opportunities were encountered. Note that this assumption is in line with the reasoning of the classical school. Human nature is such (hedonistic) that people will offend whenever there is sufficient opportunity.

Only recently have theorists began to examine motivated offenders within this framework rather than taking their presence for granted. Note, however, that many of their findings may be more consistent with integrating positivistic ideas than with rational choice premises. Alison Sherley (2005), for example, reviewed police sexual assault files from a large Canadian city and found two primary motivations. One was the perpetrators failure to resolve past incidents (e.g., loss of an intimate relationship), and the second, a deep-seated anger toward women in general. Similarly, Scott Sasse (2005) considered the motivations of 163 male sex offenders enrolled in treatment programs in a Midwestern region. He found that those who committed offenses in their homes tended to be older, to have had younger victims, to more often have themselves been victims of abuse, and were more likely to have been under the influence of drugs when they offended. In contrast, those who victimized persons outside of their homes were, on average, younger, more likely to have targeted older victims, and to have committed their crimes under the influence of alcohol. While rational choice models, especially deterrence, have been at the basis of most sex offender laws, the fit to motivations of a heterogeneous offender population seems poor (Meloy, 2005).

The presence of *suitable targets* is the second requirement of the routine activities explanation of victimization/offending. Something of value to the potential offender must be available. It could be appealing property or it could be an outlet for emotionally satisfying activity such as an expression of anger or hatred, the pursuit of excitement or fulfilling of sexual or other drives. In short, there must be something that tempts the hedonistic calculus of the would-be offender.

The crime triangle is completed by the *absence of capable guardians*. Neither persons nor other agents are present to protect the property or vulnerable persons. Capable guardians may take many different forms, depending on the context. It might mean that a person is home, a security guard is on duty, that passers by are likely, that neighbors are at home, doors are locked, cameras are installed, or dogs are present. In short, when motivated offenders happen upon suitable targets in the absence of capable guardianship, a criminal event transpires.

Cohen and Felson contended that certain social changes had facilitated increases in suitable targets and declines in the presence of capable guardians. For example, they argued that increased levels of females in the workforce had resulted in more homes being left unoccupied (absence of capable guardians) during the day, providing increased opportunities for burglars. Similarly, increased mobility placed more persons at risk for personal victimization. At the same time, technological developments resulted in more portable, but valuable, items that could be targeted by thieves in homes, automobiles, or with persons. This tendency has exploded in more recent years with the spread of items such as cellular phones, disc players, and laptop computers.

Routine Activities of Victims. The study of victims of crime, a subfield of criminology called victimology, received quite a boost in interest as a consequence of the popularity of routine activities theory. For many years the theory focused almost exclusively on how the routines or lifestyles of persons related to their risk of becoming victims of crime. Fundamentally, the theory proposes that victimization risk is a function of how one patterns their behavior. If one stays home less often, for example, the reduction in capable guardianship of their home translates to an increased risk of crime being committed against their home property. By the same token, as one more frequently ventures away from home, the risk of victimization against their person expands due to the greater likelihood of crossing paths with a motivated offender. Thus a well recognized fact among criminologists (but seen in reverse by widespread lay myth) is that the elderly are far less frequently victims of crime than are the more youthful because they place themselves less at risk. They less often go out late at night, go out by themselves, or go to bars. Going to bars, as an example, clearly places one at higher risk of victimization. To take the point further, as did Elizabeth Mustaine and Richard Tewksbury (1998), who one goes to bars with, how long they stay, how drunk they get, and what time they leave all figure in to the quality of guardianship. In interviews with 16,000 adults across the United States, Richard Felson and Keri Burchfield (2005) found that young males were especially at risk of being physically assaulted when they were out drinking. They observed even more heightened risks of sexual assault for both males and females.

Similarly, Bonnie Fisher and her colleagues (1998:702) found "that students who partied on campus several nights per week and were more likely to take recreational drugs were more likely to be a victim of on-campus violent crime." But far less than a "night on the town" can place one at a degree of risk. Mustaine and Tewksbury's (1998) research, for example, found that just frequently eating out, leaving home to study, and belonging to more clubs and organizations significantly increased risk of both minor (less than $50) and major (more than $50) theft victimizations. Similarly, Verna Henson and William Stone (1999) found that most crimes on a college campus were thefts resulting from dormitory rooms being left unlocked. Because victimization is a function of lifestyle, those who are victims once are more likely to be targeted by offenders again.

Given that much of routine activities research has focused on the role of the victim, relevant questions you might ask yourself from this perspective would scrutinize your habits. Do you conduct yourself in such a way as to minimize risk of victimization? Or do you do things that place you at risk of victimization? Do you lock your doors when you leave home? Do you ever leave your keys in your car or car doors unlocked? Do you always lock your bicycle? Taking steps to minimize risk of your property being stolen by attending to such mechanical details is referred to as *target hardening*. This can be extended to your personal safety. Do you go out late? Do you frequent bars? Do you drink often or large amounts on some occasions? Do you know the persons with whom you socialize or do you sometimes find yourself out with people whom you really do not know? Recent cases of tragic murders of promising young women, such as those of New York criminal justice student Imette St. Guillen and high school graduate Natalie Holloway, celebrating in Aruba, highlight the ideological debate about the victim role in crime. When some commentators alluded to their late night drinking with strangers, others cried foul, saying that raising these points smacked of "blaming the victim." From a criminological routine activities perspective, while the offenders bear no less responsibility for their horrendous crimes, the victims' late night drinking without the presence of friends who might provide capable guardianship were part of the equation.

"Some scholars have avoided the study of the victim's role in violence because they anticipate an accusation that they are 'blaming the victim'" (Felson & Burchfield, 2004:855). Others tread very lightly, almost apologetically, for exploring the victim's role in the crime. In her examination of sexual assaults Sherley, for example, cautions:

> Certainly, examining the victim as attractive target should in no way imply that victims somehow contribute to their own victimization (2004:99).

She later reiterates:

> Again, it is not being suggested that sexual assault victims in any way contribute to their own victimization (2004:104).

Yet lifestyle theories seem inevitably to lead to an ideological deadlock, at least for those who are ideologically inflexible. To gain causal insight into criminal events, informed by the role of the victim, it is essential that the analyst separate causation from blame or moral accountability. While blame and accountability must remain squarely assigned to the offender, the contribution of lifestyle theories is that victim lifestyle is part of the equation. Whether a victim's lifestyle or routines causally contribute to burglary by frequent vacationing, leaving their home vulnerable, or to crimes against the person by frequenting pubs, the legal and moral responsibility of the offender is unaltered. Yet an unavoidable Catch-22 remains. Deviant lifestyles bear more risk of victimization than do conforming ones. This is why the elderly are the least victimized, and young adults the most victimized, groups in our society. Recognizing these facts regarding the distribution of victimization is not necessarily "blaming the victim," and certainly removes no responsibility (legally or morally) from the offender. At some point, however, degrees of blame or personal responsibility can be inferred by the victim's actions, triggering an ideological debate about "blaming the victim." For example, the victim's behavior may reflect gaps in judgment, low self-control, risk-taking or other flawed characteristics. In that vein, it can be argued that young men are at high risk of physical assault when drinking because "intoxicated men are more provocative" (Felson & Birchfield, 2004:848). Or others may conclude that with the majority of prostitutes reporting physical assaults (e.g., Dalla, 2002), such work is too risky. As criminologists, however, our work "should be based on 'causal analysis' and should leave 'blame analysis' to the criminal justice system" (Felson & Burchfield:856). Likewise, while ideological weighting of victim behaviors may be inevitable, it is not an appropriate task for the criminologist in seeking to explain criminal events.

Routine Activities of Offenders. Of late, criminologists have examined the routines of offenders with the idea that this may help to explain patterns of offending, just as lifestyle activities of potential victims might identify victimization risk levels. In fact, it there is a strong correlation between being a victim and a perpetrator of crime. That is, deviant lifestyles are predictive of both victimization and offending.

Elizabeth Mustaine and Richard Tewksbury (1999) examined their sample of college students to determine the role of lifestyle or routine activities in explaining drunk driving. Note that this shift in focus, from victim to offender, suggests skepticism regarding the first premise of routine activities theory—the assumption that there are ample motivated offenders, only needing to come in contact with a suitable target in the absence of capable guardianship. Mustaine and Tewksbury's approach suggests that motivated offenders are not just randomly distributed, but rather that they too are products of particular situations that are created by lifestyle choices and other factors influencing people's routines. Demographic characteristics account for some of the differences in patterns of drinking and driving, especially gender, with males reporting higher rates. More directly relevant to the motivation to offend, however, are lifestyle choices. Both males and females were more likely to drive drunk when they drank away from home, were more tolerant of other illegal behavior, drank more frequently, and engaged in other forms of illegal behavior.

A study of property and violent offenses by Icelandic adolescents also applied a routine activities framework, integrating it with social control and learning theories (see Chapter 8). The authors of the study, Jon Gunnar Bernburg and Thorolfur Thorlindsson (2001) urged that the motivation of offenders not be taken for granted, but that criminologists seek to determine if motivation is shaped by the social context in which the offender is located. They specifically examined factors like having delinquent friends (learning theory) and lack of attachment with authority figures such as parents and teachers (control theory) as rendering youth who encounter opportunities for delinquency more likely to be motivated to pursue them. In other words, they found that delinquency was more a result of certain learning experiences and inadequate social bonding, combined with routine activities that present opportunities for misconduct, than just delinquent opportunities alone. This suggests two important things about routine activities; first, that it may shed light on offending as well as victimization, and second, that routine activities can be enhanced by combining or integrating it with other perspectives.

A similar approach was taken by Martin Schwartz and his colleagues (2001) in analyzing Canadian data on male sexual victimization of females among college and university students. Somewhat differently, however, they construed peer attitudes not as a learning component to be combined with routine activities, but rather as an "index of motivation." In this vein, they concluded that "motivated offenders exist because they have developed certain attitudes and behaviors as a result of encouragement and support by other males" (2001:646). They also found that offenders were more likely to be heavy drinkers. Reviewing the victimization patterns among women, they found that those who drank more, used recreational drugs more frequently, and those who partook of these activities with dating partners, had increased risk of victimization. In short, males who had been encouraged by peers to victimize females (emotionally or physically), who drank more, and who drank with dating partners were more likely to be motivated offenders, and to view females who were drinking and/or consuming drugs in the course of dating as suitable targets for sexual victimization.

Hate crimes have also been analyzed from a routine activities framework. The practice of "Claping" Amish minorities examined by Bryan Byers and Benjamin

Crider (2002) serves as an example. Claping is a verb for predatory crimes perpetrated against the Amish by non-Amish persons, usually adolescents, rooted in anti-Amish biases. The term is the counterpart to "Clape," a derogatory noun of unknown origin used in reference to Amish persons by the offenders. Typical illustrations of Claping offered by Byers and Crider are "dusting," speeding past Amish buggies to irritate the occupants with a cloud of dust, "flouring," the unleashing of a bag of flour on Amish buggies as driving past, and vandalism directed at Amish property such as blowing up mailboxes and turning over outhouses.

Utilizing a methodology of interviewing offenders in a U.S. community with an appreciable Amish population, the authors argued that Claping fit all three elements of routine activities theory. Motivation was particularly reflected in anti-Amish bias, a view that they were different and that their conduct was sometimes perceived by the offenders as provocative. Claping was also spontaneously motivated as an exciting activity to relieve boredom. Access to an automobile was essential, and in the context of adolescents driving around seeking fun, the pattern of offending could be interpreted as a youthful bonding experience to relieve boredom and act upon anti-Amish biases. Thus motivation appears not to be just random, but a product of other social forces.

The Amish were depicted as suitable targets because they were perceived by offenders as "easy" targets, as they would do little to protect themselves and were readily identifiable because of their distinct appearance and practices. The lack of capable guardianship was explained by the low likelihood of the Amish reporting victimization and the perceived social acceptance of Claping. Because Claping seemed widely viewed as mischievousness rather than crime, the expectation was that social sanctions were unlikely.

Some lifestyle choice present conceptual problems for routine activities theory. Richard Spano and his fellow researchers (2008) recently pointed this out in regard to gang membership, carrying guns and employment. While the dominant view is that gang membership is part of a deviant identity that increases risk of victimization (and offending), some have argued that it can also provide capable guardianship. Some gang members identify a need for protection as a key motivation in electing to join. Similarly, as Spano et al. (2008) note, carrying a gun is viewed by most criminologists as part of a risky deviant lifestyle. Yet it can be construed as enhancing guardianship. Conversely, conventional wisdom long held that employment insulated youth from a variety of troubles, but recent research has belied this assumption. Regarding victimization, routines such as transportation and late hours can place one at more risk and the earnings may render them a more suitable target. Data for impoverished urban minority youth collected by Spano et al. (2008) reinforced the complex nature of how these three domains of routine activity relate to risk of victimization.

How Rational Is Choice?

Economists analyze economic behavior from a rational choice perspective. They presume, whether one is buying toothpaste or a new car, that each individual will make the decision that is most favorable to them. In classical terms the consumer will maximize utility. It is assumed that the purchase decision will be rational and very predictable. That is, two different persons will typically make the same choice. If the same brand and size of toothpaste is available at two stores, and the same car at two dealerships, the two businesses with the lowest prices will make the sales. Gary Becker (1968) was one of the first economists to apply this model to the study of crime, but he has been followed by many others. Moreover, many criminologists have accepted the economic model. But can we safely assume that potential offenders (or consumers, for that matter) are rational beings who will make like decisions? On reflection, this seems to be a rather bold assumption.

In a highly regarded book on the rational choice perspective, Kenneth Tunnell (1992) points out that cognitive psychologists have adopted a different model of human decision-making. People are seen as less than fully rational. Oftentimes they do not make decisions that would appear to be in their own best interest for a variety of reasons. First, people do not always have all of the information they need to make informed decisions, and even if they do, may not have the capacity to optimally process that information. Their analytical abilities may be impaired by drugs or alcohol, by cognitive deficiencies or negative learning experiences. Moreover, they may assess things quite differently than some of us, given their life experiences. As Alfred Blumstein (1998:134) noted, "This problem of differential deterrability is particularly acute for crimes involving individuals who see no particular options in the legitimate economy, for whom life in the street is very risky anyway, and who have not been effectively socialized against committing crime. . . . Even though prison may not be a very attractive option, its disutility is likely to be far less than it is to middle-class populations." The personalities, experiences and options that we all bring to bear on a given choice in life are so diverse that it is quite naive to assume that we will all assess the situation similarly and arrive at similar choices.

How much variation is there in the availability of choices or options from one person to the next? If one person has far less options than the next, are they making choices in the same sense as that next person? As one of the authors frequently asks of students, "how many of you chose to attend this university?" Almost all will assert that they did, but what does it say that most are from the immediate region, that most work while going to school, and that many are first generation college students? When asked what opportunities to attend more prestigious schools were declined within that decision-making process, most have the same answer: none. Upon closely examining the route to the particular university it turns out that, for many, there were not a lot of decisions, but rather a path of many forces that propelled them to that particular place at that point in time. Yet that is not to say there were no choices made along the way and, in the final analysis, a decision was made to complete the admission application and to come to campus. The question here may be, can we best understand their enrollment by looking at where they are from, what kind of family influences they experienced in their formative years, and their financial standing? Or can we best explain their presence at the university in terms of those final rational decisions to complete an application and drive to the campus? Virtually every human being makes some rational choices, but the question would seem to be what is the relative weight of those choices and the many factors that shape the context of decisionmaking.

There is a distinction between rationally choosing and just doing something. It is a distortion of the concept of choice to say that a duck chooses to go to water and swim. It may also be a stretch to explain, say Mary Kay Letourneau's conviction for the rape of a 13-year-old boy as a rational choice, or to construe the conduct of many offenders as the outcome of thoughtful deliberation. More insight into these and many crimes can be gained by examining the forces that limit choices, render the offender less able to analyze situations than would a more conforming citizen, and why society chooses to react as it does to particular behaviors. It has been argued that the shortcoming of the rational choice perspective has been its failure to reconcile rationality with the observation that criminals often display impulsiveness, moral ambiguity and expressive motivations to offend (de Haan & Vos, 2003). In short, much criminal behavior, while rational steps may be taken, is far more reflective of emotional drives that seem to fly in the face of what many people would consider rational and deliberate choices.

Table 5.3 summarizes media reports of what most of us might cynically dismiss as the acts of "stupid criminals." Indeed, many of these crime news releases are of the caliber to earn mention in outlets such as the Charlotte-based "John-Boy and Billy" radio show's "Dumb Crook News," *The Stupid Crook Book* (Gregory, 2002), or Butler and Ray's (2000) *The World's Dumbest Criminals.* They are, however, real and in some cases very tragic. Clearly, each of these crimes were less than fully rational, or at least rewards and sanctions were weighted quite differently than they would be by more law-abiding citizens. If indeed, these are stupid crimes, can we still assume, as

---

TABLE 5.2
Rational Crimes or Stupid Crimes?

- A 24-year-old city police officer in Tennessee who was assigned to teach in the Drug Abuse Resistance Education (DARE) program pleaded guilty to contributing to the delinquency of a minor. This was based on an incident in which the car he was riding in was stopped by a state trooper at 2:30 a.m. on Main Street of a nearby small town. He was a passenger in the car with two 17-year-old's, one of whom was consuming beer that he had purchased.

- A Seattle, Washington woman was arrested for dancing topless for two hours on top of an electrical tower along a busy commuting thoroughfare during the morning rush hour. She was drinking vodka as she danced, spitting it and lighting it on fire. It was later reported that she was formerly a male, but was undergoing sex change surgery. Indecent exposure and trespassing charges were filed.

- An Ohio man was arrested on drug trafficking charges after depositing $300,000 cash, contained in grocery bags, in a bank account, and declaring himself unemployed on routine depository papers.

- A Toronto, Canada man, on trial for murder, elected to serve as his own attorney. He had told a prison guard, "You guys are always picking on me because I killed some white bitch."

TABLE 5.2 Continued

- Murder charges were filed against an ex-policeman in Detroit in the 1999 slaying of his wife and son. In 1975 he had been found not guilty by reason of insanity in the deaths of his first wife and their two children.

- A Tennessee community college astronomy teacher was convicted of stealing an antique telescope lens from a Cincinnati observatory. He had donated it to the college where he was employed.

- One of four armed robbers was killed and six customers wounded in a foiled attempt to rob a bar filled with off-duty policemen. They were gathered to hear a performance of the "Pigs in a Blanket" band, comprised of police officers.

- A Bristol, Tennessee man arrived an hour and a half late at his hearing on auto theft and drug charges. He was arrested because he drove to the hearing in a stolen car.

- A 32-year-old Newport, Tennessee man was arrested on the courthouse lawn right after kissing his 17-year-old bride to seal their wedding vows. A passing deputy recognized the groom as an individual with an outstanding theft warrant. He approached the newlyweds, handcuffed the groom and escorted him in to the jail. The official conducting the wedding observed that the bride was left "standing at the altar" and was "really upset." The Circuit Judge released him on bond the following day so that the couple could go on their honeymoon.

- The Circuit Judge alluded to in the above scenario was charged a few months later with public intoxication and destruction of county property. Enraged over the County Commission's investigation of a friend's trash disposal company, the judge ransacked the office of the County Executive while he and others stood by in dismay. Police officers finally escorted the judge out the back door. Friends noted that he had been under a lot of stress, as his mother had recently died and his home had burnt. He was hospitalized for depression after the incident.

- A 36-year-old Tennessee man pled guilty to a charge of voluntary manslaughter. The charge arose from an incident in which he and his wife were drinking with another man and the defendant fell asleep. When he awoke and found his wife having sex with the other man, he shot him four times.

- A Florida man shot and killed his wife's lover in a Starbucks coffee shop, then fatally shot himself. His wife had been planning to leave him for the victim.

- A Tennessee sheriff was charged with burglarizing the home of, and assaulting the son of, his chief deputy. The event occurred during a night that the sheriff's niece was spending in the home of the alleged victim, who claimed that the sheriff was in uniform at the time. The 19-year-old niece's father was charged, along with the sheriff.

do deterrence and rational choice theorists, that crimes are a product of rational (or at least bounded rational) choice?

Note that several threads of commonality run through these crime scenarios. Most involved emotionally charged issues. Some involved alcohol impairment. Clearly, most of the offenders displayed a distorted focus on potential benefits of their crime (whether financial or emotional satisfaction) to the neglect of likely costs in any calculations they made. In some cases it is difficult to imagine that even minimal calculation took place. It would appear that like the duck going to water, they just did it. Would a highly (or even minimally) rational actor have made choices such as those reflected in Table 5.3? Alas, a plethora of episodes are potential material for stupid/dumb criminal shows and books. The next three chapters offer some insight regarding these rather widespread, but relatively unthinking offenders.

Summary

In seeking to explain crime, one of the most debated issues is the role of choice and the issue of how rational is any decisionmaking on the part of offenders. The concept of deterrence, with its origins in the classical school of criminology, assumed a high degree of rationality. It was intended to be a general theory of crime, that is, one that explains all types of crime and offenders. Contemporary deterrence theory and the broader rational choice framework envision choice in somewhat more relative terms, a bounded rationality, that recognize variations in levels of choice and rationality. Criminology is a relatively new field of inquiry. Explanations of crime as a natural phenomenon began only with the classical school in the eighteenth century. Before that, crime was viewed as a supernatural occurrence. Response to it often was irrational. Church and state joined forces to produce a period of gruesome and barbaric responses to crime and deviance. Throughout Europe, people were tortured and executed for all manner of offenses, real and imagined. It was this epoch of atrocities that provided the backdrop for the beginning of criminology: a reform movement referred to as the classical school of criminology. Classical criminology emerged in the latter part of the eighteenth century as part of the Enlightenment. Led by Cesare Beccaria and Jeremy Bentham, it stressed a fair and rational response to crime, asserting that human beings could thereby be deterred from criminal behavior. Beccaria and Bentham asserted that this could be accomplished through assuring relative certainty, celerity, and severity of punishment. Most criminologists emphasize the contributions of the classical school of criminology to humanitarian reform of the administration of justice more than to theoretical ideas. The school's work led to substantial mitigation of the harshness of punishment and established most of the rights and protections of the accused now regarded as fundamental to Western justice. It also provided the theoretical premises of Western legal codes and the Peelian principles of policing that have dominated both England and America for more than 150 years. Deterrence theory was neglected in the United States in favor of sociological positivism for nearly 100 years, although it had provided the theoretical foundation for the practice of criminal justice for more than two centuries. The last one-third of the twentieth century witnessed a re-examination of the deterrence doctrine and initiation of research to test it. The long delay in subjecting the perspective to scientific scrutiny can be attributed to its ideological ingredients. The notion of deterrence pits those sympathetic to punitive responses to crime against others with a distaste for punishment. The decline of faith in rehabilitation that characterized the 1970s, along with a generally more conservative political climate, however, increased receptivity to research regarding deterrence.

Deterrence doctrine identifies certainty, severity, and celerity of punishment as key elements in a rational decision-making process aimed at deciding between criminal and noncriminal paths of conduct. With renewed conceptual attention, this central thesis has been expanded to incorporate a range of further contingencies for deterrent effects. One view that has been increasingly emphasized is the importance of distinguishing perceptions from objective characteristics of punishment, with more importance attributed to the former as an element in the deterrence of crime. Another important differentiation is between general and specific deterrence, the former consisting of punishment designed to influence decisions of persons other than the punished individual, while the latter is intended to modify the behavior of that person. Third, recognition of degrees of deterrence is now deemed possible. Absolute deterrence, the complete avoidance of criminal behavior due to fear of punishment, is one extreme, while restrictive or marginal deterrence recognizes modifications of criminal conduct short of abstention. Finally, the role of informal sanctions and other extralegal variables has been given particular attention and now is being widely credited as more important to potential deterrent processes than legal factors. This contemporary perspective on deterrence is actually part of a broader rational choice framework for understanding crime. While threats of punishment sometimes deter criminal behavior, such effects can vary according to both types of crimes and persons. In fact, individual deterrability is now conceptualized as falling along a continuum. While some of us are good candidates for sanctions because we are potentially deterrable, others are incorrigible (undeterrable) while still more are acute conformists who never require threats of sanctions to insure conformity. The more deterrable crimes probably include acts that are more rational, instrumental (designed to meet goals), nonviolent, mala prohibita in nature, and those that must be committed in public. Examples of previously studied potentially deterrable offenses reviewed in this chapter include professors violating parking regulations and cheating college students. Woman battering, on the other hand, has generated mixed evidence, but largely favorable towards the deterrence doctrine. Almost all research examining the effects of capital punishment has failed to find general deterrent effects. Persons thought more deterrable include those with low commitment to crime as a way of life, amateurs, and those that see themselves as having more to lose, such as their employability. A number of personality and demographic factors also have been suggested as relevant to deterrence.

Rational choice theory includes more than just deterrence. Perspectives rooted in rational choice, however, are not theories in the conventional sense of explaining crime. Routine activities or lifestyle theory, for example, is widely viewed as an analytical framework for understanding victimization patterns. It conceptualizes victimization as the result of convergence of motivated offenders, attractive targets, and a lack of capable guardians at some point in space and time. Recent research, however, has also examined the effect of lifestyle routines in terms of prospects for offending. Whether crime is largely a product of choices and, if so, how those choices are made is a major topic of debate within criminology. Many criminal events appear not to be very rational choices at all, or at least reflect patterns of decision making quite different from those more typically seen among law-abiding citizens. Positivistic theories reviewed in the following three chapters are quite at odds with the rational choice approach.

Key Terms and Concepts

Absence of Capable Guardians
Absolute Deterrence
Acute Conformists
Anti-Rehabilitation Movement
Backlash Effect
Base Rate Fallacy
Blood Feuding
Bounded Rationality
Brutalization Effect
Certainty, Severity, and Celerity
Classical Criminology
Crime Displacement
Crime Triangle
Criminogenic
Deterrable
Deterrence Theory
Embarrassment
Enlightenment
Expressive Crimes
Free Will
General Deterrence
Hedonistic
Holy Inquisition
Incorrigible
Instrumental Crimes
Justice Model

London Metropolitan Police Act
Mala in Se
Mala Prohibita
Marginal (Restrictive) Deterrence
Minneapolis Domestic Violence Experiment
Motivated Offenders
Normative Validation
Objective Punishment Properties
Panopticon
Perceptions of Punishment
Positive Criminology
Preclassical Criminology
Quartering
Rational
Rational Choice
Routine Activities Theory
Shaming
Specific (Special) Deterrence
Suitable Targets
Target Hardening
Tiger Prevention Fallacy
Utilitarianism
Victimology
Visceral States
Warden's Survey

Key Criminologists

Cesare Beccaria
Jeremy Bentham
Lawrence Cohen
Marcus Felson
Robert Martinson
Raymond Paternoster

Sir Robert Peel
Alex Piquero
Greg Pogarsky
Sir Samuel Romilly
Charles Tittle

Case

Furman v. Georgia, 428 U.S. 238 (1972)

References

Amnesty International, "Facts and Figures on the Death Penalty," http://www.amnesty.org

Andenaes, J. (1968). "Does Punishment Deter Crime?" *Criminal Law Quarterly*, 11:76-93.

Andenaes, J. (1966). "The General Preventive Effects of Punishment." *University of Pennsylvania Law Review*, 114:949-983.

Andenaes, J. (1952). "General Prevention—Illusion or Reality?" *Journal of Criminal Law, Criminology, and Police Science*, 43:176-198.

Anderson, L.S., T.G. Chiricos & G.P. Waldo (1977). "Formal and Informal Sanctions: A Comparison of Deterrent Effects." *Social Problems*, 25:105-115.

Applegate, B.K., F.T. Cullen, B.G. Link, P.J. Richards & L. Lanza-Kaduce (1996). "Determinants of Public Punitiveness Toward Drunk Driving: A Factorial Survey Approach." *Justice Quarterly*, 13:57-79.

Bailey, W.C. (1998). "Deterrence, Brutalization and the Death Penalty: Another Examination of Oklahoma's Return to Capital Punishment." *Criminology*, 36:711-733.

Bailey, W.C. (1966). "Correctional Outcome: An Evaluation of 100 Reports." Journal of *Criminal Law, Criminology, and Police Science*, 57:153-160.

Bailey, W.C. & R.D Peterson (1999). "Capital Punishment, Homicide, and Deterrence: An Assessment of the Evidence." In M.D. Smith & M.A. Zahn (eds.) *Studying and Preventing Homicide*. Thousand Oaks, CA: Sage.

Barnes, H.E. & N.K. Teeters (1951). *New Horizons in Criminology*, Second Edition. New York, NY: Prentice-Hall.

Beccaria, C. (1764/1963). *On Crimes and Punishments*, trans. H. Paolucci. Indianapolis, IN: Bobbs-Merrill.

Becker, G. (1968). "Crime and Punishment: An Economic Approach." *Journal of Political Economy*, 76:493-517.

Bedau, H.A. (1997). *The Death Penalty in America: Current Controversies*. New York, NY: Oxford University Press.

Belknap, J. & K.D. McCall (1994). "Woman Battering and Police Referrals." *Journal of Criminal Justice*, 22:223-236.

Bentham, J. (1789/1973). *Political Thought*. New York, NY: Barnes and Noble.

Berk, R.A., A. Campbell, R. Klap & B. Western (1992). "A Bayesian Analysis of the Colorado Springs Spouse Abuse Experiment." *Journal of Criminal Law and Criminology*, 83:170-200.

Bernasco, W. & R. Block (2009). "Where Offenders Choose to Attack: A Discrete Choice Model of Robberies in Chicago." *Criminology*, 47: 93-130.

Bernburg, J.G. & T. Thorlindsson (2001). "Routine Activities in Social Context: A Closer look at the Role of Opportunity in Deviant Behavior." *Justice Quarterly*, 18:543-567.

Bien, D.D. (1960). *The Calais Affair*. Princeton, NJ: Princeton University Press.

Bishop, D.M. (1984). "Legal and Extralegal Barriers to Delinquency: A Panel Analysis." *Criminology*, 22:403-419.

Blackwell, B.S., H.G. Grasmick & J.K. Cochran (1994). "Racial Differences in Perceived Sanction Threat: Static and Dynamic Hypotheses." *Journal of Research in Crime and Delinquency,* 31:210-224.

Blumstein. A. (1998). "U.S. Criminal Justice Conundrum: Rising Prison Populations and Stable Crime Rates." *Crime & Delinquency*, 44:127-135.

Bouffard, J.A. (2002). "The Influence of Emotion on Rational Decision Making in Sexual Aggression." *Journal of Criminal Justice*, 30:121-134

Bowers, W.J. (1988). "The Effect of Executions is Brutalization, Not Deterrence." In K.C. Haas & J.A. Inciardi (eds.) *Capital Punishment: Legal and Social Science Approaches*. Newbury Park, CA: Sage Publications.

Braithwaite, J. (1989). *Crime, Shame and Reintegration*. Cambridge, UK: Cambridge University Press.

Brown, D.W. (1978). "Arrest Rates and Crime Rates: When Does a Tipping Effect Occur?" *Social Forces*, 57:671-681.

Brown, S.E. (1990). "Police Responses to Wife Beating: Five Years Later." *Journal of Criminal Justice*, 18:459-462.

Brown, S.E. (1984). "Police Responses to Wife Beating: Neglect of a Crime of Violence." *Journal of Criminal Justice*, 12:277-288.

Brown, S.E. (1981). "Deterrence and the Tipping Effect." *Southern Journal of Criminal Justice*, 6:7-15.

Butler, D. & A. Ray (2000). *The World's Dumbest Criminals*. Rutledge Hill Press.

Buzawa, E.S. & A.D. Buzawa (2008). "Courting Domestic Violence Victims: A Tale of Two Cities." *Criminology & Public Policy*, 7:671-685.

Byers, B.D. & B.W. Crider (2002). "Hate Crimes against the Amish: A Qualitative Analysis of Bias Motivation Using Routine Activities Theory." *Deviant Behavior*, 23:115-148.

Carmichael, S., L. Langton, G. Pendell, J.D. Reitzel & A.R. Piquero (2005). "Do the Experiential and Deterrent Effect Operate Differently Across Gender?".*Journal of Criminal Justice*, 33:267-276.

Chambliss, W.J. (1967). "Types of Deviance and the Effectiveness of Legal Sanctions." *Wisconsin Law Review*, 1967:703-719.

Chambliss, W.J. (1966). "The Deterrent Influence of Punishment." *Crime & Delinquency*, 12:70-75.

Chesney-Lind, M. (2002). "Criminalizing Victimization: The Unintended Consequences of Pro-arrest Policies for Girls and Women." *Criminology & Public Policy*, 1:81-90.

Cohen, A.K. & M. Felson (1979). "Social Change and Crime Rates: A Routine Activities Approach." *American Sociological Review*, 44:214-241.

Choi, A. & J.L Edelson (1995). "Advocating Legal Intervention in Wife Assaults: Results from a National Survey of Singapore." *Journal of International Violence*, 10:243-258.

Cochran, J.K. & M.B. Chamelin (2000). "Deterrence and Brutalization: The Dual Effects of Executions," *Justice Quarterly*, 17:685-706.

Cochran, J.K., M.B. Chamelin & S. Mark (1994). "Deterrence or Brutalization? An Impact Assessment of Oklahoma's return to Capital Punishment." *Criminology*, 32:107-134.

Cochran, J.K., M.B. Chamelin, P.B. Wood & C.S. Sellers (1999). "Shame, Embarrassment, and Formal Sanction Threats: Extending the Deterrence/Rational Choice Model to Academic Dishonesty." *Sociological Inquiry*, 69:91-105.

Copes, H. & L.M. Vieraitis (2009). "Bounded Rationality of Identity Thieves: Using Offender-Based Research to Inform Policy." *Criminology and Public Policy*, 8: 237-262.

Critchley, T.A. (1972). *A History of Police in England and Wales*. Montclair, NJ: Patterson Smith.

Dalla, R.L. (2002). "Night Moves: A Qualitative Investigation of Street-Level Sex Work." *Psychology of Women Quarterly*, 26(1):63-74.

Davis, R.C., C.S. O'Sullivan, D.J. Farole & M. Rempel (2008) "A Comparison of Two Prosecution Policies in Cases of Intimate Partner Violence: Mandatory Case Filing Versus Following the Victim's Lead." *Criminology & Public Policy*, :633-662.

de Haan, W. & J. Vos (2003). "A Crying Shame: The Over-Rationalized Conception of Man in The Rational Choice Perspective." *Theoretical Criminology*, 7:29-54.

Dixon, J. (2008). "Mandatory Domestic Violence Arrest and Prosecution Policies: Recidivism and Social Governance." *Criminology & Public Policy*, 7:663-670.

Dunford, F.W. (1992). "The Measurement of Recidivism in Cases of Spouse Assault." *Journal of Criminal Law and Criminology*, 83:120-136.

Ehrlich, I. (1975). "The Deterrent Effect of Capital Punishment: A Question of Life and Death." *American Economic Review*, 65:397-417.

Exum, M.L. (2002). "The Application and Robustness of the Rational Choice Perspective in the Study of Intoxicated and Angry Intentions to Aggress." *Criminology*, 40:933-966.

Felson, M. (2002). *Crime & Everyday Life*, Third Edition. Thousand Oaks, CA: Sage.

Felson, M. (1998). *Crime & Everyday Life*, Second Edition. Thousand Oaks, CA: Pine Forge Press.

Felson, M. (1994). *Crime and Everyday Life: Insights and Implications for Society*. Thousand Oaks, CA: Pine Forge Press.

Felson, R.B., J.M. Ackerman & C.A. Gallagher (2005). " Police Intervention and the Repeat of Domestic Assault." *Criminology* 43:563-584.

Felson, R.B., E.P. Baumer & S.F. Messner (2000). "Acquaintance Robbery." *Journal of Research in Crime & Delinquency*, 37:284-305.

Felson, R.B. & K.B. Burchfield (2004). "Alcohol and the Risk of Physical and Sexual Assault Victimization." *Criminology*, 42:837-859

Ferri, E. (1901/1968). "Three Lectures Given at the University of Naples, Italy—April 22, 23, and 24, 1901." In S. Grupp, *The Positive School of Criminology*. Pittsburgh, PA: University of Pittsburgh Press.

Finken, L.L., J.E. Jacobs & K.D. Laguna (1998). "Risky Drinking and Driving/Riding Decisions: The Role of Previous Experience." *Journal of Youth and Adolescence*, 27:493-512.

Fisher, B.S., J.J. Sloan, F.T. Cullen & L. Chunmeng (1998). "Crime in the Ivory Tower: The Level and Sources of Student Victimization." *Criminology*, 36:671-710.

Geerken, M. & W.R. Gove (1977). "Deterrence, Overload and Incapacitation: An Empirical Evaluation." *Social Forces*, 56:424-427.

Geis, G. & I. Bunn (1997). *A Trial of Witches: A Seventeenth-Century Witchcraft Prosecution*. London: Routledge.

Geis, G. & I. Bunn (1981). "Sir Thomas Browne and Witchcraft: A Cautionary Tale for Contemporary Law and Psychiatry." *International Journal of Law and Psychiatry*, 4:1-11.

Geis, G. (1972). "Jeremy Bentham." In H. Mannheim (ed.) *Pioneers in Criminology*. Montclair, NJ: Patterson Smith.

Gibbs, J.P. (1989). *Control: Sociology's Central Notion*. Champaign, IL: University of Illinois Press.

Gibbs, J.P. (1975). *Crime, Punishment, and Deterrence*. New York, NY: Elsevier.

Gibbs, J.P. (1968). "Crime, Punishment, and Deterrence." *Southwestern Social Science Quarterly*, 48:515-530.

Gibson, C.L., D. Khey & C.J. Schreck (2008). "Gender, Internal Controls, and Academic Dishonesty: Investigating Mediating and Differential Effects." *Journal of Criminal Justice Education*, 19: 2-18.

Grasmick, H.G., B.S. Blackwell & R.J. Bursik, Jr. (1993). "Changes in Sex Patterning of Perceived Threats of Sanctions." *Law and Society Review*, 27:679-705.

Grasmick, H.G. & R.J. Bursik, Jr. (1990). "Conscience, Significant Others, and Rational Choice: Extending the Deterrence Model." *Law and Society Review*, 24:837-861.

Grasmick, H.G. & E. Kobayashi (2002). "Workplace Deviance in Japan: Applying an Extended Model of Deterrence." *Deviant Behavior*, 23:21-43.

Gregory, L. (2002). *The Stupid Crook Book*. Andrews McMeel Publishing.

Griffiths, J. (1970). "The Limits of Criminal Law Scholarship." *Yale Law Journal*, 79:1388-1474.

Guerette, R.T., V.M.K. Stenius & J.M. McGloin (2004). "Understanding Offense Specialization and Versatility: A Reapplication of the Rational Choice Perspective." *Journal of Criminal Justice*, 33:77-87.

Gustavo, M.S. (2000). "Perception of Risk, Lifestyle Activities, and Fear of Crime." *Deviant Behavior*, 21:47-62.

Hay, C. (1998). "Parental Sanctions and Delinquent Behavior: Toward Clarification of Braithwaite's Theory of Reintegrative Shaming." *Theoretical Criminology*, 2:419-443.

Hagan, F. (1982). *Research Methods in Criminal Justice and Criminology*. New York, NY: Macmillan.

Hagan, J., J.H. Simpson & A.R. Gillis (1979). "The Sexual Stratification of Social Control." *British Journal of Sociology*, 30:25-38.

Heath, J. (1982). *Torture and English Law: An Administrative History*. Westport, CT: Greenwood.

Henson, V. & W.E. Stone (1999). "Campus Crime: A Victimization Study." *Journal of Criminal Justice*, 27:295-307.

Hilton, N.Z. (1993). "Police Intervention and Public Opinion." In N.Z. Hilton (ed.) *Legal Responses to Wife Assaults*, pp. 37-61. Newbury Park, CA: Sage Publications.

Hobbes, T. (1651/1962). *Leviathan*. London, UK: Collier-MacMillan.

Holland, J.J. (2000). "'Intimate Partner' Attacks on Decline." Associated Press, *Johnson City Press*, May 18

Hood, R.G. (1971). "Research on the Effectiveness of Punishments and Treatments." In L. Radzinowicz & M.E. Wolfgang (eds.) *Crimes and Justice*, Vol. 3. New York, NY: Basic Books.

Johnson, G. (2000). "Repeal: New Hampshire Votes to Abolish Death Penalty." Associated Press: *Johnson City Press*, May 19.

Johnson, H.A. (2003). *History of Criminal Justice*, Third Edition. Cincinnati, OH: Anderson Publishing Co.

Kassebaum, G., D.A. Ward & D.M. Wilner (1971). *Prison Treatment and Parole Survival: An Empirical Assessment*. New York, NY: John Wiley and Sons.

Kleck, G., B. Sever, S. Li & M. Gertz (2005). "The Missing Link in General Deterrence Research." *Criminology*, 43:623-659.

Kramer, H. & J. Sprenger (1486/1928). *Malleus Maleficarum*. London, UK: John Rodker.

Kruttschnitt, C. (2008). "Editorial Introduction: The Effect of 'No-Drop' Prosecution Policies on Perpetrators of Intimate Partner Violence." *Criminology & Public Policy*, 629-632.

Labriola, M., M. Rempel & R.C. Davis (2008). "Do Batterer Programs Reduce Recidivism? Results from a Randomized Trial in the Bronx." *Justice Quarterly*, 25:252-282.

Lacroix, P. (1963). *France in the Middle Ages*. New York, NY: Frederick Ungar.

LaFree, G., L. Dugan & R. Korte (2009). "The Impact of British Counterterrorist Strategies on Political Violence in Northern Ireland: Comparing Deterrence and Backlash Models." *Criminology*, 47:17-46.

Langbein, J. (1977). *Torture and the Law of Proof*. Chicago, IL: University of Chicago Press.

Lea, H.C. (1887/1955). *A History of the Inquisition of the Middle Ages*. New York, NY: Russell Sage Foundation.

Lea, H.C. (1866/1973). *Torture*. Philadelphia, PA: University of Pennsylvania Press.

Loewenstein, G., D. Nagin & R. Paternoster (1997). "The Effect of Sexual Arousal on Expectations of Sexual Forcefulness." *Journal of Research in Crime and Delinquency*, 34(4):443-473.

Lyman, J.L. (1964). "The Metropolitan Police Act of 1829." *Journal of Criminal Law, Criminology and Police Science*, 55:141-154.

Maestro, M. (1973). *Cesare Beccaria and the Origins of Penal Reform*. Philadelphia, PA: Temple University Press.

Martinson, R. (1974). "What Works?—Questions and Answers about Prison Reform." *Public Interest*, 35:22-54.

Matsueda, R.L., D. Huizinga & D.A. Kreager (2006). "Deterring Delinquents: A Rational Choice Model of Theft and Violence." *American Sociological Review*, 71:95-122

Maxwell, C.D., J.H. Garner & J.A. Fagan (2002). "The Preventive Effects of Arrest on Intimate Partner Violence: Research, Policy and Theory." *Criminology & Public Policy*, 1:51-80.

Meloy, M.L. (2005). "The Sex Offender Next Door: An Analysis of Recidivism, Risk Factors, and Deterrence of Sex Offenders on Probation." *Criminal Justice Policy Review*, 16:211-236.

Mendes, S.M. (2004). "Certainty, Severity, and Their Relative Deterrent Effects: Questioning the Implications of the Role of Risk in Criminal Deterrence Policy." *Tennessee Electronic Library*; 1-15.

Miller, J.L. & A.B. Anderson (1986). "Updating the Deterrence Doctrine." *Journal of Criminal Law and Criminology*, 77:418-438.

Monachesi, E. (1972). "Cesare Beccaria." In H. Mannheim (ed.) *Pioneers in Criminology*. Montclair, NJ: Patterson Smith.

Montesquieu, C.L. (1748/1900). *The Spirit of the Laws*. New York, NY: Appleton.

Morris, N. (1973). "Foreword." In M. Maestro, *Cesare Beccaria and The Origins of Penal Reform*. Philadelphia, PA: Temple University Press.

Mustaine, E. E. & R. Tewksbury (1999). "Assessing the Likelihood of Drunk Driving: Gender, Context and Lifestyle." *Journal of Crime and Justice*, 22:57-93.

Mustaine, E.E. & R. Tewksbury (1998). "Predicting Risks of Larceny Theft Victimization: A Routine Activity Analysis Using Refined Lifestyle Measures." *Criminology*, 36:829-858.

Nagin, D.S. & G. Pogarsky (2003). "An Experimental Investigation of Deterrence: Cheating, Self-Serving Bias, and Impulsivity." *Criminology*, 41:167-194.

Narayanan, G. (2005). " Theorizing Police Response to Domestic Violence in the Singaporean Context: Police Subculture Revisited." *Journal of Criminal Justice*, 33:429-439.

Newman, G. (1983). *Just and Painful. A Case for the Corporal Punishment of Criminals*. New York, NY: Macmillan Publishing Company.

Newman, G. (1978). *The Punishment Response*. Philadelphia, PA: J.B. Lippincott.

Paternoster, R. & L. Iovanni (1986). "The Deterrent Effect of Perceived Severity: A Reexamination." *Social Forces*, 64:751-777.

Paterson, E.J. (1979). "How the Legal System Responds to Battered Women." In *Battered Women*, D.M. Moore (ed.), pp. 79-99. Thousands Oaks, CA: Sage.

Phillipson, C. (1923/1970). *Three Criminal Law Reformers*. Montclair, NJ: Patterson Smith.

Piliavin, I., R. Gartner, C. Thornton & R.L. Matsueda (1986). "Crime, Deterrence, and Rational Choice." *American Sociological Review*, 51:101-119.

Piquero, A. & S.G. Tibbetts (1996). "Specifying the Direct and Indirect Effects of Low Self-Control and Situational Factors in Decision-Making: Toward a More Complete Model of Rational Offending." *Justice Quarterly*, 13:481-510.

Pogarsky, G. (2002). "Identifying 'Deterrable" Offenders: Implications for Research on Deterrence." *Justice Quarterly*, 431-452.

Pogarsky, G. & A.R. Piquero (2004). "Studying the Reach of Deterrence: Can Deterrence Theory Help Explain Police Misconduct?" *Journal of Criminal Justice*, 32:371-386.

Pratt, T. (2008) "Rational Choice Theory, Crime Control Policy, and Criminological Relevance." *Criminology & Public Policy*,7:42-52.

Radelet, M.L. & R.L. Akers (1996). "Deterrence and the Death Penalty: The View of the Experts." *Journal of Criminal Law & Criminology*, 87:1-16.

Reckless, W.C. (1967). *The Crime Problem*, Fourth Edition. New York, NY: Appleton-Century-Crofts.

Redmon, D. (2002). "Testing Informal Social Control Theory: Examining Lewd Behavior during Mardi Gras." *Deviant Behavior*, 23:363-384.

Reppetto, T.C. (1976). "Crime Prevention and the Displacement Phenomenon." *Crime & Delinquency*, 22:166-177.

Rousseau, J. (1762/1948). *The Social Contract*. London, UK: Oxford University Press.

Sasse, S. (2005). "'Motivation' and Routine Activities Theory." *Deviant Behavior*, 26:547-570.

Schafer, S. (1976). *Introduction to Criminology*. Reston, VA: Reston.

Scheff, T.J. (1988). "Shame and Conformity: The Deference-Emotion System." *American Sociological Review*, 53:395-406.

Scheider, M.C. (2001). "Deterrence and the Base Rate Fallacy: An Examination of Perceived Certainty." *Justice Quarterly*, 18:63-86.

Schwartz, M.D., W.S. DeKeseredy, D. Tait & S. Alvi (2001). "Male Peer Support and a Feminist Routine Activities Theory: Understanding Sexual Assault on the College Campus." *Justice Quarterly*, 18:623-649.

Scott, G.R. (1938/1959). *The History of Corporal Punishment*. London, UK: Torchstream.

Sellin, T. (1952). "Murder and the Death Penalty." *Annals of the American Academy of Political and Social Science*, 284:1-166.

Sherley, A.J. (2005). "Contextualizing the Sexual Assault Event: Images from Police Files." *Deviant Behavior*, 26:87-108.

Sherman, L.W. & R.A. Berk (1984). "The Specific Deterrent Effects of Arrest for Domestic Assault." *American Sociological Review*, 49:261-272.

Sherman, L.W., J.D. Schmidt, D.P. Rogan, D.A. Smith, P.R. Gartin, E.G. Cohn, D.J. Collins & A.R. Bacich (1992). "The Variable Effects of Arrest on Criminal Careers: The Milwaukee Domestic Violence Experiment." *Journal of Criminal Law and Criminology*, 83:170-200.

Silberman, M. (1976). "Toward a Theory of Criminal Deterrence." *American Sociological Review*, 41:442-461.

Spano, R., J.D. Freilich & J. Bolland (2008). "Gang Membership, Gun Carrying, and Employment: Applying Routine Activities Theory to Explain Violent Victimization Among Inner City, Minority Youth Living in Extreme Poverty." *Justice Quarterly*, 25:381-410.

Spohn, C. & D. Holleran (2002). "The Effect of Imprisonment on Recidivism Rates of Felony Offenders: A Focus on Drug Offenders." *Criminology*, 40:329-358.

Stack, S. (1998). "The Effect of Publicized Executions on Homicides in California." *Journal of Crime and Justice*, 21:1-16.

Stalans, L.J. (1996). "Family Harmony of Individual Protection? Public Recommendations About How Police Can Handle Domestic Violence Situations." *American Behavior Scientist*, 39:433-448.

Sugarman, D. & S. Boney-McCoy (2000). "Research Synthesis in Family Violence: The Art of Reviewing the Research." *Journal of Aggression, Maltreatment & Trauma*, 4:55-82.

Sutherland, E.H. (1925). "Murder and the Death Penalty." *Journal of Criminal Law and Criminology*, 15:522-529.

Tibbetts, S.G. & D.C. Herz (1996). "Gender Differences in Factors of Social Control and Rational Choice." *Deviant Behavior*, 17:183-208.

Tibbetts, S.G. & D.L. Myers (1999). "Low Self-Control, Rational Choice, and Student Test Cheating." *American Journal of Criminal Justice*, 23:179-200.

Tittle, C.R. (1980). *Sanctions and Social Deviance: The Question of Deterrence*. New York, NY: Praeger.

Tittle, C.R. (1969). "Crime Rates and Legal Sanctions." *Social Problems*, 16:408-423.

Tittle, C.R. & A.R. Rowe (1974). "Certainty of Arrest and Crime Rates: A Further Test of the Deterrence Hypothesis." *Social Forces*, 52:455-462.

Tittle, C.R. & A.R. Rowe (1973). "Moral Appeal, Sanction Threat, and Deviance: An Experimental Test." *Social Problems*, 20:488-498.

Tunnell, K.D. (1992). *Choosing Crime: The Criminal Calculus of Property Offenders*. Chicago, IL: Nelson-Hall.

Vollmer, A. (1936). *The Police and Modern Society*. College Park, MD: McGrath.

Walker, L. (1979). *The Battered Woman*. New York, NY: Harper and Row.

Wilkins, L.T. (1969). *Evaluation of Penal Measures*. New York, NY: Random House.

Williams, F.P., III (1985). "Deterrence and Social Control: Rethinking the Relationship." *Journal of Criminal Justice*, 13:141-151.

Wilson, O.W. & R.C. McLaren (1972). *Police Administration*, Third Edition. New York, NY: McGraw-Hill.

Wright, B.R.E., A. Caspi, T.E. Moffitt & R. Paternoster (2004). "Does the Perceived Risk of Punishment Deter Criminally Prone Individuals? Rational Choice, Self-Control, and Crime." *Journal of Research in Crime and Delinquency*, 41:180-213.

Zimring, F.E. & G.J. Hawkins (1973). *Deterrence: The Legal Threat in Crime Control*. Chicago, IL: University of Chicago Press.

6
Individual Theories
of Crime: Biological and
Psychological Perspectives

The previous chapter examined the emergence of criminology with the classical school, heavily identified with the Italian reformer, Cesare Beccaria. This school of thought emerged in the context of the Western world's revolution against the dominance of royalty and the church with burgeoning Enlightenment thought. As the first natural explanation of crime, it represented what Thomas Kuhn (1970) called a *paradigm revolution*. This is a dramatic shift in the theoretical orientation, and especially the underlying assumptions, for explaining a phenomenon. This rational choice or free will outlook dominated criminological thought for about a century before another paradigm revolution occurred. This chapter begins with a review of the social context that set the stage for a paradigm shift into *positivism*.

It was dramatic scientific developments in the late nineteenth century that provided fertile ground for the emergence of positive criminology. Charles Darwin's *On the Origin of Species* (1859) and *The Descent of Man* (1871) set the intellectual tone. The Darwinian context cannot be overstated. There was optimism that science could provide the answers to many questions and solutions to diverse human problems. Darwin's works were widely read and very influential examples of this emerging scientism. Thus it is not surprising that criminologists turned to science or that the earliest positivists emulated Darwin's theories. Cesare Lombroso is typically recognized as the father of modern or positivistic criminology and one of the key ideas in his earlier works was that of *atavism*, a view of criminals as a throwback to an earlier and more primitive evolutionary stage. In seeking to explain crime in terms of biological evolution Lombroso was clearly following in the footsteps of the giant figure that Darwin represented in scientific study.

The shift to positivism as a new paradigm for understanding crime is of far greater importance than any specific theories within that framework. Initially, positivism embraced biological variables, attempting to explain crime in terms of biological makeup predisposing some people to commit crime. It later incorporated psychological variables, and as Chapters 7 and 8 reveal, ultimately came to be dominated by social factors for most of the twentieth century. Thus positivism takes many different forms, and oftentimes positivists with different disciplinary identities will disagree sharply over what variables might explain crime. Generally, we can divide positivist thinking into biological, psychological and sociological camps. Recognizing that the theories falling into the positive criminological paradigm are so diverse, it is important to understand what they have in common.

The common ground of all positivistic theories can be seen more clearly by focusing on two aspects of the concept: *empiricism* and *determinism*. First, positivism presumes that knowledge can be discovered only by means of observation and experience. It insists that criminologists employ the scientific method to seek answers to their questions. Thus positivism is rooted in the collection of empirical data, thereby shifting the focus from crime to criminals. Classical criminologists, by contrast, were philosophers. They only had to engage in armchair theorizing about crime because they assumed there were no individual differences between criminals and noncriminals in need of explanation. Differences in the criminal justice system were what were thought to matter. This leads to the second element within positivism. It assumes that individual differences are rooted in factors beyond, or at least not entirely within, the control of individuals. Thus the offender's behavior is "determined" by something other than her or his free-willed choice. In other words, there are forces that shape people and their behavior. As positivism came to life in criminology, the view was that offenders were products of biological deficiencies.

Every theory offers a prescription for dealing with crime. Positivism and rational choice are characterized not only by antithetical assumptions, but also by diverse policy implications. Given the positivists' dismissal of free will, punishing criminal behavior becomes both morally objectionable and unfruitful. Positivism instead, calls for the medicalization of criminality. Following this *medical model*, the causes of crime are sought, and once identified, a cure is within reach. As with disease, it is assumed that discovery of cause is the first step toward cure. Thus, while deterrence theorists advocate the fashioning of punishments to fit the crime, positivists favor the tailoring of treatments to fit the criminal.

Positivism dominated American criminology for most of the twentieth century and provided the rationale for many policy developments. It had wide effects on the practice of penology, even leading to the adoption of the more contemporary "corrections" title that is consistent with criminological applications within the medical model framework. It gave rise to the *indeterminate* (open-ended) *sentence* which calls for release of the offender once deemed cured or rehabilitated. *Community corrections*, including the practices of probation and parole, are also part and parcel of positivism. Prediction tables used by parole boards are an empirical tool for helping to determine when an offender is likely rehabilitated, meriting release. Moreover, the wide ranges of treatments that have been tried in correctional settings are rooted in positivistic theories of crime.

Positivism obviously can be used to justify greater intervention in the lives of offenders than is the case with rational choice theories because the express goal of

FIGURE 6.1
Comparison of Positive and Rational Choice Paradigms

Positive	Rational Choice
focuses on criminals	focuses on crime
assumes individual differences	assumes no individual differences
assumes deterministic forces	assumes free will
rooted in biology, psychology, or sociology	rooted in philosophy, especially utilitarianism
applicable at individual level to address differences rooted in biology, psychology, or social environment	applicable at group-level only (no individual differences)
calls for medical model applications (treatment) to individuals	calls for criminal justice system applications (punishment) to individuals

the positive doctrine is to help, not punish, the individual. This is a concern regarding contemporary positivism, given some lessons of history. It raises moral and political questions regarding the limits of intervention in the name of rehabilitation. The question is, even given the knowledge that a strategy is effective, what is morally permissible? Group counseling? Psychotherapy? Administration of drugs or hormones? Dietary controls? Monitoring of associations with other persons? Lobotomies? Sterilization? As Stanley Grupp (1968:8) noted more than three decades ago, "the problems posed by the potential tyranny of the expert remain as ominous today as ever." Many criminologists continue to echo this caution. Figure 6.1 highlights some of the differences between positivism and classical rational choice thinking.

Reviewing the history of rational choice thinking, we saw that deterrence, the foremost theory derived from the paradigm, emerged in the late eighteenth century. It was then largely supplanted by positivism about 100 years later, only to reemerge in the last three decades of the twentieth century, and continues to thrive today. A similar fate befell biological, and to a large degree psychological, positivism. Biologically based criminology emerged as the foremost perspective for conceptualizing crime with the publication of Cesare Lombroso's *The Criminal Man* in 1876. Although this work was not translated to English until 1911 (Lombroso-Ferrero), and then not fully, the influence of Lombroso was quickly felt throughout the Western world, including the United States (Rafter, 1992). He ushered in positivistic thinking under the umbrella of *criminal anthropology*, which he defined as the study of the "organic and psychic constitution" of abnormal (criminal) persons (Lombroso-Ferrero, 1911/1972:5). Biological criminology began to loose ground in the eyes of U.S. criminologists, however, in the 1920s and 1930s. The death knell of the perspective was rung by two factors. First, the close association of biological explanations of human behavior, including crime, with the Nazi and Fascist movements led to their being inextricably tied to racist ideology. The fact that extreme biological positivism was advocated by Hitler and

Mussolini and used as the basis for genocidal policies established a political climate that rejected and remained unreceptive to biological variables and crime for decades. This is a debate that, as will be seen, persists yet today. Secondly, any study of the history of the discipline of criminology must acknowledge the crucial role played by Edwin Sutherland in shaping the field. He was a sociologist who sought to elevate criminology to a respectable status within that discipline and to disassociate it from biology, psychology, and other disciplines. He was very successful on both counts, steering mainstream criminology down a sociological path from the 1940s through the remainder of the twentieth century. As a result of these two factors, it has been noted that, "By mid-century, biological explanations for crime were pass8E, disreputable, and perhaps even taboo. They were unthinkable and even unmentionable." (Wright & Miller, 1998). Sociological variables still dominate criminology, but it has increasingly become interdisciplinary in recent years.

The early history of biological positivism is reviewed before turning to contemporary biological theories of crime. That early story begins with a more detailed look at the life and works of Cesare Lombroso, credited with founding criminological positivism.

Cesare Lombroso (1835-1909)

CORBIS-BETTMAN

Cesare Lombroso

Cesare Lombroso was born in Verona, Italy, one of the few cities of the era that allowed a Jewish boy to attend high school. He went on to obtain a medical degree from the University of Pavia in 1858. The early part of his career was spent as an army physician, followed by work in several hospitals for the insane. From 1876 until his death he was a professor at the University of Turin. He led a peaceful life as a productive scholar, with the devoted following of two daughters (Gina and Paola), a son-in-law (William Ferrero) and many students.

It is important to reemphasize that Lombroso's development of biological positivism was, as we see with most theorists and theories, a logical extension of the intellectual thought of his time. Not only did he follow Darwin's model, but also built upon the earlier work of others who had addressed crime within a biological framework. Franz Joseph Gall (1758-1828), for example, preceded Lombroso in popularizing phrenology, which associated criminality with abnormalities in the brain that they believed could be identified externally, earning them the nickname of "skull-feelers."

Lombroso's daughter, Gina, noted after his death a turning point in his career. While performing an autopsy on a violent criminal, Lombroso observed an unusual cranial depression, similar to that found in rodents, birds, and lower types of apes. His daughter later would describe the impact of this discovery on her father:

> 'At the sight of the skull,' says my father, 'I seemed to see all at once, standing out clearly illumed as in a vast plain under a flaming sky, the problems of the nature of the criminal, who reproduces in civilized times characteristics, not only of primitive savages, but of still lower types as far back as the carnivora' (Lombroso-Ferrero, 1911/1972:6-7).

This discovery laid the foundation for Lombroso's subsequent theoretical work. Adopting a social Darwinian perspective, he maintained that humans demonstrate different levels of biological development. Certain characteristics, such as the cranial depression he had found, marked for Lombroso an atavistic person, that is, a person possessing qualities of more primitive ancestors. Lombroso classified such biological throwbacks as a *born criminal*, and in his earliest work, he insisted that all criminals were atavistic. By the time of his death, though, he had backed away, saying that born criminals accounted for about one-third of the law-breaking population. The other two-thirds were *criminaloids*, or minor offenders.

The following list offers a brief sample of the wide range of characteristics set forth by Lombroso to identify atavistic criminals:

- The criminal skull tends to be larger or smaller than the average skull common to the region or country from which the criminal hails;

- Prominent frontal sinuses and excessive development of the femoral muscles, a characteristic common for primates and carnivores;

- Excessively large jaws and cheekbones;

- An asymmetrical physiognomy in which eyes and ears are frequently situated at different levels, or are of unequal size.

- Shifty eyes or hard expression in eyes;

- Unusually large or small ears, or ears standing out from the face as in chimpanzees;

- A flattened nose is common among thieves while murderers showed an aquiline nose, like the beak of a bird of prey; and

- Rapists and murderers are likely to have fleshy, swollen, and protruding lips. Swindlers have thin, straight lips (Excerpted from Lombroso-Ferrero, 1911/1972:24).

In one study, Lombroso compared two groups of criminals to presumptively noncriminal Italian soldiers. He reported that only 11 percent of the soldiers had three or more of the anomalies indicative of biological inferiority, while 35 and 40 percent of the criminal groups had three or more such defects (see Figure 6.2).

FIGURE 6.2
Percentage Distribution of Skull Anomalies Found by Lombroso

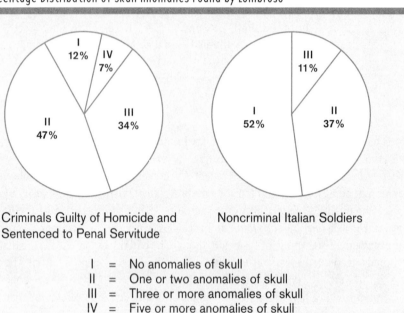

Criminals Guilty of Homicide and   Noncriminal Italian Soldiers
Sentenced to Penal Servitude

I   =   No anomalies of skull
II =   One or two anomalies of skull
III =   Three or more anomalies of skull
IV =   Five or more anomalies of skull

Charles Thomas and John Hepburn (1983:146) argue that history has been far too generous with Lombroso, that he "had the effect of blocking our progress for more than a quarter of a century." Although sociological positivism ultimately supplanted the biological (and psychological) versions, a *Statistical School* preceded Lombroso with initiation of the scientific study of crime by nearly a half a century. A.M. Guerry (1802-1866), a French social statistician, was the first to analyze ecological (geographic-based) data in a search for relationships between crime and social characteristics. The best known representative of this school was Adolphe Quetelet (1796-1874), a Belgian who is revered as the "father of modern statistics." Quetelet refuted the notion of free will and sought explanations of crime, or what he called propensities for crime, through analysis of social data (Quetelet, 1833/1984). A third major figure in this largely unheralded school was Henry Mayhew (1812-1887), an Englishman who took essentially a sociological approach in analyzing both official data and detailed observations. It is one of the ironies of history that individual-based positivism, led by a Lombrosian biological perspective and later psychological factors, won out over the socially oriented statistical school that closely paralleled mainstream twentieth century criminology.

Lombroso and The Female Offender

Unlike the relatively rapid development in this period of theories to explain the behavior of male offenders, there were few facts and ideas about female offenders.

Lombroso, however, with his son-in-law, William Ferrero, in 1895, became a pioneer in the study of crime by women when he published *The Female Offender*, employing the same analytical framework used in his earlier work.

The authors measured various body parts and noted physical irregularities in women in prison and before the courts. They associated female offending with features such as occipital irregularities, narrow foreheads, prominent cheekbones, and a "virile" form of face.

Lombroso and Ferrero reported fewer degenerative physical characteristics among female offenders than they had found among men. Prostitutes were said to have more atavistic qualities than other female offenders, because they mostly offended against what Lombroso believed to be "female decency." The "evil tendencies" of women offenders were said to be more numerous and varied than those of men (1895:151). Their "maternal instincts" and "ladylike" qualities were said to be suppressed and they were depicted as more merciless in their violent offenses than their male counterparts. Female criminals were believed by Lombroso and Ferrero to be overgrown children with no moral sense.

The study by Lombroso and Ferrero of female offenders has deservedly received harsh criticism, and both their methods and theoretical assumptions have been attacked. Among other things, they generalized from small numbers of offenders and control groups. They failed to consider more plausible explanations for the alleged findings on body build and criminal behavior. A deformed physique, for instance, can make it difficult to obtain a job and to form satisfactory personal relationships which, in turn, can encourage crime. They also confused biological and environmental factors, grouping under biology such matters as tattooing, drinking, and overeating. In addition, their assumptions regarding women had no scientific basis. That the female offender was declared to be more ruthless and merciless than the male had much more to do with the fact that she had deviated from her stereotypical sex-role identity than with her actual behavior. The observation of Paul Topinard, a French contemporary of Lombroso, that pictures of Lombroso's supposedly atavistic criminals looked much like those of his own academic friends succinctly pinpointed the inadequacy of Lombroso's work (cited in Tarde, 1912:270).

Enrico Ferri (1856-1928)

Enrico Ferri was born the son of a poor Italian shopkeeper and was a politically active member of the Socialist party for most of his life. A pivotal point in his career came when he sent Lombroso a copy of his dissertation, which critiqued the classical school and its assumption of free will. Lombroso's response, Ferri reminisced years later, had been complimentary, but qualified; Lombroso insisted that "Ferri isn't positivist enough!" Ferri, upon being informed by a friend of this, retorted, "What! Does Lombroso suggest that I, a lawyer, should go and measure the heads of criminals in order to be positivist enough!?" (Cited in Sellin, 1968:17-18). The two men soon became close colleagues, and Ferri ultimately incorporated anthropometric methods into his positive approach to criminology.

Under Ferri's influence, positivism developed into a multiple factor approach, seeking many different causes for a single criminal act, an approach that had an immense impact on American criminology (Grupp, 1968). Ferri also argued, in opposition to the classical tradition, that different punishments should be accorded criminals committing similar crimes, with the penalty to be tailored to the background and traits of the offenders as these are seen to predict future acts.

Ferri's study of crime in France and Italy showed that, with the exception of infanticide (the killing of an infant) and patricide (the murder of one's own father), crimes against the person occur with greatest frequency during the summer months. He attributed the higher summer rate chiefly to three circumstances: (1) the physiological effects of heat, which leave a large surplus of energy; (2) the better nourishment of the population in the summer; and (3) an enhanced irritability due to oppressive temperatures and humidity (Ferri, 1917). Ferri (1917:54) also joined with Lombroso and his fellow positivists in challenging the free will assumption that largely underlay the work of the classical theorists:

> How can you still believe in the existence of a free will, when modern psychology, armed with all the instruments of positive modern research denies that there is any free will and demonstrates that every act of a human being is the result of an interaction between the personality and the environment of man? . . . The positive school of criminology maintains . . . that it is not the criminal who wills: in order to be a criminal it is rather necessary that the individual should find himself permanently or transitorily in such personal, physical, and moral conditions, and live in such an environment, which become for him a chain of cause and effect, externally and internally, that disposes him toward crime.

Although Ferri succeeded in chronicling the strength of the positive approach to criminology, his career, ironically exemplified what became the downfall of biological positivism. Ferri displayed a naive faith in the promise of scientism to address crime, failing to question whether scientists and politicians might abuse such power. Ferri ended his career as a Fascist, declaring that "the Fascist government . . . has accepted and is putting into effect some of the principles and the most characteristic practical proposals of the positive school" (cited in Sellin, 1968:32).

Raffaele Garofalo (1852-1924)

Raffaele Garofalo rounded out the trio of pioneering Italian criminological positivists. Garofalo rejected the legal definition of crime for a sociological approach. He thought offenders against the person lacked the natural moral sentiment of "pity," while property offenders were deficient in "probity" (honesty), a conclusion easy enough to reach after the crime has occurred, but singularly difficult to demonstrate in regard to particular individuals prior to the offense. Garofalo believed in ridding society of criminal offenders (those "inassimilable to the particular conditions of the environment") and thereby helping along the Darwinian thesis of selection of the fittest (Allen, 1960:329). The peril of such extreme views is reflected in the fact that Garofalo, like Ferri, became an activists in the Italian Fascist movement under Benito Mussolini. He viewed it as legitimate for the state to intervene in the natural evolutionary process, as depicted by Darwin, and to execute, imprison or transport inferior criminally inclined persons.

Charles Goring (1870-1919)

Though it also highlighted biological determinism, Charles Goring's *The English Convict* (1913), the result of 13 years of work, undermined Lombroso's ideas about "born criminals." Goring criticized Lombroso for relying on observations rather than instruments for measurement, and he provided quotations from Lombroso's work to demonstrate its recourse to nonscientific language. One such observation was a story of a woman accused of poisoning her victims with arsenic. "The bust which we possess of this criminal," Lombroso had written, "so full of virile angularity, and above all, so deeply wrinkled, with its Satanic leer, suffices of itself to prove that the woman in question was born to do evil, and that, if on one occasion to commit it had failed, she would have found others" (Goring, 1913:15). Such Lombrosian hyperbole led Goring to conclude that "as a result of this attitude of mind, of its haphazard method of investigation, of its desire to adjust fact to theory, rather than to formulate a theory by observation of fact—as a result of all this, we have . . . an organized system of self-evident confusion whose parallel is only to be found in the astrology, alchemy, and other credulities of the Middle Ages" (Goring, 1913:15).

For his part, Goring, a medical officer in the English prisons, collaborated with the famous statistician Karl Pearson to study 3,000 recidivist convicts and a large number of noncriminals. Goring summarized his work in the following terms:

> The preliminary conclusion reached by our inquiry is that [the] anthropological monster has no existence in fact. The physical and mental constitution of both criminal and law-abiding persons, of the same age, stature, class, and intelligence, are identical. There is no such thing as an anthropological criminal type (Goring, 1913:370).

Nonetheless, Goring found support for the position that persons of different constitutional types were likely to commit certain kinds of crimes, and in this regard, as Piers Beirne (1993:8) writes: "The English Convict advanced an ambiguous argument about Homo criminals not in opposition to Lombrosianism but in parallel to it." Goring claimed, for instance, that offenders convicted of crimes of violence were characterized by strength and "constitutional soundness" considerably above the average of that of other criminals, and that burglars, thieves, and arsonists "as well as being inferior in stature and weight, are also relative to other criminals and the population at large, puny in their general bodily habit" (Goring, 1913:200). Goring also found that convicts were one to two inches shorter than noncriminals and weighed three to seven pounds less. He thought these results were a general indication of hereditary inferiority. Scholars today would want to know, among other things, whether the relative shortness and lesser weights were the result of poor nutrition, itself associated with class position. They would challenge the idea that the results indicate hereditary inadequacy and would point out that innumerable short people and those who weigh less than the average person never commit crimes.

Earnest A. Hooton (1887-1954)

The next major entrant into the debate regarding physiological causation in crime was Earnest A. Hooton, a Rhodes Scholar and Harvard University physical anthropologist, who published *The American Criminal: An Anthropological Study* (1939a) and *Crime and the Man* (1939b). Hooton was a renowned, but very controversial figure, even in his own time. He was convinced that crime could only be understood through biology and therefore was adamantly opposed to social and cultural anthropology and to the emergence of sociology as the leading criminological framework. He summarized his view of the criminal offender in the following way:

> Criminals are organically inferior. Crime is the resultant of the impact of environment upon low grade human organisms. It follows that the elimination of crime can be effected only by the extirpation of the physically, mentally, and morally unfit, or by their complete segregation in a socially aseptic environment (Hooton, 1939a/1969:309).

Such words, suggesting the killing off of those alleged to be unfit on the highly arguable ground that they would inevitably commit criminal acts, would echo ominously when soon afterwards a similar reasoning provided the rationale for the genocidal tactics of the Nazi regime in Germany (Kuhl, 1994).

Hooton arrived at his conclusions from a massive study of more than 17,000 persons, including 14,000 prisoners. He offered innumerable distinctions between those caught for committing crime and his control group, a listing quite reminiscent of Lombroso's atavists. There were, however, very serious methodological flaws in Hooton's work. As did Lombroso, he confused inherited traits with conditions that are the result of environmental influences, such as tattooing. Besides, the group to which he compared the prisoners was a haphazard collection of firefighters, sunbathers, and hospital outpatients. In addition, it is illogical to maintain that because certain traits are observed in a studied population these traits are the cause of their behavior.

Nicole Rafter's review of Hooton's career depicts him as "an offbeat eugenicist." While eugenics was at the heart of his view, leading him to favor birth control, sterilization and even euthanasia, he distanced himself from racism, taking the position that crime was committed by "morons and other degenerates who could be found in every race (Rafter, 2004:757). It was striking that, though a staunch eugenicist, he not only decried Nazi's as "vicious subhumans," but served on the editorial board of the National Association for the Advancement of Colored People. Perhaps Hooton's most lasting contribution was to keep the pulse of biological criminology beating, however slightly, through the middle portion of the last century. This was accomplished primarily through his influence on other criminologists, particularly Sheldon and Eleanor Glueck and William Sheldon, all on the Harvard faculty as well.

William Sheldon (1898-1977)

Constitutional Psychology was the name attached to the biological approach developed by William Sheldon in *Varieties of Delinquent Youth* (1949), a study of 200 young men referred to a Boston rehabilitation facility. Sheldon (1949:5) argued that the body is really "an objectification, a tangible record, of the most long-standing and most deeply established habits that have been laid down during a long succession of generations."

Sheldon built upon the work of Ernst Kretschmer (1925), who believed that there were three distinctive bodily forms—*somatotypes*—and that persons with particular types were likely to behave in particular ways. The types were labeled *endomorph* (soft and round), *mesomorph* (muscular), and *ectomorph* (lean). Specific temperaments were said to be associated with each body type: endomorphy, for instance, "is manifested by relaxation, conviviality, and gluttony for food, for company and for affection and social support" (Sheldon, 1949:25).

Sheldon found delinquents to be decidedly high in mesomorphy and low in ectomorphy. His sample was too small to be used to relate body types to specific offenses, but

---

FIGURE 6.3
Somatotypes

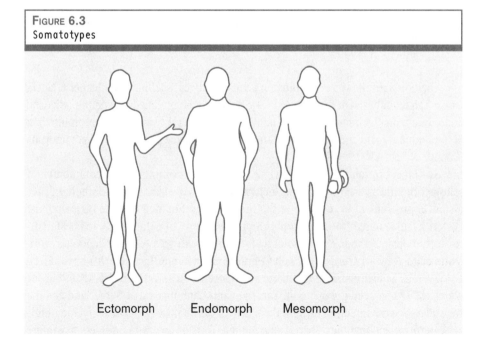

Ectomorph   Endomorph   Mesomorph

HIGHLIGHT 6.1
Nude Posture Studies of Students Create Stir

All college freshmen from several Ivy League and other prestigious schools were required to pose nude for photos, from the 1940s through the 1960s. They were taken by William H. Sheldon, who believed there was a relationship between body shape and intelligence and other traits. Sheldon's work has since been dismissed by most scientists as quackery.

Much of Sheldon's work has been destroyed by participating schools, but it was recently revealed that the Smithsonian Institution retains a collection of nude photos, including pictures of Hillary Rodham Clinton, George H.W. Bush, and Diane Sawyer. A spokesperson for the Smithsonian indicated that they are now sealed, but previously were made available to students and researchers. At issue now is whether they should be destroyed or retained for their historical value. The stir was created when alumni of schools such as Yale and Mount Holyoke read a report in the *New York Times Magazine* about the collection. They then began calling their alma maters, some distraught and others mildly amused, to find out what would become of the photos.

Source: Adapted from AP report by B. Greenberg in the *Johnson City Press*, January 21, 1995.

Sheldon argued in colorful language that he had substantiated Hooton and further demonstrated the significance of criminal anthropology for understanding lawbreaking:

> Hooton is one of a small group of contemporaries who have resolutely persisted in the retention of common sense in the formula for academic science. He considers it a datum of common sense that there are structurally superior and inferior organisms, and that a relationship must exist between structural and behavioral inferiority (Sheldon, 1949:752).

Sheldon's results were supported in a 1950 study by Sheldon and Eleanor Glueck, a research team based at the Harvard Law School, who matched 500 delinquents and nondelinquents. Delinquents were found to be considerably more mesomorphic than nondelinquents and their ranks contained a much lower proportion of ectomorphs (Glueck & Glueck, 1950:196).

Scathing critiques from within the mainstream criminological community of scholars met the work of William Sheldon and the Gluecks. Edwin Sutherland, for instance, preeminent in the field at the time, faulted Sheldon on nine major points. His criticisms ranged from Sheldon's sloppy definition of delinquency to his statistical techniques. Orthodox criminological thought continues to give Sheldon's work low marks. Recently, however, Robert Sampson and John Laub (1990) have raised a revisionist voice, insisting that there was more to these early efforts than that for which they have been given credit. Sampson and Laub insist that Sutherland and the sociologists were intent on turning the study of crime into an exclusively sociological enterprise and that they overreacted to the efforts of potential intruders to capture some of what they regarded as their intellectual turf.

Criminal Heredity: The Bad Seed Theory

Efforts have been made to link genetic traits to criminal behavior by studying families in which criminal activity was widespread through generations, an approach called *eugenics* in its early days of popularity. In the closing decades of the nineteenth century and opening decades of the last century, there was a strong premise that nature played a stronger role than did nurture. Thus observation of widespread deviant behavior within a family was viewed as explicable by genetics, with little thought given to environmental influences or the need to control for other factors that might cause both deviance and particular biological characteristics. No one stopped to think, for example, that both stunted growth and deviance could be products of social disadvantage. It was concluded by many biological theorists that differences in the physiques of offenders must be the cause of observed patterns of deviance.

One of the early classics in the study of "degenerate" families is Henry Goddard's *The Kallikak Family* (1912/1955). Goddard traced two lineages of Martin Kallikak (a fictitious name), a member of an upstanding family. While a militiaman during the American Revolution, Kallikak met a *feeble-minded* (then the label for a person functioning below the normal intellectual range, but above the level designated "idiot") girl by whom he became the father of a feebleminded son. This child was given the name of the father in full, and "thus has been handed down to posterity the father's name and the mother's mental capacity" (Goddard, 1912/1955:18). Of the 480 descendants that Goddard could trace from the union, 36 were illegitimate, 33 prostitutes, 24 alcoholics, 3 epileptics, 82 died in infancy, 3 were criminals, and 8 kept houses of prostitution. The 496 descendants from Martin's marriage to a "respectable" woman of "good family" all were described as "normal" except for two alcoholics and one person said to be sexually promiscuous.

The difficulty with this study, of course, is that it proclaims the significance of heredity as the cause of the problems, but is quite unable to separate nature from nurture. Goddard attended to this problem but never appreciated how his words undercut his own argument. He observed that the feebleminded offspring "married into families, generally of about the same type" while "all of the legitimate children of Martin, Sr., married into the best families in their state, the descendants of colonial governments, signers of the Declaration of Independence, soldiers, and even founders of a great university" (Goddard, 1912/1955:19-30). That Goddard had demonstrated that good genes and good homes are likely to produce law-abiding citizens and that the reverse is also true is beyond question. But he was far from documenting satisfactorily that genetic make-up predestines any person to any particular fate, absent a host of other circumstances.

Another widely cited early study of family history is Richard Dugdale's *The Jukes: A Study in Crime, Pauperism, Disease and Heredity* (1877). Dugdale began his work with Ada Jukes (fictitious name) and located more than 1,000 of her descendants, including 140 criminals, 280 paupers, 40 persons with venereal disease and assorted other deviants. In short, the name of the Jukes, like the Kallikaks, has lived in infamy for generations. In 1911 Dugdale's research was revised and expanded by a eugenicist, Arthur H. Estabrook, whose work was published in *The Jukes in 1915*. Highlight 6.2

HIGHLIGHT 6.2
Bad Seed or Bad Science: Reflecting on the Jukes Family as Victims of Ideological Bias

The Jukes family has stood in social science history for more than one century as the epitome of a genetically flawed family, teeming with crime, mental illness, poverty, and a host of other social defects. They were used to provide the academic evidence of the power of genetics in transmitting such defective character, leading eugenisists' calls for sterilization, lobotomies, isolation, and even extermination.

The recent finding of archives from the original studies of the fictitiously named Jukes, undertaken first by Richard Dugdale and updated by Arthur Estabrook, cast a dark cloud over the Jukes research. The work appears to have been ideologically driven to bolster the views of the eugenics movement that was a craze in the early 1900s. Dugdale's work was often misrepresented as purely supporting a biological explanation of the Juke's deviance, while Estabrook has been accused of knowingly misrepresenting the data. He did not, for example, point out that some of the lineage became lawyers, real estate brokers, and fulfilled other respectable roles. He also withheld the information that Ada Juke's husband was a descendant of a governor. Estabrook did reveal that the Jukes were not comprised of a single family, but rather were a composite of several families, including such surnames as Miller, Bank, and Bush.

Source: Adapted from S. Christianson (2003). *The New York Times*, February 8. Books and Arts Section.

points to the ideological bias that played a part in driving the family studies approach and the inhumane policies for which they ultimately provided support.

Family pedigree studies such as those of the Jukes and the Kallikaks fueled the eugenics movement that blossomed in the late nineteenth and early twentieth centuries. These ideas informed government policy for contending with crime, mental health, and other social ills. The U.S. Supreme Court case of *Buck v. Bell, Superintendent* (1927) exemplifies the impact of the eugenics movement on law. In an opinion delivered by the renowned and progressive Justice Oliver Wendell Holmes, Jr., the court ruled that the State of Virginia had the authority to administer involuntary surgical sterilization on "feebleminded" and other "unfit" persons if the superintendent of a state institution deemed it in the best interest of society. The subject of the appeal before the court was Carrie Buck, a young woman who was the offspring of a feebleminded woman and who had already given birth to a feebleminded illegitimate child. In Justice Holmes' words, "It is better for all the world, if instead of waiting to execute degenerate offspring for crime, or to let them starve for their imbecility, society can prevent those who are manifestly unfit from continuing their kind . . . Three generations of imbeciles are enough" (*Buck v. Bell*, 1927). The law permitting involuntary sterilization of humans continued in Virginia until 1974.

As the twentieth century unfolded, criminologists became increasingly uncomfortable with biological explanations of crime. By mid-century, biological accounts were in disrepute and a sociological approach came into dominance. The rejection of genetics and other biological factors in explaining crime was more a reflection of ideology than science. The abuse of human rights, supported on the grounds of eugenic interpretations of social problems, reached a dreadful height with the rise of the Nazi and Fascist parties in Europe and eruption of World War II. Because biological theorizing was used as an intellectual justification for denying human rights and even for seeking extermination of peoples, the perspective was spurned by most in the criminological community. The overwhelming rejection of a biological criminological perspective was not the result of cumulative scientific research, but primarily an ideological response to horrific abuses of science. An unfortunate consequence was the stymieing of progress in objective understanding of the role that biological factors play in the generation of crime and deviance.

Contemporary Biological Perspectives

Criminology, many believe, is once again in the midst of a dramatic shift insofar as the role it extends to biology in understanding crime. As Nicole Rafter (2004:736) recently concluded, "today biological explanations are again gaining credibility and are joining forces with sociological explanations in ways that may soon make them equal partners." A recent review of "the genetic turn in sociology," published in the widely circulated Chronicle of Higher Education (Shea, 2009), painted a similar picture of a growing acceptance of biological factors in the well established "parent" discipline. The Chronicle article noted that leading sociology journals have recently published papers that focus on the role of biology in understanding human behavior and that even a subfield of gene-environment interactions is emerging in the sociology departments of some universities. Some, however, are less optimistic about the progress that has been made toward including modern biological insights within criminological circles. John Wright and his colleagues (2008) reviewed the prevalence of biological focus among the faculty and dissertations of doctoral programs in criminology and criminal justice, finding little scholarly focus in the area. Similarly, they lamented, only four percent of the articles published in four premier criminology journals over the past dozen years were biologically informed. Their concern is that a wealth of new (biological) knowledge is being excised from the body of criminological knowledge that is transmitted through graduate study and the journals of our field. Wright and his colleagues worry that this "biological ignorance" stifles our ability to explain criminal behavior and, worse yet, that it reinforces an anti-biological ideological bias.

Delightfully, Richard Wright and Mitchell Miller (1998:14) identified an earlier edition of this text as meriting "praise for unusually good coverage of biocriminology." They only faulted the presentation for its mention of association of the perspective with racism. Similarly, Wright et al. (2008:327) object that "To this day, introductory criminology textbooks link biological theorizing with the repulsive practices that accompanied Hitler and Mussolini…" Still, individual level explanations of crime and deviance, whether biological or psychological, do hold the potential for human rights deprivations of those at statistical risk of misconduct. These abuses are part of history, forewarning criminologists to remain on guard to prevent new ethical misuses of science. Yet at the same time, as reviewed below, striking advances in knowledge about biology and human behavior have been discovered in recent years. The science of criminology is obligated to incorporate these emerging findings in our quest to explain crime and deviance.

Though many of the same debates persist, and others have emerged, the differences have narrowed substantially. Perhaps the most important change is that few theorists now propose to explain crime and deviance solely through biological variables. Those who incorporate biological variables are unlikely to consider themselves biocriminologists, eugenicists or criminal anthropologists. The more common identities are as biosocial, biopsychological, sociobiological or psychobiological criminologists, or as interdisciplinary criminologists. This reflects a growing tendency to incorporate or "integrate" (see Chapter 10) variables within theories that are derived from a much wider range of "parent disciplines," including biology.

Along with becoming far more multidisciplinary, biologically inclusive criminology has moved in a less deterministic direction. The debate is framed not so much in a *nature v. nurture* format, but rather in a nature *and* nurture perspective. Well-known biosocial criminologist John Wright noted in a Visiting Scholar lecture delivered at Western Carolina University that there is "no single gene for crime," but rather "that for the vast majority of people, it is always a combination of their genetic architecture, their experiences and what they have been socialized to do." (Wright lecture, 2009). Biological theories no longer see crime as biological destiny, but as outcomes that are the sum of biological *risk factors*, combined with a wide range of environmental influences. These risk factors impact the statistical probability of criminal behavior, while recognizing a complex path between biology and crime. Clearly, not all persons who suffer from bouts of depression, have high testosterone levels, or who are genetically programmed to be aggressive will become involved in crime. The more risk factors present, however, the greater the odds of criminal behavior. The environment, in turn, can either further enhance risk of criminality or may serve to insulate the biologically at-risk person from a criminal path.

Although criminology has been decidedly moving in a multidisciplinary direction, some resistance in mainstream criminology (the more sociologically oriented) to theories of criminal behavior that rely upon physiological variables continues. This is partly based on ethical concerns, a fear that identification of biological deficiencies may be more likely to lead to unacceptable interventions in the lives of subjects than if they displayed only social risk factors. Although some researchers focusing on physiological factors have emphasized that we can identify those at risk and devise policies to do "good" things for them (e.g., develop programs for prenatal care, provide opportunities that will help insulate genetic "time bombs," etc.), concern remains that biology tends to hold more implications for doing "bad" things to people. This is where the historical abuses of eugenicists and racists haunt criminological research. It is difficult to discount a history that includes sterilization, lobotomies, institutionalization of persons classified as "feebleminded," and political agendas to annihilate races of people politically designated as inferior. Even Paul Billings, himself a clinical geneticist at Stanford University, echoes such concerns: "It's not the genes that cause violence in our society. It's our social system" (Stolberg, 1993: A18). Highlight 6.3 examines the controversy that continues over the role of biology in explaining problem behavior, including crime.

HIGHLIGHT 6.3
Genetic Controversy Reigns

How controversial are genetics in explaining human behavior? Nikolas Rose (2000), an expert on biology and crime, has pointed out that we exist in a "biologized culture"—one that increasingly turns to genetics to explain human diversity in all dimensions. From athletic performance to intellectual capacity to artistic talent, human performances are increasingly linked to genetics, raising concerns about genetic alterations being employed to produce the ideal offspring. But of concern to criminologists is the other end of the continuum, the role of genetics in producing "problem" behaviors. Thus geneticists have claimed genetic links to schizophrenia, bipolar disorder (manic depression), alcoholism, aggression, and various forms of crime.

Does the focus on genetic predisposition alarm you? It does alarm some people. In 1992 a conference entitled "Genetic Factors in Crime: Findings, Uses, and Implications" was funded by the National Institute of Health (NIH). It was to bring together researchers from many disciplines on the campus of the University of Maryland to share their research findings on genetics and crime. But it did not take place as scheduled. In the face of accusations by some leaders of African-American groups that this could facilitate racism, NIH suspended funding. The conference finally went forward, still under protest, in 1995.

The difficulty is that persons displaying traits (social, psychological, or biological) placing them at risk for delinquent and criminal behavior can always be discriminated against, potentially even before displaying the "problem" behavior. The search for a biological precursor of criminal activity is fueled by a desire to locate characteristics that will effectively identify the potential lawbreaker. If low intelligence or high testosterone levels are likely to lead to illegal behavior, it might make sense to locate people with such traits and seek to remedy them or to isolate or more carefully monitor those who have them. Unfortunately, ideology bears heavily on the identification of risk factors. When the risk factors are located in genetics, suspicions, some of them also rooted in ideology, come to the forefront.

Controversy notwithstanding, recent advances in the biological sciences have produced a new generation of research that has revived biocriminology. Thus much contemporary biological research on the causes of crime is far more sophisticated and rests upon quite new and rapidly evolving knowledge and technology. Some of it remains highly controversial, while other portions have been positively received by the criminological community as a whole. One thing for certain, however, is that biologically oriented criminological research has become very diverse. Interest has been generated by focus on topics such as the following:

- intelligence, family, twin, and adoption studies for assessing genetics

- genetic influence on male parenting commitment

- The xyy syndrome, or males with an extra y in their chromosomal structure;

- the "premenstrual syndrome," or PMS, among females;

- male testosterone levels;

- impact of steroid hormone use, primarily among athletes;

- nutrition and diet;

- functioning of neurotransmitters such as serotonin, dopamine, and norepinephrine;

- minimal brain dysfunction;

- attention deficit disorder;

- DNA screening, e.g., location of genetic markers for manic depression;

- Environmental neurotoxins such as tobacco and lead

In addition to having become more multidisciplinary and less deterministic, biologically informed criminology has become quite diverse, as the sampling of topics listed above suggests. Contemporary biological criminology incorporates a wide range of variables that are genetic, prenatal, and environmental. It is genetics, however, that has been at center stage in the nature and nurture debate.

The "nature" or genetics premise is that propensities for human behavior are transmitted through genetic structures. The concept is that musical talent, athleticism, intelligence, creativity, and any other observable human traits (called *phenotypes*) are heritable in much the same manner as height, hair color and skin tone (physical phenotypes). The criminological focus is on behavioral phenotypes such as aggression, violence, and criminality. Unlike Lombrosian reasoning, the modern biological perspective searches for degrees of heritability, expressed in terms of a *heritability coefficient*, h^2, that is analogous to the squared correlation coefficient, r^2, commonly calculated by researchers. Both coefficients range from 0 to 1.0 and reflect the amount of "explained variance" in the dependent variable. To illustrate variability in heritability coefficients, it would be 0 for explaining the language that people speak because linguistic abilities are not inherited at all, but rather are acquired through learning from ones environment. Near the other end of the heritability continuum, height yields a coefficient of approximately .90, reflecting the fact that it is about 90 percent determined by our genetic structure (Rowe, 2002).

The broad research question for *behavioral genetics* is the relative contribution of genetics and environment to any given phenotype. Aside from considering the independent effects of genetics and environment on human behavior, the impact of nature x nurture interaction is sought. Much of the focus of behavioral genetics research is on the interaction of a particular genetic structure, called a *genotype*, with various environmental influences. The behavioral genetics paradigm, however, incorporates a much broader array of environmental influences than do the more traditional sociological models of crime causation. Potential environmental influences are further subdivided into shared and nonshared categories. *Shared environmental influences* are the common social experiences within a family such as their standard of living, neighborhood experiences, and patterns of familial interaction. Each member of the family also experiences environmental interactions specific to them, referred to as *nonshared environmental influences*. Examples are prenatal events such as oxygen deprivation or exposure to toxins entering the mother's bloodstream, accidental injuries sustained during delivery or after birth, influences from peers, or unique treatments within the family and so forth. One recent study, for example, found that identical twins whose mother's were disengaged from one of the pair were more likely to have self-control problems ad to become involved in delinquency (Beaver, 2008).

Genetic predispositions or risk factors are a function of an infinite array of possible genetic composites. Many patterns of imbalanced genetic structures, called *polymorphisms*, however, have been identified by geneticists. Various polymorphisms placing people at risk for heart disease, different forms of cancer, Alzheimer's disease, and many other physical ailments are being discovered. Similarly, polymorphisms contributing to behaviorally related outcomes such as bipolar disorder (Leon et al., 2005), Attention Deficit Hyperactivity Disorder (ADHD), Conduct Disorders (CD), Oppositional Defiant Disorder (ODD) (Gordon & Moore, 2005; Kirley et al., 2004), and the body's ability to regulate neuro-transmitters such as serotonin (Rowe, 2002) have revolutionized psychiatry. These behavioral disorders, in turn, are significant predictors of delinquent and criminal behavior.

There are two broad methodological approaches for examining criminal phenotypes (Rowe, 2002). Dramatic technological advances in recent years have provided geneticists with the tools for quickly and economically analyzing DNA samples from blood and saliva. Identifying genetic structures in this manner allows comparison of genotypes across persons to determine if they are associated with behavioral/criminal phenotypes. The second general approach is to compare phenotypes across ranges of biologically related people. Studies of twins and adopted children have provided two sorts of natural experiments that have greatly enhanced our understanding of genetics and crime.

Twin Studies and Genetic Research

The study of twins when comparing phenotypes across biologically related persons adds an important methodological dimension. We know that, on average, siblings share 50 percent of their genes, 25 percent in the case of half-siblings. The same is true for dizygotic (DZ) or "non-identical" twins, as they are the product of two separate eggs being fertilized and developing simultaneously. Biologically, they are siblings sharing a birth date. Monozygotic (MZ) or "identical" twins, however, have the same genetic makeup because they are the result of a single egg splitting, being fertilized, and developing at the same time. Since identical twins share 100 percent of their genes, theoretically they should be exactly the same once nonshared environmental influences are controlled.

This knowledge of the genetic composition of biological relatives enables researchers to test hypotheses regarding behavioral outcomes. The key concept in twin studies is *concordance*, referring to the portion of cases wherein both twins display the same behavioral outcome. Thus the genetics or "nature" prediction is that identical twins will display twice the concordance as their fraternal counterparts. That is, if a subject has a twin falling in a criminal phenotype, the risk of criminality should be twice as high for an MZ as compared to a DZ twin. Efforts are made to control for shared environments by grouping related subjects according to whether they were reared in the same family or were separated at birth.

Johannes Lange's *Crime as Destiny* (1930) pioneered in the exploration of criminal concordance. He found much more concordance for MZ than for DZ twin brothers, consistent with genetic explanations of criminality. Probably the most cited twin study is Karl O. Christiansen's (1977) work undertaken in Denmark. He examined records for a large cohort and found the following rates of criminal concordance: 35 percent for identical males; 13 percent for nonidentical male twins; 21 percent for identical females; and 8 percent for nonidentical female twins.

Twin studies have become a mainstay in efforts to assess genetic influence among biological relatives. One recent study sought to explain the phenotype of youth's selection of friends who smoke and drink (Cleveland et al., 2005). They found concordance correlations of .70 for a large American sample of high school boys who were MZ twins, compared to .30 for DZ twins, .27 for full siblings and .07 for half siblings. A similar pattern was observed for females. Because concordance was more than doubled for identical versus fraternal twins and siblings as well as for full versus half siblings, their conclusion was that the selection of substance abusing friends is overwhelmingly genetically rather than socially influenced.

The classic twin study design was deployed in another recent study seeking to explain conduct disorders (Jaffee et al., 2005). Again the correlations for the identical twins were more than twice the value of those for fraternal twins. The researchers estimated that 72 percent of the variance in conduct disorders could be attributed to genetics, leaving about 28 percent explained by a combination of shared and non-shared environmental influences. They found that physical maltreatment was one of those environmental factors contributing to conduct disorders. In addition, they found an interaction effect between the genetic risk and maltreatment. Specifically, for those with the lowest genetic risks the maltreatment led to only a 1.6 percent increase in conduct disorders, while high genetic risk was associated with a 27.5 percent increase in identification of conduct disorders.

Adoption Studies

Adoption studies provide another particularly attractive way to test the effect of biology on behavior. They involve infants adopted soon after birth by non-family members, thereby reducing confounding effects. Anecdotal accounts of reunions of adoptees with relatives, revealing very similar life courses despite environmental differences, are quite common nowadays.

An early study by R.R. Crowe (1972) determined that adopted children whose biological mothers had criminal records displayed higher levels of criminal involvement

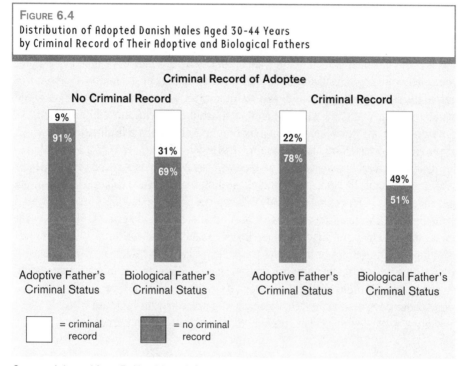

FIGURE 6.4
Distribution of Adopted Danish Males Aged 30-44 Years
by Criminal Record of Their Adoptive and Biological Fathers

Source: Adapted from B. Hutchings & S.A. Mednick (1977). "Criminality in Adoptees and Their Adoptive and Biological Parents: A Pilot Study." In S.A. Mednick & K.O. Christiansen (eds.) *Biosocial Bases of Criminal Behavior*, pp. 127-141. New York, NY: Gardner Press.

than those whose biological mothers had no such records. In a larger study of adopted persons, Barry Hutchings and Sarnoff Mednick (1977), using Danish data, found an increasing tendency for males to have criminal records if their fathers (adoptive or biological) had criminal records, with the tendency more pronounced if the biological father was the offender. Figure 6.4 displays a portion of their findings. Hutchings and Mednick suggest that poor heredity may make people more vulnerable to endangering social circumstances because they suffer from a genetic disadvantage that places them in a position in society in which they are more likely to succumb to crime.

Testosterone and Aggression

Testosterone, the main hormone that produces male secondary sex characteristics, has been frequently studied in regard to criminal violence; individual differences in testosterone levels are known to be heritable. Reiss and Roth (1993) report that such studies find a high prevalence of elevated testosterone levels in violent male sex offenders, but that the correlation is often confounded by alcohol abuse, which modifies testosterone levels in complex ways and is also associated with violent behavior.

A study of 4,462 military personnel in the Vietnam War period by Alan Booth and D. Wayne Osgood (1993) found a strongly significant relationship between testosterone levels and adult deviance. They suggested that the influence is mediated by the effect of testosterone on social integration and prior involvement with juvenile delinquency; or, put another way, that proneness toward violence creates for a person a social world in which ultimately the latent propensity to violence is called into play. A youngster with a high testosterone level, for instance, may push and shove classmates during his early school years and, as a result, may be isolated from the well-behaved members of the class and will find companionship only with those like himself. As part of this outcast group, the person may find himself involved in situations in which his propensity to use force is given rein, as in a gang fight.

One of the best known sources of excessive testosterone is associated with the use of anabolic steroids by competitive athletes seeking every edge to enhance their strength and endurance. There is a sizable body of scientific evidence that these steroids, a synthetic derivative of testosterone, have a host of deleterious side-effects. Most relevant are the mood swings and aggressiveness that are manifested in what is popularly termed "steroid rage." An array of anecdotal cases also suggest that such artificial boosts in testosterone lead to violent outbursts, in some cases culminating in murders perpetrated by young men who did not have a history of violence. With estimates of use among high school boys as high as 10 percent, and extraordinarily high use in some sport subcultures, testosterone and aggression may be of growing concern.

Premenstrual Syndrome (PMS)

The premenstrual syndrome (PMS) experienced by some women is said to be characterized by physical and psychological symptoms that spark uncontrollable rages and violent acts. About one in seven women is believed to suffer difficulties prior to her menstrual period severe enough to interfere with daily activities. Among the symptoms associated with PMS are: abdominal bloating, backaches, headaches, skin rashes, weight gain, breast tenderness, irritability, tension, insomnia, lethargy, and fatigue.

PMS is a recognized excuse from criminal culpability in France and has been introduced with varying degrees of success in both English and American courts. The leading British case is that of Christine English, who killed her lover by driving her car over him after he threatened to end their affair. An expert witness testified that English has suffered from PMS for 13 years; the jury acquitted her.

It remains controversial whether PMS difficulties are a problem associated with contemporary civilization or present-day social attitudes. One set of writers believes that PMS is as much a political issue as it is a medical issue. Those writers suggest that one might just as well label a condition to be known as "pre-breakfast syndrome." This syndrome would be found among people who stagger out of bed, depressed at the dawn of a new day, feeling wobbly and uncertain, at least until they have had some food. PMS exists, but it is not notably important, these authors insist, arguing that PMS has been accorded too much significance because it allows chauvinist males to label female behavior at times as uncontrollably erratic (Laws, Hey & Eagan, 1985).

Nutrition and Crime

Just as some learning theorists maintain that our behaviors are a reflection of our learning experiences, nutritionists often warn that "you are what you eat." Evidence, in fact, has accumulated to support the importance of diet as a variable to help explain behavior, including deviant and criminal acts. All of us find that our moods are affected by hunger, increasing aggression and the likelihood of poor judgment, for example. Persons suffering from hypoglycemia or low blood sugar levels are more likely to evidence behavioral responses ranging from inattentiveness to impulsivity and violence. It has been suggested that the sugar present in junk foods can trigger reactive hypoglycemia, contributing to violent behavior. We now know that ADHD is a widespread disorder among youth and that it is strongly linked to substance abuse and adult criminality (Gordon and Moore, 2005). The first, and often only necessary, step in controlling hyperactivity is regulation of dietary intake. Evidence of the power of diet in alleviating misconduct was generated in an experiment undertaken by Stephen J. Schoenthaler (1991) in a juvenile institution. The sugar served to an experimental group was covertly reduced, resulting in 45 percent fewer incidents of reported violence in the next three months, even though the staff did not know who had the reduced sugar diet. Figure 6.5 shows the "before" and "during" diets fed to boys in the experimental group.

FIGURE **6.5**
Diet of Inmates Before and During Experiment

Before	During
Afternoon Snacks	
two soft drinks	fruit juice
potato crisps	mixed nuts
sweets	peanut butter/honey
cupcakes	wholegrain bread
	crackers
Dinner	
cheese and onion pizza	Lasagna
shredded lettuce	tossed salad with dressing
biscuits	toasted garlic buns
ice cream	sherbet
Kool-Aid or sweetened	skimmed milk or
iced tea	unsweetened iced tea
Evening Snacks	
ice cream	popcorn
soft drinks	peanuts and other nuts
sweets	cheeses and cold meat
pastries	fruit
potato crisps	sugar-free soft drinks

Source: S.J. Schoenthaler (1991:7). *Improve Your Child's IQ and Behavior*. London: BBC Books.

The infamous "Twinkie defense" has brought derision to the causal interpretation of nutrition and crime. The phrase refers to the defensive strategy employed by the attorney of Dan White who was charged with the 1978 shooting deaths of Mayor George Moscone and Harvey Milk, whom the mayor had appointed to fill a position on the Board of Supervisors as a replacement for White. While the role of nutrition in the case was greatly exaggerated, it has persisted in infamy because White's "diminished capacity"mitigated the offense from a premeditated murder to manslaughter, resulting in a seven and one-half year sentence and only five years of prison time. While the junk food component (it was actually Ding Dongs, Ho Hos, and Cokes rather than Twinkies) was barely mentioned, that is where the press focused (Pogash, 2003). The "Twinkie defense" has since been an ideologically loaded anti-deterministic catch-phrase, often used to suggest that we have a system that allows blame to be shifted from offenders to ridiculous causal claims. Yet evidence of White's "diminished capacity" was rather compelling. He was suffering from a bipolar swing into depression and a drastic change in his dietary regimen was only one of many extreme personality changes that were symptomatic of clinical depression. He was ordinarily a fitness buff and extremely healthy eater, but in his depressed state was devouring large quantities of junk food. In a one-liner his attorney alluded to the possibility that his poor diet may have further exacerbated his depression. Clearly, however, there was a complex combination of psychobiological forces that propelled White to commit the two murders. Perhaps the more appropriate debate should not surround the criminological question of causality, but the legal and ethical issues of what should be done with such an offender.

Environmental Neurotoxins

Inherent in the nature vs. nurture debate is the difficulty of distinguishing mere correlates of deviance from causal factors. Recall that scientific studies must always control additional variables that may account for both the dependent variable (crime or deviance for us) *and* for what we presume to be the independent or causal variable(s). Biological researchers have heightened our sensitivity in recent years to the possibility that there may be biological variables that impact both the criminal behavior we are seeking to explain and the heretofore dominant social variables (e.g., Moffitt, 2005). It is quite plausible that social class, for example, could be propelled downward due to biological problems, while the same biological characteristics increase crime involvement. Consequently, the negative correlation between social class and crime could be an inflated or entirely spurious function of biological characteristics. Another possibility is that social and biological forces may interact to become stronger than the sum of their individual impact (Caspi et al., 2005; Jaffee et al., 2005).

Following the lead of behavioral geneticists and considering the total environment, another block of variables that need to be taken into consideration are *environmental neurotoxins* such as nicotine and lead. As with other biological variables, it is possible for environmental neurotoxins to reveal spurious correlations, additive effects, or to interact with other variables. In a recent assessment of the effects of nicotine on fetal development, Chris Gibson and Stephen Tibbetts (2000) found support for additional effects when considered along with father absence. Onset of delinquent behavior was significantly greater for youth whose mothers had smoked during pregnancy and for those whose father was absent during their childhood years. Smoking by pregnant women, it appears, introduces nicotine into the fetal bloodstream, resulting in damage to the central nervous system and, in turn, lowering serotonin available to the brain. The social disadvantage of absent fathers was found to place the youth at further risk of delinquency. In addition, Gibbons and Tibbetts found that the interaction of prenatal smoking and father absence was significant with an effect that exceeded that of father absence. That is, those youth whose mothers smoked during pregnancy and with absent fathers as children were at especially high risk of delinquent involvement.

Another widespread environmental neurotoxin is lead. The neurological effects of lead are well documented and provide the basis for federal legislation that has required its' removal from gasoline, paint, and other products consumed on a mass level. More recently, studies have linked exposure to lead with delinquent and criminal behaviors (Dietrich et al., 2001; Needleman et al., 1996; Needleman et al., 2002).

The ongoing Cincinnati Lead Study (CLS) has followed a cohort of persons born in impoverished neighborhoods characterized by extremely high levels of environmental lead concentrations, resulting in extraordinary rates of lead poisoning in residents (Wright et al., 2008). They measured blood lead levels at the prenatal stage, at age six, and an average level across childhood to age six. These lead exposure levels were then statistically assessed for their association with later arrest rates for various categories of crime and for imprisonment. The study controlled for a host of crime correlates, including social class, gender, maternal IQ, and various other neurotoxins.

The findings of the CLS are quite sobering. From among 248 subjects followed, 800 arrests were generated, most among males. Nearly two-thirds of them had at least one arrest with a mean of 5.2 each. Less than 20 percent of them were responsible for a majority of arrests, consistent with the "career criminal" findings reported in Chapter 10. A lead increase of just one microgram per deciliter of prenatal blood was associated with a 7.8 percent increase in arrests, while a one microgram increase at age six corresponded with 5.2 percent more arrests. The strength of this relationship between lead exposure and misconduct bodes poorly for children born to communities heavily polluted by lead. The overwhelming majority of subjects in the CLS displayed prenatal through age six levels of lead in the bloodstream that were 10 or more micrograms per deciliter above safe levels.

Lead poisoning damages the brain by stifling synapse formation. This reduces the travel of neurotransmitters, and correspondingly, lowers arousal of the cerebral cortex. The role of neurotransmitters and arousal of the brain are two of the biological issues at the forefront of contemporary research.

Neurotransmitters and Crime

Neurotransmitters are the chemical messengers in the brain that allow neural cells to communicate with one another. Four of the 50 or so known neurotransmitters have been studied most thoroughly in relation to violent crime—dopamine, norepinephrine, serotonin, and GABA.

Consider *serotonin* (pronounced SER-uh-TOE-nin) as perhaps the most widely known neurotransmitter. Serotonin is a naturally occurring chemical produced in the brain from one of the essential amino acids derived from food (Rowe, 2002). It is one of the 50 or so chemicals that serve as messengers from the estimated 10 billion to 100 billion of the body's nerve cells (neurons). Carriers of such messages are called axions; those which receive the messages are known as dendrites. Serotonin must jump the synapse, a space between axions and dendrites, for successful communication of the brain. The process is analogous to spark plugs in gasoline engines. If the spark cannot quickly and consistently fire across the gap, the engine will not run smoothly. This process in the human brain can be undermined by a shortage of serotonin, damage to the brain, or by genetic polymorphisms. Research has shown that people with low serotonin levels are prone to impulsive violent acts, depression, and suicide.

The discovery of neurotransmitters such as serotonin, and resulting progress in their regulation, has been at the basis of a revolution in psychopathology. Although controversy remains, and by all accounts we are far from a complete understanding of neurotransmitters and their regulation, results have been encouraging. Prozac is a widely discussed and controversial example of antidepressants that work, in part, by regulating serotonin (Rowe, 2002). Despite issues that have been raised with such psychotherapeutic drugs it is now clear, however, that communications within the brain provide an important link to understanding and treating at least some antisocial behaviors.

Arousal and Crime

Another theoretical perspective that sees functioning of the brain as central to understanding deviant patterns of behavior posits variation in the level of stimulation necessary for arousal of the cerebral cortex. *Arousal theory* asserts that those with low arousal of the brain require a lot of neurological stimulation to achieve a feeling of emotional balance. The individual with a low state of arousal will seek out stimulation through exciting activities. While this need can be satisfied by legitimate hobbies and occupational pursuits, it can also be met with delinquent and criminal behaviors. One would therefore expect that those who ride motorcycles, engage in martial arts, or enjoy rock climbing would have low arousal. Conversely, those who choose to pursue hobbies such as stamp collecting, playing chess, or photography are likely to display high arousal. In short, much of variation that we routinely see in personality may be rooted in arousal differences among persons. Low arousal becomes a problem when the individual seeks thrills and excitement to stimulate them through illegal channels. Delinquent and criminal behavior may be quite satisfying because they stimulate the brain to a pleasing level.

One interesting application of low arousal theory by Lee Ellis (1996) is suggestive of the wider potential of the concept for explaining both deviant and conforming conduct. Ellis notes that religiosity has rather consistently been found negatively associated with criminal behavior. He argued that both might be explained through arousal theory. While those with low arousal of the cerebral cortex will be inclined to seek stimulating and exciting social activity, they will not only be more likely to be caught up in risk-taking deviant activities, but less likely to seek involvement in religious ceremonies. These would typically be very boring occasions to the suboptimally aroused, ones that would be quite uncomfortable. The exception would lay with rare, but exciting, religious services such as those that pass snakes, play loud music, or provide other very exciting activities. Conversely, the superoptimally aroused are easily overloaded. For them, the conventional and serene church service would provide for optimal stimulation and therefore, they would more likely seek church attendance.

Ellis summarized five findings related to cortical arousal of criminals. Note that these are physiological features that tend to accompany low neurological arousal:

- recording of lower EEG brain wave patterns

- more frequent history of Attention Deficit Hyperactivity Disorder (ADHD)

- less response to threats of pain

- slower recovery to baseline arousal

- low levels of monoamine oxidase (MAO) in the blood, in turn related to serotonin neurotransmitter levels

While the evidence is far from in, research on arousal is at least highly suggestive of a biological link between personality and behavior. Since low arousal can be accommodated by, and even highly functional, for some socially approved activities, however, the theory probably requires merging with social variables. It is the social environment that most likely distinguishes between persons with low arousal who turn to criminal "thrills" and those who channel their arousal needs into socially acceptable activities.

Evolutionary Psychology

Another biological perspective is both more controversial and more difficult to empirically test. Called *sociobiology* or more recently, *evolutionary psychology*, the concepts are rooted in Charles Darwin's evolutionary concepts, but applied to human behavior. There are two fundamental phases of the evolutionary process. First, mutations of genes occur on a random basis, and secondly, those that contribute to the survival of the species endure and thrive (Rowe, 2002). Thus organisms continuously evolve. One variation of evolutionary psychology asserts that male pursuit of reproductive privileges, a natural survival instinct, has facilitated the evolution of male "cheaters."

According to this cheater theory, there are two basic models of male behavior in the competition for female attention. A species' survival is dependent upon reproduction and each member's participation in this process is determined by their ability to attract or dominate members of the opposite sex. How do females select prospective sexual partners or mates? One criterion is the impression the female has regarding the male's ability or inclination to help raise offspring. The cheater theory suggests that some males have evolved "with genes that incline them toward an extremely low parental investment reproductive strategy" (Ellis & Walsh, 1997:245). This could potentially inhibit the male's participation in reproduction because females will be more likely to mate with males exhibiting behavior more characteristic of good nurturers. In order not to be excluded from sexual activity, these low investing males have developed strategies to seduce women. They mimic the behaviors of high investing males up to the point of impregnation. The "cheaters," those with low parental investment, are society's criminals. They will deceive, steal, and do whatever it takes to engage in reproduction. These characteristics are also manifested in their general lifestyles, leading them to engage in criminal activities.

Psychogenic Theories of Crime

The role of psychology in explaining crime can be quite confusing. Both students and professors sometimes find themselves frustrated by the gap between accounts of crime offered by mainstream criminologists versus those offered by psychologists with an interest in crime. For that reason, some psychologists have written texts that present the psychological perspective on crime (e.g., see Andrews & Bonta, 1994; Bartol, 1999). The frustration of psychologists faced with the larger body of criminological theory and research is sometimes evident, as for example when Andrews and Bonta proclaimed "that the rational empiricism of PCC [psychology of criminal conduct] had been under severe attack for years by criminologists who placed higher value on social theory and political ideology than rationality and/or respect for evidence" (1994;1) and that "No student of the psychology of criminal behavior can afford to ignore the fact that the . . . antipsychology rhetoric continues even today in textbook criminology" (1994:25). Likewise, many criminology professors have felt the sting of hearing some of their psychology colleagues assert in their classrooms that all criminals are psychopaths.

So what leads to such different perspectives? On the one hand, a thesis such as the relativity of crime emphasized in this book is entirely incompatible with the notion that all criminals are psychopaths. All offenders cannot be psychopaths, or otherwise mentally or biologically distinct, to the extent that "criminals" are defined by actions or reactions of others. So one disciplinary difference lies in the degree to which it is assumed that criminals are different from noncriminals. Here there is room for a middle ground, for example, that some are quite different, while others are not at all different. One researcher may be particularly interested in, say serial killers, who are overwhelmingly likely to display individual differences. Another researcher may be interested in a category of offenders such as speeding violators, who are quite unlikely to be distinct.

Level of explanation is another variation of this. Psychologists are more inclined to attribute differences to internal individual factors, but more criminologists will look at external forces that lead to any differences. Again, both views may be right in different cases, or as integrative models explore, they may both be right at the same time. For example, a person might commit an assault because their personality places them at risk for doing so *and* because their social circumstances shaped that personality disorder in the first place. As noted at several points in this chapter, social circumstances may trigger behaviors for which a person is already genetically at risk.

Another source of confusion is rooted in the bounds of psychological explanations. Psychology is a very large field and what some consider psychology others may label biology. Psychology is the study of the functioning of the mind, so criminal psychology seeks to understand the mind of the criminal. Many psychological theories incorporate genetics or other biological variables in the quest to understand functioning of the mind, so that it becomes difficult to distinguish psychological from biological explanations. Similarly, many mainstream criminological theories contain measures of the learning process, thereby becoming almost indistinguishable from psychological accounts of learning.

Psychologists played a major role in crime theorizing in the early decades of the twentieth century, but were then supplanted by sociologists. The last couple of decades have seen rapid growth of theoretical integration and increased multidisciplinary study of crime. Thus psychology has reentered the criminological enterprise in this context. The remainder of this chapter provides a modest sampling of the more purely psychogenic theories. Given the breadth of psychology and psychiatry, however, this coverage is very shallow. Nevertheless, many psychological variables do appear in other chapters presenting mainstream criminological theories of crime. Overall, modern criminological theories often incorporate psychological variables, rather than psychological theories being applied to criminal behavior.

Psychoanalytic Theories

The psychological perspective often receives an unfair assessment within criminological corners by failing to distinct between psychology and psychiatry. The differences, however, are substantial. Traditional psychiatry is associated with the work of Sigmund Freud (1856-1939), who was born in Moravia and completed his medical training in Vienna, Austria. His work was brilliant, but very controversial. He came close to discovering the value of cocaine as an anesthetic for eye operations. Freud himself used cocaine, sometimes heavily, for about 10 years, but stopped completely in 1896.

At the foundation of the Freudian psychoanalytic perspective is the assumption that the human personality is driven by unconscious forces, many of them related to sexual desires. As such, they are not directly observable, but purportedly can be inferred by a skilled analyst. The Freudian psychoanalyst has been trained to believe that the personality consists of a triad of unconscious forces. The *id* consists of biological drives that underlie all human behavior. The *libido*, for example, is the sex drive. The id is an unconscious aspect of personality that drives people to seek self-satisfaction. The problem, from this perspective, is simple. An uncontrolled libido will result in rapes or other deviant behaviors to fulfill the sex drive. The *superego* consists of the conscience, representing the moral standards of society. The *ego* is the mediating force, often called the conscious personality. In a normal person, these three personality components will balance conflict. The personality is well adjusted so that the person is neither a rapist nor celibate.

Freud determined that conflicts between the id and superego generally result in guilt. The individual wants to "rape, pillage, and plunder" but the superego says "no." There are appropriate and inappropriate ways in which individuals can deal with the guilt imposed by the desires of the id. According to Freud, *sublimation* is a healthy response to the guilt. In such instances, the individual channels his or her drives into socially approved activities. A workaholic, for example, may be channeling "excessive" sexual desires into work. An unhealthy reaction to guilt may be to deny that the desires even exist. This *repression* may result in additional problems. *Projection* refers to when a person with repressed drives believes that many other people possess these drives. A common example provided for such repressed individuals is the homophile, a person that sees and fears homosexual tendencies in others, but is actually projecting their own repressed desires. Another possible unhealthy response to guilt is *reaction formation*, the exaggeration of a persons own behavior to the opposite extreme. Here, for example, the person with strong sexual drives may declare celibacy.

Freud contended that conflicts between the id and superego occur throughout life, but are particularly important during childhood. If not appropriately resolved then, these unresolved conflicts will increase the odds of problem behavior in later years. Freud went on to suggest that the criminal may suffer from an overdeveloped superego, leading to constant feelings of guilt. For this reason the criminal may actually do things, such as leaving clues at crime scenes, because of their unconscious desire to be caught and punished. The "stupid crimes" presented in Table 5.3, to the Freudian, would be proof of these unconscious desires for punishment. The solution to these unresolved and unconscious id-superego conflicts is to dig deep into the mind and pull them out through psychoanalysis. The problem is that we cannot see or measure them and therefore, cannot empirically test this theory. Moreover, the skills that psychiatry lays claim to are highly subjective. How can we support or reject a claim that the criminal seen committing a crime was driven by an unconscious desire to be caught and punished, as opposed to being driven by angry emotions that led him or her to act irrationally? How can we be confident that psychiatric labels, such as "sex addiction" or "workaholism" are not more a reflection of value differences of the labeler than the mental health of the subject?

The Freudian system is in many ways seductive, because it is a closed framework of thought; that is, once the premises are granted it becomes impossible to rebut a Freudian conclusion. In this sense, it is not science, but a different paradigm for explaining behavior. For this reason, the eminent philosopher of science Karl Popper dismissed Freudian psychoanalysis (along with Marxism and astrology) as made up of self-confirming, nonscientific tenets. For Popper, the difficulty was that the theories could not be falsified—that is, there was no conceivable behavior that would contradict them.

The self-confirming aspect of Freudian theory is exemplified by the diagnosis of a probation officer that a delinquent under her supervision showed "neurotic tendencies." The boy had been late for his appointment with the officer, who interpreted the tardiness as "hostility," with the alleged hostility forming the basis for a diagnosis of neurosis. But had the boy been precisely on time, the officer, using a Freudian approach, might well have interpreted this as "compulsivity," and had he been early this could have been viewed as "defensiveness"—and both of these could also be translated into neurotic manifestations.

The major scientific problem with the Freudian system as it applies to criminology is that it is not predictive. It is one thing to proclaim, after the fact, that a boy who killed his father after the father had beaten his mother was acting out an unresolved Oedipal fixation. It is quite another thing to *predict* which boys will murder their fathers. Science calls for careful measurement, prediction and replication. Psychotherapy calls for interpretive insight.

Traditional psychiatric thinking is not very compatible with criminological explanations of crime, yet there appears to be some value and face validity to many of its concepts. For example, we have all displayed and seen others engage in reaction formations, and we shall see in Chapter 8 that this concept can be deployed from a social psychological framework. Perhaps the most telling problem with psychiatry, however, is that studies have found no difference in outcomes with persons who received psychotherapy from those who received no treatment at all (Schwitzgabel, 1979). Moreover, even if there were some degree of success, it would be impractical for most criminological purposes. Psychoanalysis, according to its practitioners, requires hundreds of hours of time to deploy. Such investments are unfortunately not realistic for the typical offender.

Personality Theories

Psychological theories of crime rely on the view that something within individuals causes them to behave in certain ways (for a sampling of studies, see Farrington, 1994). Arnold Binder's (1988) comprehensive review of research on juvenile delinquency found that the following personality characteristics were reported in early studies to be more common among delinquents than nondelinquents: sadism and a lack of compassion, emotional immaturity, insensitivity to others, and hyperactivity. More recently, tests employing the *Minnesota Multiphasic Personality Inventory* (MMPI), a 556-item test consisting of 10 clinical scales, are said to show a relationship between measures of psychopathic deviancy, schizophrenia, and hypomania (unproductive hyperactivity) and later delinquency (Hathaway & Monachesi, 1953; Megargee & Bohn, 1979).

A study of the link between personality traits and crime propensity undertaken by psychologist Robert F. Krueger and his colleagues (1996) attempted to merge strengths of traditional psychology and mainstream criminology. They capitalized on what they saw as a failure of criminologists to incorporate personality measures, while using the more sophisticated measures of crime that criminologists have developed, but that psychologists have neglected to use. They administered the Multidimensional Personality Questionnaire (MPQ) and three delinquency measures to a birth cohort of 862 male and female 18-year-olds. They concluded that the personalities of those who abstained from delinquency could best be described (1996:334) in terms of "a preference for conventionality, planfulness, meek nonaggressive behavior, and a nonassertive interpersonal style." Conversely, they characterized the youths who engaged in delinquency (1996:332) as persons who "preferred rebelliousness over conventionality, behaved impulsively rather than cautiously, and said they were likely to take advantage of others."

Hans Eysenck was a British psychobiologist who spent a number of years developing one of the more sophisticated psychological theories of crime. His *conditioning theory* asserts that criminals have personalities that differ from those of noncriminals (e.g., see Eysenck & Gudjonnson, 1989). He felt that mainstream criminological theories emphasizing social variables held little value in explaining crime. Conversely, he placed a lot of emphasis on the heritability of neurological predisposition for criminality. He concluded in one of his last publications (Eysenck,1996:146) that "genetic causes play an important part in antisocial and criminal behaviour. This simple fact is no longer in doubt."

At the root of Eysenckian theory are two major shaping forces: one's inherited nervous system and environmental conditioning forces. These impact three critical personality features or temperaments: extraversion, neuroticism and psychoticism. Each is claimed to be associated with norm-violating behavior. The *extravert* (a quality measured by various scales and corresponding to conventional use of the term) is outgoing, risk-taking, impulsive and requires a lot of activity. While these needs certainly can be accommodated through law-abiding activities, they predispose the individual to seek out excitement, which oftentimes can be found in deviant or criminal activity. The source of this extraversion lies in the persons central nervous system. Persons with lower arousal levels of the cerebral cortex require more stimulation to achieve optimal arousal. The *introvert*, by contrast, requires only very low levels of stimulation. To add to this problem, the person who has low cortical arousal is also more difficult to indoctrinate with a conscience through a conditioning process. Their low arousal results in less absorbency of social lessons and response to sanctions. *Neuroticism* (distinct from the more typical clinical mental disorder) refers to ones degree of emotionality. It is how excitable one is, which is proffered to be a function of the autonomic nervous system. The more neurotic individual is thought more likely to engage in deviance, due to lack of control. Finally, psychotocism (extreme insensitivity, cruelty, etc.) was thought to be a function of testosterone, serotonin, and monoamine oxidase levels, but has been considered far less than the extraversion and neuroticism continua.

Mental Disorders and Crime

Other writers of the psychological school have focused on persons who once were labeled *psychopaths*, but now are declared to have *antisocial personalities* (Feldman, 1993), which are characterized by high impulsivity, an inability to form lasting relationships with others, and the trait of experiencing little or no guilt when inflicting harm. Psychopaths tend to be narcissistic and motivated by self-gratification (McCord & McCord, 1964). They often are described as loners and as persons incapable of demonstrating love or showing compassion; at the same time, their behavior is marked by "glibness and superficial charm" (Hare & Hart, 1993:105). The crimes of psychopaths are said to be rarely planned beforehand; McCord (1983) believes that psychopathy is largely the result of early childhood rejection by parents that often is compounded by brain damage or brain dysfunction.

Other forms of mental illness involve less sweeping claims regarding connections to criminality, but have accumulated massive bodies of evidence that afflicted persons are at high risk for criminal and other antisocial behavior. The *bipolar disorder* or manic depression is one such form of mental illness. It is estimated that about one percent of the general population has the bipolar disorder (Barondes, 1997; Papolos & Papolos, 1999). The consensus is that the condition is caused by deficiencies in the autonomic nervous system's ability to regulate emotion. There are thought to be inappropriate levels of or an imbalance between neurotransmitters such as serotonin, norepinephrine, and dopamine, causing emotions to alternate from one extreme to another. In effect, the bipolar individual can fluctuate from having a very low to a very high arousal threshold. Bipolar disorder is a heritable trait, with at least the potential for its development being genetically transmitted. Studies have identified polymorphisms that place persons at risk for bipolar and other mood disorders by disrupting neurotransmission (Leon et al., 2005). Durand and Barlow (2000), for example, found a concordance rate of 80 percent for identical twins, compared to 16 percent for fraternal twins. A flawed gene responsible for some cases of bipolar disorder was recently discovered (Kelsoe et al., 2003). Like other biological predictors of criminality, the bipolar disorder is a "time bomb" that may be detonated by stressful life events. Once triggered, the disorder becomes a cyclical process, with wide variation in the timing of relatively normal, manic and depressive stages.

While most agree that great strides have been made in controlling the disorder with drugs, recurring patterns of deviance are quite common among bipolar persons. Unfortunately, medications have side effects and very frequently the individual will discontinue their use, while hiding the change from others. Much of the deviant behavior thought to result from bipolar disorder is not designated criminal at any given time or place, but nevertheless, is very disruptive of relationships. The disorder, for example, is associated with poor judgment, deceit, and manipulation of others. Sexual deviance and financial irresponsibility are common domains of misconduct, with infidelity or excessive spending causing the collapse of many personal relationships. Bipolar individuals typically follow a line of rational argumentation to support even the most bizarre patterns of behavior and often lead secretive lives. Consequently, patterns of deviance are frequently successfully hidden, even from close family members, for extended periods of time. Moreover, deviant episodes are separated by periods of relatively normal behavior and exceptional levels of creativity or other forms of productivity are widespread among bipolar individuals. Many gifted artists, actors, and intellectuals, for example, have been afflicted with the illness.

Left untreated, and particularly in combination with other characteristics predictive of criminal behavior, the bipolar disorder is associated with even the most serious forms of crime. Figure 6.6 summarizes news media reports of recent serious crimes attributed to offenders suffering from bipolar disorder.

FIGURE 6.6
Serious Crimes Attributed to Subjects Suffering From Bipolar Disorder

Offender	Crime
Alice Faye Redd	Swindled dozens of mostly elderly persons out of their life savings in a pyramid scheme that netted her millions of dollars. She was a former Republican fund-raiser and church activist, married to a pediatrician. Sentenced to 15 years in prison in 1995, released in 1998 to die of spine cancer in her Florida home.
Steven Abrams	Intentionally drove his Cadillac Eldorado onto a California playground in 1999, killing two young children. He claimed that he wanted to kill innocent people because of rejections he had experienced. He had been convicted of stalking a woman who had rejected his advances in 1994, serving two months in jail and being required to take lithium for a three-year probationary period.
Brandon Wilson	A 21-year-old Wisconsin drifter who slit the throat of a 9-year-old boy in a California public restroom in 1999. He was delusional and a user of LSD and other hallucinogenic drugs.
Jeffrey Hutchinson	A former Army Ranger killed the woman he was living with and her three children in their Florida home in 2001. He was sentenced to death. He was diagnosed with Gulf War Syndrome as well as bipolar disorder.
Christa Gail Pike	Mutilated and killed another 19-year-old woman in the Job Core when the two were competing in a romantic relationship with a male in the program. She is still appealing a death sentence and her attorneys argue that being on death row has caused further deterioration of her mental health, characterized by both bipolar and obsessive-compulsive disorders.

Schizophrenia also effects about one percent of the population (Lachenmeyer, 2000), but is much more disruptive to the persons life-course and more associated with crime. The illness usually begins early in life and is characterized by dramatic misperceptions of the world and inappropriate emotions. It is not a well understood disease, but the consensus is that it also is rooted in neurobiology. Zacarias Moussaoui, the bumbling al-Qaeda operative convicted in conjunction with the infamous 9/11/01 attacks, is one of the most recent well-known criminals diagnosed as schizophrenic.

Both schizophrenia and manic depression are considered by some psychologists as psychotic disorders because they represent degrees of departure from reality (Andrews & Bonta, 1994).

Integrating Psychological Explanations

Some recent studies have been considerably more sophisticated than those considered above. Terrie Moffitt, Donald Lynam, and Phil Silva (1994), for instance, conducted a longitudinal study in which they secured "neuropsychological scores" from a cohort of several hundred New Zealand males from age 13 to age 18. Such scores are said to "support inferences that observable behavior is linked to the physical health of the brain"; they are based on an array of items, such as memory tests, motor skill tasks, and measures of self-control as well as ability to process language and to synchronize information with action. The scores also drew upon electroencephalogram and brain-imaging technology.

The authors identify two distinct groups of delinquents: a relatively small group that engages in antisocial behavior of some sort at every life stage and a larger group that does so only during adolescence. On the basis of their testing, they found a significant difference in neuropsychological scores for males only and only for those who begin delinquency at an early age and persist in such behavior through adolescence. In regard to omnibus intelligence tests, they discovered that the "active ingredient" in predicting delinquency from such tests was poor verbal ability:

> Children who have difficulty expressing themselves and remembering information are significantly handicapped. Dysfunctional communication between a child and his parents, peers, and teachers may be one of the most critical risk factors for childhood conduct problems that grow into persistent antisocial behavior in young adulthood. Neuropsychological deficits interfere with school performance and educational attainments; both are proven risk factors for offending. Moreover research (Kandel et al., 1988) has shown that exceptionally strong verbal skills can be an asset for resisting the effects of criminogenic environments.

Like all responsible psychogenic researchers today, Moffitt and her colleagues (1994) grant that such deficiencies can be associated with law-abiding behavior as well as crime, depending upon the life circumstances of the individual. The need to explore the possible contribution of biological and psychogenic explanations of crime as part of overarching integrative theories of crime (see Chapter 10) seems to represent an important and worthwhile intellectual task. Researchers are continuing to have successes through such theoretically integrated frameworks. Stephen Tibbetts and Alex Piquero (1999), for example, found interaction effects for neuropsychological risk (measured as low birth weight) and environmental disadvantages (socioeconomic status and family structure) in producing early delinquency, especially among males.

Similarly, Chris Gibson, working with Tibbetts (2000) found that maternal smoking and father's absence was associated with later delinquency. Such interdisciplinary efforts will undoubtedly continue.

Summary

This chapter tells the story of a second major paradigm shift in the history of criminology. It began in an era of scientific revolution, with Charles Darwin at the forefront. This led to the adoption of the positive paradigm, marked by its adherence to the scientific method and presumption of determinism. Positive criminology first took the biological route, soon to be followed by the closely allied psychological. The history of biogenic and psychogenic criminology was traced, followed by an overview of contemporary biogenic and psychogenic theory and research.

Biological explanations of the causes of criminal behavior got off to a poor start because of the crude methods of measurement, their ethnocentric biases, and the primitive theoretical thinking. Some of these problems, of course, can be attributed to the nature of scientific tools at the time—just as, 100 years from now, thinkers undoubtedly will wince at some of the notions that we today regard as truth or our best approximation of that condition.

The positivist tradition in criminology that began with Cesare Lombroso, with all its shortcomings, traditionally has been credited with turning the field away from armchair theorizing toward the employment of field inquiry to determine the accuracy or falsity of hypotheses. Even this credit, however, has recently been challenged by Piers Beirne (1993), who believes that scholars have overlooked a considerable emphasis in the writings of the classical school on the scientific search for truth. Beirne maintains that scientific criminology really began with the work of early French and Belgian scholars—particularly Adolphe Quetelet and A.M. Guerry—who resorted to ecological tactics, plotting on maps the distribution of crime and other social conditions in the attempt to learn which situations were associated. Lombroso's later work, translated and heralded in the United States, pushed into the background these pioneering empirical efforts by other scholars.

Lombroso's writing led to further exploration of the relationship between genetic factors and crime. Goring's work rebutted Lombroso's idea, though it advanced biological arguments of its own that can be regarded as equally spurious. The approach was resurrected by Earnest A. Hooton, William Sheldon, and Sheldon and Eleanor Glueck during the 1940s and early 1950s, but rebuttals from criminologists consigned this work to near-oblivion. As a result of ties between biological explanations of human behaviors, the rise of Nazi and Fascist powers and the scathing attacks of Edwin Sutherland and other sociologically oriented criminologists, the perspectives were replaced by a social version of positivism.

In the closing years of the twentieth century, changes in the criminological land-scape began to provide much more room for biogenic/psychogenic variables. First, the areas themselves changed markedly. They became much less deterministic and far more interdisciplinary. At the same time, mainstream criminology was moving in an interdisciplinary direction. The result is an emerging body of criminological theory substantially incorporating biological and psychological variables.

In the biological arena, studies of twins and adoption records have led to seri-ous consideration being extended to the role of genetics. Both the biologically and psychologically oriented have focused much of their work on genetics. The result has been the uncovering of evidence linking genetics to such diverse characteristics as intelligence, athleticism, hyperactivity, and serious mental disorders such as schizo-phrenia and bipolar disorder. Biocriminologists have examined the effects of numer-ous categories of variables, including hormones, diet and toxic metallic elements.

Psychology is a diverse field and often difficult to distinguish from the biologi-cal perspective. Most people are familiar with the basic tenets of the psychoanalytic school, reviewed in this chapter, but it represents only a small portion of the field and is adamantly rejected by many psychologists. A number of personality theories have been developed. Eysenck's was developed specifically to explain crime and incorporates both biological and socialization variables. Others have developed mental illness constructs, such as the bipolar disorder and schizophrenia, intended to account for the bizarre behavioral patterns of mentally ill persons that often become involved in crime.

It is clear that at least the immediate direction for criminology will include the integration of more variables from a wider range of categories, including the psycho-logical and biological realms. The coming years almost surely will see more attempts to develop general theories of crime that are quite interdisciplinary.

Key Terms and Concepts

Antisocial Personality
Arousal Theory
Atavism
Behavioral Genetics
Bipolar Disorder
Born Criminal
Community Corrections
Concordance
Constitutional Psychology
Conditioning Theory
Criminal Anthropology
Criminaloids
Determinism
Ectomorph
Ego
Empiricism
Endomorph
Environmental Neurotoxins
Eugenics
Evolutionary Psychology
Extravert
Feebleminded
Genotype
Id
Indeterminate Sentence
Introvert
Jukes Family
Kallikak Family

Libido
Medical Model
Mesomorph
MMPI
Nature vs. Nurture
Neuroticism
Neurotransmitters
Nonshared Environmental Influences
Paradigm Revolution
Phrenology
PMS
Polymorphisms
Positivism
Projection
Psychopath
Reaction Formation
Repression
Risk Factors
Schizophrenia
Serotonin
Shared Environmental Influences
Sociobiology
Somatotypes
Statistical School
Sublimation
Superego
Testosterone

Key Criminologists

Karl O. Christiansen
Charles Darwin
Richard Dugdale
Lee Ellis
Arthur H. Estabrook
Hans Eysenck
William Ferrero
Enrico Ferri
Diana H. Fishbein
Sigmund Freud
Raffaele Garofalo
Eleanor & Sheldon Glueck

Henry Goddard
Charles Goring
A.M Guery
Earnest Hooton
John Laub
Cesare Lombroso
Henry Mayhew
Terrie Moffitt
Adolphe Quetelet
Robert Sampson
William Sheldon
Edwin Sutherland

Case

Buck v. Bell, Superintendent, 274 U.S. 200 (1927)

References

Allen, F.A. (1960). "Raffaele Garofalo." In Hermann Mannheim (ed.) *Pioneers in Criminology*, pp. 254-276. London, UK: Stevens.

Andrews, D.A. & J. Bonta (1994). *The Psychology of Criminal Conduct*. Cincinnati: Anderson.

Barondes, S.H. (1997). *Mood Genes; Hunting for Origins of Mania and Depression*. New York: WH. Freeman.

Bartol, C.R. (1999). *Criminal Behavior: A Psychosocial Approach*, Fifth Edition. Upper Saddle River, NJ: Prentice Hall.

Beaver, K.M. (2008). "Nonshared Environmental Influences on Adolescent Delinquent Involvement and Adult Criminal Behavior." *Criminology*, 46: 341-370.

Beirne, P. (1993). *Inventing Criminology: Essays on the Rise of "Homo Criminals."* Albany, NY: State University of New York Press.

Binder, A. (1988). "Juvenile Delinquency." *Annual Review of Psychology*, 39:253-282.

Booth, A. & D.W. Osgood (1993). "The Influence of Testosterone on Deviance in Adulthood: Assessing and Explaining the Relationship." *Criminology*, 31:93-117.

Caspi, A., T.E. Moffitt, M. Cannon, J. McClay, R. Murray, H. Harrington, A. Taylor, L. Arseneault, B. Williams, A. Braithwaite, R. Poulton & I.W. Craig (2005). "Moderation of the Effect of Adolescent-Onset Cannabis Use on Adult Psychosis by a Functional Polymorphism in the Catechol-O-Methyltransferase Gene: Longitudinal Evidence of a Gene X Environment Interaction." *Biological Psychiatry*, 57; 1117-1127.

Christiansen, K.O. (1977). "A Preliminary Study of Criminality among Twins." In S.A. Mednick & K.O. Christiansen (eds.) *Biosocial Bases of Criminal Behavior*, pp. 89-108. New York, NY: Gardner.

Christianson, S. (2003). "Bad Seed or Bad Science: The Story of the Notorious Jukes Family." *The New York Times*, Feb 8.

Cleveland, H.H., R.P. Wiebe & D.C. Rowe (2005). "Sources of Exposure to Smoking and Drinking Friends among Adolescents: A Behavioral-Genetic Evaluation." *The Journal of Genetic Psychology*, 166(2); 153-169.

Crowe, R.R. (1972). "The Adopted Offspring of Women Criminal Offenders: A Study of their Arrest Records." *Archives of General Psychiatry*, 27:600-603.

Darwin, C. (1871/1964). *The Descent of Man*. New York, NY: D. Appleton.

Darwin, C. (1859/1964). *On the Origin of the Species*. Cambridge, MA: Harvard University Press.

Denno, D. (1990). *Biology and Violence: From Birth to Adulthood*. Cambridge, MA: Cambridge University Press.

Dietrich, K.N., M.D. Ris, P.A. Succop, O.G. Berger & R.L. Bornschein (2001). "Early Exposure to Lead and Juvenile Delinquency." *Neurotoxicol Teratol*, 23; 511.

Dugdale R.L. (1877/1910). *The Jukes: A Study in Crime, Pauperism, Disease, and Heredity*. New York, NY: G.T. Putnam's Sons.

Durand, V.M. & D.H. Barlow (2000). *Abnormal Psychology: An Introduction*. Scarborough, Ontario: Wadsworth.

Ellis, L. (1996). "Arousal Theory and the Religiosity-Criminality Relationship." In P. Cordell & L. Siegel. *Readings in Contemporary Criminological Theory*. Boston, MA: Northeastern University Press.

Ellis, L. & A. Walsh (1997). "Gene-Based Evolutionary Theories in Criminology." *Criminology*, 35:229-276.

Estabrook, A.H. (1916). *The Jukes in 1915*. Washington: The Carnegie Institute of Washington.

Eysenck, H.J. (1996). "Personality and Crime: Where Do We Stand?" *Psychology, Crime and Law*, 2:143-152.

Eysenck H.J. & G.H. Gudjonnson (1989). *The Causes and Cures of Crime*. New York, NY: Plenum.

Farrington, D.P. (ed.) (1994). *Psychological Explanations of Crime*. Aldershot, Hants: Dartmouth.

Feldman, P. (1993). *The Psychology of Crime: A Social Science Textbook*. Cambridge, MA: Cambridge University Press.

Ferri, E. (1917). *Criminal Sociology*, trans. J.I. Kelly & J. Little. Boston, MA: Little, Brown.

Gibson, C.L. & S.G. Tibbetts (2000). "A Biosocial Interaction in Predicting Early Onset of Offending." *Psychological Reports,* 86:509-518.

Glueck, S. & E. Glueck (1950). *Unraveling Juvenile Delinquency*. Cambridge, MA: Harvard University Press.

Goddard, H.H. (1912/1955). *The Kallikak Family*. New York, NY: Macmillan Publishing Company.

Gordon, J.A. & P.M. Moore (2005). "ADHD among Incarcerated Youth: An Investigation on the Congruency with ADHD Prevalence and Correlates among the General Population." *American Journal of Criminal Justice*, 30(1); 87-97.

Goring, C.B. (1913). *The English Convict: A Statistical Study*. London, UK: His Majesty's Stationery Office.

Grupp, S. (1968). *The Positive School of Criminology: Three Lectures by Enrico Ferri*. Pittsburgh, PA: University of Pittsburgh Press.

Hare, R.D. & S.D. Hart (1993). "Psychopathy, Mental Disorder, and Crime." In S. Hodgins (ed.) *Mental Disorder and Crime*, pp. 104-115. Newbury Park, CA: Sage Publications.

Hathaway, S.R. & E. Monachesi (1953). *Analyzing and Predicting Juvenile Delinquency with the MMPI*. Minneapolis, MN: University of Minnesota Press.

Hooton, E.A. (1939a/1969). *The American Criminal: An Anthropological Study*. Westport, CT: Greenwood.

Hooton, E. A. (1939b). *Crime and the Man*. Cambridge, MA: Harvard University Press.

Hutchings, B. & S.A. Mednick (1977). "Criminality in Adoptees and Their Adoptive and Biological Parents: A Pilot Study." In S.A. Mednick & K.O. Christiansen (eds.) *Biosocial Bases of Criminal Behavior*, pp. 127-141. New York, NY: Gardner.

Jaffee, S.R., A. Caspi, T.E. Moffitt, K.A. Dadge, M. Rutter, A. Taylor & L.A. Tully (2005). "Nature X Nurture: Genetic Vulnerabilities Interact with Physical Maltreatment to Promote Conduct Problems." *Development and Psychopathology*, 17; 67-84.

Kandel, E., S.A. Mednick, L. Kirkegaard-Sorensen, B. Hutchings, J. Knop, J.R. Rosenberg & F. Schlesinger (1988). "IQ as a Proactive Factor for Subjects at High Risk for Antisocial Behavior." *Journal of Consulting and Clinical Psychology*, 56:224-226.

Kirley, A., N. Lowe, C. Mullins, M. McCarron, G. Daly, I. Waldman, M. Fitzgerald. M. Gill & Z. Hawi (2004). "Phenotype Studies of the DRD4 Gene Polymorphisms in ADHD: Association with Oppositional Defiant Disorder and Positive Family History." *American Journal of Medical Genetics Part B*, 131B; 38-42.

Kretschmer, E. (1925). *Physique and Character*. New York, NY: Harcourt Brace.

Krueger, R.F, A.Caspi, T.E. Moffitt, P.A. Silva & R. McGee (1996). "Personality Traits Are Differentially Linked to Mental Disorders: A Multitrait-Multidiagnosis." *Journal of Abnormal Psychology*, 105:299-312.

Kuhl, S. (1994). *The Nazi Connection: Eugenics, American Racism, and German National Socialism*. New York, NY: Oxford University Press.

Kuhn, T.S. (1970). *The Structure of Scientific Revolution*, Second Edition. Chicago, IL: University of Chicago Press.

Lachenmeyer, N. (2000). *The Outsider*. New York, NY: Broadway.

Lange, J. (1930). *Crime as Destiny*, trans. C. Haldane. New York, NY: Boni.

Laws, S., V. Hey & A. Eagan (1985). *Seeing Red: The Politics of Premenstrual Tension*. London, UK: Hutchinson.

Leon, S.L., E.A. Croes, F.A. Sayed-Tabatabaei, S. Claes, C.V. Broeckhoven & C.M. van Duijn (2005). "The Dopamine D4 Receptor Gene 48-Base-Pair_repeat Polymorphism and Mood Disorders: A Meta-Analysis." *Biological Psychiatry*, 57; 999-1003.

Lombroso, C. & W. Ferrero (1895). *The Female Offender*. London, UK: Unwin Fisher.

Lombroso-Ferrero, G. (1911/1972). *Criminal Man*. Montclair, NJ: Patterson Smith.

McCord, W. (1983). "Psychopathy." In S.H. Kadish (ed.) *Encyclopedia of Crime and Justice*, Vol. 4, pp. 1315-1318. New York, NY: The Free Press.

McCord, W. & J. McCord (1964). *The Psychopath: An Essay on the Criminal Mind*. Princeton, NJ: Van Nostrand.

Megargee, E.I. & M.J. Bohn (1979). *Classifying Criminal Offenders: A New System Based on the MMPI*. Beverly Hills, CA: Sage Publications.

Moffitt, T.E. (2005). "The New Look of Behavioral Genetics in Developmental Psychopathology: Gene-Environment Interplay in Antisocial Behaviors." *Psychological Bulletin*, 131(4):533-554.

Moffitt, T.E., D.R. Lynam & P.A. Silva (1994). "Neuropsychological Tests Predicting Persistent Male Delinquency." *Criminology*, 32:277-300.

Needleman, H.L., C. McFarland, R.B. Ness, S.E. Feinberg, M.J. Tobin (2002). "Bone Lead Levels in Adjudicated Delinquents: A Case Control Study." *Neurotoxicol Teratol*, 24:711.

Needleman, H.L., J.A. Riess, M.J. Tobin, G.E. Biesecker, J.B. Greenhouse (1996). "Bone Lead Levels and Delinquent Behavior." *Jama*, 275; 363.

Papolos, D.F. & J. Papolos (1999). *The Bipolar Child*. New York, NY: Broadway Books.

Pogash, C. (2003). "Myth of the 'Twinkie Defense'." *San Francisco Chronicle*.

Quetelet, A. (1833/1984). *Research on the Propensity for Crime at Different Ages*. Translated by S.F. Sawyer. Cincinnati, OH: Anderson Publishing Co.

Rafter, N.H. (1992). "Criminal Anthropology in the United States." *Criminology*, 30:525-545.

Rafter, N.H. (2004). "Earnest A. Hooton and the Biological Tradition in American Criminology." *Criminology*, 42:735-771.

Reiss, A.J., Jr. & J.A. Roth (1993). *Understanding and Preventing Violence*. Washington, DC: National Academy Press.

Rose, N. (2000). "The Biology of Culpability: Pathological Identity and Crime Control in a Biological Culture." *Theoretical Criminology*, 4:5-34.

Rowe, D.C. (2002). *Biology and Crime*

Sampson, R.J. & J.H. Laub (1990). "Crime and Deviance over the Life Course: The Salience of Adult Social Bonds." *American Sociological Review*, 55:609-627.

Sellin, T. (1968). "Enrico Ferri: Pioneer in Criminology." In Stanley Grupp (ed.) *The Positivist School of Criminology: Three Lectures by Enrico Ferri*. Pittsburgh, PA: University of Pittsburgh Press.

Schoenthaler, S.J. (1991). *Improve Your Child's IQ and Behavior*. London, UK: BBC Books.

Schwitzgabel, R.K. (1979). "The Right to Effective Treatment." *California Law Review*, 62:936-956.

Shaw, S.H., Z. Mroczkowski-Parker, T. Shekhtman, M. Alexander, R.A. Remick, A.D. Sadovnick, S.L. McElroy, P.E. Keck, Jr. & J.R. Kelsoe (2003). "Linkage of Bipolar Disorder Susceptibility Laws to Human Chromosome 13q32 in a New Pedigree Series." *Molecular Psychiatry*, 8:558-564.

Shea, C. (2009). "The Nature-Nurture Debate, Redux." *The Chronicle of Higher Education*, B6-9.

Sheldon, W. (1949). *Varieties of Delinquent Youth*. New York, NY: Harper and Row.

Stolberg, S. (1993). "Fear Clouds Search for Genetic Roots of Violence." *Los Angeles Times*, (Orange Cty. ed.) (Dec. 30): Al, A18.

Tarde, G. (1912). *Penal Philosophy*, trans. R. Howell. Boston, MA: Little, Brown.

Thomas, C.W. & J.R. Hepburn (1983). *Crime, Criminal Law, and Criminology*. Dubuque, IA: William C. Brown.

Tibbetts, S.G. & A.R. Piquero (1999). "The Influence of Gender, Low Birth Weight, and Disadvantaged Environment in Predicting Early Onset of Offending: A Test of Moffitt's Interactional Hypothesis." *Criminology*, 37:843-878.

Wright, J.P. (2009) Visiting Scholar Lecture at Western Carolina University: "Who is Winning the Nature/Nurture War? Insights From the Study of Violence." Posted at: http://fpamediaserver.wcu.edu/~static/johnwright.mov Summarized in: *The Carolina Criminologist*, 1,2:1-3,10-11.

Wright, J.P., K.N. Dietrich, M.D. Ris, S.D. Wessel, B.P. Lanphear & R.W. Hornung (2008). "Association of Prenatal and Childhood Lead Concentrations With Criminal Arrests in Early Adulthood." *PLoS Medicine*, 5.

Wright, J.P., K.M. Beaver, M. DeLisi, M.G. Vaughn D. Boisvert and J. Vaske (2008). "Lombroso's Legacy: The Miseducation of Criminologists." *Journal of Criminal Justice Education*, 19: 325-338.

Wright, R.A. & J.M. Miller (1998). "Taboo Until Today?: The Coverage of Biological Arguments in Criminology Textbooks, 1961 to 1970 and 1987 to 1996." *Journal of Criminal Justice*, 26:1-19.

7
Social Structure Theories of Crime

The preceding chapter reviewed two theoretical traditions (the biological and psychological) that locate the cause of crime in individual human differences. This chapter and the two that follow present the sociological orientation that has dominated American criminology since the 1920s.

Sociologists envision crime, delinquency, and deviant behavior as the product of social forces rather than of individual differences. Most sociological theories fit the positivist mode in that they contend that these social forces push or influence people to commit crime. Even at this broad level of categorization, however, the perspectives are not pure. Sociobiology, for instance, combines social and biological variables to explain crime. Many sociologists incorporate psychological factors in their theories; and both economists and sociologists are currently pursuing classical explanations of crime. So despite the general dominance of sociology in criminological theory construction, all manner of cross-disciplinary perspectives and hybrid theories can be found. A major trend is toward integration of various theoretical perspectives, a matter considered in Chapter 10.

Classification of theories within the sociological perspective is a knotty task. We have elected to use the term "social structure" to characterize the theories reviewed in this chapter, "social process" for those in Chapter 8, and "social reaction" in reference to the theories considered in Chapter 9. We do not contend that this organization scheme is necessarily the correct one, only that it provides a useful framework for contrasting sociological explanations of crime and their underlying assumptions.

The social structure genre provides the purest sociological explanation of crime and delinquency. It links the key troubles of individuals to the social structural origins of these difficulties (Mills, 1956). Theories that are most appropriately characterized as social structural depict crime as a product of characteristics of society. Structural features that contribute to poverty, unemployment, poor education, and racism are viewed as indirect or root causes of high crime rates among members of socially

235

deprived groups. Theories of this variety, however, are not intended to imply that only poor people commit crimes, nor do they mean that people located in the lower levels of the social structure have no choices or are devoid of responsibility for misconduct. These theories do, however, assume that crime is primarily a lower-class problem and point to flaws within the social structure that increase the odds of a person within that social stratum resorting to illegal behavior. Social structure theorists draw attention to the primarily lower-class status of the clientele of our criminal justice system. This perspective also is frequently used to explain the disproportionate involvement of minorities in crime and delinquency (e.g., Martinez, 2003; Messner et al., 2001; Peterson et al., 2000) and the effect of unemployment and other economic hardships on crime rates (e.g., Britt, 1997; Hill & Crawford, 1990; Messner & Rosenfeld, 2007). Many criminologists, however, reject the assumption that crime is primarily a lower-class phenomenon, attributing the disproportionate lower-class representation in the criminal justice system to discrimination.

Social structure theories are macro-theories. They are designed specifically to account for the higher rates of crime that the perspective assumes to characterize the lower echelon of the American class structure. Consequently, some criminologists maintain that social structure theories may be properly tested only with data collected at the group level (e.g., Bernard, 1987; Messner & Rosenfeld 2007), while others (e.g., Agnew, 1987, 1999; Menard, 1995) counter that individual-level data satisfactorily mirror the group problems that social structure theories portray.

Social structure theories provided the dominant explanation of crime in the 1950s and 1960s, but they were largely supplanted in the 1970s with the rise of control (see Chapter 8) and deterrence (see Chapter 5) theories. The focus on underlying structural defects was consistent with the reformist ideal of the era. Social structure theories reflect a fundamental faith in the social system, but they seek to identify structural flaws that contribute to the genesis of crime. Social structure theorists typically fit the traditional liberal image; they tend to be persons looking for means of reform without radically altering the basic social structure. They assume consensus regarding the legitimacy of laws and seek only adjustments to assure fairness. Charles Thomas and John Hepburn (1983) illustrate this orientation by comparing social structure theorists and automobile mechanics. The mechanics, they point out, strive to restore the automobile to a level of efficiency defined in terms of its original design. This is attempted by cleaning, adjusting, tuning, and replacing parts of the engine. The mechanic does not critique the basic premise of an internal combustion engine, but rather accepts it as the optimal powerhouse for the vehicle. Likewise, social structure theorists do not question the foundation of our social structure, but they suggest how the social structure can be optimized by identifying and correcting deficiencies. Other explanations of crime, however, adopt a conflict perspective and offer fundamental critiques of our social system (for examples, see Chapter 9).

There are two major variations of social structure theories. Strain theories most frequently reflect the notion that crime is an outgrowth of weaknesses in the social structure. The social ecology tradition, though it does not fit quite so neatly, is incorporated in the present chapter because its analyses of the social and economic conditions of neighborhoods contributed to the foundation of the social structure tradition.

Strain Theories

Strain theories are at the heart of the sociological bid to account for crime. The thrust of this theoretical agenda is that stress, frustration, or strain (hence the name), generally a product of failed aspirations, increase the prospects for norm violation. These theories maintain that norms are violated to alleviate the strain that accompanies failure. Blockage of legitimate goal attainment is said to encourage deviant solutions. Key objectives of strain theories, therefore, are the specification of sources of strain and of deviant adaptations. Most strain theorists reason that the structure of American society creates the greatest pressure within the lower social echelons, and consequently, these theorists focus on explaining lower-class crime. Strain also tends to be associated with distorted aspirations, unrealistic desires for attainment, and crass materialism. This goal distortion sets the stage for individual failure and the search for deviant solutions.

Emile Durkheim, an early French sociologist, stimulated the strain tradition for explaining crime and other deviant behavior. Robert Merton's revision of Durkheim's theory, thereafter, provided the foundation for contemporary understanding of this perspective in the context of American culture. Theorists such as Richard Cloward, Lloyd Ohlin, Robert Agnew, Steven Messner, and Richard Rosenfeld further extended the concept. The collective works of these scholars delineate the central tenets of strain theory.

Emile Durkheim—
Origins of Social Structure Theory

Born in 1858 in France, Emile Durkheim was exposed to the confusion and turmoil of a nation adjusting to a new social order. The French Revolution of 1789 had supplanted a repressive monarchy with a representative-based republic. Following closely upon this political upheaval were the social and economic transformations brought about by the industrial revolution. Nineteenth-century France was a country in transition. The classical notion of free will was being challenged and Cesare Lombroso (see Chapter 5) had introduced his biological determinism in the middle of the nineteenth century. Toward the end of the century, Durkheim brought focus upon how the organization of society can propel people toward violating norms. In other words, Durkheim, as a sociologist, saw behavior as socially rather than individually determined.

In 1892, Durkheim received the first doctoral degree in sociology awarded by the University of Paris. His most important contribution to criminology lies in his reviving the concept of anomie, delineated most clearly in Suicide (1897/1951). Although the term can be traced to ancient Greeks, among whom it meant "lawlessness," for Durkheim anomie represented a state of "normlessness." Because it is norms, or socially expected behavior, that control how people act, their breakdown represents a threat to social control. Durkheim hypothesized that anomie contributes to suicide. Many contemporary theorists speculate that it also is a vital factor in many types of crime.

Because sociology was a new discipline, Durkheim felt it necessary to demonstrate the utility of this perspective so that it could gain credibility. What, critics asked, could be gained by examining social institutions and group behavior that could not be understood through the analysis of individuals? To test his belief that individual behavior was shaped by larger social phenomena, Durkheim examined the most individual of all forms of deviance: the taking of one's own life. His proposition was that the basic determinants of suicide are social variables such as religion, marital status, and economic conditions. He approached the explanation of deviance on a group (or macro) level (attempting to account for rates of suicide), but the fact that his brother had taken his own life suggests that Durkheim was interested in interpreting behavior at the individual (or micro) level as well. Occasionally, he drew analogies in Suicide that reflected his concern with bridging a macro-theory with micro-level explanations.

To test his proposition, Durkheim examined suicide data from nineteenth-century Europe and descriptive data about preliterate societies. Among his findings were:

- the rate of suicide is much lower in purely Catholic countries;

- Jews showed lower suicide rates than both Catholics and Protestants;

- single persons (including those divorced and separated) are more likely to commit suicide than are married persons;

- suicide rates increase steadily with age;

- suicides are more numerous during periods of economic crisis than during periods of stability;

- periods of crisis such as war and revolution are associated with higher-than-normal suicide rates;

- the number of suicides in the military is greater than among civilians; and

- suicide is found in some preliterate societies where norms stipulate that wives take their own lives when their husbands die and that servants kill themselves when their masters die.

Durkheim divided these findings into four categories of suicide related to the social configuration of society: egoistic, altruistic, fatalistic, and anomic. These categories are on a macro-theoretical level because Durkheim explained deviance in terms of the organization of society and social institutions. His conclusions were supported by data showing higher rates of suicide in geographical areas reflecting the social configurations specified by the theory.

It was Durkheim's research on suicide that laid the foundation for anomie or strain theory. Anomic suicide, he postulated, occurs when rapid or extreme social change or crisis threatens group norms. People become uncertain of the appropriateness of their behavior. This results in a state of confusion or "normlessness." Durkheim's examples referred to the higher suicide rates during wars and revolutions as well as during periods of economic recession, depression, or advancement. Durkheim considered fatalistic and anomic suicide as opposites, that is, the former reflecting over-control while the latter represents a lack of normative control. Criminologists have extended the idea of anomie or strain to account for the genesis of crime.

Durkheim's four types of suicide are:

- Egoistic—suicide resulting from a weakening of commitment to group values and goals, especially when the individual has come to rely primarily upon his or her own resources;

- Altruistic—suicide precipitated by an over-commitment to group values and norms;

- Fatalistic—suicide derived from excessive regulation (e.g., slavery or imprisonment); and

- Anomic—suicide that occurs when rapid or extreme social change or crisis threaten group norms.

Anomie

Anomie refers to a state or a condition in society in which the norms are no longer effective in regulating behavior. How is it that norms are disrupted or the willingness to conform to norms is attenuated? In addition to crises, such as wars, Durkheim indicated that anomie also is the result of a disjunction between people's aspirations and their ability to achieve these goals. This may be brought about by rapid social change such as drastic economic growth. In nineteenth-century French society, Durkheim speculated that such economic expansion would be more likely to affect the upper and middle classes, whose expectations and aspirations expand to an insatiable level. As Durkheim (1897/1951:253) wrote:

> With increased prosperity, desires increase. . . . Overweening ambition always exceeds the results obtained, great as they may be, since there is no warning to pause here . . . since this race for an unattainable goal can give no other pleasure but that of the race itself . . . once it is interrupted the participants are left empty-handed. . . . How could the desire to live not be weakened under such conditions?

Durkheim noted a lower suicide rate among the lower classes and suggested that poverty insulated the poor from experiencing anomie and, thus, suicide.

Aspirations, Durkheim felt, are class related, with the upper classes having higher goals than those below them. While stating that aspirations varied, Durkheim believed that the French Revolution had created an egalitarian society in which all members had a similar opportunity to succeed or fail. Thus, what later strain theorists referred to as the opportunity structure was considered to be a constant. Figure 7.1 illustrates Durkheim's presentation of the relationship between social class and anomie.

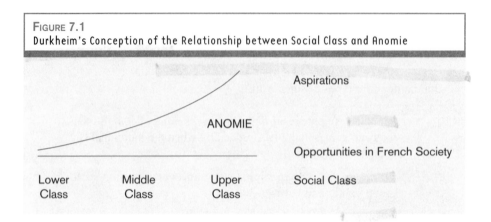

FIGURE 7.1
Durkheim's Conception of the Relationship between Social Class and Anomie

Durkheim felt that a successful social structure defines reasonable limits for desires, but that when social organization falters, insatiable desires are unleashed. Unlimited aspirations create pressure for deviant solutions. Recent instances of "creative accounting" practices that lead to criminal charges (e.g., Enron, WorldCom and Madoff) serve as examples of the effect of such unlimited aspirations.

Robert K. Merton— Social Structure and Anomie

Robert K. Merton's 1938 version of anomie theory has been acclaimed as one of the most influential developments in the study of crime and deviance. At a time when crime seemed rampant in American society, Merton presented an explanation that seemed enlightening: social conditions place pressures on people differentially throughout the class structure, and people react individually to these conditions. While Durkheim assumed that humans are naturally inclined to have unlimited desires that must be socially controlled, Merton felt that such desires are socially generated.

Merton postulated that all societies have a cultural system that denotes socially approved values and goals and that details acceptable norms or institutionalized means for achieving these goals. Not only do these prescribed goals and means enable people to pursue success in appropriate ways, but at times they also exert pressure on some segments of the society to engage in nonconforming behavior in an effort to achieve success. This happens when the goals of success are emphasized more than acceptable ways of seeking that success.

American society, according to Merton, espouses one overriding goal: the acquisition of wealth. The "almighty dollar" is something for which most Americans are taught to strive. While there are culturally approved means for obtaining wealth, they are given less emphasis, and of course, not everyone succeeds through legitimate endeavors. This may result in shortcuts or in nonconforming behavior to obtain money.

The institutionalized means for pursuing wealth and status are clearly set forth in American society, but these means are not feasible for most of those at the bottom of the social structure. The "Protestant work ethic" espouses traditional middle-class values that have been popularized by American folklore. Ben Franklin's maxims, passed on from generation to generation, highlight the means to success (e.g., a penny saved is a penny earned, a stitch in time saves nine, honesty is the best policy, don't put off until tomorrow what you can do today). The means include frugality, diligence, deferred gratification, hard work, honesty, and success through self-improvement (i.e., education). Though access to the opportunity structure is not uniformly available to all, it is expected that with hard work, anyone in America can be successful. It is not uncommon for grade school students to be told that if they work hard, they have the potential to become president. Success stories of the "self-made man" are put forth as examples of the validity of the claim that perseverance will be rewarded. The problem, however, is that many people try to achieve success but fail. Little emphasis is placed on the intrinsic rewards of adhering to the socially approved means whether or not these produce success. The attainment of wealth, Merton argued, has become such an overriding concern that little satisfaction is derived from merely playing the game honestly. Winning is what it's all about. Vince Lombardi, a revered Green Bay Packer football coach, declared, "Winning isn't everything; it's the only thing." A business writer (Tauby, 1991:59) illustrates how this theory might explain recent marked increases in crimes such as embezzlement by women. White-collar crimes, she wrote, "are sometimes a by-product of the American dream gone haywire, a warped form of ambition."

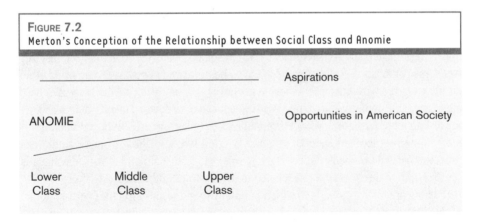

FIGURE 7.2
Merton's Conception of the Relationship between Social Class and Anomie

The legitimate means for obtaining wealth are differentially available throughout the class structure. Members of the upper class have greater access to education, important interpersonal contacts that will enhance their opportunities, and socialization that prepares them for competition in the struggle to achieve wealth and status (Mills, 1956; Domhoff, 1967; Dye, 1976). Members of the lower-class experience greater stress or strain in their attempts to make money legitimately. That is also why, Merton argued, they are found in disproportionate numbers among the criminal population, the mentally disturbed, and other deviant groups. This conflict between the institutionalized means and the culturally specified goals is what causes anomie (see Figure 7.2). It is an inequitable social structure, evaluating success similarly at all social levels, that produces lower-class strain and that ultimately leads to crime and delinquency. Merton (1938:680) summarized his argument in this manner:

> It is only when a system of cultural values extols, virtually above all else, certain common symbols of success for the population at large while its social structure rigorously restricts or completely eliminates access to approved modes of acquiring these symbols for a considerable part of the same population, that antisocial behavior ensues on a considerable scale.

How accurate is Merton's depiction of American society? Do you think we measure the success of ourselves and others primarily in materialistic terms? Do we value ends above means? If other concerns rival or exceed the value placed on monetary success, the notion of strain or pressure toward deviant routes to success is called into question. Similarly, if American culture emphasizes the value of following the rules as much or more than attaining success, the theory will not hold up. To speculate on our cultural values, consider questions such as the following: Is more emphasis placed on the status and income of occupations or on whether the occupations themselves are intrinsically satisfying? Do sports revolve more around fair play or winning? Does our educational system place a higher premium on grades and diplomas or on hard work and perseverance? Does the business community more keenly prize profits or integrity in business practices? Answers to such questions help to evaluate Merton's premise that goals and means are poorly integrated in our society.

To assess the applicability of Merton's version of anomie to American society, we must consider at least one other empirical issue. Are the means made available to the lower class inadequate for the goals to which society leads the lower class to aspire? Are some persons so severely handicapped by being reared in poverty, slums, and other disadvantaged environments that they do not have, or do not perceive themselves as having, reasonable opportunities to become well educated, to develop talents, and to acquire rewarding jobs? Can cultural background block people from effectively competing for the common symbols of success of which Merton wrote? If both of these conditions (overemphasis on monetary success and denial of opportunities) are met, the stage is set for strain in the lives of those located in lower strata of the social structure.

There are different ways in which people respond to this structural stress, not all of them deviant. Merton identified five individual modes of adaptation: conformity, innovation, ritualism, retreatism and, rebellion. They are depicted in Figure 7.3.

From the standpoint of criminal behavior, *conformists* are of little concern. They accept the culturally specified goals and adhere to the institutional means in their attempts to succeed, and they will continue to do so regardless of their success or failure. These are the people who hold a society together; society must be largely constituted of conformists in order to continue functioning.

Innovation is probably the most common form of adaptation to structural stress induced by the inability to legitimately achieve cultural goals. It is primarily innovators who become the focus of criminologists. Innovators aspire to attain conventional goals but use illegal means to succeed because they do not perceive themselves as having legitimate opportunities. The Wall Street broker who engages in insider trading, the

---

FIGURE 7.3
Merton's Individual Modes of Adaptation

Modes of Adaptation		Culture Goals	Institutionalized Means
I	Conformity	+	+
II	Innovation	+	−
III	Ritualism	−	+
IV	Retreatism	−	−
V	Rebellion	±	±

Reprinted with permission of The Free Press, a Division of Simon & Schuster, Inc., from SOCIAL THEORY AND SOCIAL STRUCTURE, Revised and Enlarged Edition by Robert K. Merton. Copyright A9 1968, 1967 by Robert K. Merton.

individual who burglarizes homes, the person who sells his or her body, and the student who cheats on a test are examples of people that use illegitimate means to obtain desired ends. As a social structure theory, this explanation of crime points disproportionately to the lower class, for whom legitimate opportunities for success are less available.

Ritualists can be thought of as the opposite of innovators; they abide by the rules but have abandoned pursuit of the goals. Ritualists go through the motions but lack commitment to the attainment of wealth or status. In the authors' years of teaching, students have been encountered who could be classified as ritualists. They attend classes, read assignments, and play the role of student, with the exception that they seem oblivious regarding grades and graduation. Whether they get an "A" or a "D" on a test makes no difference. The professor who routinely comes to class, but makes few demands on students to excel, demonstrates no up-to-date knowledge of subject matter, no new approaches to teaching, and lacks enthusiasm also exemplifies the ritualist. Outside of academe, the bureaucratic worker who always follows rules to the letter but seems to have forgotten the goals of the work group demonstrates ritualism. This adaptation precludes the possibility of failure. It is a "safe" approach to life.

A fourth mode of adaptation is that of the *retreatists* or societal dropouts. These people neither aspire to cultural goals nor abide by the institutionalized means. Their dropout status is characterized by transiency, drug addiction, and homelessness. While this mode of adaptation is viewed as deviant and some of the behaviors have been criminalized (e.g., vagrancy and public drunkenness), retreatists for the most part engage in crimes that have no victims except, of course, themselves. Retreatists represent the antithesis of the Protestant work ethic and middle-class values.

Rebellion is the final mode of adaptation identified by Merton. This occurs when a person rejects the goals and the means of society. Unlike the retreatist, however, the rebel substitutes a new set of values and norms for the discarded ones. Examples include the street-gang member who seeks a "rep" instead of money and uses violence and intimidation instead of hard work and honesty to achieve the goal, and the political revolutionary who employs subversive and violent acts rather than participating in the existing political system. While Merton refers to rebellion as an individual mode of adaptation, rebels are essentially societal dropouts who form a subculture with its own values and norms.

These five modes of adaptation, Merton suggested, are ways in which people respond to anomic conditions. From a criminal justice perspective, conformists and ritualists do not pose a problem. It is the innovators, retreatists, and rebels who get into trouble with law enforcement agents.

Whereas Durkheim maintained that it was the insatiable aspirations of people that led to social strain, Merton believed that it was the differential access to the means necessary for attaining success that caused stress. This focus on the opportunity structure of society shifted attention to the lower classes and to instrumental crimes such as burglary, robbery, larceny, and other crimes that would produce an economic gain. Subsequent criminologists extended this perspective, most notably, to explanations of juvenile delinquency and gang activity.

Richard A. Cloward and Lloyd E. Ohlin— Opportunity Theory

Approximately 20 years after the publication of Merton's classic work on anomie, Richard Cloward and Lloyd Ohlin (1960) proposed a model explaining gang delinquency that expanded upon Merton. Their extension of anomie is called *opportunity theory*. Cloward and Ohlin agreed with Merton in large measure, but they believed that he had failed to acknowledge the role of illegitimate opportunity structures in the development of deviant adaptations to anomic conditions. They suggested that, just as the availability of legitimate means varies across social groups, so does access to illegitimate opportunity structures. They argued that the delinquent activities in which one becomes immersed are a function of the delinquent opportunities that are available to that person.

Illegitimate opportunity structures, like legitimate ones, presuppose social organization or integration in order to offer illegal opportunities. "Just as the unintegrated slum cannot mobilize legitimate resources for the young, neither can it provide them with access to stable criminal careers, for illegitimate learning and opportunity structures do not develop" (Cloward & Ohlin, 1960:173). According to Cloward and Ohlin, a community is considered well-organized against crime if, for example, it has an active parent-teacher association (PTA), a high level of citizen involvement in local politics, a community-watch program, and groups such as the Elks Club and Daughters of the American Revolution. Conversely, the words of "Stanley," a delinquent youth who traced his career for Clifford Shaw in *The Jack-Roller: A Delinquent Boy's Own Story* (1930/1966:54), illustrate a community well-organized for aberrant behavior:

> Stealing in the neighborhood was a common practice among the children and approved by the parents. Whenever the boys got together they talked about robbing and made more plans for stealing. I hardly knew any boys who did not go robbing. The little fellows went in for petty stealing, breaking into freight cars, and stealing junk. The older guys did big jobs like stick-up, burglary, and stealing autos. The little fellows admired the "big shots" and longed for the day when they could get into the big racket.

Cloward and Ohlin maintained that persons seeking innovative solutions to their strained circumstances must learn the necessary values and skills to take advantage of the opportunity structure within their community. Traits that produce success or failure in capitalizing on legitimate opportunity structures also apply to illegitimate opportunity structures. The process by which one is rejected from illegitimate endeavors is no more fair or forgiving than are the avenues through which legitimate success is sought. Those lacking the proper skills and potential will confront failure in their efforts to become, say, drug pushers.

To illustrate opportunity structures, imagine concluding that you are doomed to failure no matter how diligently you work; therefore, you seek an illegal route to success. What criminal solution would you select? The most frequent response of college students is that they would "push drugs." This answer reflects the opportunity rationale of Cloward and Ohlin. Selling illicit drugs is one of the more salient illegal opportunities available to college students. There are two reasons for this fact. First, the college community is an organized and well-integrated environment that provides an opportunity for a profitable illicit drug venture. Second, as a college student you already have or presume that you can readily accumulate the necessary knowledge, skills, and interpersonal contacts essential to conducting such an enterprise on a college campus.

Frustrated college students, on the other hand, would be unlikely candidates for running a loan-shark operation in an urban setting or managing a "chop shop" (recycling stolen cars) in a rural community. Although these are profitable activities in a community organized for criminal activity, most college students lack the requisite skills and personality attributes to take advantage of these illegal opportunities.

Adaptation to anomie, Cloward and Ohlin argued, is associated with the environment in which an individual lives. If there are no pawn shops, fences, or willing buyers of stolen goods, then it is much less attractive to a burglar to continue to steal. There are only so many iPods and DVD players that one person can use. If the ecological area lacks an illegitimate opportunity structure, persons may turn to petty and unprofitable forms of crime or resort to retreatism or rebellion. The ecological studies of Clifford Shaw and Henry McKay and other scholars in the Chicago School laid the groundwork for an analysis of community organization and disorganization as elements of opportunity structures. Edwin Sutherland (1937:211) likewise anticipated the concept of differential opportunity, noting that "selection and tutelage are the two necessary elements" in becoming a professional thief. That is, success within a particular criminal subculture requires access to learning structures to allow demonstration of aptitude and acquisition of the pertinent skills. Cloward and Ohlin (1960:151) explicitly acknowledged their debt to Shaw and McKay and to Sutherland, noting that their version of strain theory contains elements of both the structure (strain) and process (learning) traditions:

> The concept of differential opportunity structures permits us to unite the theory of anomie, which recognizes the concept of differentials in access to legitimate means, and the "Chicago tradition," in which the concept of differentials in access to illegitimate means is implicit. We can now look at the individual, not simply in relation to one or the other system of means, but in relation to both legitimate and illegitimate systems.

Concerned with explaining gang delinquency, Cloward and Ohlin identified three different types of gangs: criminal, conflict, and retreatist (see Figure 7.4). Each gang type represents a specific mode of adaptation to perceived anomie. The criminal gang, similar to Merton's innovator, aspires to the conventional goals of society. Its access to the legitimate means for achieving success are blocked, but there is an illegitimate opportunity structure, in the form of community organization for crime, that permits the gang to achieve money and status through illegal or nonconventional means. An example would be the inner-city youth exposed to older gang members who are operating a theft ring. The youth learns the appropriate behavior and justifications from these older youths and sees them achieve success through their illegal operations. As a consequence, the youth joins the gang and ultimately moves up through its ranks. The "Gang Feature" provided in this chapter highlights the importance attributed to the availability of legitimate opportunities.

FIGURE 7.4
Cloward and Ohlin: Group Adaptations to Anomie

Types of Adaptation	Conventional Goals	Legitimate Means	Illegitimate Means
Criminal	+	−	+
Retreatist	−	−	−
Conflict	±	±	±

Source: Adapted from R.A. Cloward and L.E. Ohlin (1960). *Delinquency and Opportunity*. New York, NY: The Free Press.

Cloward and Ohlin (1960:171) described the neighborhood providing illegitimate opportunity structures in this way:

> [T]he criminal subculture is likely to arise in a neighborhood milieu characterized by close bonds between different age-levels of offenders, and between criminal and conventional elements. As a consequence of these integrative relationships, a new opportunity structure emerges which provides alternative avenues to success-goals. Hence the pressures generated by restrictions on legitimate access to success-goals are drained off. Social controls over the conduct of the young are effectively exercised, limiting expressive behavior and constraining the discontented to adopt instrumental, if criminalistic, styles of life.

When an illegitimate opportunity structure exists, Cloward and Ohlin postulated that individuals confronted with blocked legitimate opportunity structures will gravitate toward the illegitimate means and engage in behavior that will result in the attainment of conventional goals. In the event that an illegitimate opportunity structure does not exist, as when a community is disorganized, a conflict gang will develop (see Figure 7.5). Conflict subcultures are characterized by destructive and violent

GANG FEATURE

Gangs and Social Structure in International Perspective

During the 1990s it became increasingly evident that the youth gang problem experienced by the United States was also occurring in Europe. Not only were gangs emerging in rural and small-town America, they were emerging in previously gang-free cities of Europe. While some of these gangs were influenced by the media (van Gemert, 2001), others developed in response to perceived structural problems associated with a lack of access to legitimate opportunities (e.g., Lien, 2001; Mares, 2001).

Four relatively recent studies conducted by anthropologists employing qualitative methodologies have documented the presence of youth gangs in the Netherlands, Norway, Great Britain, and Germany. Results from these four projects will be summarized in this Gang Feature. For a broader discussion of the emergence of gangs throughout Europe, consult the recent publication by Malcolm Klein and his colleagues (2001).

Frank van Gemert, a Dutch anthropologist studied violent youth groups in The Hague and Rotterdam and, while he acknowledged the role of structural and cultural factors, his research led him to emphasize the impact of juvenile life style that is transmitted largely through the media. The groups he studied were involved in violent offenses but often times avoided violence through the art of intimidation. Members of these groups, the Eight Tray Crips and the Eastside Crips in The Hague and the Southside First Tray Crips in Rotterdam, had not only adopted the names of a well-known American gang, they had adopted their symbols (i.e., bandanas, clothing, and hand signs). The cultural diffusion of youth culture through the media is captured in the following quote from van Gemert's work (2001:145):

> Over the past few years, Dutch youths have been attracted to video clips and compact discs with gangsta rap, in which the scene is set by young African-Americans with big cars and fat gold chains, and in the company of sensual ladies. The language of these youths is characterized by hyperbole and contains many references to competi-

tion and violence. The fact that famous rappers like Tupac Shakur, Notorious B.I.G. and Stretch not only talked about the hard life of the 'hoods, but actually were killed as gangsters in drive-by shootings, takes nothing away from their intentions.

Dennis Mares, another Dutch anthropologist, conducted his research in Manchester, England. Here he studied three youth groups over a four month period in 1997-1998. Two of these gangs, the Gooch and the Doddington, were located in the most impoverished sections of the city. Each gang had approximately 90 members, most of whom were African-Caribbean. The third gang was located in a working class section of Manchester and all of the members were white. With the exception of location and racial composition, the three gangs were remarkably similar—they were involved in a number of illegal activities ranging from drug use and sales to violent confrontations. The gangs were not organized around drug dealing nor were they well organized. In explaining the presence of gangs in Manchester, Mares invokes Wilson's (1987) notion of the underclass. For example, he writes (2001:165):

> In the gangs it is a way of coming to terms with, not necessarily a conscious rebellion against, structural class differences, but at the same time reproducing and mocking these legitimized dissimilarities on a more localized scale. . . . To explain why gangs in Moss Side and Salford have developed . . . it is necessary to take a closer look at the impact of the process of de-industrialization that has hit Manchester since the 1970s. . . . Apart from being geographically located, these economic changes also had a greater impact on youths than on adults, as youngsters became more excluded from economic participation because of declining demand for industrial laborers.

In her study of gangs in Oslo, Norway, Inger-Lise Lien (2001:169) provides evidence of the cultural diffusion of youth culture

Gang Feature, *continued*

described by van Gemert. The gang youth "watch American gangster movies and give themselves gangster names like Cash Money Brothers, Black Mafia Society, Mafia Sisters." Like Mares, though, she suggests that is the desire to obtain material goods without the legitimate means to attain them that has led to the formation of the Oslo gangs. Interviews with gang members painted a picture of pessimism about the future and concern about not finding jobs through legal channels. Additionally, many of the gang-involved youth were immigrants who felt limited in their ability to succeed in the Norwegian economy. One member of the Young Guns, for example, stated: "We were poor, and we were newcomers to Norway. . . . The boys in the Killers were second-generation immigrants. They drove around in BMWs and Mercedes. They thought they were better than us (sic), but we wanted to show them who we were, and put them in their place. This is how all this gang business started. We taught them how to respect us, and when they saw us they would tremble. We were happy."

behavior. The conventional goals are abandoned and supplanted by alternative values usually emphasizing physical prowess and cunning. Conflict gangs often have been sensationalized by the media, as in movies such as *West Side Story*, *Colors* and *Boyz in the Hood*. Cloward and Ohlin (1960:172) wrote the following about conflict gangs:

> First, an unorganized community cannot provide access to legitimate channels to success goals. . . . Secondly, access to stable criminal opportunity systems is also restricted. . . . Finally, social controls are weak in such communities. These conditions, we believe, lead to the emergence of conflict subcultures.

The last of the delinquent subcultures identified by Cloward and Ohlin is the retreatist, which is composed of social dropouts (e.g., drunkards, drug addicts). While this form of behavior may be seen as individualistic, Cloward and Ohlin argue that drug users, for example, must establish contacts with others if for no other reason than to obtain drugs. In the authors' scheme, therefore, retreatism is seen as a group adaptation to the blocked opportunity structure. As with the conflict subculture, retreatists experience the double frustration of having access to neither legitimate

FIGURE 7.5
Level of Community Organization, Availability of Illegitimate Means, and Type of Delinquent Gangs

Level of Community Organization	Availability of Illegitimate Means	
	Yes	No
Organized	Criminal	Retreatist
Disorganized	Criminal	Conflict

nor illegitimate means. They are double losers. They may be found in unorganized communities, but are more likely to exist in organized communities. This is because (1) without illegitimate means, a criminal subculture cannot persist, and (2) in an organized community, the destructive and malicious behaviors associated with conflict gangs will not be tolerated. Thus, Cloward and Ohlin argued, youths in such a situation will resort to withdrawal and drug or alcohol use.

Recent Developments in Strain Theory

Robert Agnew— General Strain Theory

Although social strain has been the dominant American sociological theory of crime during the twentieth century, it came under increasing attack during the 1970s (e.g., Hirschi, 1969; Kornhauser, 1978; Bernard, 1984). According to Robert Agnew (1992), the decline in the popularity of social strain theory can be attributed to four major criticisms:

- the focus on lower-class delinquency;

- the neglect of goals other than middle-class status and financial gain;

- the failure to consider barriers to achievement other than social class; and

- the inability to account for why only some people who experience strain turn to criminal activity.

Agnew proposes a general strain theory (GST) that addresses these criticisms.

Strain theory has historically been class-bound; that is, lower-class crime is explained as a result of blocked opportunities. In his general strain theory, Agnew broadens the perceived sources of strain by identifying three types of strain-inducing stimuli: (1) the failure to achieve one's goals; (2) the removal of positively valued stimuli; and (3) the presence of negatively valued stimuli. Virtually everyone experiences one or more of these types of strains, but it is the individual's interpretation of the source of the strain that is the determining factor of whether illegal activity will occur. It is when these strains are seen as unjust, too great, or uncontrollable that criminal behavior is more likely to result. Agnew suggests that strain produces anger, frustration, and/or depression and that these negative emotions are the source of illegal responses to strain.

In response to empirical tests of GST and in attempts to refine the perspective, Agnew (2001; 2004; 2006) provided expanded discussions of the role of various types of strain that contribute to criminal behavior. First, he distinguished between *objective* strains, "events or conditions that are disliked by most members of a given group" (Agnew, 2001:320), and *subjective* strains, "events or conditions that are disliked by the people who are experiencing (or have experienced) them" (Agnew,

2001:321). Acknowledging that not all people respond to the same condition in the same manner, Agnew emphasizes the need to account for the individual's subjective assessment of the strain in order to understand its role in offending. A second component of Agnew's elaboration of GST consists of delineating four characteristics of strain related to crime: (1) when strain is seen as unjust, it is more likely to cause anger; (2) when strain is high in magnitude or severity it is more likely to result in a criminal response (for instance, "it is more difficult to legally cope with a large rather than small financial problem" (Agnew, 2001:332); (3) strains associated with low social control (unemployment and homelessness) are more likely to lead to crime; and (4) strain is associated with a criminal outcome when criminal activity is seen as a means to reduce strain (for instance, the bullied child sees bullying others as a way to cope with the strain).

A third point in Agnew's (2001) elaboration of GST is the specification that while some strain will result in criminal activity, not all strain is expected to produce a criminal response. For instance, he indicates that the following types of strains should increase the likelihood of criminal activity: parental rejection; the failure to achieve core goals that are not the result of conventional socialization and that are easily achieved through crime (e.g., thrill, excitement, money); child abuse; homelessness; criminal victimization; child abuse or neglect; and abusive peer relations. On the other hand, the following types of strain should NOT increase the likelihood of crime: unpopularity or isolation from peers; excessive demands of conventional jobs that are well rewarded (long hours associated with many professional jobs); failure to achieve goals that result from conventional socialization and that are difficult to achieve through illegitimate channels (e.g., educational or occupational success); burdens associated with the care of conventional others to whom one is strongly attached, like children and sick/disabled spouses.

The failure to achieve goals includes blocked opportunity due to a person's location in the class structure, but it also can involve the failure to realize desired goals due to individual weakness or inadequacies. The fact that a 4'6" lower-class youth is unable to make the high school basketball team may have more to do with her height than with her social class standing. Agnew also suggests that strain may occur when an individual perceives the reward to be inadequate relative to the effort, especially when compared to others. Criminology professors often hear students complain, "But, I studied 10 hours for this exam, why didn't I get an A?" Does this question indicate strain? Not in the traditional sense, but under Agnew's general strain theory we can now appreciate why this same student was caught cheating on the next exam. Agnew also postulates that criminal behavior can result from experiencing stressful life events—both the removal of positively valued stimuli and the exposure to negative stimuli. While psychologists have studied the effects of the removal of positively valued stimuli such as divorce, moving, changing schools, switching jobs, and death of a family member, criminologists generally have failed to consider the impact of such events on behavior. Agnew argues that such life events can contribute to social strain. Victimization, for instance, is one negative stimuli that has been linked to offending. Child abuse or wife battering also may cause stress that the individual will ultimately seek to relieve through criminal activities.

Deviance is but one possible consequence of strain. Agnew identifies a number of cognitive, emotional, and behavioral adaptations that will minimize negative outcomes and thus reduce the probability of criminal behavior resulting from strain. For instance, people can invoke one of three cognitive coping strategies: minimizing the importance of goals (i.e., it's not that important); minimizing negative outcomes (i.e., it really isn't all that bad); or accepting responsibility (i.e., it's my fault). Persons who learn to reduce the relevance of strain will be less likely to resort to antisocial behavior.

Steven Messner and Richard Rosenfeld— Crime and the American Dream

In a different vein from Agnew, Steven Messner and Richard Rosenfeld (1994; 2007) propose an explanation of social strain theory that rekindles the macro-level perspective offered by Robert Merton more than 50 years ago. America, as we pointed out in Chapter 4, has a violent crime rate higher than most other nations. Messner and Rosenfeld maintain that the American Dream is the root cause of this high volume of crime. The American Dream consists of a broad cultural ethos that entails a commitment—in fact, an over-commitment—to material success through individual competition. In one of his later works, Robert Merton (1968) indicated that the American Dream is a double-edged sword—the very elements that contribute to America's success at the same time foster that "cardinal American vice, deviant behavior" (1968:200).

An emphasis on individual success tends to undermine the collective sense of community and the glorification of monetary success tends to limit aspirations to economic success. "Tasks that are primarily non-economic in nature tend to receive meager cultural support, and the skillful performance of these tasks elicit little public recognition" (Messner & Rosenfeld, 1994:8). As an example, Messner and Rosenfeld cite education, which is largely viewed as a means to achieve economic or occupational success an end in itself. How many students reading this text, for example, are attending college for the sole or primary purpose of learning and "expanding their horizons?" And how many are in college to obtain credentials necessary for a prestigious, high-salaried job?

Messner and Rosenfeld suggest that the American Dream has created an anomic society, one in which the attainment of goals has superseded the need to conform to legitimate means. They summarize their view in the following manner:

> Our basic thesis is that the American Dream itself exerts pressures toward crime by encouraging an anomic cultural environment, an environment in which people are encouraged to adopt an "anything goes" mentality in the pursuit of personal goals (2001:61).

This cultural environment is dominated by the economy and its interconnection with other social institutions. Messner and Rosenfeld maintain that four cultural values underscore the American Dream: achievement, individualism, universalism, and materialism.

- achievement is considered the "defining feature of American culture." The emphasis is not on good sportsmanship, fair play, and effort; it is on winning.

- individualism identifies the American focus on the rights of the individual to think and do as they see fit. Infringement on these rights, as detailed in the Bill of Rights, would be seen as un-American.

- universalism connotes the American ethos and the culturally shared values described by Merton in his anomie theory. Americans are encouraged to aspire to success, generally measured in terms of economic success. The pursuit of upward mobility and the evaluation of success or failure produces considerable stress throughout the society.

- materialism, or the fetishism of money, is a distinctive American phenomenon. Money, especially the accumulation of large amounts, has become a measure of success in American society. Messner and Rosenfeld explain that "monetary success is inherently open-ended. It is always possible to have more money. Hence, the American Dream offers 'no final stopping point.' It requires 'never-ending achievement'" (2001:63-64).

This cultural emphasis on achievement, individualism, universalism, and materialism interacts with social institutions of family, education, and the polity. The pre-eminent role of economic considerations in the pursuit of success unduly affects American society in three interrelated ways:

- devaluation of noneconomic institutional functions and roles;

- accommodation to economic requirements by other institutions; and

- penetration of economic norms into other institutional domains (Messner & Rosenfeld 2001:70).

Devaluation of noneconomic goals is notably present in the educational arena. Education is seen by most as a means to an end—job acquisition or job promotion. Rarely is education seen as an end in itself. Students are encouraged to study to get good grades, not to learn for the sake of learning. Accommodation to economic requirements is evident within the family. Rarely must a parent find time for work; the trick is finding time for one's family. For instance, rather than supporting a pro-family policy that encourages and promotes parental involvement with their children, the Unites States, unlike most other industrialized nations, has no mandatory paid maternity or parental leave law. In fact, parents generally must take un-paid leave upon the birth of a child and are then criticized for their inappropriate priorities, placing family before work. The influence of the economy has also penetrated other aspects of American life. Business leaders have become frequent participants in the pursuit of electoral office, usually with no prior political background or experience.

The assumption is that government would be better run like a business. A similar trend is also occurring in higher education where increasingly university governing bodies are turning to corporate America for recruitment of chancellors and university presidents. The glorification of the business model ignores the unique roles of government and education and succumbs to the cultural value of defining achievement through monetary success.

Anomic societies tend to have relatively weak and/or ineffective social control as a result of the emphasis on ends rather than means. At a local high school track meet, one of the authors observed a T-shirt with an inscription characteristic of the winning at all cost mentality—"Second place is the first loser." With this emphasis, it becomes increasingly difficult for social institutions such as the family and education to exert counterbalancing effects. "Innovation" or the use of illegitimate or illegal means (e.g., steroid use among athletes) has become common throughout society.

Assessing Strain Theories

At the heart of the strain paradigm is the assumption that crime, delinquency, and other forms of deviance are essentially problems located in the lower strata of our social structure. The advent of self-report measures, however, brought this axiom into question. On the basis of self-report data, criminologists increasingly have attacked strain theory, suggesting that it is founded upon a "myth of social class and criminality" (Tittle, Villemez & Smith, 1978). This myth, it is argued, is a product of inherent biases in official statistics. The justice system creates a lower-class crime problem through a class-biased enforcement response. Others have turned the coin, contending that such criticisms represent an inaccurate myth of classlessness (Braithwaite, 1981).

The relationship between class and crime is critical to strain theory, and is indeed a complex issue. The difficulty (broached in Chapter 4) lies in how to measure both class and crime. Some researchers maintain that the conclusion that crime is not associated with class is rooted in deficient measures of the two variables (e.g., Clelland & Carter, 1980; Johnson, 1980; Brown, 1985; Brownfield, 1986). They argue that class-based theoretical traditions such as strain are premised on "a two-class model comprised of the really lower class and of everyone else" (Brown, 1985:213). The lower class in such a model is termed the underclass, the disreputable poor, or the surplus population. It consists of people who are chronically unemployed and typically subsist on welfare benefits (Wilson, 1987). This is a much different collectivity from the one comprised of persons who have attained less than a high school education and whose jobs pay poorly. People who are lower-class by these latter criteria, but who nonetheless are in the mainstream of American culture because they work and bring home wages, may feel deprived, but they experience a lesser or qualitatively different strain than members of the former group. Thus, how social class is measured has implications for the outcome of tests of strain theory.

Self-reports that do not show more delinquency among the lower-class have been depicted as deficient because they include trivial offenses. Status offenses (conduct prohibited only due to juvenile status), for example, are included in most self-report scales. It has been argued that listing items such as skipping school and disobeying parents skews the delinquency measure and distorts the relationship between social class and delinquency. It is asserted that delinquency will prove to be related to social class if it is measured to reflect serious misconduct.

Findings by both David Brownfield (1986) and Stephen Brown (1985) support the criticism that evidence refuting the lower-class concentration of delinquency is due to flawed conceptualization of the class and delinquency variables. Both found violent offenses to be associated with "disreputable poverty" or underclass affiliation. James DeFronzo (1983) also found poverty to be positively related to burglary and larceny, and public assistance levels to be negatively related to homicide, rape, and burglary. Following Thomas Bernard's (1987) contention that strain theories may be appropriately tested only at the macro-level, DeFronzo's results lend particular support to strain suppositions.

In an interesting study of 200 "homeless" men in Edmonton, Alberta, Stephen Baron and Timothy Hartnagel combined in-person interviews with observational data to examine the relationship between homelessness and crime. They sought to determine how these homeless men accounted for their failure. From a strain theory perspective, the attribution of failure should be placed on the social structure rather than on oneself. In support of this perspective, Baron and Hartnagel (1997:425) report that "long-term unemployment and sparse employment histories tend to undermine perceptions of equal opportunity and lead the youths to blame the government, private industry, and the economy for their condition." In a similar vein, Paul Vowell and David May (2000:56) found that "perceived blocked opportunity significantly predicted gang membership and violent behavior" in a study of more than 8,000 adolescents in a southern state. Contrary to theoretical expectation, however, poverty status increased the perceptions of blocked opportunities for the European American youths but not for the African-American youth.

Hoffman and Ireland (2004) undertook a study to assess the ability of Cloward and Ohlin's opportunity theory to explain differences in rates of delinquency. Utilizing data from the National Education Longitudinal Study (NELS), they were able to measure both school- and individual-level measures for a sample of more than 12,000 students enrolled in 883 schools across the United States. Their findings are supportive of the role of anomie in explaining differences in delinquency; that is, they found that the disjunction between economic aspirations and educational expectations was associated with increased levels of delinquent involvement. However, contrary to the theoretical premise of opportunity theory that illicit opportunity structures help to account for variations in illegal activity, Hoffman and Ireland found no support for school-level effects on delinquency.

A more fundamental question, however, is whether strain theory must focus exclusively on the lower class. Scott Menard contends that while strain may be felt more strongly among the lower class, this does not mean that anomie "varies within the social structure. Instead, it means that the effects of anomie may be felt differently by individuals with different positions in the social structure" (Menard, 1995:137). In his investigation of Merton's anomie theory, Menard (1995) found that an individual's mode of adaptation, combined with a measure of social class, was better able to explain variations in some types of offending. Agnew's General Strain Theory serves as an example of a theoretical attempt to explain the presence of criminal activity within all social class levels. The question, however, still remains; do members of the lower class necessarily experience greater strain? Perhaps lower-class persons are not motivated by materialistic aims or middle-class success standards and, consequently, do not undergo strain. Or even if they do, might not persons of other classes experience strain as a product of other social structural features?

In their 2005 publication, Travis Pratt and Francis Cullen report on findings from a meta-analysis of 214 articles published between 1960 and 1999. They examined the extent to which empirical assessments of macro-level theories supported the underlying assumptions of those theories. Included in their macro-level assessment were the following seven perspectives: social disorganization; resource/economic deprivation; anomie/strain; social support/altruism; routine activity; rational choice/deterrence; and subcultural. Of relevance for the material discussed in the current chapter, Pratt and Cullen concluded that the overall support for social disorganization theory was "fairly strong" while "anomie/strain theory has not been adequately tested to confirm its empirical status" (Pratt and Cullen 2005:410).

The keystone foundation of contemporary strain theory, Mertonian anomie, is often criticized for limiting its focus to property crimes. To the extent that Merton's position is read in this manner, the extension of the strain paradigm by Cloward and Ohlin has alleviated the problem, as noted by Francis Cullen (1988:233):

> [B]ecause scholars have shown that any given strain state (e.g., frustrated aspirations) can lead to a range of responses, the relationship between strain and any one form of deviance or crime is indeterminate, not etiologically specific or determinate; hence the need for a theory of intervening variables—opportunity theory—that explains why people pursue one wayward path and not another.

To a considerable extent, Messner and Rosenfeld's Institutional Anomie Theory (IAT) addresses both the debate about the location of strain in the class structure and the concentration on property crime. Their theoretical formulation refocuses attention to macro-level conditions and societal effects on violent offending. Mitch Chamlin and John Cochran (1995) used data from all 50 states to examine the extent to which institutional anomie theory could explain and predict rates of instrumental crime. Their findings were consistent with Messner and Rosenfeld's model, reporting that "it is the interplay between economic and other social institutions that determines the level of anomie within a collectivity and, in turn, the level of crime" (Chamlin & Cochran, 1995:423). In a subsequent assessment of the underlying assumptions of IAT, Chamlin and Cochran (2007) suggest that this theory is best suited for explaining crime in advanced western nations.

Other tests of IAT are generally supportive of the perspective. Micheel Maume and Matthew Lee (2003:1168) found that IAT explained variations in homicide rates "across macrosocial units within the United States." To what extent, however, do these findings hold across nations? Remember, Messner and Rosenfeld contend that adherence to the American Dream is the source of America's high violent crime rate relative to those found in other countries. Two studies comparing homicide rates cross-culturally also report findings consistent with institutional anomie theory. Jukka Savolainen (2000) and Steven Messner and Richard Rosenfeld (1997) found that nations with higher levels of social welfare support systems had lower homicide rates. In further efforts to assess the robustness of institutional anomie theory, William Pridemore (2002) examined the effects of structural factors on homicides in transitional Russia. His findings of a strong correlation between negative socio-economic change and homicide were consistent with Messner and Rosenfeld's predictions. However, in a subsequent examination of the relationship between socio-economic change and serious property crime in transitional Russia, Kim and Pridemore (2004) failed to find a relationship.

The past decade has witnessed a number of empirical tests of GST, beginning with one conducted by Robert Agnew and Helene White (1992). They found that measures of general strain theory did a moderately good job of explaining delinquency and drug use. Measures of family, school, and neighborhood strain were significant predictors of delinquency, while the traditional measures of failure to achieve valued goals were not. They also found that these strain variables had different effects. Adolescents with delinquent friends, for example, were more susceptible to the negative effects of strain than were adolescents with pro-social peers. Paternoster and Mazerolle (1994) also found strain was associated with higher rates of delinquency when they controlled for the effect of social control and differential association variables.

Subsequent researchers have tested different aspects of GST. Mazerolle and Piquero (1998) for example found that, in a sample of college students, some types of strain were related to feelings of anger, and that anger was predictive of violent behavior but not of other offenses (see also Mazerolle et al., 2003). Similarly, utilizing a sample of offenders, Piquero and Sealock (2000) found that of the coping strategies identified in general strain theory, anger was predictive of interpersonal violence. Depression, on the other hand, was not predictive of offending. Brezina (1996), utilizing both cross-sectional and longitudinal data, found that strain produced negative feelings of anger and resentment that were related to increased rates of delinquent involvement. Broidy (2001), on the other hand, reported mixed support for GST. Consistent with GST, she found that strain is related to anger and other negative emotions but that the results varied by the type of strain experienced by the individual. In an investigation of gender differences, Mazerolle (1998) did not find differential effects of the GST variables for males and females. He did, however, report slight gender differences for violent offenses. In a subsequent test the extent to which GST accounts for both male and female offending, Piquero and Sealock (2004:146) found that the "underlying theoretical process articulated in GST may be the same and apply equally well across gender." In their examination of gender differences, however, Broidy and Agnew (1997) stated that anger, on the part of males, was more likely to result in violent offending.

Agnew's (2001; 2004) extension of his General Strain Theory articulates the importance of controlling for the type of strain: some forms of strain are likely to lead to crime while others are not. In a recent study of street youth in Vancouver, Canada, Stephen Baron examined the effect of specific types of strain on offending and drug use. He conducted interviews with more than 400 youths between the ages of 15 and 24 and found that various aspects of general strain theory explained violent crime, property crime and total crime. However, "the strains Agnew outlined were not successful in predicting drug use" (Baron 2004:474). To summarize this growing body of research dedicated to assessing the efficacy of GST in explaining diverse forms of offending, while some mixed results have emerged, there is growing support for the ability of general strain theory to account for variations in some types of criminal offending (e.g., Agnew et al., 2002; Baron, 2004, 2007; Mazerolle & Maahs, 2000; Mazerolle et al., 2000; 2003).

Policy Implications

Strain theories have straightforward implications for combatting crime. Reductions in structurally induced strain, the perspective implies, will be accompanied by declining rates of crime. A variety of approaches may serve to curtail strain, but the traditional interpretation fuses with liberal ideology. The administrations of both John F. Kennedy and Lyndon B. Johnson in the 1960s incorporated a social activism perspective that included a delinquency prevention component (Binder & Polan, 1991). Attorney General Robert Kennedy was strongly influenced by *Delinquency and Opportunity*, written by Cloward and Ohlin; Kennedy adopted it as the blueprint for the federal response to crime during his brother's presidential administration and Ohlin was appointed as a special assistant to Kennedy's President's Commission on Juvenile Delinquency and Youth Crime. After all, "Ohlin's opportunity theory was a natural for the biases of the Kennedys (particularly Robert) because it connected delinquency to problems stemming from race and poverty" (Binder & Polan, 1991:249). Upon assuming the presidency, Lyndon Johnson continued this tradition, declaring a "war on poverty" in 1964. Johnson's Great Society vision was translated into specific programs, such as Project Headstart, VISTA, Job Corps, and Upward Bound, which were designed to enhance the opportunity for poor youths to succeed in school. Similarly, the Mobilization for Youth project in the lower east side of New York City provided educational and job opportunities for deprived youths.

It is widely conceded that the programs of the 1960s designed to alleviate poverty and enhance opportunities failed. The only parties said to profit from many of these programs were "poverty pimps," that is, persons who derived a living from operating the bureaucratic structure that was ostensibly designed to fight poverty. Stephen Rose (1972) has argued that the failure of the programs was in part due to misdirecting the effort from restructuring society to attempting to change the poor. The programmatic shortcomings of strain-derived policies may have been more a failure of implementation than theory. Others, however, contend that the programs had positive effects on participants (see, for example, Schweinhart, 1987; Reynolds et al., 2001).

The goals-means disjuncture delineated by Merton and adopted by other strain theorists can also be translated into policy by seeking to implement changes that lower aspirations (Kornhauser, 1978). Recall that Merton asserted that it is the disproportionate American emphasis on success, coupled with restricted opportunity that generates deviance. It follows that a society de-emphasizing upward social mobility would generate less strain. This type of society, of course, is not desirable to the majority because it defies the American ideology that anyone's child can grow up to be president, or at least to be rich, if only he or she strives hard enough.

Unlike other social strain theorists, Messner and Rosenfeld call for a more drastic social policy change than that described above. Because criminal activity is a product of the anomic cultural conditions brought about by the dominance of the economy and the pursuit of monetary success, crime reduction policies need to concentrate on the underlying cultural and structural causes. That is, crime reduction policies should seek to "vitalize families, schools, and the political system." This includes such policies as: the provision of family leave; job sharing for mothers and fathers; flexible work schedules; affordable child care; de-emphasis on economic role of education; enhanced use of intermediate sanctions in the criminal justice system; and implementation of social policies that "ensure that material well being is not strictly tied to economic functions and to guarantee that noneconomic roles receive meaningful financial support from collective resources" (Messner & Rosenfeld, 2001:106). More modest policy suggestions might include greater efforts at modifying teacher training to inculcate tolerance of a wider range of class-based youth characteristics. Academic and extracurricular activities could likewise be altered to enhance the odds for successful competition by lower-class youth. In short, any measures aimed at attenuation of strain induced by the social structure are policy relevant to the strain perspective.

Social Ecology

Ecology is defined as "the study of the relation of the organism to its environment" (Voss & Petersen, 1971:viii). Social ecology focuses on the person's relation to the social environment. For criminology, this entails study of the spatial distribution of crime and delinquency.

The social ecology approach to the study of crime grew out of research conducted by members of the Department of Sociology at the University of Chicago during the first half of the twentieth century. The Chicago School, as it became known, emphasized the interrelationship between research and policy, which in many instances involved getting out of university offices and into the field. The idea, derived from plant ecology, was that people must be studied in their natural habitat. Robert Park, an early Chicago sociologist whose work had an impact upon criminological research and theory, viewed the city as a social organism that contains "natural areas," that is, areas characterized by ethnic groupings, homogeneous income levels, and by certain kinds of commerce or industry. Natural areas include such well-known communities as San Francisco's Chinatown, Boston's North End, and New York's Harlem. Park claimed that symbiotic relationships exist among the inhabitants of such areas and between the areas (e.g., the commercial areas depend on the residential areas for business and the residents rely on the merchants to provide food and other amenities).

Park teamed with his colleague Ernest Burgess to describe the growth of American cities. They claimed that cities expand radially from a central business area. This concentric zone model of city growth is depicted in Figure 7.6. Five zones, each growing gradually and invading the adjacent zone, are identified. The only limits to the concentric zones are boundaries such as lakes, rivers, highways, and railroad tracks. Zone I is the central business district, characterized by few residents and dominated by commercial establishments. Zone II is the transitional zone. It contains deteriorated housing, factories, and abandoned buildings. Generally, the poorest persons in the city live in zones of transition, including the most recent immigrant groups. Zone III is the working-class area, where people escaping from the transitional zone settle. Typically, this zone has single-family tenements lining the streets. Zone IV lies in the outskirts of the city, where single-family homes with yards and garages abound. Beyond this is the commuter zone, i.e., the suburbs. Park and Burgess claimed that all cities expand and grow in this manner. As one zone becomes too confining, it encroaches upon the next zone until the original inhabitants move to the next zone. The closer they are to the central business district, the lower the quality and rental price of housing. Residents seek to migrate to outer zones as their economic positions improve. This migration pattern was adopted from the biological branch of ecology, which identified patterns of invasion, dominance, and succession.

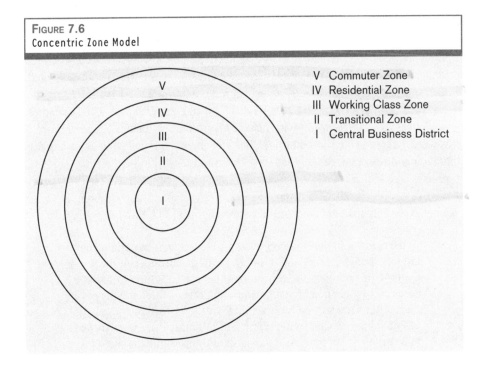

FIGURE 7.6
Concentric Zone Model

V Commuter Zone
IV Residential Zone
III Working Class Zone
II Transitional Zone
I Central Business District

Clifford Shaw and Henry McKay— Social Disorganization and Cultural Transmission

Clifford Shaw and Henry McKay built upon the work of Park and Burgess to study delinquency in Chicago. Using three different types of maps, Shaw and McKay (1942) plotted rates of male delinquency in Chicago between 1900 and 1933. "Spot" maps pinpointed the residences of all juveniles arrested, "rate" maps reported the percentage of juveniles with arrest records in each of 431 census tracts, and "zone" maps provided delinquency rates for each of the five zones in the concentric zone model.

Shaw and McKay examined the relationships between a number of community variables and delinquency. They found that areas with high delinquency rates were characterized by:

- a decreasing population;

- a high percentage of "foreign born" and "Negro" heads of families;

- a high percentage of families on relief;

- a low rate of home ownership; and

- low median rental values.

Additionally, the authors located other behaviors and social phenomena common to the high-delinquency areas. Among these were high rates of truancy, infant mortality, tuberculosis, mental disorders, and adult criminality. Shaw and McKay also examined trends over time. Despite changes in the ethnic nature of the groups inhabiting the different areas, the rates of delinquency and other social problems remained relatively constant. This demonstrated that the high delinquency rates could not be attributed to the groups occupying the inner zones, but rather that the rates were related to the ecological features of those zones. For every year, the zone map of social maladies showed an inverse relationship with distance from the city center. In other words, rates were highest in the central business district and transitional zone, lowest in the commuter and residential zones, and in between in the working-class zone.

Shaw and McKay concluded that delinquency is associated with the physical structure and social organization of the city. They claimed that differential value systems existed in different communities. They wrote (1942:170-172):

> In the areas of high economic status where the rates of delinquency are low there is, in general, a similarity in the attitudes of the residents with reference to conventional values. . . . In contrast, the areas of low economic status where the rates of delinquency are high, are characterized by wide diversity in norms and standards of behavior. . . . Children living in such communities are exposed to a variety of contradictory standards and forms of behavior rather than to a relatively consistent and conventional pattern.

Shaw and McKay argued that this exposure to a multitude of different values meant that boys in these areas would come into contact with individuals involved in criminal or deviant activities.

In addition to the differential association within high delinquency neighborhoods, Shaw and McKay described the areas as being socially disorganized, which is a concept that Cloward and Ohlin later incorporated into opportunity theory and one that has received greater attention from criminologists than have other aspects of the social ecology school. Social disorganization centered around three variables: poverty, residential mobility, and racial heterogeneity. These factors, depicted in Figure 7.7, are conceptualized as independent variables that generate social disorganization, which in turn contributes to crime and delinquency. The idea is that poor communities foster social disorganization because they lack the resources to address their problems. Funds are unavailable for developing viable recreation areas, for example. High levels of residential mobility contribute to anonymity. Social control declines because people do not know who belongs and who does not, inhibiting development of a sense of community. This is further exacerbated in heterogeneous communities where, because people do not come to know one another, common values fail to emerge. This absence of community values allows a tradition of delinquent behavior to develop that is handed down from one generation to the next through a process called cultural transmission. The breakdowns in community social control have been viewed as "a group-level analog of control theory" (Bursik, 1988:521), a perspective discussed in the following chapter.

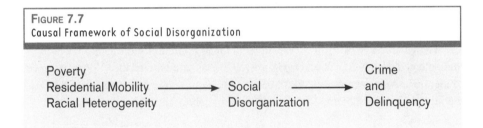

FIGURE **7.7**
Causal Framework of Social Disorganization

Poverty
Residential Mobility ⟶ Social ⟶ Crime and
Racial Heterogeneity Disorganization Delinquency

Another characteristic of the high-delinquency areas is the presence of numerous service agencies funded and staffed by groups external to the community. To Shaw and McKay, this situation reflected a lack of community organization and led them to launch their Chicago Area Project (CAP), a delinquency prevention program. Shaw was an activist who felt an obligation to integrate research and practice. The CAP was based upon results of the ecological research as well as the biographical studies conducted by Shaw (1930/1966).

The Chicago Area Project was conducted from 1932 to 1957 in three high-delinquency areas. A field worker from Shaw and McKay's Institute for Juvenile Research organized local residents to improve the community. Originally privately funded, CAP ultimately was taken over by the state of Illinois as part of its delinquency prevention program.

> The CAP stressed the importance of maintaining the autonomy of the community. An effort was made to avoid the imposition of Anglo-Saxon, middle-class standards on residents. The aim was to "stimulate" community organization without engineering and controlling it and to "spark" the latent potential for community control (Snodgrass, 1976:12).

Snodgrass describes Shaw's conception of "community" as that of a "folk-idealist waging an imaginary war with urban-industrial reality" (1976:13). Shaw based his model on his own experience growing up in a rural Indiana town. He believed that crime was bred in the slums of the city and that a development of community would lead to a reduction in delinquency.

While the purpose of the CAP was loosely articulated, Shaw felt that the program would be successful if it did nothing more than unite residents and reinstate the bonds of social control. In his summary of the CAP, Solomon Kobrin (1959:22), who had worked with Shaw and McKay at the Institute for Juvenile Research, wrote:

> The theory on which the Area Project program is based is that, taken in its most general aspect, delinquency as a problem in the modern metropolis is principally a product of the breakdown of the machinery of spontaneous social control. . . . [D]elinquency was seen as adaptive behavior on the part of male children of rural migrants acting as members of adolescent peer groups in their efforts to find their way to meaningful and respected adult roles essentially unaided by the older generation and under the influence of criminal models for whom the inner city areas furnish a haven.

The Chicago Area Project was a precursor to community prevention programs implemented during the 1960s. Snodgrass (1976) has summarized the CAP as designed to inculcate American middle-class values into slum residents in the belief that this would reduce the problems found disproportionately in these inner-city areas.

Contemporary Social Ecology

Following empirical tests of social disorganization theory in the 1950s and 1960s, there occurred a relative decline in theoretical and methodological interest in the social disorganization perspective. Criminologists turned largely to the labeling and conflict theories (see Chapter 9) and to social psychological perspectives such as Hirschi's social control theory, Akers' social learning theory (both discussed in Chapter 8), and increasingly to integrated theoretical models (see Chapter 10). A testament to the durability of the social disorganization perspective, however, is provided in the following conversation reported by Bursik and Grasmick: "during an annual meeting of the American Society of Criminology during the mid-1980s, we were informed that social disorganization was the 'herpes of criminology . . . once you think it is gone for good, the symptoms flair up again" (1993:30). As suggested by this quote, criminologists have continued to promote the importance of community-level factors in the etiology of crime. Robert J. Bursik, Jr., who received his Ph.D. from the Department of Sociology at the University of Chicago, has been one of the stronger proponents of this perspective. In 1993, he and his colleague, Harold G. Grasmick, published their widely acclaimed book, *Neighborhoods and Crime*, detailing their systemic theory of crime. In that work, they emphasize the role of social control in regulating criminal activity within the neighborhood. As the following discussion of "contemporary" social disorganization theory reflects, the work of Shaw and McKay was instrumental in stimulating a rich tradition of macro-level research examining the community context of crime.

A number of sociologists replicated the Shaw and McKay Chicago study (Lander, 1954; Bordua, 1958-1959; Chilton, 1964; Quinney, 1964). These studies generally focused on variables available from the U.S. Census Bureau's decennial surveys. Representative of factors believed to be indicative of social disorganization were: low median monthly rental rate, low percentage of owner-occupied homes, high percentage of nonwhites, high percentage of overcrowded homes, and high percentage of foreign-born individuals. Despite some discrepancies among the studies, the general conclusion was that social disorganization was associated with rates of officially recorded crime and delinquency.

A major criticism of the work of Shaw and McKay and the four cited replications has been their dependence upon police or court records to measure delinquency. Would those same results hold for self-report data? Studies utilizing the self-report method reported contradictory conclusions. Robert Kaspis (1978) found that delinquency was higher in communities with high migration rates, but he did not find higher delinquency rates in neighborhoods where there was a higher probability of contact with adult criminals and delinquent friends, or where there was greater exposure to norms supportive of illegal behavior. Thus, Kaspis discovered only partial support for the social disorganization model.

In a study of Chicago youth, John Johnstone (1978) reported that community-level characteristics proved to be the least useful in explaining delinquency rates and that there was no evidence to suggest that crime was higher for groups in economically depressed areas. A subsequent study by Johnstone (1983) examined gang behavior. In this study, he did find community poverty to be highly correlated with gang recruitment. Youth gangs were found primarily in communities characterized by social and economic deterioration. Johnstone noted that "the opportunity to gang is established by the external social environment, but the decision to do so is governed by social and institutional attachments and by definitions of self" (1983:296). In a similar vein, Anne Cattarello (2000) found that individuals who lived in socially disorganized neighborhoods were more likely to associate with delinquent peers than were youth who lived in organized communities. Furthermore, relying upon longitudinal data collected as part of an evaluation of the DARE program in Lexington, Kentucky, she concluded that all of the neighborhood variation in delinquency was mediated by the peer variables. That is, neighborhood characteristics explained variations in association with delinquent peers which in turn accounted for differential involvement in criminal activity.

A comprehensive study of violent offenders in four cities (New York, Chicago, Miami, and Dallas) reported results similar to those of Johnstone. Jeffrey Fagan, Elizabeth Piper, and Melinda Moore (1986) interviewed violent (according to police and court records) offenders as well as comparison groups of high school students and dropouts. Analysis of both neighborhood and individual level data led Fagan and his colleagues (1986:462) to conclude:

> Despite the disproportionate concentration of violent and serious juvenile delinquency in inner-city neighborhoods, most adolescents living in conditions of relative deprivation avoid the predictable consequences of peer, family, and social influences with respect to criminality. . . . Apparently, social and economic conditions in inner cities amplify the social processes which contribute to delinquency.

In 1989, Robert Sampson and Byron Groves published what has become a widely cited test of social disorganization theory. This classic work relied upon data from the 1982 British Crime Survey (BCS) and tested the efficacy of social disorganization theory to explain both self-reported offending and victimization. They found that "communities characterized by sparse friendship networks, unsupervised teenage peer groups, and low organizational participation had disproportionately high rates of crime and delinquency" (Sampson and Groves 1989:799). Importantly for subsequent development of this theoretical framework, Sampson and Groves noted that the levels of community organization mediated the effects of community structural characteristics. A subsequent replication of Sampson and Groves' work, utilizing data from the 1994 BCS, concluded that the earlier findings were robust and supported the social disorganization perspective (Lowenkamp et al., 2003).

Other relatively recent studies utilizing self-reports have found community-level effects on rates of offending. Without exception, however, these studies find that individual-level factors have a larger effect on self-reported crime than do the macro-level (i.e., measures of social disorganization) factors (e.g., Elliott et al., 1995; Oberwittler, 2004). This was also found to be the case in an examination of self-reported drug use (Esbensen & Huizinga, 1990).

Another trend in recent ecological studies has been toward the inclusion of extra-community dynamics in the study of delinquency. Janet Heitgard and Robert Bursik (1987) examined the effects of neighborhood racial change and other indicators of social disorganization upon delinquency rates in adjoining areas. Their analysis showed that delinquency rates increased as a consequence of rapid compositional changes in adjoining neighborhoods.

Interesting empirical questions are still being explored by researchers utilizing the social ecology/social disorganization framework. Criminologists have incorporated new techniques (e.g., self-report and victimization data) and new approaches (e.g., examination of extra-community dynamics and a combination of individual and community-level data). Other developments include the expanded use of factor analysis, a complex statistical technique that allows consideration of a larger number of community variables (see, for example, Simcha-Fagan & Schwartz, 1986; Scheuerman & Kobrin, 1986) and other advanced statistical tools to better examine trends over time (e.g., Bursik, 1986). The social disorganization hypothesis requires longitudinal data because it predicts that community changes will be followed by shifts in rates of crime and delinquency. In a recent study of a decade of changes in two Baltimore neighborhoods, for example, Ralph Taylor and Jeanette Covington (1988) found that increased social disorganization was followed by increases in violent crime.

The popularity of social ecology declined concomitantly with increases in the popularity of strain and, particularly, of control and deterrence theory. Much of the initial decline of criminological focus on the ecological perspective can be attributed to W.S. Robinson's (1950) clarification of a significant inferential error that often plagued ecological studies. Robinson aptly pointed out that ecological (group-level) correlations cannot substitute for individual-level correlations. Because, for example, the economic resources of communities are associated with rates of crime in those communities does not necessarily mean that the same statistical relationship holds on an individual level. This problem, termed the ecological fallacy, may have unduly discouraged criminologists from analyzing ecological data because of their abiding interest in explaining and predicting criminality on an individual level (Bursik, 1988). During the past 20 years, however, the potential for integrating macro-level with micro-level theories has been given more attention (e.g., Hagan, 1989; Short, 1989). The social ecology framework is experiencing a significant resurgence in efforts to understand the causes of crime and delinquency (Sampson 2002; Sampson et al., 2001; Wikstrom & Loeber, 2000).

Summary

This chapter has examined social structure theories. The theories subsumed under this category have three common characteristics. They portray crime as a product of deficiencies in the social structure, such as poverty and the lack of educational opportunity. Another feature is their focus on the lower-class milieu as the source of crime. Because they view crime as a lower-class problem, social structure theorists examine only the lower-class segments of society in seeking to explain crime. Some criminologists, however, have applied strain theories to white-collar offenses and others to explain increases in crimes by women. Third, this is a macro-theory tradition. Social structure theories are designed to account for variations in rates of crime among groups, not to explain individual-level criminality.

Strain theory is one of the purest sociological approaches to understanding crime. It is rooted in Emile Durkheim's concept of anomie, or normlessness, but was given its contemporary usage by Robert Merton. Strain or frustration is considered a product of failure that is likely to be disproportionately experienced within the lower class due to structural limitations on opportunities. This failure may elicit innovative or deviant responses to meet culturally emphasized success goals, primarily the goals of material acquisition and higher status. Richard Cloward and Lloyd Ohlin extended the concept with their opportunity theory, pointing out that resorting to illegitimate means to success is not always a readily available option. Instead, they argued, illegitimate opportunity structures are governed by factors such as social organization in a manner similar to legitimate opportunities.

Strain theories were very popular in the 1960s and provided the basis for many social programs. The success of policies derived from the strain tradition, however, has been marginal at best. In addition, the assumption that crime is a lower-class problem has sparked a major debate within criminological circles. Questions have also been raised regarding the picture of delinquency as portrayed by each of the major strain theories. Criminologists such as Robert Agnew with his general strain theory and Steven Messner and Richard Rosenfeld in *Crime and the American Dream*, however, have re-energized the strain tradition. It appears that this theoretical perspective will continue to contribute to the evolution of our understanding of crime for some time.

The social ecology school laid much of the framework for strain theories, but also contributed to the formulation of theories that can be classified primarily as social process ideas. Social ecology is patterned after the study of plants and their environment, applying the principles from that field to the study of humans and their social environment. The concept of social disorganization is one of the primary contributions of this perspective. A disorganized community lacks the stability and resources to formulate or accomplish collective goals, leading to higher rates of crime. This has implications both for the social structure and for cultural deviance, a variation of social process theory considered in the following chapter.

Key Terms and Concepts

Altruistic Suicide
Anomie
Chicago Area Project
Chicago School
Concentric Zone Model
Conflict Gang
Conformity
Criminal Gang
Cultural Transmission
Ecological Fallacy
Goals and Means
Innovation
Institutional Anomie Theory

Myth of Classlessness
Opportunity Theory
Reaction Formation
Rebellion
Retreatism
Retreatist Gang
Ritualism
Social Disorganization
Social Ecology
Social Organization
Social Structure Theories
Sociobiology
Strain Theories

Key Criminologists

Robert Agnew
Robert J. Bursik, Jr.
Richard Cloward
Emile Durkheim
Henry McKay
Robert Merton

Steven Messner
Lloyd Ohlin
Richard Rosenfeld
Robert J. Sampson
Clifford Shaw
Edwin Sutherland

References

Agnew, R. (2006). *Pressured into Crime: An Overview of General Strain Theory*. Los Angeles, CA: Roxbury Publishing Company.

Agnew, R. (2004). "A General Strain Theory Approach to Violence." Pp. 37-50 in M.A. Zahn, H.H. Brownstein, and S.L. Jackson (eds.) *Violence: From Theory to Research*. Cincinnati, OH: LexisNexis/Anderson Publishing.

Agnew, R. (2001). "Building on the Foundation of General Strain Theory: Specifying the Types of Strain Most Likely to Lead to Crime and Delinquency." *Journal of Research in Crime and Delinquency*, 38:319-361.

Agnew, R. (1999). "A General Strain Theory of Community Differences in Crime Rates." *Journal of Research in Crime and Delinquency*, 36:123-155.

Agnew, R. (1992). "Foundation for a General Strain Theory of Crime and Delinquency." *Criminology*, 30:47-87.

Agnew, R. (1987). "On 'Testing Structural Strain Theories.'" *Journal of Research in Crime and Delinquency*, 24:281-286.

Agnew, R., T. Brezina, J.P Wright & F.T. Cullen (2002). "Strain, Personality Traits, and Delinquency: Extending General Strain Theory." *Criminology*, 40:43-71.

Agnew, R. & H.R. White (1992). "An Empirical Test of General Strain Theory." *Criminology*, 30:475-499.

Baron, S.W. (2007). "Street Youth, Gender, and Financial Strain and Crime: Exploring Broidy and Agnew's Extension of General Strain Theory." *Deviant Behavior*, 28:273-302.

Baron, S.W. (2004). "General Strain, Street Youth and Crime: A Test of Agnew's Revised Theory." *Criminology*, 42:457-483.

Baron, S.W. & T.P. Hartnagel (1997). "Attributions, Affect, and Crime: Street Youths' Reactions to Unemployment." *Criminology*, 35:409-434.

Bernard, T.J. (1987). "Testing Structural Strain Theories." *Journal of Research in Crime and Delinquency*, 24:262-280.

Bernard, T.J. (1984). "Control Criticisms of Strain Theories: An Assessment of Theoretical and Empirical Adequacy." *Journal of Research in Crime and Delinquency*, 21:353-372.

Binder, A. & S.L. Polan (1991). "The Kennedy-Johnson Years, Social Theory, and Federal Policy in the Control of Juvenile Delinquency." *Crime & Delinquency*, 37:242-261.

Bordua, D.J. (1958-1959). "Juvenile Delinquency and Anomie." *Social Problems*, 6:230-238.

Broidy, L.M. (2001). "A Test of General Strain Theory." *Criminology*, 39:9-35.

Broidy, L.M. & R. Agnew (1997). "Gender and Crime: A General Strain Theory Perspective." *Journal of Research in Crime and Delinquency*, 34:275-306.

Braithwaite, J. (1981). "The Myth of Social Class and Criminality Reconsidered." *American Sociological Review*, 46:36-37.

Brezina, T. (1996). "Adapting to Strain: An Examination of Delinquent Coping Responses." *Criminology*, 34:39-60.

Britt, C.L. (1997). "Reconsidering the Unemployment and Crime Relationship: Variations by Age Group and Historical Period." *Journal of Quantitative Criminology*, 13:405-428.

Brown, S.E. (1985). "The Class-Delinquency Hypothesis and Juvenile Justice System Bias." *Sociological Inquiry*, 55:213-223.

Brownfield, D. (1986). "Social Class and Violent Behavior." *Criminology*, 24:421-438.

Bursik, R.J., Jr. (1988). "Social Disorganization and Theories of Crime and Delinquency: Problems and Prospects." *Criminology*, 26:519-551.

Bursik, R.J., Jr. (1986). "Ecological Stability and the Dynamics of Delinquency." In A.J. Reiss & M.H. Tonry (eds.) *Crime and Community*, pp. 35-66. Chicago, IL: University of Chicago Press.

Bursik, R.J., Jr. & H.G. Grasmick (1993). *Neighborhoods and Crime*. New York: Lexington Books.

Cattarello, A.M. (2000). "Community-Level Influences on Individuals' Social Bonds, Peer Associations, and Delinquency: A Multilevel Analysis." *Justice Quarterly*, 17:33-60.

Chamlin, M.B. & J.K. Cochran (2007). "An Evaluation of the Assumptions that Underlie Institutional Anomie Theory." *Theoretical Criminology* 11:39-61.

Chamlin, M.B. & J.K. Cochran (1995). "Assessing Messner and Rosenfeld's Institutional Anomie Theory: A Partial Test." *Criminology*, 33:411-429.

Chilton, R.J. (1964). "Continuity in Delinquency Area Research: A Comparison of Studies for Baltimore, Detroit, and Indianapolis." *American Sociological Review*, 29:74-83.

Clelland, D. & T.J. Carter (1980). "The New Myth of Class and Crime." *Criminology*, 18:319-336.

Cloward, R.A. & L.E. Ohlin (1960). *Delinquency and Opportunity: A Theory of Delinquent Gangs*. New York, NY: The Free Press.

Cohen, A.K. (1955). *Delinquent Boys: The Culture of the Gang*. New York, NY: The Free Press.

Cullen, F.T. (1988). "Were Cloward and Ohlin Strain Theorists? Delinquency and Opportunity Revisited." *Journal of Research in Crime and Delinquency*, 25:214-241.

DeFronzo, J. (1983). "Economic Assistance to Impoverished Americans." *Criminology*, 21:119-136.

Domhoff, G.W. (1967). *Who Rules America?* Englewood Cliffs, NJ: Prentice Hall.

Durkheim, E. (1897/1951). *Suicide: A Study in Sociology*, trans. J.A. Spaulding & G. Simpson. New York, NY: The Free Press.

Dye, T.R. (1976). *Who's Running America?* Institutional Leadership in the United States. Englewood Cliffs, NJ: Prentice Hall.

Elliott, D.S., W.J. Wilson, D. Huizinga, R.J. Sampson, A. Elliott & B. Rankin (1995). "The Effects of Neighborhood Disadvantage on Adolescent Development." *Journal of Research on Crime and Delinquency*, 33:389-426.

Esbensen, F.-A. & D. Huizinga (1990). "Community Structure and Drug Use: From a Social Disorganization Perspective." *Justice Quarterly*, 7:691-709

Fagan, J., E. Piper & M. Moore (1986). "Violent Delinquents and Urban Youth." *Criminology*, 24:439-471.

Felson, M. (1994). *Crime and Everyday Life: Insights and Implications for Society*. Thousand Oaks, CA: Pine Forge Press.

van Gemert, F. (2001). "Crips in Orange: Gangs and Groups in the Netherlands." In M.W. Klein, H-J. Kerner, C.L. Maxson & E.G.M. Weitekamp (eds.) *The Eurogang Paradox: Street Gangs and Youth Groups in the U.S. and Europe*, pp.145-152. Dordrecht, Netherlands: Kluwer Academic Publishers.

Hagan, J. (1989). "Micro and Macro-Structures of Delinquency Causation and a Power-Control Theory of Gender and Delinquency." In S.E. Messner, M.D. Krohn & A.E. Liska (eds.) *Theoretical Integration in the Study of Deviance and Crime*. Albany, NY: State University of New York Press.

Hagedorn J. & P. Macon (1988). *People and Folks Gangs: Crime, and the Underclass in a Rustbelt City*. Chicago, IL: Lake View Press.

Heitgard, J.L. & R.J. Bursik, Jr. (1987). "Extracommunity Dynamics and the Ecology of Delinquency." *American Journal of Sociology*, 92:775-787.

Hill, G.D. & E.M. Crawford (1990). "Women, Race, and Crime." *Criminology*, 28:601-626.

Hirschi, T. (1969). *Causes of Delinquency*. Berkeley, CA: University of California Press.

Hoffman, J.P. & T.O. Ireland (2004). "Strain and Opportunity Structures." *Journal of Quantitative Criminology*, 20:263-292.

Johnson, R.E. (1980). "Social Class and Delinquent Behavior." *Criminology*, 18:86-93.

Johnstone, J.W.C. (1983). "Recruitment to a Youth Gang." *Youth and Society*, 14:281-300.

Johnstone, J.W.C. (1978). "Social Class, Social Areas, and Delinquency." *Sociology and Social Research*, 63:49-72.

Kaspis, R.E. (1978). "Residential Succession and Delinquency." *Criminology*, 15:459-486.

Kim, S.-W. & W. Pridemore (2004). "Social Change, Institutional Anomie and Serious Property Crime in Transitional Russia." *The British Journal of Criminology*. 4:81-97.

Klein, M.W., H-J. Kerner, C.L. Maxson & E.G.M. Weitekamp (2001). *The Eurogang Paradox: Street Gangs and Youth Groups in the U.S. and Europe*. Dordrecht, Netherlands: Kluwer Academic Publishers.

Kobrin, S. (1959). "The Chicago Area Project—A 25-Year Assessment." *Annals of the American Academy of Political and Social Science*, 322:19-29.

Kornhauser, R.R. (1978). *Social Sources of Delinquency*. Chicago, IL: University of Chicago Press.

Lander, B. (1954). *Towards an Understanding of Juvenile Delinquency*. New York, NY: Columbia University Press.

Lien, I.-L. (2001). "The Concept of Honor, Conflict and Violent Behavior Among Youths in Oslo." In M.W. Klein, H-J. Kerner, C.L. Maxson & E.G.M. Weitekamp (eds.) *The Eurogang Paradox: Street Gangs and Youth Groups in the U.S. and Europe*, pp.165-174. Dordrecht, Netherlands: Kluwer Academic Publishers.

Lowenkamp, C.T., F.T. Cullen & T.C. Pratt (2003). "Replicating Sampson and Grove's Test of Social Disorganization Theory: Revisiting a Criminological Classic." *Journal of Research in Crime and Delinquency*, 40:351-373.

Mares, D. (2001). "Gangstas or Lager Louts? Working Class Street Gangs in Manchester." In M.W. Klein, H-J. Kerner, C.L. Maxson & E.G.M. Weitekamp (eds.) *The Eurogang Paradox: Street Gangs and Youth Groups in the U.S. and Europe*, pp.153-164. Dordrecht, Netherlands: Kluwer Academic Publishers.

Martinez, Jr., R. (2003). "Moving beyond Black and White Violence: African American, Haitian, and Latino Homicides in Miami." In D.F. Hawkins (ed.) *Violent Crime: Assessing Race & Ethnic Differences*. New York, NY: Cambridge University Press.

Mazerolle, P. (1998). "Gender, General Strain, and Delinquency: An Examination." *Justice Quarterly*, 15:65-91.

Mazerolle, P. & J. Maahs (2000). General Strain and Delinquency: An Alternative Investigation of Deviant Adaptations." *Justice Quarterly*, 17:73-778.

Mazerolle, P. & A. Piquero (1998). "Linking Exposure to Strain with Anger: An Investigation of Deviant Adaptations." *Journal of Criminal Justice*, 26:195-211.

Mazerolle, P., V.S. Burton, Jr., F.T. Cullen, T.D. Evans & G.L. Payne (2000). "Strain, Anger, and Delinquency Adaptations: Specifying General Strain Theory." *Journal of Criminal Justice*, 28:89-101.

Mazerolle, P., A. Piquero & G.E. Capowich (2003). "Examining the Links between Strain, Situational and Dispositional Anger, and Crime: Further Specifying and Testing General Strain Theory." *Youth & Society*, 35:131-157.

Maume, M.O. & M.R. Lee (2003) "Social Institutions and Violence: A Sub-national Test of Institutional Anomie Theory." *Criminology*, 41:1137-1172.

Menard, S. (1995). "A Developmental Test of Mertonian Theory." *Journal of Research in Crime and Delinquency*, 32:136-174.

Merton, R.K. (1968). *Social Theory and Social Structure*. New York, NY: The Free Press.

Merton, R.K. (1938). "Social Structure and Anomie." *American Sociological Review*, 3:672-682.

Messner, S.F. & R. Rosenfeld (2007). *Crime and the American Dream*, Fourth Edition. Belmont, CA: Wadsworth.

Messner, S.F. & R. Rosenfeld (2001). *Crime and the American Dream*, Third Edition. Belmont, CA: Wadsworth.

Messner, S.F. & R. Rosenfeld (1997). "Political Restraint of the Market and Levels of Criminal Homicide: A Cross-National Application of Institutional Anomie Theory." *Social Forces*, 75:1393-1416.

Messner, S.F. & R. Rosenfeld (1994). *Crime and the American Dream*. Belmont, CA: Wadsworth.

Messner, S.F., L.E. Raffalovich & R. McMillan (2001). "Economic Deprivation and Changes in Homicide Arrest Rates for White and Black Youths, 1967-1998: A National Time-Series Analysis." *Criminology*, 39:591-613.

Mills, C.W. (1956). *The Power Elite*. New York, NY: Oxford University Press.

Oberwittler, D. (2004). "A Multilevel Analysis of Neighbourhood Contextual Effects on Serious Juvenile Offending: The Role of Subcultural Values and Social Disorganization." *European Journal of Criminology* 1:201-235.

Paternoster, R. & P. Mazerolle (1994). "General Strain Theory and Delinquency: A Replication and Extension." *Journal of Research in Crime and Delinquency*, 31:235-263.

Peterson, R.D., L.J. Krivo & M.A. Harris (2000). "Disadvantage and Neighborhood Violent Crime: Do Local Institutions Matter?" *Journal of Research in Crime and Delinquency*, 37:31-63.

Piquero, N.L. & M.D. Sealock (2004). "Gender and General Strain Theory: A Preliminary Test of Broidy and Agnew's Gender/GST Hypotheses." *Justice Quarterly*, 21:125-158.

Piquero, N.L. & M.D. Sealock (2000). "Generalizing General Strain Theory: An Examination of and Offending Population." *Justice Quarterly*, 17:449-484.

Pridemore, W.A. (2002). "Vodka and Violence: Alcohol Consumption and Homicide Rates in Russia." *American Journal of Public Health*, 92:1921-1930.

Quinney, R. (1964). "Crime, Delinquency, and Social Areas." *Journal of Research in Crime and Delinquency*, 1:149-154.

Reynolds, A.J., J.A. Temple, D.L. Robertson & E.A. Mann (2001). "Long-Term Effects of an Early Childhood Intervention on Educational Achievement and Juvenile Arrest: A 15-Year Follow-up of Low-Income Children in Public Schools." *Journal of the American Medical Association*, 285:2339-2378.

Robinson, W.S. (1950). "Ecological Correlations and the Behavior of Individuals." *American Sociological Review*, 15:351-357.

Rose, S.M. (1972). *The Betrayal of the Poor: The Transformation of Community Action*. Cambridge, MA: Schenkmann.

Sampson, R.J. (2002). "Transcending Tradition: New Directions in Community Research, Chicago Style—The American Society of Criminology 2001 Sutherland Address." *Criminology*, 40:213-230.

Sampson, R.J. (1985). "Structural Sources of Variation in Race-Age-Specific Rates of Offending Across Major U.S. Cities." *Criminology*, 23:647-673.

Sampson, R.J. & W.B. Groves. (1989). "Community Structure and Crime: Testing Social-Disorganization Theory." *American Journal of Sociology*, 94:774-802.

Sampson, R.J., J.D. Morenoff & T. Gannon-Rowley (2002). "Assessing 'Neighborhood Effects': Social Processes and New Directions in Research." *Annual Review of Sociology*, 28:443-478.

Savolainen, J. (2000). "Inequality, Welfare State, and Homicide: Further Support for the Institutional Anomie Theory." *Criminology*, 38:1021-1042.

Scheuerman, L.A. & S. Kobrin (1986). "Community Careers in Crime." In A.J. Reiss & M.H. Tonry (eds.) *Crime and Community*, pp. 67-100. Chicago, IL: University of Chicago Press.

Schweinhart, L.J. (1987). "Can Preschool Programs Help Prevent Delinquency?" In J.Q. Wilson & G.C. Loury (eds.) *From Children to Citizens*, Vol. 3, pp. 135-153. New York, NY: Springer-Verlag.

Shaw, C.R. (1930/1966). *The Jack-Roller: A Delinquent Boy's Own Story*. Chicago, IL: University of Chicago Press.

Shaw, C.R. & H.D. McKay (1942). *Juvenile Delinquency in Urban Areas*. Chicago, IL: University of Chicago Press.

Short, J.F., Jr. (1989). "Exploring Integration of Theoretical Levels of Explanation: Notes on Juvenile Delinquency." In S.E. Messner, M.D. Krohn & A.E. Liska (eds.) *Theoretical Integration in the Study of Deviance and Crime*. Albany, NY: State University of New York Press.

Short, J.F., Jr. & F.L. Strodtbeck (1965). *Group Process and Gang Delinquency*. Chicago, IL: University of Chicago Press.

Simcha-Fagan, O. & J.E. Schwartz (1986). "Neighborhood and Delinquency: An Assessment of Contextual Effects." *Criminology*, 24:667-699.

Smith, D.A. & G.R. Jarjoura (1988). "Social Structure and Criminal Victimization." *Journal of Research in Crime and Delinquency*, 25:27-52.

Snodgrass, J. (1976). "Clifford R. Shaw & Henry D. McKay: Chicago Criminologists." *British Journal of Criminology*, 16:1-19.

Sutherland, E.H. (1937). *The Professional Thief*. Chicago, IL: University of Chicago Press.

Tauby, L.A. (1991). "Other Women's Money." *Working Women*, (December):56-59.

Taylor, R. & J. Covington (1988). "Neighborhood Changes in Ecology and Violence." *Criminology*, 26:553-589.

Thomas, C.W. & J.R. Hepburn (1983). *Crime, Criminal Law and Criminology*. Dubuque, IA: William C. Brown.

Tittle, C., W. Villemez & D. Smith (1978). "The Myth of Social Class and Criminality: An Empirical Assessment of the Empirical Evidence." *American Sociological Review*, 43:643-656.

Voss, H.L. & David M. Petersen (eds.) (1971). *Ecology, Crime and Delinquency*. New York, NY: Appleton-Century-Crofts.

Vowell, P.R. & D.C. May (2000). "Another Look at Classic Strain Theory: Poverty Status, Perceived Blocked Opportunity, and Gang Membership as Predictors of Adolescent Violent Offending." *Sociological Inquiry*, 70:42-60.

Wikstrom, P.O. & R. Loeber (2000). "Do Disadvantaged Neighborhoods Cause Well-Adjusted Children to Become Adolescent Delinquents?" *Criminology*, 38:1109-1142.

Wilson, W.J. (1987). *The Truly Disadvantaged: The Inner City, the Underclass, and Public Policy*. Chicago, IL: University of Chicago Press.

8

Social Process
Theories of Crime

While social structure theories address variations in rates of crime across structural conditions, *social process theories* most commonly attempt to explain how individuals become law violators. This focus on social interactions or processes experienced by individuals, as opposed to structural matters, represents a shift from macro-theory to micro-theory. Social process theories redress errors that arise when social structure theories are applied at the individual level. Traditional strain theories, for instance, are rooted in the premise that the social structure generates disproportionate pressure upon members of the lower- class to violate norms. The implication is that individuals subjected to economic disadvantage will resort to criminal or delinquent solutions, while the well-to-do, because of the absence of structurally induced strain, will not. This clearly can be misleading, because most people subjected to the stress of poverty do not become criminals, while some people who do not experience poverty become offenders.

Unlike social structure theories, social process theories typically do not approach crime and delinquency as primarily a lower-class problem; one of their strengths is that their explanatory power cuts across social classes and economic strata. The social process perspective is bolstered by self-report findings, reviewed in Chapter 4, which suggest that both delinquency and crime are more equally distributed across social classes than official data indicate.

At the same time, social process theories are consistent with a pattern of crime and delinquency weighted toward members of the lower-class. Features of the social structure may unevenly expose members of the lower-class to adverse social processes, which in turn could translate to higher rates of deviance. It is the interactions of individuals with more immediate groups, such as family and peers, however, that may push those individuals toward or pull them away from lawbreaking. In the social process framework, these are the key to explaining behavior. Each individual will learn values of either conformity or deviance through these social processes. Some theories within this tradition assert that the social processes one experiences may provide, or fail to provide, restraints against norm violations. The emphasis is on the interactions experienced within groups significant to the individual.

Three forms of social process theories are discussed in this chapter: *learning*, *culture conflict*, and *social control.* These approaches share the premise that groups influence the individual. They are often termed *social psychological theories* (as an alternative to the social process label) because they incorporate both group (social) and individual (psychological) variables. This perspective, then, seeks to integrate macro-level and micro-level explanations of crime, and social and psychological explanations, and also to account for crime across all social classes.

Attempts to categorize theories, however, are rarely endorsed with unanimity. A recent debate between Barbara Costello (1997; 1998) and Ross Matsueda (1997) illustrates the problem. Following the lead of Ruth Kornhauser (1978), Costello (1997:405) asserted that "differential association theory is the best known variation of the cultural deviance perspective." In response, Matsueda (1997:447) asserted that Kornhauser, and thus Costello, "faltered seriously when she reduced differential association theory to the ridiculous assumptions of 'cultural deviance theory'." The issue is embedded in how Edwin Sutherland's theory of differential association is read. His work is outlined in the following section.

Learning Criminal Behavior

The first group of social process theories is rooted in the notion that criminal behavior is learned in a social context. The learning perspective assumes that law-breaking values, norms, and motives are acquired through interaction with others. The requisite skills and techniques are likewise learned, although their content varies widely with the complexity of the crime. Because these theories envision criminal behavior as a product of the same learning processes as noncriminal behavior, crime is construed as "normal" rather than "pathological." The task of learning theories is to detail the process through which criminal patterns are cultivated. In the 2005 Presidential address to the American Society of Criminology, Julie Horney (2006) proposed that a broad version of Skinnerian rooted learning theory holds potential to organize much of our knowledge about criminal behavior.

Edwin H. Sutherland— Differential Association

Edwin Hardin Sutherland (1883-1950) was born in Nebraska and, after earning a Ph.D. in sociology at the University of Chicago, held professorial appointments at William Jewell College (Liberty, Missouri), the University of Illinois, the University of Minnesota, the University of Chicago, and served as department head at Indiana University (Odum, 1951). Sutherland is probably the most widely known criminologist, and *differential association* is the most prominent theory of criminal behavior. Sutherland's theory can be considered the first truly sociological effort to explain crime. His intent was to displace the biological and psychological explanations that were dominant early in the twentieth century. Independent of the merit of differential association as an explanation for crime, its role in bringing the field of criminology under the sociological umbrella is of immense importance.

Differential association was influenced by several intellectual traditions. First, the theory was an extension of the French criminologist Gabriel Tarde's (1843-1904) "laws of imitation," a social explanation of the origins of crime formulated late in the nineteenth century in response to the Lombrosian accounts (Vine, 1972).

Three other lines of thought had substantial influence on Sutherland's development of differential association: symbolic interactionism, cultural transmission, and culture conflict. Studying under George Herbert Mead (1863-1931) at the University of Chicago sensitized Sutherland to the *symbolic interaction* premise that people conduct themselves according to the meaning that things have for them. Consequently, Sutherland thought in terms of the meanings that individuals assign criminal conduct or, in other words, in terms of the emergence of value systems. Symbolic interactionism led him to consider how values favorable or unfavorable to criminal behavior are learned and interpreted in interaction with others.

Edwin Sutherland

Courtesy: Indiana University Archives

The tradition of ecological research at Chicago contributed to the conceptualization of differential association by suggesting that the community environment plays a key role in crime and delinquency. The findings of Shaw and McKay (see Chapter 7) that crime and delinquency tend to appear in neighborhoods with particular physical and social features, and that criminal values are transmitted just as are language and other cultural traits (i.e., *cultural transmission*), set the stage for explaining law-violating conduct as a product of learning. Their idea of social disorganization as the failure of a community to support crime-inhibiting conditions also was consistent with a learning explanation of criminal misconduct. Sutherland shifted the focus from the community (macro) to an individual (micro) level by addressing in differential association the process through which a person learns the criminal behavior patterns found in the community.

Culture conflict theorists such as Thorsten Sellin (1938) added to the Chicago ecological data an interpretation that subcultures such as those in the impoverished and socially disorganized neighborhoods studied by Shaw and McKay are characterized by their own conduct norms. These norms are contrary to those of the larger culture and become a source of conflict because behavior that is normal in the context of some subcultures constitutes crime in the eyes of the larger society. Sutherland drew upon this idea, along with those of cultural transmission and social disorganization, to develop differential association as an explanation for crime. Extending Figure 7.7, Figure 8.1 summarizes the framework underlying differential association. It depicts

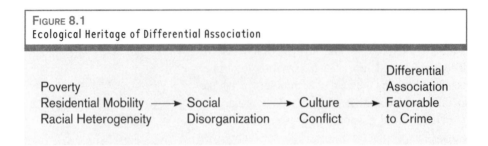

FIGURE 8.1
Ecological Heritage of Differential Association

factors such as poverty, residential mobility, and racial heterogeneity as contributing to social disorganization, which in turn, engenders culture conflict. Values and behavioral patterns culturally transmitted in socially disorganized neighborhoods produce culture conflict.

Differential association suggests that persons socialized in disorganized neighborhoods are likely to have associations that will encourage criminal adaptations. In contrast, individuals from socially organized neighborhoods are more likely to experience noncriminal associations. In later versions of differential association, Sutherland substituted differential social organization for social disorganization, noting that community organization represents a continuum rather than a dichotomy. What he drew from his close association with the Chicago School was an awareness that crime is socially distributed and a belief that it is learned behavior. The need was to understand that learning process.

Finally, Sutherland's own research endeavors contributed to differential association. In *The Professional Thief* (1937), he identified the careful tutelage necessary for both admittance to and practice of the trade. Best known of Sutherland's works is *White Collar Crime* (1949), which demanded that crime be defined to include offenses of persons in the upper socioeconomic class (see Chapters 11 and 12 for elaboration and examples). He pointed out that the crime picture was skewed by the neglect of such offenses in the justice process and in official crime statistics. He observed, "This bias is quite as certain as it would be if the scholars selected only red-haired criminals for study and reached the conclusion that redness of hair was the cause of crime" (1949:9). This concern goes to the heart of differential association because the theory is intended to account for all crime, including both the white-collar and street varieties. This was made explicit in the characterization of the goal of the theory as the development of a set of scientific "interrelated general propositions, to which no exceptions can be found" (Sutherland & Cressey, 1974:72). Differential association seeks to explain factors associated with crime (e.g., age, race, gender, socioeconomic status) but not causally related to it. Sutherland sought to identify processes common to offenders who are old and young, African-American and white, male and female.

Differential association was expounded primarily in Sutherland's classic textbook, which extended through 11 editions during a period of nearly 70 years. The first edition was published in 1924 as *Criminology*. Differential association first appeared in a crude form in the second (1934) edition, entitled *Principles of Criminology*. The theory was made explicit in the form of seven principles in the third (1939) edition. The final version of the theory, comprised of nine principles, was presented in the fourth (1947) edition. Following Sutherland's death, his student, Donald R. Cressey (1919-1987), revised the next six editions (1955-1978), but never modified Sutherland's last statement of differential association. Cressey felt that the theory should be tested extensively prior to subjecting it to modification. The final edition was published in 1992 with a revision by David Luckenbill.

Principles of Differential Association

The nine principles of differential association theory, are presented in Figure 8.2. These propositions specify "the process by which a particular person comes to engage in criminal behavior" (Sutherland & Cressey, 1974:75).

The principle that criminal behavior is learned provides the foundation for differential association. This expressly rules out heredity, human nature, and innovation as causes of aberrant behavior. Persons are not, as George Thorogood sings, "born to be bad," nor do they invent deviant behavior. They are taught how to behave, or misbehave, in a social context. This provides a sharp contrast with some other theories. Classical criminology and its deterrence propositions assume that human nature moti-

---

FIGURE 8.2
Principles of Differential Association

1. Criminal behavior is learned.

2. Criminal behavior is learned in interaction with other persons in a process of communication.

3. The principal part of the learning of criminal behavior occurs within intimate personal groups.

4. When criminal behavior is learned, the learning includes:
   (a) techniques of committing the crime, which are sometimes very complicated, sometimes very simple;
   (b) the specific direction of motives, drives, rationalization, and attitudes.

5. The specific direction of motives and drives is learned from definitions of the legal codes as favorable or unfavorable.

6. A person becomes delinquent because of an excess of definitions favorable to violation of law over definitions unfavorable to violation of law.

7. Differential associations may vary in frequency, duration, priority, and intensity.

8. The process of learning criminal behavior by association with criminal and anticriminal patterns involves all of the mechanisms that are involved in any other learning.

9. While criminal behavior is an expression of general needs and values, it is not explained by those general needs and values, since noncriminal behavior is an expression of the same needs and values.

Source: Adapted from E.H. Sutherland and D.R. Cressey (1974). *Criminology*, Ninth Edition, pp. 75-76, Philadelphia, PA: J.B. Lippincott.

vates the offender and focuses on how that proclivity might be curtailed. Likewise, control theory, which we shall turn to later in this chapter, rests on the premise that people will engage in crime or delinquency if not controlled. Which do you regard as the most plausible starting point for explaining crime? Are we destined to offend if not discouraged by external forces or are we disinclined to commit criminal acts until we are taught to do so? Each theory of crime rests on certain assumptions that may not be scientifically resolvable.

The second and third principles of differential association specify that criminal behavior is learned primarily in interaction with significant others such as family and friends. The emphasis placed on parental influence in child rearing illustrates widespread endorsement of these points. It is taken for granted that children will learn language, eating habits, personal hygiene, and a host of other behaviors from their parents. Differential association extends this learning process to the realm of crime. As the associations of youth (i.e., their circle of significant others) expand, it is expected that conduct initially shaped by parents will increasingly come under the influence of peers, often arousing concern of the parents about the company kept by their offspring.

Media influence upon learning is minimized in Sutherland's theory. Contemporary thought questions this, but the nature of media has changed dramatically since the formulation of differential association. Television, for example, was not introduced until after the birth of the theory. Given this contextual shift, it may not be inconsistent to incorporate media influences into the third principle. Highlight 8.1 reviews a recent media issue that received a lot of attention.

In the fourth principle, learning techniques of committing crime are said to be much less important than learning the mindset (motives, drives, rationalizations, attitudes) conducive to criminal behavior. While a particular mindset is essential, familiarity with technique relates to the type of crime perpetrated and to success in completing it without detection. Some crimes entail learning complex techniques. Studies of white-collar criminals (Sutherland, 1949), confidence men (Maurer, 1974), and professional thieves (Sutherland, 1937) illustrate the considerable skills that must be mastered to pursue these criminal paths. Many offenses, however, require little or no skill. Learning the motives and drives, which results in "a relatively constant desire or persistent urge to do illegal things" (Tittle et al., 1986:414) is, on the other hand, a requisite of criminal behavior. Similarly, criminal behavior is supported by learning rationalizations and attitudes that define it as acceptable. Persons may, for example, steal or rape because they have been taught specific attitudes and rationalizations, but the skills necessary for such crimes usually are minimal.

Definitions favorable and unfavorable to violations of the law, identified in the fifth statement, provide the key to differential association because they determine the values or mindset of the individual. We all are exposed to some mixture of definitions regardless of with whom we associate. Definitions favorable to violation of the law may be learned from law-abiding persons and, conversely, values supportive of legal codes may be acquired from convicted criminals. All of us as children received from our parents or parental figures some definitions favorable to law violation. Examples include observing parents ignoring speed limits, discussing ways to cheat on income tax returns, bringing materials home from the workplace, and failing to return excessive change dispensed by

HIGHLIGHT 8.1
Mass Media and Violence

Do rock lyrics cause violent behavior? This question is hotly debated in numerous circles, from the family kitchen to the halls of Congress. Tipper Gore, wife of former Vice President Al Gore, lobbied to institute a process of labeling songs and videos on the assumption that these lyrics have a negative impact on youth. In 1993 the rap song, "Cop Killer," by Ice-T was banned in a number of jurisdictions. Did this song promote and cause kids to kill cops, as its critics proclaimed? According to Dennis R. Martin, President of the National Association of Chiefs of Police, 144 U.S. police officers were killed in the line of duty during 1992. Did "Cop Killer" contribute to any of these deaths? Martin seems to think so and bases his opinion on a brief review of a case involving the wounding of two police officers by four juveniles in Las Vegas. Given that at least 1.5 million persons had listened to the original cut prior to its banning, Mark Hamm and Jeff Ferrell point out the absurdity of establishing a cause and effect relationship between the song and police deaths. They comment that this argument "intentionally engineers self-serving moral panic around rap music, and obstructs solutions to the sorts of problems which rap portrays."

They point out that Ice-T is not the first artist to include a "cop killer" theme in music. Eric Clapton's recording of "I Shot the Sheriff" had far greater sales and never suffered any sort of moral or political condemnation. A number of other songs have been equally graphic of violence toward police without public censure.

Source: Mark S. Hamm and Jeff Ferrell (1994). "Rap, Cops, and Crime: Clarifying the 'Cop Killer' Controversy." *ACJS Today*, Vol. 13, No. 1 (May/June).

cashiers. Accompanying these offenses are attitudes and rationalizations: "The traffic is light and the posted speed limit is too low"; "Taxes are too high"; "Nobody at work was going to use these materials"; "They shortchanged me plenty of times."

A definition unfavorable to legal codes does not require that a violation occur. Conveyance of values, even some that are intended to be positive, may be sufficient to constitute such a definition. The law-abiding parent who maintains that stealing to feed one's children is acceptable is providing a definition favorable to law violation, even though the intent is probably to bolster a sense of commitment to family. A parent confined to a penitentiary, on the other hand, may impress upon his or her visiting offspring that stealing is always wrong. In both circumstances, the young person would receive a mix of definitions.

The sixth statement of differential association specifies that an excess of definitions favorable to violation of law over definitions unfavorable embodies "the principle of differential association" (Sutherland & Cressey, 1974:75). It is the weight of definitions favorable to law violation, which may be construed as a ratio, that determines learning of criminal patterns:

$$\frac{\text{definitions favorable to violation of law}}{\text{definitions unfavorable to violation of law}}$$

These definitions are virtually illimitable and occur throughout life, with a person becoming delinquent (criminal) when the ratio exceeds unity.

It is not clear whether Sutherland meant to provide a single ratio incorporating all definitions favorable and unfavorable to crime or specific ratios for each type of crime (Tittle et al., 1986). Both the general and specific interpretations have been adopted to test the theory. While the general interpretation seems to be more widely entertained, it is evident that one may also learn only specific types of crime. A college student, for example, may be exposed to an excess of definitions favorable to smoking marijuana, but may have little association with definitions favorable to robbery.

All associations do not carry equal weight. The theory projects variation in terms of frequency, duration, priority, and intensity. Frequency refers to how often exposure to definitions occurs, and duration refers to the length of each exposure. Priority specifies the time that particular associations are initiated. Definitions absorbed in early childhood are said to have greater impact than those in later life. Intensity reflects the degree of identification with particular associations. The more a child identifies with a person, the more weight will be attributed to the definitions provided by that person. To bring the ratio specified by statement six into accord with proposition seven, it would be necessary to weight the formula by these factors; this task is one that admittedly "would be extremely difficult" (Sutherland & Cressey, 1974:76).

The final two statements of differential association provide further linkage to general learning principles. They emphasize that criminal behavior is learned in the same manner as other behavior, and that both types of behavior are products of similar needs and values. It is meaningless, for example, to attribute theft to desire for high income because many law-abiding persons also aspire to high incomes.

Criticisms of Differential Association

The major criticisms of differential association have focused on the theory's testability, causal framework, and breadth. Perhaps the most serious criticism is that the theory is not verifiable through empirical testing. Concepts incorporated in the theory (e.g., definitions, association, excess) were vaguely and imprecisely explained, leaving researchers to generate their own operational definitions (Tittle et al., 1986). There have been notable disparities both in operational definitions of the theory's concepts and in the research findings seeking to test the theory. Similarly, as noted above, measuring the ratio of definitions favorable to violation of the law to those unfavorable is impracticable (Tittle et al., 1986; Matsueda, 1988).

Charles Tittle and his colleagues (1986) focused on deficiencies in the causal framework set out by Sutherland. Differential association presumes, for example, that definitions acquired in association with others lead to behavioral patterns. In other words, some associations were thought to cause criminal behavior and others to cause noncriminal behavior. The reverse, however, is also plausible. Persons may engage in criminal conduct, for whatever reasons, and then seek out particular associations to match their criminal values and activities; this is a "birds of a feather" interpretation. Another possibility is that the relationship between associations and behavior may be reciprocal, that is, both may influence one another simultaneously. The causal nexus is also complicated by the possibility of intervening variables. Tittle et al. (1986) found, for example, that excess associations with criminal definitions led to criminal behavior only through intermediary factors such as criminal motivations.

Differential association is widely criticized as being so broad that, in attempting to explain all criminal behavior, the theory succeeds in explaining none. Ironically, other critics have faulted the theory for not attempting to answer enough questions. Specifically, some criminologists object that differential association fails to account for why people form the associations that they do. This criticism, however, overlooks the evolution of differential association, which shows that while it was formulated to account for individual criminal behavior, it was closely wed to macro-level explanations of crime. Sutherland learned from his professors at Chicago that features of the social structure generate normative conflict and that this determines a person's associations. Differential association theory examines the impact of those associations. Craig Reinarman and Jeffrey Fagan summarized Sutherland's view by noting "that while crime is caused by differential association with others from whom one learns an excess of definitions favorable to law violation, the probability of such differential association is a function of differential social organization" (1988:311).

Testing Differential Association

Despite the difficulties, many criminologists have attempted to test differential association. These efforts have established that deviance of one's friends is among the strongest and most consistent predictors of delinquent and criminal behavior identified to date. This finding has held up fairly consistently across a number of offense categories: age, gender, and a range of cultural settings. Misconduct has also been observed whether the "friend" variable was measured as total number of deviant friends, their proportion or the total number of offenses reported by friends. The key concept proposed by Sutherland and echoed by many other learning theorists is one of *balance*. That is, as the level of exposure to deviant influences increases, risk of learning or absorbing the values underlying those behaviors increases.

This notion of balance in learning from peers was recently expanded and tested by Jean Marie McGloin (2009). In her work, peer influence balance was conceptualized as the *deviance gap* between a subject and whom they identified as their best friend. It was hypothesized that it is the span of that gap, or relative deviance imbalance between the two, that exerts a delinquency influence. In short, and consistent with Sutherland's original ideas, the expectation was that individuals will seek to balance their levels of deviant activities with those of their best friend. A series of such propositions were tested with a sample of 1,170 students in grades 7-12, providing evidence of a reciprocal relationship between the delinquency of the youth and that of their best friends. In other words, each party to the friendship dyad tends to gravitate toward the behavioral pattern of their counterpart across time.

Social learning theorists have expanded and modified differential association to incorporate the principles of B.F. Skinner's operant conditioning (e.g., Glaser, 1956;

Jeffery, 1965; Adams, 1973; Akers, 1973). Daniel Glaser's (1956) *differential identification* is a variation of learning theory that specifies the degree of identity with a person, real or imaginary, as the key to adoption of values predisposing a person to criminal or law-abiding behavior. This modification allows a learning role for the media. A public figure such as an athlete, according to differential identification, might have more influence on a person than individuals with whom the person interacts directly. A film character, "Rambo," for instance, may be the source of greater value inculcation than real persons with whom the individual has face-to-face interaction.

Charles Tittle and his colleagues (1986) tested a causal model of differential association depicting the influence of six variables on self-reported prediction of criminal behavior by adults. The model incorporated reciprocal causation and the intervening variables discussed above. Fear of sanctions also was included in the model, which specifically posed an "experiential effect" (see Chapter 5) whereby associations with those providing definitions favorable to crime could serve to reduce fear of sanctions by teaching that certainty and severity of punishment is relatively low. Although no support for this segment of the model was found, the model represents careful consideration of the prospects for theoretical integration that are addressed in Chapter 10. Overall, the writers concluded: "Our analyses on the whole support Sutherland's main contention: that differential association with crime-favorable definitions is a central factor in explaining criminal behavior" (1986:425).

Ronald Akers—
Social Learning Theory

Ronald Akers (1985) expanded Sutherland's differential association theory by adding components of operant (voluntary response) and respondent (involuntary response) conditioning. While implied in Sutherland's sixth proposition, Akers formalized the extent to which learning is the result of exposure to both conforming and criminal behavior and definitions. Akers assumes that criminal behavior does not differ as behavior from normative conduct and both forms of behavior can be explained by his *social learning theory*. Accordingly, Akers identifies four key elements that help to shape behavior:

- differential associations;
- definitions;
- differential reinforcement; and
- imitation.

Differential associations refer to the process detailed by Sutherland, including the learning of definitions favorable or unfavorable to the law through a process of social interaction. Definitions apply to one's own attitudes; including orientations, rationalizations, definitions of the situation, and other evaluative aspects of right and wrong. These definitions include both general (i.e., religious and other moral values and norms that are unfavorable to nonconforming behavior) and specific beliefs (i.e., definitions that direct the person to commit particular acts). For example, a person may believe in the general validity of the legal order while at the same time disagree with rules regulating "victimless" crimes. This person can rationalize that while it may be illegal to smoke marijuana, it is a matter of individual choice with no victim and, therefore, it is acceptable.

Differential reinforcement consists of the actual or anticipated consequences of engaging in specific behavior. Rewards or other positive consequences will reinforce the desirability of the behavior whereas punishments will serve as a deterrent. In addition to direct rewards, Akers includes "the whole range of actual and anticipated, tangible and intangible rewards. . . . Social rewards can be highly symbolic . . . fulfilling ideological, religious, political, or other goals" (Akers, 1994:99).

Imitative behavior may also occur independent of the learning process. In some situations, observation of behavior committed by a revered role model (and observed consequences of the behavior) may result in imitative behavior. This possibility, however, is more pronounced for first-time or exploratory behavior than it is for explaining continued behavioral patterns.

Akers suggests that these components are part of a complex learning process and that criminal behavior can be expected when it has been differentially reinforced and defined as desirable. This social learning process is summarized as:

> one in which the balance of learned definitions, imitation of criminal or deviant models, and the anticipated balance of reinforcement produces the initial delinquent or deviant act. The facilitative effects of these variables continue in the repetition of acts, although initiation becomes less important than it was in the first commission of the act. After initiation, the actual social and non-social reinforcers and punishers affect whether or not that act will be repeated and at what level of frequency. Not only the behavior itself, but also the definitions are affected by the consequences of the initial act. Whether a deviant act will be committed in a situation that presents the opportunity depends on the learning history of the individual and the set of reinforcement contingencies in that situation (Akers, 1994:99).

One can see that Akers' version of social learning theory includes aspects of Sutherland's differential association as well as a number of characteristics of rational choice theory (see Chapter 5). In fact, Akers has made the argument that rational choice theory is no more than a variant of social learning theory and that it has nothing new to offer (Akers, 1990).

Tests of Social Learning Theory

Two main criticisms have been leveled at social learning theory: (1) the reinforcement proposition is tautological; and (2) the temporal sequencing of peer association and delinquency is poorly specified. The argument is that reinforcement occurs when behavior has been strengthened. This is true by definition and cannot be disproved, because if the behavior has not been strengthened, then it has not been reinforced. Akers counters this criticism by stating that the social learning proposition is non-tautological because "the theory would be falsified if it is typically the case that positive social approval or other rewards for delinquency . . . more often reduce than increase its occurrence" (Akers, 1990:103).

With regard to the temporal ordering criticism, Akers points out that the theory presumes a reciprocity between association with delinquent friends and delinquency. In some instances, individual delinquency will precede association with delinquent friends, while in others the association will precede initiation into deviance. This criticism would have merit, he insists, only if delinquency occurred prior to association with delinquent friends in the majority of instances.

To date, research has supported the social learning hypothesis with regard to the temporal sequencing issue. First, association with delinquent peers or with those who are tolerant of deviance occurs. Next, definitions favorable to illegal activity are learned. Then nonconforming behavior is positively reinforced by others, and finally the individual engages in the learned behavior (Krohn et al., 1985; Sellers & Winfree, 1990; Winfree et al., 1993; 1994; Menard & Elliott, 1994; Akers & Lee, 1996;). Research on social learning theory in general has produced consistent support for the propositions and when competing models have been tested using the same data sets, the social learning model receives the most empirical support (Akers & Cochran, 1985; Deschenes & Esbensen, 1999; Elliott et al., 1985; Esbensen & Deschenes, 1998; Matsueda & Heimer, 1987)

Social learning theory has fared well in explaining youthful marijuana use and theft (Bauer, 2009), partner violence (Sellers et al., 2005) and closely reflects the intergenerational character of family violence. Social learning theory has also been recently applied to account for police deviance (Chappell & Piquero, 2004). In short, social learning theory and other versions of the learning framework have been successfully applied to a wide range of behaviors.

Culture Conflict and Crime

Culture conflict theory is closely allied with versions of learning theory. The focus is on the normative content of cultures and how members of groups are trained through a learning process. Norms are seen as being passed down in the same manner as other cultural traits. When behaviors rooted in the values of one subculture conflict with those of society at large, problems arise. This conflict of values and the behaviors motivated by those values can cause criminal or delinquent behavior; this effect represents a perspective on the origins of crime called *culture conflict or cultural deviance*.

Because the basic framework of culture conflict is anchored in the learning process, we have included it in this chapter. Culture conflict, however, is one of the most difficult perspectives to categorize. Contrary to the tradition, culture conflict largely depicts crime as a lower-class problem by focusing on what is learned in subcultural settings. Three of the variations of culture conflict discussed below (Wolfgang and

Ferracuti's "subculture of violence;" Anderson's "code of the street," and Miller's "focal concerns") describe law violation exclusively as a lower-class phenomenon, while the third (Sellin's "culture conflict") implicates social class as a major source of culture conflict and crime. In addition, the perspective readily lends itself to macrotheoretical conceptualization and analysis, though social process theories ordinarily are limited to the micro-level. Like differential association, the origins of culture conflict theory are linked to the ecological findings of the Chicago School. The discovery of Shaw and McKay that crime and delinquency persisted in impoverished

GANG FEATURE

Birds of a Feather?

Two relatively recent studies have tested the efficacy of social learning theory in explaining gang delinquency. Thornberry and his colleagues conducting the Rochester Youth Development Survey tested two competing models of gang activity: social facilitation and selection. The social facilitation model, what we would label social learning, indicates that gang members are no different from non-gang members but that "the normative structure and group processes of the gang are likely to bring about high rates of delinquency and drug use" (Thornberry et al., 1993:58). The selection model is derived from social control theory and suggests that gang members are inherently different from non-gang members. This model "posits that gangs recruit their members from adolescents who are already delinquent, or at least who have a high propensity for delinquency" (Thornberry et al., 1993:57). They also questioned whether an "enhancement" model may better explain gang behavior. The enhancement model maintains that gang members are recruited from delinquent youth but that the gang environment exacerbates their delinquency. Using their longitudinal data, Thornberry et al. compared rates of delinquency across time while controlling for gang membership. They found that "(R)esults for the transient members—those who were gang members for only one year and presumably less committed to the gang—are most involved [and] consistent with the social facilitation model. . . . Results from the stable gang members—those who remain as gang members for at least two years and who are presumably

more committed to the gang—are slightly more consistent with the enhancement model. . . . But even for them, delinquent involvement is greatest during their years of active gang membership. None of these results is consistent with the pure selection model" (Thornberry et al., 1993:70-71).

Utilizing a different strategy, Winfree and his colleagues surveyed 197 ninth-grade students. A number of questions derived from Akers social learning theory were developed and asked of the students. For example, to measure differential association, they computed the proportion of one's best friends who were involved in gang activity. To measure the concept of differential reinforcement, they asked respondents about what good and bad things would be associated with gang membership. In their analyses, they attempted to classify the respondents according to responses to the survey questions. They found that "Gang members were distinguishable from nongang youths more in terms of variables derived from social learning than personal-biographical characteristics, including ethnicity, gender, and place of residence" (Winfree et al., 1994:167).

Both of these studies relied upon self-report methodologies and used school-based samples. While the Rochester study was longitudinal in design, the New Mexico study was cross-sectional. Different measures were used and different analysis strategies were conducted. Yet, despite these study differences, the authors report similar results; general support for the efficacy of social learning theory in explaining adolescent gang membership.

and socially disorganized neighborhoods, despite the different ethnic backgrounds of new waves of inhabitants, suggested subcultures as a source of law-violating behavior. Both the ecological and culture conflict perspectives display features that cross the social structure and process boundaries, and for that reason, these perspectives might best be conceptualized as bridging theories (Williams & McShane, 1998).

Like strain theories described in the previous chapter, culture conflict theories locate the cause of crime and delinquency in subcultural features. The causal schemes delineated, however, are quite distinct. While strain theorists see deviance as a product of frustration experienced by lower-class persons upon failure to reach goals derived from the dominant middle-class culture, the culture conflict perspective views deviance as conformity to norms of a subculture that run counter to those of the dominant group. Because law-breaking behavior is learned as part of the content of a subcultural code, it is construed as normal rather than pathological.

The popularity of culture conflict theories has declined in recent years. While there are a number of reasons for this decline, J. Mitchell Miller and his colleagues (1997) identify ideology as the primary factor. The first blow to their position came from the rise of conflict-based theories in the 1970s (see Chapter 9). This perspective located the crime problem with the state and the elite who dominate it, a position quite contrary to identifying subcultures as being at the root of the problem. More recently, calls for "political correctness" have implied that attributing crime to subcultural differences is labeling the subcultures as inferior, drawing focus away from social conditions, and perhaps reflecting racism.

Thorsten Sellin—
Conflict of Conduct Norms

Thorsten Sellin (1897-1994) first stressed culture conflict as an explanation of crime and delinquency, drawing liberally from ideas of the Chicago School and those of Sutherland. Sellin (1938:62) noted that Shaw's ecological studies identified neighborhood characteristics that "give rise to social attitudes which conflict with the norms of the law." He also credited Sutherland's concept of differential association with providing the sociological framework for culture conflict theory. Sutherland had served on the delinquency subcommittee of the Social Science Research Council. Under the auspices of the council, Sellin's major statement on culture conflict was issued in his 1938 monograph, *Culture Conflict and Crime*.

Sellin was born in Sweden but emigrated to North America with his family at the age of 17. He earned a Ph.D. in sociology at the University of Pennsylvania and taught there from 1921 to 1968 (Laub, 1983). He served as mentor to a number of accomplished criminologists, most notably Marvin Wolfgang, with whom Sellin collaborated on several research projects. Aside from his seminal work on culture conflict, Sellin has made major contributions in a wide range of areas, including crime statistics and capital punishment.

In a 1979 interview, Sellin said that he had not offered culture conflict as a theory to explain crime, but rather as "an attempt to give a new slant, a new inspiration . . .

to the field" (Laub, 1983:174). It was Sellin's concern with the development of the scientific stature of criminology that led him in this direction. His work succeeded in moving criminology away from a legalistic and toward a normative definition of crime (see Chapter 1). Noting that the legal definition of crime was inadequate to develop laws of human behavior, as social science requires, Sellin argued that the task of criminology is to explain violation of conduct norms. The Catch-22 is that conformity to the norms of many subcultures may contradict norms of the dominant culture, placing members of those subcultures in the position of violating the norms of some social group no matter how the members conduct themselves. Sellin's concept of culture conflict sensitized criminology to the relativity of conduct norms and, therefore, of crime. Crime, then, may be explained in terms of conduct norms learned in a subculture that does not shape legal codes.

Given the context of the times, Sellin often focused on the immigration of persons to America. He cited, for example, a case in which a "Sicilian father in New Jersey killed the 16-year-old seducer of his daughter, expressing surprise at his arrest since he had merely defended his family honor in a traditional way" (1938:68). This illustrates *primary culture conflict*, the collision of norms from distinct cultural systems. Sellin's work also delineated *secondary culture conflict*, which occurs with the evolution of subcultures in a heterogeneous society. This type of conflict of conduct norms is characteristic of contemporary America, exemplified by the law violations of groups such as juvenile gangs in urban ghettos, drug-oriented subcultures, outlaw motorcycle gangs (see Quinn & Koch, 2003), and racist cliques (see Pridemore & Freilich, 2006).

Marvin Wolfgang and Franco Ferracuti— Subculture of Violence

Sellin's protégé, Marvin Wolfgang (1925-1998), teamed with the Italian criminologist Franco Ferracuti to extend the concept of culture conflict in their *subculture of violence* theory (Wolfgang & Ferracuti, 1967). The theory is not intended to explain all violent behavior, but only assaults and homicides that occur spontaneously or in what is popularly termed the heat of passion. Most violence is of this variety rather than of a premeditated nature or of psychotic origin. Spontaneous violence is particularly prevalent among late adolescent to middle-age males in lower-class settings.

Wolfgang and Ferracuti's efforts represent an early attempt to integrate theoretical explanations for crime into a single framework. Wolfgang contributed the sociological perspective characteristic of North American criminology, drawing heavily from culture conflict, ecological studies, and a variety of learning theories. Ferracuti, on the other hand, brought to their collaborative effort the medical and biological paradigms that have dominated European criminology. Their theory also draws freely on psychological variables, combining them with social factors, as is characteristic of social process theories.

The theory contends that the subculture of violence "is only partly different from the parent culture. . . . It cannot be *totally* different from the culture of which it is a part" (Wolfgang & Ferracuti, 1967:100). A subculture need not display violence as "the predominant mode of expression," but a "potent theme of violence" differentiates the subculture from the larger culture. A subculture of violence exists when, in some social situations, "a violent and physically aggressive response is either expected or required" (1967:159). Members of the subculture are obliged to resort to violence to defend their "honor." An attack on one's manliness, that is, on a man's physical prowess or sexuality, for example, demands violent retaliation. A formative influence on the subculture of violence theory can be seen in Wolfgang's earlier homicide research, as reflected in the concluding chapter of *Patterns in Criminal Homicide* (1958/1975:329):

> Our analysis implies that there may be a subculture of violence which does not define personal assaults as wrong or antisocial; in which quick resort to physical aggression is a socially approved and expected concomitant of certain stimuli. . . . A conflict or inconsistency of social norms is most apparent, and the value-system of the reference group with which the individual differentially associates and identifies, determines whether assaultive behavior is necessary, expected, or desirable in specific social situations. When an insult or argument is defined as trivial and petty by the prevailing culture norms, but as signals for physical attack by a subcultural tradition, culture conflict exists.

Wolfgang and Ferracuti conceded that social structure or other factors may be responsible for the emergence of the subculture, but they explained the continuity of the subculture through a learning process. Learning is facilitated by positive reinforcement of violent behavior and, conversely, imposition of negative sanctions upon failure to respond violently to the appropriate stimuli. Lower-class males who inhabit the locale of a subculture of violence and who are not hesitant to respond to perceived insults with skillfully deployed violence are accorded prestige, while those males who use nonviolent means of conflict resolution are scorned and ostracized. Because members of the subculture learn violence as a normal way to manage interpersonal conflict, guilt is obviated. Social control strategies of the dominant culture, therefore, are circumvented by the learned values and norms of the subcultures. This suggests that the spontaneous violent behavior generated by subcultural values might best (or only) be contained by decomposing the subculture. Urban renewal efforts to disperse low-income housing over wider areas are designed, in part, for this purpose.

Sandra J. Ball-Rokeach (1973) undertook one of the first empirical tests of the subculture of violence thesis. She found little relationship between stances on "machismo" values delineated by Wolfgang and Ferracuti and self-reported participation in interpersonal violence, leading to the conclusion "that values play little or no role as determinants of interpersonal violence" (1973:742-743). Noting the lack of empirical support for any of the subcultural theories of violence, Thomas Bernard (1990) recently tested a variation not rooted in violence. He drew on prior research suggesting that "angry aggression" develops among the "truly disadvantaged" as a consequence of racial discrimination and low social position in the urban environment. The violent subcultural setting described by Wolfgang and Ferracuti, in other words, might be attributable to the social structure rather than value systems unique to that environment.

Elijah Anderson—
Code of the Street

A more recent approach to explaining the disproportionate violence among young African-American males living in impoverished areas has been proposed by Elijah Anderson (1999). The *code of the street* that he details sounds very similar to the "honor" that Wolfgang and Ferracuti described. As Anderson explains, the individual committed to the street code feels compelled to risk their life in violent confrontations if "dissed" (disrespected). The code, like the subculture of violence, requires the resident to project toughness, engage in violent posturing, and to be willing to resort to violence. Abiding by this code provides the otherwise unsuccessful young man with a sense of self-worth. The attitudes and posturing, in turn, feed a cycle of violence. Young men who are "strapped" (carrying firearms) or conceal "blades" (knives) are primed for violence, as are those they encounter.

Where Anderson's code of the street differs from the subculture of violence and other culture conflict theories that preceded it is in identifying the origins of the cultural content. Anderson offers a connection to social structure theories, reasoning that the street code develops in response to poverty, discrimination, family disruption, and other structural problems. That is, social structural deficiencies lead to adoption of the street code as an alternative set of values, while they, in turn, lead to increased levels of violence. Tests of this theoretical framework have already lent some empirical support to these connections between social structures and the street code (Brezina et al., 2004; Stewart & Simons, 2006).

Like many other contemporary perspectives, a particular strength of the street code is its connection of social structure and culture conflict traditions. Note that the values incorporated in the cultural component of the street code hold a strong resemblance to those identified in Walter Miller's earlier culture conflict theory.

Walter Miller—
Lower-Class Focal Concerns

Walter Miller's (1958) focus on features of lower-class culture also attributed deviance to a distinct normative structure that conflicts with norms of the dominant culture. As with other theories falling within the culture conflict tradition, Miller's theory is grounded in learning theory and ecological data. To the extent that the norms learned in lower-class settings depart from those of the dominant middle-class culture, the stage is set for culture conflict.

Miller, a cultural anthropologist, employed an ethnographic (descriptive) research strategy to observe lower-class male gang members in their natural habitat. Seven social workers directed by Miller spent three years with members of delinquent gangs in Roxbury, Massachusetts, near Boston.

The field observations led Miller to conclude that lower-class persons display a set of *focal concerns* that distinguish them from the mainstream of American society. While similar to values, these focal concerns have the scientific advantage of being directly observable in the behavior of subjects and, at least arguably, of being more descriptively neutral. The six focal concerns identified by Miller are summarized in Figure 8.3.

| FIGURE 8.3 |
| Walter Miller's Lower-Class Focal Concerns |

Dimension	Definition
Trouble	Interference from official social control agents of the dominant culture
Toughness	Distorted image of masculinity
Smartness	Skill and ability to dominate verbal exchanges pertinent to the lower-class environment
Excitement	Relieving the monotonous routine of lower-class existence through emotion-arousing entertainment that often violates norms of the dominant culture
Fate	Belief in little control over the forces shaping one's life
Autonomy	Ambivalence regarding freedom from external control reflected in overt resentment of control, but covert pursuit of control

Source: Adapted from W.B. Miller (1958). "Lower-Class Culture as a Generating Milieu of Gang Delinquency." *Journal of Social Issues*, 14, 3:5-19.

Trouble

Miller concluded that members of the lower class are preoccupied with the prospect of their activities leading to *trouble*, which results in unwanted interference from representatives of the dominant culture. This concern with "getting into trouble" does not reflect identification with the norms of middle-class culture, but rather trepidation about the potential complications for life that deviation from such norms brings. Truancy, for example, may lead to threatening inquiry from school officials or human service professionals. Cohabitation, if discovered by social workers, may lead to the withholding of welfare benefits. At the heart of trouble, however, is the potential for arrest, fines, court appearances, jail sentences, and similar inconveniences generated in response to drinking sprees, fights, or other illegal behavior. The behavior may conform to subcultural expectations, but trouble represents its undesirable consequences. A lower-class male recurrently involved in law-violating behavior may be revered as a "good old boy" or a "stand-up guy," but at the same time decried as "always in trouble." Individuals have to decide whether to conduct themselves as the subcultural standards encourage or to avoid trouble. Miller noted that potential for trouble serves as a negative criterion for mate selection in the lower-class, in contrast to the potential for success and achievement that are accorded priority in the middle-class. Trouble, then, is met with ambivalence in lower-class culture.

Toughness

The *toughness* dimension of lower-class focal concerns, Miller suggested, may be a reaction to the female-dominated households that are prominent in the lower-class environment. Lacking male role models, lower-class boys develop patterns of behavior that distort masculinity. Strength, physical skills and prowess, and bravery in the face of threats are emphasized, while intellectual and cultural foci of the upper classes are actively disdained. Boys who are upwardly mobile, scholastically successful, or who develop artistic talents are labeled "queer," "sissy," or "pansy," while tattoos are considered masculine. Homophobia (irrational fear of, aversion to, or discrimination against homosexuality or homosexuals) is rampant among lower-class males; characteristics of males that depart from a narrow perception of masculinity are labeled pejoratively. Overt expression of affection among males is taboo; bantering and roughhousing are encouraged.

Trouble may be a sequel to preoccupation with toughness. Determination to demonstrate one's masculinity through physical combat typically generates behavior defined by legal codes as disruptive, disorderly, or assaultive. This and other dimensions of lower-class focal concerns can be seen as inherently contradictory to the codified norms of the middle-class.

Smartness

While intellectual accomplishment, as reflected by formal education or command of traditional and organized bodies of knowledge, is met with contempt in the lower-class, being streetwise is highly valued. The lower-class male is provided an opportunity to learn particular skills or to foster *smartness* in the lower-class milieu and is judged by his success in cultivating those "smarts." Smartness is the ability to manipulate and outwit others through skillful deployment of verbal and psychological skills. The lower-class male, for example, takes pride in out-maneuvering the police and other representatives of the dominant culture in verbal exchanges, making their antagonists appear naive and foolish. There is a continuous flow of aggressive repartee in the ribbing, kidding, and teasing that transpires. These exchanges often consist "of increasingly inflammatory insults, with incestuous and perverted sexual relations with the mother a dominant theme" (Miller, 1958:10). Mastery of these skills can place an individual even higher in social rank than the "tough guy." The "smart guy" is also admired as one who reaps benefits from others with a minimum of physical effort. Con men, card sharks, and persons in similar roles fit this perception of success or "having it made."

Excitement

While the daily routine of lower-class existence can be exceedingly boring, the humdrum of "hanging out" or monotonous jobs are interspersed by a periodic "night on the town," particularly on weekends. Thrill or *excitement* is actively sought on these occasions. Toughness and smartness are acted out and the tediousness of daily routine is replaced with use of alcohol and drugs, gambling, music, and sexual quests. An evening filling the expectation of excitement typically consists, though not in any predetermined order, of getting high, becoming boisterous, having sexual encounters, and demonstrating toughness through verbal exchanges or fighting. Fixation on excitement permeates lower-class culture and generates ambivalence because of its potential for trouble.

Fate

Lower-class culture depicts the future as a matter of *fate* rather than a product of education, hard work, saving, and other paths subsumed under the middle-class focus on deferred gratification. One is "lucky" or "unlucky" and, although luck is seen as prone to shift, the future is not seen as subject to control. Belief in fate complements smartness; both, for example, support gambling while denigrating the value of work. Preoccupation with fate is reflected in the prominence of gambling in lower-class settings (e.g., playing pool, rolling dice, booking bets) and in the content of many body tattoos (e.g., "lucky," "born to lose"). Fate also interfaces with the other focal concerns of the lower-class; gambling and tattooing, for example, may also exemplify toughness and excitement, while raising prospects of trouble.

Autonomy

The final dimension of Miller's lower-class focal concerns is reflected in "a strong and frequently expressed resentment of the idea of external controls, restrictions on behavior, and unjust or coercive authority" (Miller, 1958:12). This control theme runs rampant through country music, exemplified in songs such as Johnny Paycheck's "Take This Job and Shove It" and a plethora of prison songs, including Johnny Cash's "Folsom Prison Blues" and "Doin' My Time." Ironically, *autonomy* or freedom from external intervention and control is precluded by enactment of the other focal concerns. A lifestyle revolving around the lower-class focal concerns almost inevitably leads to trouble and the intervention of social control agents representing the dominant culture. Autonomy, in other words, reflects the resentment of the lower-class toward culture conflict.

Analysis of Focal Concerns

Do you see evidence of these focal concerns in lower-class environments? Are they different from the values or concerns of the middle-class? If so, does preoccupation with these concerns frequently lead to conflict with the law? These are some of the empirical questions that must be addressed before accepting or rejecting Miller's theory. Miller's perspective offers a sharp contrast with the strain tradition's premise that lower-class and middle-class persons subscribe to essentially the same values, but that lower-class persons resort to crime and delinquency out of frustration resulting from failure to live up to those expectations.

Both perspectives also have important philosophical implications. Strain theory's presumption that middle-class values must logically be coveted by the lower-class might be considered presumptuous and chauvinistic. Conversely, Miller's lower-class focal concerns resemble stereotyping and bigotry. Miller's proposition is also a radical notion rooted in conflict rather than consensus theory. The fundamental idea is that different social classes subscribe to contradictory norms and that the more powerful classes impose their moral views on the less powerful through legal channels.

A number of criticisms have been leveled at Miller's theory. Some have noted that it is difficult for middle-class persons to observe lower-class settings without injecting class bias. Second, this theory, like most others, only addresses male delinquency. Others have concluded that the theory is tautological. Miller observed the behavior of persons in a lower-class milieu to identify their focal concerns and then used those focal concerns to account for their behavior. Little research has been undertaken to test the theory and, given the difficulty of observing and interpreting focal concerns or other value-related phenomena, it will be difficult to do so. Nevertheless, the unique assumptions of the theory have ensured its prominent place in discussions of the causes of crime and delinquency.

Social Control and Crime

Social control, like learning and culture conflict theories, revolves around the process of socializing people. For these theories, propensity for crime or delinquency is a function of social processes that are assumed or delineated. The common ground, however, ends here. *Control Theories* represent a sharp contrast with other theoretical approaches, even those similarly classified as social process explanations.

Each variation of the control perspective rests on the premise that, if left alone, people will pursue self-interests rather than those of society. Only by intervening and nurturing persons into a controlled social existence can they be fashioned into conformity. Other social process theories, including learning and culture conflict explanations, however, take the opposing view: that human nature is good and deviance only emerges as a product of negative environmental experience. Control theory, however, views crime as predictable behavior that society has failed to bridle. Learning theories and the related culture conflict perspective depict crime as a product of criminogenic forces, while the control approach sees crime as a consequence of the failure of social constraints.

A notion of free will is relied upon to accommodate the shift in focus from criminogenic forces to social controls. As in the classical accounts of criminal behavior, control theory depicts choice as relevant to behavior. This perspective, along with the classical (Chapter 5) views, departs from positivist criminology. Because it assigns choice and responsibility to the offender, the control approach is often considered a conservative account of crime and deviance.

Value consensus also lies at the basis of control theory. It is assumed that most people believe essentially in a common set of values, even if they violate those values. Obtaining social conformity is a matter of applying measures to prevent people from violating the norms to which they initially are committed. Each variation of control theory depicts the controls necessary for conformity or explains how those controls are circumvented. Two major contributions to the control perspective are examined in the remainder of this section: neutralization and social bond theories.

Gresham M. Sykes and David Matza— Techniques of Neutralization

The original point of departure for *techniques of neutralization* as a theory of delinquency was Sutherland's assertion that learning criminal or delinquent behavior includes values and rationalizations as well as techniques of committing offenses. Gresham Sykes and David Matza (1957) contended that learning excuses that may be situationally invoked allow boys to engage in behavior that violates the value system to which they basically subscribe. To support this assertion, Sykes and Matza cited anecdotal evidence that offenders typically experienced feelings of guilt and shame. In addition, they observed that offenders display some selectivity in their choice of victims, tending to avoid those who more closely reflect mainstream values of society and seeking out disvalued targets. Priests and nuns, for example, enjoy relative immunity from victimization, while robbery victims are actively sought among homosexuals ("queer baiting") or alcoholics ("rolling drunks"). The point is buttressed by comments made to one of the authors by a prison inmate in regard to child molesters. He noted that while we, on the outside of prisons, saw inmates as the "scum of society," molesters within the prison were viewed by other inmates as the "scum of the scum" and were often assaulted, robbed, and abused in other ways.

Note that it can be acceptable to violate norms while still holding to their validity if such norms are seen as conditional. Although one is expected, for example, to be on time for social engagements and is committed to that behavioral norm, some circumstances may excuse tardiness. Norms that are codified in criminal codes, in contrast, are quite explicit in identifying excuses and mitigating circumstances. "The criminal law, more so than any comparable system of norms, acknowledges and states the principled grounds under which an actor may claim exemption. The law contains the seeds of its own neutralization" (Matza, 1964:61). These seeds lie in concepts such as intent, self-defense, insanity, and accident. According to the theory of neutralization, such juridical precepts are extended well beyond their legal bounds to serve as mechanisms to relieve guilt, thus freeing a person to violate norms. Figure 8.4 lists the five techniques of neutralization originally set forth by Sykes and Matza.

To allow violation of laws in which one essentially believes, while preserving self-image, neutralization must *precede* the offense. Rationalizations are excuses that *follow* norm violation and therefore do not account for the offense. This distinction raises an important methodological issue, as it disvalues the testimony of offenders following their violations as causally related to their lawbreaking.

FIGURE 8.4
Gresham Sykes and David Matza's Techniques of Neutralization

Technique	Definition
Denial of Responsibility	disclaiming personal accountability for law violation
Denial of Injury	claiming that the prohibited behavior is absent the element of harm
Denial of the Victim	transforming the victim of illegal behavior into a justifiable target
Condemnation of the Condemners	denouncing the persons that allege law violation
Appeal to Higher Loyalties	justifying law violation by conforming to the moral demands of another group affiliation

Source: Adapted from G.M. Sykes and D. Matza (1957). "Techniques of Neutralization: A Theory of Delinquency." *American Sociological Review*, 22:664-670.

Denial of Responsibility

The *denial of responsibility* extends the legal concept of intent to dismiss responsibility for deviant actions. The strategy is echoed in assertions that the outcome was "an accident," was "not my fault," or that "I couldn't help it." Other variables allegedly beyond the offender's control are interjected to deny or mitigate responsibility for the conduct. The strategy extends beyond circumstances immediately surrounding a particular incident, enveloping factors in the social environment "such as unloving parents, bad companions, or a slum neighborhood. In effect, the delinquent approaches a 'billiard ball' conception of himself in which he sees himself as helplessly propelled into new situations. . . . By learning to view himself as more acted upon than acting, the delinquent prepares the way for deviance from the dominant normative system without the necessity of a frontal assault on the norms themselves" (Sykes & Matza, 1957:667). The inequities of our social structure can be incorporated into a mentality that is then available to neutralize norm violation by claiming a lack of personal responsibility.

Denial of Injury

A claim that no real harm was done reflects the denial of injury. This is shown in assertions such as: "They could afford it;" "I was just borrowing it;" and "They've got insurance." *Denial of injury* can be thought of as an extension of the legal category of offenses *mala prohibita*; that is, the neutralizer claims that the offense was merely a technical violation, not a moral wrong. The delinquent is only exaggerating, not departing from, the larger societies' exceptions for "kid's stuff," "a little hell-raising" or "sewing wild oats."

Denial of the Victim

By denying existence of a victim, the offender dismisses the wrongfulness of the illegal conduct under the particular circumstances of its occurrence. *Denial of the victim* actually has two meanings, with distinctive implications (Minor, 1981). First, the existence of a victim is denied by the assertion that the targets of the offense are blameworthy. The victims "got what they deserved" and thus are not appropriately regarded as victims. Con men, for example, often assert that "you can't take an honest man;" he must have "larceny in his veins" (Maurer, 1974:101). Stealing from allegedly crooked merchants, defending turf from rival gangs, or assaulting homosexuals all exemplify the blameworthy victim as an excuse for transgression. Groups as notoriously deviant as the Hell's Angels stand ready to excuse law violation by assertions such as: "If any girl claims she was raped by the Angels, it was most likely because she came up and asked for it" (Thompson, 1966:246).

The second form of denial of the victim is much less extreme. "Insofar as the victim is physically absent, unknown, or a vague abstraction (as is often the case in delinquent acts committed against property), the awareness of the victim's experience is weakened . . . and it is possible that a diminished awareness of the victim plays an important part in determining whether or not this process is set in motion" (Sykes & Matza, 1957:668). The victim in this instance is not actively reputed, but does not emerge as a factor to be contended with explicitly.

Condemnation of the Condemners

By repudiating the motives and behaviors of their accusers, law violators are asserting that their own misconduct, by comparison, is less blameworthy. They shift focus from actions contemplated or undertaken to those of the group responding to the deviance, particularly agents of social control. Offenders often deride police, judges, and prosecutors as "corrupt" or "getting away with worse." To the extent that he or she is successful in changing the subject to the actions of accusers, the criminal has successfully neutralized the norms that would control his or her behavior. Sykes and Matza term this process the *condemnation of the condemners*.

Appeal to Higher Loyalties

A dilemma is encountered when a person seeks to abide by the norms of the larger society but those norms are in conflict with the behavioral demands of a smaller, but more intimate, group with which the person is affiliated. Violation of the rules of society may be neutralized by claiming loyalty to the more pressing demands of the immediate group, an *appeal to higher loyalties*. Thus, the offender may claim that the offense was necessary "to help a friend" or "for my family." This dilemma of dual loyalties, like the other techniques of neutralization, has its seeds in culturally condoned excuses. Few would blame a father who stole a drug he could not afford or otherwise acquire in order to treat his very sick infant.

The Context of Neutralization

In *Delinquency and Drift* (1964), Matza elaborated on the neutralization process. His critique of positivism assigns motivations to delinquency a lesser role than they have assumed in theories such as differential association, differential opportunity, reaction formation, or lower-class focal concerns. Matza noted that these positivistic theories account for "too much delinquency"; most youth exposed to the conditions that the theories specify do not become delinquent and, of those who do, most grow out of it without experiencing environmental change. He argued that this overprediction or "embarrassment of riches" undermines the deterministic assumption of the theories and he offers in its place a *soft determinism* that represents a middle ground between the classical and positivist schools. Matza contended, "Most men, including delinquents, are neither wholly free nor completely constrained but fall somewhere between" (1964:27). The delinquent is depicted as one who is largely committed to the dominant normative structure, but is freed to *drift* into delinquency when social controls are loosened. Neutralization provides one means of intermittently denying the rules to which a person generally is committed.

Matza denied that there are delinquent subcultures that shape the behavior of their members. Instead, he depicts subcultures of delinquency populated by young males experiencing anxiety over status, masculinity, and membership. These insecurities, he argued, render the boys highly receptive to the opinions of others. This contributes to *shared misunderstandings* and erroneous beliefs that their peers are committed to delinquency. As boys grow older, anxiety is reduced as they more comfortably adopt the male role and assume new affiliations. Consequently, most boys mature out of delinquent behaviors rather than moving into the criminal careers that positivistic explanations imply.

Analysis of Neutralization

Despite frequent citation in the literature, neutralization has been subjected to scant empirical scrutiny and the studies that have been undertaken do not offer strong support. W. William Minor's analysis of neutralization among incarcerated adults led him to conclude that "it would be premature at this time to attempt an assessment of the validity of neutralization theory" (1980:106). In a later (1981) longitudinal study conceptualizing neutralization as compatible with subcultural theories, however, Minor found some support for it. Richard Ball (1983) also found partial support for neutralization among "rurban" (an area blending rural and urban features) boys. Attributed neutralization (perception of others' commitment to these excuses) provided a better prediction of self-reported delinquency than did personal neutralization, suggesting that delinquency may be a product of the shared misunderstanding that Matza described. That this was evident only for sixth-grade, and not for ninth-grade, boys indicates that the misunderstanding may dissipate early rather than late in adolescence.

John Hamlin (1988) argued that the lack of support for neutralization may indicate that the theory is incorrect. He believed that establishing a causal order between excuses and law-violating behavior "is near impossible to prove conclusively" (1988:430). An explanation that people excuse their behavior ex post facto (rationalization) is, after all, at least as plausible as an interpretation that the excuse precedes, and thus allows, commission of the illegal act (neutralization). Although an abundance of anecdotal illustration of neutralization (or rationalization) is available, these accounts are tainted by the problem of causal order.

Some recent studies have reinvigorated neutralization theory. Robert Agnew (1995) argued that the meager and inconsistent empirical support for the perspective might be due to the manner in which most tests have been conceptualized. He pointed out that the theory did not actually predict that neutralization would lead directly to delinquency, only that it would allow it. Thus, he argued, neutralization may have a strong effect on delinquency for some but little or none for others. This could account for the relatively weak support for the theory to date. He went on to longitudinally examine a large sample from the National Youth Survey. His analysis revealed that violence (fighting with peers) had a "moderately large" effect on violence for those who had a lot of delinquent peers and for those who were generally quite opposed to violence.

A study relying on qualitative interview data undertaken by Dean Dabney (1995) concluded that theft of drugs and supplies by hospital nurses is widespread and well accounted for by the social learning of techniques of neutralization within the workplace. The Agnew and Dabney studies combined suggest that neutralization theory warrants more detailed examination, incorporating both various conditions under which it might have greater effects and strategies to address the causal order problem. Barbara Costello's (2000) test of neutralization theory, along with social bond theory, found that police-related neutralizations (condemnation of the condemners) among juveniles were particularly strong.

Agnew's suggestion that neutralization may vary across types of persons set the stage for recent examinations of different uses of neutralizations, depending on societal attachments. Sykes and Matza's neutralization theory predicts that those who have more social attachments, such as youth having concern about how their parents view them or persons having job responsibilities, will be more likely to use neutralizations. Since neutralization assumes that persons are committed to the established order, it will be more necessary to neutralize norm violations as one becomes more attached to conventional life. Those who are unattached would not feel guilt for violating conventional norms because of their lack of connection to them and therefore would have no need to neutralize their violations. Hirschi's social bond theory, examined in the following section, predicts just the opposite; that only unattached or low-attached individuals will neutralized the norms. Findings on this point, as with more basic neutralization hypotheses, have been mixed. Heith Copes' (2003) interviews of adult male auto thieves revealed that the high-attached subjects (employed, married, more educated) more often resorted to neutralization and used more types than did the low-attached respondents. Costello (2000), in contrast, found that delinquents who reported more attachment to their parents resorted to less neutralization.

While most tests of neutralization theory have been applied to street crimes or to more bizarre forms of deviance, it follows that if high-attached deviants neutralize more often than their low-attached counterparts, the theory should be particularly applicable to white-collar crime. In a recent study of Medicare/Medicaid fraud among speech, occupational, and physical therapists, Rhonda Evans and Dianne Porche (2005) found strong support for this reasoning. They found that 81 percent of the therapists in their sample were engaging in over-billing fraud. Interviews with their subjects revealed endemic guilt-neutralizing statements. The "everybody else does it" rationale suggested by Coleman (1994) to supplement the original five techniques was most common and reflected in numerous statements such as, "Well I know that everyone I work with does it. So I guess that makes it pretty acceptable" (Evans & Porche, 2005:260). Denial of responsibility (e.g., "Sometimes my patients are sick and coughing all over so I cut the session short. Other times they are just uncooperative," 2005:262) was the next most frequently expressed neutralization. Denial of injury was also cited in comments such as "It's not like the patients care when I end their session 5 or 10 minutes early" (2005:265). While this study did not address the causal order problem, the neutralization (or rationalization) strategies were so widespread among these healthcare professionals that it does lend some support to the theory.

Quite a few applications of neutralization have been offered for behaviors that some deem deviant, but involve no violation of legal codes. One example assessed the behavior of mother's in subjecting daughters to child beauty pageant careers (Heltsley & Calhoun). The study followed several months of highly negative press coverage of child beauty pageants in the aftermath of the 1996 murder of young beauty queen JonBenet Ramsey. They suggested that the mothers were depicted as deviant for subjecting daughters to the regimen of beauty pageant competition. Comments solicited from the mothers reflected considerable resort to neutralization. The most frequently deployed was condemnation of the condemners. This neutralization often followed a theme that those suggesting that the children were being sexualized by the activities, thereby placing them at risk of sexual victimization, must themselves be perverts to think such a thing. A distant second most frequently used neutralization was denial of injury, the argument being along lines that the activities were far from harmful to the young girls, but, in fact, very positive experiences.

A behavior even more vehemently argued to be abusive, degrading, and humiliating to women is "hogging," the practice of targeting overweight women for sexual exploitation. Jeannine Gailey and Ariane Prohaska (2006) examined the trend of such behavior among young men and the propensity to neutralize it. They observed that the activity unfolds in a group context when large amounts of time are spent in bars. It incorporates humor, betting, and sexual conquest, all revolving around efforts expended toward "picking up" overweight and unattractive women. Most of the "hoggers" (the deviant males) interviewed in this study thought their behavior was "normal and funny." They all offered comments that could be construed as expressions of one or more of Sykes and Matza's neutralizations. All five techniques were exemplified, with denial of victim (e.g., "she was desperate"). Most commonly followed by denial of responsibility ("I was drunk" or "I was really horny").

Neutralization theory has provided provocative concepts for half a century and continues to be researched. The empirical support, however, has been weak and mixed. Recent findings, however, suggest that it may have something to offer in understanding crime and deviance, especially by combining it with other ideas and examining differences in very specific contexts.

Travis Hirschi—
Social Bond Theory

The leading social control explanation of crime is Travis Hirschi's *control* or *social bond theory*. Like the work of Matza, Hirschi's work rests upon the assumption that "a person is free to commit delinquent acts because his ties to the conventional order have somehow been broken" (1969:3). Rather than pointing at offenders and asking "why do they do it?" (as do strain and culture conflict theories), Hirschi inquires why the conformist does *not* violate the law. His answer is that people do not break laws to the extent that they have internalized law-abiding norms or developed social bonds. Hirschi believes that it is not necessary to identify motivations to deviance, although he acknowledges that certain forces or pressures hold the potential to be integrated with a control perspective. Humans, like other animals, will violate rules if those rules have not been socially indoctrinated as part of a moral code:

> [W]e are all animals, and thus all naturally capable of committing criminal acts. . . . The chicken stealing corn from his neighbor knows nothing of the moral law; he does not want to violate rules; he wants merely to eat corn. . . . No motivation to deviance is required to explain his acts. So, too, no special motivation to crime within the human animal . . . [is] required to explain his criminal acts (Hirschi, 1969:31).

Assuming normative consensus, weakened or broken social bonds reduce a person's "stakes in conformity." With deficient ties to the social order, deviant impulses that most or all people have are likely to be acted upon. The weaker the ties, the more likely deviance is to transpire. Social bonds do not reduce motivations to offend; they only reduce the chance that a person will succumb to those motivations. Hirschi (1969:27) identified four interrelated elements of the social bond, concluding that "the more closely a person is tied to conventional society in any of these ways, the more closely he is likely to be tied in other ways."

Attachment

Sensitivity to the opinions of others is at the heart of the *attachment* element of bond theory. "The essence of internalization of norms, conscience, or superego thus lies in the attachment of the individual to others" (Hirschi, 1969:18). To the extent that an individual cares about the opinions of conventional others, she or he is controlled. A potent test of conformity of youths is their response to the query: "Do you care what your parents think?" If the answer is "no," and it is really meant, the person is relatively free to deviate from the laws of society. Attachment to parents is particularly important. Originally, Hirschi (1969) asserted that this can insulate the individual from delinquency regardless of relative parental conformity. Empirical findings, however, have established that only attachment to conventional parents will insulate one from delinquency. Karen Knight and Tony Tripodi; (1996), for example, found a positive relationship between attachment to family and delinquency for a sample in which more than 70 percent of the subjects had other family members who had been in jail. For them, family attachment was associated with more delinquency, the opposite of what control theory predicts for attachment.

A fear that the parent will learn of a violation is not essential to control behavior. It is necessary only that the person considers what the parent(s) would think of deviant actions. Only a psychological presence, in other words, is required. This trial question can be extended to include other relatives, teachers, coaches, peers, and neighbors.

If attachment to one parent reduces the likelihood of delinquency, will attachment to two parents be better yet? Hirschi's (1969) findings and reasoning suggested not. Consequently, most research has not examined the role of one versus two parents in the attachment bond. The research of Joseph Rankin and Roger Kern (1994) raises interesting questions in this regard. First, they found "that strong attachment to both parents . . . has a greater preventive effect on delinquency than strong attachment to either one or no parent" (1994:507). This has clear implications for the quality of family relationships. Second, they found that if there is a strong attachment to only one parent, it does not matter whether it is to the father or mother. This contradicts the "tender years" legal presumption of some states that assumes children's ties to mothers are more important than those to fathers. Third, their examination of broken homes revealed findings at odds with Hirschi's argument. While Hirschi asserted that attachment to one parent in a single-parent home provides the full benefit of attachment, Rankin and Kern found less delinquency in intact homes where the youth was strongly attached to both parents.

Attachment has been accorded the most attention of Hirschi's four elements. Although the bulk of tests have examined juvenile attachments to parents and schools, others are of potential importance. Spousal attachments, for example, have been scrutinized. Michael Maume and his colleagues (2005) found that marital attachment was associated with cessation of marijuana use. John Hepburn and Marie Griffin (2004) even found that attachments were associated with reduced likelihood of recidivism among child molesters on probation. Another recent study (Thaxton & Agnew, 2004) found that attachments are nonlinear. They discovered that attachments were not only weak, but negative, for highly delinquent youth. Consequently, the effects of attachment may have been underestimated by much prior research because a linear relationship between attachment and delinquency was assumed.

Commitment

Given the assumption that people are rational, they will contemplate the consequences of actions before acting. Hirschi considered such calculations to be a *commitment* to the conventional order. Conformity is encouraged by fear of losing what you have or expect to acquire. Prospects for employment and educational opportunities, reputation, and other valued conditions will discourage delinquent behavior. The more ambitious a person is, therefore, the less likely he or she is to commit criminal offenses. The high-school athlete may follow all of the coach's rules to avoid risk of suspension from competition. The college student aspiring to a career in law or criminal justice may avoid experimenting with drugs out of fear of imperiling career prospects. Even nonconventional commitments may encourage conventional conformity, as when youths who aspire to organized crime affiliation avoid forms of criminal behavior deemed inappropriate by those whose judgment is important to them. Hirschi characterized commitment as "common sense" because abiding by social rules helps to maintain and advance one's status in society.

Involvement

The notion that remaining busy in conventional activities insulates persons from unconventional behavior is commonplace. The platitude that "idle hands are the devil's workshop" echoes the idea of *involvement*. Discussing the impact of involvement, Hirschi (1969:22) noted, "To the extent that he is engrossed in conventional activities, he cannot even think about deviant acts, let alone act out his inclinations." Despite the widespread common sense assumption that involvement in legitimate activities will reduce delinquency, little empirical support has been found. The findings with sports involvement have been mixed at best and the effects of youth employment have been found to be associated with *more* delinquency rather than less, particularly as the number of work hours increase (Wright & Cullen, 2000). Not surprisingly, there has been ideological resistance to this finding. When John Wright was presenting to the American Society of Criminology early evidence of the positive relationship between youth employment and delinquency, contrary to control theory predictions, his research was greeted with a firestorm of objections that this could not be so. While the reasons appear to be quite complex (e.g. disposable income that can be used for alcohol or drugs; mixtures of different age groups; lack of supervision after work), the finding has now been replicated several times.

Belief

Hirschi's control theory postulates that, although people have been socialized into a common set of beliefs, there nevertheless is variation in the strength of their beliefs. The stronger that peoples' *belief* in the conventional order is, the less likely they are to offend. For persons with weaker belief in the law, Hirschi contends that neutralization is not essential.

Analysis of Social Bond

Hirschi is one of the few theorists to have proposed a theory of crime or delinquency that was subjected to substantial empirical testing during its developmental stages. In *Causes of delinquency* (1969), he presented the results of self-report, police, and school data for 3,605 boys involved in the Richmond (California) Youth Project. The data supported his new version of control theory (Hirschi, 1969). The theory has since been buttressed by empirical testing undertaken by many criminologists (e.g., Hindelang, 1973; Conger, 1976; Hepburn, 1977; Cernkovich, 1978; Krohn & Massey, 1980; Wiatrowski et al., 1981; Lasley, 1988). While the basic framework of the theory has been challenged by only a few criminologists, it has frequently been noted that its' explanatory power is weak and that it has been applied mostly to minor offenders (e.g., Cretacci, 2003).

Hirschi's (1969) original test of social bond theory excluded females, but he noted that additional studies should examine gender. A number of criminologists have since tested control theory among females and found it to have strong explanatory power. One recent study (Li & MacKenzie, 2003), however, found differential effects of social bonds across gender for adult subjects. The theory has also been tested across various age groups, revealing varying fits (LaGrange & White, 1985). In short, social control or bond theory has fared reasonably well in empirical tests, but appears to need elaboration and more careful specification.

A major deficiency of social control or bond theory is its failure to come to grips with causal order. It proposes that social bonds relate to delinquency; weak attachments are presumed to lead to delinquency and correlations between bonds and delinquency are so interpreted. It is just as plausible, however, that delinquent behavior causes deterioration of social bonds. Virtually all tests of control theory have relied upon cross-sectional data, thus failing to address causal order; Robert Agnew (1985; 1991), however, has examined two sets of longitudinal data for juveniles and found only very weak support. Agnew (1991:150) concluded that these data "raise further doubt about the importance attributed to Hirschi's theory."

A second damaging criticism of control theory is its neglect of the origin of social bonds and their varying strength. Control theories assert that deviant behavior is a consequence of weak bonds with the conventional order. This places a scholar attempting to explain crime or conformity in a quandary. To attribute behavior, either deviance or conformity, to the strength of social bonds is only a partial answer. If social bonds are responsible for the behavior, the obvious concern is to understand those social bonds. If, as Hirschi claims, there is variation in the strength of bonds, it becomes essential to account for such differences. One study of illicit drug use among young adults failed to find bonding differences between offenders and nonoffenders (Kandel & Davies, 1991). If anything, the drug users displayed more attachments to friends than did non-users. This led the researchers to conclude that a cultural deviance rather than a control perspective best explained drug use.

Hirschi's version of control theory has also been criticized on theoretical grounds. Willem Schinkel (2002:140-141), in arguing that the theory is tautological concluded that "the idea that the criminal has a weakened bond to society tells us nothing new, since the criminal is part of the non-conventional, rather than the conventional, and a criminal, someone who commits non-conventional acts, is thus by definition someone who commits less conventional acts (since these constitute the 'bond' to conventional society)."

The assumptions underlying social bond theory are also open to question. Hirschi's portrayal of the morality of "man," for example, seems to be that humans are naturally immoral. In Hirschi's view, humans will do whatever benefits them unless they are controlled by social bonds. Schinkel (2002:126) summarizes the commitment bond as "the idea that rules are obeyed out of fear for the consequences of not doing so," then asking, "Is the only thing that prevents Travis Hirschi from shooting Gilbert Geis in the head the fact that Hirschi is afraid he will spend the rest of his life in jail?" To the contrary, Schinkel argues, morality is more than a purely oppressive force. Following Kant, he argues that morality is inherent in human nature rather than absent, as Hirschi contends, with choices at the center of human existence. Thus persons are not constrained by morality, as Hirschi argues, but potentially freed by moral choices. Yet those choices cannot be as arbitrarily classified as in social bond theory. The conventional and nonconventional are not so discrete. Persons can be strongly bonded to conventional society, yet engage in nonconventional activities. This would be quite evident, for example, among crooked politicians, white-collar criminals, or abusive clergy.

The policy impact of control theory is less direct than for strain theories. It is often construed as a "common sense" perspective. Control theory is at the core of what many people attempt to do in rearing their children. As Lamar Empey (1982:268) noted, "[W]hen most people concentrate on their own children, rather than children in general, they sound like control theorists." Attachment calls for strengthening the family, schools, and other primary institutions. Most parents strive to foster the attachment of their children to conventional persons and institutions. Similarly, involvement calls for the development of playgrounds and other recreational opportunities. Among individual families this translates to encouraging children to participate in athletics, hobbies, and various extracurricular activities. Parents also press their offspring to commit to educational, professional, and other social goals, and they attempt to foster a belief in the social order so that the children will develop a stake in conformity.

Michael Gottfredson and Travis Hirschi— A General Theory of Crime

More recently Hirschi, working with Michael Gottfredson (1990) developed *A General Theory of Crime* rooted in the notion of *low self-control*, as opposed to inadequate social controls or bonds as proposed earlier. According to this theory, crime is the result of individuals with low self-control encountering situations or opportunities in which crime will produce immediate gratification with relatively low levels of risk. They view crime as so simple, however, that opportunities are abundant, propelling anyone with low self-control into a crime-saturated abyss. Self-control is said to be taught in early childhood, implying that parental discipline and management are the only factors in explaining delinquent and adult criminal offending. Parents can instill self-control in their children by monitoring the child's behavior and recognizing and punishing misbehavior when it occurs. Failure to do this will result in low self-control.

Gottfredson and Hirschi argue that the cause of *all* crime is low self-control (thus called a *general theory*) and that this characteristic is stable across the life course and set by age eight. In other words, the individual who is prone to act out in elementary school is also likely to be involved in adolescent delinquency, adult crime, and even deviant behavior in their elder years. Low self-control, they argue, is associated not only with crime and delinquency, but also with what they call *analogous acts* or noncriminal behavior also resulting from low self-control. Examples are excessive drinking, smoking, illicit sex, and even accidents. That is, individuals with low self-control will consistently engage in behavior that causes problems for themselves and others. They will be inclined to pursue short-term pleasures at the expense of long-term goals. Health may be jeopardized by smoking and drinking; accidents may result from high-risk behaviors while under the influence of drugs or alcohol; criminal charges may follow violent responses to insults, and so on.

Low self-control is a construct that is comprised of several characteristic features. It has most been typically operationalized through the Grasmick et al. (1993) 24-item scale, consisting of six elements. Persons with low self-control are envisioned as displaying these elements. They are:

1. Impulsiveness. The person with low self-control will have an inability to delay gratification, preferring quick pleasures and rewards.

2. Simple tasks. Activities that do not require planning or intellectual investment will be preferred over those that do.

3. Risk seeking. The excitement of risky behavior will be rewarding, while safe and careful activities will bring boredom.

4. Physicality. Physical endeavors will be preferred over intellectual activities.

5. Self-centeredness. Low self-control will be characterized by insensitivity to the needs and interests of others and excessive focus on desires for the self.

6. Temper. The person with low self-control will easily lose their temper.

Gottfredson and Hirschi rule out "positivistic" sources of low self-control such as learning or cultural transmission. Who, they ask, would intentionally pass on to their offspring the trait of low self-control, given that it is a dysfunctional trait. Analogous to Hirschi's earlier social bonding theory, it is argued that self-control is more or less low in the beginning. In the absence of effective child rearing, low self-control will persist. If children's behavior is not monitored and deviance sanctioned over the first eight years of life, self-control will be set (or remain) at a low level. This will then persist throughout the individual's life.

Gottfredson and Hirschi see themselves as developing a theory that fills the gap between classical or deterrence ideas and positivism. While the theory is rooted in the classical hedonistic view of human nature, not all persons are equally deterrable due to variations in levels of self-control. Thus, as with a positivistic perspective, the motivation to crime varies, but no particular motivation *per se* is needed, only low self-control coupled with opportunity. This, however, does not compel the person to deviance (as positivists typically assert about their independent variables). It is only a trait or personality factor that shapes choices. Gottfredson and Hirschi depict all crime as exciting, requiring little skill or planning, and providing little long-term gain.

Analysis of the General Theory

The general, or low self-control, theory of crime is the most cited and tested explanation of crime at present. It has fared well with recent cross-cultural tests. Results have been similar between Whites and African-Americans (Vazsonyi & Crosswhite, 2004), Russian (Tittle & Botchkavar, 2005) and Swiss samples (Vazsonyi & Klanjšek,, 2008) and has generally held for females, though not as strongly, as well as males. The relationship between low self-control and a wide range of crimes and analogous behaviors has consistently been observed, albeit, mostly at weak to moderate levels. Low self-control has been found to be related to academic dishonesty (Cochran et al., 1998), courtship violence (Sellers, 1999), binge drinking (Gibson et al., 2004), and adolescent sexual behavior (Hope & Chapple, 2005). Many other forms of deviance have been identified as significantly related to low self-control as well, but with the researchers finding other variables equally or more strongly related (e.g., Evans et al., 1997; Gibson & Wright, 2001; Gibbs & Giever, 1995; Wright et al., 1999; Wright & Cullen, 2000)). An overall assessment of the empirical support for the theory was undertaken by Travis Pratt and Frank Cullen (2000). They also concluded that while there is widespread support for the predictive power of low self-control, other factors, particularly social learning variables play a role as well.

Recent research undertaken by Constance Chapple (2005) further supported the value of combining low self-control with variables drawn from social learning and other theoretical frameworks. She found that the presence of low self-control tends to lead to peer rejection, consistent with Gottfredson & Hirschi's contention that low self-control undermines many personal relationships, and to association with deviant peers. Both of these problems, in turn, further contribute to delinquency. Elizabeth Cauffman and her colleagues (2005) also found that while low self-control was a predictor of delinquency, so was heart rate (a biological variable) and spatial span (a Neuropsychological measure) and they continued to be after statistically controlling for the effects of low self-control. Similarly, George Higgins (2005) found value in low self-control for explaining software piracy among college students, but found moral beliefs, attitudes toward the offense, and peer behavior to all be even stronger influences.

Moral beliefs as they relate to self-control have recently been examined by Olena Antonaccio and Charles Tittle (2008). They collected self-report data from a sample of 500 Ukraine adults to contrast a new morality-based theory of crime with the self-control explanation. Morality was conceptualized in a cognitive form (that is, what *would* you do), as opposed to assessing the morality of one's actual behavior. The idea, derived from Wikström and Treiber's (2007) Situational Action Theory (SAT) is that an actor's moral framework is one of many individual and environmental factors that drive behavior. Wikström and Treiber contend that that SAT is a general theory of crime, largely obviating the need for focus on self-control. They assert that self-control is not relevant for those who have no moral compunction regarding a particular behavior nor for those with high moral restraint, but rather, only for those with more flaccid moral commitments.

Antonaccio and Tittle (2008) found that self-control had a significant impact on violent behavior and most property offenses. This held for the most part, albeit at reduced levels, after controlling for cognitive morality. However, the morality measure was an appreciably and consistently stronger predictor of all forms of crime. The Ukraine locale is one that has undergone many recent and disruptive social changes and is plagued with high levels of crime so that results cannot be generalized to the western world. Yet it provides a new lens for elaborating the role of self-control in producing deviant behavior.

Despite the widespread attention and considerable empirical support, the general theory has been subjected to much criticism (see, for example, Akers, 1994; Delisi et al., 2003; Geis, 2000; Tittle, 1995). Concerns with the theory can be conceptualized as falling into empirical and theoretical categories. The empirical issues regard how research has been conducted and its failure to find evidence supportive of the full range of claims made by Hirschi and Gottfredson. The theoretical criticisms focus on the logic of the theory.

One of the empirical matters of greatest concern is how self-control has been operationalized. The Grasmick et al. (1993) scale has been most widely used and debate has centered on whether the concept of self-control is unidimensional or best conceived as a combination of multiple factors (see Piquero et al., 2000; Delisi et al., 2003). Some researchers maintain that self-control is a unitary concept (e.g., Nagin & Paternoster, 1994; Piquero & Tibbetts, 1996; Polakowski, 1994), while others have concluded that the different predictive abilities of the subscales (e.g., impulsivity) indicate that it should not be considered unidimensional (Arneklev et al., 1993; Delisi et al., 2003; Wood et al., 1993).

The empirical findings with the self-control concept have also been criticized as being of modest value. Although there have been consistent findings that self-control is related to a wide range of deviance, the strength of that relationship is usually weak or modest. This raises a fundamental problem of criminological research: statistical versus substantive significance (see Brown, 1989 for discussions of this topic). In short, a relationship (e.g., between self-control and deviance) can be statistically significant, yet not be of great substantive importance. A statistically significant relationship inspires confidence that the relationship will be consistently found with different samples, while a substantively important relationship is a very strong one. The self-control variable has been characterized as often statistically significant, but usually of limited substantive importance (Stylianou, 2002).

There are also important empirical assertions within the general theory that are debated. For example, the general theory depicts self-control as being set by around age eight and then remaining fixed throughout ones life. Other perspectives are rooted in assertions to the contrary. The life course or developmental perspective (see Chapter 10), for example, views deviant propensity as continually changing in response to life experiences. Moreover, recent research has generated evidence that self-control is a function of a variety of factors. One analysis (Longshore et al., 2005) showed low self-control to be a function of weak bonding. A second research project observed that males and females differentially respond to their upbringing in terms of development of self-control (Blackwell & Piquero, 2005). A third effort found that adverse neighborhood conditions explained low self-control about as well as parental supervision (Pratt et al., 2004). Still another study, while largely consistent with self-control theory, differed in finding that ADHD is a major contributor to low self-control (Unnever, 2003). In fact, they concluded that low self-control is the only mechanism by which the ADHD youth is placed at risk for delinquency. Similarly, Kevin Beaver and his colleagues (2008) located considerable relationship between language skills and self-control. Finally, Michael Turner and his fellow researchers (2005), while finding that the origins of self-control lay primarily in parenting, noted that it could still be enhanced by school socialization, at least in the less disadvantaged neighborhoods. They summed up the complexity of shaping self-control nicely:

> This research suggested that the sources or genesis of self-control, contrary to the assertions made by Gottfredson & Hirschi (1990), were more complex than simple parental socialization experiences. It therefore might be argued that Gottfredson & Hirschi sacrificed theoretical precision for theoretical parsimony, a position that potentially underestimated the complexity of the sources of self-control and, in turn, delinquency and crime (Turner et al., 2005:336).

Another interesting explanation of the theory relates it to victimization. Researchers have tested the proposition that low self-control places people at risk of victimization. This nicely blends victimization studies, which find a great deal of crossover between victims and offenders, with efforts of a general theory to explain offending. Among the studies that have taken this approach, Eric Stuart and his colleagues (2004), looking at female drug users, found that very low self-control contributed to their violent victimization even after controlling for lifestyle (see Chapter 5 discussion of lifestyle theories). Alex Piquero and his colleagues (2005) found low self-control to be associated with both violent offending and homicide victimization (see discussion of victim precipitation, Chapter 11). Similarly, Kathleen Fox and her colleagues (2009) found stalking victimization of women was related to low self-control. These findings are consistent with Gottfredson & Hirschi's claim that persons with low self-control will encounter an array of problems, including unemployment, few long-term relationships, criminal activity, and accidents. These tests indicate that risk of victimization is another lifetime risk that can be added to the plight of persons with low self-control.

Theoretical concerns lie more at the heart of critiques of the general theory. One of the most widespread criticisms of the theory is that it is tautological, meaning that the logical path followed is a circular one. The issue is that self-control and the propensity toward criminal behavior/analogous acts are not independently defined, but rather, are one and the same. That is, low self-control is defined in terms of persons committing deviant acts, while the theory maintains that low self-control is the cause of deviance. Thus the hypothesis seems to be that low self-control causes low self-control. Some researchers, in fact, have used deviant behaviors as the proxy for low self-control, finding that they are predictive of other deviant behaviors (e.g., Evans et al., 1997; La Grange & Silverman, 1999; Redmon, 2003; Wright et al., 1999). Stelios Stylianou (2002:536), however, asserts that "one cannot use crime and analogous behavior as measures of low self-control. Correlations among different criminal and analogous acts are evidence of versatility, not of causation." Such correlations can also be readily be interpreted as support for learning theories rather than self-control. "A correlation between a variety of deviant behaviors could simply mean that certain social contexts are associated with learning the attitudes and techniques required for a variety of deviant behaviors (Stylianou, 2002).

Another concern has been Gottfredson and Hirschi's relative neglect of the opportunity variable. The opportunities for crime that one encounters may be more important than his or her self-control. In the absence of opportunity, low self-control may not be very predictive of crime or analogous behaviors. Carter Hay and Walter Forrest (2008) argue that this over-simplification attenuates the explanatory power of the theory. Adding a routine activities component they found that unsupervised and peer association time both independently contributed and amplified the effects of low self-control on a variety of delinquent behaviors. Others have found support for an additive effect; individuals with low self-control and with greater opportunity for engaging in criminal activity report higher levels of offending (Cochran et al., 1998; Grasmick et al., 1993; Piquero & Tibbetts, 1996; Sellers, 1999).

Other theories that have claimed to explain all crime and delinquency (e.g., classical deterrence, differential association) have encountered the criticism that they better fit some forms of behavior than others. Gottfredson and Hirschi's theory encounters this problem as well. While research has found low self-control predictive of a variety of criminal behaviors, questions remain regarding the viability of the theory for explaining all crime, especially the white-collar variety (Reed & Yeager, 1996). Returning to the logic of the theory, Gottfredson and Hirschi maintain that all crime is spontaneous rather than planned, requires little skill, and is not very profitable. These assumptions seem to largely defy criminological understanding of white-collar, organized, and perhaps other forms of crime. It is quite plausible that low self-control could turn out to be an important concept in the understanding of some, but not all, forms of crime as the theory asserts. That is, evidence may be marshaled to support low self-control, while not supporting the general application of the theory.

Other theorists have been less generous in assessing the theoretical contributions of general/low self-control theory. Davis Redmon (2002), for example, recently formulated a harsh theoretical indictment. He sought to determine if low self-control could explain lewd conduct (exposure or public sex acts) that persons self-reported at Mardi Gras. He found that two of five criminal/analogous behaviors (numbers of fistfights and drug use) were predictive of the lewd conduct. He concluded, however, that qualitative interviews of subjects were not supportive of low self-control. The most frequent account offered for the lewd behaviors was "discontent with the 'daily grind'." The argument developed was that low self-control was not the cause of the deviance because, in fact, the subjects overwhelmingly led lives characterized by self-control. As Redmon (2002:381) summarized, "respondents believe that performing lewd behavior temporarily liberates them from self-control." He concludes (2002:384-

385) that "people are not performing lewd conduct because they lack self-control, but because they are expected to have too much of it. Performing lewd conduct is a response to maintaining self-control, not a consequence of lacking it." In other words, the reported lewd conduct, fist fights, and drug use are seen as the outcomes of excessive demand for self-control rather than the result of inadequate self-control.

Redmon's (2002) critique goes beyond the empirical validity and logical structure of the theory of low self-control to consider its ideological foundation. He depicts the theory as "a form of expert knowledge that intends to subject people to discipline and label them with the stigma of low self-control in an effort to manage them more effectively. The power of self-control is that it produces stigmatized people who monitor, watch and discipline themselves" (2002:387-388). This is done "at the expense of eliminating spontaneity, pleasurable emotions, and short-term behaviors" (2002:389). The general theory of crime or low self-control theory clearly does reflect a more conservative policy agenda, depicting a very wide range of behaviors as symptomatic of an underlying lack of self-control. Moreover, this deficiency that is not remediable, but requires that such individuals not be extended opportunities for engaging in deviant behaviors.

Summary

This chapter has examined social process theories. Those theories reviewed in this grouping analyze the social processes or interactions associated with crime. Social process theories tend to have a micro-theoretical focus; that is, the theories look at how individuals become law violators. A social psychological label is often ascribed to the theories because they combine sociological and psychological variables. Unlike social structure theories, most social process perspectives do not limit focus to any segment of the class structure. Three groups of theories have been subsumed under the social process category in this chapter: social learning, culture conflict, and social control.

Edwin H. Sutherland, author of the theory of differential association, is generally viewed as the prime mover of learning theory. In its final form, differential association was comprised of nine principles. The key one asserted that persons become criminal offenders through an excess of definitions favorable to violation of the law. This theory is of particular importance because it helped bring the sociological perspective to a dominant position in criminological studies in the United States. Ronald Akers' social learning theory broadened this perspective through incorporation of additional learning principles.

Culture conflict or cultural deviance theory is derived from learning theory. Its basic idea is that crime and delinquency are learned as normal behavior in a subcultural setting. Thorsten Sellin took the lead in this theoretical tradition, while Marvin Wolfgang and Franco Ferracuti followed with their "subculture of violence" theory. Walter Miller focused on the lower class, and postulated distinct focal concerns that predispose persons in that class to violate legal codes.

Control theories, as do learning and cultural deviance theories, view crime as a reflection of failure of social constraints rather than as a product of criminogenic forces. The theories are rooted in both value consensus and free will assumptions.

At the heart of Walter Reckless' containment version and Gresham Sykes and David Matza's neutralization version of control theory, is the idea that because people fundamentally believe in the law, they must generate a rationale to excuse law violation prior to violating. Travis Hirschi's social control or bond theory is the most highly regarded version of this perspective. Hirschi proposed four elements of a bond to society that serve to control people. He maintained that the weaker the social bonds of the law, the less the individual is constrained by the law.

Gottfredson and Hirschi's general theory of crime is one of the more recent and widely discussed. They see self-control at the heart of not only crime and delinquency, but also analogous behaviors. It is contended that self-control is fixed by the age of eight. While the theory has been tested considerably and support has been rather consistent, self-control explains a relatively small portion of variance in crime rates. It has also been vigorously criticized on theoretical grounds.

Key Terms and Concepts

Analogous Acts
Appeal to Higher Loyalties
Attachment
Autonomy
Balance
Belief
Code of the Street
Commitment
Condemnation of the Condemners
Control Theories
Cultural Deviance
Cultural Transmission
Culture Conflict
Denial of Injury
Denial of Responsibility
Denial of Victim
Deviance Gap
Differential Association
Differential Identification
Drift
Excitement
Fate

Focal Concerns
General Theory of Crime
Hogging
Involvement
Learning Theories
Low Self-Control
Primary Culture Conflict
Secondary Culture Conflict
Shared Misunderstandings
Smartness
Social Bond Theory
Social Control Theories
Social Learning Theory
Social Process Theories
Social Psychological Theories
Soft Determinism
Subculture of Violence
Symbolic Interaction
Techniques of Neutralization
Toughness
Trouble

Key Criminologists

Ronald Akers
Donald R. Cressey
Franco Ferracuti
Daniel Glaser
Michael Gottfredson
Travis Hirschi
David Matza

Walter Miller
Thorsten Sellin
Edwin H. Sutherland
Gresham Sykes
Gabriel Tarde
Charles Tittle
Marvin Wolfgang

References

Adams, L.R. (1973). "Differential Association and Learning Principles Revisited." *Social Problems*, 20:458-470.

Agnew, R. (1995). "The Techniques of Neutralization and Violence." *Criminology*, 32:555-580.

Agnew, R. (1991). "A Longitudinal Test of Social Control Theory and Delinquency." *Journal of Research in Crime and Delinquency*, 28:126-156.

Agnew, R. (1985). "Social Control Theory and Delinquency: A Longitudinal Test." *Criminology*, 23:47-61.

Akers, R.L. (1994). *Criminological Theories: Introduction and Evaluation*. Los Angeles, CA: Roxbury.

Akers, R.L. (1990). "Rational Choice, Deterrence, and Social Learning Theory: The Path Not Taken." *Journal of Criminal Law and Criminology*, 81:653-676.

Akers, R.L. (1985). *Deviant Behavior: A Social Learning Approach*, Third Edition. New York, NY: Wadsworth.

Akers, R.L. (1973). *Deviant Behavior: A Social Learning Approach*. Belmont, CA: Wadsworth.

Akers, R.L. & J.K. Cochran (1985). "Adolescent Marijuana Use: A Test of Three Theories of Deviant Behavior." *Deviant Behavior*, 6:323-346.

Akers, R.L. & G. Lee (1996). "A Longitudinal Test of Social Learning Theory: Adolescent Smoking." *Journal of Drug Issues*, 26:317-343.

Anderson, E. (1999). *Code of the Street: Decency, Violence, and the Moral Life of the Inner City*. New York: W.W. Norton.

Antonaccio, O. & C.R. Tittle (2008). "Morality, Self-Control, and Crime." *Criminology*, 46, 479-510.

Arneklev, B.J., H.G. Grasmick, C.R. Tittle & R.J. Bursik (1993). "Low Self-Control and Imprudent Behavior." *Journal of Quantitative Criminology*, 9:225-247.

Ball, R.A. (1983). "Development of Basic Norm Violation." *Criminology*, 21:75-94.

Ball-Rokeach, S.J. (1973). "Values and Violence: A Test of the Subculture of Violence Thesis." *American Sociological Review*, 38:736-749.

Beaver, K.M., M. Delisi, M.G. Vaughn, J.P. Wright & B.B. Boutwell (2008). "The Relationship Between Self-Control and Language: Evidence of a Shared Etiological Pathway." *Criminology*, 46:939-970.

Bernard, T.J. (1990). "Angry Aggression among the 'Truly Disadvantaged.'" *Criminology*, 28:73-96.

Blackwell, B.S. & A.R. Piquero (2005). "On the Relationships between Gender, Power Control, Self-Control, and Crime." *Journal of Criminal Justice*, 33:1-17.

Brauer, J.R.(2009). "Testing Social Learning Theory Using Reinforcement's Residue: A Multilevel Analysis of Self-Reported Marijuana Use in the National Youth Survey." *Criminology*, 47: 929-970.

Brezina , T., R. Agnew, F.T. Cullen & J.P. Wright (2004). "The Code of the Street: A Quantitative Assessment of Elijah Anderson's Subculture of Violence Thesis and its Contribution to Youth Violence Research." *Youth Violence and Juvenile Justice*, 2: 303-328.

Brown, S.E. (1989). "Statistical Power and Criminal Justice Research." *Journal of Criminal Justice*, 17:115-122.

Cauffman, E., S. Steinberg & A.R. Piquero (2005). "Psychological, Neuropsychological and Physiological Correlates of Serious Antisocial Behavior in Adolescence: The Role of Self-control." *Criminology*, 43(1):133-176.

Cernkovich, S.A. (1978). *The American Occupational Structure*. New York, NY: John Wiley and Sons.

Chappell, A.T. & A.R. Piquero (2004). "Applying Social Learning Theory to Police Misconduct." *Deviant Behavior*, 25:89-108.

Chapple, C.L. (2005). "Self-Control, Peer Relations, and Delinquency." *Justice Quarterly*, 22(1):89-106.

Cochran, J.K., P.B. Wood, C.S. Sellers, W. Wilkerson & M.B. Chamlin (1998). "Academic Dishonesty and Low Self-Control: An Empirical Test of a General Theory of Crime." *Deviant Behavior*, 19:227-255.

Coleman, J.W. (1994). *The Criminal Elite: The Sociology of White Collar Crime*. New York: St. Martin's Press.

Conger, R.D. (1976). "Social Control and Social Learning Models of Delinquent Behavior." *Criminology*, 14:17-39.

Copes, H. (2003). "Societal Attachments, Offending Frequency, and Techniques of Neutralization." *Deviant Behavior*, 24:101-127.

Costello, B. (2000). "Techniques of Neutralization and Self-Esteem: A Critical Test of Social Control and Neutralization Theory." *Deviant Behavior*, 21:307-29.

Costello, B. (1998). "The Remarkable Persistence of a Flawed Theory: A Rejoinder to Matsueda." *Theoretical Criminology*, 2:85-92.

Costello, B. (1997). "On the Logical Adequacy of Cultural Deviance Theories." *Theoretical Criminology*, 1:403-428.

Cretacci, M. (2003). "Religion and Social Control: An Application of a Modified Social Bond on Violence." *Criminal Justice Behavior*, 28(2):254-277.

Dabney, D. (1995). "Neutralization and Deviance in the Workplace: Theft of Supplies and Medicines by Hospital Nurses." *Deviant Behavior*, 16:313-331.

Delisi, M., A. Hochstetler & D.S. Murphy (2003). "Self-Control Behind Bars: A Validation Study of the Grasmick et al. Scale." *Justice Quarterly*, 20:241-263.

Deschenes, E.P. & F.A. Esbensen (1999). "Violence and Gangs: Gender Differences in Perceptions and Behavior." *Journal of Quantitative Criminology*, 15:313-331.

Elliott, D.S., S.S. Ageton & D. Huizinga (1985). *Explaining Delinquency and Drug Use*. Beverly Hills, CA: Sage Publications.

Empey, L.T. (1982). *American Delinquency: Its Meaning and Construction*. Homewood, IL: Dorsey Press.

Esbensen, F.A. & E.P. Deschenes (1998). "A Multisite Examination of Youth Gang Membership: Does Gender Matter?" *Criminology*, 35:475-495.

Evans, D.T., F.T. Cullen, V.S. Burton, Jr., R.G. Dunaway & M.L. Benson (1997). "The Social Consequences of Self-Control: Testing the General Theory of Crime." *Criminology*, 35:475-495.

Evans, R.D. & D.A. Porche (2005). "The Nature and Frequency of Medicare/Medicaid Fraud and Neutralization Techniques among Speech, Occupational, and Physical Therapists." *Deviant Behavior*, 26:253-270.

Fox, K.A., A.R. Grover & C. Kaukinen (2009). "The Effects of Low Self-Control and Childhood Maltreatment on Stalking Victimization among Men and Women." *American Journal of Criminal Justice*, 34:181-197.

Gailey, J.A. & A. Prohaska (2006). "'Knocking off a Fat Girl:' An Exploration of Hogging, Male Sexuality, and Neutralizations." *Deviant Behavior*, 27:31-49.

Geis, G. (2000). "On the Absence of Self-Control as the Basis for a General Theory of Crime." *Theoretical Criminology*, 4:35-53.

Gibbs, J.J. & D. Giever (1995). "Self-Control and Its Manifestations among University Students: An Empirical Test of Gottfredson and Hirschi's General Theory." *Justice Quarterly*, 12:231-255.

Gibson, C., C.J. Schreck & J.M. Miller (2004). "Binge Drinking and Negative Alcohol-Related Behaviors: A Test of Self-Control Theory." *Journal of Criminal Justice*, 32:411-420.

Gibson, C. & J.P. Wright (2001). "Low Self-Control and Coworker Delinquency: A Research Note." *Journal of Criminal Justice*, 29:483-492.

Gottfredson, M. & T. Hirschi (1990). *A General Theory of Crime*. Stanford, CA: Stanford University Press.

Glaser, D. (1956). "Criminality Theories and Behavioral Images." *American Journal of Sociology*, 61:433-444.

Grasmick, H.G., C.R. Tittle, R.J. Bursik, Jr. & B.J. Arneklev (1993). "Testing the Core Empirical Implications of Gottfredson and Hirschi's General Theory of Crime." *Journal of Research in Crime and Delinquency*, 30:5-29.

Hamlin, J.E. (1988). "The Misplaced Role of Rational Choice in Neutralization Theory." *Criminology*, 26:425-438.

Hay, C. & W. Forrest (2008). "Self-Control Theory and the Concept of Opportunity: The Case for a More Systematic Union." *Criminology*, 46:1039-1072.

Heltsley, M. & T.C. Calhoun (2003). "The Good Mother: Neutralization Techniques Used by Pageant Mothers." *Deviant Behavior*, 24:81-100.

Hepburn, J.R. (1977). "Testing Alternative Models of Delinquency Causation." *Journal of Criminal Law and Criminology*, 67:450-460.

Hepburn, J.R. & M.L. Griffin (2004). "The Effect of Social Bonds on Successful Adjustment to Probation: An Event History Analysis." *Criminal Justice Review*, 29(1):46-75.

Higgins, G.E. (2005). "Can Low Self-Control Help with the Understanding of the Software Piracy Problem?" *Deviant Behavior*, 26:1-24.

Hindelang, M.J. (1973). "Causes of Delinquency: A Partial Replication and Extension." *Social Problems*, 20:471-487.

Hirschi, T. (1969). *Causes of Delinquency*. Berkeley, CA: University of California Press.

Hope, T.L. & C.L. Chapple (2003). "Maternal Characteristics, Parenting, and Adolescent Sexual Behavior: The role of Self-Control." *Deviant Behavior*, 26:25-45.

Horney, J. (2006). "An Alternative Psychology of Criminal Behavior." *Criminology*, 44(1):1-16.

Jeffery, C.R. (1965). "Criminal Behavior and Learning Theory." *Journal of Criminal Law*, Criminology and Police Science, 54:294-300.

Kandel, D. & M. Davies (1991). "Friendship Networks, Intimacy, and Illicit Drug Use in Young Adulthood: A Comparison of Two Competing Theories." *Criminology*, 29:441-469.

Knight, K.W. & T. Tripodi (1996). "Societal Bonding and Delinquency: An Empirical Test of Hirschi's Theory of Control." *Journal of Offender Rehabilitation*, 23:117-129.

Kornhauser, R.R. (1978). *Social Sources of Delinquency: An Appraisal of Analytic Methods*. Chicago, IL: University of Chicago Press.

Krohn, M.D. & J.L. Massey (1980). "Social Control and Delinquent Behavior: An Examination of the Elements of the Social Bond." *Sociological Quarterly*, 21:529-544.

Krohn, M.D., W.F. Skinner, J.L. Massey & R.L. Akers (1985). "Social Learning Theory and Adolescent Cigarette Smoking: A Longitudinal Study." *Social Problems*, 32:455-473.

LaGrange, R.L. & H.R. White (1985). "Age Differences in Delinquency: A Test of Theory." *Criminology*, 23:19-45.

LaGrange, T.C. & R.A. Silverman (1999). "Low Self-Control and Opportunity: Testing the General Theory of Crime as an Explanation for Gender Differences in Delinquency." *Criminology*, 37:41-72.

Lasley, J.R. (1988). "Toward a Control Theory of White-Collar Offending." *Journal of Quantitative Criminology*, 4:347-362.

Laub, J.H. (1983). *Criminology in the Making*. Boston, MA: Northeastern University Press.

Li, S.D. & D.L. MacKenzie (2005). "The Gendered Effects of Adults Social Bonds on the criminal Activities of Probationers." *Criminal Justice Review*, 28(2):278-298.

Longshore, D., E. Chang & N. Messina (2005). "Self-Control and Social Bonds: A Combined Control Perspective on Juvenile Offending." *Journal of Quantitative Criminology*, 21(4):419-437.

Matsueda, R.L. (1997). "'Cultural Deviance Theory': The Remarkable Persistence of a Flawed Term." *Theoretical Criminology*, 1:429-452.

Matsueda, R.L. (1988). "The Current State of Differential Association Theory." *Crime & Delinquency*, 34:277-306.

Matsueda, R.L. & K. Heimer (1987). "Race, Family Structure, and Delinquency: A Test of Differential Association and Social Control Theories." *American Sociological Review*, 47:489-504.

Matza, D. (1964). *Delinquency and Drift*. New York, NY: John Wiley and Sons.

Maume, M.O., G.C. Ousey & K. Beaver (2005). "Cutting the Grass: A Reexamination of the Link between Marital Attachment, Delinquent Peers and Desistance from Marijuana Use." *Journal of Quantitative Criminology*, 21(1):27-53.

Maurer, D.W. (1974). *The American Confidence Man*. Springfield, IL: Charles C Thomas.

McGloin, J.M. (2009. "Delinquency Balance: Revisiting Peer Influence." *Criminology*, 47:439-478.

Menard, S. & D.S. Elliott (1994). "Delinquent Bonding, Moral Beliefs, and Illegal Behavior: A Three-Wave Panel Model." *Justice Quarterly*, 11:173-178.

Miller, J.M., A.K. Cohen & K.M. Bryant (1997). "On the Demise and Morrow of Subculture Theories of Crime and Delinquency." *Journal of Crime and Justice*, 20:167-178.

Miller, W.B. (1958). "Lower-Class Culture as a Generating Milieu of Gang Delinquency." *Journal of Social Issues*, 14:5-19.

Minor, W.W. (1981). "Techniques of Neutralization: A Reconceptualization and Empirical Examination." *Journal of Research in Crime and Delinquency*, 18:295-318.

Minor, W.W. (1980). "The Neutralization of Criminal Offense." *Criminology*, 18:103-120.

Nagin, D.S. & R. Paternoster (1994). "Personal Capital and Social Control: The Deterrence Implications of a Theory of Individual Differences in Criminal Offending." *Criminology*, 32:581-606.

Odum, H.W. (1951). "Edwin H. Sutherland—1883-1950." *Social Forces*, 29:348-349.

Piquero, A., R. MacIntosh & M. Hickman (2000). "Does Self-Control Affect Survey Response? Applying Exploratory, Confirmatory, and Item Response Theory Analysis to Grasmick et al.'s Self-Control Scale." *Criminology*, 38:897-930.

Piquero, A.R., J. MacDonald, A. Dobrin, L.E. Daigle & F.T. Cullen (2005). "Self-Control, Violent Offending, and Homicide Victimization: Assessing the General Theory of Crime." *Journal of Quantitative Criminology*, 21(1):55-71.

Piquero, A. & S. Tibbetts (1996). "Specifying the Direct and Indirect Effects of Low Self-Control and Situational Factors in Offenders' Decision Making: Toward a More Complete Model of Rational Offending." *Justice Quarterly*, 13:481-510.

Polakowski, M. (1994). "Linking Self- and Social Control With Deviance: Illuminating the Structure Underlying a General Theory of Crime and its Relations to Deviant Activity." *Journal of Quantitative Criminology*, 10:41-78.

Pridemore, W.A. & J.D. Freilich (2006). "A Test of Recent Subcultural Explanations of White Violence in the United States." *Journal of Criminal Justice*, 34:1-16.

Pratt, T.C. & F.T. Cullen (2000). "The Empirical Status of Gottfredson and Hirschi's General Theory of Crime: A Meta-Analysis." *Criminology*, 38:931-964.

Pratt, T.C., M.G. Turner & A.R. Piquero (2004). "Parental Socialization and Community Context: A Longitudinal Analysis of the Structural Sources of Low Self-Control." *Journal of Research in Crime and Delinquency*, 41(3):219-243.

Quinn, J. & S. Koch (2003). "The Nature of Criminality within One-Percent Motorcycle Clubs." *Deviant Behavior*, 24:281-305.

Rankin, J.H. & R. Kern (1994). "Parental Attachments and Delinquency." *Criminology*, 32:495-515.

Redmon, D. (2003). "Examining Low Self-Control Theory at Mardi Gras: Critiquing the General Theory of Crime within the Framework of Normative Deviance." *Deviant Behavior*, 24:373-392.

Reed, G.E. & P.C. Yeager (1996). "Organizational Offending and Neoclassical Criminology: Challenging the Reach of a General Theory of Crime." *Criminology*, 34:357-382.

Reinarman, C. & J. Fagan (1988). "Social Organization and Differential Association: A Research Note from a Longitudinal Study of Violent Juvenile Offenders." *Crime & Delinquency*, 34:307-327.

Schinkel, W. (2002). "The Modernist Myth in Criminology." *Theoretical Criminology*, 6:123-144.

Sellers, C.S. (1999). "Self-Control and Intimate Violence: An Examination of the Scope and Specification of the General Theory of Crime." *Criminology*, 37:375-404.

Sellers, C.S. & L.T. Winfree (1990). "Differential Associations and Definitions: A Panel Study of Youthful Drinking Behavior." *International Journal of Addictions*, 25:755-771.

Sellers, C.S., J.K. Cochran & K.A. Branch (2005). "Social Learning Theory and Partner Violence: A Research Note." *Deviant Behavior*, 26:379-395.

Sellin, T. (1938). *Culture Conflict and Crime*. New York, NY: Social Science Research Council.

Stewart, E.A., K.W. Elifson & C.E. Sterk (2004). "Integrating the General Theory of Crime into an Explanation of Violent Victimization among Female Offenders." *Justice Quarterly*, 21(1):159-181.

Stewart, E.A. & R.L. Simons (2006). "Structure and Culture in African American Adolescent Violence: A Partial Test of the "Code of the Street" Thesis." *Justice Quarterly*, 23(1):1-33.

Stylianou, S. (2002). "The Relationship between Elements and Manifestations of Low Self-Control in a General Theory of Crime: Two Comments and a Test." *Deviant Behavior*, 23:531-557.

Sutherland, E.H. (1949). *White Collar Crime*. New York, NY: Dryden.

Sutherland, E.H. (1939). *Principles of Criminology*, Third Edition. Philadelphia, PA: J.B. Lippincott.

Sutherland, E.H. (1937). *The Professional Thief*. Chicago, IL: University of Chicago Press.

Sutherland, E.H. & Donald R. Cressey (1974). *Criminology*, Ninth Edition. Philadelphia, PA: J.B. Lippincott.

Sykes, G.M. & D. Matza (1957). "Techniques of Neutralization: A Theory of Delinquency." *American Sociological Review*, 22:664-670.

Thaxton, S. & R. Agnew (2004). "The Nonlinear Effects of Parental and Teacher Attachment on Delinquency: Disentangling Strain from Social Control Explanations." *Justice Quarterly*, 21(4):763-791.

Thompson, H. (1966). *Hell's Angels*. New York, NY: Ballantine.

Thornberry, T.B., M.D. Krohn, A.J. Lizotte & D. Chard-Wierschem (1993). "The Role of Juvenile Gangs in Facilitating Delinquent Behavior." *Journal of Research in Crime and Delinquency*, 30:55-87.

Tittle, C.R. (1995). *Control Balance: Toward a General Theory of Deviance*. Boulder, CO: Westview Press.

Tittle, C.R. & E.V. Botchkovar (2005). "Self-Control, Criminal Motivation and Deterrence: An Investigation Using Russian Respondents." *Criminology*, 43(2):307-352.

Tittle, C.R., M.J. Burke & E.F. Jackson (1986). "Modeling Sutherland's Theory of Differential Association: Toward an Empirical Clarification." *Social Forces*, 65:405-432.

Turner, M.G., A.R. Piquero & T.C. Pratt (2005). "The School Context as a Source of Self-Control." *Journal of Criminal Justice*, 33:327-339.

Unnever, J.D., F.T. Cullen & T.C. Pratt (2003). "Parental Management, ADHD, and Delinquent Involvement: Reassessing Gottfredson and Hirschi's General Theory." *Justice Quarterly*, 20(3):471-500.

Vazsonyi, A.T. & J.M. Crosswhite (2004). "A Test of Gottfredson and Hirschi's General Theory of Crime in African American Adolescents." *Journal of Research in Crime and Delinquency*, 41(4):407-432.

Vazsonyi,, A.T. & R. Klanjšek (2008. "A Test of Self-Control Theory Across Different Socioeconomic Strata." *Justice Quarterly*, 25:101-131.

Vine, M.S.W. (1972). "Gabriel Tarde (1843-1904)." In H. Mannheim (ed.) *Pioneers in Criminology*. Montclair, NJ: Patterson Smith.

Wiatrowski, M.D., D.B. Griswold & M.K. Roberts (1981). "Social Control Theory and Delinquency." *American Sociological Review*, 46:525-541.

Wikström, P.H. & K. Treiber (2007). "The Role of Self-Control in Crime Causation." *European Journal of Criminology*, 4:237-264.

Williams, F.P., III & M.D. McShane (1998). *Criminology Theory: Selected Classic Readings*, Second Edition. Cincinnati, OH: Anderson Publishing Co.

Winfree, L.T., C.S. Sellers & D.L. Clason (1993). "Social Learning and Adolescent Deviance Abstention: Toward Understanding the Reasons for Initiating, Quitting, and Avoiding Drug Use." *Journal of Quantitative Criminology*, 9:101-125.

Winfree, L.T, G.L. Mays & T. Vigil-Backstrom (1994). "Youth Gangs and Incarcerated Delinquents: Exploring the Ties between Gang Membership, Delinquency, and Social Learning Theory." *Justice Quarterly*, 11:229-256.

Winfree, L.T, T. Vigil-Backstrom & G.L. Mays (1994). "Social Learning Theory, Self-Reported Delinquency, and Youth Gangs." *Youth and Society*, 26:147-177.

Wolfgang, M.E. (1958/1975). *Patterns in Criminal Homicide*. Montclair, NJ: Patterson Smith.

Wolfgang, M.E. & F. Ferracuti (1967). *The Subculture of Violence*. London, UK: Social Science Paperbacks.

Wood, P.B., B. Pfefferbaum & B.J. Arneklev (1993). "Risk-Taking and Self-Control: Social Psychological Correlates of Delinquency." *Journal of Crime & Justice*, 16:111-130.

Wright, B.R.E., A. Caspi, T.E. Moffit & P.A. Silva (1999). "Low Self-Control, Social Bonds, and Crime: Social Causation, Social Selection, or Both?" *Criminology*, 37:479-514.

Wright, J.P. & F.T. Cullen (2000). "Juvenile Involvement in Occupational Delinquency." *Criminology*, 38:863-896.

9
Social Reaction
Theories of Crime

The preceding four chapters have examined explanations of crime in terms of the offending individual. Rational choice theorists, for example, employ the concept of free will, and argue that people are rational beings who decide whether or not to violate the law. Biogenic and psychogenic theorists assume that genetic or other differences place some people at high risk of law violation. Psychoanalysts claim that aberrant behavior is attributable to some traumatic early experience unsatisfactorily resolved. Social structure and process theorists view the individual as acting within the specific contexts of his or her environment. Depending upon the nature of these contexts, persons are thought to have varying probabilities of becoming involved in criminal activity.

Contrary to these emphases, social reaction theorists focus upon social and institutional responses to the individual. These theorists are not as interested in the initial delinquency or crime as they are in the way in which the act is responded to by social control agents. Social reaction approaches view the individual as a largely passive being who is forced into the role of a criminal by societal definitions or by the reactions of others. As John Curra (2000:viii) asserts at the outset of *The Relativity of Deviance*, "deviance cannot be understood apart from its social context." The social context of crime is indeed important, serving as one of the themes of this book.

Following the introduction and proliferation of self-report methods of studying crime and delinquency, the *labeling perspective* grew both in appeal and acceptance as an explanation of crime and deviance. Labeling theorists maintain that official reactions to law violations label people as criminals and ensnare them in this deviant identity. These theorists further contend that it is not the behavior alone that affects official response, but that the physical characteristics and demeanor of the individual also play major roles in fashioning the response. An interesting study, for instance, conducted by Darrell Steffensmeier and Robert Terry (1973), found that people were much more willing to attribute illegal intentions to individuals fitting a common stereotype. The researchers had four students (two males and two females) pretend to shoplift in a department store (with the manager's knowledge and approval), and recorded witnesses' reactions to the observed behavior. A student of each sex dressed the part of a "preppy," the other pair dressed in "hippie" fashion. As you might guess, people were more likely to report the "shoplifting" of the male hippie than that of any of the others. In decreasing likelihood of being reported were the acts of the female hippie, male preppy, and finally, the female preppy. When questioned, witnesses indicated their willingness to overlook the behavior of the preppy-looking shoplifters because it was inconsistent with the witnesses' pre-established ideas, but they expected no better from "hippies."

The labeling perspective was widely endorsed by scholars during the 1960s and 1970s. Since then, attempts have been made to evaluate the labeling approach and to better specify its theoretical parameters (e.g., Gove, 1980; Dotter & Roebuck, 1988; Matsueda, 1992; Huizinga & Henry, 2007). By the end of the 1980s, the early promises of the labeling perspective had been battered by research results, and the theory subsequently lost much of its theoretical glitter (Wellford, 1987).

What has come to be known as *critical criminology* also experienced a surge in popularity among American criminologists beginning in the early 1960s, then grew rapidly in the 1970s. As Ray Michalowski (1996) suggests, critical criminology is best viewed as an intellectual movement. The latter part of this chapter briefly reviews the development of critical criminology. This perspective has had substantial impact on criminological thought, even though its fundamental premises may not be widely accepted in totality. Critical criminology, however, is now widely recognized as a competing perspective from which crime may be analyzed and has its own division within the American Society of Criminology. As will be seen, however, it has evolved into a very broad perspective encompassing a variety of theories.

As with each theoretical perspective, it is important to recognize the context within which it grew. The social climate in the United States in the 1960s and 1970s was dramatically shaped by the civil rights movement, the Vietnam War, the riots in Watts, Newark, and Detroit, the protests at the 1968 Democratic National Convention in Chicago, the assassinations of President John Kennedy, civil rights leader Martin Luther King, Jr., and presidential candidate Robert Kennedy, and the corruption of the Nixon administration culminating with the Watergate scandal. The political and social turmoil of the times created a pervasive mistrust of government and other social institutions. It was a time of wide-scale questioning of authority.

Discriminatory practices against racial minorities and women by the criminal justice system, the educational system, and the business sector were also brought to light. Given this climate, and the active role many educators and students played in the civil rights and anti-war movements, it is not surprising that social scientists began to focus on the role played by political, economic, and other social institutions in shaping societal definitions of legal and illegal behaviors. While the U.S. Department of Justice was investing billions of dollars in law enforcement and corrections, criminologists such as William Chambliss, Austin Turk, and Richard Quinney were insisting that those in power manipulated the law for their own interests. Others, including non-conflict theorists, were documenting the deleterious societal effects of white-collar and corporate crime.

Labeling Theory

Labeling and social conflict theories provide a critical perspective for the examination of major assumptions in criminology. Labeling theory has its foundation in the works of George Herbert Mead and Charles Horton Cooley. These early twentieth-century sociologists are associated with symbolic interactionism, a perspective emphasizing individual levels of behavior, as opposed to the group-level emphasis of the social structure theorists. Cooley is best known for his development of the "looking-glass" self concept. He argued that our understanding of ourselves is primarily a reflection of our perception of how others react to us. That is, we see ourselves through others. George Herbert Mead elaborated upon this concept by focusing attention on the interaction between an emerging self and the perceptions of others' reactions to that self. According to Mead, this dynamic interplay between the individual and others leads to the development of a self-concept that affects subsequent behavior.

Labeling theory is built upon this foundation. Its proponents argue that the individual is a constantly changing being who responds to others' reactions. A formal response by the criminal justice system, labeling theorists contend, forces the individual to re-assess his or her personal identity. Additionally, others who become aware of the apprehension and official response re-evaluate their opinions about the individual. This process of re-assessment is the basis of the labeling perspective. Note that this is precisely the opposite of deterrence theory. Deterrence proposes to reduce future criminal or delinquent behavior through application of punitive responses, while those same punishments will cause more aberrant behavior according to labeling theory.

Consider the example of Lisa, a recent high school graduate who plans to enroll at the state university in the fall. A week after graduation, Lisa attends a party at which cocaine and marijuana are available. She tries both drugs for the first time and a friend gives her a small vial of cocaine for later use. On her way home, Lisa encounters a police sobriety checkpoint. While she is getting her driver's license out of her purse, the vial of cocaine accidentally falls into Lisa's lap. She is arrested on suspicion of possession of a controlled substance. After being formally processed, Lisa receives six months probation on the condition that she enroll in a drug treatment clinic. In the eyes of the law, she is now a convicted criminal. The personal and social ramifications of the labeling process are far greater, however, than the mere acquisition of the label "criminal." Lisa's parents, friends, neighbors, and high school teachers now see her in a different light. No longer is Lisa perceived as the intelligent, motivated young woman they had known; now she is suspect, and is viewed as a potentially bad influence on "decent" kids. Lisa's self-image also may undergo a transformation. She perceives others as avoiding her, or talking behind her back; she begins to view herself as an outsider and moves toward the acceptance of those going to the drug clinic as her true friends. The labeling process is complete: the formal label has been applied, significant others have reacted to the official label, and Lisa has accepted the label and adjusted her self-concept and peer affiliations.

While this hypothetical case may be extreme, it highlights major issues identified by labeling theorists. First, of primary importance to labeling theorists is what transpires after an act, not what caused or precipitated the act. Second, deviance is a

You may not initially be the label but you become the label.

property conferred upon an act; it is not something inherent in the act (Erikson, 1962). That is, Lisa's experimentation with cocaine and possession of the vial was not deviant until it was officially tagged as such by the arresting officer and others. Third, the labeling of an individual is a process of symbolic interaction between the "deviant" and significant others. Edwin Lemert (1951) referred to this as *secondary deviance*. Fourth, the labeling process is affected by who does the labeling and by how the labeled person reacts to the label. Fifth, the act of labeling may lead to *retrospective interpretation* of the individual's prior behavior. For example, the fact that Lisa got a punkish haircut two weeks before her arrest will now be seen as "another" indication that she is indeed a drug abuser; before the haircut had been regarded as "kinda cute." Sixth, a deviant label such as that of "criminal" or "drug abuser" becomes a pivotal status that overrides other personal attributes. In our example, Lisa is now defined as a drug abuser first and foremost, and this label affects how others will respond to her. Consequently, the probability of further criminal behavior (secondary deviance) is enhanced. A deterrence theorist, on the other hand, would predict less likelihood of future misconduct by Lisa as she should have learned the consequences.

Frank Tannenbaum— Dramatization of Evil

While the 1960s and 1970s saw a proliferation of books and articles advocating the labeling perspective (e.g., Kitsuse, 1962; Becker, 1963; Goffman, 1963; and Schur, 1973) its origins can be found in Frank Tannenbaum's 1938 publication, *Crime and the Community*. Tannenbaum sought to expand the ability of existing theories to explain criminal behavior by focusing on what transpired after an individual had been caught and identified as having violated a law. Tannenbaum termed this process of social reaction to illegal behavior the *dramatization of evil*. He contended that criminals are not inherently different from the rest of the population, but that specific acts in a person's overall repertoire of behaviors are singled out and brought to public attention. The following excerpt highlights how a person who commits a single deviant act is transformed:

> There is a gradual shift from the definition of the specific act as evil to a definition of the individual as evil, so that all his acts come to be looked upon with suspicion. . . . From the community's point of view, the individual who used to do bad and mischievous things has now become a bad and unredeemable human being. From the individual's point of view, there has taken place a similar change. . . . The young delinquent becomes bad because he is not believed if he is good (Tannenbaum, 1938:17-18).

Dramatization of evil is related to *legal relativism*, another concept introduced by Tannenbaum. Acts, he insisted, are neither inherently good nor evil; there are varying degrees of good and evil, and the social audience influences the label placed upon specific behavior. The same behavior engaged in by individuals of different social status or in varying settings may be responded to quite differently. Being drunk at a fraternity party, for example, is not treated in the same manner as drunken behavior during a final exam. What is appropriate or at least tolerable behavior in one situation may be frowned upon in another.

Edwin M. Lemert— Primary and Secondary Deviation

The next major contribution to the labeling perspective was made by Edwin Lemert in his 1951 publication, *Social Pathology*. Lemert is known particularly for distinguishing between primary and secondary deviation. Primary deviation refers to occasional or situational behavior that may be excused or rationalized by the actor and/or the social audience. Driving 45 miles per hour in a 30 miles-per-hour zone, for example, can be rationalized by statements such as: "Everybody else is going that fast." Being drunk in public and making obscene comments is excused when the audience is told that the group is returning from a "bachelor's party." However, when such behaviors become a regular and prominent part of the actor's identity, the situation is no longer primary deviation.

Lemert wrote that "when a person begins to employ his deviant behavior or a role based upon it as a means of defense, attack, or adjustment to the overt and covert problems created by the consequent societal reaction to him, his deviation is secondary" (1951:76). *Secondary deviation* is the result of a dynamic interaction between the individual's deviation and the societal response to the deviation. Lemert described this process in the following manner (1951:77):

The sequence of interaction leading to secondary deviation is roughly as follows:

1. primary deviation;

2. social penalties;

3. further primary deviation;

4. stronger penalties and rejection;

5. further deviation, perhaps with hostilities and resentment beginning to focus upon those doing the penalizing;

6. crisis reached in the tolerance quotient, expressed in formal action by the community stigmatizing of the deviant;

7. strengthening of the deviant conduct as a reaction to the stigmatizing and penalties;

8. ultimate acceptance of deviant social status and efforts at adjustment on the basis of the associated role.

Once the process of secondary deviation results in the labeling of an individual, it becomes extremely difficult for the person to escape classification as a deviant. Lemert maintained that official reactions such as arrests, court hearings, and investigations by public welfare agencies usually exacerbate the situation and often cause dramatic redefinitions of the self. Thus, the process of formally responding to a criminal or deviant act, Lemert would argue, is likely to cause further criminal activity.

Howard S. Becker— Secret Deviants and the Falsely Accused

Howard S. Becker was one of the more prominent proponents of labeling theory to emerge during the 1960s. His now classic work, *Outsiders: Studies in the Sociology of Deviance*, first published in 1963, delineated several key elements of labeling theory as it is known today. Among these is his assertion that deviants and criminals are themselves not a homogeneous group. Aside from the fact that someone who commits a burglary may be very different from a rapist, some individuals are labeled deviant even though they have never committed a deviant or criminal act. Still others commit law violations but are never apprehended or even detected. By grouping the vast assortment of criminals together and by including what Becker called the "*falsely accused*," we wind up with quite a heterogeneous collection of people. Along these lines, Becker wrote (1963:9):

> [S]ocial groups create deviance by making the rules whose infraction constitutes deviance, and by applying those rules to particular people and labeling them as outsiders. From this point of view, deviance is not a quality of the act the person commits but rather a consequence of the application by others of rules and sanctions to an "offender." The deviant is one to whom that label has successfully been applied; deviant behavior is behavior that people so label.

To amplify this belief that criminal and deviant behavior are social artifacts, Becker presented a typology depicting four different types of deviants and nondeviants. Figure 9.1 presents these types. The *conformist* and the *pure deviant* are both accurately perceived by society in terms of their actual behaviors. The other two types, however, are often misjudged. The *falsely accused* have been identified as deviants or criminals, perhaps due to their sex, age, race, social status, peer group affiliation, or physical appearance. While these incorrectly placed labels may be more frequently found in nonlegal settings, studies also have documented the existence of falsely accused individuals on death row (Bedau & Radelet, 1987; Huff, 2002).

According to what we know from self-report studies, *secret deviants* comprise a large group; many criminal violations are never brought to the attention of the police. These individuals are able to avoid detection or witnesses may fail to impose a criminal or deviant label on the actions.

These four criminal types can cause analytical problems for criminologists. The falsely accused individual, for instance, may appear in official records as a criminal and criminologists may attempt to explain the causes of this person's criminality in

---

Figure 9.1
Adaptation of Becker's Typology of Deviant Behavior

	Conforming Behavior	Norm-Violating Behavior
Perceived as Deviant	Falsely Accused	Pure Deviant
Not Perceived as Deviant	Conformist	Secret Deviant

---

the same manner as they do that of the pure deviant. Labeling theorists would contend that it is appropriate to examine the effects of the label once it has been placed, irrespective of its accuracy. This, in part, can be attributed to the conceptualization of deviance as a *master status*. Borrowing from an article by Everett C. Hughes, Becker suggested that a deviant or criminal label becomes a master status with a number of assumed auxiliary statuses. A doctor, for example, is generally assumed to be male, white, upper-middle class, and Protestant or Jewish. In the same vein, a criminal is assumed to be an undesirable person who has no respect for the law and is likely to commit any number of offenses in order to obtain what he (being male is an auxiliary status of criminals) wants.

Another concept introduced by Becker is that of *moral entrepreneurs*, that is, individuals who either serve as rule creators or rule enforcers. Becker identified the prototype of these rule creators as a moral crusader, a person who "feels that nothing can be right in the world until rules are made to correct it" (Becker, 1963:148). Prohibitionists in their campaign against alcoholic beverages are good examples of moral entrepreneurs who wanted to impose their standards upon others. While they sometimes are viewed as busybodies, many moral crusaders are motivated by a humanitarian drive. They believe that their moral values are superior to those of others and that adoption of their positions will produce a better or more decent life for all.

We must ask, as do labeling theorists: Who creates rules and who is regulated by those rules? Becker maintained that moral entrepreneurs tend to be members of the upper classes who typically want to help those beneath them to achieve a better status. That those beneath them do not always like the means proposed for their salvation is another matter. Moral entrepreneurs seek to regulate morals—be they within the realm of alcohol, drugs, sexual activity, human reproduction (e.g., abortion), child rearing practices, or work habits. As is central to the social reaction perspective, it is not the objective behavior of "deviants" that varies and requires explanation. It is the relative success of moral entrepreneurs in controlling deviance through redefining it to coincide with their moral perspective. One successful strategy for redefining or creating deviance is to cultivate a "moral panic"—a public perception of behaviors or groups of persons that greatly exaggerate their potential for harm to the larger society. Such a response to contemporary gangs serves as an example of moral panic as described in this chapter's "Gang Feature."

GANG FEATURE

Moral Panic!

In their article, "Moral Panic and the Response to Gangs in California," Jackson and Rudman examined California's response to the growing youth gang problem of the 1980s. As discussed in earlier chapters (see especially the "Gang Features" in Chapters 2 and 5), the primary response to gangs has been suppression. Jackson and Rudman attempt to account for this public policy response based on a belief in the deterrability of these behavioral patterns.

Gangs and their members garnered the attention and interest of the media during the mid 1980s. "Gangsta rap" and "wannabe" became part of the common vernacular as MTV and VH1 exposed the world to the gang lifestyle. Gangs such as the Crips, Bloods, Vice Lords, and Gangster Disciples were featured in the evening news and in the local papers. Hollywood also joined this media frenzy, producing feature-length movies depicting the gang lifestyle, usually with an emphasis on the violence and drug dealing aspects that would appeal to movie-goers. Local, state, and federal government agencies responded to this publicity. A number of initiatives in law enforcement and in research endeavors were promoted in response to this gang phenomenon.

The popular image of gangs presented by the mass media and furthered by law enforcement was that of juveniles possessing a cache of high-power weapons and engaging in a lucrative drug trade. "These gangs were characterized either as instrumental groups or vaguely defined youth street gangs whose overriding purpose was to make large amounts of money through the distribution and sale of crack and other drugs" (Jackson & Rudman, 1993:258). The general public was left with the belief that vast profits and luxurious lifestyles were common to these "gang bangers" and that because of the money available, gang members were drawn primarily from poor and minority youth with limited legitimate employment opportunities.

Jackson and Rudman provided the following examples of how media coverage spread this image of gang members:

- With the added pressure being put on gangs dealing drugs in the Los Angeles area, we're going to see a further increase in their dealing drugs in Sacramento (Sacramento Mayor's Task Force Final Report on Drug Abuse, 1988).

- Entire Sacramento neighborhoods are now at risk of becoming the Northern California rendition of south-central L.A. because of the rock cocaine plague and the gangs that brought it here. Residents of some areas . . . contend with almost daily drive-by shootings, brawls, fights, and vandalism, not to mention the devastation wrought by those hooked on rock; prostitution, child abandonment and abuse, theft and drug-induced insanity (*Sacramento Bee*, 1988).

Due also in part to deaths of innocent bystanders (frequently killed in gang "drive-bys"), the public willingly and eagerly believed reports about "the intimidation of potential witnesses to gang-related activities, reports of increasing gang violence in schools, gang graffiti, drug-related commitments to local facilities, and drug-related arrests" (Jackson & Rudman, 1993:259). This perception was associated with a concern that gangs would continue to increase in size and power unless additional resources were provided to law enforcement. There appeared to be a belief that gangs were more heavily armed than the police, and that the only way to respond to the gang problem was to increase the budgets and staff of the police.

Jackson and Rudman examined California's legislative response to gangs, concluding that the "evidence to date suggests that the nature of the reaction to the 'gang problem' in California is similar to other instances of what has been referred to as 'moral panics.' Where a perceived threat of an individual or group greatly surpasses their actual threat the setting is ripe for the characterization of it as a 'moral panic'" (Jackson & Rudman, 1993:271).

Edwin M. Schur—
Radical Nonintervention

A controversial book by Edwin Schur epitomized the labeling perspective's position regarding the effect of processing juveniles through the justice system. Published in 1973, *Radical Nonintervention* argued that nothing should be done with or to children who violate the law. He argued that most adolescent rule-breaking is petty in nature and that punishment is unnecessary. Society should take a more tolerant stance and allow adolescents to experiment with a wide array of behavioral alternatives. To do otherwise, Schur maintained, serves only to label and to isolate youth from legitimate roles.

Schur agreed with Becker that the label "delinquent" is a master status and difficult to overcome. Furthermore, due in part to the alleged discriminatory practices of the justice system, Schur contended that lower-class, African-American males are more likely to be officially labeled than are other youths. This occurs in part because of the lack of power among juveniles in general and lower-class, African-American males in particular. These individuals are, for instance, unable to pay for legal counsel or to argue effectively with the police not to press charges.

Schur also discussed the concept of retrospective interpretation, which was introduced by John Kitsuse (1962), another early advocate of the labeling perspective. Retrospective interpretation refers to the process by which people re-interpret an individual's behavior in light of new information concerning that individual. Schur and others have argued that a delinquent label serves as a prompt for others to re-evaluate things that a child has said or done in the past and then redefine these matters so they are made consistent with the new information (e.g., the new punk haircut of our hypothetical Lisa is reinterpreted in light of her arrest for possession of a controlled substance).

Overview of Labeling Perspective

Drawing on the seminal works reviewed above, we can summarize the labeling perspective. Because it incorporates such a wide range of thought, many view it as a general perspective for understanding crime and delinquency rather than as a concise theory. It is also seen by many to be more applicable to juveniles than to adults based upon the assumption that youth are, for better or worse, more malleable than are adults. In other words, just as it is often argued that a youth may be more amenable to rehabilitative intervention than an adult, the labeling perspective holds that interventions also have more potential for backfiring and creating a delinquent self-image among them. The labeling process is a circular one as depicted in Figure 9.2.

First, as efforts of moral entrepreneurs are successful in redefining more conduct as criminal or delinquent, the deviance net is broadened. Successful criminalization of more behaviors will expand the ranks of offenders. More behaviors will be construed as primary deviance and will lead to initiation of the labeling process. The process will

FIGURE 9.2
The Labeling/Deviance Spiral

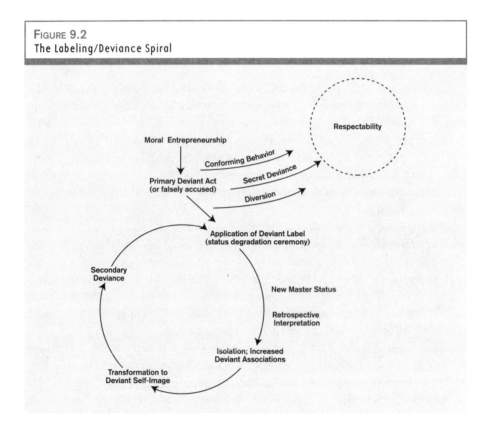

be applied to others who are falsely accused. Otherwise, those who are conformists and secret deviants will retain respectability, while diversion programs are intended to preserve respectability for identified deviants. Those to whom the label is otherwise successfully applied become deviants as a result of status degradation ceremonies. The juvenile who is adjudicated at the conclusion of a hearing, for example, assumes the new master status of "juvenile delinquent." As a consequence of the successful labeling, the deviant is isolated from "respectable" influences and resorts to increased associations with similarly situated persons. This contributes to transformation of the person's self-image to a deviant one, setting the stage for secondary deviance. From this point, a spiral away from respectability and moving more deeply into deviance continues.

Once again, it may be helpful to frame the labeling hypothesis in terms of personal experiences and observations. Have you ever engaged in any behaviors that, if detected, could have labeled you a delinquent? Did any of your friends do so? Self-report data suggest that we would have difficulty finding anyone who did not! Perhaps you committed a few delinquent acts, got caught, were punished, and were better off for it. If not caught and adjudicated delinquent, maybe it would have been best if you had been. That is, punishment might keep one out of future trouble by teaching him or her a lesson, what we have termed specific deterrence. On the other hand, it might be that being caught and officially labeled would have made you or your friend more, rather than less, likely to commit additional delinquent acts. Labeling theory maintains

HIGHLIGHT 9.1
Is a "Sex Offender" Label Worth Dying For?

Thomas Varnum, a convicted sex offender in Maine, concluded in 1997 that it was worth dying for a "sex offender" label. He had served three and a half years in prison for befriending a nine-year-old boy and having sex with him repeatedly over a six-month period. Paroled for a year and a half, he was employed in construction and working as a mechanic on weekends. His landlord did not know of his conviction, but said he was a good tenant. While the new Megan's Law, a version of which had passed in Maine and some 40 other states, could not be applied to him retroactively, the sheriff's department found a way. Based on an old law that allowed the release of information about convictions, deputies circulated fliers about Varnum on the road where he lived. They included his mug shot, address and notice that he was convicted of gross sexual assault. Following neighbors calls, Varnum's landlord asked that he move. The next evening he used a shotgun to blow the top of his head off.*

Another convicted sex offender, Nate Sims, chose to pack his bags and run . . . again. Sims had been convicted of the rape and sodomy of a woman and served a twenty year prison term. Upon returning to his hometown of Danville, Kentucky, he found his picture and the "sex offender" label in the newspaper. This cost him the job he had just obtained and was arrested for violating parole by living in his car rather than his registered address. But his luck briefly changed when a local born-again Christian family offered him a bedroom in their affluent home. The couple asked, "What would Jesus do?" But their neighbors asked how they could do that and deluged them with flyers, anonymous letters, phone calls and visits to their business. When camera crews arrived, Nate packed his bags and left his new home and another new job.

These results of aggressive labeling strategies raise many questions. What are the moral rights of persons concerned with protection of their families from "risky" residents? What are the rights of "sex offenders" to reestablish their lives—to work and live somewhere?

Sources: Adapted from *Jerry Schwartz, Associated Press writer, *Johnson City Press*, 3-22-98. and Allen G. Breed, Associated Press writer, *Johnson City Press*, 9-2-99.

that kids will misbehave, but that most will outgrow it without official intervention. To the contrary, it is argued, official labeling may inject a typical young person into that downward spiral of deviance.

Research on Labeling Theory

Charles R. Tittle (1980) has identified two basic problems with labeling theory. First, propositions are not clearly specified so as to allow researchers to study the relationship between key variables. Second, there is an absence of data to adequately test the labeling perspective. Very few direct tests have been made, and Tittle argued that the vagueness of the labeling concept further exacerbates the problem by making it difficult to glean information from studies conducted for other purposes.

Tittle noted that two propositions can be generated from the labeling literature. First, labeling, especially by formal agents of social control, is said to result in negative reactions by others once they become aware of the official label. This response is often associated with the "attribution of bad character and stereotypical behavioral expectations" (Tittle, 1980:247). Second, labeling theorists posit that official processing is more heavily influenced by personal and social characteristics than by actual norm violations.

With respect to the first hypothesis, Richard Schwartz and Jerome Skolnick (1962) examined the effect of official criminal justice processing on future job employment. Four folders were prepared describing a single, 32-year-old male with a history of short-term jobs as kitchen helper, maintenance worker, and handyman. The only difference in the four folders was the applicant's reported record of criminal court involvement. Folder 1 indicated that the applicant had been convicted and sentenced for assault. Folder 2 stated that he had been tried and acquitted, while folder 3 included a letter from a judge certifying the applicant had been found not guilty. The fourth folder made no mention of a criminal record.

Twenty-five copies of each folder were sent to a sample of 100 prospective employers in a resort area. Results tended to confirm the labeling perspective. Nine positive responses were received from the folders indicating no criminal justice system involvement. This compared to lower responses for the folders with letters (six), with acquittal (three), and with a conviction (one). Schwartz and Skolnick (1962:335) commented upon this result in the following manner:

> From a theoretical point of view, the finding leads toward the conclusion that conviction constitutes a powerful form of "status degradation" which continues to operate after the time when, according to the generalized theory of justice underlying punishment in our society, the individual's "debt" has been paid. A record of conviction produces a durable if not permanent loss of status.

In an interesting application of the labeling perspective Shadd Maruna and his colleagues (2004) turned their attention to desistance from crime, focusing less on the reactions of others than to the self-identity of the offender. While prior work has tended to examine the effects of labeling on subsequent life chances, these authors were interested in the process of desistance from crime and the establishment of an offender's credentials, or self-image, as a reformed person. One interesting outcome of their interviews with counselors and clients at a treatment facility in upstate New York was that "like social scientists, neither the clients nor counselors we interviewed had an agreed upon standard for determining whether a person has 'rehabilitated' or 'reformed'"(Maruna et al., 2004:276). In explaining the process of desistance, the researchers borrowed from Lemert's notion of primary and secondary deviation and introduced the concepts of *primary desistance* and *secondary desistance* to distinguish the temporary desistance all offenders experience from the "changed person" identity that only a subset experience. They suggest that desistance from crime consists of a process of negotiation that ultimately can produce a change in self-identity. This process of desistance is similar to the labeling process—only in reverse. For desistance to occur, they suggest that a "delabeling process" and "decertification" stage are important.

David Ward and Charles Tittle (1993) studied the effects of informal sanctions on the self-image and subsequent behavior of 390 junior and senior high students. In this investigation of academic cheating, they found that informal peer "sanctioning and labeling of norm violators significantly affects the likelihood that an offender will develop a deviant identity and that such identities significantly affect the likelihood of recidivism" (Ward & Tittle, 1993:60).

In a six-year longitudinal study of 2,617 California youths, Suzanne Ageton and Delbert Elliott tested two specific hypotheses stemming from labeling theory. The following questions guided their research: "Does legal processing create and/or promote an increased orientation toward delinquency?" and "What effect, if any, do other environmental and behavioral factors such as peer group affiliations and self-reported delinquent behavior play in this process?" (Ageton & Elliott, 1974:89). Their analyses showed that legal processing "creates and/or heightens an orientation toward delinquency." Furthermore, the authors also found that Anglos and males were more negatively affected by police contact than were Mexican-Americans, African-Americans, and females.

Ruth Triplett (1993) also examined informal reactions in considering factors that contribute to parents labeling their children delinquent. Triplett agreed that informal responses may be more salient than formal because of the importance the labeled actor assigns the labeler. Being viewed as delinquent by a parent may be far more traumatic than being so labeled by an official of the juvenile justice system. Examining data from a national sample of 1,324 youth, Triplett found the parental labeling to be a function of the youths' grades, delinquent friendships, relationships with parents, parental beliefs, and race as well as their delinquent activities. These findings suggest that whether parents identify their offspring as delinquents depends more on how they fit the stereotype than on the child's actual behavior. Labeling theory asserts, however, that such labeling or stereotyping may cause further delinquent behavior.

In a more recent study Eric Stewart and his colleagues (2002) explored not only the direct effect of arrest on subsequent behavior; they also examined the role of mediating factors that could explain the mechanisms by which labeling worked. They relied on in-depth interviews of rural Iowa families to test the extent to which delinquent behavior and subsequent arrest affected family relationships (specifically parenting practices). Importantly, the longitudinal data allowed these authors to examine the subsequent effect of parenting practices on delinquency. They concluded: "As expected, greater involvement in delinquency and poorer parenting behaviors at time 1 increased the probability of legal sanctions. Legal sanctions, in turn, predicted further increases in delinquency and decreases in parenting quality one year later at time 3" (Stewart et al., 2002:52).

Along the same lines as Stewart's research, Jon Gunnar Bernberg and his colleagues (Bernberg & Krohn 2003; Bernberg et al., 2006) analyzed data from the Rochester Youth Development Study. This data set also consists of longitudinal panel data (following the same people across time) and therefore allows for more thorough examination of the effect of processing on subsequent behavior than is the case with cross-sectional data. In their first article, Bernberg and Krohn (2003) found that arrest and juvenile justice intervention in early adolescence was negatively related to the likelihood of high school graduation, which in turn affected employment which was linked to adult crime. In addition to this mediating effect of juvenile justice intervention on high school graduation and employment, they also found the intervention to have a direct effect on adult crime. In their subsequent research, Bernberg and colleagues (2006) explored the extent to which arrest effected peer group affiliation. As Becker (1960) had hypothesized early in the history of the labeling perspective, they found that police arrest appears to influence social networks; arrested youth increased association with delinquent peers following an arrest. This change in social networks, in turn, led to an increase in subsequent offending. Other recent appraisals of labeling theory have also found support for the negative effects of both formal (Chiricos et al. 2007; Hagan & Palloni, 1990; Huizinga et al., 2003; Sweeten 2006) and informal labeling (Matsueda, 1992).

Contrary to the preceding studies supportive of labeling theory, several investigations have failed to substantiate the labeling hypotheses. In an early study, Jack Foster, Simon Dinitz, and Walter Reckless (1972) learned from their study of 196 boys that only a few indicated that their public image had suffered as a consequence of their contact with authorities. For the most part, the boys did not feel that their interpersonal relationships were negatively affected, although some believed that their prospective employment might be harmed due to having a police record. In an investigation into the effect of formal processing on self attitudes, Gary Jensen (1972) discovered a difference by race; African-American adolescents who have contact with the police are less likely to think of themselves as delinquents than are white adolescents. Jensen also reported that, in general, delinquents have lower self-evaluations than do nondelinquents.

The study by Steffensmeier and Terry detailed at the outset of this chapter provides firm support for the effect of personal characteristics on the decision to prosecute. In a more carefully controlled study, Lawrence Cohen and Rodney Stark

---

HIGHLIGHT 9.2
Is a Loser's Label Worth Killing Over?

Some have concluded that in the minds of Eric Harris and Dylan Klebold, it *was*. The two boys stormed Columbine High School in Colorado, killing 13 before taking their own lives. The most common account given for this horrendous action is that they were outcasts. Their targeting of specific individuals who were popular and affiliated with mainstream groups lends credence to this interpretation. In the aftermath of the tragedy, many high school students around the country were pledging efforts to not taunt, bully, or mock others (Miller, 1999). There has been a lot of agreement that labeling may trigger horrendous behavior on the part of those labeled as misfits, losers, and weirdos. Such tragedies may lead to reassessment of labeling in this context.

(1974) examined 371 shoplifting cases at a large metropolitan department store and the manager's decision whether to prosecute. Contrary to what would be predicted by labeling theorists, personal characteristics such as age, race, and sex were found to be unrelated to the decision. One variable that did help to explain the decision to prosecute was the value of the stolen merchandise. The authors concluded that deviance, at least in this setting, was not "in the eyes of the beholder."

Policy Relevance of Labeling Theory

Stemming in large measure from the labeling theory literature, changes in the rehabilitation model of the 1960s were evident by the mid-1970s. In particular, diversion programs aimed at preventing offenders from penetrating the formal process of the criminal justice system sprang up around the country.

While most of these programs targeted juvenile populations, the same rationale applies to adult groups. In addition to the labeling argument, the United States began experiencing drastic overcrowding in its juvenile and adult correctional facilities during the 1970s. Diversion programs were thus advocated on two fronts: avoidance of negative labeling associated with formal processing and cost savings from reducing the prison population. See Highlight 9.3 for an interesting cross-national examination of the effect of arrest on subsequent offending.

HIGHLIGHT **9.3**
The Effects of Arrest on Subsequent Behavior:
A Cross-National Comparison

Deterrence theorists (see Chapter 5) maintain that future criminal activity can be reduced through effective threats of sanctioning. General deterrence principles suggest that the general population will be deterred from offending if perceived sanctions are implemented with sufficient speed, certainty, and severity. Specific deterrence refers to the reduction in subsequent offending by someone who already has received a sanction as a result of prior offending. This theoretical perspective has dominated the past 25 years of American criminal justice. Three-strikes legislation, habitual offender laws, boot camps, and juvenile waiver to adult court are representative of the belief that crime can be deterred by repressive justice system strategies. In contrast to the deterrence doctrine, labeling theorists postulate that formal justice system interventions aggravate the situation and actually "amplify" deviance and other law violating behaviors. These two theoretical perspectives predict mutually contradictory effects of the same criminal justice interventions. The research reported below attempts to assess the effect of arrest on subsequent offending.

The Denver Youth Survey (see Chapter 3) is a longitudinal study of families that has followed the same group of study participants from 1988 to the present. Annual interviews provide information about each, including self-reports of arrest and offending. The Bremen School-to-Work

HIGHLIGHT **9.3** Continued
The Effects of Arrest on Subsequent Behavior:
A Cross-National Comparison

Study is a similar study conducted in Bremen, Germany. Data from both of these studies were used to examine arrest and sanctioning patterns among 14-24 year old males and females (see Huizinga et al., 2003).

The justice system in Bremen is quite lenient in its treatment of 14- to 17-year-olds in that more than 90 percent of cases referred to the prosecutor are dismissed or diverted. In the Denver study, arrest is a relatively common phenomenon with 73 percent of the males and 43 percent of the females had been arrested by age 18. The arrest figures for Bremen were 34 percent and 9 percent respectively for males and females. Confinement is rare in Bremen in contrast to Denver where 10-20 percent of cases result in confinement. Despite quite different justice philosophies, the prevalence of delinquency in the two cities is remarkably similar (between 62 and 69% of juveniles are involved in delinquent activity during the adolescent years). David Huizinga and his colleagues (2003) state; "given the substantial difference in orientation of the two systems, it is surprising that there is not a greater difference in offending."

Huizinga and colleagues were interested in the extent to which these different justice system orientations effected adolescent offending. Four different analysis strategies (cross-tabulations, multinomial regression, event history models, and a precision control group matching analysis) produced the same results. "In all the analyses, there was very little effect of arrest on subsequent delinquent behavior. When there was an effect, arrest resulted either in maintaining the previous level of delinquency (persistence) or increasing subsequent delinquent behavior. There was essentially no indication at the individual level at either site that arrest resulted in a decrease in delinquent behavior" (Huizinga et al., 2003:3).

The fact that very similar findings regarding the effect of arrest on subsequent offending were obtained in two sites with such different justice systems, one characterized as lenient and the other as punitive, suggests that the findings are quite robust. Arrest does not produce the deterrent effect that proponents of specific deterrence would predict. The authors of the study call for "greater concern about and discussion of the current U.S. orientation toward increased criminalization of behaviors and increased severity of sanctions" (Huizinga et al., 2003:5).

Debate soon arose about the value of diversion as a means of avoiding formal processing. A number of studies concluded that diversion resulted in *net widening* of the social control process (e.g., Klein et al., 1976; Dunford, 1977; Blomberg, 1980). Edwin Lemert, for example, wrote: "What began as an effort to reduce discretion in juvenile justice became a warrant to increase discretion and external control where none existed before" (1981:45). And, in a summary of studies examining the net-widening issue, James Austin and Barry Krisberg (1981:170) concluded that "diversion programs have been transformed into a means for extending the net, making it stronger, and creating new nets."

This net-widening phenomenon refers to what diversion critics see as a bastardization of the intent of diversion program. Instead of placing offenders who previously would have been incarcerated into diversion programs, officials put into the programs offenders who previously would have been released or would have been placed on probation, thus widening the net of official processing. Timothy Bynum and Jack Greene, for example, found that "[w]ith a 32 percent decrease in the use of consent and dismissal decisions, it is evident that a number of youth whose cases would have formerly been dismissed or handled in a consent fashion were now receiving diversion" (1984:141). Not all evaluations, however, support this conclusion. In his analysis of the flow of youth through three metropolitan juvenile justice systems, Finn Esbensen (1984:126) found that "[t]wo metropolitan diversion programs that apparently were implemented in good faith and not subverted by opponents succeeded in reducing the number of youths penetrating and being maintained in the criminal justice system."

Another criticism of diversion programs attacks the premise that negative labeling will be avoided if an individual is placed in a community treatment facility. Malcolm Klein and his colleagues (1976:110) claimed that diversion "is equally or even more encapsulating" than justice system penetration. The debate about the effect of diversion and what role it should play continues, although somewhat abated. Little research on the topic has been presented since 1984, when Arnold Binder and Gilbert Geis argued that "diversion remains a flourishing mode of serving young offenders, as indeed it must so long as the present juvenile justice system remains in operation" (1984:624).

The late 1990s witnessed policy directions diametrically opposed to the premises of labeling theory, generally in the form of substantial increases in the harshness of responses to juvenile misconduct. In the United States, for example, legislation facilitated the transfer of juveniles to the criminal court at younger ages, for less serious offenses, and with less extensive records of delinquency. Harsher legislation was introduced in Britain as well. In his participant observation study of the juvenile justice process in a British town, Ruggiero (1997:344) concluded that the wave of more punitive juvenile delinquency legislation had the effect of generating a "climate of increased intolerance against young offenders." This more punitive legislation, in turn, served "as a catalyst for measures which were even tougher than those it established" (1997:351). That is, the "get tough on kids" message sent by the new laws led teachers, social workers, and juvenile justice personnel to resort more frequently to official sanctions to control youth. Similarly, "zero tolerance" policies in American schools spawned cases of suspensions for use of over-the-counter medications for common ailments such as menstrual cramps and headaches. One honor student was suspended for carrying a spreading knife in her lunch pail, and on several occasions, young elementary school boys were sanctioned for arguably innocuous kisses or pats that were construed as sexual harassment. In short, the trend leans toward official labeling of a broad array of youthful behaviors as delinquent.

Roots of Critical Criminology

The theories presented in the preceding chapters are representative of a broad conceptual orientation referred to as the *consensus view* (see Chapter 1). This approach to interpreting society and social reality rests on the assumption that "a consensus of values among its members" exists and that "the state is organized to protect the general public interest" (Vold et al., 1998:235). In the event of conflict among persons or groups, the state is seen as serving as a mediator to bring about a resolution that best suits the interests of society at large.

The *conflict perspective* posits that society is composed of groups that have opposing values and interests and that the state represents the values and interests of the groups with the most power. Among the earliest systematic treatments of conflict were those by Karl Marx in the latter half of the nineteenth century. One of the applications to crime that set the stage for emergence of radical criminology in the 1960s and 1970s was George Vold's publication of *Theoretical Criminology* in 1958. These two important works are reviewed below.

Karl Marx— Conflict Theory

Much of contemporary conflict theory can be traced back to the writings of the German economist and social philosopher Karl Marx. While Marx and his colleague, Friedrich Engels, had little to say regarding crime per se, their theoretical statements about capitalist society and the history of human civilization laid the foundations for subsequent development of conflict theories in criminology.

Marx believed that the dominant feature of all societies was the mode of production, that is, the way in which people develop and produce material goods. He argued that the economic base of society shaped all social arrangements: "The mode of production of material life determines the general character of the social, political, and spiritual processes of life. It is not the consciousness of men that determines their being but, on the contrary, their social being determines their consciousness" (Marx, 1964:51). This emphasis upon the economic arena led Marx to focus much of his attention on the relationship between the producers (i.e., workers) and those who owned the means of production. Under capitalism, Marx maintained, the bourgeoisie is the dominant class that owns the means of production and the proletariat are forced to work for (or in Marxian terms, sell their labor to) the bourgeoisie. This division of labor has led to the alienation of workers.

Alienation of the proletariat from the products of their labor is indicative of an unequal distribution of property and power in society. This unequal access to property and power lays the foundation for an inevitable class conflict that Marx believed to prevail throughout all of social history. In every society, according to Marx, there exist two opposing groups: one wishing to preserve the status quo and the other attempting to modify existing relationships. This theory of social organization has provided the foundation for the conflict school of criminology in that "contemporary Marxists wish to explore ways in which law, as a form of social control, has been used to contain class struggle and maintain class divisions at different times in different societies" (Lynch & Groves, 1986:7).

Michael Lynch and Byron Groves elaborated further upon the role of contemporary Marxist criminologists:

> They also seek to uncover ways in which historically generated systems of social inequality contribute to the production of specific forms of crime. In other words, Marxists attempt to make sense of crime and criminal justice by examining each in its specific social and historical context. For example, there is no reason to assume that a Roman or feudal social and economic system would produce the same types of crime as we find in our society. . . . Significant societal changes such as urbanization, industrialization, bureaucratization, and the social and technological changes that accompany them, have spawned a whole range of new behaviors (including criminal behaviors such as auto theft, computer crime, and skyjacking) and new forms of law and social control (1986:7).

The relationship between the elite and the state are viewed in two alternative ways by contemporary Marxist criminologists. Instrumental Marxism sees the state and criminal law as intricately linked to the bourgeoisie. That is, the economic elite use the power of the state as an instrument for the maintenance of their own power. Police, courts, and prisons serve the interests of the elite by controlling those who pose threats to the status quo. Others view this version of Marxism as naive and conspiratorial. They point out that the state, including the criminal justice system, sometimes takes actions that arguably violate the interests of the power elite. *Structural Marxism* sees the state as semi-autonomous from the power elite. While the state typically supports the power elite, thereby protecting the capitalist system, it does not always do so. In fact, occasional support of the proletariat builds credibility for the state, thus strengthening it in the long run.

Group Conflict Perspective

George Vold—
Group Conflict Theory

George Vold introduced his formulation of *group conflict theory* in 1958. Vold's conceptualization is rooted in the tradition of social interaction and collective behavior theories. He viewed humans as group oriented and society as a collection of groups, each with its own interests. These groups form because members have common interests and needs that can best be met through collective action. Students in a class, who feel that they have been mistreated by their instructor, for example, would be more likely to obtain redress if they banded together than if they worked individually. Their group grievances probably would carry more weight with the instructor, department head, or dean than would individual complaints.

Vold maintained that groups come into conflict with one another as the interests and purposes they serve begin to overlap and encroach. When this occurs, each group tends to defend itself. To carry the above-mentioned example further, let us assume that a professor has neither distributed a syllabus nor described the grading system to the class. After the second exam, a number of students are told that they are failing the course. Students who received scores in the 70s on the first test and in the 50s on the second test are shocked and assume an error was made. The instructor then informs them that any score of less than 60 is treated as a zero. Thus a "76" and a "0" equals a 38 average, which translates into a letter grade of F. This grading policy offends these students and they band together to preserve their "rights." Note that it was not until the power of the instructor to determine the grading system conflicted with the interests of the students who failed was there a need for the students to "defend" themselves. Vold stated that "conflict between groups tends to develop and intensify the loyalty of the group members to their respective groups" (Vold, 1958:206).

Another element of Vold's group conflict theory pertains to the distribution of power. Who, for example, enacts laws and who enforces them? Vold claimed that "those who produce legislative majorities have control over the police power and dominate the policies that decide who is likely to be involved in violation of the law" (Vold, 1958:209). Former President Reagan was able to shape the U.S. Supreme Court in his conservative image. The liberal Warren Court was largely comprised of appointees from the Kennedy and Johnson administrations. During the Rehnquist Court, we witnessed decisions that overturned or modified those made by the Warren Court. Such changes in laws alter our definitions of crime and criminals. Doctors, for instance, who perform abortions, as well as women who get abortions, possibly would be perceived and treated as criminals if the U.S. Supreme Court were to overturn the *Roe v. Wade* (1973) decision.

An interesting aspect of Vold's theory is that he viewed crime and delinquency as minority group behavior. This represents an extension of his belief that human behavior is dominated by group behavior that is often characterized by conflict. Vold wrote (1958:211): "The juvenile gang is nearly always a 'minority group,' out of sympathy with and in more or less direct opposition to the rules and regulations of the dominant majority; that is, the established world of adult values and power." Youth gangs are in large part a result of intergenerational conflict, which adults are destined to win, given their control of the legal apparatus.

Vold cautioned that, while his theory pertained to crime in general, it was most appropriate for explaining four kinds of crime:

- crimes arising from political protest;

- crimes resulting from labor disputes;

- crimes arising from disputes between and within competing unions; and

- crimes arising from racial and ethnic clashes.

While these four crime types fit quite neatly into Vold's general theoretical framework, the more individual-based crimes, such as rape, embezzlement, robbery, and fraud do not mesh as well. The growth of "radical criminology" in the 1970s as a phase in the critical perspective, however, fleshed out the notion of power much more clearly.

The Radical Era—1960s and 1970s

Austin Turk—
Crime and the Legal Order

Turk proposed a conflict analysis of crime that closely resembles the labeling perspective. In his 1969 publication, *Criminality and Legal Order*, he wrote that "[n]othing and no one is intrinsically criminal; criminality is a definition applied by individuals with the power to do so, according to illegal and extralegal, as well as legal criteria" (Turk, 1969:10). He maintained that the label or status of criminal is conferred upon individuals in subordinate or powerless positions in society. Conflict between groups seeking to gain or maintain control over one another characterizes society. Turk noted that "one is led to investigate the tendency of laws to penalize persons whose behavior is more characteristic of the less powerful than of the more powerful and the extent to which some persons and groups can and do use legal processes and agencies to maintain and enhance their power position vis-à-vis other persons and groups" (Turk, 1969:18).

For Turk, it is important not only to examine the behavior of the police and other enforcers, but also to scrutinize the actions of the person being apprehended. Turk wrote that "people, both eventual authorities and eventual subjects, learn and continually re-learn to interact with one another as, respectively, occupants of superior and inferior statuses and performers of dominating and submitting roles" (1969:41-42). Lawbreaking occurs when there is a failure in the system, that is, when subjects feel able to test the strength of the ability of the authority figure to control their behavior.

Criminalization, the process of being labeled criminal, requires more than lawbreaking behavior. It results from the interaction between the enforcers and the alleged violators. This interaction is shaped by five social factors:

- the congruence of cultural and social norms;
- the level of organization of the subjects;
- the degree of sophistication in the interpretation of behaviors;
- the power differential between enforcers and violators; and
- the realism of moves during the conflict.

While the congruence of norms is the key variable, the other factors interact to affect the probability of conflict and of criminalization. By definition, most authority figures are part of an organized system, so it is with the violators that variation occurs. "An individual who has group support for his behavior is going to be more stubborn in the face of efforts to make him change than is someone who has only himself as an ally" (Turk, 1969:58). Thus, conflict is more likely to occur when the offender is part of an organized group.

The degree of sophistication refers to the basis or rationale used to justify behavior. Authorities generally rely upon legal norms to interpret a situation. Subjects, on the other hand, may rely upon nonlegal interpretations of behavior. They are more likely to make use of abstract justifications such as "justice" or, in the case of unsophisticated offenders, to resort to rationalizations. Conflict, Turk argued, is more likely to occur when subjects are less sophisticated. Delinquent gangs are usually organized unsophisticates, which may account for their high rate of conflict with authorities.

The fourth factor affecting the probability of criminalization is the power differential between the enforcers and violators. While enforcers generally have greater power than violators, this is not always the case. Witness, for example, the ability of certain white-collar offenders and politically connected individuals to beat the criminal justice system. Turk proposed that, in general, "the greater the power difference in favor of norm enforcers over resisters, the greater the probability of criminalization" (1969:70).

The remaining mediating factor affecting criminalization is the realism of moves made by enforcers and subjects during a conflict. This refers to the appropriateness or suitability of the behavior of individuals during their interaction. A key here is the extent to which each party engages in what may be called unrealistic moves. Resisters, for example, engage in unrealistic moves when they increase the visibility or offensiveness of the behavior that initiated conflict with authorities. A marijuana user, for example, is more likely to be detected and to bring about conflict if the marijuana smoking is flagrant. The pot smoker who smokes at home and uses a breath mint prior to going out in public is engaging in realistic behavior. On the other hand, the individual who rolls a joint at the mall and goes window shopping while smoking it is engaging in what Turk would call unrealistic moves. In this latter scenario, the open disregard for current laws regulating marijuana use make it difficult for a law enforcement official to disregard the behavior. Authorities, for instance, can be accused of making unrealistic moves if they deviate from normal legal procedures (e.g., use of excessive force during arrest).

Based upon these dichotomies, Turk suggested that it is possible to predict the relative probability of criminalization. He claimed that the highest probability exists when:

- both enforcers and resisters have a high congruence between cultural and social norms,

- both groups engage in unrealistic moves, and

- the power difference clearly favors the enforcers.

Richard Quinney—
The Social Reality of Crime

Richard Quinney (1970) proposed a slightly different explanation of crime and criminal behavior. Borrowing from Vold's earlier statements as well as from social interaction and learning theories, Quinney developed six propositions and associated axioms that outline his *social reality of crime* theory. These six propositions, as noted by Quinney (1970:15-23), are:

Proposition 1	(Definition of Crime): Crime is a definition of human conduct that is created by authorized agents in a politically organized society.
Proposition 2	(Formulation of Criminal Definitions): Criminal definitions describe behaviors that conflict with the interests of the segments of society that have the power to shape political policy.
Proposition 3	(Application of Criminal Definitions): Criminal definitions are applied by the segments of society that have the power to shape the enforcement and administration of criminal law.
Proposition 4	(Development of Behavior Patterns in Relation to Criminal Definitions): Behavior patterns are structured in segmentally organized society in relation to criminal definitions, and within this context persons engage in actions that have relative probabilities of being defined as criminal.
Proposition 5	(Construction of Criminal Conceptions): Conceptions of crime are constructed and diffused in the segments of society by various means of communication.
Proposition 6	(The Social Reality of Crime): The social reality of crime is constructed by the formulation and application of criminal definitions, the development of behavior patterns related to criminal definitions, and the construction of criminal conceptions.

Quinney, like the labeling theorists, views crime as the product of social definition. An important aspect of proposition 1, however, is that the definition of crime is imposed by authority figures in society. Quinney asserted that crime is a function of a stratified social system in which the actions of one group are judged and categorized by the dominant group.

Propositions 2 and 3 are similar to Vold's group conflict theory. Their emphasis is upon the political power that is necessary to establish definitions of criminal behavior as well as to label individuals as criminals. Throughout American history, for example, alcohol has been, with but few exceptions, a socially accepted drug. Even in today's society, where drug abuse has been identified as the nation's number one problem and politicians campaign on "get tough on drugs" platforms, alcohol is still seen as an appropriate, and even a glamorous, drug. After newscasters discredit the use of steroids by athletes and the consumption of cocaine by entertainers, the newscast is interrupted by advertisements promoting the use of alcohol. How is it that a drug that is responsible for far more deaths and health-related problems than all of the illegal "street drugs" combined can continue to be legal and socially approved? The first three propositions of Quinney's theory provide a possible explanation.

Proposition 4 is derived from social learning theory, more specifically from Sutherland's differential association theory. It is from an individual's interaction with others that definitions of behavior, as well as behavioral patterns, are developed. And, depending upon one's location in the class structure, there is a differential probability that the behaviors in which a person engages will be defined as criminal. An excellent example of this can be found in William Chambliss' (1973) article, "The Saints and the Roughnecks." Chambliss compared the illegal and delinquent behavior of two groups of high-school boys, one comprised of middle-class student leaders and the other of lower-class boys. While the latter had a reputation for being involved in delinquent activity, it was the "saints" who engaged in greater amounts and more serious illegal behavior.

Quinney's final two propositions summarize his theory of the social reality of crime. Behavior is criminalized through the exercise of power and the use of the media to foster support for the definitions of crime set forth by the powerful sector of society. Returning to our alcohol example, as long as alcohol producers and politicians can use their power to promote the glamorous and social aspects of alcohol, little will be done to outlaw this drug. True, some groups, such as Mothers Against Drunk Driving (MADD), have been able to increase awareness concerning drunk driving, but recent polls show that alcohol consumption among high school students is rising. With respect to defining behavior as criminal, we can be certain that when politicians talk about law and order and getting tough on crooks, they are referring to crimes of the street, not "crimes in the suites."

William Chambliss and Robert Seidman— Law, Order, and Power

William Chambliss and Robert Seidman presented a Marxian analysis of the American justice system in their 1971 publication *Law, Order, and Power*. They examined subsystems involved in the creation and enforcement of the law (i.e., the legislature, courts, and the police), concluding that "the legal order . . . is in fact a self-serving system to maintain power and privilege" (1971:4).

The popular view of the organization of society, they argued, inhibits the majority from reaching this same conclusion. They summarized this popular view in the following manner (Chambliss & Seidman, 1971:502):

- the law represents the values of society;

- if it does not represent the values of everyone, then it at least expresses the best common denominator of the society and operates through a value-neutral governmental structure, which is ultimately controlled by the choice of the people; and

- in the long run the law serves the best interests of the society.

This myth of how the law operates, the authors claimed, is easily discredited when one examines how it works on a day-to-day basis.

Chambliss and Seidman traced the law in action by examining the legislative processes leading to rule creation. They wrote:

[E]very detailed study of the emergence of legal norms has consistently shown the immense importance of interest-group activity, not "the public interest," as the critical variable in determining the content of legislation. To hold to the notion of natural laws emerging from the needs of society requires that we accept the highly questionable assumption that somehow interest groups operate in the best interests of society. It may be true that "what's good for General Motors is good for society," if all the members of society benefit from the triumph of special interests. Rarely does this happen. Laws inevitably improve things for some people and make things worse for others (1971:73).

In addition to the legislature, appellate courts are a primary source of rulemaking. Decisions written by appellate judges serve as precedents for future court cases. Are these cases decided by neutral judges in the best interests of society? Chambliss and Seidman claimed that they are not. Judges bring to their role as decisionmakers their own biases and values. They undergo a socialization process that advocates the value consensus orientation. Furthermore, judges are selectively recruited from the upper echelons of American society. Chambliss and Seidman concluded that appellate judges "are necessarily biased in favor of ensuring that courts are more available to the wealthy than to the poor, and tend to produce solutions in the interests of the wealthy" (1971:113).

With respect to the role of law enforcement, Chambliss and Seidman emphasized the bureaucratic nature of the police and their connection to the political structure. The authors summarized the process of law enforcement in complex societies with the following six propositions (1971:269):

- The agencies of law enforcement are bureaucratic organizations.

- An organization and its members tend to substitute for the official goals and norms of the organization ongoing policies and activities which will maximize rewards and minimize the strains on the organization.

- This goal substitution is made possible by:

    - the absence of motivation on the part of the role-occupants to resist pressures towards goal-substitution;

    - the pervasiveness of discretionary choice permitted by the substantive criminal law, and the norms defining the roles of the members of the enforcement agencies; and

    - the absence of effective sanctions for the norms defining the roles in those agencies.

- Law enforcement agencies depend for resource allocation on political organizations.

- It will maximize and minimize strains for the organization to process those who are politically weak and powerless, and to refrain from processing those who are politically powerful.

- Therefore it may be expected that the law enforcement agencies will process a disproportionately high number of the politically weak and powerless, while ignoring the violations of those with power.

In summary, Chambliss and Seidman conducted an analysis of the law in action. They claimed that the law does not represent the "public interest"; rather, it represents the interests of those in power. Chambliss' (1964) analysis of the emergence of vagrancy laws (see Chapter 2) is a classic illustration of this.

Contemporary Critical Thought

While all critical criminology is based on a conflict premise, it has become considerably more diverse over the past two decades, incorporating "a growing multiplicity of critical theoretical approaches" (Michalowski, 1996:13). All explain crime as a function of the distribution of power and they are "all 'radical' in the sense that they are associated with political agendas that involve deep and fundamental social change" (Vold et al., 1998). Three important contemporary critical streams of thought are *left realism, feminism,* and *postmodernism.*

Left Realism

Radical criminologists have highlighted the crimes committed by the powerful and the effect of these "suite crimes" (i.e., white-collar offenses such as insider trading, embezzlement, and abuse of power) on the poor and working class. One problem with this perspective, however, is the lack of attention paid to "street crimes" (e.g., crimes included in the UCR Index classification). Left realists have criticized the earlier radical perspective by emphasizing the violent and costly aspects associated with conventional intra-class and intra-race crime. They maintain that while crimes of the powerful have a deleterious effect on society, so do street crimes.

Radical criminologists historically have glamorized traditional street offenders either as modern-day Robin Hoods or as leaders of the proletarian revolution. Left realists view this romanticization as naïve and unrealistic. They claim that "street crime is 'real,' and not a moral panic created by elite opinion makers such as the media" (Schwartz & DeKeseredy, 1991:51). As such, crime control policies need to address not only the crimes of the wealthy but also the crimes committed by the poor against the poor.

The left realist movement has been most successful in establishing itself in Britain (see, for example Young, 1988). Walter DeKeseredy and Martin Schwartz (1991) suggest that left realism has failed to develop as thoroughly in the United Stated because of (1) the marginalization of socialists and socialist thought in America and (2) the failure to establish a dominant center of radical criminological theory at American universities.

According to two leaders of British left realism, John Lea and Jock Young (1984), the perspective is based on the following four premises:

- street crime is a serious problem for the working class;

- working-class crime is primarily perpetrated against other members of the working class;

- it is relative poverty, not absolute poverty, that breeds discontent and this discontent without a political solution creates crime; and

- crime can be reduced through implementation of practical, socialist policies.

These assumptions identify poor and working-class people as those most likely to be victimized not only by the policies of the rich and powerful, but also by their similarly situated neighbors. Crime control policies, therefore, need to address both social inequality and individual depravity. Left realists have proposed a number of alternatives to conservative crime control policies. In order to reduce the further marginalization of prisoners, they recommend greater use of community service programs, victim restitution, community placements, and an overall reduction in the reliance on prison. Left realists acknowledge the importance of policing society and deterring prospective offenders, but they call for stricter civil and democratic control of the police. In addition to these specific crime control policies, Raymond Michalowski (1983) suggests that economic policies that shift the burden of the welfare state from consumers to producers would further reduce conventional crime. Among the recommended strategies are: tax surcharges on industries trying to close plants or reduce a community's work force; laws mandating the retraining of workers displaced by new technologies; and a minimum wage that is 50 percent above the poverty level.

Feminism

Feminist criminologists highlight the fact that the social world is fundamentally gendered; that is, men and women encounter different life experiences that are a product of cultural, historical, and societal processes interwoven with race and class inequalities. Feminist criminologists maintain that it is important for criminologists "to situate the study of crime and justice in the recognition that gender is an organizing principle of institutions, including criminal justice policies and practice" Miller 2003:4).

Critical forms of feminism have assumed three major variations. *Radical feminism* identifies a patriarchal social order in which men dominate women as the fundamental issue. This power imbalance is the product of sexist patterns of socialization that instill a belief in male superiority. Both males and females come to accept differential gender roles that place men in positions of relative power. The solution, following this perspective, would be to alter those socialization patterns in order to equalize power among genders.

HIGHLIGHT 9.4
An Example of the Creation of a Social Problem

An interesting example of additional pressures on today's adolescents is the phenomenon of teenage sex. Today we are bombarded with mass media messages about teenage pregnancy and teenage motherhood and all of the associated social problems. Why does society suddenly have this new social problem? If we go back 150 years in history, were teenagers not engaging in sexual activity? Were teenage females not getting pregnant? It may be that society has not experienced change in adolescent behavior but that the social context has changed. In the early 1800s, many women were married and having babies by age 16. Since these babies were born within the confines of marriage, there was no problem. Today, however, while adolescents are entering puberty at younger and younger ages and are being exposed to increasingly explicit sexual stimulation by the larger culture, they are being told to wait until marriage before engaging in sexual activity. The mean ages at first marriage for American women and men, meanwhile, have increased steadily to the current 23 and 25 years respectively. Due, then, to social structural changes in the marital, labor, and education arenas, contemporary adolescents are expected to refrain from engaging in behavior that their great-grandparents practiced at the same age.

Marxist feminism sees women as dominated by men as a result of the disproportionate location of economic power among the men. As with pure Marxism, it is ownership of the means of production that underlies an imbalance of power. This serves the interest of the dominant male elite because it subjugates females to roles of sexual and domestic service. Following this perspective, the solution would be in the form of a broad redistribution of wealth that would include women as well as male proletariat.

Socialist feminism sees capitalism as inevitably flawed, producing a range of oppression, including that experienced by women. Biology also has played a role, however, in the sense that the reproductive function placed most of the burden of child bearing and rearing on women. This contributed to the formation of male dominance, and capitalism has perpetuated it. Thus the solution is both wealth redistribution and freeing women from their disproportionate burden of child-rearing responsibilities.

Postmodernism

While the paradigm shift to classicism led to a call for rationalism, and the later emergence of positivism brought science into the equation, postmodernism rejects the notion that rationalism and science merit a superior position in explaining the way things are. "Modern" thinking saw science as the method that holds the potential to understanding. Postmodernists believe that it is time to move on to a new way of understanding. The argument is that "truth" is not purely objective. There are many equally valid ways to pursue truth, the scientific method being only one. In fact, the scientific approach is viewed as troubling because scientists generally view themselves as "experts," thereby creating a "privileged" knowledge (Einstadter & Henry, 1995). Knowledge, from a postmodernist perspective, is viewed in egalitarian terms. Equal consideration is extended to anyone's understanding of the world. Over the past decade, this perspective has begun to appear in criminology.

The source of inequitable distribution of power is identified as language. Those who control language control the "truth." By illustration, the legalese that serves as the only acceptable language in legal proceedings does not objectively present the full truth (Milovanovic, 1994). One hires an attorney to use the necessary language to win. The defendant in a criminal case cannot simply tell his or her version of the truth. Instead, the defendant relies on a lawyer to present his or her case in legalese, which may tell a very different story. To sift through these different stories or versions of the truth, postmodernism employs a method referred to as discourse analysis. This process calls for looking not only at what is said, but how and why.

The story told by any actor is heavily influenced by particular social institutions that must be included in analysis of their story. The "truth" about educational issues, for example, as espoused by your criminology professor, will be heavily influenced by the existing institution of higher education. Your professor most likely would insist that you complete a course in criminological theory (so here you are!) and probably one in statistics. She or he would probably hold to the view that these are necessary learning experiences to enable you to really understand crime. This would not be surprising, as it is the mainstream perspective within the academic discipline of criminology. The postmodernist, however, would believe that your nonexpert views are just as valid, though you might see that the "truth" about crime could only be grasped by living in a neighborhood like yours, and that courses in criminology and statistics would add nothing. Applied to criminological issues, the "truth" as seen by a police officer, for example, would be largely shaped by the contemporary police institution and might be quite different from "truth" in the eyes of a citizen viewing the same scenario. Thus police may not see a particular incident as brutality, even though it is seen as such by many citizens.

Central to postmodernism is the concept of *deconstructionism*. Since conventional wisdom is primarily a product of modern rational ways of generating knowledge, primarily the scientific method, the validity of that knowledge is rejected. Thus the task comes to be deconstructing or tearing down existing bodies of knowledge. Because postmodernism calls for deconstruction of knowledge rather than creation of knowledge it is criticized as nihilistic. As Werner Einstadter and Stuart Henry (1995:280) ask, "If truth is not possible, how can we decide anything?"

Research on Conflict Theory

A number of studies have assessed the utility of the conflict perspective. These investigations generally take one of two approaches:

- case studies testing the hypothesis that laws are formulated in the interests of those in power; and

- empirical works examining the extent to which individuals are subject to differential processing by the criminal justice system based upon their race or socioeconomic status (SES).

With respect to the former approach, Frank Williams concluded in his review of the literature that "findings would appear to support the conflict notion that many laws are, in fact, formulated to benefit power groups" (1980:215). This conclusion is supported by the following studies of:

- vagrancy laws (Chambliss, 1964);

- the enactment of the Marijuana Tax Act (Becker, 1963);

- the development of laws regulating theft (Hall, 1952); and

- the Prohibition movement (Sinclair, 1964).

The evidence regarding differential processing is not as supportive of the conflict perspective as it is for the development of laws. Studies have examined differential processing by race and SES for both juveniles and adults at various levels of the justice system. In an analysis of juvenile court records in a southeastern city, Timothy Carter and Donald Clelland (1979) distinguished between two types of offenses to see if the disposition received varied by the nature of the misconduct. They found greater discrimination in court dispositions for moral as opposed to traditional offenses. Moral offenses are status offenses such as incorrigibility, truancy, and runaway, as well as victimless offenses such as drug and alcohol use and sexual activity. These moral offenses, they maintained, challenge the existing social system and consequently receive harsher treatment than traditional offenses.

Robert Sampson and John Laub (1993) investigated the judicial processing of 580,000 juvenile cases in 21 states. They found that for personal, property, and drug offenses, underclass African-American males had higher rates of out-of-home placements than did white males. This pattern of juvenile justice response, they believe, is "consistent with the idea that underclass African-American males are viewed as a threatening group to middle-class populations, and thus will be subjected to increased formal social control by the juvenile justice system" (Sampson & Laub, 1993:306).

Studies of adult treatment reveal the inconsistencies encountered when testing conflict theories. In their study of police use of deadly force, David Jacobs and David Britt (1979) found that states with the greatest economic disparities experienced the largest number of police killings, while the percentage of African-Americans in each state had no relationship to police killings. Similarly, Alan Lizotte (1978) found in his study of court processing in Chicago that both African-American and white laborers received longer prison terms than did white-collar workers. This finding held even when he controlled for such variables as number of prior arrests, seriousness of the case, and strength of the evidence. Contrary to Lizotte, Theodore Chiricos and Gordon Waldo (1975) reported that socioeconomic status was unrelated to sentence severity in their study of more than 10,000 inmates in three southern states.

Frank Williams' review of the literature on the relationship between race and/ or SES and justice system processing showed that while some of this research did support the conflict perspective, the vast majority—more than 80 percent—did not (Williams, 1980). William Wilbanks (1987) examined the literature dealing with race and the criminal justice system. Although he conceded that there may be some discrimination on the part of individuals working in the system, Wilbanks concluded that "there is insufficient evidence to support the charge that the system is racist today" (Wilbanks, 1987:8).

Cassia Spohn provides evidence to refute Wilbanks assertion and suggests that researchers "who simply test for the direct effect of defendant race may incorrectly conclude that race does not affect sentence severity" (1994:265). Her evaluation of sentencing decisions involving a sample of all felony cases in Detroit during 1976 through 1978 found that the relationship between race and sentencing requires examination of a number of variables. Of particular importance were the observed interactions among offender race, victim race, relationship between offender and victim, and the type of crime that combined to produce different sentencing outcomes. Representative of the complexity of these interactive effects are the following specific results:

- blacks who murder white strangers or acquaintances receive longer sentences than other defendants;

- blacks who sexually assault white strangers, white acquaintances, or black strangers are sentenced to longer sentences than others; and

- offenders who victimized strangers, regardless of their race or the race of their victims, were sentenced to prison at the same rate; among non-strangers, the incarceration rate was significantly higher for black-on-white crimes than for intra-race crimes (Spohn, 1994:264).

So where does all this leave the conflict perspective? There exist some compelling arguments as well as data supportive of the hypothesis that laws are made to benefit the rich. Contradictory findings, however, underlie the question of differential treatment of the powerless within the justice system. Recent research, though, suggests that part of the inconsistency in findings may be attributable to overly simplified tests of the effect of race or class and that possible interaction effects with other key variables must be scrutinized.

Policy Relevance of Conflict Theory

To date, conflict theory per se has had little impact on the criminal justice system. Despite this, there are clear policies that can be derived from this perspective, not all of which are clearly linked with popular notions of crime fighting. Conflict theorists might maintain that President Obama's best crime fighting proposal is his call for health care reform. Elliott Currie's (1985; 1989) policy recommendations reveal the emphasis of the conflict perspective on "fighting crime" through changes in social institutions other than alteration in the criminal justice system.

In his 1989 article, Currie provided 12 recommendations for confronting crime in the twenty-first century. Of these, only two emphasize justice system policies. The remaining recommendations deal with the larger socio-political environment. Citing the failure of the conservative neoclassical approach that dominated the criminal justice system during the 1970s and 1980s, the author suggested that American criminology is experiencing an "etiological crisis." A new way of thinking about crime is necessary.

Currie cited an increasing abundance of research to substantiate his recommendations. He referred to his position as a "social environmental" or "human-ecological" perspective, which is one that involves policy interventions on the individual and family level as well as on the larger social context. Currie's recommendations (1989:11-21) are:

- expand high-quality, intensive early education along the model of Head Start;

- expand health and mental health services for high-risk children and youth and for their parents, including high-quality prenatal and post-natal care;

- establish a greater commitment to family support programs, especially real rather than rhetorical support for comprehensive programs against child abuse and domestic violence;

- insist that prison time be used more constructively so that offenders leave a little smarter, a little healthier, and a little more sober;

- establish a commitment to accessible, nonpunitive drug abuse treatment for those who need it;

- move toward reducing inequality and social impoverishment by, among other things, increasing the minimum wage, which has fallen 30 percent in real terms during the 1980s, and raise women's earnings closer to those of men;

- move toward an active labor market policy aimed at upgrading the work available to disadvantaged Americans;

- develop a genuinely supportive national family policy that would include, for example, paid leave at the birth of a child;

- assume greater responsibility for the economic and social stability of local communities;

- provide a more careful research plan to examine what works for individuals at risk;

- learn more about how to create comprehensive, preventive strategies for "high-risk" communities; and

- attempt to understand more about why some societies have low or relatively low crime rates, while others, including our own, suffer such pervasive violence.

While not all conflict criminologists would agree with Currie's agenda, most would applaud his attempt to identify short-term as well as long-term recommendation for confronting crime in American society. His emphasis upon the causes as opposed to the consequences of behavior is not as "radical" as it was 25 years ago. From the conflict perspective, it is clear that there is more to fighting crime than merely fighting criminals.

Summary

In this chapter we have examined two broad theoretical perspectives that differ from theories discussed in Chapters 5 through 8. The labeling approach focuses attention on the societal reaction to behavior and is concerned with understanding the consequences of this social response. In a similar fashion, conflict theory is interested in understanding how the social and criminal justice systems respond differentially to persons suspected of violating the law. Additionally, conflict theorists question the legitimacy of the existing social structure, maintaining that the laws and the enforcement procedures are structured to benefit the rich and punish the poor.

The labeling perspective grew in popularity through the 1960s and 1970s but lost much of its appeal as research findings failed to substantiate its claims. Self-report studies did indicate that most people commit at least minor offenses, but subsequent evaluations did not yield substantial evidence that differential social response was responsible for the disparate rates of prosecution and incarceration.

The conflict perspective has experienced a resurgence in support since the 1960s. Many attribute its renewed popularity to the social turmoil of the 1960s and 1970s. The "new criminology," as the conflict theories have labeled their work (Taylor et al., 1973), actually consists of diverse and relatively distinct theoretical strains. All are based on the conflict perspective rooted in the works of Karl Marx and are founded on the general notion that society is comprised of groups in conflict. George Vold's development of group conflict theory preceded the 1960s resurgence of conflict criminology.

Conflict theory provided the foundation for a much broader critical criminology, beginning with the radical era of the 1960s and 1970s. Works of such theorists as Quinney, Turk, and Chambliss represent this exciting period. In the past decade, critical thought has become more diverse yet. Left realism, several feminist lines of thought, and postmodernism are all vibrant segments of contemporary criminological thought.

Both the broad conflict/critical and labeling perspectives discussed in this chapter have necessitated that criminologists question some of the underlying assumptions of traditional theories. As a result, criminology texts, journal articles, and papers presented at the annual meetings of the American Society of Criminology and the Academy of Criminal Justice Sciences today reflect a more critical analysis of crime and societal and criminal justice response.

Key Terms and Concepts

Conflict Perspective
Conformist
Consensus View
Criminalization
Critical Criminology
Deconstructionism
Deviance Amplification
Dramatization of Evil
Falsely Accused
Feminism
Group Conflict Theory
Instrumental Marxism
Labeling Perspective
Left Realism
Legal Relativism
Marxist Criminology
Marxist Feminism

Master Status
Moral Entrepreneurs
Net Widening
Postmodernism
Primary Deviation
Pure Deviant
Radical Criminology
Radical Feminism
Radical Nonintervention
Retrospective Interpretation
Secondary Deviation
Secret Deviant
Social Conflict Theory
Social Pathology
Socialist Feminism
Structural Marxism

Key Criminologists

Howard S. Becker
William Chambliss
Edwin Lemert
Karl Marx
Richard Quinney
Edwin M. Schur

Robert Seidman
Frank Tannenbaum
Charles R. Tittle
Austin Turk
George Vold

Case

Roe v. Wade, 410 U.S. 113 (1973)

References

Ageton, S.S. & D.S. Elliott (1974). "The Effects of Legal Processing on Delinquent Orientations." *Social Problems*, 22:87-100.

Austin, J. & B. Krisberg (1981). "Wider, Stronger, and Different Nets: The Dialectics of Criminal Justice Reform." *Journal of Research in Crime and Delinquency*, 18:165-196.

Becker, H.S. (1963). *Outsiders: Studies in the Sociology of Deviance*. New York, NY: The Free Press.

Bedau, H.A. & M.L. Radelet (1987). "Miscarriages of Justice in Potentially Capital Cases." *Stanford Law Review*, 40:21-179.

Bernburg, J.G. & M.D. Krohn (2003). "Labeling, Life Chances, and Adult Crime: The Direct and Indirect Effects of Official Intervention in Adolescence on Crime in Early Adulthood." *Criminology*, 41:1287-1318.

Bernburg, J.G., M.D. Krohn & C.J. Rivera (2006). "Official Labeling, Criminal Embeddedness, and Subsequent Delinquency." *Journal of Research in Crime and Delinquency*, 43:67-88.

Binder, A. & G. Geis (1984). "Ad Populum Argumentation in Criminology: Juvenile Diversion as Rhetoric." *Crime & Delinquency*, 30:624-647.

Blomberg, T.G. (1980). "Widening the Net: An Anomaly in the Evaluation of Diversion Programs." In M.W. Klein & K.S. Teilman (eds.) *Handbook of Criminal Justice Evaluation*. Beverly Hills, CA: Sage Publications.

Bynum, T.S. & J.R. Greene (1984). "How Wide the Net? Probing the Boundaries of the Juvenile Court." In S.H. Decker (ed.) *Juvenile Justice Policy: Analyzing Trends and Outcomes*. Beverly Hills, CA: Sage Publications.

Carter, T. & D. Clelland (1979). "A Neo-Marxian Critique, Formulation and Test of Juvenile Dispositions as a Function of Social Class." *Social Problems*, 27:96-108.

Chambliss, W.J. (1988). *Exploring Criminology*. New York, NY: Macmillan Publishing Company.

Chambliss, W.J. (1973). "The Saints and the Roughnecks." *Society*, 11:24-31.

Chambliss, W.J. (1964). "A Sociological Analysis of the Law of Vagrancy." *Social Problems*, 12:67-77.

Chambliss, W.J. & R.B. Seidman (1971). *Law, Order, and Power*. Reading, MA: Addison Wesley.

Chiricos, T.G., K. Barrick, W. Bales & S. Bontrager (2007). "The Labeling of Convicted Felons and Its Consequences for Recidivism." *Criminology*, 45:547-581.

Chiricos, T.G. & M. DeLone (1992). "Labor Surplus and Punishment: A Review and Assessment of Theory and Evidence." *Social Problems*, 39:421-446.

Chiricos, T.G. & G. Waldo (1975). "Socioeconomic Status and Criminal Sentencing: An Empirical Assessment of a Conflict Proposition." *American Sociological Review*, 40:753-772.

Cohen, L.E. & R. Stark (1974). "Discriminatory Labeling and the Five-Finger Discount: An Empirical Analysis of Differential Shoplifting Dispositions." *Journal of Research in Crime and Delinquency*, 11:25-39.

Curra, J. (2000). *The Relativity of Deviance*. Thousand Oaks, CA: Sage.

Currie, E. (1989). "Confronting Crime: Looking Toward the Twenty-First Century." *Justice Quarterly*, 6:5-25.

Currie, E. (1985). *Confronting Crime: An American Challenge*. New York, NY: Pantheon Books.

DeKeseredy, W. & M. Schwartz (1991). "British and U.S. Left Realism: A Critical Comparison." *International Journal of Offender Therapy and Comparative Criminology*, 35:248-262.

Dotter, D.L. & J.B. Roebuck (1988). "The Labeling Approach Re-examined: Interactionism and the Components of Deviance." *Deviant Behavior*, 9:19-32.

Dunford, F.W. (1977). "Police Diversion: An Illusion." *Criminology*, 15:335-352.

Einstadter, W. & S. Henry (1995). *Criminological Theory: An Analysis of its Underlying Assumptions*. Fort Worth, TX: Harcourt Brace.

Erikson, K.T. (1962). "Notes on the Sociology of Deviance." *Social Problems*, 9:307-314.

Esbensen, F. (1984). "Net-Widening? Yes and No: Diversion Impact Assessed Through a Systems Processing Rates Analysis." In S.H. Decker (ed.) *Juvenile Justice Policy: Analyzing Trends and Outcomes*. Beverly Hills, CA: Sage Publications.

Foster, J.D., S. Dinitz & W.C. Reckless (1972). "Perceptions of Stigma Following Public Intervention for Delinquent Behavior." *Social Problems*, 20:202-209.

Goffman, E. (1963). *Stigma*. Englewood-Cliffs, NJ: Prentice Hall.

Gove, W.R. (1980). *The Labelling of Deviance*. Beverly Hills, CA: Sage Publications.

Hagan, J. & A. Palloni (1990). "The Social Reproduction of a Criminal Class in Working-Class London, circa 1959-1980." *American Journal of Sociology*, 96:265-300.

Hall, J. (1952). *Theft, Law and Society*. Indianapolis, IN: Bobbs-Merrill.

Huff, C.R. (2002). "Wrongful Conviction and Public Policy: The American Society of Criminology 2001 Presidential Address." *Criminology*, 40:1-18.

Huizinga, D. & K. L. Henry (2007). "The Effect of Arrest and Justice System Sanctions on Subsequent Behavior: Findings from Longitudinal and Other Studies." In A.M. Liberman (ed.) *The Long View of Crime: A Synthesis of Longitudinal Research*. New York: Springer.

Huizinga, D., K. Schumann, B. Ehret & A. Elliott (2003). "The Effect of Juvenile Justice System Processing on Subsequent Delinquent and Criminal Behavior: A Cross-National Study." Paper presented at the Annual Meeting of the Western Society of Criminology, Vancouver, British Columbia, February.

Jackson, P. & C. Rudman (1993). "Moral Panic and the Response to Gangs in California." In S. Cummings & D.J. Monte (eds.) *The Origins and Impact of Contemporary Youth Gangs in the United States*. Albany, NY: State University of New York Press.

Jacobs, D. & D. Britt (1979). "Inequality and Police Use of Deadly Force: An Empirical Assessment of a Conflict Perspective." *Social Problems*, 26:403-412.

Jensen, G.F. (1972). "Parents, Peers, and Delinquent Action: A Test of the Differential Association Perspective." *American Journal of Sociology*, 78:562-575.

Kitsuse, J.I. (1962). "Societal Reaction to Deviant Behavior: Problem of Theory and Method." *Social Problems*, 9:247-256.

Klein, M.W., K.S. Teilman, J.A. Styles, S.B. Lincoln & S. Labin-Rosensweig (1976). "The Explosion of Police Diversion Programs." In M.W. Klein (ed.) *The Juvenile Justice System*. Beverly Hills, CA: Sage Publications.

Lea, J. & J. Young (1984). *What Is To Be Done About Law and Order?* Harmondsworth, UK: Penguin.

Lemert, E.M. (1981). "Diversion in Juvenile Justice: What Hath Been Wrought." *Journal of Research in Crime and Delinquency*, 18:35-46.

Lemert, E.M. (1951). *Social Pathology*. New York, NY: McGraw-Hill.

Lizotte, A. (1978). "Extra-Legal Factors in Chicago's Criminal Courts: Test of the Conflict Model of Criminal Justice." *Social Problems*, 25:564-580.

Lynch, M.J. & W.B. Groves (1986). *A Primer in Radical Criminology*. Albany, NY: Harrow and Heston.

Maruna, S., T.P. Lebel, N. Mitchell & M. Naples (2005). "Pygmalion in the Reintegration Process: Desistance from Crime through the Looking Glass." *Psychology, Crime, and Law*, 10:271-282.

Marx, K. (1964). *Selected Writings and Social Philosophies*. London, UK: McGraw-Hill.

Matsueda, R.L. (1992). "Reflected Appraisals, Parental Labeling, and Delinquency: Specifying a Symbolic Interactionist Theory." *American Journal of Sociology*, 97:1577-1611.

Michalowski, R. (1996). "Critical Criminology and the Critique of Domonation: The Story of an Intellectual Movement." *Critical Criminology*, 7:9-16.

Michalowski, R. (1983). "Crime Control in the 1980s: A Progressive Agenda." *Crime and Social Justice*, 19:13-23.

Miller, J. (2003). "Gender, Crime, and (In)Justice: Introduction to the Special Issue." *Journal of Contemporary Ethnography*, 32:3-8.

Miller, K. (1999). "Students Make Pledge Not to Taunt Outcasts." Associated Press release, *Johnson City Press*, 5-30.

Milovanovic, D. (1994). *A Primer in the Sociology of Law*. Albany, NY: Harrow and Heston.

Pelfrey, W.V. (1980). *The Evolution of Criminology*. Cincinnati, OH: Anderson Publishing Co.

Quinney, R. (1970). *The Social Reality of Crime*. Boston, MA: Little, Brown.

Ruggiero, V. (1997). "Punishing Children: The Manufacture of Criminal Careers in Hellion Town." *Theoretical Criminology*, 1:341-361.

Sampson, R.J. & J.H. Laub (1993). "Structural Variations in Juvenile Court Processing: Inequality, the Underclass, and Social Control." *Law and Society Review,* 27:285-311.

Schur, E.M. (1973). *Radical Nonintervention: Rethinking the Delinquency Problem*. Englewood Cliffs, NJ: Prentice Hall.

Schwartz, M.D. & W.S. DeKeseredy (1991). "Left Realist Criminology: Strengths, Weaknesses, and the Feminist Critique." *Crime, Law and Social Change*, 15:51-72.

Schwartz, R.D. & J.H. Skolnick (1962). "Two Studies of Legal Stigma." *Social Problems*, 10:133-142.

Sinclair, A. (1964). *Era of Excess: A Social History of the Prohibition Movement*. New York, NY: Harper and Row.

Spohn, C. (1994). "Crime and Social Control of Blacks: The Effect of Offender/Victim Race on Sentences for Violent Felonies." In G. Bridges & M. Myers (eds.) *Inequality, Crime, and Social Control*. Boulder, CO: Westview Press.

Steffensmeier, D.J. & R.M. Terry (1973). "Deviance and Respectability: An Observational Study of Reactions to Shoplifting." *Social Forces*, 51:417-426.

Stewart, E.A., R.L. Simons, R.D. Conger & L.V. Scaramella (2002). "Beyond the Interactional Relationship between Delinquency and Parenting Practices: The Contribution of Legal Sanctions." *Journal of Research in Crime and Delinquency*, 39:36-59.

Sweeten, G. (2006). "Who Will Graduate? Disruption of High School Education by Arrest and Court Conviction." *Justice Quarterly* 23: 547-581.

Tannenbaum, F. (1938). *Crime and the Community*. Boston, MA: Ginn.

Taylor, I., P. Walton & J. Young (1973). *The New Criminology: For a Social Theory of Deviance*. New York, NY: Harper and Row.

Tittle, C.R. (1980). "Labelling and Crime: An Empirical Evaluation." In W.R. Gove (ed.) *The Labelling of Deviance: Evaluating a Perspective*. Beverly Hills, CA: Sage Publications.

Triplett, R. (1993). "The Conflict Perspective, Symbolic Interactionism, and the Status Characteristics Hypothesis." *Justice Quarterly*, 10:541-556.

Turk, A. (1969). *Criminality and Legal Order*. Chicago, IL: Rand McNally.

Vold, G.B. (1958). *Theoretical Criminology*. New York, NY: Oxford University Press.

Vold, G.B., T. Bernard & J. Snipes (1998). *Theoretical Criminology*, Fourth Edition. New York, NY: Oxford University Press.

Ward, D. & C.R. Tittle (1993). "Deterrence or Labeling: The Effects of Informal Sanctions." *Deviant Behavior*, 14:43-64.

Weidner, R.R. & W. Terrill (2005). "A Test of Turk's Theory of Norm Resistance Using Observational Data on Police-Suspect Encounters." *Journal of Research in Crime and Delinquency*, 42:84-109.

Wellford, C.F. (1987). "Delinquency Prevention and Labeling." In J.Q. Wilson & G.C. Loury (eds.) *From Children to Citizens, Volume III: Families, Schools, and Delinquency Prevention*. New York, NY: Springer-Verlag.

Wilbanks, W. (1987). *The Myth of a Racist Criminal Justice System*. Monterey, CA: Brooks-Cole.

Williams, F.P., III (1980). "Conflict Theory and Differential Processing: An Analysis of the Research Literature." In J. Inciardi (ed.) *Radical Criminology: The Coming Crisis*. Beverly Hills, CA: Sage Publications.

Young, J. (1988). "Radical Criminology in Britain: The Emergence of a Competing Paradigm." *British Journal of Criminology*, 28:159-183.

Zhang, L. (1997). "Informal Reactions and Delinquency." *Criminal Justice and Behavior*, 24:129-150.

10
Recent Developments in Criminological Theory

The preceding five chapters discussed theoretical paradigms that have an established history in criminological theory. In this chapter, we review several approaches to the understanding of crime that are currently eliciting considerable attention in the criminological journals. During the past 30 years, integrated theoretical models, criminal careers research, and developmental criminology have emerged as new perspectives.

Three major factors are associated with the development of these theoretical orientations. First, there has been a growing acceptance among criminologists of the limitation of existing theories. Rather than viewing the theories as competing explanations of behavior, the movement has been toward considering them as complementary. There may not be a single cause of crime; in fact, there may be multiple paths (e.g., Elliott et al., 1985; Huizinga et al., 1991; Simons et al., 1994) or different trajectories for different types of people (Moffitt, 1994; Nagin et al., 1995). Theoretical integration combines elements of the traditional perspectives to provide a more comprehensive understanding of criminal behavior.

A second development has been closely associated with the incapacitation model and the "get tough" on crime orientation of the Reagan and Bush administrations of the 1980s and early 1990s. Research findings have consistently pinpointed a violent and criminally active group of offenders that account for more than one-half of all street crimes. The criminal career approach has sought to identify these high rate offenders and to isolate factors associated with their high rates of offending. Specific guidelines for incapacitating these offenders for longer periods of time (often for life) than other offenders have been proposed in numerous jurisdictions as a way to reduce the crime rate. For example, "three-strikes" legislation (providing more punitive sentences for felons upon their third conviction) was introduced at the federal and state levels. While some legal challenges to these punitive laws have been made, the U.S. Supreme Court, in two separate decisions handed down in March 2003, upheld the constitutionality of the California legislation.

A third factor can be seen as a combination of the two preceding approaches, resulting in the formation of developmental or life-course criminology (Loeber & LeBlanc, 1990). During the past 20 years, developmental criminology has experienced substantial growth and holds considerable promise for theoretical development (e.g., Bartusch et al., 1997; Benson, 2002; Farrington, 2002; Hawkins & Weis, 1985; Moffitt, 1994; Paternoster & Brame, 1997; Piquero & Tibbetts, 2001; Sampson & Laub, 1993b; Simons et al., 2002; Thornberry et al., 2003).

Integrated Theoretical Models

The integrated approach to theory construction combines existing theories in order to better explain the causes of crime. The theories discussed in earlier chapters have not accounted for much of the variation in crime rates among subgroups of the population. Social structural theories, for example, help to explain the disproportionate representation of minorities and members of the lower classes in official measures of crime and delinquency. But they fail to explain adequately why middle- and upper-class people break the law. Travis Hirschi's social control theory attempts to account for individual variations in criminal activity, but it does not explain why members of certain groups have fewer "bonds" to conventional society. While the conflict perspective claims that the laws are enacted by the rich and powerful to their benefit, there is no consistent evidence to suggest that these statutes cause people to violate the law or that different standards are applied when processing rich or poor offenders through the justice system. A new perspective may be needed.

The writings of Clifford Shaw and Henry McKay (1942) represent an early attempt at integrating social disorganization and social learning theories. For Shaw and McKay, the organization and physical structure of the community was of major importance in terms of affecting behavior and interaction patterns. It was the diversity of values and behaviors in communities, however, that was instrumental in exposing youths to deviant alternatives. (See Chapter 7 for a more thorough discussion of Shaw and McKay's work.)

Richard Cloward and Lloyd Ohlin's (1960) theory of differential opportunity combines traditional strain theory with social learning theory. Societal goals can be attained through the use of legitimate or illegitimate means, depending, in part, on a person's access to different opportunity structures. A criminal subculture, for example, will develop when legitimate opportunities for success are blocked or unavailable and illegitimate means are available. This is a classic statement of strain theory: a person deviates because of some external stress. Cloward and Ohlin built upon this strain perspective; they wrote that delinquency is group behavior requiring social support and confirmation. This social learning component maintains that behavior, as well as definitions and rationalizations for the behavior, are learned in interaction with similarly situated individuals.

The foundation for integrating different theoretical orientations thus has a history dating back to the 1940s. It was not until the 1970s, however, that the movement toward the integration of competing theoretical models was referred to in such terms and began to command interest from criminological theorists. Not all theorists, however, were receptive to this trend; some argue that the theories are incompatible because of their contradictory assumptions about the causes of behavior.

Can Theories Be Combined?

At the root of the debate about the appropriateness and utility of the integrated approach lies the issue of whether the assumptions of strain, control, and learning theories are incompatible. In her widely acclaimed book, Ruth Kornhauser (1978:23-25) provided a classification and description of the underlying assumptions of these three major theoretical models. She suggested that social structural theories assume that a general consensus exists with regard to basic values expressed in the criminal law. Violation of the law is not the result of an innate desire or tendency, but is caused by frustration brought about by barriers blocking the attainment of social goals. The source of crime, therefore, is to be found in the organization of society and in the distribution of access to legitimate means for attaining socially approved and desired objectives. Remember, for instance, the theory of anomie put forth by Robert Merton (reviewed in Chapter 7). The disjunction between cultural values and societal norms placed individuals in a state of anomie or normlessness. People responded differently to this structural stress and became conformists, innovators, ritualists, retreatists, or rebels. It is the structure of society, not a specific character trait that places the individual in the position to deviate.

In direct contrast to this assumption of the social structuralist, Kornhauser contended that social control theorists assume that humans are inherently hedonistic, self-serving creatures who will "rape, pillage, and plunder" to their hearts' content unless otherwise restrained. She maintained that these control theorists assume that all segments of the population experience the same amount of strain, in that our desires can be met only by foregoing the gratification of certain other desires. Thus, to get an "A" on your criminology exam, you will need to forego the pleasure of attending the big social event of the semester. It is your "stake" or belief in conformity that will dictate whether you study or party. Likewise, control theorists argue, it is through the development of this stake in conformity that involvement in criminal behavior is mediated (Hirschi, 1969). This, Kornhauser wrote, is especially the case with criminal activity because illegal means are usually a faster way to satisfy our desires than the legal approach of the normative structure.

These two major theoretical orientations are diametrically opposed to one another in terms of their assumptions about the motivating factors or causes of criminal behavior. Social learning theory presents a third approach. It postulates that deviance or offending behavior is always normative, at least within some subcultural group. Stealing cars may be against the law in society at large, but within a juvenile gang studied by one of the text authors, stealing a car each week was required to maintain one's status in the group. Social learning theorists make no assumptions about the innate qualities of humans; instead, they maintain that a person is born with a "clean slate" and learns to conform to or deviate from the larger societal norms. The cause of delinquency is found in the conflicting subcultures that inevitably result in some individuals being socialized into subcultural values that conflict with what has been defined as legal by society at large. (Table 10.1 provides a summary of the underlying assumptions of these three perspectives.)

TABLE 10.1 Major Theoretical Models and Assumptions	Strain Theory	Control Theory	Learning Theory
Assumption:	Humans are innately good.	Humans are innately evil, hedonistic.	Humans are neither good nor evil.
Cause of Crime:	Frustration brought about by structural malfunction.	Unfulfilled wants fulfilled through illegal avenues due to a lack of "controls" or "bonds" to society.	Socialization into a subculture in which violation of the legal code is normative.
Question posed:	Why do people deviate from the norms?	Why do people conform to the norms?	How are norms learned?

Some theorists argue that it is impossible to combine or integrate these theories into one theoretical model. Travis Hirschi (1979:34), for example, maintained that "separate is better" and wrote that the assumptions of strain, control, and differential association theories are fundamentally incompatible." Delbert Elliott, on the other hand, represents the integrationists in claiming that "there is nothing inherent in the form or approach to integration that precludes the reconciliation of different assumptions" (1985:132). This debate surrounds the integration perspective.

Approaches to Integration

Most attempts to integrate theories have generally sought to explain individual levels of behavior through a combination of social psychological theories (Conger, 1976; Cernkovich, 1978; Aultman & Wellford, 1979; Elliott et al., 1979; Johnson, 1979; Segrave & Hasted, 1983; Thornberry, 1987; Winfree et al., 1996). These models, when tested, have generally relied upon self-report measures and thus have been largely confined to explanations of delinquency.

The most common attempts at integration have involved social control and social learning theories. Less common has been the integration of social control and strain theories, and even less common have been attempts to integrate all three of the major perspectives. Still other attempts at integration have included the labeling approach, social disorganization, conflict, and deterrence theories. The most common approach is to combine the theories in a sequential model so that one theoretical perspective is temporally more proximate to the actual behavior than are the other perspectives in the model. This approach is referred to as the end-to-end model (Hirschi, 1979) and suggests that one of the theories better explains early or prior causes of delinquency while another is more proximate to actual precipitating factors in criminal activity.

Let us look at an example of this approach. Assume that a friend of yours, Al, has just been arrested for armed robbery. You want to understand why he would do such a thing, so you go to your criminology professor to discuss it with her. Your professor asks you a lot of questions about Al, and you wind up presenting the following information.

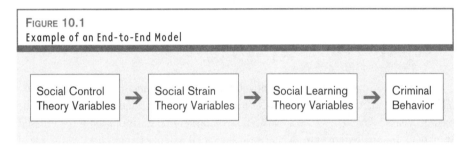

FIGURE 10.1
Example of an End-to-End Model

Social Control Theory Variables → Social Strain Theory Variables → Social Learning Theory Variables → Criminal Behavior

Ever since you have known Al, he has had a bad home life and preferred hanging out with friends to being at his own home. It seemed as if his parents did not want to have anything to do with him. His parents were relatively poor and did not buy Al many presents. In school, Al did all right for a while but by sixth grade he started getting in trouble with teachers for not doing his homework. You seem to remember him ditching school beginning about then. By the time you both were in high school, you had grown apart; Al started smoking and drinking. He occasionally got in trouble at school and got suspended at least once a semester for his antics. His grades were just barely above passing, he did not study, and he did not seem to understand the need to get good grades. The kids that Al hung around with were much like him. After school and on weekends, Al and his friends would hang out and party. You had heard that they occasionally would steal things from cars and sell them to buy beer and pot. Since graduation from high school you had seen Al on occasion, and it seemed that he was still doing the same things he had done in high school.

Your professor now asks you to think about the theories that you have studied this semester. Control theory focuses on the extent to which an individual is attached to conventional adults and involved in conventional activities. We see that Al was not emotionally attached to his parents. Thus, control theorists would say that Al had a low stake in conformity. Furthermore, it appears that Al was not much involved in school. Control theorists would conclude that these facts were what caused Al to commit armed robbery.

Alternatively, strain theorists would concentrate on the fact that Al grew up in poverty and did not have many material goods as a potential source of his law violating behavior. This situation was further aggravated by his inability to perform well in school, leading to more strain in his young life. His response to this strain was, in Merton's terminology, to become an "innovator." Learning theorists, on the other hand would emphasize the importance of Al's peer group. As his peer group changed, there was now mutual support among this group for smoking, drinking, and skipping school.

Proponents of an integrated approach would seize upon the diversity of possible explanations to account for Al's ultimate arrest. For instance, the initial weak bonds were further weakened by Al's school failure; his school failure either lowered his aspirations or he accepted the fact that he would not be able to attain the goals he had as a young child; and when Al started hanging out with a bad crowd, he found reinforcement for his own behavior. While any one of these explanations can be invoked to account for Al's criminal activity, the integration of multiple theoretical perspectives can be seen as a way of enhancing our overall understanding of criminal behavior.

Objectives of Integration

Why has criminological theory development turned to the integration approach, and why was there a relative explosion of different integrated models during the past 30 years? Answers to these questions can largely be attributed to the increased statistical sophistication introduced into the social sciences since the 1950s. Early theories were usually limited to the examination of relationships between two variables; the connection, for example, between social class and crime. On occasion, a third or controlling variable would be introduced to see if there were different patterns of association. The question might be: what is the relationship between social class and crime when researchers control for race? In other words, is there a difference in crime rates for middle-class whites and middle-class African-Americans? This did not permit criminologists to talk about causes of crime, only correlates. When testing theories, often with the objective of suggesting policies, it is vital that the causes or precursors of the particular behavior be identified.

While it is not essential for you, at this stage, to understand fully the following discussion of statistics, a general overview will help you to appreciate the integrated models approach. The introduction of multiple regression analysis and path analysis in the social sciences provided criminologists with the statistical tools to begin to address causality. Three conditions generally must be met before it can be said that "X" causes "Y":

- the two variables must be correlated;

- X must precede Y temporally; and

- alternative hypotheses must be eliminated.

Diagrams of causal relationships generally use the following format:

$$X \longrightarrow Y$$

The independent variable, the one hypothesized to be the cause of some phenomenon, is represented by "X" and appears to the left of the schematic representation.

The dependent variable, the thing affected by the independent variable, is represented by "Y" and is to the right of "X."

A simple explanation of crime might be that social class position is a cause of criminal behavior. This would be depicted in the following manner:

Social Class ⟶ Criminal Behavior
(X1)   (−)   (Y)

This example reflects the strain theory hypothesis that there is an inverse or negative relationship between social class and criminal behavior, that is, that persons in the lower class will have higher rates of criminal behavior.

The introduction of a third variable, one representing social learning theory, produces an example of an integrated model:

Social Class ⟶ Criminal Associations ⟶ Criminal Behavior
(X1)   (−)   (X2)   (+)   (Y)

The integration of strain and social learning specifies the following two hypotheses:

- a negative relationship between social class and the number of friends involved in criminal activities; and

- a positive relationship between criminal associates and involvement in criminal behavior.

Remember the example of Al. He was from a relatively poor or lower-class home, he associated with a "bad crowd," and he wound up committing an armed robbery.

Models such as the one just presented can be tested empirically using multiple regression analysis. This method allows the researcher to determine the amount of variation in the dependent variable that is explained by the independent variables in the model. In a self-report survey of college students, for example, a criminologist would ask questions about:

- the student's social class background;

- the number of the student's friends that engage in criminal behavior; and

- the number of crimes that the student has committed during some time period.

Highlight 10.1 provides a sample of questions that might be used in such a survey. These questions would be asked of a sample of students. The researcher could conduct a multiple regression analysis on the data and present information regarding the strength of relationships between each variable and the extent to which all of the independent variables helped to explain criminal behavior.

Criminologists often use this statistical procedure to test the utility of their theoretical models. The explained variance of the various theories ranges from 15 percent (Cernkovich, 1978) to 52 percent (Elliott et al., 1985). The relative strengths

---

HIGHLIGHT 10.1
Sample Questions for a Survey to Test an Integrated Model

1. Which of the following best describes your social class?
   a. lower class   d. middle class
   b. working class   e. upper middle class
   c. lower middle class   f. upper class

2. How many of your friends have done something that could have gotten them in trouble with the law during the past year?
   a. none of them   c. most of them
   b. a few of them   d. all of them

3. How many times during the past year have you done each of the following things?
   a. stolen something worth more than $5
   b. hit someone with the idea of seriously hurting them
   c. used a credit card without the owner's permission
   d. used illegal drugs

---

of the theoretical models in explaining criminal behavior and of variables representing specific theoretical perspectives are influenced, in part, by the particular combinations of theories.

Social strain theory, for example, has little if any power in explaining individual differences in rates of criminal offending when combined with social learning or labeling predictors (Elliott & Voss, 1974; Aultman & Wellford, 1979; Simons et al., 1980). Compared to when each perspective is tested separately, the total explained variance of the models is increased when perspectives are combined.

In addition to the increased power of new statistical procedures, another reason for the surge of interest in the integrated approach is the inadequacy of each of the dominant perspectives to account adequately for the variation in crime rates. During the 1970s, criminology was dominated by a struggle to prove that one theory was better or more powerful than another. Elliott (1985:126) commented on this debate:

> Researchers came to recognize that these crucial tests rarely provided evidence that justified a conclusion that one hypothesis was correct and the other incorrect. At best these tests provided evidence that one hypothesis was more plausible or more powerful than the other. . . . The observation that both hypotheses might be correct and might account for independent portions of the variance in crime was typically overlooked by researchers focusing upon crucial tests, because the objective was to prove one theory right and the other wrong.

The integration approach abandons this competition between theories in favor of seeking more complete understanding of the processes leading to criminal behavior. Three examples of integrated models are described in the following pages.

Delbert Elliott, Suzanne Ageton, and Rachelle Canter— An Integrated Theoretical Perspective

A widely cited example of the integrated model approach is the work of Delbert Elliott, Suzanne Ageton, and Rachelle Canter, which incorporates aspects of strain, social learning, and social control perspectives into a single explanatory paradigm. Their model "avoids the class bias inherent in traditional perspectives and takes into account multiple causal paths to sustained patterns of delinquent behavior" (1979:3).

As proponents of the self-report method of measuring delinquent and criminal behavior, Elliott and colleagues believe that it is not only possible, but preferable, to be able to identify individuals that are involved in habitual criminal activity. Early self-report studies found that almost all people surveyed had violated the law and that there were no race and social class differences in rates of offending. With improvements in self-report techniques, more recent studies have been able to identify serious or career offenders (e.g., Elliott, Huizinga & Morse, 1987; Farrington, 1987; Horney & Marshall, 1991; Howell 2003; Loeber et al., 2005; Thornberry et al., 2003). Refinements in self-report measures have also resulted in the identification of race and class differences once researchers controlled for both the frequency and seriousness of reported offenses (Huizinga & Elliott, 1987). Members of the lower class and racial minorities tend to report greater levels of involvement in delinquent activities. Elliott and his colleagues maintain that it is important to focus on patterned delinquent activity when discussing the causes and correlates of delinquency. While most people are law violators, only a minority are heavily involved in criminal activity; that minority accounts for the majority of all crime. Their model, therefore, seeks to explain patterned delinquent behavior.

The Elliott et al. theoretical model is an example of the end-to-end approach. First, the authors identify early socialization experiences as resulting in strong or weak bonds. The ideas and terminology of this stage of the integrated model are borrowed directly from Travis Hirschi's social control theory. During childhood, children develop varying levels of attachment to parents, teachers, and other conventional adults. Levels and strengths of attachments are related to the child's involvement in and commitment to conventional activities such as school, church, community athletics, and service or hobby clubs. This early socialization process determines, to a large degree, the extent to which the child will be integrated into society or, in the terminology of social control theorists, have a stake in conformity.

Second, Elliott and his colleagues argue that these early socialization outcomes are tested in late childhood and adolescence, as the child is exposed to a greater array of social institutions and experiences. During this stage, youths experience success or failure in conventional contexts such as school, clubs, work, and athletics that subsequently strengthen or attenuate the early bonds. The peer group begins to play an increasingly more important role in the life of the child. The types of peer groups to which the child is exposed serve to weaken or reinforce the early bonds as well as other social experiences. Exposure to conventional peer groups promotes conventional behaviors that lessen the probability of involvement in patterned delinquent behavior. Conversely, exposure to delinquent peer groups reinforces negative social experiences and results in a high probability of involvement in delinquent behavior patterns. These last two stages of the model reflect the strain and learning perspectives.

An important element of the model is the notion that there are multiple paths leading to delinquent or nondelinquent behavior (Elliott et al., 1985, 1989; Huizinga et al., 1991; Moffitt, 1993; Simons et al., 1994; 2002; Thornberry et al., 2003). For example, a child who starts out with weak bonds may experience success in conventional social contexts and be exposed to conventional peers and subsequently not engage in delinquent activities. Conversely, a child who develops strong attachments to conventional society in the home may experience failure in school and other social contexts and interact with delinquent peers. Such a path would lead to a high probability of involvement in patterned delinquent activity. Figure 10.2 summarizes this model and the multiple paths leading to delinquency.

FIGURE 10.2
Adapted from the Integrated Theoretical Model of Elliott, Ageton, and Canter (1979)

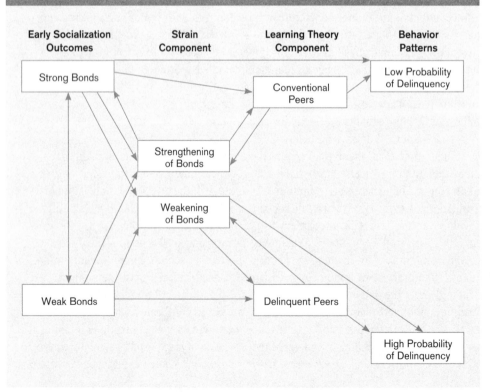

Mark Colvin and John Pauly—An Integrated Structural-Marxist Theory of Delinquency Production

In their 1983 critique, Mark Colvin and John Pauly faulted existing theories of juvenile delinquency for being too social-psychological, that is, focusing too heavily upon micro-sociological levels of explanation. The dominant theories identify conditions that tend to be precursors to delinquent behavior but they do not explain how these variables are distributed in the social systems. Colvin and Pauly introduced a structural-Marxist theory that integrates elements of the micro-sociological theories. They maintain that capitalism and its accompanying social relations to the means of production produce different attitudes toward authority. Based upon the type of social control found in the workplace, workers develop respect and willingness to comply with the power and authority structures, or they develop hostility and alienation. The more coercive the control is, the more extreme the alienation.

Workers' experiences in the workplace are reproduced at home and subsequently affect children's socialization experiences within the family, school, and peer group. Colvin and Pauly (1983:514-515) wrote that:

> family compliance structures are class differentiated and that parent-child relations are profoundly shaped by parents' encounters with workplace compliance structures. The relations of workplace control, which take various class-related forms under capitalism, shape the consciousness, and behavior of parents who repeatedly produce and reproduce control relations with children. The specific nature of these early controls . . . strongly influences the type of control structure the child will encounter when entering school. . . . [P]eer groups develop control relations of their own. . . . [P]eer groups, through their various structures of control, can reinforce either conventional or delinquent behavior.

The key variables in this structural Marxist theory of delinquency are the parents' social class and the coerciveness of the workplace social control structure. Colvin and Pauly argued that these two structural factors affect social psychological variables such as parents' and children's alienation and that these factors are in turn associated with the type of peer groups selected by the children (Sutherland, 1947). Next, the authors borrowed from opportunity theory (Cloward & Ohlin, 1960) and maintained that the type of delinquency is shaped by the availability of illegitimate opportunity structures. (See Figure 10.3 for a schematic representation of this model).

Charles Tittle— Control Balance Theory

In 1995 Charles Tittle proposed an integrated theory of deviance that combines elements of control and routine activities theories. This theory is of significance for

FIGURE 10.3
A Structural-Marxist Integrated Model-Summary of Colvin and Pauly (1983)

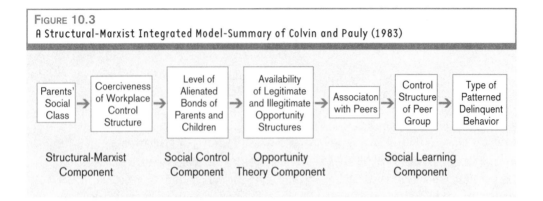

several reasons. First, Tittle maintains that this model explains both conventional criminal behavior and white-collar crime. Second, he claims that the theory accounts for not only the occurrence of deviance but also the type of deviance. At the heart of this perspective is the notion of "control balance;" that is, deviance occurs when there is an imbalance between the amount of control that one can exercise and the amount of control to which one is subjected.

All humans, according to Tittle strive to be autonomous, yet most people have a number of constraints placed upon them that restricts their autonomy. Additionally, all people possess a variable number of resources upon which they rely to attain their needs. Conformity occurs as long as peoples' abilities to fulfill their desires are not overly constrained. Tittle refers to a "control ratio" to account for the probability of deviance occurring. This control ratio refers to the amount of control a person can exercise divided by the amount of control to which he or she is subjected. When this control ratio is balanced, the probability of deviance is low and the probability of conformity is high. When this control ratio produces a surplus of control (the individual has the resources to exercise more control than that to which they are subjected), the probability of deviance is increased. Conversely, and perhaps more intuitively, when this control ratio produces a deficit, deviance is also likely to result. While both types of control imbalance produce deviance, the nature of the control imbalance affects the type of deviance that is most likely to result. Tittle (1995:124) defines deviance as "any behavior that the majority of a given group regards as unacceptable or that typically evokes a collective response of a negative type." Within this broad definition of deviance, Tittle delineates six different types of deviance; three types (exploitation, plunder, and decadence) are more common when there is a control surplus. The other three types of deviance are more likely to result from a control deficit—predation, defiance, and submission.

The following six types of deviance are intended to represent the spectrum of human conduct that produces a negative collective response (Tittle, 1995:137-140):

- **predation**, which includes such diverse acts as theft, rape, homicide, assault, fraud, and sexual harassment;

- **exploitation**, which involves indirect predation and includes the following deviant behaviors—"corporate price-fixing,

> profiteering from manufacturing processes that endanger work-
> ers, influence peddling by political figures . . . and employment
> of religious injunctions to solicit financial contributions for the
> personal use of evangelists;"

- **defiance**, including such acts as curfew violations, vandalism, and political protests;

- **plunder**, which refers to individuals or organizations pursuing their own interests without much regard for how their behavior affects others (e.g., pollution by oil companies with subsequent price increases to cover the costs of cleanup);

- **decadence**, including such acts as "group sex with children, cruel debauchery such as humiliating people for entertainment and nonsensical pleasure seeking or destruction, as in sadistic torture;"

- **submission**, which consists of passive obedience to the expectation, commands, or desires of others (helping to repress others, allowing oneself to be physically abused or sexually degraded).

Control imbalance is just one aspect, albeit a central one, of Tittle's theory. Borrowing from routine activities theory, Tittle also maintains that deviance is a product of predispositional and situational motivations, constraints, and opportunity. Two tests of control balance have reported support for the perspective (Piquero & Hickman, 1999; Baron & Forde, 2007). Control imbalance and motivation to deviate, however, do not necessarily produce deviance. Tittle maintains that "an individual with 100 units of behavioral motivation to do a particular thing is not likely to do it if he or she also faces 100 comparable units of constraint, whereas an individual with 10 units of motivation but only 1 unit of constraint has a much better chance of committing the act" (Tittle, 1995:168). Constraint refers to the probability, or perceived probability, that potential control will actually be exercised. "The control ratio indicates the extent to which control efforts can potentially be brought to bear against a person; constraint refers to the actual probability that potentially controlling reactions will be forthcoming" (Tittle, 167-168).

One last element of the theory is opportunity. Without the opportunity to deviate, there will be no deviation. If, for example, there is no alcohol available, there will be no drunkards. If there are no possessions, there will be no theft. As Tittle (1995:169) states "No matter how favorable the motivational and constraint configuration, the actual likelihood of deviance occurring depends on there being an opportunity for it to happen."

John Braithwaite (1997) has provided one early response to Tittle's work. He commends Tittle for proposing a theory that explains both street and suite crime. He notes "If it can be shown that both control surpluses and control deficits explain deviance, it may be that crime in the suites can be explained by control surplus, crime in the streets by control deficit, so that control imbalance structured into a society becomes a common cause of both types of crime" (Braithwaite, 1997:78).

Tests of Integrated Models

Researchers have compared the relative explanatory power of competing theories and then combined them into an integrated theoretical framework. In most instances, this has resulted in an increase in the explained variance. Another objective has been to determine if certain models are better predictors than others of specific types of behaviors. Integrated models, for example, have been used to explain general delinquency, assaultive behavior, property offenses, female delinquency, and various types of drug use. Findings reveal that the ability of a given model to explain behavior varies with the type of behavior in question.

One of the most frequent combinations of theories involves social control and social learning perspectives. Rand Conger (1976) found control variables to be important but learning theory variables to be better predictors of delinquent behavior. He concluded that social control theory is incomplete, not incorrect. "By combining the notion that individuals are 'bonded' to others with certain principles of social learning theory, the groundwork for a stronger theory is developed. Essentially, the social learning model clarified how attachments will influence deviant behavior by including to whom one is attached in the analysis" (Conger, 1976:37).

Other studies have found similar results; each of the theoretical perspectives makes an independent contribution to the explained variance while combining them increases the total explained variance (Linden, 1978; Johnson, 1979; Johnstone, 1983; and Thornberry et al., 1991, 1994). One study of delinquency, however, found that when differential association theory is properly operationalized (i.e., the theoretical concepts are properly specified through questionnaire items), it accounts for more than one-half of the variation in reported delinquency and mediates the effects of the social control variables (Matsueda, 1982). In a test of interactional theory (an integration of social control and learning theories in which the authors stipulate that there are "feedback" loops between variables), Thornberry and colleagues reiterate the need to understand how both perspectives promote criminal behavior. They write:

> Theoretically, the long-standing debate between differential association or learning theory on the one hand and social control on the other may have unnecessarily occupied the time of theoretical criminology. The issue should not be posed as a question of whether association with delinquent peers causes delinquency, or whether adolescents, once having committed delinquent behavior, seek out and associate with others who engage in similar behaviors…. The present results suggest the need to specify how the reciprocal relationship between these variables develops as adolescents proceed from the initiation of delinquency to its maintenance and eventual cessation (1994:75).

Criminologists also have tested models combining social strain and social control theories. These models generally account for less of the variation in delinquency or crime rates than do the social learning/social control approaches (Cernkovich, 1978; Segrave & Hasted, 1983). Still other theorists have integrated three or more of the dominant theoretical perspectives. While findings from these studies vary slightly,

GANG FEATURE

Once in a Gang, You're in for Life

The title of this "Gang Feature" is a statement commonly heard when listening to gang members on talk shows or in interviews with the media. The gang is a life-long commitment. To what extent is this an accurate picture? Not very, if the research literature is any indication. Several observational and qualitative studies (e.g., the research with New York City gang girls conducted by Anne Campbell and the qualitative interviews with St. Louis gang members reported by Scott Decker and Barrik Van Winkle) include discussions about members leaving the gang, surprisingly little attention has been given to this aspect of gang life. Most attention has been to the recruitment process and the activities of the gang. Leaving the gang, as with desistance of criminal activity in the criminal career debate, deserves greater attention.

Recent longitudinal surveys, The Denver Youth Survey and the Rochester Youth Development Survey, have allowed researchers to examine the "career" of gang members. These surveys interviewed the same youth over a period of time and were able to document gang membership across time. Somewhat surprising was the finding that most gang members claim membership for one year or less. Gang membership turns out to be a fluid phenomenon, not all that dissimilar from other adolescent peer group associations.

In the Denver Youth Survey, Esbensen and Huizinga examined the relationship between gang membership and involvement in serious delinquent offending. As part of this analysis, they identified the years of actual gang membership. Of the 90 gang members in their study, only 18 of them reported being in the gang for two or more consecutive years, and only eight of these youth were in the gang for three or more years. Another 12 were members for two nonconsecutive years. In other words, 60 of the 90 gang members reported being in the gang during only one year of the four-year study.

With respect to serious delinquency, Esbensen and Huizinga report that gang membership is associated with higher rates of offending. Interestingly, the increase in offending begins in years prior to joining, but increases drastically during the year of membership. They report that gang members are more likely to commit serious crimes and, importantly, to commit them more frequently. In recent publications, Thornberry has reported similar results from the Rochester study, and Hill and colleagues have replicated these findings with a sample of Seattle youth.

the general results consistently support the enhanced explanatory power of these integrated models (Elliott et al., 1985, 1989; Simons et al., 1980; Winfree et al., 1981).

Policy Relevance of Integrated Models

Policy recommendations are implicit in these integrated theoretical models. Two of the models presented in this chapter emphasize the role of early parenting in developing the child's social bond to society. A number of researchers have evaluated proposals and programs for improving the ability of parents and parents-to-be to be effective (Loeber & Dishion, 1983; Farrington, 1987; Greenwood, 1987; and Hawkins et al., 1987; Larzelere & Patterson, 1990; McCord, 1991). These ideas generally involve either the instruction of high school students in effective parenting or the provision of training for parents of children already enrolled in school. David

Hawkins and his colleagues at the University of Washington are involved in a longitudinal study evaluating a program that seeks to teach parents how better to discipline, monitor, and in general socialize their children. Other efforts to improve the child's early social bond include preschool programs such as Head Start. A longitudinal study of the Perry Pre-school Program, an experimental program to assess both short- and long-term effects of preschool participation, found that program participants not only had fewer school-related problems than the control group, but also had lower levels of involvement in delinquent and criminal behavior (Schweinhart, 1987). Integration theorists who support elements of social control theory would advocate these preventive measures.

For individuals already in the criminal justice system, rehabilitation programs incorporating efforts to strengthen the offender's attachment to society are recommended. This would include educational and vocational training as well as counseling for drug dependency and other problems. Other policy recommendations depend upon the specific model. The "Structural-Marxist Model," for instance, would advance many of the same changes discussed by Elliott Currie in his 1989 essay. These include reducing inequality in society and improving the conditions currently found in the labor market. (These recommendations are discussed in detail in Chapter 9.)

The Criminal Career Debate

A relatively heated controversy in criminology concerns whether criminals comprise a distinctive group within the general population. Proponents of the criminal career concept (Blumstein et al., 1988a, 1988b; Barnett et al., 1992) maintain that individuals can be dichotomized into active offenders and non-offenders. Critics (Gottfredson & Hirschi, 1990; Rowe et al., 1990) suggest that this is an artificial and erroneous distinction. They posit that humans possess different levels of "crime proneness" or varying propensities for crime. While this may appear to be an academic debate about the nature of crime, it has major policy ramifications. The "three strikes" statutes enacted during the 1990s underscore its importance.

Public opinion polls continually reveal that crime is one of the major concerns reported by Americans. Media reports of random violence, gang disputes, and drug abuse appear daily and apparently contribute to the general perception that crime in America is out of control. As discussed in Chapter 4, however, while the crime rate increased from 1972 to 1991, crime has actually declined each year since 1992. Given the public concern with crime and the fear of victimization, a common political theme has been to "get tough on crime." During the 1992 presidential election, George H. Bush, Bill Clinton, and Ross Perot each tried to be the "tough guy" on crime. Former President Clinton fulfilled his campaign promise by recommending the hiring of 100,000 more police officers and by promoting an incapacitation model to lock up for life any person convicted of a third federal felony. This recommendation was part of the criminal career debate. If it is correct that individuals can be categorized as active offenders or non-offenders, then the argument can be made that crime rates will decrease if we identify the active offenders and imprison them. During the 1980s, we witnessed the introduction of habitual offender laws also based on the premise that life sentences for repeat offenders would protect society and reduce crime. Given the prominence of such policies in the current era, it is important that we examine their theoretical and empirical underpinnings.

The criminal career paradigm dates back to the pioneering work of Eleanor and Sheldon Glueck during the 1930s and 1940s. In their widely cited study of 500 delinquent boys and a matched sample of 500 nondelinquents, the Gluecks found that the delinquent boys continued their illegal activity into adulthood. Investigation of official records and interviews with the study participants when they were 31 years old found that 62 (14%) of the 442 nondelinquents located had adult convictions. Of the 438 delinquents located, 354 (81%) had been arrested as adults. The Gluecks found the following characteristics to be more descriptive of the delinquent than nondelinquent sample:

> . . . they are less adequate than the non-delinquents in capacity to operate on a fairly efficient level and have less emotional stability. . . . they are more dynamic and energetic, much more aggressive, adventurous, and positively suggestible, as well as stubborn. . . . more inclined to impulsive and non-reflective expression of their energy-drives. . . . Such temperamental equipment is in itself highly suggestive of the causes for their greater inclination to ignore or readily break through the bonds of restriction imposed by custom or law. (Glueck & Glueck, 1950:251-252)

This early career research was largely ignored by American criminologists, in part due to the emphasis on nonsociological explanatory factors. However, as will be discussed below, the recent past has seen a resurrection of the Gluecks' research.

Research conducted by Marvin Wolfgang and his colleagues (1972) at the University of Pennsylvania also provided early fuel for the criminal career debate. Their study of a cohort of males born in Philadelphia in 1945 found that six percent of the 9,945 boys accounted for more than 50 percent of the officially recorded delinquent acts. More importantly, this same six percent accounted for 63 percent of all Index offenses. With all the caveats about relying upon official arrest data aside, the policy relevance of this finding is clear—identify and isolate this criminal six percent and reduce crime. For instance, several recent studies report that youth gang members account for approximately 75 percent of all violent offenses (Howell, 2003; Huizinga, 1997; Thornberry et al., 2003).

The criminal career research, according to Daniel Nagin and Kenneth Land (1993), was fueled by the work of two engineers concerned about the high levels of crime in New York City. They applied their mathematical training to model the effect of incapacitating offenders for varying lengths of time. In their analyses they considered both the onset and termination of criminal activity, clearly implying that criminals are distinguishable from noncriminals.

As the most vocal proponents of the career paradigm, Alfred Blumstein and his colleagues have argued that there may well be different explanatory models for the initiation, maintenance, and termination of criminal activity. Research examining criminal behavior (Blumstein & Graddy, 1982) and drug use (Esbensen & Elliott, 1994) has indeed found different explanatory factors associated with initiation and termination of the respective activities.

Widespread agreement exists regarding the sequence of illegal activity from adolescence to adulthood, and there is virtually no disagreement about the positive relationship between past and future criminal behavior. The controversy revolves around whether various types of criminals exist who have different crime histories. Michael Gottfredson and Travis Hirschi argue that crime is the product of a single underlying construct—a criminal propensity—identified as low self-control (1988; 1990). Consequently, for them, it is nonsensical to discuss criminal careers and different paths to crime. On the other hand, Arnold Barnett and his associates (Alfred Blumstein, Jacqueline Cohen & David Farrington) contend that criminal career research allows for:

> the separate examination of (1) participation in offending (the distinction between those who engage in crime and those who do not); (2) characterization of the continuing criminal career, represented by the individual frequency of offending; and (3) termination of offending. Our approach allows for the possibility that different factors could influence these different facets of a criminal career, whereas the single-factor approach presumes that all aspects of a criminal career are influenced by the same factors in the same way (1992:133).

Given these diametrically opposing viewpoints, it should come as no surprise that this has been at times a heated dispute. While agreeing to comment on the two positions, Kenneth Land (1992:149) wrote that it "would be somewhat like trying to referee a fight between King Kong and Godzilla—with a substantial likelihood of being crushed in the middle, regardless of what I say." A different approach to the criminal career debate has been proposed by David Rowe, Wayne Osgood, and Alan Nicewander. They propose that an unobservable yet relatively stable set of factors accounts for an individual's "crime proneness." This latent trait approach assumes that there is some trait associated with the individual that determines the likelihood that the person will engage in crime. Their position:

> ... largely falls on the side of the current debate that is articulated by Hirschi and Gottfredson. Nevertheless, we do not join Hirschi and Gottfredson in the wholesale rejection of the criminal career approach. Instead, we see merit in studying the distribution of criminal acts over individuals' lives, and we believe that a latent trait approach provides the most appropriate basis for such research (1990:238).

According to Blumstein and his colleagues, "the concept of criminal career refers to the longitudinal sequence of offenses committed by an offender who has a detectable rate of offending during some period" (1988a:2). It could be said that a one-time experimenter in crime has a criminal career spanning that one instance. Generally, however, a more restrictive interpretation is accepted. A criminal career consists of a beginning (referred to as initiation), a period of offending (duration) at some measurable level (frequency or lambda), and a period of inactivity (variably referred to as discontinuity or termination). The term criminal career signifies the sequence of offending during some time period, not an assumption that an individual earns a livelihood through criminal activity. Blumstein and colleagues (1988b) also suggest that the criminal career paradigm does not imply that there is any special progression of behaviors or any specialization of behaviors, as Gottfredson and Hirschi (1988) have attributed to the criminal career position. In a relatively recent issue of the Crime and Justice series published by the University of Chicago Press, Alex Piquero, Al Blumstein, and David Farrington (2003) provide a comprehensive review of the current state of criminal career theory and research. The "Gang Feature" in this chapter reports on findings from the longitudinal studies being conducted in Denver and Rochester, examining the degree to which gang membership fits into the criminal career debate.

A number of commentators have confused the criminal career research with that regarding career criminals (or habitual offenders). The latter would be supportive of an incapacitative model while the former would only limitedly support incapacitation. As stated previously, criminal careers have a beginning and some period of active offending. But, importantly, they also have periods of low offending or non-offending. The career criminal conception assumes that the criminal activity is relatively constant. The criminal career perspective does not support the three strikes notion as life events such as marriage, divorce, parenthood, employment, and unemployment have significant impacts on patterns of offending (Horney et al., 1995). Thus, it is possible that incarceration of a three-time offender may *not* have any significant effect on the crime rate.

Policy Relevance of the Criminal Career Paradigm

The criminal career paradigm suggests that a policy of selective incapacitation will affect the crime rate. The objective is to identify career offenders, incarcerate them during their periods of high offending, and thus reduce crime. In response to this, Gottfredson and Hirschi write, "the common expectation that short-term changes in the probabilities of punishment (such as arrest) or in the severity of punishment (such as length of sentence) will have a significant effect on the likelihood of criminal activity misconstrues the nature of self-control" (1990:255-256).

In the current atmosphere of "get tough" on crime, the criminal career paradigm has attracted considerable attention. The call for more prisons, longer sentences, mandatory minimum sentences, and habitual offender laws (also referred to as "three strikes") rests largely on the belief that criminal activity can be reduced through incapacitation of offenders, especially high-rate offenders. If judges can correctly identify those individuals variably referred to as habitual offenders and career criminals, then some identifiable number of crimes can be prevented. The issue then becomes one of cost (of building and incarcerating offenders) weighed against the benefits (of crimes and social damage prevented).

The objectives of criminal career research are threefold: (1) to accurately identify the high-rate offender; (2) to identify factors associated with onset, maintenance, and termination; and (3) to determine the average number of offenses committed by each offender during some period of time. To date, the last objective has received the most attention from criminologists involved in the criminal career debate.

In 1982, Peter Greenwood co-authored the RAND Report, a survey of prisoners in three states. Greenwood determined that the average number of offenses committed by these inmates per year, while varying considerably, could be estimated at much more than 100. Thus, for every offender imprisoned, more than 100 crimes would be prevented. In a subsequent publication, Edwin Zedlewski (1987) estimated that 187 felonies are committed each year by the typical "career criminal." Other researchers have determined the offending rate to be considerably less than either of these estimates. Alfred Blumstein and Jacqueline Cohen (1979) suggest that the number of felonies committed by adult offenders is approximately 10 per year. In their investigation of Nebraska prisoners, Julie Horney and Ineke Marshall (1991) found that the estimates provided by Zedlewski overestimated lambda, (the frequency of offending), by 72 percent. The Horney and Marshall data rely upon an elaborate month-by-month interview schedule that allowed for finer measurement than the earlier surveys that produced higher estimates. A more recent examination of offending differences between imprisoned and free offenders is provided by Jose Canela-Cacho and his colleagues, Alfred Blumstein and Jacqueline Cohen (1997). They report substantial differences between these two groups of offenders, with the incarcerated offenders committing from 10 to 50 times as many offenses a year as the free offenders. While this may seem to be a purely academic question, serious policy implications are associated with the size of lambda. Using Zedlewski's estimate, for example, led to the conclusion that spending $25 million to build more prisons to incarcerate more prisoners for longer periods of time would produce a social savings of $430 million in terms of crimes prevented. If, however, the estimates provided by Canela-Cacho and his colleagues and those reported by Horney and Marshall are correct, then the benefits of the incapacitation model reported by Zedlewski are considerably overstated.

Among criminologists, little disagreement exists regarding the futility and inappropriateness of the "three strikes" policy. This cannot be attributed to a liberal "soft on crime" orientation but rather to empirical research. Despite the overwhelming criminological opposition, politicians and many in the general public support the three strikes approach. Why are the supposed experts being ignored? Is the politician's support based merely on re-election concerns? Why is the public so intent to put its fellow citizens away for life? These are important and interesting questions.

Developmental and Life-Course Criminology

Developmental, alternatively referred to as life-course, criminology "is the study, first of the development and dynamics of problem behaviors and offending with age. . . . The second focus . . . is the identification of explanatory or causal factors that predate, or co-occur with, the behavioral development and have an impact on its course" (Loeber & LeBlanc, 1990:377). While psychologists have embraced the developmental perspective and examined within-*individual* change, criminologists have been reticent to study criminal behavior from a life-course perspective. The vast majority of criminological research has focused on scrutinizing macro-level correlates of crime, which has, of necessity, led to an emphasis on cross-sectional studies of within-*group* differences. This emphasis on the macro-level can be attributed to three factors: (1) longitudinal panel data sets that allow for examination of individual change over time are exceedingly rare; (2) criminologists have traditionally believed in the stability of personality over time; and (3) a reliance on official measures of criminal behavior has resulted in a left-handed censoring of important information—that is, little is known about law violators and their behavior prior to official notice thus making it difficult to discuss causes of the behavior. Also, as Terrie Moffitt (1994) has noted, it is difficult to distinguish between early and late onset since, given available data sets, "early" has been artificially defined as mid-adolescence— thus childhood violations or problem behaviors have been ignored.

Criminologist's reliance upon cross-sectional research designs has limited the research questions that can be addressed. While some theorists maintain that theory should drive questions and subsequently determine the research design, practical concerns such as time, money, and personnel frequently lead to cross-sectional research designs (i.e., these designs are easier to conduct than are longitudinal ones). As a result of this focus on cross-sectional designs, life-course research has been precluded from entering the mainstream of criminological thought. While there has not been an abundance of life-course research, the past 50 years have seen some notable efforts: Eleanor and Sheldon Glueck (1951; 1968), Joan McCord (1979), Lee Robins and P. O'Neal (1958; 1966; 1978), Rowell Huesmann et al. (1984), Monroe Lefkowitz et al. (1977), Phil Silva (1990) and Delbert Elliott and associates (1985; 1989). The past 10 years, however, have been witness to an increase in the number of longitudinal data sets that allow for examination of developmental perspectives (e.g., Huizinga et al., 2003; Loeber et al., 1998; Thornberry et al., 2003). A recent publication by Terence Thornberry and Marvin Krohn (2003) provides an excellent overview of the major findings from seven longitudinal studies.

Michael Gottfredson and Travis Hirschi are among the most vocal opponents of developmental criminology. In their general theory of crime, they argue that life events have virtually no effect on behavior. Criminal activity declines as a result of maturation regardless of whether the person gets married, has a child or becomes employed. They also maintain that personal characteristics (e.g., impulsivity, aggression, self-control) remain stable over time and that longitudinal research is not needed to study criminal behavior. While there is considerable evidence to support their assumptions, consensus on these issues remains elusive.

In a comprehensive review of the literature on childhood antisocial acts, Rolf Loeber (1982) found considerable stability in the antisocial behavior of children. Those who initially displayed high levels of antisocial behavior were more likely to persist in the behavior than were those children who had initial low rates. Likewise, Rowell Huesmann and colleagues found early aggression to be an important predictor of later problem behavior, including criminal activity.

One concern with the stability hypothesis, however, is that it leads to an erroneous conclusion because not all antisocial children grow into antisocial adults. In fact, "MOST antisocial children do not become antisocial as adults" (Gove 1985:123—emphasis added). The research of Lee Robins and P. O'Neal (1958; 1966; 1978), Joan McCord (1979), and others also concludes that there is far less stability in behavioral patterns than has been suggested. Many delinquents do not become adult offenders and many adult offenders do not have a juvenile record.

The age-crime relationship poses an important question for developmental criminologists. Does the drastic increase in crime during adolescence represent higher prevalence rates (more persons in the population) or higher individual offending rates? Longitudinal studies in both England and the United States (Wolfgang et al., 1987) have provided evidence that the increase is almost entirely attributable to an increase in the number of offenders rather than an increase in the criminal activity of a small number of offenders. These results beg the question, why this drastic increase in offenders? Delinquency researchers have long suggested that some phenomena unique to adolescent development may account for this increase, be it physiological changes, sociocultural changes such as increasing role of peer groups and separation from families of origin, or some combination of the two.

Moffitt proposes that there may exist "two qualitatively distinct categories of individuals, each in need of its own distinct theoretical explanations" (Moffitt, 1994:4). She distinguishes between adolescent-limited and life-course-persistent antisocial behavior. Adolescent-limited antisocial behavior occurs when generally healthy teens mimic antisocial behavior in ways that are normative and adaptive to the adolescent experience. The life-course-persistent behavior is the product of "individual differences in child neuropsychological health . . . culminating in a pathological adult antisocial personality structure" (Moffitt, 1994:3). Both of these behavior types have distinct etiologies that require separate analyses. Otherwise, Moffitt warns, "disinformation" will be obtained. For example, if research is conducted among 16- and 17-year-olds (the peak participation years) to seek a better understanding of serious, predatory, and persistent antisocial behavior, then a number of adolescent-limited offenders would be included in the sample. This would result in biased estimates of relationships between etiological factors and behavior. If Moffitt is correct in her assertion that different etiologies exist for these two groups, then inconsistencies reported by juvenile delinquency researchers can perhaps be better understood.

A well-documented body of research exists to support Moffitt's position. Researchers have consistently found a small group of individuals (approximately 5%) who display consistently high rates of antisocial behavior across time. Wolfgang and his colleagues (1972) found a violent six percent in their Philadelphia cohort accounted for more than one-half of all the crimes committed by the entire sample. Elliott and his associates reported that four percent of the male adolescents could be classified as serious violent offenders during a five-year period (Elliott et al., 1986). And, in a recent investigation, Moffitt and colleagues tested her model on a birth cohort from the Dunedin multi-disciplinary health and development study in New Zealand. They found that "poor neuropsychological status predicted specifically male offending that began before age 13 and persisted thereafter . . . . neuropsychological status was unrelated to delinquency that began in adolescence" (Moffitt et al., 1994:277). Clearly, these adolescent-limited offenders may well be substantively different from the life-course-persistent types. It may be that contemporary criminology has become overly concerned with criminal *behavior* at a time when criminologists should be examining criminal *behaviors*. Cross-sectional research and studies focusing on incarcerated offenders look at only a very small part of the overall picture. Different etiologies may well exist for the two delinquent types identified by Moffitt. It may be that life events affect these types differently and that different policies may need to be implemented for intervention or prevention purposes.

A symposium focused on life-course/developmental criminology was convened at the University of Albany in April 2005. This symposium featured presentations by Robert Sampson and John Laub (2005), Daniel Nagin and Richard Tremblay (2005), and Terrence Thornberry (2005). Each of these presentations was then critiqued by distinguished criminologists who were asked to comment on the theoretical and empirical implications of the presentations. These presentations and critiques were subsequently published in the November 2005 issue of the Annals of the American Academy of Political and Social Sciences (Sampson & Laub, 2005) and provide a current assessment of this line of criminological theory development. It is interesting to note the extent to which the criminal career paradigm and developmental criminology have converged during the past 20 years, with life-course criminologists concentrating on initiation, escalation, maintenance, frequency of offending, and desistance, terms that are at the core of the criminal career literature. In his concluding remarks to the symposium, Al Blumstein (2005) highlighted the value of longitudinal research designs that allow for within-individual examination of the developmental trajectories of criminal careers. Importantly, he points out that the various stages of the criminal career, such as onset of crime, have different antecedents depending upon when in the life cycle they occur. Developmental and life-course criminology hold much promise for the understanding of crime and Blumstein encouraged those attending the symposium to engage in more collaborative work that would allow for a cumulative body of work to evolve. In his remarks he emphasized the importance of collaboration: "One would hope that these important streams of research would join up in some ways so that the results would be stronger than that resulting from each of the authors alone" (Blumstein, 2005:253).

Sampson and Laub's Developmental Model

Robert Sampson and John Laub (1990; 1993; 2003; see also Laub & Sampson, 1993; 2003) have formulated a developmental model of criminal behavior based upon their re-analysis of the Gluecks' *Unraveling Juvenile Delinquency* data. Their model considers within-individual change over time (as recommended by Loeber & LeBlanc, 1990), while acknowledging the importance of life transitions to understand behavioral patterns. They presume that certain transitions are more important or relevant during specific developmental periods.

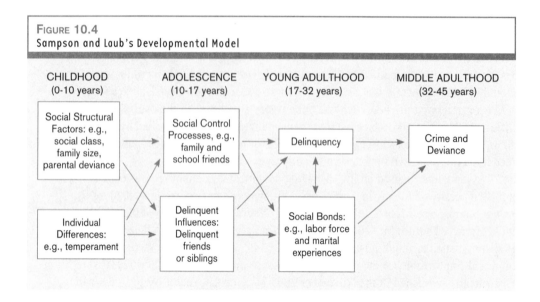

FIGURE 10.4
Sampson and Laub's Developmental Model

Sampson and Laub's theoretical model (presented in Figure 10.4) is grounded in social control theory: criminal behavior is the result of weak or attenuated bonds to society. The model indicates the importance of both stability and change over the life course. Two main hypotheses derived from their theory are:

- childhood antisocial behavior (e.g., juvenile delinquency, conduct disorder, violent temper tantrums) is linked to a wide variety of troublesome adult behaviors, including criminality, general deviance, offenses in the military, economic dependency, educational failure, and marital discord. These long-term relationships are posited to occur independent of traditional variables such as social class background and race/ethnicity.

- . . . social bonds to adult institutions of informal social control (e.g., family, education, neighborhood, work) influence criminal behavior over the life course despite an individual's delinquent and antisocial background (Sampson & Laub 1990:611).

Sampson and Laub's model postulates that some persons who develop strong conventional bonds in childhood may later have these bonds attenuated and be set on a path to criminal involvement. One could also infer the reverse trajectory—that some of those individuals emerging from childhood with very weak conventional bonds may have positive prosocial experiences, either at school with a conventional peer group or in some community group or activity, which subsequently strengthens their conventional bonds and sets them on a noncriminal path. This same sequence can be initiated at any point during the life span, even after some adolescent involvement in delinquent behavior. The person that had serious difficulties during adolescence but then successfully makes the transition into prosocial roles and develops strong bonding to new social roles and contexts (e.g., marriage and employment) is quite likely to terminate his or her involvement in criminal behavior. The model thus accounts for variation in the termination as well as in the initiation of criminal behavior. This dynamic view of bonding is supportive of Moffitt's developmental taxonomy that suggests that many of those evidencing antisocial behavior in childhood do not continue this behavior into adolescence and that a significant number of adolescents with no evidence of childhood problems become involved in delinquency during their adolescent years (Robins & O'Neal, 1958; Lefkowitz et al., 1977; Loeber, 1982; Mitchell & Rosa, 1981). The developmental approach also helps explain why a majority of delinquents cease their illegal activity during their early adult years and why a significant proportion of adult criminals have no record of delinquency during their adolescent years (Glueck & Glueck, 1968; McCord, 1979; Shannon, 1981; Sampson & Laub, 1993a; Moffitt, 1994; Bartusch et al., 1997; Paternoster & Brame, 1997). In a recent publication, Cohen and Vila (1996) contrasted the competing theoretical orientations of developmental criminology and Gottfredson and Hirschi's general theory. While empirical studies have tended to support the Sampson and Laub model, Cohen and Vila suggest that there actually is no greater support for one over the other; it is a matter of traditional positivists being less threatened by the interpretation of criminal activity set forth by Sampson and Laub.

Policy Implications of Developmental Criminology

Developmental criminology produces a multitude of recommendation for policymakers. The theoretical and empirical works suggest that interventions can occur at a number of points in the life course. In their test of the Seattle Social Development Model, for example, Huang and associates (2001:100) make five recommendations. First, intervening at only one point in the model may be a "weak" strategy. Second, due to the finding that there are multiple pathways, suggests that multiple intervention strategies may be required. Third, interventions should target not only "risk" factors, but should also address "protective" factors (that is, factors that are associated with a lower prevalence of problem behavior). Fourth, research has consistently found that prior behavior influences current and future behavior. This highlights the need for early prevention and intervention strategies to reduce adult offending. Fifth, the role of the peer group is vital. Research has documented the effect of delinquent peer groups on individual behavior. Thus, disrupting these antisocial groups early in life or teaching resistance skills to negate these influences should be encouraged. The recent U.S. Surgeon General's Report on Youth Violence (2001) highlighted a number of programs that have been identified as effective in reducing risk factors associated with subsequent offending.

Summary

Integrated theoretical models have proliferated since the 1970s. Several factors underlie this theoretical development. First, the refinement of self-report methods of data collection has enabled researchers to obtain data directly from law violators. This has allowed for examination of direct links between personal characteristics and behavior. Second, the increased sophistication of statistical methods has permitted researchers to look simultaneously at the effect of a number of variables upon behavior. As a result, researchers have been able to examine not only the correlates but also the causes of behavior. Third, the results of evaluations of individual theoretical perspectives failed to show high levels of explanatory power. By combining theories, criminologists have achieved a higher level of understanding of the paths or processes that produce criminal behavior.

The criminal career debate has been fueled by concern with high crime rates. Incapacitation and selective incapacitation provide quick-fix solutions to a complicated question. Unfortunately, these quick-fix solutions have failed to produce a reduction in crime. The criminal career research has identified a violent and/or highly criminal group of five or six percent of offenders. It has not produced any prediction instrument to identify these individuals, although research suggests the importance of social events on the rate of offending among these individuals (e.g., Horney et al., 1995).

Developmental and life-course criminology hold considerable promise. This branch of research transcends the traditional static examination of adolescence and young adulthood and focuses on life-course trajectories. It allows for closer examination of the interplay between childhood experiences and adult behavior. A number of longitudinal panel studies have provided the type of data necessary to test developmental models (e.g., the reconstructed Glueck data, the National Youth Survey, the Dunedin Health Survey, the OJJDP studies, and the Chicago Neighborhood Study).

Key Terms and Concepts

Adolescent-Limited	Lambda
Career Criminal	Latent Trait
Criminal Career	Life-Course Persistent
Discontinuity	Maintenance
Duration	Onset
End-to-End Model	Patterned Delinquent Activity
Frequency	Termination
Initiation	Three Strikes
Integrated Model Approach	

Key Criminologists

Alfred Blumstein	Rolf Loeber
Jacqueline Cohen	Ross Matsueda
Mark Colvin	Joan McCord
Delbert Elliott	Terrie Moffitt
David Farrington	John Pauly
Michael Gottfredson	Lee Robins
Travis Hirschi	Robert Sampson
Julie Horney	Terence Thornberry
David Huizinga	Charles R. Tittle
Marvin Krohn	Marvin Wolfgang
John Laub	

References

Aultman, M.G. & C.F. Wellford (1979). "Towards an Integrated Model of Delinquency Causation: An Empirical Analysis." *Sociology and Social Research*, 63:316-327.

Baron, S.W. & D.R. Forde (2007). "Street Youth Crime: A Test of Control Balance Theory." *Justice Quarterly* 24:335-355.

Barnett, A., A. Blumstein, J. Cohen & D.P. Farrington (1992). "Not All Criminal Career Models Are Equally Valid." *Criminology*, 30:133-140.

Bartusch, D.J., D.R. Lynam, T.E. Moffitt & P.A. Silva (1997). "Is Age Important? Testing a General Versus a Developmental Theory of Antisocial Behavior." *Criminology*, 35:13-48.

Benson, M.L. (2002). *Crime and the Life Course*. Los Angeles, CA: Roxbury Publishing Company.

Blumstein, A. (2005). "An Overview of the Symposium and Some Next Steps." *The Annals of the American Academy of Political and Social Science*, 602:242-258.

Blumstein, A. & J. Cohen (1979). "Estimation of Individual Crime Rates from Arrest Records." *Journal of Criminal Law and Criminology*, 70:561-585.

Blumstein, A., J. Cohen & D. Farrington (1988a). "Criminal Career Research: Its Value for Criminology." *Criminology*, 26:1-35.

Blumstein, A., J. Cohen & D. Farrington (1988b). "Longitudinal and Criminal Career Research: Further Clarifications." *Criminology*, 26:57-74.

Blumstein, A. & E. Graddy (1982). "Prevalence and Recidivism in Index Offenses: A Feedback Model." *Law and Society Review*, 16:265-290.

Braithwaite, J. (1997). "Charles Tittle's Control Balance and Criminological Theory." *Theoretical Criminology*, 1:77-97.

Campbell, A. (1988). *The Girls in the Gang*, Second Edition. New York, NY: Basil Blackwell.

Canela-Cacho, J.A., A. Blumstein & J. Cohen (1997). "Relationship between the Offending Frequency of Imprisoned and Free Offenders." *Criminology*, 35:133-171.

Cernkovich, S.A. (1978). "Evaluating Two Models of Delinquency Causation: Structural Theory and Control Theory." *Criminology*, 16:335-352.

Cohen, L.E. & B.J. Vila (1996). "Self-Control and Social Control: An Exposition of the Gottfredson-Hirschi/Sampson-Laub Debate." *Studies in Crime and Crime Prevention*, 5:125-150.

Cloward, R.A. & L.E. Ohlin (1960). *Delinquency and Opportunity*. New York, NY: The Free Press.

Colvin, M. & J. Pauly (1983). "A Critique of Criminology: Toward an Integrated Structural-Marxist Theory of Delinquency Production." *American Journal of Sociology*, 89:513-551.

Conger, R.D. (1976). "Social Control and Social Learning Models of Delinquent Behavior." *Criminology*, 14:17-40.

Currie, E. (1989). "Confronting Crime: Looking Toward the Twenty-First Century." *Justice Quarterly*, 6:5-25.

Decker, S.H. & B. Van Winkle (1996). *Life in the Gang: Family Friends, and Violence*. New York, NY: Cambridge University Press.

Elliott, D.S. (1985). "The Assumption that Theories Can Be Combined with Increased Explanatory Power: Theoretical Integrations." In R.F. Meier (ed.) *Theoretical Methods in Criminology*. Beverly Hills, CA: Sage Publications.

Elliott, D.S., S.S. Ageton & R.J. Canter (1979). "An Integrated Theoretical Perspective on Delinquent Behavior." *Journal of Research in Crime and Delinquency*, 16:3-27.

Elliott, D.S., D. Huizinga & S.S. Ageton (1985). *Explaining Delinquency and Drug Use*. Beverly Hills, CA: Sage Publications.

Elliott, D.S., D. Huizinga & S. Menard (1989). *Multiple Problem Youth: Delinquency, Substance Use, and Mental Health Problems*. New York, NY: Springer-Verlag.

Elliott, D.S., D. Huizinga & B.J. Morse (1987). "Self-Report Violent Offending: A Descriptive Analysis of Juvenile Violent Offenders and Their Offending Careers." *Journal of Interpersonal Violence*, 1:472-514.

Elliott, D.S. & H.L. Voss (1974). *Delinquency and Dropout*. Lexington, MA: D.C. Heath and Company.

Esbensen, F. & D.S. Elliott (1994). "Continuity and Discontinuity in Illicit Drug Use: Patterns and Antecedents." *Journal of Drug Issues*, 24:75-97.

Esbensen, F. & D. Huizinga (1993). "Gangs, Drugs, and Delinquency in a Survey of Urban Youth." *Criminology*, 31:565-589.

Farrington, D.P. (2002). "Developmental and Life-Course Criminology: Key Theoretical and Empirical Issues." The Sutherland Award Address, Annual Meeting of the American Society of Criminology, Chicago, IL. November.

Farrington, D.P. (1987). "Early Precursors of Frequent Offending." In J.Q. Wilson & G.C. Loury (eds.) *From Children to Citizens Volume III: Families, School, and Delinquency Prevention*. New York, NY: Springer-Verlag.

Glueck, S. & E. Glueck (1968). *Delinquents and Non-Delinquents in Perspective*. Cambridge, MA: Harvard University Press.

Glueck, S. & E. Glueck (1950). *Unraveling Juvenile Delinquency*. Cambridge, MA: Harvard University Press.

Gottfredson, M. & T. Hirschi (1990). *A General Theory of Crime*. Stanford, CA: Stanford University Press.

Gottfredson, M. & T. Hirschi (1988). "Science, Public Policy, and the Career Paradigm." *Criminology*, 26:37-55.

Gove, W.R. (1992). "Comparing Criminal Career Models." *Criminology*, 30:141-147.

Gove, W.R. (1985). "The Effect of Age and Gender on Deviant Behavior: A Biopsychosocial Perspective." In A.S. Rossi (ed.) *Gender and the Life Course*. New York, NY: Aldine.

Greenwood, P.W. (1987). "Care and Discipline: Their Contribution to Delinquency and Regulation by the Juvenile Court." In Francis X. Hartman (ed.) *From Children and Citizens Volume II: The Role of the Juvenile Court*. New York, NY: Springer-Verlag.

Greenwood, P.W. & A. Abrahamse (1982). *Selective Incapacitation*. Santa Monica, CA: RAND Corporation.

Hawkins, J.D., R.F. Catalano, G. Jones & D. Fine (1987). "Delinquency Prevention through Parent Training: Results and Issues from Work in Progress." In J.Q. Wilson & G.C. Loury (eds.) *From Children to Citizens Volume III: Families, School, and Delinquency Prevention*. New York, NY: Springer-Verlag.

Hawkins, J.D. & J.G. Weis (1985). "The Social Development Model: An Integrated Approach to Delinquency Prevention." *Journal of Primary Prevention*, 6:73-97.

Hirschi, T. (1979). "Separate and Unequal Is Better." *Journal of Research in Crime and Delinquency*, 16:34-38.

Hirschi, T. (1969). *Causes of Delinquency*. Berkeley, CA: University of California Press.

Horney, J. & I.H. Marshall (1991). "Measuring Lambda Through Self-Reports." *Criminology*, 29:471-495.

Horney, J., D.W. Osgood & I.H. Marshall (1995). "Criminal Careers in the Short-Term: Intra-Individual Variability in Crime and Its Relation to Local Life Circumstances." *American Sociological Review*, 60:655-673.

Howell, J.C. (2003). *Preventing and Reducing Juvenile Delinquency: A Comprehensive Framework*. Thousand Oaks, CA: Sage Publications.

Huang, B., R. Kosterman, R.F. Catalano, J.D. Hawkins & R.D. Abbott (2001). "Modeling Mediation in the Etiology of Violent Behavior in Adolescence: A Test of the Social Development Model." *Criminology*, 39:75-107.

Huesmann, L.R., L.D. Eron & M.M. Lefkowitz (1984). "Stability of Aggression over Time and Generations." *Developmental Psychology*, 20:1120-1134.

Huizinga, D. (1997). "Gangs and the Volume of Crime." Paper presented at the Annual Meeting of the Western Society of Criminology, Honolulu, February.

Huizinga, D. & D.S. Elliott (1987). "Juvenile Offenders: Prevalence, Offenders, and Arrest Rates by Race." *Crime & Delinquency*, 33:206-223.

Huizinga, D., F. Esbensen & A.W. Weiher (1991). "Are There Multiple Paths to Delinquency?" *Journal of Criminal Law and Criminology*, 82:83-118.

Huizinga, D., R. Loeber & T.P. Thornberry (1994). *Urban Delinquency and Substance Abuse*. Washington, DC: U.S. Department of Justice.

Jensen, G.F. (1972). "Parents, Peers, and Delinquent Action: A Test of the Differential Association Perspective." *American Journal of Sociology*, 78:562-575.

Johnson, R.E. (1979). *Juvenile Delinquency and Its Origins: An Integrated Theoretical Approach*. New York, NY: Cambridge University Press.

Johnstone, J.W.C. (1983). "Recruiting to a Youth Gang." *Youth and Society*, 14:281-300.

Kornhauser, R.R. (1978). *Social Sources of Delinquency*. Chicago, IL: University of Chicago Press.

Land, K.C. (1992). "Models of Criminal Careers: Some Suggestions for Moving Beyond the Current Debate." *Criminology*, 30:149-155.

Larzelere, R.E. & G.R. Patterson (1990). "Parental Management: Mediator of the Effect of Socioeconomic Status on Early Delinquency." *Criminology*, 28:301-324.

Laub, J.H. & R.J. Sampson (2003). *Shared Beginnings, Divergent Lives: Delinquent Boys to Age 70*. Cambridge, MA: Harvard University Press.

Laub, J.H. & R.J. Sampson (1993). "Turning Points in the Life Course: Why Change Matters to the Study of Crime." *Criminology*, 31:301-326.

Lefkowitz, M.M., L. Eron, L. Walder & L.R. Huesmann (1977). *Growing Up to Be Violent: A Longitudinal Study of the Development of Aggression*. New York, NY: Pergamon.

Linden, R. (1978). "Myths of Middle-Class Delinquency: A Test of the Generalizability of Social Control Theory." *Youth and Society*, 9:407-432.

Loeber, R. (1982). "The Stability of Antisocial and Delinquent Behavior: A Review." *Child Development*, 53:1431-1446.

Loeber, R., L. Homish, E.H. Wei, D. Pardini, A.M. Crawford, D.P. Farrington, M. Stouthamer-Loeber, J. Creemers, S.A. Koehler & R. Rosenfeld. (2005). "The Prediction of Violence and Homicide in Young Males." *Journal of Consulting and Clinical Psychology* 73:1074-1088.

Loeber, R. & M. LeBlanc (1990). "Toward a Developmental Criminology." In M. Tonry & N. Morris (eds.) *Crime and Justice*, Vol. 12. Chicago, IL: University of Chicago Press.

Loeber, R. & T.J. Dishion (1983). "Early Predictors of Male Delinquency: A Review." *Psychological Bulletin*, 94:68-99.

Loeber, R., D.P. Farrington, M. Stouthamer-Loeber, T. Moffitt & A. Caspi (1998). "The Development of Male Offending: Key Findings from the First Decade of the Pittsburgh Youth Study." *Studies in Crime and Crime Prevention*, 7:121-172.

Matsueda, R.L. (1982). "Control Theory and Differential Association: A Causal Modeling Approach." *American Sociological Review*, 47:489-504.

McCord, J. (1991). "Family Relationships, Juvenile Delinquency, and Adult Criminality." *Criminology*, 29:397-417.

McCord, J. (1979). "Some Child Rearing Antecedents of Criminal Behavior in Adult Men." *Journal of Personality and Social Psychology*, 9:1477-1486.

Messner, S.E., M.D. Krohn & A.E. Liska (1989). *Theoretical Integration in the Study of Deviance and Crime*. Albany, NY: State University of New York Press.

Mitchell, S. & P. Rosa (1981). "Boyhood Behavior Problems as Precursors of Criminality: A Fifteen-Year Follow-up Study." *Journal of Child Psychology and Psychiatry*, 22:19-33.

Moffitt, T. (1994). "Natural Histories of Delinquency." In E.G.M. Weitekamp & H. Kerner (eds.) *Cross-National Longitudinal Research on Human Development and Criminal Behavior*. Boston, MA: Kluwer Academic Publishers.

Moffitt, T. (1993). "Adolescent-Limited and Life-Course Persistent Antisocial Behavior: A Developmental Taxonomy." *Psychological Review*, 100:674-701.

Moffitt, T., D.R. Lynam & P.A. Silva (1994). "Neuropsychological Tests Predicting Persistent Male Delinquency." *Criminology*, 32:277-300.

Nagin, D.S. & R.E. Tremblay (2005). "What Has Been Learned from Group-Based Trajectory Modeling? Examples from Physical Aggression and Other Problem Behavior." *The Annals of the American Academy of Political and Social Science* 602:82-117.

Nagin, D.S., D.P. Farrington & T.E. Moffitt (1995). "Life-Course Trajectories of Different Types of Offenders." *Criminology*, 33:1111-1139.

Nagin, D.S. & K.C. Land (1993). "Age, Criminal Careers, and Population Heterogeneity: Specification and Estimation of a Nonparametric, Mixed Poisson Model." *Criminology*, 31:327-362.

Paternoster, R. & R. Brame (1997). "Multiple Paths to Delinquency: A Test of Developmental and General Theories of Crime." *Criminology*, 35:49-84.

Piquero, A. D.P. Farrington & A. Blumstein (2003). "The Criminal Career Paradigm." In M. Tonry (ed.) *Crime and Justice: Review of Research*. Chicago, IL: University of Chicago Press.

Piquero, A. & P. Mazerolle (2001). *Life-Course Criminology: Contemporary and Classic Readings*. Belmont, CA: Wadsworth.

Piquero, A. & M. Hickman (1999). "An Empirical Test of Tittle's Control Balance Theory." *Criminology*, 37:319-341.

Robins, L. & P. O'Neal (1978). "Sturdy Childhood Predictors of Adult Antisocial Behavior." *Psychological Medicine*, 8:611-622.

Robins, L. & P. O'Neal (1966). *Deviant Children Grown Up*. Baltimore, MD: Williams and Wilkens.

Robins, L. & P. O'Neal (1958). "Mortality, Mobility, and Crime: Problem Children Thirty Years Later." *American Sociological Review*, 23:162-171.

Rowe, D.C., D.W. Osgood & W.A. Nicewander (1990). "A Latent Trait Approach to Unifying Criminal Careers." *Criminology*, 28:237-270.

Sampson, R.J. & J.H. Laub (2005). "Developmental Criminology and Its Discontents: Trajectories of Crime from Childhood to Old Age." *The Annals of the American Academy of Political and Social Science*, Volume 602. Thousand Oaks, CA: Sage Publications.

Sampson, R.J. & J.H. Laub (2005). "A Life-course View of the Development of Crime." *The Annals of the American Academy of Political and Social Science*, 602:12-45.

Sampson, R.J. & J.H. Laub (2003). "Life-course Desisters? Trajectories of Crime among Delinquent Boys Followed to Age 79." *Criminology*, 41:301-339.

Sampson, R.J. & J.H. Laub (1993). *Crime in the Making: Pathways and Turning Points through Life*. Cambridge, MA: Harvard University Press.

Sampson, R.J. & J.H. Laub (1990). "Crime and Deviance over the Life Course: The Salience of Adult Social Bonds." *American Sociological Review*, 55:609-627.

Schweinhart, L.J. (1987). "Can Preschool Programs Help Prevent Delinquency?" In J.Q. Wilson & G.C. Loury (eds.) *From Children to Citizens Volume III: Families, School, and Delinquency Prevention*. New York, NY: Springer-Verlag.

Segrave, J.O. & D.N. Hasted (1983). "Evaluating Structural and Control Models of Delinquency Causation: A Replication and Extension." *Youth and Society*, 14:437-456.

Shannon, L.W. (1981). Assessing the Relationship of Adult Criminal Careers to Juvenile Careers. Report to NIJJDP and OJJDP: Iowa Urban Community Research Center, University of Iowa.

Shaw, C.R. & H.D. McKay (1942). *Juvenile Delinquency in Urban Areas*. Chicago, IL: University of Chicago Press.

Silva, P.A. (1990). "The Dunedin Multidisciplinary Health and Development Study: A Fifteen-year Longitudinal Study." *Pediatric and Perinatal Epidemiology*, 4:96-127.

Simons, R.L., E. Stewart, L.S. Gordon, R.D. Conger & G.H. Elder, Jr. (2002). "A Test of Life-Course Explanations for Stability and Change in Antisocial Behavior from Adolescence to young Adulthood." *Criminology*, 40:401-434.

Simons, R.L., C. Wu, R.D. Conger & F.O. Lorenz (1994). "Two Routes to Delinquency: Differences between Early and Late Starters in the Impact of Parenting and Deviant Peers." *Criminology*, 32:247-275.

Simons, R.L., M.G. Miller & S.M. Aigner (1980). "Contemporary Theories of Deviance and Female Delinquency: An Empirical Test." *Journal of Research in Crime and Delinquency*, 17:42-53.

Sutherland, E.H. (1947). *Principles of Criminology*, Fourth Edition. Philadelphia, PA: J.B. Lippincott.

Thornberry, T.P. (2005). "Explaining Multiple Patterns of Offending across the Life Course and Generations." *The Annals of the American Academy of Political and Social Science* 602:156-195.

Thornberry, T.P. (1987). "Toward an Interactional Theory of Delinquency." *Criminology*, 25:863-891.

Thornberry, T.P. & M.D. Krohn (2003). *Taking Stock of Delinquency: An Overview of Findings from Contemporary Longitudinal Studies*. New York, NY: Kluwer Academic/Plenum Publishers.

Thornberry, T.P., M.D. Krohn, A.J. Lizotte, C.A. Smith & K. Tobin (2003). *Gang and Delinquency in Developmental Perspective*. New York, NY: Cambridge University Press.

Thornberry, T.P., A.J. Lizotte, M.D. Krohn, M. Farnworth & S.J. Jang (1994). "Delinquent Peers, Beliefs, and Delinquent Behavior: A Longitudinal Test of Interactional Theory." *Criminology*, 32:47-83.

Thornberry, T.P., A.J. Lizotte, M.D. Krohn, M. Farnworth & S.J. Jang (1991). "Testing Interactional Theory: An Examination of Reciprocal Causal Relationships among Family, School, and Delinquency." *Journal of Criminal Law and Criminology*, 82:3-35.

Tittle, C.R. (1997). "Thoughts Stimulated by Braithwaites' Analysis of Control Balance Theory." *Theoretical Criminology* 1:99-110.

Tittle, C.R. (1995). *Control Balance: Toward a General Theory of Deviance*. Boulder, CO: Westview Press.

Winfree, L.T.,F.-A. Esbensen & D.W. Osgood (1996). "Evaluating a School-Based Gang Prevention Program: A Theoretical Perspective." *Evaluation Review*, 20:181-203.

Winfree, L.T., H.E. Theis & C.T. Griffiths (1981). "Drug Use in Rural America: A Cross-Cultural Examination of Complementary Social Deviance Theories." *Youth and Society*, 12:465-489.

Wolfgang, M.E., R. Figlio & T. Sellin (1972). *Delinquency in a Birth Cohort*. Chicago, IL: University of Chicago Press.

Wolfgang, M.E., T.P. Thornberry & R. Figlio (1987). *From Boy to Man: From Delinquency to Crime*. Chicago, IL: University of Chicago Press.

Zedlewski, E.F. (1987). *Research in Brief: Making Confinement Decisions*. Washington, DC: National Institute of Justice.

PART III

Types of Crime

Having examined theoretical explanations of crime, we now are ready to discuss different forms of criminal activity. The chapters in this section consider three types of crime: violent, economic, and victimless.

Violent and economic crimes, discussed in Chapters 11 and 12, include offenses that the average citizen most often envisions when thinking of the crime problem: robbery, burglary, rape, and the like. These "street crimes" are important both because they are relatively widespread and because they incite fear among the populace. Many offenses of lesser public concern that fit the categories of violent and economic crimes, however, are more widespread, costly, and harmful. Human and financial losses attributable to street crimes pale in comparison to losses caused by what are most commonly called "white-collar crimes." The plea bargain of financier Bernard Madoff in 2009, for instance, indicated that he had bilked investors out of $65 billion (Sander, 2009)

An important issue for criminology is how wide the net of criminal law should be cast. "Crimes without victims" are said by some to be the result of an overextension of the criminal law, although others argue that criminalization of behaviors within this category such as drug use and prostitution protects the larger society. Chapter 13 discusses these offenses and the manner in which they are handled.

11
Violent Crime

What reasonably can be said to constitute a "crime of violence"? The uncertainty of a precise definition was demonstrated when the United States Supreme Court confronted the case of Josue Leocal. Leocal, a native of Haiti, living legally in Florida, had been convicted of driving under the influence of alcohol and injuring two persons in an accident. He pled guilty and received a two-year prison term. Based on a Florida statute that declared that the use of physical force against a person or property was a crime of violence and that an alien who perpetrated such an offense could be deported. Leocal was ordered back to Haiti by the immigration authorities. But a unanimous Supreme Court decreed that while the consequences of Leocal's actions were violent, he himself had not been proven to have manifested intent to employ physical force; therefore his deportation was illegal because he had not committed a "crime of violence" (*Leocal v. Ashcroft*, 2004).

Generally, when people express fear about crime, it is almost always the obviously violent crimes—the murders, robberies, rapes, and assaults—that frighten them. Since the catastrophic crashes on September 11, 2001 of two hijacked planes into the World Trade Center in New York City and of a third commandeered jet into the Pentagon in Washington, D.C., terrorist activities also have assumed a prominent place on the roster of feared crimes.

Crime victims may be deeply angered when they are swindled or their house is burglarized, but these emotions pale against the thought of death or serious injury from a crime of violence. And that fear has some factual basis. Measured in terms of other industrialized countries, America is a very violent society. As one writer has observed: "The country was built on brutal violence, revels in it, and shows every evidence of clinging to it with the crazed destructive strength of an obsessive lover" (Herbert, 2006: A25). That judgment may be overblown, but because of anxiety about the threat of violence, many people in the United States alter the way they arrange their lives. They may pass up activities that necessitate returning home after dark. They refuse to open their door to unknown callers or to stop and offer help to a stranger seemingly confused about where he (and it is almost invariably a "he" who is feared) is going.

Nonetheless, all violence is not bad. Violence directed against enemies, such as that which put down the Nazi scourge in World War Two, may forestall greater harm. Violence as part of competition may prove personally and socially enabling. As Mary Jackman (2002:387) has noted, in many instances violence is not driven by "malicious intent" nor is it "socially repudiated." The difficulty becomes that of encouraging "useful" aggression and discouraging criminal violence.

Violence has long been part of our literary tradition. The classic stories of childhood are often grim and gory. Captain Hook waves a spiked hook at Peter Pan. And Hansel and Gretel are about to be placed in the witch's oven. It has been argued, however, that fairy tales teach children not to imitate violence, but to overcome it (Shattuck, 1996). Murder also occurs early in the Bible when Cain slays his brother (Barmash, 2005), and theatre-goers need only count the corpses in Shakespeare's *Hamlet* to appreciate the dramatic potentialities of violence (Foakes, 2003).

Of more concern are current presentations of violence on television and in motion pictures. Events that are reasonably true to life suddenly erupt into fight sequences defying credence, with individuals seemingly inflicting punishment on each other that no human being could survive for more than a few minutes. In rapid sequence, chairs bashed over heads will be ignored and ferocious punches to the jaw will be absorbed by the hero with only a grunt. The mayhem will proceed until at last the villain succumbs.

It is easier to caricature such proceedings than to assay their impact. Recent research indicates that violence portrayed on television is most likely to induce aggressive responses in individuals who bring to the viewing personal problems such as unsatisfactory social relationships (Eriksen & Jensen, 2009). But to determine definitively media influence on violent behavior would involve an intricate kind of research: ideally, one group would be exposed to portrayals of violence while another would not have such an experience. Then subsequent recourse to violence by members of the two groups would be compared. But it would be enormously complicated to establish two such distinctive groups for purposes of research.

Ethnographic studies document preliterate tribes whose members find no pleasure in dominating other persons or in hunting and killing. All they ask is to be left in peace, a state they usually can achieve only by retreating to inaccessible territories. Anthropologist Geoffrey Gorer (1966) found that the distinguishing trait of peace-loving tribes is an enormous gusto for sensual pleasures—eating, drinking, sex, and laughter. Such tribes make little distinction between the social characteristics of men and women. No child grows up being told that "All men do X" or that "No proper woman does Y."

Violence will be controlled only when societies no longer insist that virility and similar masculine status symbols be tied to demonstrations of aggression. The paradox is that avoidance of violence either will have to be universal or the violent will prevail. The alternative, asking for violence to be expressed toward only real enemies, but to be controlled in terms of criminal acts, is a condition no contemporary industrialized society has been able to achieve.

Johan Galtung (1990) suggests that attention ought to be paid to reducing any aspect of a culture that can be used to legitimize violence. He points to the principle of *herrenvolk* that prevailed in Nazi Germany and allowed its people to define themselves as above the dictates of moral law. Symbols such as stars, crosses and crescents, flags, anthems, military parades, and ubiquitous portraits of the leader—these often are relied upon to support violent behavior directed against those defined as outsiders.

In a recent comprehensive review of violence patterns, Randall Collins concludes that it is the exception, not the rule, and does not occur easily or automatically. Collins maintains that antagonists by nature are fearful and tense and that their anxieties typically result in atrocities against the weak, ritualized exhibitions before audiences, and clandestine acts of terrorism and murder (Collins, 2008).

Index Crimes: Homicide, Assault, and Rape

Three behaviors generally are viewed as serious violent crimes in America—homicide, assault, and rape. But we would stress that what is labeled "violent crime," as we noted in earlier chapters, varies by ideology, time, locale, and observer. We consider assault a serious violent crime, while failure to provide medical treatment to a pregnant woman who does not have health insurance is defined as an acceptable consequence of a market economy. The assault may involve nothing more than a pushing bout between adolescents, while the failure to provide the medical care may result in what could have been an avoidable death of the woman or of the fetus that she was carrying.

Besides, many forms of interpersonal violence receive little attention. Violence that takes place within families and among acquaintances rarely becomes known to the criminal justice system. In addition, there are more than 100,000 deaths each year from work-related accidents, many of which result from illegal workplace conditions. About 30,000 deaths yearly are believed to be caused by faulty consumer products (Coleman, 2002).

Homicide

The unlawful killing of one human being by another constitutes homicide. The killing must have occurred after, not before or during the birth of the victim. The criminal act need not be the sole cause of death, but only a recognizable causal factor. The legal definition of homicide also requires that the death occur within a year and a day from the time the injury was inflicted. In the United States there is no statute of limitations for homicide; that is, no matter how much time has elapsed since the killing, the offender still can be prosecuted.

Homicide traditionally is broken down into four categories: murder, manslaughter, excusable homicide, and justifiable homicide. First-degree murder includes the attributes of premeditation and malice aforethought, the intent to kill. Premeditation refers to the prior formation of that intent; even a moment of such intent antecedent to the act fulfills the requirement. Malice aforethought is the manifestation of a deliberate intention to take the life of a fellow creature. In New York, after the 9/11 disaster the legislature added "killing in the furtherance of an act of terrorism" to the embrace of first-degree murder.

Second-degree murder includes malice aforethought but not premeditation. An excusable homicide is a death that occurs as a consequence of an accident perpetrated by a person performing a lawful act with ordinary caution. A boxer whose punch kills his opponent has committed an excusable homicide, as has a driver who operates his vehicle safely but runs over a child who recklessly dashed out in front of the car. Justifiable homicide involves a legal act, such as the infliction of the death penalty on a convicted felon or a killing in self-defense. In recent years, many states have abandoned the requirement that a threatened person retreat if possible and enacted "stand your ground" self-defense statutes which legalize killing a person who is seen as endangering you. Opponents label these "Shoot First Laws" (Fontaine, 2010).

There also is a felony-murder doctrine, which holds that if a death occurs during the commission of a felony (say, for instance, a burglary), the perpetrator of the felony is chargeable with first-degree murder. A person setting fire to a barn might unintentionally burn to death a vagrant sleeping inside. If so, the arsonist can be charged with murder although the criminal act lacked both homicidal premeditation and malice aforethought. The felony-murder doctrine has been said to be the "most persistently and widely criticized feature of American law" (Binder, 2004:84; see also Binder, 2008).

In 2005, the Colorado Supreme Court remanded the case of Lisl Auman, who had been imprisoned for eight years on a felony-murder charge. Auman and two male companions burglarized the house of her ex-boyfriend, retrieving some of her belongings as well as taking other things. After a wild chase, she was arrested and handcuffed in the back seat of a patrol car. Five minutes later, one of the men who had been with her shot a policeman and then killed himself. Auman was convicted of first-degree murder and sentenced to life in prison without the possibility of parole. The appellate court had no quarrel with the felony-murder element in her case, but found that the jury should have been instructed to determine whether she knowingly had entered the dwelling intending to steal or only to retrieve her own possessions (*Auman v. People,* 2005). Rather than holding a new trial, the authorities entered a bargain with Auman that led to her parole with supervision and a reporting requirement for the next nine years.

Today, some states specify only a limited number of the more serious crimes as coming under the felony-murder doctrine. Highlight 11.1 tells of a case involving a 12-year-old tried for felony-murder in Oregon.

Manslaughter lacks the requirement of malice aforethought. In first-degree manslaughter, often called voluntary manslaughter, death results from conditions under which a fatality might reasonably have been anticipated, as in a knife fight. Illustrating first-degree manslaughter was the sentencing of two 20-year-old men and a 21-year-old woman in Florida to 15-year prison terms for having removed stop signs from a road intersection as a prank. Soon afterward, three teenagers entering the intersection drove into the path of an eight-ton truck and were killed.

Second-degree, or involuntary manslaughter, involves circumstances less closely related to the lethal outcome, as when a person dies from injuries sustained in a fall during a fist fight. A recent four-year sentence for involuntary manslaughter involved a woman and her husband whose dog broke its leash and mauled a resident of their apartment building to death (*People v. Noel,* 2005). Negligent manslaughter is used in some jurisdictions to prosecute driving fatalities.

Highlight 11.1
Boy, 12, Is Found Guilty of Murder in Fire

HILLSBORO, Ore., (Reuters). A State Judge today found a 12-year-old boy guilty of murder for setting an apartment house fire that killed eight Mexican immigrants last year.

The boy, Ray DeFord, who was 11 at the time of the fire, was found guilty of one count of arson and eight counts each of felony murder and criminally negligent homicide. He spent much of the trial doodling and showed no reaction when the verdict was pronounced by Judge Timothy Alexander of the Washington County Circuit, who heard the juvenile case without a jury.

Source: *New York Times*, August 22, 1997, p. 14. Article reproduced with the permission of Reuters.

Homicide Correlates

In the United States, the South shows the highest rate of murder, a matter that has led commentators to tag the region as marked by a "subculture of violence." Others insist that poverty and ethnic inequality, not regional culture, are the major contributors to the higher level of violence in the South (Huff-Corzine, Corzine & Moore, 1991).

Lifetime murder-risk probabilities are based on the likelihood that a person born in a particular year will become a murder victim over the course of that person's lifespan, assuming that the murder rate remains stable. It is sobering to realize that the danger for an African-American urban male, a member of the highest risk group, is on the order of one chance in 24 of being murdered. Native-American males are also at a high lifetime risk (one chance in 57) as are African-American females (one chance in 98). Despite media attention to the killings of adolescents and young adults, less than one-fourth of a person's lifetime homicide risk is experienced before the person's 25th birthday, except for Native-American males. The annual (in contrast to the lifetime) risk for the "average" person of being a homicide victim is about 1 in 10,000 (Reiss & Roth, 1993:62-63).

Trends in Homicide

Homicide—especially murder—is regarded as the most reliable measure of criminal activity because almost all the offenses become known to the police. This is not to say that every murder is discovered. Some killings may go into the record books as suicides or accidents. A husband or a wife may "accidentally on purpose" back out of the garage and run over an out-of-favor spouse. Another difficulty with homicide rates lies in the usual failure to discriminate among the kinds of events. There are infanticides, organized crime slayings, and lethal juvenile gang drive-by shootings, among many other forms. And there are definitional issues. Should the more than 3,000 persons killed by terrorists in the 9/11 World Trade Center disaster be counted as murder victims?

The record shows no consistent pattern for homicide in the United States. In recent times, the peak homicide rate (10.2 per 100,000 population) appeared in 1980. It had fallen to 7.9 per 100,000 by 1985. It then climbed 24 percent to 9.8 in 1991 but dropped markedly in later years, reaching a level of 5.5 in 2000, and in 2008 it achieved a new low of 5.4, the lowest rate since 1967.

The best guess regarding the reasons for the decline was that the market for crack cocaine, which produced numerous killings, had fallen off and dealers had become more secretive and less combative (Jacobs, 2000). As Alfred Blumstein and Richard Rosenfeld (1999:1211-1212) put the matter: "Whatever the drawbacks of flipping hamburgers or bagging groceries, kids are far less likely to kill or be killed working in a fast food restaurant than in selling crack on the street corner outside." Blumstein and Rosenfeld note wryly that, when homicide rates go down, politicians and law enforcement agencies point to their programs as responsible for the good news. But when the rates go up, the same sources maintain that conditions beyond their control, such as the age structure of the population and the disintegration of traditional family life, caused the increase.

Changes in domestic living arrangements also have contributed to the downturn in the homicide rate. There has been a sustained drop in killings during the past two decades that involve spouses, ex-spouses, and domestic partners. This decrease has been especially pronounced among African-Americans and appears to be related to a corresponding drop in "domesticity," that is, declining marriage rates, increasing age at marriage, and high divorce rates (Dugan, Nagin & Rosenfeld, 1999). Finally, higher rates of incarceration likely have played a role in lowering homicide rates by removing from street life some persons who were more likely than most others to kill.

Patterns in Criminal Homicide

The classic study of murder was conducted by Marvin Wolfgang (1958), who examined police records for all homicides (588) in Philadelphia for a five-year period. The study's general conclusions remain valid today. Offenders were 75 percent African-American and 82 percent male. Saturday was the most likely day for murder, and more than one-half of the offenses occurred between 8 p.m. and 2 a.m.

Men were likely to be homicide victims on the street, while women usually were killed at home, most often in the bedroom. Men most frequently were victims of fatal domestic attacks in the kitchen, and most often were killed with a kitchen knife. Alcohol was present in 64 percent of all homicide cases, and 44 percent involved alcohol consumption by both the victim and the offender.

Of the offenders, 64 percent had a previous arrest and two-thirds of those arrests were for violent offenses. Almost two-thirds of the homicides were between acquaintances, including many between close friends or relatives (a percentage that has declined somewhat over the years). When the victim was a female, 84 percent of the assailants were friends, relatives, or acquaintances. Wolfgang's data also indicated that homicide is an intraracial event—94 percent of the cases involved victims and offenders of the same race; 35 years later precisely the same figure was reported for intraracial homicides in St. Louis (Decker, 1993).

Wolfgang (1958:245) introduced the concept of victim-precipitation to suggest that "the victim may be a major precipitating causes of his own demise." The victim-precipitated cases are those in which the victim was the first to show and use a deadly weapon or to strike a blow in an altercation. Wolfgang found that about one-quarter of the Philadelphia homicides were victim-precipitated.

A concern with saving face is an important factor in homicides. So long as each party responds to an increase in the level of violence instigated by the other, a spiral of violence culminating in death can be the ultimate outcome. Homicides reflect personal values, most notably those derived from the masculine culture. "Nobody can say that to me and get away with it!" is a common expression before the escalation of a confrontation that ends in death. Some men, however, are able to avoid such situations by a repertoire of tactics. They may walk away from the threat or divert it with a joke or some other gambit that takes the bite out of the confrontation. For others, such avoidance would be regarded as intolerable cowardice.

Recently, police in medium-sized cities were declaring that many more murders than in the past were resulting from petty disputes. In Milwaukee, in 2006, the following circumstances marked various murders: One woman killed a friend after they argued over a silk dress. A man killed a neighbor whose 10-year old son had mistakenly used his dish soap. Two men argued over a cell phone and, pulling out their guns, killed a 13-year-old girl in the crossfire (Zernke, 2006).

Serial Killings and Mass Murder

Serial killings and mass murders get far more attention than their frequency merits, undoubtedly because they are so shocking. Serial killers commit repeat murders over a period of time. They account for only four-tenths of one percent of the annual homicide rate (Schlesinger, 2001) and they generally murder their victims within an hour after they abduct them (Godwin & Rosen, 2005). Researchers distinguish a subgroup of serial killers that they designate as "spree killers," persons who kill three or more victims at different locations within a period of hours or a few days (Hickey, 2009).

Mass murderers are those who kill multiple victims in a single episode; they claim even fewer victims than serial murderers (Duwe, 2007). Jane Caputi advises that we ought to cease our "aggrandizing focus" on such monsters. To do so, she claims, "would not be a self-defeating kind of response that pretends that they don't exist, but an active denial, one that negates their lure, and does not perpetuate, but diminishes their reality" (Caputi, 1990:11). It has been maintained that the attention that serial killers can anticipate is a strong prod to their death-dealing behavior.

Others also have deplored the public frenzy associated with multiple killings. Sociologist Barry Glassner (1999) labels public apprehension about serial and mass murderers as one of the "false fears" in regard to crime. He argues that spectacular offenses divert public concern from much more serious problems. Instead of worrying about X-raying Halloween candy to detect evidence of tampering, for instance, he believes that people should worry about the millions of persons in their midst without health insurance.

HIGHLIGHT 11.2
COLOMBIA Serial Killer Murders 140 People

A 42-year-old Colombian man, Luis Alfredo Garavito, confessed to having killed 140 children, usually between the ages of 8 and 16. Garavito had posed as a beggar, a cripple, and a monk at various times to gain the confidence of his victims. Their bodies later were discovered with their throats slit and showing signs of beatings and mutilation. Twenty-five skeletons of youngsters he had killed were dug up in the city of Pereira, where a mural carved into the side of an overlooking hillside now commemorates the victims.

The children were mostly from poor families and worked as street vendors. They were allowed by their parents to roam freely, often with instructions that they beg money from tourists.

Mass murders, unlike serial killings, usually are readily resolved because the offense typically is perpetrated in an open setting and ends with the offender committing suicide or being shot by the police. The mass killer may have been propelled into the murderous foray by a stressful event, such as being fired from a job. An examination of 102 incidents of what was termed "rampage homicides" found that in at least one-half of the cases the assailant had shown earlier signs of mental disturbance. The killers were likely to have military backgrounds, to kill strangers, to be white (by a large margin), and to be older than the average murderer (Fessenden, 2000).

The deadliest episode of mass murder in the United States took place on the campus of Virginia Tech University in Blacksburg, West Virginia, on April 5, 2007, when Seung-Hui Cho slaughtered 32 persons and wounded 23 others before killing himself. Cho, a senior majoring in English, had a history of mental problems (Roy, 2009).

Serial killers tend to be highly mobile. Their murders usually lack an obvious motive since there had been no prior association between the victims and the offender. They frequently will prey upon drifters, teenage runaways, and others whose disappearance is less likely to provoke investigation (see Highlight 11.2 for a serial killing report from Colombia). Perpetrators of mass murders and serial killings range from the sadist who stalks prostitutes to the disgruntled employee who resolves workplace grievances with an AK-47e to armed robbers who kill witnesses to their crimes (Levin, 2008; Shon & Milovanovic, 2006). In 2002, the Canadian police arrested a 52-year-old nightclub owner on whose suburban property they discovered the bodies of 15 women, mostly drug addicts and prostitutes. It was suspected that he had killed an additional 48 women and fed their bodies to pigs on his farm (Krauss, 2002).

Explaining Homicide

The newcomer to criminology sometimes proclaims that those who kill must be "sick"; murderers must be driven by irrational forces. This description is not an accurate characterization of the run-of-the-mill killer. As alien as murder may seem to most of us, it preponderantly is a product of circumstances that generally make sense to the perpetrator. Donald Black (1993) insists that murder typically is a form of "self-help," the method a person who feels beleaguered uses to resolve the situation. Jack Katz (1988) interprets murder as an act of "righteous slaughter," done because the perpetrator believes that the killing is essential to achieve or to maintain a certain position, such as one of self-respect. The killer typically believes that the victim deserves his or her fate. "If we stick to the details of the events," Katz (1988:12) writes, "we can see offenders defending the good, even in what initially appears to be crazy circumstances." But Kenneth Polk noted that, while there is an element of truth in Katz's point, it falls short of explaining most homicides. What Katz did, Polk (1993:194) maintains, was to "first theorize about the nature of homicide, then [he] selectively sought out illustrations of his point to 'verify' his idealized conception of how the act proceeds."

Actor Sidney Poitier in his autobiography offers the observation that "people who kill aren't evil twenty-four hours a day." He adds: "The dark side in each of us operates behind masks of varying complexity, coming to the fore when we elect to use its services. We all have a reservoir of rage, dissatisfaction, self-loathing, unhappiness, intolerable feelings of inadequacy. They make us capable of terrible things" (Poitier, 2000:220-221).

Five postulates are said by sociologist Leonard Beeghley to offer the best theoretical construct for interpreting murder. He maintains that the high rate of homicide in the United States reflects the impact of (1) greater availability of guns; (2) the illegal drug market; (3) greater racial discrimination; (4) greater exposure to violence; and (5) greater economic inequality (Beeghley, 2003).

These contemporary explanations of murder, however, have been challenged by recent research that calculates murder rates over the centuries. Murder was much more common in the Middle Ages than it is today (Dean, 2007), but the rate dropped precipitously in the seventeenth, eighteenth, and nineteenth centuries. Most theories would predict that the opposite would have happened, that murder was supposed to rise as family and community bonds in rural areas broke up and urbanization took hold. One of the more plausible explanations of the decrease in crime after the Middle Ages can be found not in urbanization patterns or patterns of economic growth but in an internal, psychological shift in attitudes toward crime. In the Middle Ages most killings occurred in front of many witnesses and were carried out to settle disputes. Other means to resolve differences, such as civil suits, would come to replace violent actions (Johnson & Monkkenon, 1996).

Subculture of Violence: Jerry

Jerry is a prison inmate serving time for murder who has been visited by one of the authors of this text. Jerry's imprisonment was the outcome of a trivial altercation. He had been sharing a trailer with another man who was moving out. Both had been drinking and when they disagreed about the ownership of a small table, the victim-to-be threatened Jerry with a gun. Jerry convinced him to put away the weapon, and then proceeded to beat him to death, explaining that the man should have known better than to point a gun at him if he was not going to use it. When Jerry was released on bail, several relatives of the victim appeared at his trailer and fired weapons at him. Jerry caught one of them after he had exhausted his ammunition. He held the man down with his foot and shot him to death. He expressed respect for this victim, concluding that those who initiated the attack against him were "doing what they had to," because he had killed a member of their family. Shortly after his admission to prison, Jerry killed an inmate he said had stolen something from him, proclaiming that "they wasn't going to make no girl of me. You let somebody steal your stuff and they will try anything."

By outward appearance, Jerry is a pleasant man. He often displayed qualities, such as loyalty, honesty, candor, and humor that were admired by visiting criminology students. Jerry says he regrets his acts and feels some sorrow for the victims, but that he would do nothing differently under similar circumstances.

Insult and Homicide

Equally telling is the story of the homicide that led to the first instance in the United States of a survivor receiving state-paid victim compensation. Robert Harris's (names have been changed) telephone call to a woman he had been seeing was answered by her neighbor, Roberta Jansen, who asked him to stop annoying the woman. Harris told Ms. Jansen, she later would write in her police report, that she was "a hoor." She informed her husband that she had been insulted, and when Harris appeared that evening, her husband demanded an apology. When Harris refused to apologize, Jansen removed his belt and moved toward him. Harris had gotten a job that day as a security guard and been given a revolver. He pulled it out and killed Jansen.

The public defender believed that Harris might win an acquittal on grounds of self-defense, but he knew that he would make a terrible witness. Harris's only concern was that a jury might believe, as the police claimed, that he had shot twice at Jansen, a matter that he regarded as an unacceptable reflection on his marksmanship. The public defender had to negotiate a plea of manslaughter and the long prison term that went with it rather than risk a trial (Geis, 1998). The case illustrates the ready recourse to violence by both men involved in it, as well as the more subtle role Ms. Jansen played in seeking redress rather than letting the matter drop without informing her volatile husband.

Homicide Theory

Subcultural theories such as Miller's (1958) focal concerns and Wolfgang and Ferracuti's (1967) subculture of violence are consistent with the bulk of data regarding homicide (see Chapter 8 for a review of these perspectives). But both theories are susceptible to charges of being a circular argument that at its core declares that violent people are people who commit violent acts (Brookman, 2005:109).

Structural explanations of homicide maintain that economic inequality leads to violence through a process of relative deprivation. A person resents that his or her share of material resources is slight relative to others. Violence triggered by relative deprivation typically is directed against those close at hand rather than at the real but more distant oppressors. Ramiro Martinez (1996) found that as there is an increase in the income gap within the Hispanic population (though not necessarily between Hispanics and the general population), the rate of killings increases, with low educational attainment being the strongest predictor of homicide.

A study that sought to explain the striking difference between African-American, Latino, and white non-Latino homicide rates concluded that all of the white-Latino differential and about half of the white-black gap could be reduced if the social situation of minorities was raised to a level currently enjoyed by mainstream whites. Julie Phillips (2002:353) found that "if white Americans were subjected to the same social pressures and structural disadvantages faced by minority populations, they would exhibit correspondingly high rates of homicide." The handicaps examined included unemployment, poverty, income inequality, substandard housing, and inferior education.

A notable series of studies of the impact of immigration into the United States by minority groups found that the influx of newcomers into Miami and El Paso did not result in a higher rate of homicide. The existence of large welcoming minority populations eased the transition for the immigrants. So too did the fact the new arrivals felt that they had better prospects in the United States than they did in their own countries (Lee, 2003; Martinez, Lee & Nielsen, 2004).

Lower rates of violence have been found to exist in urban neighborhoods that show a strong sense of community and shared values, neighborhoods in which most parents discipline children for missing school or scrawling graffiti and confront those who are creating disturbances in public space. The best predictor of the violent crime rate was labeled "collective efficacy," a term used to indicate a sense of trust, common values, and cohesion in neighborhoods (Sampson et al., 1997:918). The essential element of "collective efficacy" was a willingness by residents to intervene in the lives of their children to halt behaviors such as truancy and loitering on street corners. The study results were said to undercut theories that focus exclusively on poverty, unemployment, single-parent households, or racial discrimination, although such circumstances clearly can feed into the nature of neighborhood life. Some of the neighborhoods studied by Sampson and his co-workers were largely African-American and poverty-stricken but showed low rates of violence. John Hepp, building on the theme, discovered that the greater the income inequality in a neighborhood the higher the rate of violence. Presumably the unequal distribution of wealth also contributes to reduced collective efficacy (Hepp, 2007).

In another study, R. Maria Garcia and two colleagues sought to determine more exactly an element of efficacy as it relates to violent crime. Residents in 45 Philadelphia neighborhoods were asked if they agreed or disagreed with the statement: "Most people in my neighborhood can be trusted." Not unexpectedly, those neighborhoods showing the greatest level of such trust showed the lowest rates of violence (Garcia, Taylor & Lawton, 2007). It is not clear whether the absence of trust was brought about by the local violence or vice versa, but the results contradict the theme that street crime tends to unite a neighborhood against predators in its midst.

Though they themselves do not use drugs, people are 11 times more likely to be killed if they live in homes where drugs are present. When alcoholism exists in a home, non-drinkers living there are 70 percent more likely to be killed than non-drinkers in a home without alcoholism present (Rivara et al., 1997).

Marital status is one of the stronger correlates with homicide. Kevin Breault and Augustine Kposowa (1997) found that divorced women are more likely to be homicide victims than married females, while single women do not differ from married women in their victimization rate. The major changes in female roles and status since the 1970s have had no discernible impact on female homicide victimization rates or on the number of women killed by partners (Marvell & Moody, 1999). For males, single men are 91 percent more likely to die from murder than married men. For divorced men the rate is 72 percent higher than for married men. Routine activities theorists maintain that the low rate for single women occurs because they are much less involved in domestic violence and because they less often engage in the kinds of risky behavior that gets men killed. Examining routine activities theory in terms of homicides, Terance Miethe and his co-workers faulted the theory because data showed no notable changes in homicide patterns despite significant alterations in activity patterns over time (Miethe, Regoeczi & Drass, 2005).

All criminology theories attempt to provide an understanding of forms of violence, including homicide and the other behaviors considered in this chapter. Each has virtues; each deficiencies. Looking at the full spectrum, Margaret Zahn and her colleagues concluded:

> These theories are difficult to integrate into a parsimonious explanation because they define the phenomenon differently; use multiple levels of analysis and multiple variables that frequently do not cross over from one theory to another; the underlying assumptions differ; and evidentiary bases exist in various bodies of literature that are not easily linked to each other or to existing theories (Zahn, Brownstein & Jackson, 2004:260).

They also point out that the theories fall short because they focus only on violence that is illegal or deviant rather than on all forms of violence that inflict harm.

Assault and Battery

Broadly defined, assault is a threat or an attempt to do bodily harm to another while battery is the actual conduct, though in common usage the distinction usually is between simple and aggravated assault, with battery being implied if the act has been carried out. The Uniform Crime Reports annually show about one million aggravated assaults, which easily qualifies assault as the most serious violent crime. There are far more cases of simple assault, which do not involve the use of dangerous weapons, such as guns, knives, and tire irons, but these are not recorded in the UCR. Victim surveys indicate that about one-half million assault cases are not reported to the authorities each year. Eric Baumer (2002) found that the more affluent and the most disadvantaged segments of society are least likely to report simple assaults, and suggests that they probably are more tolerant of such incidents.

The typical aggravated assault closely parallels homicides in terms of the conditions causing it. The distinction is whether the injuries turn out to be fatal. That outcome can be influenced by factors such as the speed and quality of available emergency medical services (Smith, 2000).

Terrorism

Terrorism has four significant elements. First, it involves an act of violence intended to create fear in those exposed to it. It targets both active opponents as well as innocent victims, and it has a political purpose. The U. S. Department of State declares that terrorism is "premeditated, politically motivated violence perpetrated against non-combatant targets by substantial groups or clandestine agents, usually intended to influence an audience." Cindy Combs (2006:1) offers a more expansive definition. Terrorism, she observes, is "a synthesis of war and theater, a dramatization of the most proscribed kind of violence—that which is perpetrated on innocent victims—typically played before an audience in the hope of creating a mood of fear for political purposes."

Victims of terrorism usually belong to an entity that the terrorist believes represents a force that must be overcome. The victims are seen as symbols; the aim is to send an ideological message by killing or harming them. History teaches us that terrorism acts often will produce counter-terrorism, retaliation of a similar or more devastating kind.

Terrorism has elements that differ from other law violations. Richard Rosenfeld (2002) observes that terrorism deserves a high priority in criminology research because it is qualitatively different from the common forms of violence and does not fit easily with many current criminological theories, such as the development and life-course perspective, social control theories, or those stressing self-control. (See also Savelsberg, 2006).

Terrorism remains a particularly difficult concept to pin down. One writer notes: "This has never been, since the topic began to command serious attention, some golden age in which terrorism was easy to define, or, for that mater, to comprehend." (Cooper, 2001:881). Cooper points out that one person's terrorist will be another person's freedom fighter. He put forth his own definition: "Terrorism is the intentional generation of massive fear by human beings for the purpose of securing or maintaining control over other human beings" (Cooper, 2001:883; for other definitions and a discussion titled "Why Is Terrorism So Difficult to Define?" Whitaker, 2001; see also Young, 2006).

Victims of terrorism, as David Shichor points out, "might feel more helpless than victims of street crimes because they have less control over their own fate. They cannot identify anything that they have don wrong or could have done better to avoid victimization and they do not have clear guidelines for protecting themselves from further attacks" (Shichor, 2007:275).

Terrorists often invoke divine approval for their behavior. The United States' war in Iraq had been pressed on the ground that Iraq's leader had accumulated a record of murderous genocide against the Kurdish minority in his country. Iraq was also said to be stockpiling nuclear armaments and lethal poisons and that these could be used against the United States or Israel, America's close ally, or sold to others who would so employ them. Iraq also was said to have aided the terrorists who attacked the World Trade Center. When the allegation of Iraqi involvement in the September 11, 2001 assaults and the possession of weapons of mass destruction proved to be inaccurate, the rationale for the war was redefined as an effort to bring peace and democracy to the Middle East by establishing Iraq as a model of what could be achieved.

In waging war against Iraq, the United States itself and its leaders were regarded by some people as launching a preemptive terrorist campaign (Falk, 2003; Pious, 2006). There are several important criminological lessons here. The first is that it often depends on where you live and the values that you hold how you will decide who the terrorists truly are. During the second World War, Germany's leaders engaged in the cold-blooded slaughter of six million Jews, the most awful national act in the history of mankind (Friedrichs, 2000). Yet, Nazi sympathizers in France denounced the underground resistance against the Germans as "terrorism" (Kaplan, 2000:54).

Rape

An older definition defined rape as sexual knowledge of a female forcibly and against her will. This definition has given way in most states to gender-neutral statutory definitions that embrace homosexual rape, sexual assault of females upon males, and nonconsensual sexual activity other than penile-vaginal intercourse. All states now outlaw marital rape—sex between a woman and her husband induced by force or fear; none had criminalized this act 40 years ago (Martin, Taft & Resick, 2007). Ten to fourteen percent of married women are believed to have been victims of marital rape. They typically do not leave the marriage until they see an increase in the frequency and severity of the aggression they suffer (Bergen, 1996).

Reports from South Africa indicate a growing focus on the rape of males by males, a "hidden crime" which is said to occur beyond institutional settings and often in connection with car hijackings and burglaries (Davis & Klopper, 2002). Virtually all criminologists now regard rape as a crime of violence rather than a sexual crime, although sexual degradation often is an essential component of the offense.

Rape may have increased, paradoxically, because of the greater degree of sexual license now in evidence. Eugene Kanin (1985) found that in the past men were more likely to desist from aggressive sexual acts against women they deemed to be chaste or who otherwise desired to refrain from sexual intercourse. Today, some men assume that all women are "fair game," that all beyond a certain age are willing to engage voluntarily in sexual intercourse and that the rejection of their overture represents a rejection of them and not of the behavior. This may produce anger and frustration that could have been diverted in earlier times by blaming social standards rather than personal rejection. Women emphasize, and the law clearly agrees, that they always retain the right to say "no," and that men must learn at their peril to heed such a response.

A recent comprehensive national study of the experiences of 4,446 college women found 27.7 percent agreeing to the statement that during the past seven months "someone made you have sexual intercourse by using force or threatening to harm you." The result extrapolates to 350 rape episodes in somewhat less than a full school year on a campus of 10,000 students. The incidents divided about evenly between completed rapes and attempts. Though what happened to them fits the legal definition of the crime of rape, about half of the women did not see it that way. This was a function of factors such as embarrassment, a failure to clearly understand what rape is, self-blame, and/or not wanting to define someone they know as a criminal. Nine of ten of the assailants, the study found, were persons known to the victims, such as a boyfriend, a former boyfriend, a classmate, or a co-worker (Fisher, Cullen & Turner, 2000). Another study found that alcohol use was a paramount ingredient in sexual assaults against college women (Combs-Lane & Smith, 2002).

Catharine MacKinnon (1992:189) has pointed out that rape differs from other offenses in one notable aspect: When you are walking down the street and "somebody jumps you and takes your money, the law does not assume you were a walking philanthropist, nor do the police question how many times this has happened to you or whether you gave to United Charities last week," MacKinnon (1992:189) notes sarcastically. MacKinnon is absolutely correct in her analysis, but the difficulty with rape prosecutions is not notably with the "jumping out" cases of sexual assault but those involving circumstances in which it becomes difficult to prove beyond a reasonable doubt whether the sexual act was, in MacKinnon's term, "charitable" or whether it was forced.

Some people see a growing antagonism between men and women as contributing to the rape rate. As women strive for equality in the workplace, some men feel threatened and displaced, and may take out such feelings by aggressive acts (Barnett, 2004). The reported increase in rape rates also may be a function of more

HIGHLIGHT 11.3
ITALY Rape and Blue Jeans

Italy's Supreme Court overturned the conviction of a 45-year-old driving instructor who had allegedly raped his 18-year-old student. A lower court ruling had sentenced the man to two years and eight months in prison. The appellate ruling was based on the ground that the woman was wearing blue jeans. The court reasoned that "it is a fact of common experience" that tight blue jeans cannot be removed "without the active cooperation of the person who is wearing them" and that, therefore, the sexual intercourse must have been consensual. The court also made note of the fact that neither the accused nor the alleged victim showed bruising.

The decision met with indignation. One observer pointed out that the ruling had done something very rare in Italian life: it has united virtually all people, albeit in opposition to the court decision. The female members of the national legislature, all dressed in blue jeans, staged a protest, and talk show hosts and others sarcastically labeled blue jeans as the modern chastity belt (Calavita, 2001).

sensitivity by law enforcement officials to the plight of the rape victim. In early days (and to some extent today), there was a strong tendency by the criminal justice system to shift blame onto the victim and to subject her to further stress and embarrassment. Victims of rape were twice violated, first by the rapists and then by the justice system. The prospect of insensitive police questioning, courtroom attacks on their character and previous behavior, and innuendos regarding their consent to sexual relations deterred women from reporting rapes (for an example of such a situation see Highlight 11.3). The growing willingness to report also has been brought about by a greater frankness about sexual matters as well as the establishment of rape crisis centers, the use of female officers to interview victims, and the passage of rape shield laws that bar inquiry in court into the sexual history of the complainant (Caringella, 2009).

Men are responsible for virtually all of the rape offenses. The one percent of women accused of rape almost invariably are accessories; they may, for instance, hold a gun on the victim while their male companion rapes her. The 20- to 24-year-old group contributes the largest number of offenders. Overwhelmingly, victims and offenders share racial identification. When rape crosses racial lines, it is dictated primarily by opportunity for interpersonal contact. Rape most certainly reflects attitudes toward women as Highlight 11.4, a report from China, illustrates.

HIGHLIGHT 11.4
CHINA A Case of Rape

> Rape usually remains unreported in China because to bring forward a complaint may seriously damage the reputation of the accuser, however innocent. Gil and Anderson (1999) tell of the forcible rape of Alice, a young woman who secured a summer job in an ice-cream factory before beginning college. Her employer relied on her traditional Chinese respect for older persons and people in authority to rape her when other employees had gone home for the two-hour lunch break and she stayed behind rather than venture outside into a heavy rain.
>
> The next day Alice visited a nurse she knew to ask if she might be pregnant. "You were right in not telling," the nurse said. "There is a law against rape, but it would be very difficult for you to prove that this man did it. And you would have been shamed and, too, your family. Forget it ever happened" (Gil & Anderson, 1999:1160).

Date rape concerns have increased with the growing involvement of several drugs, including GHB (gamma hydroxybutyrate) and Rohypnol (the trade name for flunitazepam, sometimes called "roofies") that can render the person who ingests them unconscious. In large or poorly synthesized doses, the drugs can be lethal (Adams, 2007) Three young men were convicted in Detroit in 2000 of involuntary manslaughter for spiking the drink of a 15-year-old girl with a "date rape" drug; she died afterwards. Girls and women have been advised to cap bottles between sips, never to leave their drink unattended, and not to accept a drink from someone they do not completely trust.

Explaining Rape

Forcible rape is an offense typically interpreted in terms of the offenders' personal pathologies. Psychological profiles of rapists find them to be driven by a quest for power, by anger, or by sadism. A publication issued by the American Psychological Association notes that "rape is part of a general antisocial, aggressive, and risk-tolerant lifestyle" (Lalumiere et al., 2005:184).

Rape is perpetrated disproportionately by lower-class, minority, urban youth, who experience an environment hospitable to crimes of violence. Some men learn to use violence to achieve goals and to view females as sexual objects. They see access to sexual contact as a test of virility and regard force to attain this goal as acceptable.

Other scholars adopt a very different position. William Sanders believes that rapists by and large are inadequate males, whose feelings of inferiority push them toward anger and aggression against weaker targets. Sanders' (1983:273) view of "the rapist as wimp" relies on the following reasoning:

> In the world of violent men, rapists are considered punks and generally low life. We find this in prison where robbers, killers, and other violent characters hold rapists in very low esteem, about one rung above child molesters who are at the bottom of the heap.

Studying rape in Sweden, a country known for its sex-role equality, Gilbert Geis and Robley Geis (1979) concluded that the high frequency of rape in Stockholm was an artifact of the greater number of "rape-enabling" situations characteristic of the lifestyles of Swedish women who are much less reluctant than American women to invite a person they barely know to their apartment. The researchers suggest that the ratio of rapes per at-risk conditions rather than the number of rape incidents per population is a more relevant measure. They also note that culture conflict may account for part of the rape situation in Sweden. A large proportion of rapes are perpetrated by foreign males who misread friendly acts by Swedish women as sexual invitations.

Explanations for rape noted by Lee Ellis (1989) include feminist theory, social learning theory, and evolutionary theory.

Feminist theory considers rape to be the result of long and deep-rooted traditions in which males have dominated political, social, and economic life. Women are viewed as little more than property and as such they have to depend upon particular men for protection against other men.

Social learning theory portrays rape as part of a pattern of aggressive behavior by men that is learned and reinforced through four interrelated processes: (1) by imitating rape scenes and other acts of violence toward women that are seen in person, conveyed by others, or depicted by the mass media, (2) by associating sexuality and violence, (3) by adopting "rape myths," such as "No means Yes" and "Women secretly desire to be raped," and (4) by desensitizing men to the pain, fear, and humiliation of sexual aggression.

The evolutionary or sociobiological theory maintains that the lower degree of certainty that fathers (in contrast to mothers) have that they are a child's parent induces a tendency in men to evolve traits that increase their chances to have a large number of children rather than to take diligent care of a few. By way of illustration, the greatest known number of offspring fathered by a human male is 888, while 69 is the greatest number of children ever borne by a human female (Daly & Wilson, 1978). According to evolutionary theorists, the tension between different approaches to sex by males and females is responsible for much of the frustration, compromise, and deception that both sexes exhibit during courtship and, in some ways, throughout life.

Family Violence

Sentimentalists typically think of the family as a bastion of love, support, and nurturing and, most assuredly, there are families that show an abundance of all of these characteristics. On the other hand, a person is most likely to be subjected to interpersonal violence within his or her own family. Moreover, it tends to be an intergenerational problem whereby children reared in violent homes are at risk of violence plaguing their adult family relationships. Because they transpire in private space, such offenses are substantially less likely than more public law-breaking to be reported to and pursued by the criminal justice system.

Child Abuse

Children are easy targets of violence because they are incapable of offering much resistance. All of us have heard stories from friends (if we have not had the experience ourselves) of how they were persistently beaten by their father (or, less often, their mother) until they realized that they were strong enough to fight back—and either did so or said so. Thereafter, the beatings often stopped. Children can, at least at times, be a frustrating burden, emotionally and financially, and frustration often is a precursor to violence. Finally, of course, they are handy targets. The more parents and children are able to separate themselves during periods of tension—in houses with many rooms--the less likely parents are to take out their aggravations on a child.

A "cycle of violence" appears to be associated with child abuse. Cathy Widom and Michael Maxfield (2001), following 1,575 persons from childhood through young adult-hood, discovered that children who had been abused or neglected had a 30 percent higher adult criminal record for violent offenses than those who had not been so treated.

For most parents in the United States, the traditional attitude was that they had the right (even the obligation) to use physical punishment to control and train their children. In the 1960s, however, the social problem of violence toward children was "discovered." Brian Corby (1993) believes that the climate was ripe for a greater focus on the care of children. He pinpoints the affluence that allowed people to attend more closely to the quality of parent-child relationships. The publicity accorded the battered-child syndrome led to the passage of child abuse laws in all 50 states and produced a rapid rise in reports. There also was a striking increase in court cases in which, prodded by mental health workers, persons in treatment "recalled" (often unreliably) their abuse as youngsters and initiated a criminal prosecution against a parent or sued for psychological damages (Loftus & Ketcham, 1996).

The political battles that can be launched by criminological research is illustrated by the hullabaloo created when a published review of 59 studies of college students who had been sexually abused as youngsters concluded that the consequences of such incidents are not as severe as most people presume, with men reacting much less negatively than women (Rind, Bauserman & Tromovitch, 1998). The finding produced a barrage of criticism, including a statement from a Congressional leader who said that it trivialized the impact of sexual abuse and was "pedophile propaganda masquerading as science" (Dallam, 2002:112). The American Psychological Association, which publishes the journal in which the article appeared, felt obliged to announce that the Association had "always condemned the sexual abuse of children" and that it was taking steps to see that "journal editors will fully consider the social policy implications of articles on controversial topics," although in the same breath it indicated that it did not endorse censorship of scholarly research. The authors of the article declared that "lack of harmfulness does not imply lack of wrongfulness."

Wife Battering

Violence against women perpetrated by husbands and live-in male companions for a long time was regarded by the male-dominated realm of law enforcement and the equally male-dominated realm of social science as a private affair, best left in the shadows. There was a myth that women enjoyed being hit, interpreting it as attention, and therefore a sign of caring. It is true that some women who are beaten do not see themselves as real victims, but merely as suffering the usual lot of females. The popular country song "Stand by Your Man" reflects an element of sex role socialization (Brown, 1986:280).

By capitalizing on the expansionist interests in the social work, mental health, and the legal profession, and offering a good subject for the media, feminists were able to demonstrate that there was a problem demanding serous attention (Tierney, 1982). Hundreds of shelters for battered women that provide an alternative to remaining with abusive males soon were operating (Merry, 2009; Walker, 2009). At the same time research determined that there was no difference in recidivism rates if an assailant was assigned to a batterer program or put under judicial control with reporting requirements or involved in neither of these interventions (Labriola, Rampel & Davis, 2008).

Police officers often lament that battered wives get to the station house before the officers arrive with the husbands they have arrested, saying that they now forgive their mates and want them back home. The problem often is that the woman is unable to support herself and her children without the male income and that she fears even greater aggression if she pursues criminal charges. Deborah Sontag (2002:54) points out that the wife or live-in partner "oftentimes stays for the same reasons that people in other kinds of imperfect relationships do: because of the kids, because of her religion, because she doesn't want to be alone, or simply because she loves him." Linda Mills (2008) maintains that the mandatory arrest of male batterers required in some jurisdictions fails to take into account the dynamics of the particular marital relationship and can be more destructive than helpful. The title of a recent article by Drew Humphries (2002) sums up the situation in regard to domestic violence: "No Easy Answers: Public Policy, Criminal Justice, and Domestic Violence."

There are contradictory statements and data about whether men or women act violently more often against their spouses or other domestic partners (Miller, 2005). But men hit much harder and thereby wreak considerably greater damage (Felson, 2006). Indeed, 40 percent of all calls to the police come from women endangered by their husbands. Pregnant women seem to be particular targets: 37 percent of them are physically abused by their partners (Schneider 2000). A partial explanation may lie in the fact that males have doubts about the paternity of the expected child (Waite & Gallagher, 2000:157). Michael Johnson emphasizes that there are a variety of forms of domestic violence and delineates three major types that he labels (1) intimate terrorism; (2) violent resistance; and (3) situational couple violence. He argues that failure to distinguish these different situations has led to overgeneralizations and ostensibly contradictory findings (Johnson, 2008).

Men's alcohol use and economic insecurity are particularly tied to their involvement in wife-battering. Ethnicity is only minimally related to the phenomenon. The greatest risk for women is posed by former partners after the couple has split up (Fleury, Sullivan & Bybee, 2000). Research by Leona Bouffard and her colleagues learned that women who commit domestic violence "specialize" in that kind of behavior while wife-battering men are guilty of a variety of other violent acts. They point out that treatment programs for the men that focus exclusively on domestic violence fail to address more pervasive difficulties (Bouffard, Wright, Mufftic & Bouffard, 2008).

The "battered-wife-syndrome" at times has been successfully introduced into criminal trials to excuse a woman who killed her husband after being subjected to physical abuse over a period of time. Many men take exception to such acquittals, insisting that lethal force is a disproportionate response; after all, they say, assault is not a capital offense. They also argue that the women could have departed rather than killed (Ammons, 2005). Many women take strong exception to this male position. They insist that the victims of violence had lost their self-respect, their judgment, and that they retaliate out of desperation (Chan, 2001; Hattery, 2009). A recent cartoon reflected the ever-growing use of victimization defenses in criminal cases. "I understand that he hit me because he had been abused as a child," a woman on the witness stand says. Then she adds: "And that was the same reason why I killed him."

Violence toward Siblings

Sibling abuse is said to be "the most underresearched and underrecognized form of family violence" (Hines & Malley-Morrisson, 2004:263). The largest number of domestic violence cases take place among siblings (Comstock, 2008) and the annals of such violence include biblical stories in which Cain slew his brother Abel and Joseph's brothers stripped him of his coat of many colors and threw him into a pit in the wilderness (Butler, 2006).

Most parents accept squabbling and occasional hitting among their children as part of the growing-up process. Few would consider reporting even serious violence to the police, unless they concluded that one of the children was badly out of control. A telephone survey of a national representative sample found 35 percent of the respondents reporting being "hit or attacked" by a sibling during the previous six months (Finkelhor et al., 2005).

Violence against the Elderly

Public and media attention has come to be focused on the mistreatment of the aged. Such abuse involves "intentional actions that cause harm or a serious risk of harm to a vulnerable elder by a caregiver or person who stands in a trust relationship with the elder, or failure by a caregiver to satisfy the elder's basic needs or to protect the elder from harm" (Abbey, 2009:52). Demographic trends have fed into the problem: During the past half century, life expectancy has increased 50 percent. There also are fewer children to share the burden of care for elderly parents than there were in earlier times and families tend to be more geographically dispersed than they once were.

Karl Fillemer and David Finkelhor (1988) conducted a survey of 2,000 persons over the age of 65 in Boston and found 40 victims of physical abuse, 26 of verbal abuse, and seven of neglect. If their results are extrapolated, there would be about one million abused persons over the age of 65 nationally. Most (60%) of the acts of abuse were committed by spouses, with sons rather than daughters being the most frequent offspring to abuse elderly parents. There was no difference in victimization rates by race. Men were the more likely victims in terms of rate, but, because they live longer, in total numbers there were more females abused than males. Injuries inflicted on elderly women were found to be considerably worse than those visited upon elderly men.

Explaining Family Violence

Family violence is more prominent in lower-class homes than in the other social echelons of society. This does not mean that such crimes are unique to the lower classes, but only that family violence disproportionately plagues that social stratum. The stresses of poverty, welfare existence, poor housing and education, limited opportunities, and similar aspects of life on the bottom rungs of the social ladder undoubtedly contribute heavily to family violence (Barnett, Miller-Perrin & Perrin, 2005).

Conflict theory is useful for interpreting much family violence. The primary victims of such violence, women and children, usually possess little power in relation to that of their assailants. Classical theory (see Chapter 5) also has been utilized to explain family violence; the absence of serious threats of punishment may be a factor in some cases. Perhaps holding the most explanatory power are social learning theories (chapter 8) as suggested by the intergenerational character of much family violence. In sum, a wide variety of theories seem to hold promise for understanding violence directed against family members. At the same time, it seems necessary to differentiate more clearly between the diverse forms of elderly abuse before seeking theoretical understanding (Payne, 2002).

Corporate, Government, and Professional Violence

While homicide and other violent crimes and, increasingly, forms of family violence are occupying the limelight, other types of violence, equally fearsome and more widespread, are often overlooked. White-collar crimes perpetrated by businesses, governments, and professionals kill and injure, but they get much less public attention than more flamboyant incidents of death-dealing. Notorious examples of white-collar violence include the release into public waters of the chemical pesticide Kepone, cancer-causing asbestos in homes and in the workplace, mines with inadequate safety precautions that cave in, high rates of brown-lung afflictions among cotton mill workers, and harmful levels of radiation exposure among factory workers.

In part because the victims of these forms of violence exceed those of street crimes by several fold (Reiman, 2004), some criminologists have argued that violent crime should be conceptualized to include all forms of avoidable death and injury. Some violent white-collar crime episodes represent violation of existing criminal statutes, while others, equally serious, go unheeded because of successful lobbying on the part of powerful interest groups to keep them out of penal codes. This arrangement brings us back to the centrality of the concept of the relativity of crime discussed in the opening chapters.

Each year, consumer products result in about 30,000 deaths and 20 million serious injuries, while about 14,000 lives are lost and two million persons are disabled on the job. Much of this harm is a form of violence rather than the consequence of accidental forces because the risk was unreasonable, avoidable, or associated with violation of existing regulatory or criminal law (Rosoff, Pontell & Tillman, 2007).

Corporate Violence

The following are illustrative episodes of corporate violence:

- Illegal dumping by the Veliscol Chemical Company into wells that resulted in chronic depression in several families for years until they learned that chloroform had seeped into their water, acting as a daily sedative. The truck driver who hauled Veliscol's leaking barrels of chemical waste lost his sight after continued exposure to corrosive fumes. His 24-year-old son, who worked with him, developed nerve damage. His legs began to have uncontrollable tremors; one summer, he drowned while swimming (Rosoff, Pontell & Tillman, 2007).

- There was continued exposure of workers and consumers to asbestos after conclusive scientific evidence of its lethal effects became known. "It has been shown," James W. Coleman (2002:72) observes, "that even relatively low levels of asbestos exposure can have fatal effects on some people and that hundreds of thousands of people with higher levels of exposure have died from such diseases as lung cancer, mesothelioma (a rare cancer of the lining of the lungs and stomach), and asbestosis."

- Tyler Pipe, a Texas foundry, is "a dim, dirty, hellish hot place where men are regularly disfigured by amputations and burns, where turnover is so high that convicts are recruited from local prisons" (Barstow & Bergman,2003:A1). In 2000, Rolan Hoskin, a Tyler Pipe employee, descended into a deep pit under a huge molding machine to repair a balky conveyor belt. The belt was not shut down while he worked nor did it have the required metal safety guards. Hoskin was killed, his left arm and skull crushed from being pulled between the belt and its rollers.

  Tyler Pipe is a subsidiary of McWane, Inc., a company located in Birmingham. From 1995 to the beginning of 2003, 4,600 injuries were recorded in McWane foundries, many of them serious. Nine persons, including Rolan Hoskin, were killed on the job. McWane, which employs about 5,000 workers, has been cited for some 400 federal health and safety violations, far more for the same time period than the total for their six major competitors combined.

Government Violence

Governments commit violence upon their own citizens and those of foreign countries; witness the genocidal pulverizing that Muslims have undergone at the hands of Serbs in Kosovo in what formerly was Yugoslavia, and the slaughter of the Kurds by the former Iraqi government. Subtler forms of violence at home (though not legally defined as crimes) might be alleged in the failure of the United States to provide medical care for 46 million Americans in the face of the fact that all other industrialized nations offer such care.

The Tuskegee Syphilis Experiment provides one of the ugliest illustrations of governmental violence. Between 1932 and 1972, the U.S. Public Health Service, working with local health officials, withheld treatment from more than 400 syphilitic men in an economically depressed, predominantly African-American county in rural Alabama. The aim was to compare the incidence of death and debilitation among untreated subjects with a treated sample of syphilitic men and a healthy control group.

Officials did not tell the subjects that their work involved syphilis, but only that tests were to determine "bad blood." No therapeutic intervention was offered to the subjects, nor to wives who contracted the disease, nor to children who were born with congenital syphilis. Even when penicillin was determined in 1941 to be an effective cure for syphilis, treatment still was withheld. Stephen Rosoff and his co-authors

(2007:377) note: "This is particularly troubling because the advent of penicillin seemingly obviated any rational purpose for the experiment." When details of the research finally were uncovered, an Alabama court awarded each of the 70 survivors $37,500, which worked out to $2.50 a day for the 40 years in which their medical need was flagrantly ignored.

Professional Violence: Physicians

Because of their power and position, some physicians are able to perpetrate more violence without interference than persons in other occupational areas. A report prepared by a component of the National Academy of Sciences estimates that between 44,000 and 98,000 American die each year due to preventable medical efforts (Kohn, Corrigan & Donaldson, 2000). Paul Jesilow and his colleagues (1985:153) note that "unnecessary surgery, knowingly performed, is equivalent to assault." Such assaults occur more than two million times annually. This violence results in pain, suffering, maiming, and sometimes death, in addition to fleecing the victims, insurance companies, and taxpayers. A considerable proportion of malpractice cases fall into the category of criminal behavior, although the victims or their survivors almost invariably are more intent on compensation through civil remedy than punishment through criminal process. Also thoroughly documented are sexual assaults by doctors under the guise of examination and treatment. Such behavior can be more serious than street crimes because of the violation of trust (Jacobs, 1994).

Organized Crime

Organized crime is not a statutory offense such as murder, robbery, or similar forms of lawbreaking. Some of the work of members of organized crime syndicates is perfectly legal. Owning mortuaries, for instance, is particularly attractive to organized crime groups because they can be used as a cover for a murder (organized criminals do not like the word "murder"; "whacked" is the in-term). Bodies of organized crime victims can be cremated or can be buried underneath the coffin of a person who died of natural causes.

The hallmark of organized crime is a willingness to resort to violence to gain an advantage. "Violence is a generic resource of organized crime that may well remain latent for long periods of time until it is dusted off for coercive action against those that threaten either the firm or the competitive integrity of its personnel," Dick Hobbs observes. He adds: "Violence is a feature of organized crime's power, characterizing its establishment in the market place, its dominance of a section of the market, and the method by which it resolves feuds and grievances" (Hobbs, 2003:683).

Asked what quality is most necessary for a good mob boss, author Jerry Capeci responded: "First and foremost is ruthlessness. He must have a well-earned reputation for violence that will inspire his men to do whatever he wishes" (Capeci, 2006:WK5).

Criminal syndicates got their start in the 1920s with the advent of national Prohibition when they were able to supply liquor to customers who thought the federal ban on alcoholic beverages was ill-advised (Critchley, 2009). From there the tentacles of organized crime were extended into prostitution, gambling, and, notoriously, into drug operations and labor racketeering (Jacobs, 2006). Organized crime activities also include lending money at exorbitant interest rates, and a number of extortion practices grouped generally under the heading of "rackets." Money laundering involves taking illegally gained funds and running the money through processes that make it appear to be legitimate income (and preferably non-taxable). It particularly exposes the failure of efforts to coordinate law enforcement on a global level (Kochan, 2005; Madsen, 2009).

Highlight 11.5 provides details about the way money laundering is done. Adaptability is a hallmark of organized crime activity. As Jay Albanese and his co-authors note, organized criminals are quick to respond to changes in supply, demand, law enforcement, and competition: "they move geographically, shift to another illicit product, find new partners, or take other methods to ensure profitability" (Albanese, Das & Verma, 2003:6). In response, prosecutors now employ racketeering laws (RICO) to secure restraining orders, obtain injunctions and trusteeships, and to purge the ranks of organized crime.

HIGHLIGHT 11.5
COLOMBIA Money Laundering

Franklin Jurado, a Colombian economist and Harvard University graduate, was arrested in Luxembourg, where law enforcement agents seized computer disks with records of 115 bank accounts in 16 locations from Luxembourg to Budapest. Jurado's five-stage laundering scheme was designed to clean money derived from drug trafficking. Assets were moved in a series of steps from a higher- to a lower-risk condition:

(1) The initial deposit, which is the riskiest stage because the money is still close to its origins and therefore still tainted, involved placement of funds in Panama banks.

(2) The funds were then transferred from Panama to Europe and placed into corporate accounts. This involved moving U.S. dollars from Panama banks to more than 100 accounts in nine European countries. Deposits ranged from $50,000 to $1 million.

(3) The money then was shifted to new individual accounts established under phony European names. This tactic sought to evade the heightened surveillance generally accorded Colombian and Hispanic-surnamed accounts.

(4) The money was then transferred to European-front companies that would offer no reason for suspicion.

(5) The funds were returned to Colombia through investments by the European-front companies in Colombian businesses such as restaurants, construction companies, pharmaceutical enterprises, and real estate (Blum, Levi, Naylor & Williams, 1998:39-40).

The aim of organized crime typically is to secure a monopoly on some activity that will produce large profits. The reliance on organization offers the same advantages that underlie corporate activity: diversity and specialization (Federico, 2010; Roth, 2009). Organized criminals often have their own accountants and keep one or several lawyers on retainers. It becomes crucial that nobody tells tales, jeopardizing the others; thus, the emphasis on silence in the face of police pressure and the lethal retaliation against members of the group who fail to adhere to this code.

Explaining Organized Crime

Organized crime can be interpreted most readily in terms of anomie theory. It represents recourse to illegal means to achieve ends (most notably, financial ends) that are heavily emphasized by our society. As Dick Hobbs (2000:157) puts it, organized crime offers "an alternative mode of advancement to ethnic groups who found legitimate routes blocked by the inflexibility of normative society." Organized criminals typically come from the lower echelons of the society and are handicapped by poor education or other barriers to social mobility. Recruits to organized crime often are slum neighborhood youngsters who demonstrate useful talents, and who see that the people with the expensive cars, elegant clothes, and the most opulent life styles are not the honest and the hard-working but the kingpins in the organized crime syndicate.

The careers of organized criminals, aside from the element of illegality and the use of violence, correspond closely to mythical American stories of personal achievement. The racketeer reaches for success by breaking the windows of the mansion of American society rather than entering through the front door. Organized criminals often will send their children to prestigious schools and push them toward legitimate occupations. Not surprisingly perhaps, organized crime reflects the racial prejudices of those who work in it, and until recently there has been a notable absence of African-Americans involved in crime syndicates.

Summary

Conventional forms of homicide are a by-product of social interaction; their incidence increases on weekends, holidays, and other times of more intense social activity. Although uncommon, mass and serial killers receive extensive media attention. The dynamics of aggravated assault are quite similar to homicide. A homicide often can be viewed as a completed assault and an assault as an unfinished murder.

Rape has undergone reconceptualization during the past two decades from a sex crime to a crime of violence, although it obviously has a strong sexual component. This component involves the use of sexual dominance as an indication of power and superiority.

The feminist movement is responsible for highlighting domestic violence that can result in serious harm to women and children. More recently, particularly with the graying of society, concern has been expressed about the abuse of the elderly.

Sibling violence remains a subject that largely has gone unattended, although it may play a role in socialization into the use of violence.

Business, government, and professional violence form a very large, but often overlooked, part of the roster of serious harm-inflicting offenses. Injuries are often brought about by a failure to take proper precautions or by deceit in validating tests, as with new drugs.

Finally, organized crime is a term used to categorize groups of offenders, usually of similar ethnic identification, who will use force to get their way. Organized criminals engage in activities such as extortion, drug trafficking, money laundering, and protection rackets in which for a certain payoff they will "protect" a merchant from their own willingness to wreck his or her store and from predation by other mobsters.

Key Terms and Concepts

Assault and Battery
Battered-Child Syndrome
Battered Women
Extortion
Felony-Murder
Homicide
Lifetime Murder Risk
Malice Aforethought
Manslaughter

Mass Killers
Money Laundering
Premeditation
Relative Deprivation
Serial Killers
Subculture of Violence
Terrorism
Victim Precipitation

Key Criminologists

Scott Decker
Jack Katz
Albert J. Reiss, Jr.

Robert Sampson
Marvin Wolfgang

Cases

Auman v. People, 109 P.3d 647 (Colo. 2005)

Leocal v. Ashcroft, 543 U.S. 1 (2004)

People v. Noel, 28 Cal. Rpt. 3d 369 (2005).

References

Abbey, L. (2009). "Elder Abuse and Neglect: When Home Is Not Safe." *Clinics in Geriatric Medicine*, 25 (February):47-60.

Adams, C. (2007). *"Rohypnol: Roofies—The Date Rape Drug."* New York, NY: Rosen.

Albanese, J.S., D.K. Das & A. Verma (2003). *Organized Crime: World Perspectives*. Upper Saddle River, NJ: Prentice Hall.

Ammons, L.L. (2003). "Why Do You Do the Things You Do?: Clemency for Battered Incarcerated Wives, a Decade's Review," *American University Journal of Gender, Social Policy and the Law*, 11:533-565.

Barmash, P. (2005). *Homicide in the Biblical World*. New York, NY: Cambridge University Press.

Barnett, O., C.L. Miller-Perrin & R.D. Perrin (2005). *Family Violence across the Lifespan: An Introduction*, Second Edition. Thousand Oaks, CA: Sage.

Barnett, P.E. (2004). *Dangerous Desire: Sexual Freedom and Sexual Violence Since the Sixties*. New York. NY: Routledge.

Barstow, D. & L. Bergman (2003). "At a Texas Foundry, An Indifference to Life." *New York Times*, (January 8):A1, A14.

Baumer, E.P. (2002). "Neighborhood Disadvantage and Police Notification by Victims of Violence." *Criminology*, 20:579-616.

Beeghley, L. (2003). *Homicide: A Sociological Explanation*. New York, NY: Rowman & Littlefield.

Bergen, R.K. (1996). *Wife Rape: Understanding the Response of Survivors and Service Providers*. Thousand Oaks, CA: Sage.

Binder, G. (2008). "The Culpability of Felony Murder." *Notre Dame Law Review*, 83:965-1060.

Binder, G. (2004). "The Origins of American Felony-Murder Rules." *Stanford Law Review*, 57:84-244.

Black, D. (1993). *The Social Structure of Right and Wrong*. New York, NY: Academic Press.

Blum, J.A., M. Levi, R.T. Naylor & P. Williams (1998). *Financial Havens: Banking Secrecy and Money Laundering*. New York, NY: United Nations.

Blumstein, A. & R. Rosenfeld (1999). "Explaining Recent Trends in U.S. Homicide Rates." *Journal of Criminal Law and Criminology*, 88:1175-1216.

Bouffard, L.A., K.A. Wright, L.R. Muftic & J.A. Bouffard (2008). "Gender Differences in Specialization in Intimate Partner Violence: Concerning the Gender Symmetry and Violent Resistance Perspectives." *Justice Quarterly*, 25:571-594.

Breault, K.D. & A.J. Kposowa (1997). "The Effects of Marital Status on Adult Female Homicides in the United States." *Journal of Quantitative Criminology*, 13:217-230.

Brookman, F. (2005). *Understanding Homicide*. London, UK: Sage.

Brown, S. (1986). "Police Response to Wife Beatings: Neglect of a Crime of Violence." *Journal of Criminal Justice*, 12:277-288.

Butler, K. (2006). "Beyond Rivalry, a Hidden World of Sibling Violence." *New York Times*, (February 28):D1,D6.

Calavita, K. (2001). "Blue Jeans, Rape, and 'The Deconstructive Power of Law,'" *Law & Society Review*, 35:89-116.

Capeci, J. (2006). "Will the Real Mafia Stand Up." *New York Times*, (Mar. 5):WK5.

Caputi, J. (1990). "The New Founding Fathers: The Lure and Lore of Serial Killers in Contemporary Culture." *Journal of American Culture*, 13(Fall):1-12.

Caringella, S. (2009). *Addressing Rape: Reform in Law and Practice*. New York, NY: Columbia University Press.

Chan, W. (2001). *Women, Murder, and Justice*. New York, NY: Palgrave.

Coleman, J.W. (2002). *The Criminal Elite: Understanding White-Collar Crime*, Fifth Edition. New York, NY: St. Martin's.

Combs, C.C. (2006). *Terrorism in the Twenty-First Century*, Fourth Edition. Upper Saddle River, NJ: Pearson/Prentice Hall.

Combs-Lane, A.M. and D.W. Smith (2002). "Risk of Sexual Victimization in College Women: The Role of Behavioral Intentions and Risk-Taking Behaviors." *Journal of Interpersonal Violence*, 17:165-183.

Collins, R. (2008). *Violence: A Micro-Sociological Theory*. Princeton, NJ: Princeton University Press.

Comstock, G. (2008). "A Sociological Perspective on Television Violence and Aggression." *American Behavior Scientist*, 51:1184-1211.

Cooper, H. H. (2001). "Terrorism: The Problem of Definition Revisited." *American Behavioral Scientist*, 44:881-893.

Corby, B. (1993). *Child Abuse: Toward a Knowledge Base*. Philadelphia, PA: Open University Press.

Critchley, D. (2009). *The Origin of Organized Crime in America: The New York City Mafia, 1891-1931*, New York, NY: Routledge.

Dallam, S.J. (2002). "Science or Propaganda?: An Examination of Rind, Tromovitch, and Bauman (1998)." *Journal of Child Sex Abuse*, 9:109-134.

Daly, M. & M. Wilson (1978). *Sex, Evolution and Behavior: Adaptation for Reproduction*. North Sciutate, MA: Duxbury.

Davis, L. & H. Klopper (2002). Personal communication (May 22).

Dean, T. (2007). *Crime and Justice in Medieval Italy*. London, UK: Cambridge University Press.

Decker, S.H. (1993). "Exploring Victim-Offender Relationships in Homicide: The Role of the Individual and Event Characteristics." *Justice Quarterly*, 10:585-618.

Duwe, G. (2007). *Mass Murder in the United States: A History*. Jefferson, NC: McFarland.

Dugan, L., D.S. Nagin & R. Rosenfeld (1999). "Explaining the Decline in Intimate Partner Homicide: The Effect of Changing Domesticity, Women's Status, and Domestic Violence Resources." *Homicide Studies*, 3:187-214.

Ellis, L. (1989). *Theories of Rape: Inquiries into the Causes of Sexual Aggression*. New York, NY: Hemisphere.

Eriksen, S. & V. Jensen (2009). "A Push or Punch: Distinguishing the Severity in Sibling Violence." *Journal of Interpersonal Violence*, 24:185-208.

Falk, R. (2003). *The Great Terror War*. New York, NY: Olive Branch Pres.

Federico, V. (2010). *Organized Crime*. New York, NY: Routledge.

Felson, R.B. (2006). "Is Violence Against Women About Women or About Violence?" *Context*, 5:21-25.

Fessenden, F. (2000). "They Threaten, Seethe, and Unhinge. They Kill in Quantity." *New York Times*, (April 9):1.

Fillemer, K. & D. Finkelhor (1988). "The Prevalence of Elder Abuse: A Random Sample Survey." *Gerontologist*, 28:51-57.

Finkelhor, D., R. Ormond, H. Turner & S.L. Hanley (2005). "The Victimization of Children and Youth: A Comprehensive National Survey." *Child Maltreatment*, 10:5-25.

Fisher, B.S., F.T. Cullen & M.G. Turner (2000). *The Sexual Victimization of College Women*. Washington, DC: Office of Justice Programs, National Institute of Justice, U.S. Department of Justice.

Fleury, R.E., C.M. Sullivan & D.I. Bybee (2000). "When Ending the Relationship Does Not End the Violence: Women's Experience of Violence by Former Partners." *Violence against Women*, 6:1363-1283.

Foakes, R.A. (2003). *Shakespeare and Violence*. Princeton, NJ: Princeton University Press.

Fontaine, R.G. (2010). "An Attack on Self-Defense." *American Criminal Law Review* (forthcoming).

Friedrichs, D. (2000). "The Crime of the Century?: The Case for the Holocaust." *Crime, Law and Social Change*, 34:21-41.

Galtung, J. (1990). "Cultural Violence." *Journal of Peace Research*, 27:294-305.

Garcia, R.M., R. Taylor & B.A. Lawton (2007). "Impacts of Violent Crime and Neighborhood Structure on Trusting Your Neighbors." *Justice Quarterly*, 24:679-704.

Geis, G. (1998). "Crime Victims: From the Wings to Center Stage." In H.D. Schwind, E. Kobe & H.H. Kuhne (eds.) *Essays in Honor of Hans Joachim Schneider*, pp. 315-329. Berlin: de Gruyter.

Geis, G. & R. Geis (1979). "Rape in Stockholm: Is Permissiveness Relevant?" *Criminology*, 17:311-322.

Gil, V.E. & A. Anderson (1999). "Case Study of Rape in Contemporary China: A Cultural-Historical Study of Gender and Power Differentials." *Journal of Interpersonal Violence*, 14:1151-1171.

Glassner, B. (1999). *The Culture of Fear: Why Americans Are Afraid of the Wrong Things*. New York, NY: Basic Books.

Godwin, M. & F. Rosen (2005). *Tracker: Hunting Down Serial Killers*. New York, NY: Thunder's Mouth Press.

Gorer, G. (1966). "Man Has No 'Killer' Instinct." *New York Times Magazine*, (November 4):47ff.

Hattery, A. (2009). *Intimate Partner Violence*. Lanham, MD: Rowman and Littlefield.

Hepp, J.R. (2007). "Income Inequality, Race, and Place: Does the Distribution of Race and Class Within Neighborhoods Affect Crime Rates?" *Criminology*, 45:645-606.

Herbert, B. (2006). "An American Obsession." *New York Times*, (February 2):A25.

Hickey, E.W. (2009). *Serial Murderers and their Victims*, Fifth Edition. Belmont CA: Wadsworth.

Hines, D.A. & K. Malley-Morrison (2004). *Family Violence in the United States: Understanding and Combating Abuse*. Thousand Oaks, CA: Sage.

Hobbs, D. (2003). "Organized Crime and Violence." In W. Heitmeyer & J. Hagan (eds.) *International Handbook of Violence Research*, pp. 679-699. Dordrecht, The Netherlands: Kluwer.

Hobbs, D. (2000). "Researching Serious Crime." In R.D. King & E. Wincup (eds.) *Doing Research on Crime and Justice*, pp. 153-183. New York. NY: Oxford University Press.

Huff-Corzine, L., J., Corzine & D.C. Moore (1991). "Deadly Connections: Culture, Poverty, and the Direction of Lethal Violence," *Social Forces*, 69:715-732.

Humphries, D. (2002). "No Easy Answers: Public Policy, Criminal Justice, and Domestic Violence." *Criminology & Public Policy*, 2:91-96.

Jackman, M.R. (2002). "Violence in American Life." *Annual Review of Sociology*, 28:387-415.

Jacobs, B. (2000). *Robbing Drug Dealers: Violence beyond the Law*. New York, NY: Aldine de Gruyter.

Jacobs, J. (2006). *Mobsters, Unions, and Feds: The Mafia and the American Labor Movement*. New York, NY: N.Y.U. Press.

Jacobs, S. (1994). "Social Control of Sexual Assault by Physicians and Lawyers within the Professional Relationship." *American Journal of Criminal Law*, 19:43-60.

Jesilow, P.D., H.N. Pontell & G. Geis (1985). "Medical Criminals: Physicians and White-Collar Offenses." *Justice Quarterly*, 2:149-165.

Johnson, E.A. & E.H. Monkkenon (eds.) (1996). *The Civilization of Crime: Violence in Town and Country Since the Middle Ages*. Urbana, IL: University of Illinois Press.

Johnson, M.P. (2008). *A Typology of Domestic Violence: Intimate Terrorism, Violent Resistance, and Situational Couple Violence*. Hanover, NH: University Press of New England.

Kanin, E.J. (1985). "Date Rapists: Differential Sexual Socialization and Relative Deprivation." *Archives of Sexual Behavior*, 14:219-231.

Kaplan, A. (2000). *The Collaborator: The Trial & Execution of Robert Brasilach*. Chicago, IL: University of Chicago Press.

Katz, J. (1988). *The Seduction of Crime: Moral and Sensual Attractions of Doing Evil*. New York, NY: Basic Books.

Kochan, N. (2005). *The Washing Machine*. Mason, OH: Thomson.

Kohn, L.T., J.M. Corrigan & M.S. Donaldson (eds.) (2000). *To Err Is Human: Building a Safer Health System*. Washington, DC: National Academy Press.

Krauss, P. (2002). "Mounties Dig Up Body Parts in Serial Killing Case." *New York Times*, (November 24):A8.

Labriola M., M. Rempel & R.C. Davis (2008). "Do Batterer Programs Reduce Recidivism? Results from a Randomized Trial in the Bronx." *Justice Quarterly*, 25: 252-287.

Lalumiere, M.L., G.T. Harris, V.L. Quinsey & M.E Rice (2005). *The Causes of Rape: Understanding Individual Differences in Male Propensity for Sexual Aggression*. Washington, DC: American Psychological Association.

Lee, M.T. (2003). *Crime on the Border: Immigration and Homicide in Urban Communities*. New York, NY: LFB.

Lee, P. (2003). "Reason, Rape, and Angst in Behavioral Studies." *Science*, (July 18), 301-313.

Levin, J. (2008). *Serial Killers and Mass Murderers: Up Close and Personal*. Amherst, NY: Prometheus.

Loftus, E.F. & K. Ketcham (1996). *The Myth of Repressed Memories: False Memories and Allegations of Sexual Abuse.* New York, NY: St. Martin's Griffin.

MacKinnon, C.A. (1992). "Feminist Approaches to Sexual Assault in Canada and the United States: A Brief Retrospective." In C. Backhouse & D.H. Flaherty (eds.) *Challenging Times: The Women's Movement in Canada and the United State*, pp. 186-192. Montreal, CN: McGill-Queen's University Press.

Madsen, F.G. (2009). *Transnational Organized Crime.* London, UK: Routledge.

Martin, E.K., C. Taft & P.A. Resick (2007). "A Review of Marital Rape." *Aggression and Violent Behavior*, 12:329-347.

Martinez, Jr., R. (1996). "Latinos and Lethal Violence: The Impact of Poverty and Inequality." *Social Problems*, 34:131-145.

Martinez, Jr., R., M.T. Lee & A.L. Nielsen (2004). "Segmented Assimilation, Local Context and Determinants of Drug Violence in Miami and San Diego: Does Ethnicity and Immigration Matter?" *International Migration Review*, 38:131-157.

Marvell, T.B. & C.E. Moody (1999). "Female and Male Homicide Victimization Rates: Comparing Trends and Regressions." *Criminology*, 37:879-900.

Merry, S.E. (2009). *Gender Violence: A Cultural Perspective.* Malden, MA: Wiley-Blackwell.

Miethe, T.D. W. Regoeczi & A. Drass (2004). *Rethinking Homicide: Exploring the Structure and Process Underlying Deadly Situations.* New York, NY: Cambridge University Press.

Miller, S.L. (2005). *Victims as Offenders: The Paradox of Women's Violence in Relationships.* New Brunswick, NJ: Rutgers University Press.

Miller, W.B. (1958). "Lower-Class Culture as a Generating Milieu of Gang Delinquency." *Journal of Social Issues*, 14:5-19.

Mills, L.G. (20088). *Violent Partners: A Breakthrough Plan for Ending the Cycle of Abuse.* New York, NY: Basic Books.

Payne, B.K. (2002). "An Integrated Understanding of Elder Abuse and Neglect." *Journal of Criminal Justice*, 30:535-547.

Phillips, J.E. (2002). "White, Black, and Latino Homicide Rates: Why the Difference?" *Social Problems*, 49:349-374.

Pious, R.M. (2006). *The War on Terrorism and the Rule of Law.* New York, NY: Oxford University Press.

Polk, K. (1993). *When Men Kill: Scenarios of Masculine Violence.* Melbourne, Australia: Oxford University Press.

Poitier, S. (2000). *The Measure of Man: A Spiritual Autobiography.* San Francisco, CA: Harper.

Reiman, J.H. (2004). *The Rich Get Richer and the Poor Get Prison: Ideology, Class, and Criminal Justice*, Seventh Edition. Boston, MA: Pearson/Allyn and Bacon.

Reiss, A.J., Jr. & J. Roth (eds.) (1993). *Understanding and Preventing Violence.* Washington, DC: National Academy Press.

Rind, B., R. Bauserman & P. Tromovitch (1988). "A Meta Analytic Examination of Assumed Properties of Child Sexual Abuse Using College Samples." *Psychological Bulletin*, 124:22-43.

Rivara, F.P., B.A. Mueller, G. Spomes, C.T. Mendoza, N.B. Rushforth & A.L. Kellerman (1997). "Alcohol and Illicit Drug Use and the Risk of Violent Death in the Home." *Journal of the American Medical Association*, 278:569-575.

Rosenfeld, R. (2002). "Why Criminologists Should Study Terrorism." *The Criminologist*, 27 (November-December):1, 3-4.

Rosoff, S.M., H.N. Pontell & R.H. Tillman (2007). *Profit Without Honor: White-Collar Crime and the Looting of America*, Fourth Edition. Upper Saddle River, NJ: Prentice Hall.

Roth, M.P. (2009). *Transnational Organized Crime*. London, UK: Routledge.

Roy, L. (2009). *No Right to Remain Silent: The Tragedy at Virginia Tech*. New York, NY: Harmony Books.

Sampson, R.J., S.W. Raudenbush & F. Earls (1997). "Neighborhoods and Violent Crime: A Multi-Level Study of Collective Efficacy." *Science*, 277:918-924.

Sander, P. (2009). *Madoff: Corruption, Deceit, and the Making of the World's Most Notorious Ponzi Scheme*. Guilford, CT: The Lyons Press.

Sanders, W.B. (1983). *Criminology*. Reading, MA: Addison-Wesley.

Savelsberg, J. (2006). "Underused Potentials for Criminology: Applying the Sociology of Knowledge to Terrorism." *Crime, Law and Social Change*, 46:35-50.

Schlesinger, L. (ed.) (2001). *Serial Offenders: Current Thought, Recent Findings*. Boca Raton, FL: CRC.

Schneider, E. (2000). *Battered Women and Feminist Lawmaking*. New Haven, CT: Yale University Press.

Shattuck, R. (1996). *Forbidden Knowledge: From Prometheus to Pornography*. New York, NY: St. Martin's.

Shichor, D. (2007). "Thinking about Terrorism and Its Victims." *Victims and Offenders*, 2:269-287.

Shon. P. & D. Milovanovic. (eds.) (2006). *Serial Killer: Understanding Lust Murder*. Durham, NC: Carolina Academic Press.

Smith, D.M. (2000). "A New Era of Homicide Studies." *Homicide Studies*, 4:3-17.

Sontag, D. (2002). "Fatal Entanglements." *New York Times Magazine*, (November 12):52-62, 84.

Tierney, K.J. (1982). "The Battered Woman Movement and the Creation of the Wife Beating Problem." *Social Problems*, 29:207-220.

Walker, L.E.A. (2009). *The Battered Woman Syndrome*, Third Edition. New York, NY: Springer.

Waite, L. & M. Gallagher (2000). *The Case for Marriage: Why Married People are Happier, Healthier, and Better Off Financially*. New York, NY: Doubleday

Whittaker, D.J. (ed.) (2001). *The Terrorism Reader*. London. UK: Routledge.

Widom, C. & M.G. Maxfield (2001). *An Update on the "Cycle of Violence."* Washington, DC: Research in Brief, National Institute of Justice, U.S. Department of Justice.

Wolfgang, M.E. (1958). *Patterns in Criminal Homicide*. Philadelphia, PA: University of Pennsylvania Press.

Wolfgang, M.E. & F. Ferracuti (1967). *The Subculture of Violence*. London, UK: Social Science Paperbacks.

Young, R. (2006). "Defining Terrorism: The Evolution of Terrorism as a Legal Concept in International Law and its Influence on Definitions in Domestic Legislation." *Boston College International and Comparative Law Review*, 29:23-103.

Zahn, M.A., H.H. Brownstein & S.L. Jackson (eds.) (2004). *Violence: From Theory to Research*. Newark, NJ: LexisNexis/Matthew Bender.

Zernike, K. (2006). "Violent Crime Rising Sharply in Some Cities." *New York Times*, (February 12):B1, B28.

12
Economic Crime

Jealousy of what other people have, lust for personal possessions, and competitive striving for material goods derive from cultural emphases. These conditions give rise to the crime of theft—the illegal taking of another's possessions by stealth or force. Americans typically say that what they want for themselves and for their children is "happiness." Happiness can be had in many forms, like watching a lovely sunset, enjoying the company of friends and fellow students, or reading a good book. But very often the pursuit of what we regard as happiness becomes related to money.

When we place a heavy stress on material wealth, but limit legitimate opportunities for its acquisition, theft is particularly likely to be common. Robert K. Merton (1964) maintains that the United States does just this: we encourage—almost demand—that people be financially successful if they are to be well regarded. Steven Messner and Richard Rosenfeld (2007) argue that the high levels of property crime in the United States are tied directly to the "*American Dream*"—the relentless push toward material success.

Acquisitiveness and Theft

Almost all of us get somewhat caught up in the race to enhance our sense of self-worth by the acquisition of things. Those unable or unwilling to obtain material possessions in a legitimate manner may be impelled to resort to criminal behavior to acquire them. We call such crimes "economic crimes," but many other forms of criminal behavior also have financial considerations at their root. Murder may be committed to get an inheritance and arson may be committed to obtain an insurance payoff.

Honesty may be placed on a back burner when unemployment, under-employment, or addiction to drugs is involved. A cartoon makes fun of an attitude that can give rise to economic crime in the business world. "Honesty may be the best policy," a chief executive tells one of his middle managers. "But it is not our policy."

Theft also may be preferred to working routinely at a tedious job. Greed also can underlie economic crimes. Those who have much often desire much more. Somebody will have more than you do, a newer car, a bigger yacht. Merton noted that crime can be produced among those who are well off by the "anomia of success," which, he said, "arises when progressively heightened aspirations are fostered by each temporary success and by the enlarged expectations visited on [successful people] by associates" (Merton, 1964:225). Wants can be insatiable. Criminology students might ponder this point. What will satisfy them? At what point—if any—do they believe they might violate the law to obtain material goods? Are wants without limits?

Acquisitiveness Cross-Culturally

We know of some people for whom, though murder is not uncommon, theft and cheating are unknown. The Dakota Indians had a strong code against placing value on goods. The prestige they attached to property was derived from giving it away. In the same manner, undue wealth was regarded by the Navajos as the product of a lack of generosity, perhaps even the result of malicious witchcraft.

In both ancient Jewish and German law, stealing was viewed as more serious than many crimes of violence. It was a Hebrew belief that thieves who committed their crimes in secrecy thought themselves not to be watched by God. The German tribes regarded stealing, because it was premeditated, as more serious than crimes against the person, which tended to be impulsive. They punished theft with death, while allowing fines to be paid for maiming and murder.

Historically, Christian societies have fought a constant battle to inhibit acquisitiveness. The Bible exhorts individuals to strip themselves of worldly possessions in order to prepare for a heavenly state. It asserts that it will be more difficult for a rich man to achieve divine indulgence than for a camel to pass through the eye of a needle. Despite these dicta, few persons in nominally Christian societies appear to take this religious injunction against the accumulation of wealth very seriously.

Social Conditions and Theft

Though definitions of private property vary from culture to culture, there remains a nuclear agreement that some things must remain inviolable. It may be commendable in some societies to live modestly, but in no society is it considered desirable to allow everything that you possess to be stolen. A state of social chaos would result if persons dared not leave their home for fear that someone else might legally take possession of it, or if people dared not use their cars for fear of having them stopped and appropriated.

Automobile theft illustrates the relationship between possessions and property crime. Besides its obvious value as convenient transportation, having an automobile conveys status; the more expensive the car, the more important its owner appears to be. In the United States, car theft is a commonplace crime and over time different car models become the prime targets of thieves. In 2008, according to the Insurance Institute for Highway Safety, the Cadillac Escalade 4-door SUV was the most stolen car, with 15 theft claims per 1,000 vehicles sold.

The Law of Theft

The law of theft is one of the most complex segments of criminal codes. Some definitions may help. *Larceny*, the broadest form of theft, involves the taking of property from a person, without that person's consent and with the intent to deprive the person permanently of the use of the property. Larceny is often broken down into *grand larceny* and *petit (petty) larceny*, depending on the value of the property stolen. It can be argued that the distinction between grand and petty larceny reflects a class bias. The theft of $10 from a person who has no more money is at least as serious as the theft of thousands of dollars from a person who possesses millions. Regardless, the $10 theft in many jurisdictions is regarded as petty larceny, a misdemeanor, while the second is defined as grand larceny, a felony.

Robbery is a form of theft in which goods or money are taken from a person through the use of violence or fear. The fear must be of such a nature as to arouse a reasonable apprehension of danger in a reasonable person. Robbery is a more serious crime than larceny, regardless of the amount of money or the value of the goods involved. About three percent of robbery victims suffer personal injuries serious enough to require hospitalization (Tunnell, 2000).

Burglary generally is defined as a crime against a dwelling. A burglar under the old common-law definition was a person who broke and entered the house of another in the night with the intent to commit a felony. Statutes have greatly extended the common-law scope of burglary to include warehouses, storehouses, offices, and similar structures as "dwelling houses." "Night" in early English law, before the use of watches and clocks, was regarded as any time when there was insufficient light to make out a person's features. Contemporary statutes define the time limits more precisely. New York specifies the hours from sunset to sunrise. That state also divides burglary into three degrees: burglary three, which occurs by day and in an unoccupied site; burglary two, in which a human being is present in the dwelling; and burglary one, which is a nighttime offense, or one in which the burglar is armed with a dangerous weapon, or an offense in which the burglar commits assault while on the premises.

Even with such precise definitions, the law of burglary can present perplexing questions. How, for instance, would you define theft from graves, as described in Highlight 12.1?

Robbery

Some criminals commit robberies and burglaries as well as other offenses when they find an opportunity too appealing to pass by. Nonetheless, different patterns of offending tend to go with different criminals. Robbery is "easier" than burglary in

There exists a specialized kind of theft in Italy carried out by tom-baroli, or tomb raiders. One practitioner in the town of Ceveteri, west of Rome, scavenges for Etruscan ruins that lie buried in graves. He primarily seeks gold, bronzes, jewelry, and decorated vases.

Today, the Ceveteri graveyard thief mourns the decline in his business. "Nobody wants to do this work anymore," he complains. "Young people want money fast and without working. They don't want to go out at night, dig, [or] work hard. They content themselves in an office job with a pittance for a salary. Our experience is being lost."

The graveyard thief argues that the goods are being wasted lying in coffins. Besides, the government would put what it found into museums, under glass, whereas his patrons can always enjoy the pleasure of personal possession (Lattanzi, 1998).

the sense that there is a direct confrontation that quickly garners a payoff and there is no need to dispose of stolen goods. On the other hand, some offenders shy away from face-to-face contact with their victim and are nervous that they later can be identified. They also fear that they may have to shoot a victim who resists, thereby escalating the robbery into murder; 10 percent of all homicides occur in the context of a robbery (about one robbery in 300 ends with a murder).

A common impulse for robbery, as it is for burglary, is to meet the requirements for success in a depressed neighborhood. An incarcerated robber, talking to a custodial officer in New York's Sing Sing prison, summarized the situation: "In the ghetto you get no respect if you don't look right, have a car, a Mercedes-Benz—those things. No women will go out with you. That's reality" (Conover, 2000:292).

Robbery requires very different skills than burglary, develops at a different pace, and provides its own kind of emotional rewards, most notably the opportunity to show "courage." For many offenders, burglary is seen as boring, too slow. As one robber notes:

> Sticking up gave me a rush that I never got from B&Es [breaking and enterings]. There was an almost magical transformation in my world when I drew that gun on folks. I always marveled at how the toughest cats whimpered and begged for their lives when I stuck the barrel of a shotgun into their faces. Adults who ordinarily would have commanded my respect were forced to follow my orders like obedient kids (McCall, 1994:97)

Richard Wright and Scott Decker (1997) interviewed 86 robbers living in St. Louis. Thirty-one percent said that they had committed more than 49 robberies during their lifetime. One-third of the group had never been arrested for robbery, while another 26 percent had one or more arrests, but had never been convicted. Most (85%) usually committed street robberies; the remainder did their work in commercial establishments, most notably convenience and liquor stores, pawnshops, bars, and gas stations. Many preyed upon individuals who themselves were involved in lawbreaking; drug dealers were the likeliest victims. Dealers usually have a lot of money on them and they are unlikely to report the crime. As one robber said: "What they gonna tell the police? He robbed me for my dope?" (Wright & Decker, 1997:64; Jacobs & Wright, 2008).

A Chicago study found that robbers tend to select targets near where they live. They are wary of social barriers, that is, dissimilarities between the community where the crime is committed and their own community and themselves in regard to such matters as ethnic and racial demographics (Bernasco & Block, 2009).

A study of robbers in England who target commercial establishments notes their puzzlement when employees refuse to hand over money peacefully. "It's not their money, why should they risk their lives?" the robbers wonder (Matthews, 2002:24-25).

The expanding use of credit cards has altered robbery patterns. Robbers no longer see well-dressed persons as necessarily prime targets because they often are short of cash and heavy with credit cards. Whites are preferred victims because they are likely to offer less resistance. This is especially true of white women, though some robbers shy away from such targets because they believe that some women will respond with strong emotions, perhaps screaming, and thus jeopardize the success of the encounter. One robber explained his victim preference this way:

> Women are easy; they are so easy because they panic so quick [sic].
> Women will throw their purse to you and you just snatch it in. But
> men, they will hesitate sometimes so that you got to show them you
> are serious, shoot them in the leg (Wright & Decker, 1997:85).

One consideration in robbery is how to relieve victims of money and valuables. To ask that these things be handed over is to run the risk that victims will pass along only a portion of what they have on them. To search them means that you have to get in close to the victim and may thereby further endanger yourself. For offenders who do not use guns this possibility increases dramatically. During the Wright and Decker (1994) study, one robber told them that he had to employ a knife to pull off his robberies because no one would lend him a gun. He said that he was fearful that someone would overpower him. The interview was held in the afternoon; that night the robber was killed when an intended victim grabbed his knife and stabbed him in the chest.

The major influence on the timing of commercial robberies is the robbers' idea of the amount of money that might be on hand. The robbery rate is higher in the winter because of the longer hours of darkness, a cover: this also means that stores that stay open later are more likely robbery targets. One interesting scheme involved a robber having two of his friends shopping in the store when he held it up so that they could provide the police with false identifications of the perpetrator.

Failure to distinguish statistically between different forms of robbery often results in misleading portraits of trends. In South Africa, robberies are classified into five major categories; banks robberies, robberies of cash in transit, truck hijacking, business robbery, carjacking, and house robbery. House robberies account for about one-third of the offenses (Berg & Kimnes, 2009).

Burglary

Burglars show various degrees of ability, from those who "case" (reconnoiter) a house from which they will steal to amateurs who intrude into the most convenient target. A typology based on 456 house burglars indicated four major types of career house-breakers: those who are (1) young and versatile; (2) vagrants; (3) drug oriented burglars; and (4) sexual predators. The last group has the most serous criminal records (Vaughn et al., 2008).

Wright and Decker tell of the feeling of exaltation that comes over burglars when they find themselves inside a house: everything that they see is theirs for the taking, presuming they can carry it away without being observed. On the other hand, burglars tell of their terror when they first enter a dwelling. They know that they might be confronted by a resident with a rifle who pumps bullets into their body. Convicted burglars interviewed by Darci Barry and Stephen Brown (1997:10) documented this fear:

> You don't really fear getting caught. It's the fear of having to do something you really don't want to do. You can't never [sic] tell when someone is going to walk into you and run a stick or gun in [your] face. I mean, are you going to let them shoot you or do you try and get away? I mean, can't never tell in situations like that what you're going to do. That's what scares me; what I might do if the people or police come in.

Wright and Decker (1994) emphasize that efforts to reduce burglary through *target hardening* (better locks and windows, for instance) are not very encouraging, primarily because householders are careless about making effective use of security devices and burglars are adept at disabling them. Also, some safety devices diminish the opportunity for the resident to get out of the house in the event of a fire or earthquake. In one instance, an 11-year-old in California died of smoke inhalation when she was trapped because iron security bars covered the house windows. Her three-year-old brother had set the house ablaze while playing with a cigarette lighter.

Burglars have been known to drop identifying material, such as their wallets, in sites they enter illegally, probably out of nervousness, though professional and amateur psychiatrists are likely to say that such "mistakes" represent a desire to get caught. Folklore sometimes maintains that burglars, out of hostility toward those more affluent than they, will urinate or defecate in the houses they burglarize, but field studies report that almost never happens, except when the offenders are young kids stealing from those against whom they have a grudge.

Burglary can impose considerably more serious emotional pain on its victims than robbery where the financial loss is usually more impersonal. One burglary victim poignantly depicted his feelings:

> They stole my memories—they removed a portion of my mind. The insurance people asked how much my things were worth. I told them truthfully they were priceless. I would never look on these objects again and remember. For a period of time, I ranted

like a fanatic. Sentimental value, people said. But for me there is
no other value. If all we were talking about was money, then these
things could have been replaced and I would have had no problem
(Theroux, 2000:32).

Targets of Burglary

Virtually all burglaries are triggered by a need, real or perceived, for money.
Typically, the offenders are involved in a drinking or narcotics binge and run out of
funds to keep the party going. Or else they feel overwhelmed by debts.

Burglars will enter a house that they know is occupied only in the rarest of
circumstances. As one of Barry and Brown's (1997:14) burglars stated, "The most
thing [sic] I do not want to happen was me walking in on the resident being there."
Burglars also are concerned about neighbors. As one expressed it, "I don't want
them [sic] nosey people around where they can see me working." Common tactics
for determining occupancy include accumulated mail or newspapers, watching the
house, calling on the telephone, or just knocking on the door.

Paul Cromwell and his co-workers report that, in the Texas town where they did
research, burglars look for lawns with signs proclaiming that a member of the high
school football team lives there. The burglars presume that the occupants will be
watching the team play and choose game times to break into the residence (Cromwell,
Olson & Avery, 1991:24). In Muslim neighborhoods, religious people will leave
their shoes at the front door before entering a residence. If burglars see no footwear
there, they presume that nobody is home. Other burglars like to drive slowly through
residential neighborhoods on very hot days. Closed windows and air conditioners
that are not running are taken as signs that nobody is home.

Offenders often conclude that a house is riper for burglary when security
locks are visible because the locks indicate the likelihood that there are valuable
possessions inside.

Time and Place in Burglary

A burglar's major enemies are time, noise, and light. Their working attitude has
been well expressed by Malcolm X, who was a burglar before he became a highly
respected leader in the civil rights movement:

> I had learned from some of the pros, and from my own experience,
> how important it was to be careful and plan. Burglary, properly
> executed, though it had its dangers, offered the maximum chances
> of success with the minimum risk. If you did your job so that you
> never met any of your victims, it lessened your chances of having
> to attack or perhaps kill someone. And if through some slip-up
> you were caught, later, by the police, there was never a positive
> eyewitness (1982:141-142).

Houses on the edge of an unoccupied area are much more likely targets than those in the interior of a residential section. A study of 96 burglaries of student housing found a considerably disproportionate number of them to be from first-floor and corner units. Only 27 percent of the residences had corner locations but 53 percent of the burglaries targeted these places (Robinson & Robinson, 1997).

Police patrols are unlikely to observe a burglary in progress. Nor are burglar alarms likely to be of much value. For one thing, sophisticated burglars know how to disarm them. For another, burglars minimize the amount of time they spend in a house. A usual rule for an experienced burglar is to remain within a dwelling no more than five minutes, preferably less. If the burglar is out of a house three minutes after entering, even the fastest response to a silent alarm (unless the house is across the street or down the block from the police station) would not threaten them.

Burglars almost invariably search only places where they have learned that most people keep valuables, especially money, jewelry, electronic equipment, cameras, and weapons. Typically, burglars head first for the bedroom. Shrewd homeowners sometimes secrete their valuables in a child's room, an area rarely entered by burglars.

Big-Time Burglary

The ingenuity of career burglars is shown by a big-time jewelry theft. It took place in a Boston hotel during a national jewelry exhibit. About 9:15 each evening, exhibitors would place their wares in trunks, which were hauled to a vault where a timing device kept the doors from being opened until the following morning. Phil Cresta, a professional thief, formed a plan with two crooked Chicago jewelers that involved placing Cresta's 5-foot, 2-inch lightweight accomplice in their trunk and providing him with an air tank for breathing. The trunk was carted to the vault by the guards. Its occupant spent the next few hours transferring jewels from other trucks into his. The haul later was sold for more than half a million dollars; in addition, the Chicago jewelers filed a fake claim with their insurance company for what they alleged was their own loss (Wallace & Crowley, 2000).

Burglary Statistics

About eight percent of American households are burglarized each year. Two out of three burglaries are against residences. Burglary victims suffer losses of about $4 billion each year, with the average loss (both for resident and nonresident property) about $1,200. Burglars sometimes derive an ironic satisfaction in comparing what they have stolen with media accounts of what they are said to have stolen, a matter that feeds their belief that they were not the only crooks involved in the episode.

Slightly more than 90 percent of the persons apprehended for burglary are males. In the Wright and Decker (1994) study, the few female offenders typically worked with men, and said that, if caught, they would try to shift blame onto their male associates.

The burglary rate has dropped precipitously in the United States, going down 44 percent since 1980, so that today New York has a lower burglary rate than London, while Los Angeles shows fewer burglaries than Sydney, Australia. Those speculating on the decrease believe that the decline in crack cocaine dealing and use has been a significant factor. Crack produces a short and intense high and creates a continual need for money to maintain the drug glow. Robbery in contrast to burglary is a quick route to funds. In the United States, burglary and robbery rates paralleled each other from 1973 to 1985, when the crack epidemic began, and then robbery rates skyrocketed while burglary rates declined (Butterfield, 1997).

Perspectives on Burglary

The major explanation usually employed for burglary is "rational choice" theory (see Chapter 5), which postulates that the decision to offend is the result of a deliberate weighing, however rudimentary, of potential costs and rewards. Wright and Decker (1994), however, concluded that rational choice explanations pay too little attention to the subjective influence of emotions on burglars' decision-making process.

Wright and Decker (1994) rely on a theoretical position formulated by John and Lyn Lofland (1969). The Loflands maintained that the decision to carry out most crimes involves a three-phase process, beginning with (1) a perceived threat; moving to (2) a state of "psycho-social encapsulation," and culminating in (3) the specific criminal act. Perceived threats involve such things as the possibility of physical harm or, more likely, the risk of social disapproval in the eyes of others who are important to the person. Often men will egg each other on by "collaboratively constructed conceptions of opportunity" (Hochstetler, 2001), so that they commit a crime together that none of them would have ventured on alone.

Psychosocial encapsulation is most likely to occur when the perceived threat is immediate, when it is experienced infrequently, and when the threat occurs in circumstances in which the individual feels socially isolated, that is, unable to seek help from others. Encapsulation, the Loflands (1969:53) maintain, encourages "simple, short-term, quick, and close-at-hand" solutions, many of which are illegal.

Most burglars spend the money they gather on drugs or alcohol and status-enhancing consumer goods, such as fancy clothes, which suggests that the threat has most to do with their sense of self-worth. As Wright and Decker (1994:201) put the matter: "To be seen as hip on the street, one must be able to keep the party going." Burglary also has been interpreted as a rebellion against demands to behave like most other people, particularly to hold down a job. As Kenneth Tunnell (2000:92) observes, burglars "withdraw from participating in officially approved activities. Persistent thieves refuse to work and dislike others who do; they don't vote; they reject formal education; they don't curb their alcohol and drug use, and often maintain nomadic life styles." Burglars usually have a specific target and information about the daily routine of the site's occupants. The offense requires no equipment more sophisticated than common household utensils and tools. Importantly, there is no need for a firearm.

Shoplifting and Employee Theft

Shoplifting is sometimes referred to as the "five-finger discount." It involves theft from a retailer during the hours the store is open for business. The extent of shoplifting cannot be established accurately because most stores blend shoplifting losses into their *"inventory shrinkage"*—a figure that includes damaged merchandise that is sold at a reduced price, bookkeeping errors, breakage, and employee thefts. The best estimate is that about 80 percent of inventory shrinkage is due to theft, and that some three-quarters of that involves theft by store employees.

Stores prosecute only a relatively small percentage of the thieves they catch. This selection process is often based on factors such as the attitude of the person apprehended or the person's ethnic or racial background and financial standing. African-Americans and poor persons are more likely to be prosecuted than middle-class whites. Persons who sign a confession are sometimes then released. Those who refuse to sign are more likely to be prosecuted so that the business will not be faced with a false arrest lawsuit.

Professional shoplifters can be differentiated from amateurs, who greatly outnumber them, by the fact that they steal merchandise in order to resell it, usually to a "fence," who will pay the thief about one-third the retail value of the article (Klockars, 1974; Steffensmeier, 1986). Increasingly stolen goods are sold online: it is estimated that 70 percent of the gift cards marketed on e-bay have been stolen. Some shoplifters steal to order: customers specify their desire for certain goods and the shoplifter targets these.

Amateur pilferers flourish in department stores and in supermarkets, where they take the invitation to "self-service" literally. The height of the shoplifting season comes right before Christmas when the pressures to purchase are most intense.

Mary Owen Cameron, in her classic study of shoplifters apprehended in Chicago's Marshall Field's department store, concluded that amateur shoplifters are not compulsive, uncontrolled thieves suffering from psychological disturbances, but rather respectable people who pilfer systematically. She found that they come to the store prepared to steal and continue to steal until apprehended. Cameron maintained that the damage to the arrested amateur thief's self-concept is usually sufficient to inhibit further stealing. She notes:

> Pilferers generally do not think of themselves as thieves, and they resist being pushed to conceive of themselves in these terms. It is often quite difficult for the store staff to convince the arrested person that he has actually been arrested. Again and again the store police explain to pilferers that they are under arrest as thieves, that they will, in the normal course of events, be taken in a police wagon to jail, held in jail and tried in court before a judge and sentenced. "Yes, I took the dress," one woman sobbed, "but that doesn't mean I'm a thief" (Cameron, 1964:161).

Shoplifters employ a variety of tactics from the common ploy of "grazing" in supermarkets, that is, consuming food while strolling about the store, to fraudulent returns to department stores. Professionals may use a "*booster box*," a wrapped parcel with a hidden spring that allows the thief to reach inside and open the bottom while it is resting on merchandise to be stolen. Other techniques involve "crotching," in which goods are hidden beneath loose clothes and held between the thief's thighs, and the switching of labels from less to more expensive items. Some shoplifters plot to get arrested by stealing while in full view of a store detective, and then unloading the product surreptitiously before they are apprehended. Thereafter, they can file a suit for damages for slander, false arrest, or false imprisonment, a tactic that can be used only a limited number of times. Professionals sometimes resort to particularly blatant tactics. A couple of thieves hoisted a canoe onto their shoulders in a crowded New York department store and, unmolested, marched out the front door. Then there was the shoplifter who would set fire to a clothing rack and make off with other merchandise during the ensuing panic (Newman, 2006). A police chief in a suburban jurisdiction notes of shoplifters: "We've arrested 90-year-old grandmothers, people in wheelchairs, women pushing baby carriages, and women who walk in weighing 120 pounds and walk out looking pregnant" (Jacobs, 2005). One shoplifter observed that customers complain that they can't find anyone to wait on them in the large department stores. "I say," he observed, "Thank you. Let them keep it that way" (Trebay, 2000:A24).

Stores, for their part, now tag products with electronic sensors that set off an alarm, secure some items to the racks, and use television cameras to monitor sales areas and fitting rooms. Placing clothes on a rack with every other hanger pointing in a reverse direction forestalls shoplifters who might try to grab an armful of merchandise and flee from the store. Many stores now are built with fewer angles, so that they provide unobstructed sight lines for those on the lookout for shoplifters. But as Highlight 12.2 indicates, dedicated shoplifters are not without counter-moves.

HIGHLIGHT **12.2**
OREGON The Lego Thief

> An Oregon man specialized in shoplifting Lego equipment, the Danish building toys. Over three years, he stole more than $600,000 worth of them from dozens of stores in five western states. He counterfeited bar codes that altered the price of Lego sets from $100 to $15. Then he sold the loot to toy collectors on a web site.

Source: Zimmerman (2006).

Employee Theft

A typical employee theft tactic is to "sell" an item to a friend, say a $150 pair of shoes, but to charge for a $2 container of shoe polish. Some employees paste a bar code for an inexpensive item on their wrist and use that when making a much more expensive "sale" to friends. Employees also often take merchandise out with them when they leave work.

Retailers have sought to control thefts by establishing a national database that lists all employees caught stealing. The blacklist now contains the names of about 750,000 persons. Nobody can be placed on the list unless the store has a signed confession or the names of two persons who verify that there was an oral confession (Coleman, 2000).

Perspectives on Shoplifting

Many criminology students undoubtedly can offer their personal stories about the forces that underlie shoplifting expeditions. Lloyd Klemke (1992) found that 56 percent of the 165 college students he surveyed admitted that they had been involved in at least one shoplifting offense. Jack Katz (1988) analyzed shoplifting accounts obtained primarily from women criminology students at UCLA. He emphasizes the "seductive power of objects," the "cheap thrills," and the "profoundly moving experience." Katz believes that for the students shoplifting is a tactic in a war against boredom rather than against poverty. While granting the accuracy of Katz's insight, Bill McCarthy (1995) insists that it focuses on only one of a considerable number of correlates of shoplifting at the expense of other variables.

The "thrills" of shoplifting are noted by a persistent practitioner who indicates that "if the store manager is standing here and I could take something right under his nose, that's what I'd get because it's more of an accomplishment." Asked if he had tried legitimate employment, the shoplifter replied: "Never looked for none [sic] because there wasn't anything that I enjoyed more than shoplifting" (Tunnell, 2000:100). Judith Wallerstein and her colleagues document the appeal of shoplifting with an interview report of a practitioner:

> We loved to shoplift. That was the best. We'd go in a group to a store and someone would make a disturbance and when the authorities went to see what happened we'd take expensive cosmetics and other things that look good. I remember the feeling-my stomach would be all knotted with fear and I'd be light-headed and almost dizzy because I felt so exhilarated. Getting out and running fast even made it better. I never needed or even wanted anything we stole. What was important was the excitement (Wallerstein, Lewis & Blakeslee, 2000:118)

Theories to explain shoplifting have been compiled by Klemke (1992). The list begins with psychiatric and psychological postulations that typically blame pathological sexual conditions, and often equate the items that are stolen, like fountain pens, to sexual organs. A national survey found that 11.3 percent of 43,000 respondents could be identified as lifetime shoplifters. Thee persons were said to be characterized by deficits in impulse control, anti-social personality disorders, substance abuse, pathological gambling, and bipolar disorders (Blanco, et al., 2008).

Increases in shoplifting during periods of economic recession and especially in times of inflation are employed to verify anomie and strain theory insights. In terms of social control theory, Klemke observes that "there is rather consistent support for the proposition that weak social bonds in the family are moderately related to shoplifting," while the research results on ties to school and shoplifting "are less consistent" (Klemke, 1992:97).

Sykes and Matza's (1957) idea that neutralization is an important element in the commission of crime finds support in the shoplifting literature. A 20-year-old justified her stealing from stores in terms of what Sykes and Matza would call "denial of the victim," in which the offender insists that nobody has been hurt who did not deserve that injury:

> I felt the whole system—who owns the stores, who makes the profit—is set up by the same people, the people who have everything. I thought it served them right[;] they have more than they know what to do with. Every time I stole something, I'd say, "They rip us off every time we buy something, so I'm just getting even." (Klemke, 1992:106-107)

Telemarketing Fraud

Telemarketing becomes illegal when the seller oversteps established limits of merchandising truthfulness. It is a crime to promise a person on the other end of the telephone line that he or she will receive a 33 percent annual return if they invest in your oil drilling company if you have no legitimate basis for specifying that level of profit. The offense is even more obvious if the oil well does not exist. Victims' active involvement distinguishes telemarketing fraud from burglary and robbery.

Telemarketing scammers purchase lists of possible customers ("smooches" is what they are called in the trade) and cold-call them. The salespeople, almost always men, often will adopt aliases so that they cannot be located if there is a later complaint. Sometimes complainers are told that while the person from whom they bought the original purchase is no longer employed there, the salesman now talking to them will get their money and more back if they invest in his product.

There are an estimated 140,000 telemarketing firms at work today in the United States and they generate higher annual sales than magazines, radio, television, and direct-mail advertising. About 10 percent of telemarketers are believed to engage in illegal activities, and Americans lose about $40 billion a year to fraudulent sales pitches, though only one in 10,000 victims will report their loss to the authorities, usually because they are embarrassed by their gullibility (Stevenson, 1998).

A successful telemarketing scammer (they are called "yaks" in the business) requires verbal skills and an ability to improvise, though the basic pitch and recommended responses usually are scripted. For instance, if a customer says that she does not like doing business over the phone, the following response is in order:

> If doing business over the phone is difficult for you, I certainly can empathize with you. It is difficult for me as well. However, business lives on the phone. I know for a fact that there are literally thousands of people much like yourself who are making $50,000

and $100,000 from business conducted over the phone. A $20,000 investment is not a lot of money and it won't hurt you financially. So I'm asking you to give me just one percent of your confidence and the opportunity to earn the other 99 percent. Let me prove to you what I can do for you and base all future activity on the results I get. Fair enough?

The story is told of a new telemarketing employee who pondered a customer's response that he never did business over the telephone, and then replied with perplexity: "Not even to buy a pizza?"

Improvisation tactics are exemplified by the following story of a telemarketer selling phony investments:

When I was new in phone sales I closed an oil and gas deal, but the client asked me first, how long have you been working in oil and gas? I told him to hang on a minute, I had another call. My supervisor asked me, how long have you been driving? I said for fifteen years. He said, "Then you've been working with oil and gas for fifteen years, haven't you?"

With women, especially elderly women, salespersons will employ a considerable number of "dears" in their pitch and will call customers "sir" and "ma'am." Older people generally are more reluctant, out of what they regard as politeness, to hang up abruptly on callers, although the scammers prefer rapid turndowns if the person is not a likely purchaser, because they operate on the premise that the more calls they make the more likely they are to hook a sucker. They generally cite a ratio of one buyer to about 100 calls.

Inside the packed cubicles from which calls are made, a tape deck plays music. None of this is audible to customers because of "confidencers"—devices that screen out background noise. A favorite musical tune is Billy Joel's "Easy Money," which contains the line: "Someone's got a fortune that they're begging me to take." Inventive salespeople may create their own effects by beating on staplers to duplicate the sound of a teletype machine.

Novelist Doris Lessing (1961:52) provides a clue to the dynamics that drive many telemarketing salespersons. She writes about a con man who sought to exploit her: "His strength was—and I could feel just how powerful that strength was—this terrible, compelling anxiety that he should be able to force someone under his will." Lessing observes further: "It was almost as if he were pleading silently, in the moment when he was tricking a victim: Please let me trick you; please let me cheat you; I've got to; it's essential for me."

The self-esteem of the trickster becomes involved with the zest of combat. One telemarketing fraud manager expressed the feeling in these words:

When I make a sale, it's like woooo. It's like Yes! I got addicted to it. It's like more exciting than anything. To know that the money was on the table and it was a battle of wills and I won! Yeah! I backed the guy down. He woke up that day not expecting a call from me. The furthest thing in his mind was getting into oil and gas (Doocey et al., 2001).

Various forms of swindling such as telemarketing scams are pervasive throughout the world. Highlight 12.3 indicates a scheme used in Ghana.

HIGHLIGHT **12.3**
GHANA Street Swindling by Fast Talkers

Swindling, also called azah in Ghana, is usually perpetrated by people who are versatile in twisting words to confuse unsuspecting victims. Some swindlers were alleged to have combined magic with rhetoric, and promised to either double victims' monies, give new or superior products, help victims win fortunes, or give them potions to entice and neutralize those in authority. Generally, swindlers are interested in money, but may be content with clothing, jewelry, wristwatches, or any readily available portable valuables. Females accounted for 68 percent of the swindling victims, but 98 percent of the perpetrators were males in their mid to late thirties (Appiahene-Gyamfi, 2003:19).

Computer Crime

Consider the following criminal offense. The owner of a company which builds sets for television shows has purchased a custom-designed computer for $3,600. The new computer fails to meet his expectations, and he refuses to pay the seller. The seller retaliates by infecting the purchaser's computer system with a virus that cripples his business transactions. For doing so, the seller and one of his technicians became the first casualties of New York State's law against computer tampering.

One scam artist set up an ordinary looking but completely bogus ATM machine in a shopping mall near Hartford, Connecticut. The machine supplied customers with apologetic notes saying that some fault precluded transactions. Using the personal identification numbers (PINS) from hundreds of people attempting to withdraw money, the thieves tapped into real automated teller machines to net at least $50,000 (Shover, 1996:53).

A well-publicized computer crime involved a high school student in New Jersey who at the age of 14 began a series of what are called "pump and dump" schemes. In a typical move, he purchased 18,000 shares of Man Sang Holdings, a jewelry company, at prices between $1.37 and $2 a share. He then flooded the Internet chat rooms with messages that stated that Man Sang Holdings was on the verge of reaping great profits. Sales soared to more than a million shares at a peak price of $4.68, and the young instigator unloaded his cache. He accumulated $272,826 until he was caught by Securities and Exchange investigators. The penalty? That he return what he had made—with interest (MacFarquhar, 2000).

A typical computer fraud scheme might take the following form:

> A 25-year-old computer terminal operator arranged to receive
> pension checks under 30 different names. When notice of a
> pensioner's death came in, she was supposed to enter it on the
> computer in order to terminate the payments. Instead, she would
> enter an address change and send the check to a post office box.
> When auditors sent out letters to verify that the pensioners were
> still alive, the letters went to the fraudulent new addresses. It was
> a simple matter for the terminal operator to respond affirmatively
> (Krauss & MacGahan, 1979:10).

Computer fraud has developed its own vocabulary. Among the common terms
used for schemes are: (1) the *Trojan horse*, which involves hiding a small program
that cheats the company within a larger program; (2) the *salami technique*, involving siphoning off small amounts from each transaction; (3) *trap doors*, codes that
are inserted by programmers during the debugging phases of program development
and not eliminated thereafter. They can be used to ease later access to what should
be restricted information; and (4) *piggybacking*, which involves stealing the formula
which provides access to a system or using a system that somebody has failed to log
off on properly (Grabosky, 2007).

White-Collar Economic Offenses

The complexity and awkwardness of the concept of *white-collar crime* inheres
in the fact that there is no agreement on whether the category should be:

- restricted to the class position of people who commit certain kinds
  of offenses (Sutherland, 1949/1983), or whether it should be

- applied only to the offenses themselves, regardless of who the
  perpetrators are (Weisburd, Waring & Chayet, 2001).

For those who favor definition (1), white-collar crimes are regarded as offenses
committed by persons of high status in the course of their business, professional, or
political lives. How high such status needs to be to qualify for the category is one of the
definitional dilemmas. For those who favor definition (2) a white-collar crime is any
offense involving violations of certain laws such as those which forbid conspiracies in
restraint of trade, as well as statutes that outlaw false advertising, embezzlement, and
laws that come under the general heading of fraud. With this definition it does not matter
who violates the law; it is the nature of the law that counts. The difficulty here is that in
some categories that come to be called white-collar crime, almost one-half of the violators can be unemployed, a matter which undercuts the original intent of the concept of
white-collar crime to call attention to abuses of power by those in leadership positions.

This dilemma highlights the strong ideological element that has been part of the
idea of white-collar crime. When restricted to persons of status and power, the cat-

egory of white-collar crime serves to correct the tradition of tying the idea of crime to the activities of the poor, members of minority racial and ethnic groups, and other persons who do not share equally in the wealth of the society. Others regard such a focus as propaganda, rooted in a desire to bring about social reform by attending to the wrongs of the powerful rather than to engage in objective social science.

The usual response to this last criticism is that most definitions in criminology are ideological and that the study of crime is a reformist enterprise. Criminologists seek to understand crime and wrongdoing in order to reduce it, whether by reforming the social system or the individual.

Background of White-Collar Crime

Reformers always have complained about the crimes of persons with power who used their offices and their wealth to exploit others. In the Bible, prophets hurled ferocious denunciations at usury—the lending of money at interest—and against merchandising tricks, such as withholding commodities from the market until scarcity and near-starvation forced people to pay unconscionably high prices for the products.

Criminologists at first only glancingly attended to the phenomenon of white-collar crime. Thorstein Veblen, an iconoclastic social economist, was one of the earliest scholars to upbraid upperworld law breakers. In his *Theory of the Leisure Class*, Veblen noted that the ideal captain of industry was like the ideal delinquent in his "unscrupulous conversion of goods and persons to his own ends, and a callous disregard of the feelings and wishes of others, and of the remoter effects of his actions" (Veblen, 1912:237). Edward A. Ross, a pioneering sociologist, also unloosed some colorful invective against the crimes of the well-placed, whom he labeled *criminaloids*. Ross (1907:47) wrote: "They are not degenerates tormented by monstrous cravings. They want nothing more than what we all want—money, power, consideration—in a word, success; but they are in a hurry and they are not particular about the means."

The concept of white-collar crime was formally born in 1939 when Edwin H. Sutherland of Indiana University used the term as the title of his presidential address to the American Sociological Society. Sutherland, Nebraska-born, a product of populist politics, berated his fellow criminologists for ignoring white-collar crime. This neglect, he maintained, had led them to adopt superficial theories of crime causation. Broken homes and poverty, Sutherland insisted, cannot be causes of crime because white-collar crime is committed by persons of great affluence who typically come from intact homes (or, at least did so when Sutherland was writing). Nor do such psychiatric explanations as Oedipal fixations hold water, since corporate executives who violate the antitrust laws rarely can be found to suffer from such syndromes (Sutherland, 1940).

Concern with precise definition was not of much importance to Sutherland because he assumed that, whatever the definition, white-collar crime could adequately be explained by the theory of differential association (see Chapter 8). The definitional chaos established by Sutherland has continuously plagued the study of white-collar crime (Geis, 2007). Among proposed definitions, the one that most closely adheres to Sutherland's original concept is that offered by Albert J. Reiss, Jr. and Albert Biderman (1980:4):

> White-collar violations are those violations of law in which pen-alties are attached that involve the use of a violator's position of economic power, influence, or trust in the legitimate economic or political institutional order for the purpose of illegal gain, or to commit an illegal act for personal or organizational gain.

The relative shortage of scholarly work on white-collar offenders can be traced to the complexity of the subject, which may involve matters of criminology, civil and criminal law, organizational theory, psychology, accounting, and other special-ties. Besides, the subject does not lend itself readily to quantitative analyses which dominate the social sciences. In addition, persons who commit white-collar crimes are much less accessible to research inquiries than, say, juvenile delinquents Stephen Rosoff, who interviewed physicians convicted of defrauding Medicaid, tells of some of the issues involved in such work:

> White-collar criminals often have enjoyed great respect in the past, a respect they have unwillingly forfeited. My experience teaching in prison left me with a sense that while most convicts proclaim their "innocence," it is usually a pro forma ritual. My experience with "peculating physicians" left me with a different sense. These guys not only proclaim their innocence, they believe it—or, at least, they desperately want you to believe it. They hunger for the respect they once had.
>
> The first challenge in interviewing an elite offender is to extract information without being too adversarial. If I were interviewing a convicted burglar, I would probably call him Charlie (or whatever his first name is), while he might call me Doc. There is a role rever-sal when the offender is an elite deviant. I respectfully called the Medicaid fraud subject Dr. So-and-so. And I might well be called Steve in return—or called nothing at all. No problem. When the interview ends, I'm still the one without a parole officer (Dodge & Geis, 2006:86).

Forms of White-Collar Crime

The global economic meltdown of 2007 and 2008 involved white-collar crimes, greed, irresponsibility, and a not inconsiderable dosage of stupidity. The trigger was the out-of-control sale of home mortgages, often on the basis of false documentation or no documentation at all, to persons who could not afford what they were induced to purchase. Salesmen assured buyers that the value of their house would increase dramatically and they could then refinance, using the dwelling as if it were an ATM machine. Teaser loans carrying one or two percent interest in a few years would reset at exorbitant rates, driving payments up from, say, $800 a month to $2400. Defaults and foreclosures followed apace and Wall Street behemoths such as Bear Stearns (Bamber & Spencer, 2009; Kelly, 2009), Lehman Brothers (McDonald & Robinson, 2009), American International Group (AIG) (Cohan, 2009; Shelp & Ehbar, 2009), and Fannie Mae and Freddie Mac (Christie, 2006) found themselves over their heads in debt. These companies, whose balance sheets were saturated with so-called subprime mortgages, collapsed, were bought by competitors, or were bailed out by the federal government with huge infusions of taxpayer money. The unemployment rate soared and states were faced with staggering budget shortfalls.

Criminal charges were not common; it is not a criminal offense to be reckless with stockholders' money. Angelo Moxilo, CEO of Countryside Financial, was among the few malefactors formally charged. He had sold $129 million of his own stock in the company while at the same time telling investors that it was a marvelous investment when he well knew otherwise (Michaelson, 2009).

The most publicized offender was Bernie Madoff who had run a Ponzi scheme, paying old investors not out of profits but out of money secured from new investors. He was sentenced to 150 years in federal prison when the impossible mathematics of his situation caught up with him (Sander, 2009; Strober & Srober, 2009).

Not long before the meltdown there had been the looting of savings and loan institutions of billions of dollars. One estimate is that by the year 2021, the bailout costs for insolvent thrifts will reach $473 billion. The S & L scandals highlighted a form of white-collar crime in which officials within the corporations were not acting, as in antitrust and similar kinds of violations, to enhance company profits but rather were engaged in what has been called "collective embezzlement" in order to gain personally at the expense of the institution (Pontell, 2005; Calavita, Pontell & Tillman, 1997:177).

There also is a long roster of offenses committed by medical doctors against government benefit programs such as Medicare (for the elderly) and Medicaid (for the poor). The cost of such fraud is said to be somewhere between 10 to 25 percent of the total amount of money expended on the programs. Some of the cases are bizarre. In Illinois, a psychiatrist was found to have billed Medicaid for 4,800 hours of work during the year, or almost 24 hours each workday. Other physicians have been caught billing for visits from persons who were dead at the time of the alleged medical service. A psychiatrist billed Medicaid for sexual liaisons with a patient, claiming that he had submitted the bills for "professional services" so that his wife, who handled his accounts, would not become suspicious.

The category of white-collar crime also includes such matters as false advertising. Department stores often raise the price of a product one day and then the next day drop it back to where it had been, maintaining in their advertising that it now is "on sale" and "reduced by 70 percent." In bait-and-switch tactics, a store will advertise a specific product at a strikingly low price, but when the customer tries to buy the item, the store indicates either that it no longer is available, or a clerk demonstrates that the on-sale item is much inferior to the thing that the store really wants to sell (Blumberg, 1989).

Rationalization and White-Collar Crime

White-collar offenders, given their "respectable" backgrounds, are adept at finding soothing explanations for their crimes. Male embezzlers typically insist that they were only borrowing the money and intended to repay it after they dealt with financial demands that were vexing them. In a study of women who embezzled, Dorothy Zietz (1981) found a different set of explanations that most often concentrated on the need the women felt to supply their family—husbands and children—with financial aid.

Rarely will there appear a white-collar offender with the refreshing honesty to admit: "I was deliberately engaged in crooked business dealings." Some offenders blame their violations on personal problems such as alcoholism, drug addiction, or marital difficulties. To the extent that such thoughts precede criminal acts, they are consistent with neutralization theory discussed in Chapter 4.

Other Characteristics of White-Collar Crime

If the category of white-collar crime is confined to persons with power who commit offenses in the course of their occupational work, the definition restricts the ranks of possible perpetrators. Anybody with strength, or a gun and decent aim, or access to poison, can commit murder, but only corporate executives are in a position to violate the Sherman Antitrust Act. You and I can canvass the neighborhood and try our hand at burglary, presuming we have the nerve and are not intimidated by the risk of prison or the restraints of conscience. But only a physician (or someone who pretends to be a physician) can overservice patients enrolled in government medical benefit programs by ordering unnecessary X-rays or performing unneeded surgery.

People typically engage in forms of criminal behavior that are the most familiar to them. A bank teller, pressed for money, will try embezzling, while an unemployed minority youth, also without funds, turns to armed robbery. A bonus of social status is access to opportunities for the "more decent" kinds of crime.

At the same time, powerful persons exert pressure to make certain that harmful behaviors that they might or do engage in are not included in the penal law—or are stated in such convoluted language that it becomes unclear what is prohibited. A recent example illustrates the process. The federal Sarbanes-Oxley Act required the Securities and Exchange Commission (SEC) to adopt a rule mandating that lawyers who become aware that the company for which they work is breaking the law to notify the SEC of the situation (Fletcher & Pette, 2008; Anand, 2007).

Corporate lawyers got the SEC to back down. The original SEC rule offered a rather simple definition of the information that a lawyer would be obligated to report: "Evidence of a material violation," it read, "means information that would lead an attorney reasonably to believe that a material violation has occurred, is occurring, or is about to occur." This was too straightforward for the legal lobby. The rule was altered to read: "Evidence of a material violation means credible evidence, based upon which it would be unreasonable, under the circumstances, for a prudent and competent attorney not to conclude that it is reasonably likely that a material violation has occurred, is occurring, or is about to occur." A commentator offers the following observation on the new rule:

> Note the changes. A lawyer who reasonably believes his client is a crook can keep quiet, so long as it would not be unreasonable for someone else to fail to conclude he was right. Using the double negative did more than make the rule confusing. It made it harder for the SEC to prove a violation later (Norris, 2003:C1).

A characteristic of many kinds of white-collar crime is that its victims often are not aware that they have been harmed. Death from asbestos poisoning is likely to be slow and insidious, and victims will be hard pressed to relate their terminal illness to its precise cause, given other possible contributing factors. A factory worker with cancer cannot be certain whether it was the toxic chemicals that she handled for 15 years, the fact that she smoked too many cigarettes, poor genes, or bad luck that shortened her life.

In many white-collar crimes, the harm tends to be widely diffused and, for each person, rather insignificant. If you purchase what you believe to be orange juice, but actually get an orange concentrate diluted with water, you probably will not know the difference and, even if you do, you are not likely to make a fuss about it. But companies can earn millions of "extra" dollars by charging higher prices for products that do not meet the standards they are alleged to attain. Exceedingly few people who pay for a package of 100 thumbtacks will take the time to count the contents; it would be an easy and safe venture to put 92 thumbtacks in each package, and some merchandisers find the temptation irresistible.

Crooked Corporations and Thieving Executives

Today, the front pages of American newspapers often show a corporate executive in a business suit with handcuffs on his wrists behind his back being led into court by government agents. Crime in the corporate world seems to have become increasingly commonplace (see Glasbeck, 2002). Sometimes, the large-scale law-breaking is depicted as an unfortunate occurrence traceable to a few bad apples in an otherwise untainted orchard. But the extent and astonishing self-serving nature of business crimes in recent years has caused corporate activities to come under scathing scrutiny (DiMento & Geis, 2005; Shover & Hochstetler, 2006).

The Enron bankruptcy scandal (Eichenwald, 2005) led the parade of corporate depredations including crimes by Arthur Andersen, an accounting giant, Global Crossing, Adelphia, ImClone, and Tyco International (Tillman & Indergaard, 2005). The tactics of the Enron executives were brazen. The company accumulated huge debts that it kept off its books and out of its annual reports by transferring them to partnerships—allegedly as many as 3,000—that had been established to hide its true financial condition. These partnerships were supposed to be independent entities but actually were closely controlled by Enron executives who profited sensationally from such strategies. Andrew Fastow, a 31-year-old Enron officer, invested a few thousand dollars in the company and its affiliates after 1990 and walked away a decade later with more than $30 million. Kenneth Lay, Enron's CEO, had quietly divested himself of stock and stock options worth more than $200 million shortly before the company collapsed.

For shareholders, there was a billion dollar loss in Enron stock equity. For employees, there was fiscal catastrophe. Typical was a woman who had worked for the company for 16 years and placed 15 percent of her salary each month into Enron stock toward her retirement. She pleaded to be allowed to withdraw her investment, then at $700,000; the company refused, and she ended up with a $20,000 stake when the smoke had cleared. Fastow got a 10-year sentence, despite a plea bargain in which he agreed to supply information about other company officers.

Scholars picking through the debris of collapsed corporations often blamed the structure of corporate executives' pay incentives for the financial disasters (see Friedrichs, 2009). One writer summed up what had happened in these terms: "If the past 30 years have demonstrated anything, it is that the avarice of America's corporate leaders is practically unlimited and so is their power to run corporations in their own interest" (Cassidy, 2002:78). In 1973 the CEO of a major company was making about 45 times the average pay of the workers in that company. By 1991 the ratio had risen to 140. Today executives make about 500 times the wage of an average employee in their firm (Cassidy, 2002).

Criminological Theory and White-Collar Crime

Neil Shover (1998) believes that underlying white-collar crime are pressures to meet self-defined or externally imposed standards of successful performance. When medical scientists experience pressure to produce research breakthroughs, or when athletic coaches have a string of losing seasons, or when business owners see their profits decline, the odds are increased that they will resort to criminal resolutions.

When Sutherland first wrote of white-collar crime, he maintained that it was best explained by his theory of differential association (see Chapter 8). For Sutherland, the law-breaking behavior of businessmen, professionals, and politicians (as well as all other law violators) was the product of a learning process. Violators encountered examples of law-breaking among those with whom they worked, and they drifted or jumped into such patterns of behavior as part of their routine indoctrination into the requirements of their job. In time, they found that the definitions they encountered favorable to violation of the law overruled those encouraging law-abiding behavior.

The trouble with such an explanation, as we have seen, is that it is extremely difficult, if not impossible, to test. Controversy also exists regarding the ability of theoretical constructs to suitably interpret criminal charges against corporations rather than against individuals within them. Donald Cressey (1988) insisted that a corporation cannot form the requisite intent to allow satisfactory social psychological theorizing about its behavior. John Braithwaite and Brent Fisse (1990), rebutting Cressey, insisted that organizations possess a mind of their own (as represented, for instance, by corporate guidelines) that is distinct from the sum of the minds of those who contribute to its decisions, and that it is possible to offer theoretical interpretations of organizational acts.

The limited ability of strain theory to explain white-collar crime was recently demonstrated by Lynn Langton and Nicole Leeper Piquero (2009) who found the theory was applicable to a select group of white-collar offenders, but not likely to explain violations by corporate officers. They also noted that the strains involved differed for white-collar offenses from those of street criminals.

Summary

This chapter began with an emphasis on the fundamental cause of economic offenses, the desire to acquire money and goods and the ability and willingness to use illegal means to achieve that end. Human beings, it was pointed out, vary considerably in their devotion to material goods, their needs (real or imagined), and the likelihood that they will break the law to achieve financial ends. Some societies emphasize not acquisition but rather gift giving and plain living. Most religions deplore an undue accumulation of wealth in the face of others' poverty.

Burglary was seen to be marked by a calculation of risks and a routine that included getting into and out of a house in short order. Burglars overwhelmingly invade houses that are not occupied. They particularly choose as targets dwellings that cannot readily be seen by neighbors or passersby. The three-phase theoretical outline by John and Lyn Lofland was put forward as providing a particularly helpful interpretative scheme in regard to burglary. The Loflands maintained that burglary ensues from a perceived threat (which often is to the offender's self-esteem) that escalates into a state of encapsulation (in which the offender can think of no other way out of the dilemma) and then results in the crime.

Shoplifting, once largely a female crime, now shows a higher percentage of male offenders, a reflection of changes in shopping habits. Shoplifting by students was interpreted in a theoretical framework that focused on excitement and the seductive power of objects. It was said to be motivated more by boredom than poverty. The dynamics of employee theft are much the same as those that propel persons to shoplift.

Computer crime requires a particular kind of expertise. Computers make access to illegal economic gains much simpler.

White-collar crime, defined commonly as offenses committed by persons of power and status in the course of their occupations, has challenged many of the commonplace explanations of crime, such as those that regard broken homes as important contributors to lawbreaking. The concept of white-collar crimes nonetheless is suffused with definitional dilemmas.

Key Terms and Concepts

American Dream
Booster Box
Burglary
Criminaloid
Fence
Grand Larceny
Petit Larceny

Psychosocial Encapsulation
Robbery
Shoplifting
Target Hardening
Telemarketing Fraud
White-Collar Crime

Key Criminologists

John Braithwaite
Mary Owen Cameron
Donald Cressey
Jack Katz
John and Lyn Lofland

Henry Pontell
Edward A. Ross
Edwin H. Sutherland
Thorstein Veblen

References

Anand, S. (2007). *Essentials of the Sarbanes-Oxley Act*. Hoboken, NJ: John Wiley.

Appiahene-Gyamfi, J. (2003). "Urban Crime Trends and Patterns in Ghana: The Case of Accra." *Journal of Criminal Justice*, 31:1-11.

Bamber, B. & A. Spencer (2009). *Bear Trap: The Fall of Bear Stearns and the Panic of 2008*. New York, NY: Black Tower Press.

Barry, D. & S. Brown (1997). "Rational Choice and Environmental Cues among Residential Burglars." Paper presented at the annual meeting of the American Society of Criminology.

Berg, J. & I. Kimnes (2009). "An Overview of Crime in South Africa." *The Criminologist*, (May/June):22-24.

Bernasco, W. & R. Block (2009). "Where Offenders Choose to Attack: A Different Choice Model of Robberies in Chicago." *Criminology*, 47:93-130.

Blano, C., J. Grant, N.M. Petry, H.B. Simpson, A. Alegria, S.M. Liu & D. Hasin (2008). "Prevalence and Correlates of Shoplifting in the United States: Results from the National Epidemiological Survey on Alcohol and Related Conditions (NESARC). *American Journal of Psychiatry*, 165:905-913.

Blumberg, P. (1989). *The Predatory Society: Deception in the American Marketplace*. New York, NY: Oxford University Press.

Braithwaite, J. & B. Fisse (1990). "On the Plausibility of Corporate Crime Theory." In W.S. Laufer & F. Adler (eds.) *Advances in Criminological Theory*, 2:15-38. New Brunswick, NJ: Transaction.

Butterfield, F. (1997). "Property Crimes Steadily Decline, Led by Burglary." *New York Times*, (October 17):1,17.

Calavita, K., H. Pontell & R.H. Tillman (1997). *Big Money Crime: Fraud and Politics in the Savings and Loan Crisis*. Berkeley, CA: University of California Press.

Cameron, M.O. (1964). *The Booster and the Snitch: Department Store Shoplifting.* New York, NY: Free Press.

Cassidy, J. (2000). "The Greed Cycle: How the Financial System Encouraged Corporations to Go Crazy." *The New Yorker*, (September 23):64-77.

Christie, J. (ed.) (2006). *Fannie Mae and Freddie Mac: Scandal in U.S. Housing.* New York, NY: Nova.

Cohan, W.D. (2009). *House of Cards: A Tale of Hubris and Wretched Excess on Wall Street.* New York, NY: Doubleday.

Coleman, C. (2000). "As Thievery by Insiders Overtakes Shoplifting, Retailers Crack Down," *Wall Street Journal*, (October 4):A1, A16.

Conover, T. (2000). *Newjack: Guarding Sing Sing.* New York, NY: Random House.

Cressey, D.R. (1988)."The Poverty of Theory in Corporate Crime Research." In W.S. Laufer & F. Adler (eds.) *Advances in Criminological Theory*, 1:31-56. New Brunswick, NJ: Transaction.

Cromwell, P.F., J.N. Olson & D.W. Avery (1991). *Breaking and Entering: An Ethnographic Approach to Burglary.* Newbury Park, CA: Sage.

Dodge, M. & G. Geis (2006). "Fieldwork with the Elite: Interviews with White-Collar Criminals." In D. Hobbs & R. Wright (eds.) *The Sage Handbook of Field Work*, 79-92. London, UK: Sage.

DiMento, J.F.C. & G. Geis (2005). "Corporate Criminal Liability in the United States. In S. Tully (ed.) *Research Handbook on Corporate Legal Responsibility*, 159-176. Cheltenham, UK: Edward Elgar.

Doocey, J.H., D. Shichor, D.K. Sechrest & G. Geis (2001). "Telemarketing Fraud: Who Are the Tricksters and What Makes Them Trick?" *Security Journal*, 4:7-26.

Eichenwald, K. (2005). *Conspiracy of Fools: A True Story.* New York, NY: Broadway Books.

Fletcher, W.H. & F.N. Plette (2008). *Sarbanes-Oxley Act: Interpretation, Significance, and Impact.* New York, NY: Nova Science.

Friedrichs, D.O. (2009). "Exorbitant CEO Compensation: Just Reward or Grant Theft?" *Crime, Law and Social Change*, 51, 45-72.

Geis, G. (2007). *White-Collar and Corporate Crime.* Upper Saddle River, NJ: Prentice Hall.

Glasbeck, H. (2002). *Wealth by Stealth: Corporate Crime, Corporate Law, and the Perversion of Democracy.* Toronto, Ontario: Between the Lines.

Grabosky, P.N. (2007). *Electronic Crime.* Upper Saddle River, NJ: Prentice Hall.

Hochstetler, A. (2001). "Opportunities and Decisions: Interactional Dynamics in Robbery and Burglar Groups." *Criminology*, 39:732-767.

Jacobs, A. "As Shoplifters Sharpen Their Game, the Police Do, Too." *New York Times*, (December 24):A16.

Jacbos, B.A. & R. Wright (2008). "Researching Drug Robbery." *Crime and Delinquency*, 54:511-531.

Jesilow, P., H.N. Pontell & G. Geis (1994). *Prescription for Profit: How Doctors Defraud Medicaid.* Berkeley, CA: University of California Press.

Katz, J. (1988). *Seductions of Crime: Moral and Sensual Attractions to Doing Evil*. New York, NY: Basic Books.

Kelly, K. (2009). *Street Fighters: The Last 72 Hours of Bear Stearns, the Toughest Firm on Wall Street*. New York, NY: Portfolio.

Klemke, L.W. (1992). *The Sociology of Shoplifting: Boosters and Snitches Today*. Westport, CT: Praeger.

Klockars, C. (1974). *The Professional Fence*. New York, NY: The Free Press.

Krauss, L.I. & A. MacGahan (1979). *Computer Fraud and Countermeasures*. Englewood Cliffs, NJ: Prentice Hall.

Langton, L. & N.L. Piquero (2007). "Can General Strain Theory Explain White-Collar Crime?: A Preliminary Investigation of the Relationship between Stain and Select White-Collar Offenses." *Journal of Criminal Justice*, 35:1-15.

Lattanzi, G. (1999). "Raiders of the Lost Ark." *UTNE Reader*, (September 10):36.

Lessing, D. (1961). *In Pursuit of the English*. New York, NY: Simon and Schuster.

Lofland, J. & L.H. Lofland (1969). *Deviance and Identity*. Englewood Cliffs, NJ: Prentice Hall.

MacFarquhar, N. (2000). "Stock Swindler's Profile: Likes Wrestling, Hates Yankees, Is 15." *New York Times*, (September 22):A23.

Malcolm X. (1982). *The Autobiography of Malcolm X*. New York, NY: Grove Press.

Matthews, R. (2002). *Armed Robbery*. Cullompton, UK: Willan.

McCall, N. (1994). *Make Me Wanna Holler*. New York, NY: Random House.

McCarthy, B. (1995). "Not Just 'For the Thrill of It': An Instrumental Elaboration of Sneaky Thrill Property Crimes." *Criminology*, 33:519-538.

McDonald, L.G. & P. Robinson (2009). *A Colossal Failure of Common Sense: The Inside Story of the Collapse of Lehman Brothers*. New York, NY: Crown.

Merton, R.K. (1964). "Anomie, Anomia, and Social Integration: Contexts of Deviant Behavior." In M. Clinard (ed.) *Anomie and Deviant Behavior: A Discussion and Critique*, 213-242. New York, NY: The Free Press.

Messner, S.F. & R. Rosenfeld (2007). *Crime and the American Dream*, Fourth Edition. Belmont, CA: Thompson/Wadsworth.

Michaelson, A. (2009). *The Foreclosure of America: The Inside Story of the Rise and Fall of Countywide: Home Loans, the Mortgage Crisis and the Default of the American Dream*. New York, NY: Berkley Books.

Newman, A. (2006). "A Fire Unset Led to a Thief's Arrest." *New York Times*, (January28):B1.

Norris, F. (2003). "No Positives in this Legal Double Negative." *New York Times*, (January 24):C1.

Pontell, H.N. (2005). "Control Fraud, Gambling for Resurrection, and Moral Hazard: Accounting for White-Collar Crime in the Savings and Loan Crisis." *Journal of Socio-Economics*, 34:756-770.

Reiss, A.J. Jr. & A.D. Biderman (1980). *Data Sources on White-Collar Lawbreaking*. Washington, DC: National Institute of Justice, U.S. Department of Justice.

Robinson, M.B. & C.E. Robinson (1997). "Environmental Characteristics Associated with Residential Burglary of Student Apartment Complexes." *Environment and Behavior*, 29:657-675.

Rosoff, S.M., H.N. Pontell & R. Tillman (2003). *Looting America: Greed, Corruption, Villains, and Victims*. Upper Saddle River, NJ: Prentice Hall.

Ross, E.A. (1907). "The Criminaloid." *The Atlantic Monthly*, 99 (January):44-50.

Sander, P. (2009). *Madoff: Corruption, Deceit, and the Making of the World's Most Notorious Ponzi Scheme*. Guilford, CT: Lyons Press.

Shelp, D. & A. Ehrbar (2009). *Fallen Giant: The Amazing Story of Hank Greenberg and the History of AIG*. Second Edition. Hoboken, NJ: John Wiley

Shover, N. (1998). "White-Collar Crime." In M.J. Tonry (ed.) *Handbook of Crime and Punishment*, pp. 133-158. New York, NY: Oxford University Press.

Shover, N. (1996). *Great Pretenders: Pursuits and Careers of Persistent Thieves.* Boulder, CO: Westview.

Shover, N. & A. Hochstetler (2006). *Choosing White-Collar Crime*. New York, NY: Cambridge University Press.

Steffensmeir, D.J. (1986). *The Fence: In the Shadow of Two Worlds*. Totowa, NJ: Rowman and Littlefield.

Stevenson, R.J. (1998). *The Boiler Room and Other Telephone Sales Scams*. Urbana, IL: University of Illinois Press.

Strober, D. & G. Strober (2009). *Catastrophe: The Story of Bernard L. Madoff, the Man Who Swindled the World*. Beverly Hills, CA: Phoenix Books.

Sun-Sentinel (1989 May 4). "Alleged Thieves Willing to Pay Toll to Society." Fort Lauderdale, FL.

Sutherland, E.H. (1949/1983). *White Collar Crime: The Uncut Version*. New Haven, CT: Yale University Press.

Sutherland, E.H. (1940). "White-Collar Criminality." *American Sociological Review*, 5:1-12.

Sykes, G.M. & D. Matza (1957). "Techniques of Neutralization: A Theory of Delinquency." *American Sociological Review*, 22:664-670.

Theroux, P. (2000). *Fresh Air Fiend: Travel Writings, 1985-2000*. Boston: Houghton Mifflin.

Tillman, R.H. & M.L. Indergaard (2005). *Pump and Dump: The Rancid Rules of the New Economy*. New Brunswick, NJ: Rutgers University Press.

Trebay, G. (2000). "Shoplifting on a Grand Scale: Luxury Wear Stolen to Order." *New York Times*, (August 8):A24.

Tunnell, K.D. (2000). *Living Off Crime*. Chicago, IL: Burnham.

Vaughn, M.G., M. Delisi, K.M. Beaver & M.O. Howard (2008) "Toward a Quantitative Typology of Burglars: A Latent Profile Analysis of Career Offenders." *Journal of Forensic Sciences*, 53;1387-1392.

Veblen, T. (1912). *The Theory of the Leisure Class*. New York, NY: Macmillan.

Wallace, B.P. & B. Crowley (2000). *Final Confession: The Unsolved Crimes of Phil Cresta*. Boston, MA: Northeastern University Press.

Wallerstein, J., J. Lewis & S. Blakeslee (2000). *The Unexpected Legacy of Divorces: A 25 Year Landmark Study*. New York, NY: Hyperion.

Weisburd, D., E. Waring & E.F. Chayet (2001). *White-Collar Crime and Criminal Careers*. New York, NY: Cambridge University Press.

Wright, R.T. & S.H. Decker (1997). *Armed Robbers in Action: Stickups and Street Culture*. Boston, MA: Northeastern University Press.

Wright, R.T. & S.H. Decker (1993). *Burglars on the Job: Street Life and Residential Break-Ins*. Boston, MA: Northeastern University Press.

Zietz, D. (1981). *Women Who Embezzle or Defraud: A Study of Convicted Felons*. New York, NY: Praeger.

Zimmerman, A. (2006). "As Shoplifters Use High-Tech Scams, Retail Losses Rise." *Wall Street Journal* (October 25): A1, A12.

13
Crimes without Victims and Victims without Crimes

Most crimes create a victim, a person or an entity that suffers physical or emotional harm or the deprivation of something to which the victim has a legal right. In some instances the tie between the criminal action and the harm is inferred. Driving while intoxicated may not produce victims, but it is presumed that drunk drivers will not be in control of their vehicle as well as sober drivers and that their erratic driving may sooner or later cause harm. Some inebriated motorists may drive more carefully than they ordinarily do because they know that they are incapacitated, but they will not be able to drive as well as they could if they were equally attentive but not under the influence of alcohol. At the same time, it has to be appreciated that five out of six drunk drivers who kill in alcohol-related accidents have no previous official record for driving under the influence (Ross, 1992).

Crimes without Victims

There is a group of offenses that come under the heading of *crimes without victims* (Schur, 1965). Their common characteristic is that they involve consensual participation, that is, the parties to the illegal event engage in the behavior voluntarily. No participant complains about what occurs. It is the state in the form of the criminal law that objects and penalizes those caught in such behavior.

Prostitutes, for example, enter into sexual relationships with customers who purchase a commodity, much as someone would purchase the services and skills of a plumber or a lawyer. Indeed, in contemporary lawyer-bashing, the practice of law is sometimes equated to prostitution because many attorneys sell their wares to any party possessing the wherewithal to buy them, regardless of their own view about the guilt or innocence of the client. Illegal drug transactions also have no involuntary participants. Someone sells a product, just like people sell food, clothing, or household items, and someone else pays the asking price, bargains for a lower one, takes his or her business elsewhere, or does without.

Should They Be Crimes?

Those who believe that the roster of victimless crimes ought to be thinned or eliminated argue that an essential trait of a democracy is that it extends freedom to all citizens so long as that freedom does not infringe upon the equivalent liberty of other people. Those holding this view assert that victimless offenses are outlawed primarily on religious grounds. Prostitution violates theological dictates condemning fornication and adultery. But most Western religions, they point out, also condemn a considerable variety of other acts that the criminal law ignores, such as taking the Lord's name in vain, usury, and cursing a parent (an offense for which the Bible dictates the death penalty). Suicide also is abhorred in Catholic theology. In earlier times, suicides were declared criminal offenders, their goods confiscated, and their bodies buried in unhallowed ground at crossroads, with stakes driven through their hearts. These views no longer influence secular law. Nor, it is argued, should other facets of any group's moral or religious beliefs be imposed by law on those who do not accept the group's principles, unless it can be shown that a particular action harms others.

There is an opposing position. It holds that victimless crime is a faulty construct; that in actual fact there is no such thing. Prostitutes, it is said, degrade women in general, transmit AIDS and venereal diseases, disrupt families, rob their customers, and support pimps, men who exploit them ruthlessly. Drug addicts often are unable to engage in productive work and they steal from innocent victims in order to obtain money for their fix.

Pornography

Intense debate surrounds pornography, a purported "victimless crime." Many people maintain that pornography routinely depicts awful scenes of male brutalization of women and that it encourages acts of rape and sadism directed against women. Legislative bodies in Indianapolis and Minneapolis passed ordinances banning "sexually explicit" materials that "graphically sexually exploit subordination of women, whether in words or pictures" (MacKinnon & Dworkin, 1997). The Minneapolis ordinance declared that pornography was central to creating and maintaining the inequality of the sexes. The failure to provide a satisfactory definition of the term "sexually explicit," however, and, more basically, the conflict between the ordinances and the first amendment right to free speech led the Minneapolis mayor to veto the ordinance, and a court to rule that the Indianapolis law did not meet constitutional standards (*American Booksellers Assn. v. Hudnut*, 1985). Particularly disturbing has been the recent appearance of Webcam sites in which adults induce children to undress and perform various sexual acts that are transmitted live on computer portals (Note, 2009; Otis, 2009).

Those on the other side, while they often are hard-pressed to say much good about the product, believe that the First Amendment to the U.S. Constitution protects unpopular forms of expression, including pornography. Debate also centers on the actual consequences of exposure to pornography, and whether it reflects social values rather than introduces them. The fundamental questions are first, whether the publication and purchase of pornography is a crime without victims; second, whether innocent people suffer harmful consequences because of its legal status, and third, whether a free society is obligated to tolerate certain activities because they are part of the spectrum of constitutionally protected rights (Cothran, 2002).

Motorcycle Helmets

Ideological dispute often comes to rest on a prototypic victimless crime: riding a motorcycle without a helmet. Opponents of laws that require a helmet insist that the choice should be the motorcyclist's; if he or she elects not to wear a helmet, this should be nobody else's business. Those who advocate a law mandating the wearing of helmets say that the protection afforded the motorcyclist is also a social protection because it guards against outcomes such as might ensue if a rock strikes the unprotected head of the motorcyclist, who then loses control of the vehicle and crashes into a passing car, injuring or killing its occupants. It is stressed that the rate of motorcycle fatalities has risen for ten consecutive years. In 2007, while the deaths of people in cars and trucks and on bicycles dropped by 2,000 to 41,959, deaths of motorcyclists rose by 6.6 percent, to 5,154. The Motorcycle Safety Foundation reported that a person killed on a motorcycle was 2.5 times more likely to be under the influence of alcohol than a person killed in a car and three times more likely not to have a proper license (Wald, 2008).

The contrary argument is that all human existence is filled with risks and that we cannot handcuff every exercise of human freedom in order to try to reduce hazards. After all, nobody would seriously suggest that we cut down the heavy toll of highway deaths by banning automobiles, though many more people are killed each year in automobile accidents than are victims of homicides.

Where helmet wearing is mandatory for motorcyclists, the rationale is that the inconvenience to the rider is hardly so burdensome as to constitute an intolerable deprivation of liberty. As a legal scholar put the matter: "Any new law at all is some restriction on liberty, but not all restrictions are threats to it" (Woozley, 1983:130). Helmets assuredly save lives, although it is notable that 84 percent of those killed in motorcycle accidents in the 20 states and the District of Columbia where helmets are mandated were helmeted; lane changing is regarded as a particularly dangerous motorcycle maneuver (Mayrose, 2008).

In a notable conflict involving constitutional rights four Sikhs asked the courts for permission to ride motorcycles without helmets because the religiously-required Rishi knot into which they bind their hair under their turbans makes it impossible for them to put on a motorcycle helmet properly. A California court was not sympathetic. The motorcycle helmet law, it ruled, did not prevent a Sikh from wearing a Rishi knot and a turban and therefore did not prevent him from practicing his religion. "Rather, it prohibited him from riding a motorcycle on public highways without a helmet" (*Buhl v. Harrigan*, 1993:1616).

Pros and Cons

Opponents of the libertarian position that calls for minimum interference with human choices believe that a civilized society has a right to enforce a "common morality." In a forceful argument for this position, Patrick Devlin (1965:13), then a British high court judge, maintained that social harm results if we fail to secure adherence to a general standard of morality:

> Societies disintegrate from within more frequently than they are broken up by external pressure. There is disintegration when no common morality is observed and history shows that the loosening of moral bonds is often the first stage of disintegration, so that society is justified in taking the same steps to preserve its moral code as it does to preserve its governmental and other institutions.

Devlin's position was seconded by Robert Bork, a Yale Law School professor: "Moral outrage is a sufficient ground for prohibitory legislation," Bork declared. "Knowledge that the activity is taking place is harm to those who find it profoundly immoral" (Bork, 1991:132).

A seventeenth-century English divine used a colorful analogy to express his opposition to allowing individuals to go their own way (or, in contemporary language, to do their own thing) if what they do detracts from social well-being. Well known, because it formed the basis for the title of a novel by Ernest Hemingway, is this dictum of John Donne (1624, No. 7):

> No man is an island of itself; every man is a piece of the continent, a part of the main. Any man's death diminishes me, because I am involved in mankind. And therefore never send to know for whom the bell tolls: It tolls for thee.

Standing at the opposite end of this controversy is Friedrich Nietzsche, the German philosopher, who maintained that "morality is the best of all devices for leading mankind by the nose" (Nietzsche, 1844/1920:44).

Other counter-arguments insist that t laws must balance outcomes. To outlaw the use of narcotics, it is sometimes maintained, creates many of the situations that are then used to defend the prohibitory law. If narcotics were freely available, the argument goes, addicts would not have to steal to support their habits, and organized criminals would not be able to dominate the traffic in drugs. Similarly, prostitutes would not have to suffer the harassment of the police and their self-image might improve if they were engaged in a lawful occupation, perhaps one licensed in the same manner as other public services. In addition, the decriminalization forces argue that laws against prostitution have proven ineffective since the dawn of civilization, and that the United States now has sought to control narcotics without notable success for almost a century. Those holding the opposite position argue that, while the statutes have not eliminated or perhaps even reduced the undesirable behaviors, there is no way of knowing how much more often these behaviors would occur if they were not against the law.

The Decriminalization Drift

What is notable is the dramatic change in the way the law has come to view some victimless crimes during our own lifetime and that of our parents. Forty or so years ago, prostitution, gambling, drug use, homosexuality, and abortion were serious criminal behaviors. Today, abortion during the first trimester of pregnancy is a legal right, though fierce controversy rages about the propriety of this position. Gambling, once permitted only in Nevada, today is legal in virtually all American jurisdictions. Current debate regarding homosexuality centers on delimited issues, such as gay marriage and how overt homosexuals may be in the military. While certain drugs continue to be banned and our jails and prisons continue to overflow with inmates charged with drug law violations, marijuana possession and usage statutes have been eased and there is growing sentiment to experiment with legal distribution of drugs. Only prostitution remains under interdiction.

It has been suggested that, like much else in the society, the possession of power is the key to understanding changes in the law's approach to victimless crimes. Legalizing abortion was supported by powerful women whose lives could be distressed by unwanted pregnancies. The ranks of homosexuals also included powerful persons—lawyers, legislators, and wealthy folk—who could make an impact on the law. Gambling, besides offering a large amount of money to hard-pressed state budgets, was engaged in by people with power, and marijuana was a drug sometimes used by their children. Only prostitutes, largely powerless, catering primarily to the marginal and dispossessed, remain condemned by the criminal law throughout virtually all of the United States.

Physician-Assisted Suicide

Considerable controversy in the victimless crime realm has focused on the idea of physician-assisted suicide or, as some call it, "hastened death." Those in favor say that persons with debilitating illnesses, if they so desire, ought to be allowed to determine the time and the manner of their death. They should not have to suffer mercilessly from pain and invasive medical procedures while they move toward an inevitable demise. Their medical expenses when mortally ill can be inordinately high. Fifty percent of the total budget for Medicare is devoted to the costs for elderly people who are in their last six months of life. It is also argued that sanctioning physician-assisted suicide only makes overt the practice of many doctors who allow patients to die by giving them lethal doses of sedatives or withholding procedures that might keep them alive for a short time.

Those opposed to physician-assisted suicide say that it can be a "slippery slope" (see Wright, 2000), an entry point that will expand to allow physicians to kill persons suffering from transient bouts of depression and children who have disabilities (Lode, 1999). Laws permitting physician-induced suicide might encourage some people to give up rather than to fight to construct what could prove to be a happy and fulfilling continuing existence. Besides, to save money, pressure might be exerted to "clear the underbrush" (Nuland, 1994) by eliminating persons who are on a downward health spiral but who, if not encouraged otherwise, would prefer to remain alive. Such a measure, some say, would substitute a "duty to die" for a "right to die." That the law may be abused is illustrated by a case from Japan detailed in Highlight 13.1.

HIGHLIGHT 13.1
JAPAN Assisted Suicide without Consent

> Public opinion polls conducted by Japanese newspapers revealed up to 70 percent of respondents in favor of legalizing assisted suicide. Around 10 percent did not object to the idea of terminally ill people being killed without their consent. Nearly half of doctors questioned said they had been asked by family members to end the life of patients without the patients' consent or, in many cases, since the typical Japanese cancer patients are never told the truth about their diagnosis, without the patient ever knowing that he or she was mortally ill (Editorial, 1997:18).

Oregon was the first American jurisdiction to permit physician-assisted suicide, followed in 2009 by Washington. In both states the patient must be an adult and a state resident, must initiate the request to die (or, more literally, to kill himself or herself), show no documented depression, and be diagnosed by two doctors as having no more than six months to live. Doctors must outline for the patient alternative paths, including hospice care and pain-control medications. The laws also establish a 15-day waiting period between the patient's verbal request and the signing of a consent form. They allow the doctor to prescribe a lethal dose of drugs that the patient must take by himself or herself. Opponents of the law declare that death from some drugs being employed could require as long as three hours and that patients sometimes vomit the drugs reflexively. They also insist that the programs undercut what could be effective end-of-life palliative care: one set of writers believes this has been true in Oregon (Hendin & Foley, 2009; see also Jeffrey, 2009; an opposing conclusion is reported by Gill, 2009).

By the end of 2008 401 persons had been killed (or allowed to kill themselves, depending on how you view the issue) under the Oregon law. Those who chose the option were overwhelmingly white and, by a slight margin, males. Virtually all the deaths were brought about by the use of fast-acting barbiturates combined with an antiemetic agent. Most patients became unconscious within five minutes and most died within an hour, though one person, while unconscious, lingered for 11.5 hours (Chin, Hedberg, Higginson & Fleming, 1999). A ten-year review of the Oregon program concluded that the "weight of evidence suggests that the predictions of dire consequences were incorrect" and that the program had not "caused physicians, patients, or Oregonians in general to value life less" (Lindsay, 2009:19).

A particularly interesting analysis of physician-assisted suicide by Tania Salem (1999) points out that the Oregon law has medicalized suicide, transforming what almost always is a private act into a medical event. Salem notes that the law does not, as its supporters maintain, increase human autonomy and freedom, since competent persons always have been able to leave this life when they desired: now they must involve medical assistance; or, in Salem's words, they must "request public endorsement and legitimization of the act of suicide" (Salem, 1999:33).

Prostitution—Sex Work

Female Prostitution

What can be said of an act of female prostitution. Is it:

- An ugly and intolerable consequence of the power of males over females and the sexual exploitation of girls and women?

Or is it:

- A sensible commercial enterprise engaged in by a seller who possesses a commodity that has a market value?

For American feminists, prostitution has been a difficult and divisive issue. Some favor the second interpretation of prostitution stated above, seeing prostitutes as sex-trade workers. Others adopt the first position. They regard prostitution as the outcome of a patriarchal society in which women are defined as sex objects. Child sexual abuse, incest, and similar female victimizations are said to lie at the core of entry into prostitution. Many feminists equate prostitution to slavery, especially when pimps are involved (Holsopple, 1999). Andrea Dworkin (1997:145) took the position that "when men use women in prostitution, they are expressing a pure hatred of the female body."

Patriarchal control of prostitution is said to be reflected in the fact that many prostitutes depend upon pimps, men who take most of their earnings, and, in return, offer them protection from customers and the police and real affection or a caricature of it. For middle-class persons, the dynamics of pimping often seem difficult to comprehend. The effective pimp typically persuades several women that the only way that they can gain his love is to work the streets, bars, and hotels, seeking out customers (johns) for a sexual encounter. The pimp-prostitute roles reverse the usual (but changing) gender courtship pattern in American society in which the male must persuade the female that he is a suitable partner. Today, however, the word "pimp" appears to have replaced "cool" in popular American slang. Lisa Richardson (2000) points out that middle-class college students, chat-room denizens, and others who have nothing to do with the sex trade now designate things such as birthday presents, bikes, and clothes as "pimp." The trend illustrates the tendency of outlaw language and styles to relocate in mainstream usage.

In response to feminist protests, some police departments now use sting campaigns to arrest men who visit prostitutes, although their general belief is that the results are more symbolic than effective in reducing the level of sex trade. Some jurisdictions also revoke driving licenses of men who solicit streetwalkers and/or put the johns' photograph in public places or on the Internet. More drastic is the policy of asset forfeiture in which the vehicle that the customer used to solicit a prostitute is confiscated.

Mary Dodge and her co-workers' interviews with female police officers in sting operations found that the officers had ambivalent feelings about such work. One officer, who had participated in reverse prostitution at least once a month for six years said: "Being a decoy does feel kind of slimy, but it's an ego trip to get the johns because they're the scum of the earth." Another officer, with ten years' experience, commented: "At first, I thought: What am I doing? You get out there and you don't want to fail. It's pride. What if nobody picks me up?" (Dodge, Starr-Gimeno & Williams, 2005:76-77).

The United States is "one of the few western nations in which all forms of prostitution are illegal almost everywhere" (Anderson, 2002:748). The exceptions to the "almost everywhere" are Nevada and Rhode Island. Since 1971, Nevada law has permitted prostitution if a county with a population of less than 250,000 elects to do so. Prostitution now is permitted in 14 of Nevada's 17 counties, although it actually occurs in only 11 counties where there are 28 brothels. Nevada's legal brothels (they call themselves "ranches") are said to "offer the safest environment available for women who sell consensual sex for money." They rely on panic buttons in the assignation rooms, listening devices, and management surveillance (Brents & Hausbeck, 2005:289). Legal prostitutes in Nevada have undergone testing for AIDS since 1988 and "none has tested HIV positive since testing was mandated" (Weitzer, 2005:217).

Rhode Island offers a more limited and currently highly controversial acceptance of what is labeled "indoor prostitution" because in 1980 when the state revised its law on prostitution it outlawed brothels, streetwalking, loitering for indecent purposes, and soliciting women form a vehicle, but, probably by oversight, failed to proscribe prostitution itself (*State v. DeMagistris*, 1998). In 2009, a divided state legislature was debating whether it ought to outlaw all forms of prostitution.

Legalized prostitution, compared to unregulated illegal prostitution, results in a lower rate of AIDS because the women are in a better position than freelancers to insist that customers use condoms. Streetwalking prostitutes will not carry many condoms on their person for fear that the police will use them as evidence that they are practicing an illegal trade (Campbell, 1991).

The greatest AIDS danger for prostitutes is not from their work but from their sexual relations with men with whom they have formed a romantic attachment and with whom they do not insist on the use of condoms (Campbell, 1991). As an Australian prostitute noted: "I can't use a condom with my boyfriend. What'll he think—that I'm gonna charge him next?" (Waddell, 1996:81).

Women working in Nevada brothels usually are fingerprinted and must carry identification cards. Nevada requires that houses of prostitution not be located on a principal business street or within 400 yards of a schoolhouse or church. The women work as independent contractors. They typically turn over one-half of their receipts to the owners, and pay a daily fee for room and board. Generally, they work seven consecutive 12-hour days, then are off for two or three weeks. They average six customers daily and charge anywhere from $150 to $500, with the price varying with the time of day, the day of the week, the customer's attitude, and how drunk or high he is (Albert, 2001).

Prostitution offers a range of vocational advantages (depending, of course, on the alternative kinds of work available to the person), including flexible work hours, contact with diverse kinds of persons, a heightened sense of activity, and the opportunity to make substantial sums of money. Such benefits do not, however, accrue to all practitioners and may not endure for very long. For those women whose involvement is tawdry, prostitution represents a dangerous and dirty enterprise. They experience physical violence and earn little money (Dalla, 2007). The likely loss of self-esteem is in part a function of broader social attitudes, which in some degree are tied to the legal sanctions against the behavior. On the other hand, for some prostitutes the social definition of immorality seems rather flexible. The novelist Doris Lessing reports living in a New York apartment among a number of women engaged in the sex trade. She asked one of them if she enjoyed sex. "If you're going to talk dirty," said the prostitute, "I'm not interested" (Klein, 2000:220).

For many male customers, a prostitute represents a commodity that can be purchased and used without emotional involvement or complications. Responses solicited from 700 johns found that 47 percent found the liaison "exciting," while 43 percent indicated that they wanted "a different experience than my partner provides" and 42 percent agreed with the statement: "I am shy and awkward when I am trying to meet a woman." Smaller but significant numbers said that they did not have the time for a conventional relationship or that they did not want the responsibilities of such a relationship (Monto, 2004). As one customer put it: "I don't care about the excitement of the chase one bit. What I would really like would be a brothel where you simply go in, pay your money, and go home at a reasonable hour without any understanding on either side" (Davenport-Hines, 1995:223). A different view is offered by the Nobel Prize winning author V.S. Naipaul: "When I was young, I was a greater frequenter of prostitutes. I found them intensely stimulating. But what happened was that by the time I was in my mid-thirties, I began to feel depressed by sex with a prostitute. I felt cheated and frustrated" (French, 2008:475).

Some prostitutes have taken to the Internet, cellular phones, and the camouflage of "escort services" to carry on their sex work. The yellow pages of New York City's telephone book has more than fifty pages of listings for escort services, some of them legal businesses, others camouflages for illegal prostitution. Failure to differentiate carefully what might be called "suite prostitution" from "street prostitution" can lead to erratic conclusions about the practice (Weitzer, 2007). One study found that 75 percent of call girls, 19 percent of brothel workers, and none of the streetwalkers reported that they frequently had orgasms in their work. Almost all call girls indicated that they experienced an increase in self-esteem when they entered the trade; only eight percent of the streetwalkers gave the same response (Prince, 1986).

The possibility of decriminalizing prostitution in the United States (it is legal in many foreign countries, see Highlights 13.2 and 13.3) seems unlikely in the near future. The leading group advocating a change in the law is COYOTE (Call Off Your Old Tired Ethics), a San Francisco-based organization. It demands total removal of the criminal law's involvement with prostitution. The movement, however, continues to meet strong resistance; overwhelmingly, Americans define prostitution as immoral and, as is often the case, they believe that if it is morally wrong it ought to be outlawed.

HIGHLIGHT **13.2**
GERMANY Prostitution Reform

The German government in 2000 inaugurated a sweeping revision of laws regulating prostitution. Sex work had not been illegal in Germany, but the old law did not regard it as equivalent to other kinds of occupations. The new law eliminated the word *sittenvidrig*—meaning immoral—from the prostitution statutes, thereby allowing prostitutes to apply for health insurance and social security benefits. There are an estimated 500,000 prostitutes at work in Germany. One survey found that every day 1.2 million Germans pay for commercial sex, a figure that annually comes to nearly $7 billion.

HIGHLIGHT **13.3**
THE NETHERLANDS A Different Approach to Prostitution

Designated streetwalking zones have been established in major Dutch cities. They are said to function as safe sites in which women serve as sex workers. The zone is also said to offer the benefit of a shelter that affords prostitutes a place to meet with their colleagues, talk to health care professionals, and relax. Earlier, both the prostitutes and the police had concluded that frequent raids were only making matters worse. The women were frightened and often on the run. And the police believed that they were failing to make the streets any safer (Klinger, 2000:19).

Male Prostitution

While female prostitution is by far the most common form of the activity, young men also seek and are sought by male customers for homosexual activity. Sari van der Poel's (1992) study of male prostitutes divides them into four groups: (1) pseudo-prostitutes, boys and young men who engage in the activity if an opportunity presents itself; (2) hustlers, those who commit a wide variety of crimes, including prostitution; (3) occasionals, persons who usually lead conventional lives, but move into prostitution at times; and (4) professionals, who view prostitution as a commercial, service-oriented business. Highly valued in the work is the ability to convince a customer to spend more than he anticipated. A high percentage of the patrons of male prostitutes in The Netherlands are tourists.

Jim Cates and Jeffrey Markley (1992) report that a major goal of male prostitutes is to form a liaison with an older man—a "sugar daddy"—who will support them. As with female prostitutes, virtually all of the American male prostitutes say that financial incentives are what motivate their involvement. Martin Weinberg and his colleagues (1999) found that male prostitutes report more satisfaction from their sexual encounters than females.

One form of male prostitution involves transgender dressers, men who dress as women and solicit male customers for oral copulation. They are involved in a risky business because some customers, if they learn of the bodied gender of the prostitute, may react with violence. A study in New York found that transgender male prostitutes dressed more scantily than female streetwalkers and are more aggressive in approaching potential customers (Cohen, 1980).

Theoretical Views of Prostitution

Prostitutes were singled out for special theoretical attention in Cesare Lombroso's early writings, before he curtailed significantly his stark biological determinism (see Chapter 6). Lombroso attempted to figure out why prostitutes so often were fat. Their obesity "strikes those who look at them en masse," he declared, and he thought he knew the reason. Prostitutes were atavistic throwbacks; they were like Hottentots, who also were obese (Lombroso & Ferrero, 1895).

In today's world, prostitution is interpreted most often in sociopolitical terms. Nanette Davis (1993:viii) summarizes the prevalent view:

> Legal, social, and political patterns both generate and sustain prostitution in its various societal forms. The international focus also demonstrates the selective, gender-based, hierarchal nature of control that often exploits and damages women. Prostitution is both a social problem, linked to existing social and political structures (and hence can change only as institutions change), and, given market economies, a social opportunity for women, their male managers, and local entrepreneurs.

Drug Offenses

Illegal drug use is an activity in which a person inhales, swallows, or injects a banned pharmaceutical product that directly affects only that person, although the act can have far-reaching consequences in terms of crime, driving accidents, and illness, among other matters.

About 70 percent of the federal prison inmates now are drug offenders. In 1980, there were 41,000 persons in American prisons for drug offenses; in 2009, that figure had escalated to 500,000 prisoners. Drug sentences often exceed those for manslaughter, sexual abuse, assault, and arson, and cost taxpayers more than $20,000 annually for each inmate. At the same time, there has been a slight, but growing, movement to experiment with the decriminalization of drug transactions and usage. Since the use of alcohol and cigarettes is permitted, and both can produce devastating health consequences, people wonder why other drugs are singled out for illegal status. It also is argued that the campaign against cigarette smoking has enjoyed considerable success. Some believe that a powerful anti-drug program could prove more effective than punitive laws.

Among concerns regarding decriminalization of drug use is that there is little agreement on how the procedure might operate. Most favor some form of "medicalization" by means of which drugs would be dispensed under controlled conditions, but it is uncertain whether a black market might not spring up for those who would want to avoid official channels or would want to obtain more or different drugs than what might be available to them from licensed sources (Mosher & Akins, 2007). Highlight 13.4 portrays the approach to drug use in The Netherlands today.

HIGHLIGHT 13.4
THE NETHERLANDS A Free Drug Market

> In The Netherlands, where drugs that are illegal in the United States have been freely available since 1976, reports indicate that there has been a notable reduction in crime. The Dutch drug addiction rate is one of Europe's lowest, with an estimated 15,000 hard-core drug addicts and 600,000 marijuana users in a nation of 15 million persons. A needle-exchange program has given the Dutch one of the lowest AIDS rates in the world for intravenous drug users. But the cause-effect relationship is not that simple.. Spain, which decriminalized "soft" drugs for personal use more than a decade ago and tolerates heroin and cocaine use, has the highest AIDS death rate in Europe, with 75 percent of the mortalities stemming from intravenous drug use. Obviously, other factors besides the stance of the law feed into these diverse outcomes (Zimmer & Morgan, 1997:175; see further Korf, Bullington & Riper, 1999)

Internationally, the United Nations estimates that about 140 million people—about 2.5 percent of the world's population—smoke marijuana or hashish, a form of marijuana. At least 13 million people are believed to sniff, smoke, or inject forms of cocaine. Another eight million use heroin. The international business in illegal drugs generates an estimated $400 billion a year, amounting to eight percent of all international trade. Cultivation of opium poppies now covers more than 691,000 acres worldwide. About 300,000 million tons of coca leaves, from which cocaine is derived, are grown in Peru, Colombia, and Bolivia (Wren, 2000).

Opiate Drugs

Opiates include heroin, morphine, laudanum, and codeine, the last a less potent form than the others. The drugs are addictive in the sense that their continued use builds up a tolerance, requiring heavier dosages to obtain the same physiological response. In addition, cessation of opiate use brings on withdrawal symptoms that can involve intense physical distress. The drugs are depressants; they produce a feeling of euphoria. In this respect, addicts sometimes suffer from serious physical ailments that are masked by the effects of the drug. Opiates also blunt sexual feelings.

Before passage in 1914 of the Harrison Act, the initial federal statute outlawing opiates, the incorporation of opiates in patent medicines created addicts at all social levels. There were more female than male addicts because of the use of palliatives containing opiates for "female troubles." Narcotics could be purchased over the counter or ordered through the mail (Jonnes, 1999). Heroin was hailed as the new wonder drug, a treatment for respiratory ailments and a cough suppressant. It was produced cheaply with a high degree of purity and was usually taken orally. The name itself comes from "heroic," indicating the pharmaceutical value that the Bayer laboratories put upon it when they began marketing heroin in 1898 (Booth, 1999).

After 1914, addicts increasingly came to be concentrated in the lower socioeconomic classes, and the ratio of male to female addicts changed dramatically. Following World War II, narcotics began to be defined as a formidable public problem. The medical profession deserted the field of treatment, largely in response to threats by federal law enforcement agents based upon their agencies' arguable reading of several court decisions (Cartwright, 2001; Musto & Korsemeyer, 2002). Summarizing the situation, Paul Jesilow and his colleagues (1993:22) write:

> What is particularly notable about doctors and narcotics is the extraordinary and hasty retreat of U.S. medical practitioners from the field once the government began to regulate it. In England doctors refused to abdicate what they deemed as their responsibility for persons addicted to drugs. In the United States, there were a few prosecutions of doctors who defied or tried to evade the authority of the government, and the matter was settled. American doctors had found drug clients largely unsavory, the financial return uncertain, and the whole business not worth their trouble.

Heroin use, like most human behavior, is intended to provide the person with a satisfying outcome, at least in the short run. "It's like, the best way I can think of, sweet death," a life-long addict has said. "Because it is sweet, overpoweringly so in a lot of ways, but with an edge of real terrible danger, I guess that's why everyone has to play with it" (Hughes, 1961:124). Note that this addict presumes that "everyone" has or will flirt with heroin use, a wildly inaccurate premise. Pleasure, as the quotation suggests, has its costs and risks. It is one thing to use morphine to dull the awful pain of a terminal illness, but another to try to avoid unpleasantness in human existence. Ultimately, social values dictate the illegal status of heroin; the government will not tolerate people being lulled and dulled by a drug, but wants them to participate with as clear a mind as they can command in whatever course life lays out for them (Zimring & Hawkins, 1993).

A 33-year longitudinal study of heroin users documents decades of despair associated with the lifestyle of heroin users. Of the 581 men in the original study, 284 had died, 29.6 percent from drug overdoses or from poisoning by adulterants added to the drug. An additional 38.6 percent died from cancer or from heart or liver disease, the last often associated with hepatitis C, a contagious condition transmitted by needles used for drug injections that are not sterile. Three died of AIDS, while homicides, suicides, or accidents killed another 9.4 percent. The death rates were dramatically higher than those for an equivalent population.

The men still living were struggling. About 40 percent reported using heroin within the past year, and abuse of other illegal drugs was also frequent. Those men who had abstained from heroin use for five years were less likely to return to use, but even in this group 25 percent resumed use, some after 15 years of abstinence. Use of alcohol and illegal drugs other than heroin were common among the heroin abstainers (Hser, Hoffman, Grella & Anglin, 2001; for a similar study in Australia see Danke et al., 2009).

By 2009, Afghanistan had become the world's largest exporter of heroin, with the revenue supplying money that supported the terrorist insurgency. The massive production of heroin by Afghans had brought the price down from $251 per gram in 1990 to $75 for the same amount in 2006, thereby making the drug accessible to a larger number of people (Peters & Merlington, 2009; Shishkin & Crawford, 2006).

Perspectives on Heroin Use

There are a variety of explanations offered for heroin use, but none that has obtained a large measure of agreement within the criminological community. Since the behavior is usually done alone rather than as part of a group, psychological and psychiatric theories dominate the field. It is commonly believed that addicts tend to be passive persons, prone to dependence upon a pharmacological agent that allows them to avoid confrontation with the imperatives of "reality." But in many regards the demands of a heroin addict's existence are a great deal more "real" than the demands of life lived in more routine ways. The addict must obtain money, often on a daily basis, to buy the drug. He or she also must locate a source and evade the police: it can be a frantic lifestyle (Caputo, 2008). One writer captures this view with the observation that "what appears to be a lack of will is in fact a serious commitment to the downward spiral" (Powers, 2000:145).

Suggested psychiatric explanations seem equally superficial. "Drugs are the instant mother, the instant mother they never had," psychiatrist Bruno Bettelheim (1969:125) maintained. This observation is based on the idea that there is a necessary quantity of "mothering" required to produce "normal" behavior, and that drug use is an "abnormal" substitute for a healthy upbringing. The postulation is riddled with questionable assumptions. For one thing, the dramatic shift of drug use from middle-class women to lower-class men was not accompanied by any notable change in patterns of mothering.

Sociologists sometimes claim that heroin use is a response to the misery of slum existence and poverty, a painkiller for the distress of unemployment and a bleak pattern of life, and that therefore the most effective means to reduce addiction is to eliminate economic and social inequality. Such conditions are abhorrent as matters of social injustice, but it is not readily demonstrable that they produce addiction. Again, the fact that opiate use formerly prevailed in the middle class tends to undermine this idea.

Cocaine

Cocaine, an alkaloid derived from coca plant leaves, answers to people's demand on themselves for top performance. It is a central nervous system stimulant that results in bursts of energy and gregarious enthusiasm. Among the difficulties associated with cocaine use is that it is expensive, and after the brief initial flood of energy it at times sends users into mild to severe depression. More cocaine may be used to avoid such depression, continuing the process until, for many users, the habit becomes unmanageable.

Cocaine largely was an underground drug throughout the first half of the twentieth century. Its major devotees were jazz musicians, prostitutes, and criminals. The drug then began to be used by groups such as the Beatniks of New York's Greenwich Village and San Francisco's North Beach, and Hollywood entertainers. More recently, cocaine, cultivated in South America, has infiltrated all levels of American society.

While cocaine is not physically addictive, as heroin is, it usually creates a psychological dependence. Cocaine also can produce hyperstimulation, digestive disorders, nausea, loss of appetite, weight loss, occasional convulsions, and sometimes delusions of persecution. Repeated inhalation can erode the mucous membranes and perforate the nasal septum. A chronic "runny nose" often is the hallmark of the regular cocaine user.

Crack Cocaine

Crack cocaine costs considerably less than regular cocaine and is smoked rather than snorted or sniffed. The smoking utensil can be a special glass pipe or a makeshift device fabricated from beer and soda cans, jars, bottles, and other containers known as "stems," "straight shooters," "skillets," "tools," or "ouzies" (Inciardi et al., 1993). Crack or freebase cocaine is a different chemical product than cocaine itself, but is derived from it. It produces a rapid, potent high, and, as Inciardi and his colleagues (1993:8) note, when it arrived on the drug scene in quantity, crack "became a popular fast-food analog of cocaine because of the ease with which it could be concocted."

Crack usage has been especially pronounced among women, and the media have been prone to highlight crack-addicted newborns on the pediatric wards of county hospitals. Such media portrayals of horrific damage inflicted on their babies by crack-using mothers are contradicted by a number of scientific studies that demonstrate that prenatal cocaine use has minimal effects on newborn infants, and that such effects are primarily limited to minor growth deficits. The researchers point out that the media stories fail to separate the mother's crack use from other factors such as recourse to additional illegal substances, poor nutrition, poverty, and failure to secure adequate medical attention (Day & Richardson, 1993).

What has been marked in the realm of crack usage is the emergence of "crack-houses" in which women, desperate for crack, exchange sex for the drug. After studying the phenomenon in Miami, Inciardi and his co-workers concluded:

> The sex-for-crack phenomenon and the incredible degradation of women surrounding much of its routine enactment is like nothing ever seen in the annals of drug use, street life, prostitution, or domestic woman-battering. It entails a variety of hypersexual behaviors—high-frequency sex, numerous anonymous partners, public as well as private sex, groups as well as couples, heterosexual or homosexual or both simultaneously (Inciardi et al., 1993:39).

Tanya Sharpe points out: "A woman who shares a man's crack supply is obliged to perform a sexual act in exchange for smoking. Men who smoke with other men are not required to do so." She notes that this represents "a clear example of gender bias and is exemplary of male primacy in the crack culture" (Sharpe, 2005:65).

In New York City, during the 10 years before 2000, the police made nearly 900,000 drug arrests—more than in any other city in the world. Almost a third of these were for selling and using crack. But it does not appear to be the impact of these arrests that contributed to the recent decline in the crack trade, since nearly every other city, regardless of its law enforcement response, has shown the same or greater reduction in crack usage. The crack epidemic, as one writer observes, "behaved much like a fever. It came on strong, appearing to rise without hesitation, and then broke, just as the most dire warnings were being sounded" (Egan, 1999:A27). Crack users became defined as the biggest losers on the street, and a generational revulsion against the drug apparently developed.

Perspectives on Cocaine and Crack Cocaine

For Inciardi and his colleagues, the abuse of drugs, and most notably of cocaine and crack cocaine, is a reflection of other problems and not the cause of them. They note:

> Drug abuse is a disorder of the whole person; the problem is the person and not the drug, and addiction is but a symptom and not the essence of the disorder. In the vast majority of drug users, there are cognitive problems, psychological dysfunction is common, thinking may be unrealistic or disorganized, values misshapen, and frequently there are deficiencies in educational, employment, parenting, and other social skills (Inciardi et al., 1993:145).

They argue that what the crack-dependent person needs is not rehabilitation, which implies a return to a previously known way of life, but habilitation, which would involve the building of a positive self-image and socialization into a productive and responsible way of life (Inciardi et al., 1993).

Methamphetamine

Methamphetamine (also known as "crank, "speed," "go fast," and "meth") is a central nervous system stimulant. The term crank derives from crankcase, the site where the drug tended to be stored by truck drivers who used amphetamines to try to keep awake on long hauls. The drug was initially manufactured by biker gangs in the United States in the 1970s and then by Mexican cartels in the 1990s. The United Nations reports that methamphetamine is the most widely abused drug on earth, with almost as many addicts as for heroin and cocaine combined.

Methamphetamine is relatively easy to manufacture: other drugs required in the process, such as ephedrine, generally are smuggled into the United States from Mexico. Amphetamines are distinctive but related pharmacologically to methamphetamine. They have been widely used by persons seeking to lose weight and by students in all-night cramming sessions before exams or trying to finish a term paper on time. A relationship has been found between acts of violence and meth usage, but the writers note as well that "violence is not an inevitable outcome of chronic methamphetamine use" (Baskin-Sommers & Sommers, 2006).

Arrest figures show slightly higher usage rates for methamphetamine among females than males. Perhaps this is because most buyers of the drug do not have to deal with organized criminals; methamphetamine often is available at neighborhood bars. In Montana, meth sales and use are reported to be responsible for 80 percent of the total prison population, and 90 percent of the female inmate total. A philanthropist in the state donated millions of dollars for a media advertising campaign. The advertisements are grim:

> The camera follows the teenager as she showers for her night out and looks down to discover the drain swirling with blood. Her methamphetamine-addicted self is oozing from scabs she had picked all over her body because the drug made her think there were bugs crawling beneath her skin, and she lets out a scream worthy of [the movie] *Psycho* (Zernike, 2006:17).

In its pure form, methamphetamine is white, odorless, and bitter. Street meth tends to have a yellowish hue and to come in capsules or chunks. Users today tend to be white, lower middle-class, high-school educated, and in the 20- to 35-year age bracket (Roll, Rawson, Ling & Shoptaw, 2009). In previous years methamphetamine was injected intravenously but fear of HIV infection from contaminated needles has led to an upsurge in meth smoking. The effect of the drug will last for about ten to twelve hours, compared to the usual 45-minute effect of cocaine (Halkitis, 2009).

A 2009 a PBS television documentary, "The Meth Epidemic" offered before-and-after pictures of meth addicts. The first shots showed attractive, full-faced young persons who liked to party too much. The later images showed desiccated, toothless faces pocked with bloody sores. Sometimes less than a year had elapsed between the first and second photographs.

Marijuana

A major difficulty in the medical and criminological material regarding marijuana (or 9-THC, which stands for delta-9-trans-tetrahdrocannabinol, the drug's main ingredient) lies in the interweaving of fact and ideology. Much argument surrounds the question of the short- and long-term physical consequences of chronic marijuana usage. Some writers suggest that smoking of marijuana several times a day for a period of, say, a decade, is likely to produce deleterious organic conditions. At the moment about 0.8 percent of Americans smoke marijuana on a daily or near daily basis (Zimmer & Morgan, 1997). Marijuana smoke has been reported by the National Institute of Drug Abuse to have a higher carcinogenic content than that of cigarettes, but few marijuana users smoke the 20 or more cigarettes daily that often feed the habit of the tobacco addict.

The main physical risk from marijuana is damage to the lungs from smoking (Zimmer & Morgan, 1997:139; see generally Earlywine, 2002). There is some—but far from uniform—belief that marijuana use by pregnant women presents potential dangers for the fetus, and many point out that the better part of wisdom, given the uncertain consequences, is to be wary of the drug if pregnant. A middle-aged person's risk of heart attack increases nearly five-fold during the first hour after smoking marijuana since ingestion of the drug increases the heart rate by about 40 beats per minute (Mittelman et al., 2001). Similarly, a quartet of doctors reviewing the effect of marijuana on cardiac responses title their article, "Keep off the Grass" (Caldicott et al., 2005). Donald Jasinski, a medical professor at Johns Hopkins University and director of the Center for Chemical Dependence, answered several rhetorical questions: "Does it destroy as many lives as alcohol? No. Does it kill as many people as cigarettes? No. Does it have as many deaths associated with it as aspirin overdoses? No" (Carroll, 2002:C24).

Marijuana at one time was used in medical practice as commonly as aspirin is today, and it was known to have a relaxing effect. In 1937, the federal Marijuana Tax Act made it illegal to possess marijuana unless you had purchased a tax stamp; But there were, for all practical purposes, no stamps to be bought. Use of marijuana then was largely confined to members of underprivileged or fringe groups. The early laws were made tougher during the immediate post-World War II period as marijuana came to be grouped with heroin in the public mind.

By the late 1960s, use of marijuana (also commonly called "pot") had spread dramatically into the mainstream of American society. Along with the Vietnam War and dissent on college campuses, marijuana had become a major topic of controversy. This development triggered medical research designed to pinpoint the effects of the drug. A recent comprehensive review of all the allegations about the possible harmful effects of marijuana conducted by Lynn Zimmer and John P. Morgan, the latter a medical doctor, found little or no support for them. They point out that in 1995, *Lancet*, the highly reputable British medical journal, stated that "the smoking of cannabis [marijuana], even long term, is not harmful to health" (Zimmer & Morgan, 1997:17). The simplest summary of the research would be that marijuana has been found to be neither as dangerous as its fiercest opponents claim, nor as innocuous as its fiercest proponents insist.

It is ideology that has prevailed. Middle-class parents refused to stand by idly while their children were being confined for long prison terms for recreational marijuana use. As politicians who had used marijuana while college students moved into influential positions, they joined the campaign to reduce the penalties against users and focus enforcement on trafficking in large quantities of marijuana. In 1992,presidential nominee Bill Clinton was able to bemuse the electorate with his disingenuous explanation of his marijuana use: "I didn't inhale."

Critics of the current laws against marijuana maintain that the penal code pointlessly turns those who use the drug into criminals and in some instances generates an overall hostility toward the law and the police. They also point out that the great amounts of money that might be used for better purposes are employed to enforce the laws against marijuana. They argue that by keeping marijuana illegal, but failing to eliminate it, the society has turned over the marketing of the drug to organized crime groups that engage in a wide variety of other illegal and dangerous acts (Husak & de Marneffe, 2005).

Marijuana as Medicine

The debate regarding drug offenses as victimless crimes recently has taken another twist as persons who maintain that their medical condition could be helped and their pain alleviated if marijuana were made legally available to them joined the fray. A study of 2,400 oncologists (doctors specializing in treating cancer) found that 40 percent had recommended that their patients use marijuana. The drug also is believed to reduce eye pressure caused by glaucoma. In addition, marijuana has been claimed to lessen muscular spasms in persons with neurological disorders and to relieve migraine headaches and the pain from "phantom limb" conditions that often follow amputations. For some of these problems a synthetic capsule of THC is available by prescription, but it is not believed to be as effective for many patients as smoked marijuana, and it may produce more unpleasant side effects (Zimmer & Morgan, 1997).

Eleven states now permit physicians to prescribe marijuana when they believe it will provide pain relief. The federal Food and Drug Administration countered the movement by declaring that no sound scientific study supported the medical use of marijuana and that the government would withdraw prescription-writing privileges from doctors who took such a step, bar them from being paid for treating Medicare and Medicaid patients, and would consider prosecuting them criminally. This threat grew much stronger when the U.S. Supreme Court in 2005 by a 6-3 margin ruled that the Controlled Substance Act gave the federal government the power to outlaw the growing of marijuana for medical purposes since such activity could substantially affect interstate commerce (*Gonzales v. McClary*, 2005).

In 2002, California Judge Mary Schroeder ruled that the first amendment protected the right of physicians to discuss the use of marijuana with patients they deemed might benefit from it. The justice also voiced a view that the Supreme Court in the subsequent McClary case would decline to endorse. The rights of states, the judge declared, should prevail, "particularly in situations in which the citizens of a State have chosen to serve as a laboratory in the trial of novel social and economic experiments"(*Conant v. Walters*, 2002:639). In an editorial, the prestigious *New England Journal of Medicine* called the government's opposition "foolish," "hypocritical," and "inhumane" (Kassirer, 1997).

Opponents of medical use of marijuana challenge the view that marijuana is as effective as claimed and maintain that, even if it is, there are legal drugs that would do the job just as well or better. They also argue that the move to legalize marijuana for medical purposes is largely a camouflage for an entry point to totally decriminalize marijuana. The accuracy of this perspective is shown by a 2009 editorial in the *Washington Post* declaring that "California's medical dispensaries provide a good working example, warts and all, that legalized drug distribution does not cause the sky to fall" (Maskos & Franklin, 2009:A13). Opponents of medical marijuana also insist that once prescriptions can legally be written for marijuana there are doctors a-plenty who would authorize persons with no medical need to obtain the drug. They further maintain that marijuana use by patients with ailments such as AIDS would further damage the users' immune system and make them more susceptible to bacterial and fungal infections (Wasserman, 2005).

Marijuana Use and Criminological Theory

For Ronald Akers and Gary Jensen (2003), the most productive theoretical approach to marijuana use is to see it as the outcome of a process of differential association. The interaction between young persons and their peers, parents, and others, Akers and Jensen maintain, provides them with a social environment in which they learn ways of behaving. The peer group, particularly close friends, is the most important association for the initiation and continuing use of marijuana. Both the frequency and quantity of use are related to the number and type of current users one has as friends (see also Esbensen & Huizinga, 1993). Parents, other family members, church and religious groups, schoolteachers, authority figures, and others in the community also have an influence in determining whether marijuana will be used, and how much and for how long. Akers (1985:115) writes:

> When these [groups] act in harmony to move youngsters in the direction toward either using or not using, the chances of their behaving that way are maximized. When these sources are in conflict, adolescents will most often behave similarly to close peers. It is in peer groups that drugs typically are first made available and opportunities for use are provided.

However much insight such ideas offer about marijuana use, they leave some basic questions unanswered. Why, for instance, did the user come to develop the kinds of friendships and relationships that he or she did? Why are such peer relationships maintained by some persons but dropped by others?

Trends in Drug Use

Most high school students find illegal drugs more common at their schools than in their neighborhoods. Forty-one percent of the students in one inquiry said that they had seen drugs sold at their school, while only 25 percent had seen them being sold in their neighborhood. Twenty-five percent of the students said that they could purchase marijuana within an hour at their school.

The survey also reported that 35 percent of the teenagers identified drugs as the most important problem they face. An overwhelming majority of the teachers favored expelling a student caught with drugs at school, conducting random searches of lockers, and testing athletes for drugs. But most teachers opposed testing all students for drugs (Wren, 1999).

The initiation and progress of drug usage has been studied by Finn-Aage Esbensen and Delbert Elliott (1994), who examined data in regard to 1,172 respondents aged 11 through 30. They found that once drug use is started, it tends to be maintained for an extended time and that social learning variables are more important in accounting for initiation than demographic variables such as age and gender. Marijuana use drops on the average by more than one-third when young adults get married or cohabit and cocaine use drops by one-half. The explanation seems to be that the drug usage is no longer private, but now involves the continuing awareness of someone else. If a divorce takes place, the "marriage effect" is reversed and usage returns to about the same level as when the person was single (Bachman et al., 1997).

Victims without Crimes

Criminology by definition involves the study of illegal behavior, but as we saw in Chapter 1, crime is defined differently among criminologists. Criminology textbooks typically concentrate all or virtually all of their attention on acts that are proscribed by the criminal law. Some criminologists feel uneasy about the blinders that this approach puts upon criminological scholarship. They object that it restricts them to looking only at behavior that is defined as criminal by appointed and elected officials. Usually those who fashion the law condemn behaviors that virtually everybody regards as unacceptable—murder, robbery, car theft, and similar kinds of acts. But there are some things, such as the victimless crimes, that are outlawed for reasons that are at least arguable. And then there are other matters that seem to involve self-evident social harms that never find their way into the criminal laws. For instance, almost all continental European and South American countries have laws that mandate that persons who can aid others without risk to themselves can be criminally charged if they fail to do so. In the United States, except for five states, it is perfectly legal for a person to stand by and watch an infant drown yards away in shallow water, or for you to indifferently observe a blind man walk past and plunge over a cliff only a few feet away without you having made any attempt to stop or warn him (Schiff, 2005).

The Michigan Supreme Court spelled out the prevailing American doctrine when it overturned the conviction for manslaughter of a man who had left for dead a woman after he had observed her taking morphine and camphor tablets before she fell into a coma (*People v. Beardsley*, 1907). A leading criminal law scholar believed that the court decision—and many others like it—was abominable:

> To be temperate about such a decision is difficult. In its savage proclamation, it ignores any impulse of charity or compassion. It proclaims a morality that is smug, ignorant, and vindictive. In a civilized society, a man who finds himself with a helplessly ill person who has no other source of aid should be under a duty to summon help, whether the person is his wife, his mistress, a prostitute, or a Chief Justice. The Beardsley decision deserves emphatic repudiation (Hughes, 1955:624).

Cigarette Smoking

The manufacture and sale of cigarettes offers perhaps the best illustration of victims without crimes, and it is to put before readers the question of the legitimate reach of criminology that we dwell upon the issue here.

The tobacco story is a tale of an industry that makes extraordinary amounts of money and uses these profits in part to protect itself from regulation (Parker-Pope, 2001). The tobacco industry contributes large sums to politicians, hoping to gain their support for legislation favorable to it. Cigarette manufacturers undoubtedly do not want to kill people, but by employing tactics of obfuscation, denial, and manipulation, they have fed their financial self-interest at the expense of the lives of millions of their customers. Cigarettes are said to "cause more deaths than any other recognized lethal agents, including all the known bacteria, known viruses, bullets, wild animals, chemical poisons, and even the American automobile" (Kluger, 1996:204).

Before it yielded to lawsuits, the tobacco industry insisted that correlation was not causation: just because persons who smoked a great deal showed significantly higher rates of lung cancer did not prove that the smoking caused the cancer. In addition, many persons who smoked as much or more than those who died of lung cancer lived to a ripe old age and died of something else. And some who did not smoke died of the same diseases that killed those who smoked. In addition, people who smoke might be distinctive in some ways that leads to their demise earlier than those who do not smoke. As one physician indicated when he argued that reports of a causative connection between smoking and lung cancer were "absolutely unwarranted": "Simply because one finds bullfrogs after a rain does not mean that it rained bullfrogs" (Kluger, 1996:166).

Cigarette manufacturers maintain, as those who seek de-criminalization of narcotics use also argue, that how people choose to live their lives and contribute to their death is their own business, that life itself is a terminal disease. People have enough information to make a sensible decision, at least if we overlook that (1) strenuous advertising efforts were launched to get and keep people smoking and (2) the nicotine in cigarettes is addictive, in the sense that it is painful to give up.

The first significant development in the control of cigarette purveyance came when the government prohibited cigarette companies from advertising on television. This restriction was a considerable aid to the bigger cigarette manufacturers because, absent heavy advertising outlays, potential entrants into the market could not seriously challenge them. At the same time, the cigarette manufacturers turned to advertisements placed strategically in sports arenas so that their products would be clearly visible to television audiences.

The television ban was also welcomed by the manufacturers because the government had invoked the "fairness doctrine," which authorized rebuttal of controversial positions. The tobacco companies were being savaged during the free television time offered to those who scorned them. But notable in the decision to uphold the ban on cigarette advertising was the defense of free speech in a dissenting opinion. Judge Skelly Wright did not doubt that the attractive woman in Salem ads was in fact "a seductive merchant of death" and that the real "'Marlboro Country' is the graveyard." But the First Amendment, the jurist stated, "does not protect only free speech that is healthy or harmless" (*Capital Broadcasting Co. v. Mitchell*, 1971:582).

Subsequently, largely on the initiative of the Surgeon General, the government demanded that all cigarette packages (and, later, advertisements as well) carry a warning about the dangers of smoking. The manufacturers spent millions to get a message that was as innocuous as they could negotiate. They were not altogether displeased with the requirement of a warning because they believed that it might protect them from liability, since they could claim that they had informed people that they were engaging in risky behavior and therefore they could escape the imposition of financial damages (Brandt, 2007).

The question for criminologists remains: Is this a matter that demands their professional attention or is it outside the realm of criminal law and therefore outside their scholarly territory? A possible rule might be that if proof of inflicted harm is overwhelming criminologists might well attend to the issue, in the same way they would to illegal harms. At the same time, caution must be exercised: it is tempting to label as "crimes" matters that offend us without paying careful attention to the implications of moral judgments unsupported by unequivocal scientific backing. Thus, we again face the definitional problems posed in our opening chapter concerning the relativity of crime and the influence of ideology on its definition.

Summary

By and large, law enforcement activities have proven ineffectual for controlling victimless crimes: for instance, longstanding statutes outlawing the behaviors seem to have made little impact on the extent of drug use and prostitution (Meier & Geis, 2006). The experiment in the prohibition of the sale of alcoholic beverages in the

United States ended in shambles and resulted in the repeal of the ill-fated Volstead Act. Perhaps the most instructive lesson comes from the experience in America with cigarette smoking. Educational campaigns, appealing to medical findings and self-interest in personal health, supported by peer pressures, have made a deep indent into the extent that Americans smoke cigarettes today. Cigarette sales have fallen to their lowest level in more than 50 years. On a per capita basis the number of smokers has declined to a level last seen in the late 1930s.

Philosophers often have inveighed against attempts to use the criminal law for purposes that it cannot adequately accomplish. Two of the more famous statements are those of Baruch de Spinoza (1632-1677) and Jeremy Bentham (1748-1832). de Spinoza advocated the removal from statute books of laws restricting activities that do not injure another party on the ground that "he who seeks to regulate everybody by law is more likely to arouse vices than to reform them. It is best to grant what cannot be abolished, even though it be itself harmful" (de Spinoza, 1670/1937:141).

Bentham warned against "imaginary offenses," illustrating his position by reference to fornication and drunkenness, two acts that were outlawed in early American history. With what chance of success, Bentham asked, could a legislator seek to extirpate drunkenness and fornication by dint of legal punishment? "Not all the torture which ingenuity could invent would compass it; and before he had made any progress worth regarding, such a mass of evil would be produced by the punishment as would exceed, by a thousand fold, the utmost possible mischief of the offense." (Bentham [1798]/1948:420).

A useful set of ground rules is offered by Herbert Packer regarding behaviors that ought to be scrutinized closely in terms of the proper attitude of the criminal law toward them. These are offenses that "do not result in anyone's feeling that he has been injured so as to impel him to bring the offenses to the attention of the authorities" (Packer, 1968:151). Packer identified a number of conditions that he believed should be present before criminal sanctions are invoked, including:

- The conduct must be regarded by most people as socially threatening, and must not be condoned by any significant segment of the society;

- It can be dealt with through evenhanded and non-discriminatory law enforcement;

- Controlling it through the criminal process will not expose that process to severe qualitative or quantitative strain; and

- No reasonable alternatives to the criminal sanction exist for dealing with it.

The record shows that such considerations have led to the steady decrease in the number of "victimless" behaviors that come within the scope of the criminal law. But by no means is it certain that the process will continue or that it will proceed in the same direction. History clearly tells us that the use of the criminal law to enforce moral positions often takes a cyclical form. Today, for instance, the status of abortion under the law remains a matter of intense debate, while new aspects of the various behaviors categorized as "crimes without victims" are arousing considerable public controversy, including such matters as physician-assisted suicide and the right to use marijuana to ease a medical condition if a doctor prescribes the drug.

Finally, we can note two letters to a national newspaper that tell the story of the contradictory opinions held by thinking people regarding the preferred legal status of one of the major victimless crimes, drug use. First is an advocate of continuing to outlaw drug use:

> Legalization would be catastrophic. There are 15 million alcoholics in this country and 5 million drug addicts; do we want the 5 to become 15? Parents know that taking away the law would increase drug use and related car crashes, school dropouts and work absences. Hospital emergency rooms would be flooded, and crime would return to the crisis levels of the 1970s and '80s, when drug use was at its highest. Domestic violence and date rape would be substantially higher (Weiner, 2006:A12).

On the other side, the argument took the following form:

> Everybody knows the drug war is an abject failure. Its collateral damages is fostering anti-Americanism throughout the globe, particularly in South America, and at home it has trashed the Fourth Amendment [regarding searches and seizures] and is filling our jails with people whose only crime is to find pleasure in ways other people don't like (Padden, 2006:A12; for debates on drug legalization see Husak & de Marneffe, 2005; Huggins, 2005).

Key Terms and Concepts

Cocaine
Crack Cocaine
Crank
Crimes without Victims
Marijuana
Methamphetamines

Opiates
Physician-Assisted Suicide
Pimp
Prostitution
Status Offenses
Victims without Crimes

Key Criminologists

Ronald Akers
Elliott Currie
Nanette Davis
Finn-Aage Esbensen

Erich Goode
James Inciardi
Edwin Schur
Franklin Zimring

Cases

American Booksellers Assn. v. Hudnut, 771 F.2d 323 (7th Cir. 1985), *affirmed* 475 U.S. 1001 (1986)

Buhl v. Harrigan, 16 Cal. App. 4th 1612 (1993)

Capital Broadcasting Co. v. Mitchell, 333 F. Supp. 582 (D.C. Cir. 1971)

Conant v. Walters, 309 F.2d 693 (9th Cir. 2002).

Gonzales v. McClary, 541 U.S. 1 (2005)

People v. Beardsley, 113 N.W.2d 1128 (Mich. 1907)

State v. DeMagistris, 714 A.2d 567 (R.I. 1998).

References

Akers, R.L. (1985). *Deviant Behavior*. Belmont, CA: Wadsworth.

Akers, R.L. & G.F. Jensen (eds.) (2003). *Social Learning Theory and the Explanation of Crime*. New Brunswick, NJ: Transaction.

Albert, A.E. (2001). *Brothel: Mustang Ranch and Its Women*. New York, NY: Random House.

Anderson, S.A. (2000). "Prostitution and Sexual Autonomy: Making Sense of the Prohibition of Prostitution." *Ethics*, 112:748-782.

Bachman, J.G., K.S. Wadsworth, P.M. O'Malley, L.D. Johnson & J.F. Schulenberg (1997). *Smoking, Drinking and Drug Use in Young Adulthood: The Impacts of New Freedoms and New Responsibilities*. Mahwah, NJ: Earlbaum.

Baskin-Sommers, A. & I. Sommers (2006). "Methamphetamine Use and Violence among Young Adults." *Journal of Criminal Justice,* 34:661-674.

Bentham, J. (1802/1841). *Theories of Legislation*, Second Edition. London, UK: Trubner.

Bettelheim, B. (1969). *Children of the Dream*. New York, NY: Macmillan.

Booth, M. (1999). *Opium: A History*. New York, NY: St. Martin's.

Bork, R. (1991. *The Tempting of America: The Political Seduction of the Law*. New York, NY: Simon & Schuster.

Brandt, A.M. (2007). *The Cigarette Century: The Rise, Fall, and Deadly Persistence of the Product that Defined America*. New York: Basic Books.

Brents, B.G. & K. Hausbeck (2005). "Violence and Legalized Brothel Prostitution in Nevada." *Journal of Interpersonal Violence*, 20:270-295.

Caldicott, D.G., J. Holmes, K.C. Robers-Thomson & L. Mahar (2005). "Keep off the Grass: Marijuana Use and Acute Cardiovascular Events." *European Journal of Emergency Medicine*, 12:23-64.

Campbell, C.A. (1991). "Prostitution, AIDS, and Preventive Health Behavior." *Social Science and Medicine*, 32:1367-1378.

Caputo, G.A. (2008). *Out in the Storm: Drug-Addicted Women Living as Shoplifters and Sex Workers*. Hanover, NH: University Press of New England.

Carroll, L. (2002). "Marijuana's Effects: More than Munchies." *New York Times*, (January 29):C24.

Cartwright, D. (2001). *Dark Paradise: A History of Opiate Addiction in America*. Cambridge, MA: Harvard University Press.

Cates, J.A. & J. Markley (1992). "Demographic, Clinical, and Personality Variables Associated with Male Prostitution by Choice." *Adolescence*, 27:695-714.

Chin, E., K. Hedberg, G.K. Higginson & D.W. Fleming (1999). "Legalized Physician-Assisted Suicide in Oregon: The First Year's Experience." *New England Journal of Medicine*, 340:577-583.

Cohen, B. (1980). *Deviant Street Networks: Prostitution in New York City*. Lexington, MA: Lexington Books.

Cothran, H. (2002). *Pornography: Opposing Viewpoints*. San Diego, CA: Greenhaven.

Dalla, R.L. (2007). *Exposing the "Pretty Woman" Myth: A Qualitative Evaluation of Street-Level Prostituted Women*. Lanham, MD: Lexington Books.

Danke, S., K.L. Mills, J. Ross, A. Williamson, A. Harvard & M. Teeson (2009). "The Aging Heroin User: Career Length, Clinical Profile, an Outcome across 36 Months." *Drug and Alcohol Review*, 28:243-249.

Davenport-Hines, R. (1995). *Auden*. London, UK: Heinemann.

Davis, N.J. (1993). "Introduction: International Perspectives on Female Prostitution." In N.J. Davis (ed.) *Prostitution: An International Handbook on Trends, Problems, and Policies*, 1-13. Westport, CT: Greenwood.

Day, N.L. & G. Richardson (1993). "Cocaine Use and Crack Babies: Science, the Media, and Miscommunication." *Neurotoxicology and Teratology*, 15:293-294.

de Spinoza, B. (1670/1937). "Tractatus Theologico Politicus." Chap. XX. In A.G.A. Balz (ed.) *Writings on Political Philosophy*. New York, NY: Appleton-Century-Crofts.

Devlin, P. (1965). *The Enforcement of Morals*. London, UK: Oxford University Press.

Dodge, M.J., D. Starr-Gimeno & T. Williams (2005). "Puttin' on the Sting: Women Police Officers' Perspectives on Reverse Prostitution Assignments." *International Journal of Police Science & Management*, 7:71-85.

Donne, J. (1624). *Devotions upon Emergent Conditions and Several Steps in My Sickness*. London, UK: Augustine Matthews.

Dworkin, A. (1997). *Life and Death*. New York, NY: Free Press.

Earlywine, M. (2002). *Understanding Marijuana: A New Look at the Scientific Evidence*. New York, NY: Oxford University Press.

Editorial. (1997). "The Way We Are." *Wall Street Journal*, (January 10):A18.

Egan, T. (1999). "A Drug Ran Its Course, Then Hid With Its Users." *New York Times*, (September 19):A1, A27.

Esbensen, F. & D.S. Elliott (1994). "Continuity and Discontinuity in Illicit Drug Use Patterns and Antecedents." *Journal of Drug Use*, 24:75-97.

Esbensen, F. & D. Huizinga (1993). "Gangs, Drugs, and Delinquency in a Survey of Urban Youth." *Criminology*, 31:565-587.

French, P. (2008). *The World is What It Is: The Authorized Biography of V. S. Naipaul*. New York, NY: Knopf.

Gill, M.B. (2009). "Is the Legalization of Physician-Assisted Suicide Compatible with Good End-of-Life Care?" *Journal of Applied Psychology*, 26:27-45.

Halkitis, P.N. (2009). *Methamphetamine Addiction: Biological Foundations, Psychological Factors, and Social Consequences*. Washington, DC: American Psychological Association.

Hawkins, G. & F.E. Zimring (1988). *Pornography in a Free Society*. New York, NY: Cambridge University Press.

Hendin, H. & K. Foley (2009). "Physician-Assisted Suicide: A Medical Perspective." *Michigan Law Review*, 106:1613-1640.

Holsopple, K. (1999). "Pimps, Tricks and Feminists." *Women's Studies Quarterly*, 27:47-52.

Hser, V-I, V. Hoffman, C.E. Grella & M.D. Anglin (2002). "A 33-Year Follow-up of Narcotics Addicts." *Archives of General Psychiatry*, 58:503-508.

Huggins, L.E. (ed.) (2005). *Drug War Deadlock: The Policy Battle Continues*. Stanford, CA: Hoover Institution.

Hughes, G. (1955). "Criminal Omissions." *Yale Law Journal*, 67:590-637.

Hughes, H.M. (ed.) (1961). *The Fantastic Lodgee*. Boston, MA: Houghton Mifflin.

Husak, D. & P. de Marneffe (2005). *The Legalization of Drugs*. New York, NY: Cambridge University Press.

Inciardi, J.A., D. Lockwood & A.E. Pottieger (1993). *Women and Crack Cocaine*. New York, NY: Macmillan.

Jeffrey, D. (2009). *Against Physician Assisted Suicide: A Palliative Care Perspective*. New York, NY: Radcliffe.

Jesilow, P., H. Pontell & G. Geis (1993). *Prescription for Profit: How Doctors Defraud Medicaid*. Berkeley, CA: University of California Press.

Jonnes, J. (1999). *Hep-Cats, Narcs, and Pipe Dreams: A History of America's Romance with Illicit Drugs*. Baltimore, MD: Johns Hopkins University Press.

Kassirer, J.P. (1997). "Federal Foolishness and Marijuana." *New England Journal of Medicine*, 336(3):366.

Klein, C. (2000). *Doris Lessing: A Biography*. New York, NY: Carroll & Graf.

Klinger, K. (2003). "Prostitution, Humanism and a Woman's Choice." *The Humanist*, 63, (January-February):16-20.

Kluger, R. (1996). *Ashes to Ashes: America's Hundred-Year Cigarette War and the Unabashed Triumph of Philip Morris*. New York, NY: Knopf.

Korf, D.J., B. Bullington & H. Riper (eds.) (1999). "Symposium: Windmills in the Minds?: Drug Policy and Drug Research in the Netherlands." *Journal of Drug Issues*, 29:443-726.

Lindsay, R.A. (2009). "Oregon's Experience: Evaluating the Record." *American Journal of Bioethics*, 9:19-27.

Lode, E. (1999). "Slippery Slope Arguments and Legal Reasoning." *California Law Review*, 87:1469-1544.

Lombroso, C. & W. Ferrero (1895). *The Female Offender*. New York, NY: Appleton.

MacKinnon, C.A. & A. Dworkin (eds.) *In Harm's Way: The Pornography of Civil Rights Hearings*. Cambridge, MA: Harvard University Press.

Mascow, P. & S. Franklin (2009). "It's Time to Legalize Drugs." *Washington Post,* (August 17):A13.

Mayrose, J. (2008). "The Effect of Mandatory Motorcycle Helmet Laws on Helmet Use and Injury Patterns among Motorcyclist Fatalities." *Journal of Safety Research*, 39:429-432.

Meier, R.F. & G. Geis (2006) *Criminal Justice and Moral Issues*. New York, NY: Oxford University Press.

Mittelman, M.A., R.A. Lewis, M. Machre, J.B. Sherwood & J.E. Miller (2001). "Triggering Myocardial Interactions by Marijuana." *Circulation*, 103:2805-2809.

Monto, M. (2004). "Female Prostitution, Customers, and Violence." *Violence against Women*, 10:160-168.

Mosher, C.J. & S. Akins (2007). *Drugs and Drug Policy: The Control of Consciousness Alteration*. Thousand Oaks, CA: Sage.

Musto, D.F. & P. Korsmeyer (2002). *One Hundred Years of Heroin*. Westport, CT: Auburn House.

Nietzsche, F.W. (1844/1920). *The Antichrist*. Trans H.L. Mencken. New York, NY: Knopf.

Note. (2009). "Child Pornography, the Internet, and the Challenge of Upholding Statutory Terms." *Harvard Law Review,* 122:2206-2227.

Nuland, S.B. (1994). *How We Die: Reflections on Life's Final Chapter*. New York, NY: Knopf.

Otis, S. (2009). *Child Pornography and Sexual Grooming: Legal and Social Responses*. New York. NY: Cambridge University Press.

Packer, H.L. (1968). *The Limits of the Criminal Sanction*. Stanford, CA: Stanford University Press.

Padden, D.H. (2006). "Our Unwinnable War—Against Drugs." *Wall Street Journal*, (March 7):A12.

Parker-Pope, T. (2001). *Cigarettes: Anatomy of an Industry*. New York, NY: Public Affairs.

Peters, G. & L. Merlington (2009). *Seeds of Terror: How Heroin is Bankrolling the Taliban and al Queda*. New York, NY: Thomas Dunne.

Powers, A. (2000). *Weird Like Us: My Bohemian America*. New York, NY: DeCapo.

Prince, D.A. (1986). *A Psychological Study of Prostitutes in California and Nevada*. Ph.D. dissertation. San Diego, CA: United States International University.

Richardson, G. & N.L. Day (1992). "Maternal and Neonatal Effects of Moderate Cocaine Use During Pregnancy." *Neurotoxicology and Teratology*, 13:455-460.

Richardson, L. (2000). "The Pimp Phenomenon." *Los Angeles Times*, (December 3):E1,E3.

Roll, J.M., R.A. Rawson, W. Ling & S. Shoptaw (eds.) (2009). *Methamphetamine Addiction: From Basic Science to Treatment*. New York, NY: Guilford.

Ross, H.L. (1992). *Confronting Drunk Driving: Social Policy for Saving Lives*. New Haven, CT: Yale University Press.

Salem, T. (1999). "Physician-Assisted Suicide." *Hastings Center Report*, 20(May):30-36.

Schiff, D. (2005. "Samaritans, Good, Bad, Ugly: A Comparative Analysis. *Roger Williams University Law Review*, 11:77-141.

Schur, E. (1965). *Crimes without Victims: Deviant Behavior and Public Policy*. Englewood Cliffs, NJ: Prentice Hall.

Sharpe, T.T. (2005). *Behind the Eight Ball: Sex for Crack Cocaine Exchange and Poor Black Women*. New York, NY: Haworth.

Shishkin, P. & D. Crawford (2006). "In Afghanistan, Heroin Trade Soars Despite U.S. Aid." *Wall Street Journal* (January 18): A1).

van der Poel, S. (1992). "Male Prostitution: A Neglected Phenomenon." *Crime, Law and Social Change*, 18:259-275.

Waddell, C. (1996). "HIV and the Social World of Female Commercial Sex Workers." *Medical Anthropological Quarterly*, 10:75-82.

Wald, M. (2008). "Death of Motorcyclists Rise Again." *New York Times* (August 15):A11.

Wasserman, S. (2005). *Medical Marijuana*. Denver, CO: National Conference of State Legislatures.

Weinberg, M.S., F.M. Shaver & C.J. Williams (1999). "Gendered Sex Work in the San Francisco Tenderloin." *Archives of Sexual Behavior*, 28:503-521.

Weiner, R. (2006). "Our Unwinnable War—Against Drugs." *Wall Street Journal*, (March 7):A12.

Weitzer,R. (2007). "The Social Construction of Sex Trafficking Ideology and the Institutionalization of a Moral Crusade." *Politics & Society*, 35:447-475.

Weitzer, R. (2005). "New Directions in Research on Prostitution." *Crime, Law & Social Change*, 43:211-235.

Woozley, A.D. (1983). "A Duty to Rescue: Some Thoughts on Criminal Liability." *Virginia Law Review*, 69:1273-1300.

Wren, C.S. (2000). "Widespread Drug Use." *New York Times*, (January 23):A9.

Wren, C.S. (1999). "Study Sees Little Change in Drug Use." *New York Times*, (December 19):51.

Wright, W. (2000). "Historical Analogies, Slippery Slopes, and the Question of Euthanasia." *Journal of Law, Medicine & Ethics*, 28:176-193.

Zernike, K. (2006). "With Scenes of Blood and Pain: Ads Battles Methamphetamine in Montana." *New York Times* (February 26):17.

Zimmer, L. & J.P. Morgan (1997). *Marijuana Facts, Marijuana Myths: A Review of the Scientific Evidence*. New York, NY: The Lindesmith Center.

Zimring, F.E. & G. Hawkins (1993). *The Search for Rational Drug Control*. New York, NY: Cambridge University Press.

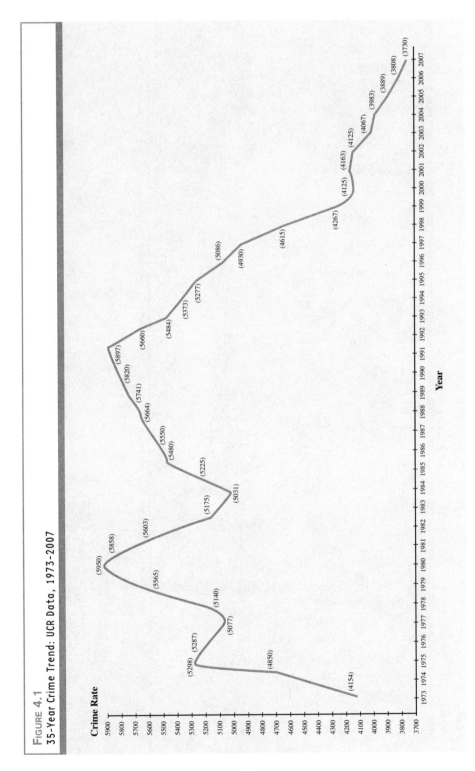

FIGURE 4.1
35-Year Crime Trend: UCR Data, 1973-2007

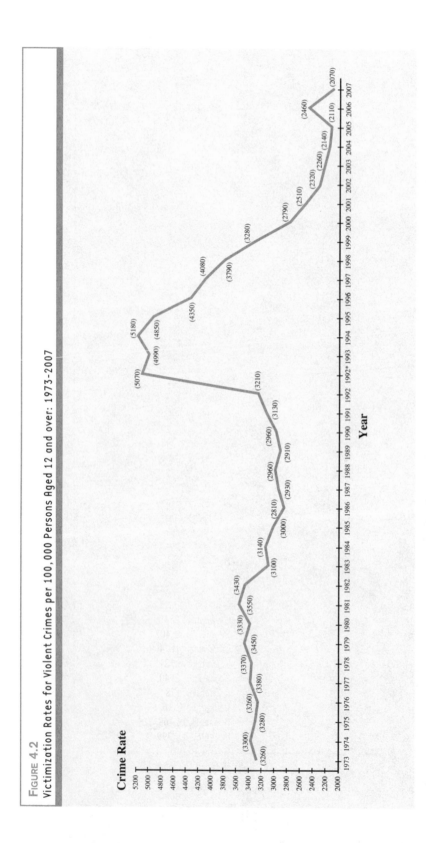

Figure 4.2

Victimization Rates for Violent Crimes per 100,000 Persons Aged 12 and over: 1973-2007

Name Index

Subject Index

About the Authors

Stephen E. Brown is a Professor of Criminology & Criminal Justice and Department Head at Western Carolina University. He received the Ph.D. in Criminal Justice and Criminology from The University of Maryland in 1979. He went through the professorial ranks at East Tennessee State University, serving as Department Chair for 11 years and leaving as Professor Emeritus in 2008.

Brown has published articles in a number of journals, including *Criminology, Journal of Criminal Justice, Journal of Criminal Justice Education, Criminal Justice Review, Youth and Society* and *Social Science Quarterly*. His areas of research interest have been broad, covering topics such as family violence, deterrence, delinquency, and application of statistics within criminology. He has served as a Trustee on the board of The Academy of Criminal Justice Sciences, and as editor of The American Society of Criminology's *The Criminologist*. He is currently working with several colleagues in assessing pedagogical challenges in teaching social science statistics.

Finn-Aage Esbensen (a.k.a. Finn) has a varied and eclectic background. Born in Denmark, the son of a baker and a nurse, he immigrated (literally "came over on the boat") first to Canada and then to the United States. After spending his teenage years in rural Massachusetts, he attended college in Boston. He received both his B.A. (German and Sociology) and M.A. (Sociology) degrees from Tufts University and his Ph.D. (Sociology) from the University of Colorado, Boulder.

Esbensen is the E. Desmond Lee Professor of Youth Crime and Violence in the Department of Criminology and Criminal Justice at the University of Missouri-St. Louis and is currently serving as Department Chair. His previous faculty positions were at Western Carolina University (1982-1986) and the University of Nebraska at Omaha (1992-2001). In addition to these academic appointments, he has held research positions at the following institutions: the Center for Criminal Justice at Harvard Law School (1974); Catholic University (1976-1977); the Behavioral Research Institute, Boulder, Colorado (1980-1981); and the Institute of Behavioral Science, University of Colorado (1987-1992).

In addition to *Criminology: Explaining Crime and Its Context* (with co-authors Steve Brown and Gil Geis), he has published a number of articles and book chapters with a major focus on youth gangs, delinquency, drug use, and prevention efforts. From 1998 through 2001, he served as Editor of *Justice Quarterly*.

Gilbert Geis is a Professor Emeritus in the Department of Criminology, Law, and Society at the University of California, Irvine. He is a former president of the American Society of Criminology and recipient of its Edwin H. Sutherland Award for outstanding research. He has also been given research awards by the Association of Certified Fraud Examiners, the Western Society of Criminology, the American Justice Institute, and the National Organization for Victim Assistance.

Geis received his undergraduate degree from Colgate University and his Ph.D. from the University of Wisconsin. He taught at the University of Oklahoma (1952-1957) and California State University, Los Angeles (1957-1972) before joining the Irvine faculty. He has held visiting appointments in the School of Criminal Justice, State University of New York, Albany; the Institute of Criminology, Cambridge University, the Faculty of Law, University of Sydney; and the College of Human Development, Pennsylvania State University. During the fall semester 1996, he was a Distinguished Visiting Professor at John Jay College in New York City.

Geis has published more than 400 articles on various aspects of crime and criminal justice. His most recent book is *White Collar and Corporate Crime* (2007).